CPA READY™
COMPREHENSIVE CPA EXAM REVIEW

6 CPA READY ONLINE
PASS IN 6 EASY STEPS, GUARANTEED

AVAILABLE BY SECTION OR COMPLETE SET

STEP 1
START WITH OUR DIAGNOSTIC CPA EXAM

The **Diagnostic CPA Exam** evaluates your level of knowledge by pinpointing your strengths and weaknesses and earmarking areas for increased (or decreased) study time. This information is passed on to the **Bisk Personal Trainer™** so that the entire course outline is color-coded, identifying your individual needs.

STEP 2
DEVELOP A STUDY PLAN WITH OUR PERSONAL TRAINER

The **Bisk Personal Trainer™** analyzes your performance on the **Diagnostic CPA Exam** by matching your weakest areas against the most heavily tested exam topics (according to AICPA specifications) and automatically develops an extensive study plan just for you. Featuring practice exams with links to over 3,400 pages of the most comprehensive textbooks on the market, this powerful learning tool even re-evaluates your needs and modifies your study plan after each study session or practice exam!

STEP 3
MASTER THE CONTENT OF THE NEW COMPUTER-BASED EXAM WITH OUR ONLINE CLASSROOMS, STREAMING VIDEO LECTURES AND SIMULATIONS TUTORIAL

- **Online Classroom** allows you to "attend class" anytime, anywhere you have access to a PC.
- **Features 50+ hours of streaming video** lectures, with in-depth coverage of the most difficult exam concepts – available to view at your convenience.
- **Practice simulation questions** just as they will appear on the computer-based exam.

www.CPAexam.com/06

NO OTHER ONLINE REVIEW IS THIS COMPLETE!

▶ GENERAL FEATURES

- Center-based navigation
- Expanded help system
- Home page with history links
- Increased settings options (including customizable content appearance)
- "Getting Started" section
- Tutorial-based help system
- Multiple-user support
- Ability to print every screen
- Audio help for all screens
- Web-based interface
- Earn up to 12 college credits

▶ STATISTICS FEATURES

- Color-coded statistical analysis by topic and microtopic
- Statistical charts compare all exams taken
- Statistics saved for every question and exam taken
- Summary details for all areas of study

▶ STUDY FEATURES

50 HOURS OF STREAMING VIDEO

- Over 200 simulation questions
- Bisk Personal Trainer™ (develops a personalized study plan based on exam performance)
- More than 4,000 actual CPA Exam questions
- Ability to mark questions for later reference
- Embedded text from our four-volume, 3,400-page textbook series
- Recently visited areas
- "Getting Started" section
- Online study guides
- Custom Study (user chooses what to study)
- Global Study (study any topic instantly)

- Study mode with correct and incorrect answer explanations
- Personal Booknotes
- Super Search
- Tutorial-based help system
- Weekly assignments, including quizzes to help keep students on track
- Video viewer guides (available weekly as a download)
- 50+ hours of streaming video lectures
- Supplemental examples help explain difficult concepts

▶ TEST FEATURES

OVER 200 SIMULATIONS

- Mirrors the actual exam
- Unlimited diagnostic exams
- Unlimited final exams (unique and timed)
- More than 4,000 actual CPA Exam questions
- Over 200 simulations
- Testlets
- Rules-based grading of essays
- Ability to mark questions for later reference
- Questions chosen and weighted from topics based on the CPA Exam
- AICPA final exam chart

▶ COMMUNICATION FEATURES

BETTER THAN LIVE

- Message boards for threaded discussions
- Weekly chat sessions with your professor
- Email interaction for one-on-one communication
- Class news to keep you up to date

MORE THAN 4,000 PRACTICE QUESTIONS!

▶ AVAILABLE BY SECTION OR COMPLETE SET

- ∗ Financial Accounting & Reporting
- ∗ Auditing & Attestation
- ∗ Regulation
- ∗ Business Environment & Concepts

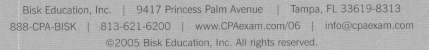
Bisk Education, Inc. | 9417 Princess Palm Avenue | Tampa, FL 33619-8313
888-CPA-BISK | 813-621-6200 | www.CPAexam.com/06 | info@cpaexam.com
©2005 Bisk Education, Inc. All rights reserved.

CPA

Comprehensive Exam Review

Business Environment & Concepts

Nathan M. Bisk, JD, CPA

ACKNOWLEDGEMENTS

We wish to thank the **American Institute of Certified Public Accountants** and other organizations for permission to reprint or adapt the following copyright © materials:

1. Uniform CPA Examination Questions and Unofficial Answers, Copyright © American Institute of Certified Public Accountants, Inc., Harborside Financial Center, 201 Plaza Three, Jersey City, NJ 07311-3881.

2. Accounting Research Bulletins, APB Opinions, Audit and Accounting Guides, Auditing Procedure Studies, Risk Alerts, Statements of Position, and Code of Professional Conduct, Copyright © American Institute of Certified Public Accountants, Inc., Harborside Financial Center, 201 Plaza Three, Jersey City, NJ 07311-3881.

3. FASB Statements, Interpretations, Technical Bulletins, and Statements of Financial Accounting Concepts, Copyright © Financial Accounting Standards Board, 401 Merrit 7, P.O. Box 5116, Norwalk, CT 06856.

4. GASB Statements, Interpretations, and Technical Bulletins, Copyright © Governmental Accounting Standards Board, 401 Merritt 7, P.O. Box 5116, Norwalk CT 06856-5116.

5. Statements on Auditing Standards, Statements on Standards for Consulting Services, Statements on Responsibilities in Personal Financial Planning Practice, Statements on Standards for Accounting and Review Services, Statements on Quality Control Standards, Statements on Standards for Attestation Engagements, and Statements on Responsibilities in Tax Practice, Copyright © American Institute of Certified Public Accountants, Inc., Harborside Financial Center, 201 Plaza Three, Jersey City, NJ 07311-3881.

6. ISB Standards, Copyright © Independence Standards Board, 6th Floor, 1211 Avenue of the Americas, New York, NY 10036-8775

PREFACE

Our texts provide comprehensive, complete coverage of <u>all</u> the topics tested on all <u>four</u> sections of the CPA Examination, including **Financial Accounting & Reporting, Auditing & Attestation, Regulation,** and **Business Environment & Concepts.** Used effectively, our materials will enable you to achieve maximum preparedness for the Uniform CPA Examination. Here is a brief summary of the **features** and **benefits** that our texts will provide for you:

1. **Information on the Computer-Based Exam...**The Uniform CPA Examination is administered at secure testing centers on computers. See Appendix B for a full discussion of this issue. This edition contains up-to-date coverage, including complete coverage of all exam changes. This edition also includes all the latest pronouncements of the AICPA and FASB, the current tax rates, governmental and nonprofit accounting, and other topics that are tested on the CPA exam. Our coverage is based on the most recent **AICPA Content Specification Outlines for the Uniform CPA Exam.**

2. **Separate and Complete Volumes...**Each volume includes text, multiple choice questions, and case-based simulations with solutions. There is no need to refer to any other volume.

3. **More than 3,400 Pages of Text...**Including a selection of more than 3,700 recent CPA Examination and exclusive Bisk Education multiple choice questions and simulations with Unofficial Answers from past exams. Solving these questions under test conditions with immediate verification of results instills confidence and reinforces our **SOLUTIONS APPROACH**™ to solving exam questions.

4. **Complete Coverage...**No extra materials are required to be purchased. We discuss and explain all important AICPA, FASB, GASB, and ISB pronouncements, including all significant ARBs, APBs, SASs, SSARs, SFACs, and FASB materials. We also cite and identify all authoritative sources including the dates of all AICPA Questions and Unofficial Answers covered in our materials.

5. **Detailed Summaries...**We set forth the significant testable concepts in each CPA exam topic. These highly readable summaries are written in complete sentences using an outline format to facilitate rapid and complete comprehension. The summaries isolate and emphasize topics historically tested by the CPA examiners.

6. **Emphasis on "How to Answer Questions" and "How to Take the Exam"...**We teach you to solve free-response questions and simulations using our unique and famous **SOLUTIONS APPROACH**™.

7. **Discussion and Development of...**AICPA grading procedures, grader orientation strategies, examination confidence, and examination success.

8. **Unique Objective Question Coverage and Unofficial Answers Updated...**We explain *why* the multiple choice alternatives are either right or wrong. Plus, we clearly indicate the changes that need to be made in the Unofficial Answers to correctly reflect current business and tax laws and AICPA, FASB, GASB, and other authoritative pronouncements.

9. **Writing Skills...**Each volume contains a section to help you brush up on your writing skills for the CPA exam.

10. **Indexes...**We have included a comprehensively compiled index for easy topic reference in all four sections.

11. **Cross References...**If you do decide to use our other materials, the software uses the same chapter numbering system as the book to allow for easy synchronization between the two formats. Our video and audio programs also are referenced to those same chapters.

12. **Diagnostic Exam to Test Your Present Level of Knowledge...**And we include a **Practice Exam** to test your exam preparedness under actual exam conditions. These testing materials are designed to help you single out for concentrated study the exam topic areas in which you are dangerously deficient.

Our materials are designed for the candidate who previously has studied accounting. Therefore, the rate at which a candidate studies and learns (not merely reads) our material will depend on a candidate's background and aptitude. Candidates who have been out of school for a period of years might need more time to study than recent graduates. The point to remember is that <u>all</u> the material you will need to know to pass the exam is here, except for the professional databases available for free from www.cpa-exam.org to candidates with a *Notice to Schedule*. All you need to do is apply yourself and learn this material at a rate that is appropriate to your situation. **As a final thought,** keep in mind that test confidence gained through disciplined preparation equals success.

OUR EDITORIAL BOARD INCLUDES THE NATION'S LEADING CPAs, ATTORNEYS AND EDUCATORS!

The Only CPA Review Texts Developed By Full-Time Experts.

YOU WILL LEARN FROM OUR OUTSTANDING EXPERTS... WITHOUT LEAVING YOUR HOME OR OFFICE.

Consulting Editor

MORTIMER M. CAPLIN, LLB, JSD, LLD, is a senior partner with the Washington D.C. law firm of Caplin and Drysdale. He served as Commissioner of the Internal Revenue Service and as a member of the President's Task Force on Taxation. He received the Alexander Hamilton Award (the highest award conferred by the Secretary of the Treasury) for outstanding and unusual leadership during service as a U.S. Commissioner of Internal Revenue. For more than 25 years, Mr. Caplin has been in private practice with his present law firm, and has served as adjunct professor for the University of Virginia Law School. He is a nationally acclaimed author of numerous articles on tax and corporate matters.

Consulting Editor

RICHARD M. FELDHEIM, MBA, JD, LLM, CPA (NY), is a New York CPA as well as an attorney in New York and Arizona. He holds a Masters in Tax Law from New York University Law School. Mr. Feldheim is a member of the New York State Society of CPAs, AICPA, New York State Bar Association, Association of the Bar of the City of New York, Arizona Bar, and American Bar Association. His background includes practice as both a CPA with Price Waterhouse & Co. and as a Senior Partner with the Arizona law firm of Wentworth & Lundin. He has lectured for the AICPA, the Practicing Law Institute, Seton Hall University, and the University of Arizona.

Consulting Editor

WILLIAM J. MEURER, CPA (FL), is former Managing Partner for both the overall operations in Central Florida and the Florida Audit and Business Advisory Services sector of Arthur Andersen LLP. During his 35-year career with the firm, Mr. Meurer developed expertise in several industries, including high technology, financial services, real estate, retailing/distribution, manufacturing, hospitality, professional services, and cable television. A graduate of Regis University, he is a member of both the American Institute of CPAs and the Florida Society of CPAs.

Consulting Editor

THOMAS A. RATCLIFFE, PhD, CPA (TX), is Director of the School of Accountancy and Eminent Scholar in Accounting and Finance at Troy University. Dr. Ratcliffe also serves as Scholar in Residence for Wilson Price (Montgomery, AL). In that role, Dr. Ratcliffe is responsible for quality control within the firm. Dr. Ratcliffe also serves as accounting/auditing technical advisor to three different associations of CPA firms (CPA America, Leading Edge, and PKF North American Network). Continuing his involvement in service roles within the accounting profession, Dr. Ratcliffe serves on the AICPA Council and is the current chair of the AICPA Accounting and Review Services Committee. He also is a member of the AICPA Private Company Financial Reporting Task Force.

Consulting Editor

C. WILLIAM THOMAS, MBA, PhD, CPA (TX), currently serves as J.E. Bush Professor and former Chair of the Department of Accounting and Business Law at Baylor University. He is a member of the AICPA, the Texas Society of CPAs, the Central Texas Chapter of CPAs, and the American Accounting Association, where he is past Chair for the Southwestern Regional Audit Section. Professor Thomas is a nationally known author and has extensive experience in Auditing CPA Review. In addition, he has received recognition for special audit education and curriculum projects he developed for Coopers & Lybrand. His background includes public accounting experience with KPMG Peat Marwick.

CHANGE ALERTS

American Jobs Creation Act of 2004

1. The maximum number of shareholders of an S corporation is increased from 75 to 100.

2. Family members (not merely a husband and wife) may be treated as one shareholder for the purposes of determination of an S corporation.

Many of the provisions of the American Jobs Creation Act of 2004 (AJCA '04) became effective October 22, 2004, and thus became eligible to be tested starting with the July-August 2005 exam window. Most of the provisions of this act are tested in the REG exam section. (Chapter 49)

BUSINESS ENVIRONMENT & CONCEPTS

VOLUME IV of IV

TABLE OF CONTENTS

The percentages refer to the proportionate values allocated to various topics in the BEC exam section, as specified in the AICPA content specification outline, presented in greater detail in the **Practical Advice** section. Bear in mind, the BEC exam section especially is designed to test integrative skills as well as content mastery. This means that information from other exam sections could be alluded to in questions and also that questions may overlap several topic areas.

QUICK TEXT REFERENCE

....

....

....

....

The editors strongly recommend that candidates read the entire **Getting Started** and **Practical Advice** sections of this volume, unless they already have read these sections in the *Financial Accounting & Reporting, Auditing & Attestation,* or *Regulation* volumes. Initially, the BEC exam section will not have simulations. When simulations are due to appear on the BEC exam section, candidates also should read the **Writing Skills** appendix of this volume. The references on this page are intended only for conveniently relocating selected parts of the volume. Add items to this list that you find yourself revisiting frequently.

FOREWORD: GETTING STARTED

Step One: Read Section One of the Practical Advice Section

Section One of the **Practical Advice** section (Appendix B) is designed to familiarize you with the CPA examination. Included in **Practical Advice** are general comments about the exam, a schedule of exam dates, addresses and numbers of state boards of accountancy, and attributes required for exam success.

Step Two: Take the Diagnostic Exam

The diagnostic exam in this foreword is designed to help you determine your strong and weak areas. This in turn will help you design your personalized training plan so that you spend more time in your weak areas and do not waste precious study time in areas where you are already strong. You can take the exams using either the books or CPA Review Software for Windows^{TM}. Don't mark answers in the book; then you can use the diagnostic as a second practice exam, if you want. The books provide you with a worksheet that makes self-diagnosis fast and easy. CPA Review Software for Windows^{TM} automatically scores your exams for you and gives you a personalized analysis of your strong and weak areas.

NOTE: If you took a previous CPA exam and passed some, but not all the sections, also analyze these exam sections to help you determine where you need to concentrate your efforts this time.

NOTE: If you purchase a package that includes software, you will also want to go through all of the software tutorials prior to beginning intensive study. They are each only a few minutes long, but they are loaded with valuable information. There is simply no better way to prepare yourself to study. The software programmers assumed candidates would take the diagnostic exam before beginning studying; take the diagnostic exam to get full benefit from the software.

Step Three: Develop a Personalized Training Plan

Based on the results from your diagnostic exams, develop your personalized training plan. If you are taking all four exam sections, are sitting for the exam for the first time, and are an "average" CPA candidate, we recommend that you train for 20 weeks at a minimum of 20 hours per week. This level of intensity should increase during the final four weeks of your training and peak at 40 hours the final week before the exam. Designed to complete your study program, our Intensive Video Series is a concentrated and effective "cram course" that targets the information you must know to pass. The videos will refresh your memory on subjects you covered weeks earlier and clarify topics you haven't yet fully grasped.

If you took the exam previously and did not condition (you will take all four sections), and you are the "average" CPA candidate, we recommend that you train for 12 weeks at a minimum of 20 hours per week. Again, this level of intensity should increase during the final four weeks of your training and peak during the final week before the exam.

The Bisk Education editors expect that most candidates will write less than four sections at once. If you are writing less than four sections, you should adjust these guidelines accordingly.

You may wonder what we mean by an "average" candidate. We are referring to a candidate who is just finishing or has just finished her/his academic training, attended a school that has a solid accounting curriculum, and received above average grades in accounting and business law courses. (An "average" candidate's native language is English.) Remember, "average" is a benchmark. Many candidates are not "average," so adjust your training plan accordingly.

Time Availability

	MON	TUES	WED	THURS	FRI	SAT	SUN
1:00 AM							
2:00 AM							
3:00 AM							
4:00 AM							
5:00 AM							
6:00 AM							
7:00 AM							
8:00 AM							
9:00 AM							
10:00 AM							
11:00 AM							
12:00 PM							
1:00 PM							
2:00 PM							
3:00 PM							
4:00 PM							
5:00 PM							
6:00 PM							
7:00 PM							
8:00 PM							
9:00 PM							
10:00 PM							
11:00 PM							
12:00 AM							

How to Find 20 Hours a Week to Study

The typical CPA candidate is a very busy individual. He or she goes to school and/or works full or part time. Some candidates have additional responsibilities such as a spouse, children, a house to take care of—the list can go on and on. Consequently, your first reaction may be, "I don't have 20 hours a week to devote to training for the CPA exam." Using the chart on the previous page, we will show you how to "find" the time that you need to develop your training schedule.

1. Keeping in mind what you would consider to be a typical week, first mark out in black the time that you know you won't be able to study. For example, mark an "X" in each block which represents time that you normally sleep, have a class, work, or have some other type of commitment. Be realistic.

2. Next, in a different color, put a "C" in each block that represents commute time, an "M" in each block that represents when you normally eat, and an "E" in each block that represents when you exercise.

3. Now pick one hour each day to relax and give your mind a break. Write "BREAK" in one block for each day. Do not skip this step. By taking a break, you will study more efficiently and effectively.

4. In a third color, write "STUDY" in the remaining blocks. Count the "STUDY" blocks. Are there 20? If not, count your "C", "M", and "E" blocks; if needed, these blocks of time can be used to gain additional study time by using Bisk Education CPA Review audio lectures and video programs. For example, our audio tutor is ideal for candidates on the go, you can listen to lectures whenever you're in the car or exercising and gain valuable study time each week.

5. If you still do not have 20 "STUDY" blocks, and you scored 70% or more on your diagnostic exams, you may still be able to pass the exam even with your limited study time. If, however, you scored less than 70% on your diagnostic exams, you have several options: (1) re-prioritize and make a block that has an "X" in it available study time; (2) concentrate on fewer exam sections; or (3) study more weeks but fewer hours per week.

How to Allocate Your 20 Weeks

Develop your overall training plan. We outline a sample training plan based on 20 hours per week and 20 weeks of study for all four sections. The time allocated to each topic was based on the length of the chapter, the difficulty of the material, and how heavily the topic is tested on the exam (refer to the exam specifications and our frequency analysis found in the **Practical Advice** section of your book). Keep in mind that this plan is for the "average" CPA candidate. You should **customize one of these plans** based on the results of your diagnostic exams and level of knowledge in each area tested. Given the AICPA examiner's stated intent to make the BEC exam section integrative, the editors recommend that candidates review for the BEC section after, or concurrently with, other exam sections. **Warning:** When studying, be careful not to fall into the trap of spending too much time on an area that rarely is tested. Note: There are Hot•Spot™ videos and audio lectures corresponding to each chapter for more in-depth study. Call 1-888-CPA-BISK.

Sample Training Plan (all 4 sections)*

		Hours
Week 1:	Read **Getting Started** and **Practical Advice** sections	1
	Take Diagnostic Exams under exam conditions (see page F-19)	10
	Read **Writing Skills** section and get organized	1
	Chapter 1—Overview	2
	Chapter 2—Cash, Marketable Securities & Receivables	6

* Candidates should make modifications to this plan to suit their individual circumstances. For instance, this plan repeats Chapter 18. Candidates may not need to return to Chapter 18, particularly those who took a governmental accounting course. Training plans for candidates sitting for one or two sections start on page F-13. The online classes incorporate different training plans within the weekly assignments posted on the online class web site. These different plans take advantage of the additional material provided online.

	Hours
Week 11: Weekly review of weeks 1 - 10	1
Chapter 18—Governmental Overview	3
Chapter 19—Governmental Funds & Transactions	9
Chapter 32—Accountant's Professional Responsibilities	3
Chapter 33—Accountant's Legal Responsibilities	4
Week 12: Weekly review of weeks 1 - 11	1
Chapter 18—Governmental Overview (after Chapter 19)	3
Chapter 20—Nonprofit Accounting	6
Chapter 34—Contracts	8
Chapter 35—Sales	2
Week 13: Weekly review of weeks 1 - 12	1
Chapter 35—Sales	4
Chapter 36—Negotiable Instruments & Documents of Title	5
Chapter 37—Secured Transactions	2
Chapter 50—Economic Theory	8
Week 14: Weekly review of weeks 1 - 13	1
Chapter 38—Debtor & Creditor Relationships	7
Chapter 42—Property	1
Chapter 51—Financial Management	11
Week 15: Weekly review of weeks 1 - 14	1
Chapter 41—Other Regulations	2
Chapter 42—Property	4
Chapter 51—Financial Management	2
Chapter 52—Decision Making	4
Chapter 53—Cost Accounting	7
Week 16: Weekly review of weeks 1 - 15	1+
Chapter 39—Agency	2
Chapter 43—Federal Taxation: Property & Other Topics	5
Chapter 44—Federal Taxation: Individuals	4
Chapter 52—Decision Making	2
Chapter 54—Planning & Control	6
Week 17: Weekly review of weeks 1 - 16	1+
Chapter 44—Federal Taxation: Individuals	6
Chapter 46—Federal Taxation: Corporations	7
Chapter 49—Corporations	6
Week 18: Weekly review of weeks 1 - 17	1
Chapter 45—Federal Taxation: Estates & Trusts	6
Chapter 46—Federal Taxation: Corporations	3
Chapter 47—Federal Taxation: Partnerships	5
Chapter 48—Partnerships	5
Week 19: Review areas in which you still feel weak	10+
Chapter 40—Federal Securities Regulation	3
Chapter 55—Information Technology	7
Week 20: Take Practice Exams under exam conditions (see page A-1)	10
Do final reviews	10+

Your Personalized Training Plan:

WEEK	TASK	DIAGNOSTIC SCORE	EST. HOURS	DATE COMPLETE	Chapter SCORE	FINAL SCORE
1						
2						
3						
4						
5						
6						
7						
8						
9						

WEEK	TASK	DIAGNOSTIC SCORE	EST. HOURS	DATE COMPLETE	Chapter SCORE	FINAL SCORE
10						
11						
12						
13						
14						
15						
16						
17						

WEEK	TASK	DIAGNOSTIC SCORE	EST. HOURS	DATE COMPLETE	Chapter SCORE	FINAL SCORE
18						
19						
20						

Step Four: Read the Rest of the Practical Advice Section

In Section Two of the **Practical Advice** section of the book, we discuss examination strategies. Section Three will familiarize you with how the CPA examination is graded and tell you how you can earn extra points on the exam simply by knowing what the grader is going to seek. In addition, in Section Four we explain our Solutions Approach™, an approach that will help you maximize your grade. In Section Five, we provide information on the AICPA exam content specifications and point distribution.

Step Five: Integrate Your Review Materials

In this step, we demonstrate how to integrate the Bisk Education CPA Review products to optimize the effectiveness of your training plan. Find and read the section that corresponds to the package that you purchased. (To facilitate easy reference to your package guidance, you may want to strike through the sections corresponding to other packages.)

Videos

The video programs are designed to supplement all of the study packages. Note how we recommend using the audio lectures in the following review plans. These recommendations also apply to the video programs. FYI: The videos have similar content as the online video lectures, but they are not exactly the same. Each of the Hot•Spot™ video programs concentrates on a few topics. Use them to help you study the areas that are most troubling for you. Each of the Intensive video programs is designed for a final, intensive review, after a candidate has already done considerable work. If time permits, use the Intensive programs at both the very beginning (for an overview) and set them aside until the final review two weeks before your exam. They contain concise, informative lectures, as well as CPA exam tips, tricks, and techniques that will help you to learn the material needed to pass the exam.

Online Package: Books, Video Lectures & CPA Review Software for Windows™

This is our most comprehensive review package. This combination provides the personal advice, discipline, and camaraderie of a classroom setting with the convenience of self-study. It is intended for those candidates who want to make sure that they pass the exam the **first** time. By using this package, you are eligible to qualify for Bisk Education's money-back guarantee. Contact a customer representative for details on the components of this package. Contact your online faculty advisor if you have questions about integrating your materials after viewing the web site guidance. (The editors strongly recommend that candidates working full-time take a maximum of 2 sections concurrently.)

Books, Audio Tutor & CPA Review Software for Windows™

This is our most comprehensive self-study review package. This combination is designed expressly for the serious CPA candidate. It is intended for those candidates who want to make sure that they pass the exam the **first** time (or *this* time, if you have already taken the exam). In addition, by using this package, you are eligible to qualify for Bisk Education's money-back guarantee.

How to Use This Package:

1. First take the diagnostic exams using CPA Review Software for Windows™. CPA Review Software for Windows™ automatically scores your exams and tells you what your strong and weak areas are. Then view the short tutorial to learn how to use the software features to their fullest.

In chapters where you are strong (i.e., you scored 65% or better on the diagnostic exam):

2. Answer the multiple choice questions using CPA Review Software for Windows™.

3. Read the subsections of the chapter that correspond to your weak areas.

4. Listen to the audio tutor for topics covered in this chapter to reinforce your weak areas and review your strong areas.

5. Now, using CPA Review Software for Windows™, answer the multiple choice questions that you previously answered incorrectly. If you answer 70% or more of the questions correctly, you are ready to move to the next chapter. If you answer less than 70% of the questions correctly, handle this chapter as if you scored less than 65% on the diagnostic exam.

6. Answer at least one simulation (if there are any) and review essay questions and solutions in any other simulations.

In chapters where you are weak (i.e., you scored less than 65% on the diagnostic exam):

2. Read the chapter in the book.

3. Listen to the audio lectures on topics covered in the chapter.

4. Re-read the subsections of the chapter that correspond to your weak subtopics.

5. Using CPA Review Software for Windows™, answer the multiple choice questions for this chapter. If you answer 70% or more of the questions correctly, you are ready to move on to the next chapter. If you get less than 70% of the questions correct, review the subtopics where you are weak. Then answer the questions that you previously answered incorrectly. If you still do not get at least 70% correct, check the exam specifications in the Practical Advice section to find out how heavily the area is tested. If this is an area that is heavily tested, continue reviewing the material and answering multiple choice questions until you can answer at least 70% correctly. Allocate more time than you originally budgeted, if necessary. If this is not a heavily tested area, move on, but make a note to come back to this area later as time allows.

6. Answer at least one simulation (if there are any) and review essay questions and solutions in any other simulations.

Books & CPA Review Software for Windows™

This combination allows you to use the books to review the material and CPA Review Software for Windows™ to practice exam questions. You can also use the books to practice exam questions when you do not have access to a computer. In addition, by using this package, you are eligible to qualify for Bisk Education's money-back guarantee.

How to Use This Package:

1. Take the diagnostic exams using CPA Review Software for Windows™. CPA Review Software for Windows automatically scores your exams and tells you what your strong and weak areas are. Then view the short tutorial to learn how to use the software features to their fullest.

In chapters where you are strong (i.e., you scored 65% or better on the diagnostic exam):

2. Answer the multiple choice questions using CPA Review Software for Windows™.

3. Read the subsections of the chapter that correspond to your weak areas.

4. Now using CPA Review Software for Windows™, answer the multiple choice questions that you previously answered incorrectly. If you answer 70% or more of the questions correctly, you are ready to move on to the next chapter. If you answer less than 70% of the questions correctly, handle this chapter as if you scored less than 65% on the diagnostic exam.

5. Answer at least one simulation (if there are any) and review essay questions and solutions in any other simulations.

In chapters where you are weak (i.e., you scored less than 65% on the diagnostic exam):

2. Read the chapter in the book.

3. Using CPA Review Software for Windows™, answer the multiple choice questions for this chapter. If you answer 70% or more of the questions correctly, you are ready to move on to the next chapter. If you get less than 70% of the questions correct, review the subtopics where you are weak. Then answer the questions that you previously answered incorrectly. If you still do not get at least 70% correct, check the exam specifications in the Practical Advice section to find out how heavily the area is tested. If this is an area that is heavily tested, continue reviewing the material and answering multiple choice questions until you can answer at least 70% correctly. Allocate more time than you originally budgeted, if necessary. If this is not a heavily tested area, move on, but make a note to come back to this area later as time allows.

4. Answer at least one simulation (if there are any) and review essay questions and solutions in any other simulations.

Books & Audio Tutor

This combination is designed for the candidate who has a strong preference for hard copy, who spends time commuting or doing other activities that could take valuable time away from studying, and for those who like to reinforce what they read by listening to a lecture.

How to Use This Package:

1. Take the diagnostic exams found in your book. Using the worksheets provided, score your exams to determine your strong and weak areas.

In chapters where you are strong (i.e., you scored 65% or better on the diagnostic exam):

2. Do the multiple choice questions for that chapter. Using the worksheet provided, analyze your strong and weak areas.

3. Read the subsections of the chapter that correspond to your weak subtopics.

4. At this point, listen to the audio tutor on topics covered in this chapter to reinforce weak areas and review strong areas.

5. Answer the multiple choice questions that you previously answered incorrectly. If you answer 70% or more of the questions correctly, you are ready to move on to the next chapter. If you answer less than 70% of the questions correctly, handle this chapter as if you scored 65% or less on the diagnostic exam.

6. Answer at least one simulation (if there are any) and review essay questions and solutions in any other simulations.

In chapters where you are weak (i.e., you scored less than 65% on the diagnostic exam):

2. First read the chapter in the book.

3. Now listen to the audio lectures covering topics in this chapter.

4. Re-read the subsections of the chapter that correspond to your weak subtopics.

5. Do the multiple choice questions and score yourself using the worksheet provided. If you answer 70% or more of the questions correctly, you are ready to move on to the next chapter. If you answer less than 70% of the questions correctly, review the subtopics that are still giving you trouble. Then answer the questions that you previously answered incorrectly. If you still do not get at least 70% of the questions correct, check the exam specifications in the Practical Advice section to find out how heavily this area is tested. If this is an area that is heavily tested, continue reviewing the material and answering questions until you can answer at least 70% of them correctly. Allocate more time than you originally budgeted, if necessary. If this area is not heavily tested, move on, but make a note to come back to this topic later as time allows.

6. Answer at least one simulation (if there are any) and review essay questions and solutions in any other simulations.

Step Six: Use These Helpful Hints as You Study

♦ MAKE FLASHCARDS OR TAKE NOTES AS YOU STUDY

Make flashcards for topics that are heavily tested on the exam or that are giving you trouble. By making your own flashcards, you learn during their creation and you can tailor them to your individual learning style and problem areas. You will find these very useful for weekly reviews and your final review. Replace flashcards of information you know with new material as you progress through your study plan. Keep them handy and review them when you are waiting in line or on hold. This will turn nonproductive time into valuable study time. Review your complete set during the last two weeks before the exam.

Make notes and/or highlight when you read the chapters in the book. When possible, make notes when you listen to the lectures. You will find these very useful for weekly reviews and your final review.

♦ DO NOT MARK THE OBJECTIVE QUESTION ANSWERS IN THE BOOK.

Do not circle the answer to objective questions in the book. You should work every multiple-choice question at least twice and you do not want to influence later answers by knowing how you previously answered.

Date your answer sheets to facilitate tracking your progress.

♦ SPEND YOUR WEEKLY REVIEW TIME EFFECTIVELY. DURING EACH WEEKLY REVIEW:

Answer the objective questions that you previously answered incorrectly or merely guessed correctly.

Go through your flashcards or notes.

Pick at least one simulation to work. Even if you are studying BEC and are sure that simulations will not appear on your exam, the practice that you gain will be useful. (Do not wait until the end of your review to attempt a simulation with an essay question.) Read the essay questions and solutions for this week's topics that you do not answer this week.

♦ MARK THE OBJECTIVE QUESTIONS THAT YOU ANSWER INCORRECTLY OR MERELY GUESS CORRECTLY.

This way you know to answer this question again at a later time.

♦ EFFECTIVELY USE THE VIDEO PROGRAMS

Watch the video lectures in an environment without distractions. Be prepared to take notes and answer questions just as if you were attending a live class. Frequently, the instructors will have you stop the program to work a question on your own. This means a 2-hour program may take 2½ hours or more to view.

♦ EFFECTIVELY USE THE AUDIO TUTOR

Use Audio Tutor to turn nonproductive time into valuable study time. For example, play the lectures when you are commuting, exercising, getting ready for school or work, doing laundry, etc. Audio Tutor will help you to memorize and retain key concepts. It also will reinforce what you have read in the books. Get in the habit of listening to the lectures whenever you have a chance. The more times that you listen to each lecture, the more familiar you will become with the material and the easier it will be for you to recall it during the exam.

Step Seven: Implement Your Training Plan

This is it! You are primed and ready. You have decided which training tools will work best for you and you know how to use them. As you implement your personalized training plan, keep yourself focused. Your goal is to obtain a grade of 75 or better on each section and, thus, pass the CPA exam. Therefore, you should concentrate on learning new material and reviewing old material only to the extent that it helps you reach this goal. Also, keep in mind that now is not the time to hone your procrastination skills. Utilize the personalized training plan that you developed in step three so that you do not fall behind schedule. Adjust it when necessary if you need more time in one chapter or less time in another. Refer to the AICPA content specifications to make sure that the adjustment is warranted. Above all else, remember that passing the exam is an **attainable** goal. Good luck!

Supplement to Step Three: Alternative Sample Training Plans

The editors strongly recommend that candidates develop personalized training plans. Several training plans are outlined for candidates to modify. The time allocated to each topic was based on the length of the chapter, the difficulty of the material for most candidates, and how heavily the topic is tested on the exam (refer to the exam specifications found in the **Practical Advice** section). You should **customize one of these plans** based on the results of your diagnostic exams and level of knowledge in each area tested.

BEC Sample Training Plan (1 exam section)

		Hours
Week 1:	Read **Getting Started** and **Practical Advice** sections (if not yet done)	1
	Take Diagnostic Exam under exam conditions (see page F-19)	3
	Read **Writing Skills** section and get organized (if not yet done)*	1
	Chapter 48—Partnerships	5
	Chapter 49—Corporations	6
	Chapter 50—Economic Theory	4
Week 2:	Chapter 50—Economic Theory	4
	Chapter 51—Financial Management	13
	Chapter 52—Decision Making	3
Week 3:	Weekly review of weeks 1 - 2	1
	Chapter 52—Decision Making	3
	Chapter 53—Cost Accounting	7
	Chapter 54—Planning & Control	6
	Chapter 55—Information Technology	3
Week 4:	Review areas in which you still feel weak	8+
	Chapter 55—Information Technology	4
	Take Practice Exam under exam conditions (see page A-1)	3
	Do final reviews and check for updating supplement	5+

* Note the BEC exam section initially will not have simulations. The AICPA plans to have BEC simulations at a future undisclosed date. This date likely will be no earlier than 2007. Bisk Education's updating supplements will notify candidates when simulations will be on the BEC exam section. If you are sure that your BEC exam will not include simulations, you need not read the Writing Skills appendix of this volume.

Regardless of whether your BEC exam will have simulations, the editors recommend that you at least answer the objective portions of simulations and read the answers to the written communication portions of simulations. These activities reinforce your mastery and provide another perspective of the content.

UPDATING SUPPLEMENTS

Bisk Education's updating supplements are small publications available from either customer representatives or our CPA review website (http://www.cpaexam.com/content/support.asp). The editors recommend checking the website for new supplements a month and again a week before your exam. Version 35 (and higher) updating supplements are appropriate for candidates with the 35th edition. Information from earlier supplements (for instance, Version 34.2) are incorporated into this edition. Supplements are issued no more frequently than every three months. Supplements are not necessarily issued every three months; supplements are issued only as information appropriate for supplements becomes available.

FAR & BEC Sample Training Plan (2 exam sections)

	Hours		Hours
Week 1:		**Week 7:**	
Read **Getting Started** and **Practical Advice** sections (if not yet done)	1	Weekly review of weeks 1 - 6	1
Take Diagnostic Exams under exam conditions (see page F-19)	5	Chapter 13—Accounting for Income Taxes	4
Read **Writing Skills** section and get organized (if not yet done)	1	Chapter 14—Statement of Cash Flows	6
Chapter 1—Overview	2	Chapter 15—Financial Statement Analysis	4
Chapter 2—Cash, Marketable Securities & Receivables	10	Chapter 52—Decision Making	5
Chapter 3—Inventory	1	**Week 8:**	
		Weekly review of weeks 1 - 7	1+
Week 2:		Chapter 16—Foreign Operations	3
		Chapter 17—Consolidated Financial Statements	8
Chapter 3—Inventory	4	Chapter 52—Decision Making	1
Chapter 4—Property, Plant & Equipment	6	Chapter 53—Cost Accounting	1
Chapter 5—Intangible Assets, R&D Costs & Other Assets	4	Chapter 54—Planning & Control	6
Chapter 6—Bonds	6	**Week 9:**	
		Weekly review of weeks 1 - 8	1+
Week 3:		Chapter 18—Governmental Overview	3
		Chapter 19—Governmental Funds & Transactions	9
Weekly review of weeks 1 - 2	1	Chapter 20—Nonprofit Accounting	1
Chapter 7—Liabilities	6	Chapter 53—Cost Accounting	6
Chapter 8—Leases	5		
Chapter 50—Economic Theory	8	**Week 10:**	
		Weekly review of weeks 1 - 9	5+
Week 4:		Chapter 18—Governmental Overview (after Chapter 19)	3
		Chapter 20—Nonprofit Accounting	5
Weekly review of weeks 1 - 3	1	Chapter 55—Information Technology	7
Chapter 9—Postemployment Benefits	5		
Chapter 10—Owners' Equity	3	**Week 11:**	
Chapter 48—Partnerships	5		
Chapter 49—Corporations	6	Review areas in which you still feel weak	10+
		Take Practice Exams under exam conditions (see page A-1)	5
Week 5:		Do final reviews	5+
Weekly review of weeks 1 - 4	1		
Chapter 10—Owners' Equity	5		
Chapter 11—Reporting the Results of Operations	1		
Chapter 51—Financial Management	13		
Week 6:			
Weekly review of weeks 1 - 5	1		
Chapter 11—Reporting the Results of Operations	11		
Chapter 12—Reporting: Special Areas	6		
Chapter 13—Accounting for Income Taxes	2		

AUD & BEC Sample Training Plan (2 exam sections)

Week 1	Hours
Read **Getting Started** and **Practical Advice** sections	1
Take Diagnostic Exams under exam conditions (see page F-19)	3
Read **Writing Skills** section and get organized	1
Chapter 21—Standards & Related Topics	4
Chapter 22—Planning	7
Chapter 23—Internal Control: General	4

Week 2:	
Chapter 23—Internal Control: General	3
Chapter 24—Internal Control: Transaction Cycles	8
Chapter 25—Evidence & Procedures	9

Week 3:	
Weekly review of weeks 1 - 2	1
Chapter 25—Evidence & Procedures	1
Chapter 26—Audit Programs	7
Chapter 27—Audit Sampling	7
Chapter 54—Planning & Control	4

Week 4:	
Weekly review of weeks 1 - 3	1
Chapter 28—Auditing IT Systems	6
Chapter 48—Partnerships	4
Chapter 54—Planning & Control	2
Chapter 55—Information Technology	7

Week 5:	Hours
Weekly review of weeks 1 - 4	1
Chapter 48—Partnerships	1
Chapter 49—Corporations	6
Chapter 50—Economic Theory	8
Chapter 51—Financial Management	4

Week 6:	
Weekly review of weeks 1 - 5	1+
Chapter 51—Financial Management	9
Chapter 52—Decision Making	6
Chapter 53—Cost Accounting	4

Week 7:	
Weekly review of weeks 1 - 6	1+
Chapter 29—Reports on Audited Financial Statements	12
Chapter 30—Other Types of Reports	3
Chapter 31—Other Professional Services	1
Chapter 53—Cost Accounting	3

Week 8:	
Review areas in which you still feel weak	5+
Chapter 31—Other Professional Services	6
Take Practice Exams under exam conditions (see page A-1)	5
Do final reviews	4+

REG & BEC Sample Training Plan (2 exam sections)

	Hours
Week 1:	
Read **Getting Started** and **Practical Advice** sections (if not yet done)	1
Take Diagnostic Exams under exam conditions (see page F-19)	5
Read **Writing Skills** section and get organized (if not yet done)	1
Chapter 32—Accountant's Professional Responsibilities	3
Chapter 33—Accountant's Legal Responsibilities	4
Chapter 34—Contracts	6
Week 2:	
Chapter 34—Contracts	2
Chapter 35—Sales	6
Chapter 36—Negotiable Instruments & Documents of Title	5
Chapter 37—Secured Transactions	2
Chapter 50—Economic Theory	5
Week 3:	
Weekly review of weeks 1 - 2	1
Chapter 38—Debtor & Creditor Relationships	7
Chapter 39—Agency	2
Chapter 50—Economic Theory	3
Chapter 51—Financial Management	7
Week 4:	
Weekly review of weeks 1 - 3	1
Chapter 41—Other Regulations	2
Chapter 42—Property	5
Chapter 43—Federal Taxation: Property & Other Topics	5
Chapter 51—Financial Management	6
Chapter 52—Decision Making	1

	Hours
Week 5:	
Weekly review of weeks 1 - 4	1
Chapter 44—Federal Taxation: Individuals	10
Chapter 45—Federal Taxation: Estates & Trusts	4
Chapter 52—Decision Making	5
Week 6:	
Weekly review of weeks 1 - 5	1
Chapter 45—Federal Taxation: Estates & Trusts	2
Chapter 46—Federal Taxation: Corporations	4
Chapter 47—Federal Taxation: Partnerships	2
Chapter 48—Partnerships	5
Chapter 49—Corporations	6
Week 7:	
Weekly review of weeks 1 - 6	1
Chapter 40—Federal Securities Regulation	3
Chapter 46—Federal Taxation: Corporations	6
Chapter 47—Federal Taxation: Partnerships	3
Chapter 53—Cost Accounting	7
Week 8:	
Review areas in which you still feel weak	7+
Chapter 54—Planning & Control	6
Chapter 55—Information Technology	7
Week 9:	
Take Practice Exams under exam conditions (see page A-1)	5
Do final reviews	15+

Exam Scheduling Strategies

Most candidates likely will split the exam between two or more windows. Sitting for all four exam sections during one exam window is preferable for candidates who want to pass the exam quickly or who travel far to take the exam.

Sitting for one exam section during one exam window is the best means of ensuring a passing score; however it does take a long time. Further, the synergy resulting from studying more than one exam section at a time is lost. The following are number of weeks from the Bisk Education one-exam-section-at-a-time study plans.

Financial Accounting & Reporting	8	Regulation	6
Auditing & Attestation	5	Business Environment & Concepts	4

Sitting for two exam sections during one exam window halves the number of exam windows and takes advantage of the synergy resulting from studying more than one exam section at a time. By scheduling one exam toward the beginning of a window and the second toward the end of a window, several weeks may separate the two exam sections.

You may want to sit for only one exam section during your first exam window to get some idea of the preparation involved for your circumstances. Bear in mind, these study plans are rigorous schedules that assume the candidate in question recently has come from a school in the United States with a strong accounting program, etc. Once you have the experience of one exam section behind you, sitting for two or even three exam sections in the next window will be facilitated by the study habits that you have developed.

The BEC exam section is designed by the examiners as an integrative section. Candidates must know the topics tested mainly in the other exam sections to answer some BEC questions with confidence. The editors generally recommend taking the BEC section after, or concurrently with, the other exam sections.

Registration Process

To sit for the exam, candidates apply to the appropriate board of accountancy. Some state boards contract with NASBA's service to handle candidate applications. Once a state board or its agent determines that a candidate is eligible to sit for the exam, the board informs NASBA of candidate eligibility and NASBA adds the candidate to its database. With a national database, NASBA is able to ensure that no candidate can sit for the same exam section more than once during a single exam window. Within 24 hours, NASBA sends Prometric a notice to schedule (NTS). At that point, a candidate can schedule a date and time to sit for the exam with Prometric.

Candidates to whom taking the exam on a particular day is important should plan to schedule their exam dates 45 days in advance. Upon receipt of the NTS, candidates have a limited amount of time to sit for the specified exam sections; this time is set by states. The exam is called on-demand because candidates may sit at anytime for any available date in the open window.

If any medical conditions exist that need to be considered during the exam, candidates should supply information about that situation when scheduling. Ordinarily, candidates may not bring anything into the exam room—including prescription medications.

Make sure that the name you use for your registration exactly matches the name on the **two** forms of identification that you will use on your examination day. Acceptable forms of identification are outlined in the AICPA's publication, *Candidate Bulletin: Information for Applicants,* available from the AICPA's exam website, www.cpa-exam.org. Contact the appropriate board of accountancy if you have any questions on what forms of identification that the examiners will accept.

DIAGNOSTIC EXAMINATION

Editor's Note: There is only one practice (or final) examination. If you mark answers for the diagnostic exam on a separate sheet of paper, these questions can be used as a second "final" exam at the end of your review.

Problem 1 MULTIPLE CHOICE QUESTIONS (120 to 150 minutes)

1. In a general partnership, which of the following acts must be approved by all the partners?
a. Dissolution of the partnership
b. Admission of a partner
c. Authorization of a partnership capital expenditure
d. Conveyance of real property owned by the partnership (7043)

2. Which of the following statements is correct regarding the division of profits in a general partnership when the written partnership agreement only provides that losses be divided equally among the partners? Profits are to be divided
a. Based on the partners' ratio of contribution to the partnership
b. Based on the partners' participation in day to day management
c. Equally among the partners
d. Proportionately among the partners (5887)

3. When a partner in a general partnership lacks actual or apparent authority to contract on behalf of the partnership, and the party contracted with is aware of this fact, the partnership will be bound by the contract if the other partners

	Ratify the contract	Amend the partnership agreement
a.	Yes	Yes
b.	Yes	No
c.	No	Yes
d.	No	No (6856)

4. Which of the following statements is correct with respect to a limited partnership?
a. A limited partner may **not** be an unsecured creditor of the limited partnership.
b. A general partner may **not** also be a limited partner at the same time.
c. A general partner may be a secured creditor of the limited partnership.
d. A limited partnership can be formed with limited liability for all partners. (2824)

5. Generally, under the Revised Uniform Partnership Act, a partnership has which of the following characteristics?

	Unlimited duration	Obligation for payment of federal income tax
a.	Yes	Yes
b.	Yes	No
c.	No	Yes
d.	No	No (5885)

6. On dissolution of a general partnership, distributions will be made on account of:

I. Partners' capital accounts
II. Amounts owed partners with respect to profits
III. Amounts owed partners for loans to the partnership

in the following order:
a. III, I, II
b. I, II, III
c. II, III, I
d. III, II, I (2345)

7. Furl Corp., a corporation organized under the laws of State X, sued Row, a customer residing in State Y, for nonpayment for goods sold. Row attempted to dismiss a suit brought by Furl in State Y, on the grounds that Furl was conducting business in State Y but had not obtained a certificate of authority from State Y to transact business therein. Which of the following actions by Furl would generally result in the court ruling that Furl was conducting business in State Y?
a. Maintaining bank accounts in State Y
b. Shipping goods across state lines into State Y
c. Owning and operating a small manufacturing plant in State Y
d. Holding board of directors meetings in State Y (7685)

8. Price owns 2,000 shares of Universal Corp.'s $10 cumulative preferred stock. During its first year of operations, cash dividends of $5 per share were declared on the preferred stock but were never paid. In the second year, dividends on the preferred stock were neither declared nor paid. If Universal is dissolved, which of the following statements is correct?
a. Universal will be liable to Price as an unsecured creditor for $10,000.
b. Universal will be liable to Price as a secured creditor for $20,000.
c. Price will have priority over the claims of Universal's bond owners.
d. Price will have priority over the claims of Universal's unsecured judgment creditors. (7134)

9. Acorn Corp. wants to acquire the entire business of Trend Corp. Which of the following methods of business combination will best satisfy Acorn's objectives without requiring the approval of the shareholders of either corporation?
a. A merger of Trend into Acorn, whereby Trend shareholders receive cash or Acorn shares
b. A sale of all the assets of Trend, outside the regular course of business, to Acorn, for cash
c. An acquisition of all the shares of Trend through a compulsory share exchange for Acorn shares
d. A cash tender offer, whereby Acorn acquires at least 90% of Trend's shares, followed by a short-form merger of Trend into Acorn (7046)

10. Under the Revised Model Business Corporation Act, which of the following statements is correct regarding corporate officers of a public corporation?
a. An officer may **not** simultaneously serve as a director.
b. A corporation may be authorized to indemnify its officers for liability incurred in a suit by stockholders.
c. Stockholders always have the right to elect a corporation's officers.
d. An officer of a corporation is required to own at least one share of the corporation's stock. (4767)

11. Which of the following rights is a holder of a public corporation's cumulative preferred stock always entitled to?
a. Conversion of the preferred stock into common stock
b. Voting rights
c. Dividend carryovers from years in which dividends were **not** paid, to future years
d. Guaranteed dividends (4768)

12. Which of the following statements is a general requirement for the merger of two corporations?
a. The merger plan must be approved unanimously by the stockholders of both corporations.
b. The merger plan must be approved unanimously by the boards of both corporations.
c. The absorbed corporation must amend its articles of incorporation.
d. The stockholders of both corporations must be given due notice of a special meeting, including a copy or summary of the merger plan. (5894)

13. The following information pertains to countries Cleo and Elin.

Disposable Income Level	Cleo Consumption	Elin Consumption
$52,000	$40,000	$39,000
$28,000	$24,000	$27,000

What is Cleo's marginal propensity to save?
a. 0.14
b. 0.23
c. 0.33
d. 1.30
e. 1.50 (7180)

14. Carlton Bank has an increase in reserves of $1,000,000. If the reserve ratio is 10%, by what amount can Carlton increase its demand deposits?
a. $ 100,000
b. $ 900,000
c. $ 1,000,000
d. $10,000,000 (7184)

15. Tea and sugar cubes are complementary goods. Tea and coffee are substitute goods. What effect does a decrease in the price of tea have?
a. Increase the price of coffee
b. Shift the supply curve for sugar cubes to the left
c. Shift the demand curve for sugar cubes to the left
d. Shift the demand curve for sugar cubes to the right (7202)

16. What is an example of a monopolistic competitive market?
a. Lawn care service industry
b. Pharmaceutical industry
c. Restaurant industry
d. Wheat market (7226)

17. A single U.S. dollar is quoted at 1.32 British pounds on the spot market and 1.353 pounds on the 60-day forward market. What is the approximate annual effect of the forward market?
a. The U.S. dollar is at a discount of 15%.
b. The U.S. dollar is at a discount of 2.5%.
c. The U.S. dollar is at a premium of 2.5%.
d. The U.S. dollar is at a premium of 15%. (7250)

18. Which of the following would **not** contribute to a high currency value?
a. Relatively high real interest rates
b. Relatively high demand for foreign goods
c. Relatively low inflation
d. Relatively stable government (7259)

19. Tremor Company has a stock price of $40, an estimated dividend at the end of the year of $2, and an expected growth rate of 10%. What is the approximate estimated cost of equity capital using the dividend growth model?
a. 15%
b. 12%
c. 10%
d. 5% (7276)

20. What is called a spontaneous financing source?
a. Chattel mortgage
b. Debentures
c. Notes payable
d. Preferred stock
e. Trade credit (7348)

21. Hardy Company must maintain a compensating balance of $50,000 in its checking account as one of the conditions of its short-term 6% bank loan of $500,000. Hardy's checking account earns 2% interest. Ordinarily, Hardy would maintain a $20,000 balance in the account for transaction purposes. What is the loan's approximate effective interest rate?
a. 5.88%
b. 6.00%
c. 6.17%
d. 6.25%
e. 6.38% (7353)

22. What is characteristic of income bonds?
a. Pay interest only if the issuer has earned it
b. Junior to subordinated debt in the event of liquidation
c. Junior to preferred and common stock in the event of liquidation
d. Guaranteed income over the security life (7326)

23. Egret Company expects next year's net income to be $2 million. Egret's current capital structure is 30% debt, 30% preferred equity, and 40% common equity. Next year, Egret's plans to issue debt and common stock as needed to maintain their 30:40 ratio, not to issue more preferred stock. Interest payments on Egret's 10,000 4%, $1,000 par value bonds are current. Egret can issue up to $1 million more 4% bonds at face value. Egret's marginal tax rate is 30%. There are no dividends in arrears on Egret's 10,000 shares of 6%, $1,000 par value cumulative preferred stock. Optimal capital spending for next year is estimated at $1.4 million. Using a strict residual dividend policy, what is the approximate estimated common stock dividend payout ratio for the next year?
a. 0%
b. 16%
c. 30%
d. 35%
e. 70% (7342)

24. For the next 2 years, a lease is estimated to have an operating net cash inflow of $7,500 per annum, before adjusting for $5,000 per annum tax basis lease amortization, and a 40% tax rate. The present value of an ordinary annuity of $1 per year at 10% for 2 years is $1.74. What is the lease's after-tax present value using a 10% discount factor?
a. $ 2,610
b. $ 4,350
c. $ 9,570
d. $11,310 (5785)

25. Which working capital policy has the greatest likelihood that a firm will be unable to meet obligations as they become due?
a. Financing all current assets with long-term debt
b. Financing all current assets with short-term debt
c. Financing fluctuating current assets with short-term debt and permanent current assets with equity
d. Financing fluctuating current assets with short-term debt and permanent current assets with long-term debt (7357)

26. Brooks Company has daily cash receipts of $400,000. Brooks' bank offers a lockbox service that will reduce collection time by two days for a $2,000 monthly fee. Brooks can earn 8% annually with any additional funds. What will be the annual increase to income before taxes from using the lockbox service?
a. $24,000
b. $32,000
c. $40,000
d. $64,000 (7361)

27. Stiffening Company is evaluating a proposed credit policy change. The proposed policy would change the average number of days for collection from 60 to 27 days and would reduce total sales by 25%, all of the decrease due to credit sales. Under the current policy, next year's sales are estimated at $128 million, with 75% of them being credit sales. Based on a 360-day year, what is the decrease in Stiffening's average accounts receivable balance of implementing the proposed credit policy change?
a. $16 million
b. $11.2 million
c. $10 million
d. $ 4.8 million   (7366)

28. Lin Co. is buying machinery it expects will increase average annual operating income by $40,000. The initial increase in the required invest-ment is $60,000, and the average increase in required investment is $30,000. To compute the accrual accounting rate of return, what amount should be used as the numerator in the ratio?
a. $20,000
b. $30,000
c. $40,000
d. $60,000   (3373)

29. Which of the following is not characteristic of venture capital?
a. Initial private placement
b. Lack of liquidity for some time period
c. Common stock issue
d. Minimum 5-year holding period   (7379)

30. Which of the following objectives is consistent with an optimal capital structure?
a. Maximum earnings per share
b. Minimum cost of debt
c. Minimum risk
d. Minimum weighted average cost of capital (7383)

31. Buff Co. is considering replacing an old machine with a new machine. Which of the follow-ing items is economically relevant to Buff's decision? (Ignore income tax considerations.)

	Carrying amount of old machine	Disposal value of new machine
a.	Yes	No
b.	No	Yes
c.	No	No
d.	Yes	Yes	(2749)

32. Mat Co. estimated its material handling costs at two activity levels as follows:

Kilos handled	Cost
80,000	$160,000
60,000	132,000

What is the estimated cost for handling 75,000 kilos?
a. $150,000
b. $153,000
c. $157,500
d. $165,000   (4641)

33. The following information is taken from Wampler Co.'s contribution income statement:

Sales	$200,000
Contribution margin	120,000
Fixed costs	90,000
Income taxes	12,000

What was Wampler's margin of safety?
a. $ 50,000
b. $150,000
c. $168,000
d. $182,000   (6645)

34. In an income statement prepared using the variable costing method, fixed factory overhead would
a. Not be used
b. Be treated the same as variable factory overhead
c. Be used in the computation of operating income but **not** in the computation of the contribution margin
d. Be used in the computation of the contribution margin   (2199)

35. A processing department produces joint prod-ucts Ajac and Bjac, each of which incurs separable production costs after split-off. Information concern-ing a batch produced at a $60,000 joint cost before split-off follows:

Product	Separable costs	Sales value
Ajac	$ 8,000	$ 80,000
Bjac	22,000	40,000
Total	$30,000	$120,000

What is the joint cost assigned to Ajac if costs are assigned using the relative net realizable value?
a. $16,000
b. $40,000
c. $48,000
d. $52,000   (6922)

36. In an activity-based costing system, what should be used to assign a department's manufacturing overhead costs to products produced in varying lot sizes?
a. A single cause and effect relationship
b. Multiple cause and effect relationships
c. Relative net sales values of the products
d. A product's ability to bear cost allocations (5462)

37. In developing a predetermined factory overhead application rate for use in a process costing system, which of the following could be used in the numerator and denominator?

	Numerator	Denominator
a.	Actual factory overhead	Actual machine hours
b.	Actual factory overhead	Estimated machine hours
c.	Estimated factory overhead	Actual machine hours
d.	Estimated factory overhead	Estimated machine hours

(2179)

38. Kerner Manufacturing uses a process cost system to manufacture laptop computers. The following information summarizes operations relating to laptop computer model #KJK20 during the quarter ending March 31:

	Units	Direct Materials
Work-in-process inventory, January 1	100	$ 70,000
Started during the quarter	500	
Completed during the quarter	400	
Work-in-process inventory, March 31	200	
Costs added during the quarter		$750,000

Beginning work-in-process inventory was 50% complete for direct materials. Ending work-in-process inventory was 75% complete for direct materials. Kerner uses a FIFO cost-flow assumption. What were the equivalent units of production with regard to materials for the quarter?
a. 450
b. 500
c. 550
d. 600

(6997)

39. Baby Frames, Inc., evaluates manufacturing overhead in its factory by using variance analysis. The following information applies to the month of May:

	Actual	Budgeted
Number of frames manufactured	19,000	20,000
Variable overhead costs	$4,100	$2 per direct labor hour
Fixed overhead costs	$22,000	$20,000
Direct labor hours	2,100 hours	0.1 hour per frame

What is the fixed overhead spending variance?
a. $1,000 favorable
b. $1,000 unfavorable
c. $2,000 favorable
d. $2,000 unfavorable

(6998)

40. The following is a summarized income statement of Carr Co.'s profit center No. 43 for March:

Contribution margin		$70,000
Manager's salary	$20,000	
Facility depreciation	8,000	
Corporate expense allocation	5,000	
Period expenses:		33,000
Profit center income		$37,000

Which of the following amounts would most likely be subject to the control of the profit center's manager?
a. $70,000
b. $50,000
c. $37,000
d. $33,000

(2683)

41. Under the balanced scorecard concept developed by Kaplan and Norton, employee satisfaction and retention are measures used under which of the following perspectives?
a. Customer
b. Internal business
c. Learning and growth
d. Financial

(7668)

42. Which of the following steps in the strategic planning process should be completed first?
a. Translate objectives into goals
b. Determine actions to achieve goals
c. Develop performance measures
d. Create a mission statement

(7675)

43. Strategic management has which of the following **two** characteristics?
a. Emphasis on accurate forecasts
b. Ideally includes a review of the entity's mission and objectives
c. Incorporates external information
d. Input primarily from top management, consultants, and employees dedicated to the planning function
e. Top-down planning (7410)

44. Much Co. has developed a regression equation to analyze the behavior of its maintenance costs (Q) as a function of machine hours (Z). The following equation was developed by using 30 monthly observations with a related coefficient of determination of .90: Q = $5,000 + $6.50Z. If 1,000 machine hours are worked in one month, the related point estimate of total maintenance costs would be
a. $11,500
b. $11,000
c. $ 6,500
d $ 5,850 (1531)

45. Bell Co. changed from a traditional manufacturing philosophy to a just-in-time philosophy. What are the expected effects of this change on Bell's inventory turnover and inventory as a percentage of total assets reported on Bell's balance sheet?

	Inventory turnover	Inventory percentage
a.	Decrease	Decrease
b.	Decrease	Increase
c.	Increase	Decrease
d.	Increase	Increase

(4655)

46. In computer processing, access time is the time that it takes
a. For data from a keyboard to reach memory
b. For data to be retrieved from memory
c. To perform a computer instruction
d. To transmit data from a remote computer to a central computer (7421)

47. Which of the following control procedures most likely could prevent IT personnel from modifying programs to bypass programmed controls?
a. Periodic management review of computer utilization reports and systems documentation
b. Segregation of duties within IT for computer programming and computer operations
c. Participation of user department personnel in designing and approving new systems
d. Physical security of IT facilities in limiting access to IT equipment (7555)

48. Which of the following is a pictorial illustration of a system's data flow and information processing, including hardware?
a. Data-flow diagram
b. Decision table
c. PERT chart
d. Program flowchart
e. System flowchart (7444)

49. Which of the following input controls is a numeric value computed to provide assurance that the original value has **not** been altered in construction or transmission?
a. Hash total
b. Parity check
c. Encryption
d. Check digit (7569)

50. What risk typically is **not** associated with outsourcing data processing?
a. Inflexibility
b. Lack of control
c. Lack of confidentiality
d. Reduction in expertise availability (7459)

51. A commonly used measure of the relative effectiveness of an online site functioning as retail store is the
a. Abandonment ratio
b. Portability ratio
c. Volatility ratio
d. Volume (7460)

52. Which of the following is a network node that is used to improve network traffic and to set up as a boundary that prevents traffic from one segment to cross over to another?
a. Router
b. Gateway
c. Firewall
d. Heuristic (6932)

53. What is the most common advantage of a compact disk (CD) over a hard disk in a personal computer system?
a. Greater access speed
b. Greater portability
c. Greater protection against surface contamination
d. Greater storage capacity (7467)

54. What stage of a system's life cycle involves hiring and training new employees and testing new procedures?
a. Analysis
b. Design
c. Implementation
d. Maintenance
e. Programming (7472)

55. What activity is **least** likely to occur during the analysis stage of system development?
a. Determine user information needs
b. Develop program specifications
c. Evaluate the current system
d. Identify problems in the current system
e. Identify system objectives   (7437)

56. What attribute is **least** descriptive of an executive information system?
a. Combines, integrates, and summarizes data from many sources
b. Designed to monitor business conditions and assist in strategic planning
c. Provides immediate and interactive access to information
d. Provides only highly aggregated information
                                                 (7435)

57. In building an electronic data interchange (EDI) system, what process is used to determine which elements in the entity's computer system correspond to the standard data elements?
a. Mapping
b. Translation
c. Encryption
d. Decoding   (7033)

58. Which of the following procedures would an entity most likely include in its disaster recovery plan?
a. Convert all data from EDI format to an internal company format
b. Maintain a Trojan horse program to prevent illicit activity
c. Develop an auxiliary power supply to provide uninterrupted electricity
d. Store duplicate copies of files in a location away from the computer center   (7021)

59. Which of the following passwords would be most difficult to crack?
a. OrCa!FISi
b. language
c. 12 HOUSE 24
d. pass56word   (7035)

60. Which of the following strategies would a CPA most likely consider in auditing an entity that processes most of its financial data only in electronic form, such as a paperless system?
a. Continuous monitoring and analysis of transaction processing with an embedded audit module
b. Increased reliance on internal control activities that emphasize the segregation of duties
c. Verification of encrypted digital certificates used to monitor the authorization of transactions
d. Extensive testing of firewall boundaries that restrict the recording of outside network traffic
                                                 (7574)

SIMULATIONS

Problem 2 (10 to 25 minutes)

In 2000, Amber Corp., a closely-held corporation, was formed by Adams, Frank, and Berg as incorporators and stockholders. Adams, Frank, and Berg executed a written voting agreement which provided that they would vote for each other as directors and officers. In 2004, stock in the corporation was offered to the public. This resulted in an additional 300 stockholders. After the offering, Adams holds 25%, Frank holds 15%, and Berg holds 15% of all issued and outstanding stock. Adams, Frank, and Berg have been directors and officers of the corporation since the corporation was formed. Regular meetings of the board of directors and annual stock-holders meetings have been held.

1. Amber Corp.'s officers ordinarily would be elected by its
A. Stockholders.
B. Directors.
C. Outgoing officers. (5404)

2. Amber Corp.'s day-to-day business ordinarily would be operated by its
A. Directors.
B. Stockholders.
C. Officers. (5405)

3. Adams, Frank, and Berg must
A. Be elected as directors because they own 55% of the issued and outstanding stock.
B. Always be elected as officers because they own 55% of the issued and outstanding stock.
C. Always vote for each other as directors because they have a voting agreement. (5406)

Mace, Inc. wishes to acquire Creme Corp., a highly profitable company with substantial retained earnings. Creme is incorporated in a state that recognizes the concepts of stated capital (legal capital) and capital surplus.

In conjunction with the proposed acquisition, Mace engaged Gold & Co., CPAs, to audit Creme's financial statements. Gold began analyzing Creme's stated capital account and was provided the following data:

- Creme was initially capitalized in 2000 by issuing 40,000 shares of common stock, 50¢ par value, at $15 per share. The total number of authorized shares was fixed at 100,000 shares.
- Costs to organize Creme were $15,000.
- During 2002, Creme's board of directors declared and distributed a 5% common stock dividend. The fair market value of the stock at that time was $20 per share.
- On June 1, 2003, the president of Creme exercised a stock option to purchase 1,000 shares of common stock at $21 per share when the market price was $25 per share.
- During 2004, Creme's board of directors declared and distributed a 2-for-1 stock split on its common stock when the market price was $28 per share.
- During 2005, Creme acquired as treasury stock 5,000 shares of its common stock at a market price of $30 per share. Creme uses the cost method of accounting and reporting for treasury stock.
- During 2006, Creme reissued 3,000 shares of the treasury stock at the market price of $32 per share.

Discuss the requirements necessary for Creme to properly declare and pay cash dividends. Set forth reasons for any conclusions stated.

(9661)

Problem 3 (15 to 25 minutes)

Scenario #1 | Response #1 | Scenario #2 | Response #2

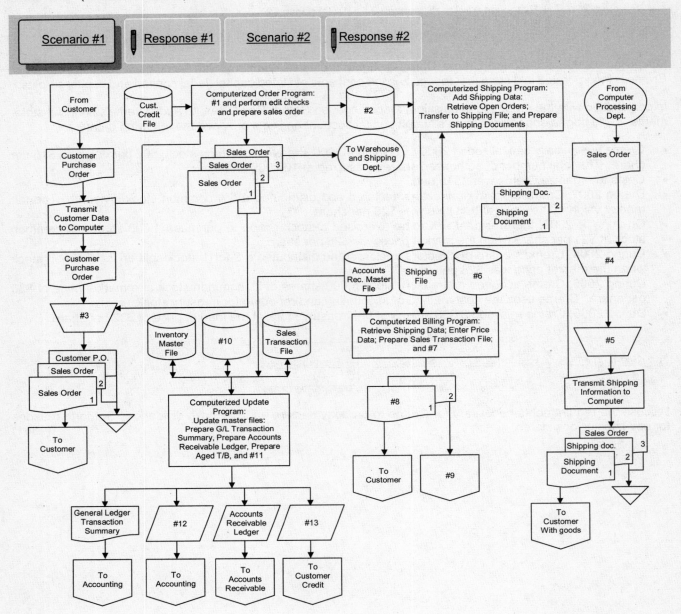

The flowchart in Scenario #1 depicts part of a client's revenue cycle. Some of the flowchart symbols are labeled to indicate control procedures and records. For each symbol labeled 1 through 13, select one response from the answer list below.

Answer List

Operations and control procedures	Documents, journals, ledgers, and files

Operations and control procedures

A. Enter shipping data
B. Verify agreement of sales order and shipping document
C. Write off accounts receivable
D. To warehouse and shipping department
E. Authorize account receivable write-off
F. Prepare aged trial balance
G. To sales department
H. Release goods for shipment
I. To accounts receivable department
J. Enter price data
K. Determine that customer exists
L. Match customer purchase order with sales order
M. Perform customer credit check
N. Prepare sales journal
O. Prepare sales invoice

Documents, journals, ledgers, and files

P. Shipping document
Q. General ledger master file
R. General journal
S. Master price file
T. Sales journal
U. Sales invoice
V. Cash receipts journal
W. Uncollectible accounts file
X. Shipping file
Y. Aged trial balance
Z. Open order file

(9911)

Software has been developed to improve the efficiency and effectiveness of the audit. Electronic spreadsheets and other software packages are available to aid in the performance of audit procedures otherwise performed manually.

Describe the potential benefits to an auditor of using software in an audit as compared to performing an audit without the use of a computer.

(9911)

ANSWERS TO MULTIPLE CHOICE QUESTIONS

The editors strongly recommend that candidates **not** spend much time on the answers to specific questions that they answered incorrectly on the diagnostic exam, particularly at the beginning of their review. Instead, study the related chapter. The numbers in parenthesis in the performance by topic chart (on this page) refer to an **explanation** of a question in the related chapters. **The question in the chapter is not necessarily the same question as in the diagnostic exam.**

1. b	6. a	11. c	16. c	21. d	26. c	31. b	36. b	41. c	46. b	51. a	56. d
2. c	7. c	12. d	17. d	22. a	27. b	32. b	37. d	42. d	47. b	52. c	57. a
3. b	8. a	13. c	18. b	23. c	28. c	33. a	38. b	43. b, c	48. e	53. b	58. d
4. c	9. d	14. d	19. a	24. d	29. d	34. c	39. d	44. a	49. d	54. c	59. a
5. d	10. b	15. d	20. e	25. b	30. d	35. c	40. a	45. c	50. d	55. b	60. a

PERFORMANCE BY TOPICS

Diagnostic exam questions corresponding to each chapter of the Business Environment & Concepts text are listed below. To assess your preparedness for the CPA exam, record the number and percentage of questions you correctly answered in each topic area. If a question has two answers, both must be correct to earn full point value. The point distribution of the multiple choice questions approximates that of the exam. To simplify candidate self evaluation, simulations are not included in the performance by topics. Explanations to the multiple choice questions are found in the corresponding chapters as referenced in parenthesis.

Chapter 48:
Partnerships

Question #	Correct	√
1 (7)		
2 (16)		
3 (20)		
4 (34)		
5 (41)		
6 (50)		
# Questions	6	
# Correct		
% Correct		

Chapter 49:
Corporations

Question #	Correct	√
7 (5)		
8 (10)		
9 (18)		
10 (19)		
11 (28)		
12 (35)		
# Questions	6	
# Correct		
% Correct		

Chapter 50:
Economic Theory

Question #	Correct	√
13 (38)		
14 (44)		
15 (62)		
16 (87)		
17 (122)		
18 (134)		
# Questions	6	
# Correct		
% Correct		

Chapter 51:
Financial Management

Question #	Correct	√
19 (6)		
20 (58)		
21 (63)		
22 (86)		
23 (103)		
24 (112)		
25 (114)		
26 (118)		
27 (124)		
28 (135)		
29 (151)		
30 (159)		
# Questions	12	
# Correct		
% Correct		

Chapter 52:
Decision Making

Question #	Correct	√
31 (16)		
32 (39)		
33 (46)		
34 (58)		
# Questions	4	
# Correct		
% Correct		

Chapter 53:
Cost Accounting

Question #	Correct	√
35 (10)		
36 (19)		
37 (35)		
38 (42)		
39 (61)		
# Questions	5	
# Correct		
% Correct		

Chapter 54:
Planning & Control

Question #	Correct	√
40 (9)		
41 (19)		
42 (32)		
43 (30)		
44 (48)		
45 (54)		
# Questions	6	
# Correct		
% Correct		

Chapter 55:
Information Technology

Question #	Correct	√
46 (21)		
47 (23)		
48 (44)		
49 (57)		
50 (59)		
51 (60)		
52 (62)		
53 (67)		
54 (72)		
55 (78)		
56 (87)		
57 (88)		
58 (97)		
59 (96)		
60 (98)		
# Questions	15	
# Correct		
% Correct		

PERFORMANCE BY AICPA CONTENT SPECIFICATION

The diagnostic exam questions are listed below by content specification category. The point distribution of the multiple choice questions approximates that of the exam. To simplify candidate self evaluation, simulations are not included.

CSO I

Question #	Correct	√
1		
2		
3		
4		
5		
6		
7		
8		
9		
10		
11		
12		
# Questions	12	
# Correct		
% Correct		

CSO II

Question #	Correct	√
13		
14		
15		
16		
17		
18		
# Questions	6	
# Correct		
% Correct		

CSO III

Question #	Correct	√
19		
20		
21		
22		
23		
24		
25		
26		
27		
28		
29		
30		
# Questions	12	
# Correct		
% Correct		

CSO V

Question #	Correct	√
31		
32		
33		
34		
35		
36		
37		
38		
39		
40		
41		
42		
43		
44		
45		
# Questions	15	
# Correct		
% Correct		

CSO IV

Question #	Correct	√
46		
47		
48		
49		
50		
51		
52		
53		
54		
55		
56		
57		
58		
59		
60		
# Questions	15	
# Correct		
% Correct		

SIMULATION SOLUTIONS

Solution 2

1. B

The Model Business Corporation Act (MBCA) provides that a corporation's officers are generally appointed by its directors.

2. C

A corporation's day-to-day business activities are generally conducted by its officers.

3. C

Adams, Frank, and Berg executed a written voting agreement providing that they would vote for each other as directors and officers. This agreement is valid and enforceable between the parties. There is no requirement in the MBCA or elsewhere that persons must be elected as directors or officers because they own a specified percentage or a majority of the issued and outstanding stock.

The initial capitalization of Creme in 2000 would result in $20,000 being allocated to stated capital. **Stated capital includes the par value of all shares of the corporation** having a par value that have been issued. Therefore, the $20,000 is calculated as follows: **40,000 shares issued × 50 cents par value = $20,000.**

The $15,000 of expenses incurred in organizing Creme would not affect stated capital. The **model Business Corporation Act permits payment of organization expenses out of the consideration received by it in payment for its shares** if the payment does not render such shares assessable or unpaid. Thus, stated capital remains at $20,000.

The 5% stock dividend would increase stated capital by $1,000 calculated as follows: **40,000 shares × 5% stock dividend = 2,000 shares × 50** cents par value **= $1,000.** The market price of the shares would have no effect on stated capital. Thus, stated capital is $21,000.

The exercise of the stock option by Crème's president would increase stated capital by $500 calculated as follows: 1,000 shares × 50 cents par value = $500. **Neither the price paid** by Crème's president **nor the market price** of the shares on the date the option was exercised **would affect stated capital.** Thus, stated capital is $21,500.

The 2-for-1 stock split would not affect stated capital. Instead the **par value** of 50 cents per share would be **reduced to 25 cents per share** and the **43,000 shares of stock issued** would be **increased to 86,000** shares. Thus, stated capital remains at $21,500.

The acquisition of 5,000 shares as treasury stock at $30 per share by Creme would have **no effect on stated capital under the cost method.** Thus, stated capital remains at $21,500.

The reissuance of the 3,000 shares of treasury stock at $32 per share would also have **no effect on stated capital under the cost method.** Thus, stated capital remains at $21,500.

Solution 3

1. M

Before preparing a sales order, the computer processing department should perform a credit check to determine that the sale will be made to a creditworthy customer. This information may be obtained from the customer credit file or from outside sources.

2. Z

Once the sales order has been prepared, it will be recorded and placed in the open order file.

3. L

This manual operation represents the process of matching customer purchase orders with sales orders for agreement.

4. B

This manual operation represents matching the shipping document with the sales order for agreement.

5. H

Once the shipping document and sales order have been matched, the goods will be released for shipment.

6. S

In order to prepare the customer bill, the computerized billing program will retrieve the shipping data from the shipping file and enter the price data from the master price file.

7. O

Once the shipping data and price data have been retrieved and the sale to the customer generated, the sales invoice will be prepared.

8. U

This document represents the duplicate copy sales invoice generated by the computerized billing program.

9. I

One copy of the sales invoice will be sent to the customer, and one will be sent to the accounts receivable department as support for the entry to the accounts receivable ledger—to be held until remittance is made by the customer.

10. Q

The computer processing department will (daily, weekly, or monthly) update the master files, such as the accounts receivable ledger, the inventory master file, the sales transaction file, and the general ledger master file.

11. N

The computer processing department will prepare, based upon the update program, an accounts receivable ledger, an aged trial balance, a general ledger transaction summary, and a sales journal.

12. T

This output function represents the sales journal which was generated by the computerized update program for the day, week, or month, depending upon the frequency of report generation established by management.

13. Y

This output report represents the aged trial balance generated by the computerized update program, which combined information from the general ledger master file, the sales transaction file, and the inventory master file.

Response #2: CAAT Advantages (6 points)

The potential benefits to an auditor of using software in an audit as compared to performing an audit without the use of a computer include the following:

1. **Time** may be **saved** by eliminating manual footing, cross-footing, and other routine calculations.

2. **Calculations,** comparisons, and other data manipulations are **more accurately performed.**

3. **Analytical procedures** calculations may be **more efficiently performed.**

4. The **scope** of analytical procedures may be **broadened.**

5. Audit **sampling** may be **facilitated.**

6. Potential **weaknesses** in a client's internal control structure may be more readily **identified.**

7. Preparation and **revision of flowcharts** depicting the flow of financial transactions in a client's structure may be **facilitated.**

8. **Working papers** may be easily **stored** and accessed.

9. **Graphics capabilities** may allow the auditor to generate, display, and evaluate various financial and nonfinancial relationships graphically.

10. Engagement-management information such as **time budgets** and the monitoring of **actual time vs. budgeted amounts** may be more easily generated and analyzed.

11. **Customized working papers** may be developed with greater ease.

12. **Standardized audit correspondence,** such as engagement letters, client representation letters, and attorney letters **may be stored and easily modified.**

13. **Supervisory-review time** may be **reduced.**

14. Staff morale and productivity may be improved by reducing the time spent on clerical tasks.

15. **Client's personnel may not need to manually prepare** as many **schedules** and otherwise spend as much time assisting the auditor.

16. Computer-generated working papers are generally more **legible** and consistent.

THE NATURE OF THE COMPUTER-BASED CPA EXAM

See the **Practical Advice** section of this volume for detailed information about the types of questions and point value of various topics. The AICPA has postponed simulations for the BEC section of the exam indefinitely.

The editors strongly encourage candidates to visit the AICPA's website (www.cpa-exam.org) and practice the free tutorial and sample exam there. The multiple choice questions in this book include letters (a, b, c, d, etc.) next to the response options. On the actual exam, these will be radio buttons, rather than letters. Candidates will click on the radio button corresponding to their answer to indicate their selection.

What will the actual exam be like? The questions throughout this book are either former exam questions or based on former exam questions. General predictions of future exams can be made based on previously disclosed exams. Specific predictions about which topics will be stressed on a particular candidate's exam are mere speculation and rather useless. (The examiners try not to make the exam predictable.) Don't waste time with mere speculation; instead, study and be prepared!

Using Videos to Study

Actively watch video classes, taking notes and answering questions as if it were a live class. If the lecturer recommends you to work an example as the video plays, write the numbers in the viewer guide, rather than merely following along. If the lecturer instructs you to stop the video to answer questions, stop the video. If the lecturer advises you to take notes, personalize your copy of the viewer guide. The lecturers provide these instructions with the insight gained from years of CPA review experience.

Each of the Hot•Spot™ videos concentrates on a few topics. Use them to help you study the areas that are most troubling for you. If you are strong in a topic, watching the video and answering the questions may be sufficient review. If your strength is moderate in a topic, you probably should read the related text before watching the video. If you are weak in a topic, one successful strategy is to watch the video (including following all of the lecturer's instructions), read the book, and then watch the video again.

Each of the Intensive videos is designed for a final, intensive review, after a candidate has already done considerable work. If time permits, use the Intensive programs at the very beginning (for an overview) and set them aside until your final review in the last two weeks before your exam. They contain concise, informative lectures, as well as CPA exam tips, tricks, and techniques that will help you to learn the material needed to pass the exam.

FYI: The Hot•Spot™ and Intensive videos have similar content as the audio tutor and online video lectures, but they are not exactly the same.

Video Cross Reference

The video programs are designed to supplement all of our study packages. They contain concise, informative lectures, as well as CPA exam tips, tricks, and techniques to help you learn the material needed to pass the exam. The **HotSpots™** videos concentrate on particular topics. Use them to study the areas that are most troubling for you. Each one of the **Intensive** video programs covers one of the four exam sections. The **Intensive** videos are designed for a final, intensive review, after you already have done considerable work. Alternatively, the **Intensive** videos may be used as both a preview and a final review. Please see the **Getting Started** section of this volume for a discussion on integrating videos into your study plan. This information, with approximate times, is accurate as we go to press, but it is subject to change without notice.

Video Title	Text Chapter	Time
Hot•Spots™ Cash, Receivables & Marketable Securities	2	3:15
Hot•Spots™ Inventory, Fixed Assets & Intangible Assets	3, 4, 5	2:45
Hot•Spots™ Bonds & Other Liabilities	6, 7	4:00
Hot•Spots™ Leases & Pensions	8, 9	2:50
Hot•Spots™ Owners' Equity & Miscellaneous Topics	10, 15, 16	3:00
Hot•Spots™ Revenue Recognition & Income Statement Presentation	1, 11, 12	4:45
Hot•Spots™ FASB 109: Accounting for Income Taxes	13	2:10
Hot•Spots™ FASB 95: Statement of Cash Flows	14	2:00
Hot•Spots™ Consolidations	2, 17	4:45
Hot•Spots™ Governmental & Nonprofit Accounting	18 - 20	5:30
Hot•Spots™ Audit Standards & Planning	21, 22	2:40
Hot•Spots™ Internal Control	23, 24, 28	1:55
Hot•Spots™ Audit Evidence	25, 26	2:45
Hot•Spots™ Statistical Sampling	27	1:30
Hot•Spots™ Standard Audit Reports	29	2:50
Hot•Spots™ Other Reports, Reviews & Compilations	30, 31	2:00
Hot•Spots™ Professional & Legal Responsibilities	32, 33	1:45
Hot•Spots™ Contracts	34	2:35
Hot•Spots™ Sales	35	2:00
Hot•Spots™ Commercial Paper & Documents of Title	36	2:00
Hot•Spots™ Secured Transactions	37	1:10
Hot•Spots™ Bankruptcy & Suretyship	38	0:55
Hot•Spots™ Fiduciary Relationships	39, 45	0:50
Hot•Spots™ Government Regulation of Business	40, 41	1:10
Hot•Spots™ Property & Insurance	42	1:20
Hot•Spots™ Property Taxation	43	1:15
Hot•Spots™ Individual Taxation	44	3:10
Hot•Spots™ Gross Income, Tax Liabilities & Credits	44, 46	2:45
Hot•Spots™ Corporate Taxation	46	3:00
Hot•Spots™ Partnerships & Other Tax Topics	45, 47	3:00
Hot•Spots™ Corporations & Partnerships	48, 49	1:00
Hot•Spots™ Economics	50	3:25
Hot•Spots™ Financial Management	51	3:00
Hot•Spots™ Cost & Managerial Accounting	52 - 54	3:20
Hot•Spots™ Information Technology	55	3:00

Intensive Video Review	FARE	AUD	REG	BEC	Total
Text Chapters	1 - 20	21 - 31	32 - 47	48 - 55	
Approximate Time	9:15	4:15	6:45	4:45	25:00

CHAPTER 48

PARTNERSHIPS

EXAM COVERAGE: The *Business Structure* portion of the BEC section of the CPA exam is designated by the examiners to be about 20 percent of the section's point value. Historically, exam coverage of corporations was slightly greater than partnerships. That relationship may not hold true under the new CSO. A slight increase in coverage of limited liability entities seems likely in the future. More information about the point value of various topics is included in the Practical Advice section of this volume.

CHAPTER 48

PARTNERSHIPS

I. Nature

A. Revised Uniform Partnership Act (RUPA)
RUPA defines a partnership as an association of two or more persons to carry on a business for profit as co-owners.

1. **Business** "To carry on a business" includes almost any type of profitable, legal activity.

2. **Co-Ownership** The persons engaged in a partnership must be co-owners. This requirement distinguishes a partnership from an agency. An agent may at times receive a share of the profits of a business. However, an agent does not have a partner's proprietary interest in the business. There is a fiduciary relationship among the partners, and between them and the partnership. Thus, each partner is an agent for the partnership and for all other partners.

3. **For Profit** Nonprofit, unincorporated associations such as religious or charitable groups, labor unions, or clubs, are not partnerships.

4. **Capacity** Generally, any person (entity) who is competent to contract may be a partner.

   a. An infant may be a partner, but only to the extent of the infant's power to contract. Therefore, an infant may at any time withdraw her/his investment unless, and to the extent that, the partnership is subject to creditors' claims. Furthermore, if liable for debts, an infant is liable only up to the amount of her/his contribution.

   b. A corporation may become a partner only where permitted by state corporation laws.

   c. A partnership may become a partner in another partnership provided all the partners agree to the arrangement.

   d. A trustee may become a partner if to do so would be prudent and in the best interest of the trust.

   e. RUPA allows general partnerships to convert to limited partnerships and vice versa. RUPA also allows general partnerships to merge with other general partnerships and with limited partnerships.

B. Partnership Theories

1. **Entity** RUPA embraces the entity theory of the partnership, for some purposes, including matters concerning title to partnership property, legal actions by and against the partnership, and continuity of existence, but RUPA does away with the marshalling of assets. All property acquired by a partnership, by transfer or otherwise, becomes partnership property and belongs to the partnership as an entity, rather than to the individual partners. RUPA abolishes the Uniform Partnership Act (UPA) concept of tenants in partnership. Generally, under RUPA, partners and third parties dealing with partnerships will be able to rely on the record to determine whether property is owned by the partnership. A partner's interest is the partner's share of the profits and losses of the partnership and the partner's right to receive distributions. This interest is personal property and can be transferred (RUPA uses the word transfer instead of assign) by the partner. The partners, by unanimous vote, may expel a partner who has transferred all of the partner's interest in the partnership.

2. **Aggregate** For some purposes, a partnership still is treated as a collection of individuals; the partnership itself is not taxed; rather, each partner pays income tax on her/his share of the profits or losses, regardless of whether cash or other property is received.

C. Distinguished From Other Entities

1. **Corporations**

   a. Advantages of a corporation as compared to a general partnership are:

   (1) The liability of stockholders is limited to the amount of their investment, whereas partners have unlimited liability.

   (2) A corporation allows continuity of business operations despite changes in ownership or management; a partnership is of limited duration (for example, the death of a partner results in a dissociation of the partnership).

   (3) A corporation may utilize a centralized management of professional managers, whereas a partnership is run co-equally by all the partners.

   (4) The ownership rights in a corporation are readily transferable; however, a partner may not transfer interest and rights in the partnership without the approval of all other partners.

   b. Advantages of a partnership as compared to a corporation are:

   (1) A partnership may be organized easily and cheaply, whereas a corporation must be organized in accordance with specific statutory procedures and must have sufficient capitalization.

   (2) A partnership generally is burdened less than a corporation by government supervision and reporting requirements.

2. **Joint Ventures** A joint venture resembles a partnership except that it is formed for only one transaction or series of transactions, rather than for a general purpose.

3. **Sole Proprietorship** A sole proprietorship is one individual engaged in business. A sole proprietorship is not a separate legal entity, distinct from its owner. A transfer of the interest of the proprietor causes a dissolution of the proprietorship. A partial transfer of a proprietor's interest requires another form of entity. A transfer of the whole interest of the proprietor in a proprietorship typically has an attendant non-competition agreement. Due to the disadvantages of the sole proprietorship form of entity, sole proprietorships tend to be small.

   a. Advantages of a sole proprietorship as compared to other forms of business are:

   (1) A sole proprietorship generally may be formed more easily and cheaply than any other entity, at the will of the proprietor. Generally, there are no requirements relating to a sole proprietorship, *per se,* although a sole proprietorship must abide by laws that relate to all businesses, such as employment, zoning, licensing, and fictitious name laws. Ordinarily, a sole proprietorship with a nationwide business need not register to do business in each state, in the manner of a corporation or limited liability company.

   (2) A sole proprietor receives all profits.

   (3) Control and accountability are centralized. A sole proprietor makes all decisions without answering to other owners. Control can change only with the proprietor's consent.

(4) The duration of a sole proprietorship is at the owner's will. The ownership rights in the entity's assets are transferable, although not always readily.

b. Disadvantages of a sole proprietorship as compared to other forms of business are:

(1) A sole proprietor has unlimited liability, placing the proprietor's personal assets at risk.

(2) By definition, a sole proprietorship's equity financing is limited to the proprietor's personal resources. Typical debt financing sources are banks and the Small Business Administration. Because a sole proprietorship is not a separate legal entity, lenders for either business or personal credit typically consider both business and personal assets and debts, which may complicate or, at least, lengthen application processes. Creditors effectively may place significant restrictions on the proprietor's financial decisions, both personal and business.

(3) A sole proprietor may lack the expertise to make sound decisions in all areas of the business. The checks and balances in more complex entities might remedy this lack or, at least, bring it to light.

(4) A sole proprietorship has no continuity of existence; it automatically terminates upon the proprietor's death.

D. **Classifications**

1. **General Partnership** An ordinary partnership formed under RUPA or common law and consists only of general partners. A general partner has the right to share in the management and profits of the partnership and has unlimited liability to partnership creditors.

2. **Limited Partnership** An arrangement specially created by the Revised Uniform Limited Partnership Act (RULPA) which consists of one or more general partners and one or more limited partners. A limited partner is one who contributes capital to the partnership but does not have any authority or voice in the management of the business. The limited partner's liability to partnership creditors is limited to the amount of capital contributed.

3. **Silent Partner** One who has unlimited liability but does not share in the management of the partnership.

4. **Ostensible or Nominal Partner** One who is not actually a partner, but who may become a partner by estoppel insofar as s/he is held out to appear to be a partner.

5. **Dormant Partner** One who is a partner with the right to management participation, but who is undisclosed and generally inactive. Once disclosed, the dormant partner has the same liability as a general partner.

6. **Secret Partner** One who actually participates in the management of the partnership but is undisclosed. If the secret partner's connection with the business is disclosed, s/he has unlimited liability.

7. **Limited Liability Partnership (LLP)** Limited liability partnerships afford liability protection to general partners. This is vastly different from traditional general partnerships. In essence, an LLP is merely a general partnership which has made an election to invoke the limited liability protection of the enabling state statute. Some states allow most professional partnerships to use LLPs; others allow most operating businesses to use LLP.

E.   Federal Income Tax Ramifications
The individual partners are taxed on their distributive shares of partnership gain and income regardless of whether the distributive share actually is distributed. The partnership's return is made on Form 1065 and is for information purposes only.

1.   **Conduit** General and limited partnerships, as well as LLCs, are not tax-paying entities. Rather, they are reporting entities which pass through distributive shares of gain and loss as well as partnership ordinary income or loss to the individual partners.

2.   **Entity Status** The general rule is that if an entity with two or more persons is formed under state law that is not a state law corporation, the entity is taxed as a partnership. A one-person LLC is disregarded for federal tax purposes and no separate return is required, yet it does not lose its liability shield.

F.   Property
All property originally brought into the partnership, or subsequently acquired by purchase or otherwise on account of the partnership, is partnership property. Included within this description is the partnership's capital, name, and goodwill. The direct property rights of a partner are the partner's interest in the partnership and the partner's right to participate in the management of the partnership.

1.   **Intent of Parties** In construing the phrase "acquired…on account of the partnership," the courts look to the intent of the parties as evidenced by the facts and circumstances surrounding each acquisition. The following are of particular importance.

a.   **Title** The fact that an asset is acquired or held in the partnership name may be considered by the court, but is not usually a major indication.

b.   **Partnership Improvement** The fact that partnership funds were used to improve an asset may be considered, but it is not a major indication.

c.   **Property Use** The fact that an asset is used in the partnership business is indicative of partnership ownership if that fact, combined with others, tends to establish the asset as partnership property.

d.   **Partnership Purpose** The fact that an asset is connected closely with the operation of a partnership is of particular importance when there is a dispute between one of the partners and the firm. In recognition of the fiduciary responsibilities inherent in a partnership, courts often view assets acquired by a partner which are necessary for or related to partnership operations as actually held in trust for the firm.

2.   **Acquisition & Conveyance** Under RUPA, any estate in real property may be acquired in the partnership name, and title so acquired may be conveyed in the partnership name. A partner may convey title to the property by a conveyance executed in the partnership name. If the partner in fact has no authority to so convey and the person with whom the partner is dealing has knowledge of the fact that s/he has no authority, the partnership may recover the property conveyed. However, when the purchaser or the purchaser's assignee is a holder for value who is without knowledge that the partner has exceeded her/his authority, then the partnership may not recover the property.

3.   **Interest in Partnership** A partner's interest in the partnership is her/his share of the profits and surplus. This interest is classified as personal property.

a.   **Profits & Losses** Profits and losses are shared equally unless the agreement specifies otherwise, even if the amount of contributed capital is not equal. If the partners agree on unequal profit sharing percentages, but are silent as to loss sharing percentages, losses are to be shared using the profit sharing proportions.

b.   **Inheritance** On her/his death, a partner's interest descends as personal property regardless of the form in which the firm's assets exist.

    c. **Assignment** Unless otherwise agreed, a partner's interest is freely assignable. The assignee is entitled only to receive the profits and capital to which the partner would have been entitled. S/he does not become a partner and is not entitled to exercise control over the partnership or use partnership property. The assignor remains liable on all partnership debts. An assignment does not cause a dissociation.

    d. **Rights of Individual Partner's Creditor to Partnership Assets** The creditor of an individual partner may not execute on or attach partnership assets. The creditor's only remedy, once her/his claim has been reduced to a judgment, is to obtain a charging order against the debtor-partner's interest. The creditor is then entitled to all future distributions of assets or surplus due the partner until the judgment is satisfied.

    e. **Family Rights** Generally, the partner's interest is treated as community property and is subject to a family allowance (statutory right of a widow to certain portions of the deceased husband's property).

4. **Right to Participate in Management** Unless there is a specific agreement to the contrary, all partners have equal rights in the management and control of the partnership business.

5. **Rights to Partnership Property** Each partner in a partnership has the right to possess and use the partnership property for partnership purposes.

    a. This right is not assignable except in connection with the assignment of rights of all the partners in the same property.

    b. This right is not subject to execution or attachment on a claim arising against the individual partner.

    c. This right is not community property, nor is it subject to family allowance or dower rights.

    d. On the death of the partner, the surviving partners are then under a duty to account to the estate of the deceased for the value of the deceased partner's rights in the property.

II. Formation

A. Overview
A partnership may be formed by either an express or implied agreement.

1. **Writing** Except in specific instances, there is no need for a partnership agreement to be in writing, and the acts of the parties alone may establish a partnership. A writing is needed in the formation of a partnership only when the partnership would otherwise be in violation of the Statute of Frauds. For example, any partnership agreement which necessitates the transfer of real property or to carry on a business for a term in excess of one year must be in writing.

2. **Articles of Partnership** Important provisions contained in the Articles of Partnership are the following.

    a. Firm name.

    b. Names and addresses of all the partners.

    c. Date the partnership becomes effective, as well as the intended duration of the partnership.

    d. Nature, purpose, and scope of partnership activity.

    e. Procedure for admission of new partners.

    f. Computation of interest on partnership capital.

g. Computation of profits and the proportionate share of profits and losses attributable to each partner.

h. Powers and duties of the partners.

i. Dissolution procedures and rights.

j. Procedure for distribution of surplus, including the disposition of the firm name and goodwill.

3. **Certificate** In most states, when a partnership is doing business under a fictitious name, it must file a certificate with the Secretary of State. This certificate must list the names and addresses of the partners and the fictitious name of the business. Failure to comply with the statutes does not invalidate the partnership, but may result in fines. The purpose of requiring registration is to allow third parties to know who is in the partnership.

4. **Filing** A statement may be filed in the state-specified office. A certified copy of a statement that is filed in the specified office of another state may be filed in the state-specified office. Either filing has the effect provided in RUPA with respect to partnership property located in or transactions that occur in that state. RUPA provides for a single, central filing of all statements (as is the case with corporations, limited partnerships, and limited liability companies). No filings are mandatory under RUPA; in all cases, the filing of such statements is optional and voluntary. Only statements that are executed, filed, and, if appropriate (such as the authority to transfer real property), recorded in conformity with RUPA have the legal consequences accorded to such statements by RUPA.

B. **Determining Partnership Existence**
The determining test is whether or not the parties intended to carry on together, as partners, a business for profit. It must appear that the parties intended joint responsibility in the management and operation of the business and intended to share in its profits and losses.

1. **Share** The sharing of gross revenues, by itself, does not establish a partnership. The receipt by a person of a share of the profits of a business is *prima facie* evidence that the person is a partner in the business, but no such inference shall be drawn if the profits were received in payment of any one of several items.

a. Of a debt by installments or otherwise.

b. As wages of an employee or rent to a landlord.

c. As an annuity to a widow or representative of a deceased partner.

d. As interest on a loan, though the amount of payment varies with the profits of the business.

e. As the consideration for the sale of goodwill of a business or other property by installments or otherwise.

2. **Ownership** Joint tenancy, tenancy in common, tenancy by the entireties, or any other type of joint ownership of property does not in itself establish a partnership. This is true regardless of whether the co-owners share any profits made through use of the property.

3. **Capital** The contribution of capital to a business endeavor does not establish a partnership, and it is not essential to the existence of a partnership that all the partners contribute capital.

4. **Designation** The designation of a business relationship as a "partnership" does not conclusively establish a partnership, nor can the parties avoid partnership liability merely by denouncing the existence of a partnership.

C. Estoppel

The relationship among the partners is governed by the express or implied partnership agreement. In dealings with third parties, however, the conduct of a party or parties may bind her/him or them as partners.

1. **Appearance** One who holds her/himself out as a partner in an actual or apparent partnership is liable to another who in good faith, and in reliance on the misrepresentation, extends credit to the apparent partner. An actual partner who either expressly or impliedly consents to a misrepresentation is likewise liable to third parties.

2. **Agent** When an actual partner represents that another is a member of the partnership, when in fact s/he is not, the partner makes the other person her/his agent. The "agent" then has the power to bind the partner to third parties as though the "agent" were actually a partner. Any liability resulting from such a misrepresentation extends only to the partners who consented to the misrepresentation.

III. Relations Among Partners

A. Fiduciary

The only fiduciary duties a partner owes to the partnership and the other partners are the duty of loyalty and the duty of care. Those duties may not be waived or eliminated in the partnership agreement, but the agreement may identify activities and determine standards for measuring performance of the duties, if not manifestly unreasonable. RUPA establishes the duty of care that partners owe to the partnership and to the other partners. The standard of care imposed by RUPA is that of gross negligence. RUPA requires a partner to refrain from competing with the partnership in the conduct of its business, but that duty is not violated merely because the partner's conduct furthers her/his own interest if certain requirements are met. RUPA also provides that partners have an obligation of good faith and fair dealing in the discharge of all their duties.

B. Mandatory Rule

Agreement cannot change certain requirements under RUPA. Some rights and duties, and implicitly the corresponding liabilities and remedies, are mandatory and cannot be waived or varied by agreement beyond what is authorized. The partnership agreement may not do any of the following.

1. Vary the requirements for executing, filing, and recording partnership statements, except the duty to provide copies to all the partners.

2. Unreasonably restrict partners' or former partners' access rights to books and records.

3. Entirely eliminate the fiduciary duties of loyalty or care, or the obligation of good faith and fair dealing. However, the statutory requirements of each can be modified by agreement, subject to limitations. Exculpatory agreements drafted by partners may be drafted in terms of types or categories of activities or transactions, but should be reasonably specific. The partners may determine the standards by which the performance of the obligation of good faith and fair dealing is to be measured. RUPA permits the partnership agreement to identify specific types or categories of partnership activities that do not violate the duty of loyalty.

4. Unreasonably reduce the partners' duty of care below the statutory standard, that is, to refrain from engaging in grossly negligent or reckless conduct, intentional misconduct, or a knowing violation of law. The standard may be increased by agreement to a higher standard of care.

5. Eliminate the obligation of good faith and fair dealing under RUPA, except the partnership agreement may prescribe the standards by which the performance of obligations is to be measured.

6. Bargain away the traditional rule that every partner has the power to withdraw from the partnership at any time. The partnership may require that the notice of withdrawal be in writing. (UPA was silent with respect to requiring a written notice of withdrawal.)

7.   Vary the right of partners to have the partnership dissolved and its business wound up.

8.   Vary the right of a court to expel a partner.

9.   Vary the requirement to wind up the partnership business in certain cases.

10.   Vary the law applicable to a limited liability partnership (LLP).

11.   Restrict the rights of third parties under RUPA.

C.   **Default Agreement**
The rights and duties of each partner in relation to the partnership are governed by any agreement among them. If there is no agreement, RUPA imposes the following rules.

1.   **Equal Rights** All partners have equal rights in the management and conduct of the partnership business. Any differences concerning ordinary matters connected with the partnership business may be decided by a majority of the partners, but no act in contravention of any agreement among the partners may be done rightfully without the consent of all the partners.

2.   **Share in Profits, Losses & Assets** A partner has a share in profits and losses and rights to assets upon dissolution of the partnership as follows.

    a.   Each partner is entitled to repayment of her/his capital contributions or advances made to the partnership. All partners are entitled to an equal share in profits and any surplus remaining after all liabilities (including those to the partners) are satisfied. A partner must contribute to the losses sustained by the partnership proportionately according to the partner's share in the profits.

    b.   The partnership must indemnify every partner for payments made or liabilities incurred by her/him in the ordinary conduct of the partnership business or in the preservation of its business or property.

    c.   A partner is entitled to interest on any sums advanced by her/him in furtherance of partnership business beyond the amount of capital the partner agreed to contribute.

    d.   A partner is not entitled to compensation for acting in the partnership business other than sharing in its profits, unless otherwise agreed. However, a surviving partner is entitled to reasonable compensation for her/his services in winding up the partnership affairs.

3.   **Books & Information** The partnership must keep its books at a central, agreed-to location. Each partner is entitled to have access to them at all times. A partner has the right to demand from the other partners full and true information of all things affecting the partnership. A partner's legal representative has the same right to such information.

4.   **Formal Accounting** Any partner has the right to a formal accounting of partnership affairs:

    a.   When the partner wrongfully is excluded from the partnership or possession of its property,

    b.   If the right is provided for under the agreement,

    c.   When another partner breaches her/his fiduciary duty, or

    d.   At any other reasonable time.

D.   **Actions Between Partner & Partnership**

1.   **Suit in Equity** The principal remedy available to a partner against her/his co-partners is a suit in equity for a dissolution and an accounting.

2.   **Action at Law** Disputes between partners almost invariably involve a conflict as to partnership assets, which necessitates an accounting of assets. Additionally, any suit by a partner against the partnership creates a conflict of interest for the plaintiff partner between her/his individual interest as plaintiff and her/his interest as a defendant member of the partnership. For these reasons, actions at law are seldom permitted except in a few situations. Typically, these situations involve controversies in which no complex accounting is necessary or in which the partner's activity is outside the scope of the partnership business. Thus, the courts will allow an action at law involving a dispute which arose at the outset of the partnership, a suit between partners not related to partnership business, or a suit for fraud or conversion of partnership assets.

IV. Relations With Third Persons

A.   Authority to Bind Partnership

Generally, the rules of agency apply in determining whether or not the partnership is bound by the dealings of one of its members with a third party. Thus, for the purpose of conducting partnership business, every partner is an agent for the partnership and for every other partner. The act of a partner committed within the scope of the partner's actual or apparent authority will, therefore, bind the partnership.

1.   **Actual**

   a.   **Express** A partner's express authority includes that authority specifically set forth in an agreement among the partners. It may also arise from decisions made by a majority of the partners regarding the conduct of the partnership business. The partnership may file a statement of authority outlining the authority that particular partner or partners may have.

   b.   **Implied** This type of authority has not been granted expressly to a partner, but instead arises from the nature and business of the partnership. It is essentially that type of authority which is reasonably necessary for a partner to perform her/his duties. For example, if a partner is in charge of the partnership's personnel, it would be reasonable and necessary to imply that s/he has the power to hire and fire employees even though this authority is not granted expressly.

2.   **Apparent** The actions of a partner which are apparently for the carrying on of the partnership's business in the usual way, but which are not actually authorized, will still bind the partnership if the third party does not know of the partner's lack of actual authority. However, if the third party knows that a partner's dealings exceed the partner's authority or is outside of the scope of the partner's apparent authority, the other partners are not liable.

   Example 1 ▶ Apparent Authority

   > A is a partner in ABC partnership and is in charge of purchasing; however, by agreement, his authority to contract is limited to $1 million. A enters into a contract on behalf of ABC with Z Company, which does not know of the limitation on A's authority. ABC still is liable on the entire contract.

3.   **Limitations** Without authorization to the contrary, no partner may do any of the following. Additional limitations may be imposed by the partnership agreement.

   a.   Assign the partnership property in trust for the benefit of creditors or on the assignee's promise to pay the debts of the partnership.

   b.   Dispose of the goodwill of the business or do any other act that would make it impossible to carry on the ordinary business of a partnership.

    c.   Confess a judgment.

    d.   Submit a partnership claim or liability to arbitration.

4.   **Termination** The majority of partners may terminate the authority of a partner, or minority of partners, unless this action would be contrary to a previous agreement. Some cases have allowed one partner to terminate the authority of a co-partner when the partnership is limited to two persons.

5.   **Notice** In regard to any matter affecting partnership affairs, notice to any individual partner is imputed to all other partners.

6.   **Knowledge** The knowledge of any partner gained while working on partnership matters is imputed to all other members of the partnership. However, any knowledge gained by a partner who is engaged in a fraud as to the partnership is not imputed to the partnership. Normally, knowledge acquired by one before s/he becomes a partner is not imputed to the partnership.

7.   **Admissions** An admission or representation made by any partner while the partner is acting within the scope of her/his authority is admissible as evidence against the partnership.

B.   **Partnership Liability**

Partners are jointly and severally liable for contracts and all actions in tort or fraud against any partnership member where the partnership is not a limited liability partnership. The other partners are liable only when the cause of action arises out of partnership business. A person with a cause of action against a partnership may sue any number of partners s/he wishes, collectively or separately. Each partner is liable for the entire amount of damages arising out of such a cause of action. However, a partner may have either a right to contribution from the other partners or a right to indemnification from a wrongdoing partner.

1.   **Contract Liability** Partners are jointly and severally liable for all debts and contract obligations of the partnership.

    a.   This liability extends to all "in fact" partners (for example, dormant partners) whether or not the creditor relied upon the fact that such a person was a partner.

    b.   An incoming partner is not personally liable for debts of the partnership incurred before the partner's admission. The partner's liability as to pre-existing claims may be satisfied only out of partnership property. Thus, an incoming partner's liability for pre-existing claims is limited to that partner's capital contribution.

2.   **Tort Liability** All partners are liable jointly and severally for actions in tort.

    a.   Tort liability may arise from the wrongful act or omission of a partner arising out of activity which was authorized by the other partners or within the partner's normal course of business. The partnership is also liable for funds misapplied by one of the partners.

    b.   Since the partners are severally liable, an action may be brought against any one of the partners.

    c.   Any partner adjudicated guilty of tortious conduct towards an outsider is liable to her/his co-partner(s). Generally, a partnership has no right to recover from third persons who inflict injuries on an individual partner.

3.   **Contract & Tort Liability** Under RUPA, adopted in a majority of states, partners are liable jointly and severally for both contracts and torts.

V. Dissociation

A. Causes

Dissociation is the result of the change in the relation of the partners when a partner ceases to be associated with the carrying on of the business. A partner's dissociation always will result in **either** a buyout of the dissociated partner's interest **or** a dissolution and winding up of the business. The partnership does not terminate on dissolution, but continues until the winding up of the partnership is complete. Dissociation may be accomplished either without violating the partnership agreement or in violation of the partnership agreement. The entity theory of partnership provides a conceptual basis for continuing the firm itself despite a partner's dissociation from the firm, if there is a buyout of that partner's interest. A dissociated partner remains a partner for some purposes and still has some residual rights, duties, powers, and liabilities.

1. Accordance With Partnership Agreement

a. **Completion of Term or Particular Project** When the partnership agreement specifies that the partnership will terminate on a certain date or when a particular project is completed, the expiration of the term or completion of the undertaking dissolves the partnership. The partners may, if they choose, continue beyond the term as partners at will.

b. **Partner's Express Decision (at Will)** When the partnership is at will, a partner may dissociate from the partnership at anytime without liability to the other partners even if the dissociation causes a loss to the firm. However, pursuant to the partner's fiduciary duty, a partner must act in good faith. Thus, if a partner chooses to exercise her/his right to dissociate from the partnership in order to exclude the partner's co-partners from a lucrative business opportunity, the act of dissociation would be wrongful, and her/his rights on dissociation would change accordingly.

c. **All Partners' Express Will** When all the partners who have not assigned their interests or had them claimed in satisfaction of a personal debt agree to dissolve, it is immaterial that the partnership is for a term and not at will.

d. **Expulsion** The expulsion of a partner from the firm must be both authorized by the agreement and bona fide. Under these circumstances, the expelling partners are not liable for any resulting damages.

2. Violating Partnership Agreement

a. **Partner's Express Decision (not at Will)** Every partner has the power to dissociate from the partnership whether or not the partner has that right under the partnership agreement. When the dissociating partner acts in violation of the agreement, the partner may be held liable for any losses caused by the dissociation. The following acts by a partner have been construed by the courts as evidencing the partner's intent to discontinue.

(1) **Assignment of Partnership Interests** A partner's transfer of her/his partnership property to a third party may be indicative, but is not conclusive, of an intent to dissociate.

(2) **Levy of Charging Order** The levy of a charging order on the partnership interest of a debtor/partner does not by itself produce a dissociation. However, the assignee or holder of a charging order can obtain a judicial dissociation of a partner from the partnership after expiration of the term or, if it is a partnership at will, whenever the interest is acquired.

b. **Illegality** Dissolution of a partnership results automatically upon the occurrence of any event that makes it unlawful for the partnership business to be conducted. The partners may change their business to avoid the illegality and thus continue the partnership relationship.

    c.   **Partner Death, Withdrawal, Bankruptcy, or Incompetency** Unless the partnership agreement provides otherwise, a partner's death, withdrawal, bankruptcy, or incompetency will result in the partner's dissociation from the partnership. The other partners may agree to continue or terminate the partnership.

    d.   **Judgment** The court has the power to adjudicate dissolution on application by or for a partner when any of the following circumstances exist.

        (1)   A partner has been declared insane in a judicial proceeding or is otherwise shown to be of unsound mind.

        (2)   A partner otherwise becomes incapable of performing her/his part of the partnership contract (generally, the incapacity must be of such a nature as to materially affect the partner's ability to discharge her/his duties).

        (3)   A partner has been guilty of conduct that tends to prejudicially affect the conduct of the business.

        (4)   A partner willfully or persistently commits a breach of the partnership agreement.

        (5)   The business of the partnership can only be conducted at a loss.

        (6)   Whenever the dissolution would be equitable.

    e.   **Charging Order** Upon the application of a partner's assignee or creditor with a charging order, the court may adjudge dissolution. Normally, the following procedures are followed when a court decrees dissolution.

        (1)   **Accounting** A suit for dissolution generally is a suit in equity for dissolution and accounting. An accounting is necessary so that the court can determine the credits or debits of each partner and supervise the distribution of partnership assets.

        (2)   **Distribution Method** Usually, the court orders a sale of all partnership assets and applies the proceeds first to satisfy debts, and then to repay each partner's capital account. Any proceeds still remaining are paid to the partners as current earnings in proportion to each partner's share of the profits.

            (a)   If there are no debts, the court may distribute the partnership assets in kind.

            (b)   If there are losses, each partner must contribute in proportion to her/his share of the profits. If one partner is insolvent or refuses to contribute, the remaining partners are liable for her/his share. They then have a cause of action against the noncontributing partner.

B.   **Continuing Business**
If a partner is dissociated from a partnership without resulting in a dissolution and winding up of the partnership business, the partnership shall cause the dissociated partner's interest in the partnership to be purchased for a buyout price. RUPA provides for a statement of dissociation.

    1.   **Authority** Every partner has apparent authority to bind the partnership by any act for carrying on the partnership business in the ordinary course, unless the other party knows that the partner has no actual authority to act for the partnership or has received a notification of the partner's lack of authority. RUPA continues that the general rule is for two years after a partner's dissociation, subject to limitations.

2. **Liability** A partner's dissociation does not, of itself, discharge the partner's liability for a partnership obligation incurred before dissociation. A dissociated partner is not liable for a partnership obligation incurred after dissociation, except as otherwise provided. In general, under RUPA, as a result of the adoption of the entity theory, relationships between a partnership and its creditors are not affected by the dissociation of a partner or by the addition of a new partner, unless otherwise agreed. RUPA provides that a dissociated partner is not liable for the debts of the continuing business simply because of continued use of the partnership name or the dissociated partner's name as a part of the partnership name.

3. **Continuing Liability** Generally, anytime a partner dissociates from a partnership and the same business is conducted by a newly formed partnership, creditors of the dissolved partnership are also creditors of the partnership continuing the business. The liability of a third person who becomes a partner in the new partnership for debts owed to creditors of the dissolved partnership may be satisfied only out of partnership property.

4. **Retiring or Deceased Partner** When a partner retires or dies and the business is continued without any settlement of accounts, the partner, her/his estate, or her/his legal representative has the option of taking the value of the partner's partnership interest as of the date of dissolution of either of the following.

   a. **Interest** Any interest accruing until the date of discharge.

   b. **Profits** Instead of interest, the profits attributable to the use of that partner's interest in continuing the business.

5. **Conversion & Mergers** RUPA Article 9 rules regarding conversions and mergers are not mandatory. Partnerships may be converted and merged in any other manner provided by law. The effect of compliance with Article 9 is to provide a "safe harbor" assuring the legal validity of such conversions and mergers. Under UPA, unanimous consent was required for conversion or merger; in certain circumstances, RUPA requires less than unanimous consent.

   a. **Conversion** RUPA authorizes the conversion of a partnership to a limited partnership and a limited partnership to a partnership. (RUPA limits the usual RUPA definition of "partnership" to general partnerships.) RUPA sets forth the effect of a conversion; the converted partnership is for most purposes the same entity as before the conversion.

   b. **Merger** RUPA provides for the merger of a general partnership and one or more general or limited partnerships and states the effect of a merger on the partnerships that are parties to the merger and on the individual partners. The surviving entity may be either a general or a limited partnership. RUPA provides that the surviving entity may file a statement of merger.

C. **Winding Up Business**
   RUPA provides that a partnership continues after dissolution only for the purpose of winding up its business, after which it is terminated. The partners who have not dissociated wrongfully may participate in winding up the partnership business. Even after termination, if a previously unknown liability is asserted, all of the partners are still liable.

   1. **Continuation** RUPA makes explicit the right of the remaining partners to continue the business after an event of dissolution, if all of the partners [including the dissociating partner(s)] waive the right to have the business wound up and the partnership terminated.

   2. **Asset Distribution** RUPA changes the distribution of assets to provide that partnership assets must be applied to discharge the obligations of partners who are creditors on parity with other creditors. Also, RUPA's distribution does not distinguish between amounts owed to partners for capital and for profit.

3. **Filing** RUPA provides that, after dissolution, any partner who has not dissociated wrongfully may file a statement of dissolution on behalf of the partnership. After 90 days, this notice gives constructive notice to creditors that the apparent authority of the partnership is ended for all purposes except winding up.

D. Partners' Rights & Authority

Unless otherwise agreed, any nonbankrupt partner who has not dissociated from the partnership wrongfully, or the legal representative of the last surviving partner, has the right to wind up the partnership affairs. Any partner, the partner's legal representative, or the partner's assignee may petition for a winding up by the court.

1. **Accordance With Partnership Agreement** As against the partner's co-partners and persons claiming through them, each partner has the right (unless otherwise agreed) to have the partnership property applied to discharge its liabilities and the surplus applied to pay in cash the amount owing to the partner. An expelled partner who is discharged from all partnership liabilities receives only the net amount due the partner from the partnership.

2. **Contravention of Partnership Agreement** Partners who have not dissociated wrongfully from the partnership have all their ordinary rights, and the right to damages from the breaching partner or partners. If all nonbreaching partners desire to continue the business in the same name, they may do so. They are entitled to possess the partnership property, but must pay the value of that partner's interest to any partner who dissociated from the partnership wrongfully.

   a. When the business is not continued, a partner who dissociated from the partnership wrongfully has the previously discussed rights and liabilities.

   b. When the business is continued by the nonbreaching partners, a partner who dissociates from the partnership wrongfully is liable for all damages to the partnership caused by the partner's action.

3. **Fraud** When a partnership contract is rescinded on the grounds of fraud or misrepresentation, the partner(s) entitled to rescission has(have) the following rights.

   a. The right to a lien on, or a right to retention of, the surplus of the partnership to secure her/his capital investment and any advances.

   b. After all liabilities to third persons have been satisfied, the right to stand in the place of creditors for her/his payments made on partnership liabilities.

   c. The right to be indemnified by the person who is guilty of the fraud or the misrepresentation. This indemnity is good against all the debts and liabilities of the partnership.

4. **Contribution From Co-Partners After Dissociation** When a partner's dissociation is caused by the act, death, or bankruptcy of a partner, each partner is liable to her/his co-partners as though the partnership had not been dissociated. However, the nondealing partners are not liable to any partner who has actual knowledge of the dissociation from the partnership before the partner acts on "behalf of the partnership."

5. **Third Persons** A partner has the power to bind the partnership as to third persons by either an act appropriate for winding up partnership affairs or completing unfinished transactions or a transaction that would bind the partnership if dissociation had not taken place, provided the third party has no knowledge of the dissociation.

6. **Acts of Partners** The partnership is not bound by any partner's acts after dissociation when either of the following apply.

   a. The partnership is dissolved because it is unlawful to carry on the business, except when the act is appropriate to wind up partnership affairs.

b. The partner is bankrupt or has no authority to wind up partnership affairs.

E. Partner's Liability

Generally, a dissociation from a partnership does not discharge the existing liability of any partner.

1. **Agreement** A partner may be discharged from any existing liability upon dissociation from the partnership by an agreement to that effect. The agreement must include as parties the partner her/himself, the partnership creditor, and the person or partnership continuing the business. The agreement may be inferred from the course of dealing between the creditor having knowledge of the dissociation and the person or partnership continuing the business.

2. **Assumption Discharges Partner's Liability** When a person agrees to assume the existing obligations of a partnership from which a former partner has dissociated her/himself, the withdrawing partner thereby is discharged from any liability to creditors who agree to the substitution.

3. **Deceased Partner's Nonpartnership Property** A deceased partner's nonpartnership property is subject to all the partnership's obligations which were incurred while s/he was a partner. However, the claims of a decedent's individual creditors have priority over those of any partnership creditors as against the nonpartnership property.

F. Asset Distribution

Subject to any agreement among the partners, the following rules apply.

1. **Priority** The partnership's assets (which are the partnership property and the contributions of the partners necessary for the payment of all liabilities) are applied in the order of partnership liabilities. The liabilities of the partnership rank in order of payment as follows.

   a. Those owing to creditors including partners.

   b. Those owing to partners other than for capital and profits.

   c. Those owing to the partners for capital.

   d. Those owing to the partners for profit.

2. **Contribution** The partners are liable for the amount necessary to satisfy all the claims. If a partner is insolvent or beyond the reach of judicial process, the other partners are responsible for her/his liabilities. Such contributing partners are liable in the proportion in which they share in the profits.

   a. An assignee for the benefit of creditors or any person appointed by the court may enforce the contributions.

   b. Any partner or the partner's legal representative may enforce the contributions, to the extent of the amount the partner has paid in excess of her/his share.

   c. The individual property of a deceased partner is liable for contributions.

3. **Sources** Once the partnership property and the property of the individual partners are in the hands of the court for distribution, the priorities are as follows.

   a. Partnership creditors have priority as to partnership property.

   b. Individual creditors generally have priority as to individual property, except for a partnership bankruptcy, wherein the partnership creditors share pro rata with partners' personal creditors.

    c.   The rights of secured or lien creditors are provided for as previously discussed.

  4.   **Partner Insolvency** If a partner becomes bankrupt or if the partner's estate is insolvent, the claims against her/his separate property rank as follows.

    a.   Those owing to personal creditors.

    b.   Those owing to partnership creditors.

    c.   Those owing to partners who have made advances for the benefit of the partnership.

VI. Limited Partnerships

A.   **Nature**
A limited partnership is a partnership formed by two or more persons having as members one or more general partners and one or more limited partners. The purpose of a limited partnership is to allow persons, who do not have the desire or ability to assume the responsibilities of a general partner, to invest in a partnership business. A limited partnership can be created only by complying with the appropriate local statute.

  1.   **General** A general partner is analogous to a partner in a general partnership. The partner is responsible for the management and control of the partnership and is personally liable for its debts. There must be at least one general partner in any limited partnership.

  2.   **Limited** A limited partner is one who makes a capital contribution to the partnership and thereby obtains an interest in that partnership.

    a.   **Services** Under the ULPA, limited partners may contribute cash or property, but not services. However, under the RULPA, limited partners are allowed to contribute services, including future services.

    b.   **Rights** A limited partner has all the rights of a general partner except that the partner has no right to manage or control the partnership. Nevertheless, the partner has the right to inspect the books, demand an accounting, and have a dissolution and winding-up decree by the court.

    c.   **Name** A limited partner's surname may not appear in the partnership name unless there is sufficient designation attached to the partner's name to indicate that s/he is a limited partner.

    d.   **Liability** A limited partner's liability ordinarily is limited to the amount of the partner's contribution in the partnership unless s/he takes part in the management of the business or violates name restrictions.

    e.   **Under Capitalization** A limited partner is liable to the partnership for any difference between her/his contribution as actually made and that which the partner agreed to make in the certificate. A limited partner holds, as trustee for the partnership, property stated in the certificate as contributed by the partner, but which in fact s/he possesses, and any money or property wrongfully paid or conveyed to the partner on account of her/his contribution.

    f.   **Withdrawals** A limited partner may receive a share of the profits or other compensation as stipulated in the certificate, provided, however, that after such payment, the partnership assets are in excess of all liabilities to creditors.

    g.   **Separate Entity** A limited partner may loan money to and transact other business with the partnership. The partner also receives payment on any resulting claims on an equal, pro rata basis with third party creditors.

h. Liquidation Generally, a limited partner may demand or receive cash in repayment of her/his contribution. However, the partner may not do so until all partnership liabilities to creditors have been paid or the partnership has sufficient assets to pay them.

i. Interest A limited partner's interest is considered personal property and it is freely assignable. A limited partner's rights are not assignable unless they are assigned to a substituted limited partner. For a person to become a substituted limited partner, all partners must be in agreement, and the certificate must be amended to reflect the substitution of limited partners.

j. Death The death of a limited partner does not dissolve the partnership.

k. Creditor Any creditor of a limited partner may obtain, through the court, a charge against the debtor's interest in the partnership.

B. Formation & Dissolution

In contrast to the formation of a general partnership, the formation of a limited partnership must be in accordance with strict statutory requirements. Additionally, limited partnerships may be formed only in those jurisdictions which have enacted enabling statutes. Some states have adopted the Uniform Limited Partnership Act (ULPA). Others have adopted the Revised Uniform Limited Partnership Act (RULPA) as amended in 1985. A limited partnership may be dissolved in any of the ways discussed for general partnerships, except the death or assignment of interest of a limited partner does not dissolve the partnership.

1. Elements The partners must execute a certificate which states the following: the name of the partnership, the character of the business, the location of the business, the term for which the partnership is to exist, a description of the capital, and the name and residence of each partner or limited partner together with a list of each member's status and rights.

2. Filing The certificate must be filed with the Secretary of State, and a copy must be filed with the clerk of the court in the county of the principal place of business. The certificate may be amended or canceled only if the above formalities are observed. The purpose of the certificate is to put creditors on notice of the limited liability of the limited partners.

3. Loss The certificate must comply substantially with the requirements. If a certificate contains a false statement, anyone who suffers a loss through reliance thereon may hold all the partners liable.

C. Revised Uniform Limited Partnership Act (RULPA)

A limited partnership is not a RUPA general partnership, but RUPA governs limited partnerships to the extent RULPA fails to provide for a circumstance. RULPA requires a limited partnership to name an office and agent for service of process. RULPA outlines how profits are to be shared if not designated in the agreement. RULPA requires foreign partnerships to register.

1. Distribution RULPA provides for the following distribution of partnership assets.

a. First, to partnership creditors including partners (general and limited) who are creditors, except for "unpaid distributions" to partners.

b. Second, to partners who previously have withdrawn from the partnership, payments to these partners for "unpaid distributions" plus the return of capital. Unpaid distributions are any distributions a partner is entitled to upon withdrawal from the firm.

c. Third, to partners (general and limited) to the extent of their capital contribution.

d. Fourth, to partners (general and limited) as to profits.

2. **Services** RULPA allows limited partners to contribute services, including future services. Section 303 of RULPA provides "safe harbors" for limited partners to participate in management, including the following.

    a. Being a contractor for, or an agent or employee of, the limited partnership or of a general partner.

    b. Consulting with and advising a general partner regarding the partnership business.

    c. Acting as a surety for the limited partnership.

    d. Voting on partnership matters such as dissolution and winding up the limited partnership or the removal of a general partner.

3. **Certificate** RULPA requires less information in the certificate than ULPA. The names of the limited partners are not required. New investors may be admitted as limited partners without amending the certificate as is required under the ULPA. The certificate need only include (a) the limited partnership's name, (b) the address of the partnership's registered office and the name and business address of its agent for service of process, (c) the name and business address of each general partner, (d) its mailing address, and (e) the latest date on which the limited partnership is to dissolve.

VII. Limited Liability Companies

A. Nature
A limited liability company (LLC) is a hybrid of corporate and partnership law.

1. **Members** An LLC is a company formed by one or more members. Owners in LLCs are usually referred to as members. Members are equivalent to partners in a general partnership. That is, they manage the company unless expressly agreed otherwise.

2. **Individual Owners** A single individual may form an LLC in many states. Formerly, most states required two or more persons to form an LLC. This was largely driven by the federal tax treatment of LLCs.

3. **Manager** The members may elect what commonly is referred to as a manager to operate the business. The manager is the equivalent of the president of a corporation. A manager does not have to be a member in the LLC.

4. **Liability Shield** There are no restrictions on members of LLCs like restrictions on limited partners. Members may be involved fully in the business and not lose the liability shield.

B. Formation & Termination
LLCs must be created in accordance with the applicable state statute.

1. **Articles of Organization** The members or organizers of the LLC must file what commonly is referred to as articles of organization. These are similar to articles of incorporation and require the name of the company, the character of the business, the location of the business, the term for which the company is to exist, and the name and address of each member. The articles or certificate normally is filed with the Secretary of State and clerk of the court in the county of the principal place of business. The articles or certificate may be amended or canceled. The purpose of the filings is to put creditors on notice.

2. **Operating Agreement** Members commonly enter into what is also known as an operating agreement, company agreement, or regulations. This is a private contract between the members which generally outlines how they will conduct the business and what rights each member in the company may have in the event a member leaves the company.

3. **Dissolution** Formerly, LLCs were dissolved upon the events that would traditionally dissolve general partnerships. Now, however, the trend is to state that such events will not dissolve the LLC. Even if there are no members, statutes provide that holders of financial rights may elect members and continue the business of the LLC.

4. **Distribution** In settling accounts after dissolution, liabilities of the LLC are paid in the following order.

   a. **Creditors** To creditors, except claims by members on account of capital contributions.

   b. **Capital** To members in respect to their capital contributions.

   c. **Profits** To members with respect to their share of undistributed profits.

CHAPTER 48—PARTNERSHIPS

Problem 48-1 MULTIPLE CHOICE QUESTIONS (80 to 100 minutes)

1. When parties intend to create a partnership that will be recognized under the Revised Uniform Partnership Act, they must agree to

	Conduct a business for profit	Share gross receipts from a business
a.	Yes	Yes
b.	Yes	No
c.	No	Yes
d.	No	No

(11/98, Law, #6, amended, 6751)

2. A general partnership must
a. Pay federal income tax
b. Have two or more partners
c. Have written articles of partnership
d. Provide for apportionment of liability for partnership debts (11/91, Law, #14, 2342)

3. For which of the following is a partnership recognized as a separate legal entity?
a. The liability for and payment of taxes on partnership gains from the sale of capital assets
b. In respect to contributions and advances made by partners to the partnership
c. The recognition of net operating losses
d. The status of the partnership as an employer for workers' compensation purposes
(11/81, Law, #20, 7131)

4. For which of the following purposes is a general partnership recognized as an entity by the Revised Uniform Partnership Act?
a. Recognition of the partnership as the employer of its partners
b. Insulation of the partners from personal liability
c. Taking of title and ownership of property
d. Continuity of existence
(5/83, Law, #3, amended, 0693)

5. A joint venture is a(an)
a. Association limited to no more than two persons in business for profit
b. Enterprise of numerous co-owners in a nonprofit undertaking
c. Corporate enterprise for a single undertaking of limited duration
d. Association of persons engaged as co-owners in a single undertaking for profit
(11/89, Law, #4, 0669)

6. Which of the following statements is correct with respect to the differences and similarities between a corporation and a limited partnership?
a. Directors owe fiduciary duties to the corporation and limited partners owe such duties to the partnership.
b. A corporation and a limited partnership may be created only pursuant to a state statute, and a copy of its organizational document must be filed with the proper state agency.
c. Shareholders may be entitled to vote on corporate matters, whereas limited partners are prohibited from voting on any partnership matters.
d. Stock of a corporation may be subject to the federal securities laws registration requirements, whereas limited partnership interests are automatically exempt from such requirements.
(11/88, Law, #5, 7132)

7. In a general partnership, which of the following acts must be approved by all the partners?
a. Dissociation of a partner from the partnership
b. Admission of a partner
c. Authorization of a partnership capital expenditure
d. Conveyance of real property owned by the partnership (R/01, Law, #8, amended, 7043)

8. Which of the following statements concerning the similarities between a general partnership and a corporation is correct?
a. Corporate stockholders and general partners have limited personal liability.
b. Corporations and general partnerships have perpetual existence.
c. Corporations and general partnership can declare bankruptcy.
d. Corporations and general partnerships are recognized as taxpayers for federal income tax purposes. (R/03, BEC, #21, 7684)

9. Which of the following statements best describes the effect of the assignment of an interest in a general partnership?
a. The assignee becomes a partner.
b. The assignee is responsible for a proportionate share of past and future partnership debts.
c. The assignment automatically dissolves the partnership.
d. The assignment transfers the assignor's interest in partnership profits and surplus.
(11/95, Law, #19, 5888)

10. The partnership agreement for Owen Associates, a general partnership, provided that profits be paid to the partners in the ratio of their financial contribution to the partnership. Moore contributed $10,000, Noon contributed $30,000, and Kale contributed $50,000. For the year, Owen had losses of $180,000. What amount of the losses should be allocated to Kale?

a. $ 40,000
b. $ 60,000
c. $ 90,000
d. $100,000   (11/94, Law, #22, amended, 5199)

11. Lark, a partner in DSJ, a general partnership, wishes to withdraw from the partnership and sell Lark's interest to Ward. All of the other partners in DSJ have agreed to admit Ward as a partner and to hold Lark harmless for the past, present, and future liabilities of DSJ. As a result of Lark's withdrawal and Ward's admission to the partnership, Ward

a. Acquired only the right to receive Ward's share of DSJ profits
b. Has the right to participate in DSJ's management
c. Is personally liable for partnership liabilities arising before and after being admitted as a partner
d. Must contribute cash or property to DSJ to be admitted with the same rights as the other partners   (11/94, Law, #23, 5200)

12. Unless otherwise provided in a general partnership agreement, which of the following statements is correct when a partner dies?

	The deceased partner's executor would automatically become a partner	The deceased partner's estate would be free from any partnership liabilities	The partner would be dissociated from the partnership automatically
a.	Yes	Yes	Yes
b.	Yes	No	No
c.	No	Yes	No
d.	No	No	Yes

(11/94, Law, #20, amended, 5197)

13. Unless the partnership agreement prohibits it, a partner in a general partnership may validly assign rights to

	Partnership property	Partnership distributions
a.	Yes	Yes
b.	Yes	No
c.	No	Yes
d.	No	No

(11/93, Law, #18, 4315)

14. Downs, Frey, and Vick formed the DFV general partnership to act as manufacturers' representatives. The partners agreed Downs would receive 40% of any partnership profits and Frey and Vick would each receive 30% of such profits. It was also agreed that the partnership would not terminate for five years. After the fourth year, the partners agreed to terminate the partnership. At that time, the partners' capital accounts were as follows: Downs, $20,000; Frey, $15,000; and Vick, $10,000. There also were undistributed losses of $30,000. Which of the following statements about the form of the DFV partnership agreement is correct?

a. It must be in writing because the partnership was to last for longer than one year.
b. It must be in writing because partnership profits would **not** be equally divided.
c. It could be oral because the partners had explicitly agreed to do business together.
d. It could be oral because the partnership did **not** deal in real estate.   (5/93, Law, #11, 3980)

15. Cobb, Inc., a partner in TLC Partnership, assigns its partnership interest to Bean, who is not made a partner. After the assignment, Bean asserts the rights to

I. Participate in the management of TLC.
II. Cobb's share of TLC's partnership profits.

Bean is correct as to which of these rights?
a. I only
b. II only
c. I and II
d. Neither I **nor** II   (5/93, Law, #15, 3984)

16. Which of the following statements is correct regarding the division of profits in a general partnership when the written partnership agreement only provides that losses be divided equally among the partners? Profits are to be divided

a. Based on the partners' ratio of contribution to the partnership
b. Based on the partners' participation in day to day management
c. Equally among the partners
d. Proportionately among the partners   (11/95, Law, #18, 5887)

Items 17 and 18 are based on the following:

Dowd, Elgar, Frost, and Grant formed a general partnership. Their written partnership agreement provided that the profits would be divided so that Dowd would receive 40%; Elgar, 30%; Frost, 20%; and Grant, 10%. There was no provision for allocating losses. At the end of its first year, the partnership had losses of $200,000. Before allocating losses, the partners' capital account balances were: Dowd, $120,000; Elgar, $100,000; Frost, $75,000; and Grant, $11,000. Grant refuses to make any further contributions to the partnership. Ignore the effects of federal partnership tax law.

17. What would be Grant's share of the partnership losses?
a. $ 9,000
b. $20,000
c. $39,000
d. $50,000   (5/92, Law, #12, 2825)

18. After losses were allocated to the partners' capital accounts and all liabilities were paid, the partnership's sole asset was $106,000 in cash. How much would Elgar receive on dissolution of the partnership?
a. $37,000
b. $40,000
c. $47,500
d. $50,000   (5/92, Law, #13, 2826)

19. Gillie, Taft, and Dall are partners in an architectural firm. The partnership agreement is silent about the payment of salaries and the division of profits and losses. Gillie works full-time in the firm, and Taft and Dall each work half-time. Taft invested $120,000 in the firm, and Gillie and Dall invested $60,000 each. Dall is responsible for bringing in 50% of the business, and Gillie and Taft 25% each. How should profits of $120,000 for the year be divided?
a. Gillie $60,000, Taft $30,000, Dall $30,000
b. Gillie $40,000, Taft $40,000, Dall $40,000
c. Gillie $30,000, Taft $60,000, Dall $30,000
d. Gillie $30,000, Taft $30,000, Dall $60,000
          (11/89, Law, #6, 0671)

20. When a partner in a general partnership lacks actual or apparent authority to contract on behalf of the partnership, and the party contracted with is aware of this fact, the partnership will be bound by the contract if the other partners

	Ratify the contract	Amend the partnership agreement
a.	Yes	Yes
b.	Yes	No
c.	No	Yes
d.	No	No

          (R/99, Law, #5, 6856)

21. Which of the following statements is correct regarding the apparent authority of a partner to bind the partnership in dealings with third parties? The apparent authority
a. Must be derived from the express powers and purposes contained in the partnership agreement
b. Will be effectively limited by a formal resolution of the partners of which third parties are unaware
c. May allow a partner to bind the partnership to representations made in connection with the sale of goods
d. Would permit a partner to submit a claim against the partnership to arbitration
          (5/97, Law, #2, 6443)

22. Under the Revised Uniform Partnership Act, which of the following statements concerning the powers and duties of partners in a general partnership is(are) correct?

I. Each partner is an agent of every other partner and acts as both a principal and an agent in any business transaction within the scope of the partnership agreement.
II. Each partner is subject to joint liability on partnership debts and contracts.

a. I only
b. II only
c. Both I and II
d. Neither I nor II
          (11/96, Law, #11, amended, 6422)

23. In a general partnership, the authorization of all partners is required for an individual partner to bind the partnership in a business transaction to
a. Purchase inventory
b. Hire employees
c. Sell goodwill
d. Sign advertising contracts
          (11/91, Law, #15, 2343)

24. Which of the following statements is(are) usually correct regarding general partners' liability?

I. All general partners are jointly and severally liable for partnership torts.

II. All general partners are liable only for those partnership obligations they actually authorized.

a. I only
b. II only
c. Both I and II
d. Neither I nor II   (11/95, Law, #17, 5886)

25. Eller, Fort, and Owens do business as Venture Associates, a general partnership. Trent Corp. brought a breach of contract suit against Venture and Eller individually. Trent won the suit and filed a judgment against both Venture and Eller. Trent will generally be able to collect the judgment from

a. Partnership assets only
b. The personal assets of Eller, Fort, and Owens only
c. Eller's personal assets only after partnership assets are exhausted
d. Eller's personal assets only
                              (11/90, Law, #12, 0666)

26. Wind, who has been a partner in the PLW general partnership for four years, decides to withdraw from the partnership despite a written partnership agreement that states, "no partner may withdraw for a period of five years". What is the result of Wind's withdrawal?

a. Wind's withdrawal automatically causes a dissociation of a partner from the partnership by operation of law.
b. Wind's withdrawal has **no** bearing on the continued operation of the partnership by the remaining partners.
c. Wind's withdrawal is **not** effective until Wind obtains a court ordered decree of dissolution.
d. Wind's withdrawal causes a dissociation of the partner from the partnership despite being in violation of the partnership agreement.
                       (R/01, Law, #7, amended, 7042)

27. The partners of College Assoc., a general partnership, decided to dissolve the partnership and agreed that none of the partners would continue to use the partnership name. Which of the following events will occur on dissolution of the partnership?

	Each partner's existing liability would be discharged	Each partner's apparent authority would continue
a.	Yes	Yes
b.	Yes	No
c.	No	Yes
d.	No	No

(11/94, Law, #24, amended, 5201)

28. On February 1, Addison, Bradley, and Carter, physicians, formed ABC Medical Partnership. Dr. Bradley was placed in charge of the partnership's financial books and records. On April 1, Dr. Addison joined the City Hospital Medical Partnership, retaining the partnership interest in ABC. On May 1, ABC received a writ of attachment from the court attaching Dr. Carter's interest in ABC. The writ resulted from Dr. Carter's failure to pay a credit card bill. On June 1, Dr. Addison was adjudicated bankrupt. On July 1, Dr. Bradley was sued by the other partners of ABC for an accounting of ABC's revenues and expenses. Which of the preceding events resulted in the dissociation of a partner from the ABC Medical Partnership?

a. Dr. Addison joining the City Hospital Medical Partnership
b. Dr. Carter's interest in the partnership being attached by the court
c. Dr. Addison being adjudicated bankrupt
d. Dr. Bradley being sued for an accounting by the other partners of ABC
                         (5/98, Law, #2, amended, 6619)

29. Park and Graham entered into a written partnership agreement to operate a retail store. Their agreement was silent as to the duration of the partnership. Park wishes to dissolve the partnership. Which of the following statements is correct?

a. Park may dissolve the partnership at any time.
b. Unless Graham consents to a dissolution, Park must apply to a court and obtain a decree ordering the dissolution.
c. Park may **not** dissolve the partnership unless Graham consents.
d. Park may dissolve the partnership only after notice of the proposed dissolution is given to all partnership creditors.   (11/95, Law, #20, 5889)

Items 30 and 31 are based on the following:

Downs, Frey, and Vick formed the DFV general partnership to act as manufacturers' representatives. The partners agreed Downs would receive 40% of any partnership profits and Frey and Vick would each receive 30% of such profits. It was also agreed that the partnership would not terminate for five years. After the fourth year, the partners agreed to terminate the partnership. At that time, the partners' capital accounts were as follows: Downs, $20,000; Frey, $15,000; and Vick, $10,000. There also were undistributed losses of $30,000.

30. If Frey died before the partnership terminated,
a. Downs and Vick would have been able to continue the partnership if the partnership purchased Frey's partnership interest
b. The partnership automatically would have continued until the five year term expired
c. The partnership would automatically dissolve
d. Downs and Vick would have Frey's interest in the partnership   (5/93, Law, #13, amended, 3982)

31. Vick's share of the undistributed losses will be
a. $0
b. $ 1,000
c. $ 9,000
d. $10,000   (5/93, Law, #12, 3981)

32. When the Revised Uniform Partnership Act applies and there is **no** general partnership agreement, which of the following events occur(s) when a partner dies?

	The partnership is dissolved	The deceased partner's estate is free from any partnership liability
a.	Yes	Yes
b.	Yes	No
c.	No	Yes
d.	No	No

(R/03, BEC, #1, amended, 7663)

33. Which of the following statements regarding a limited partner is(are) generally correct?

	The limited partner is subject to personal liability for partnership debts	The limited partner has the right to take part in the control of the partnership
a.	Yes	Yes
b.	Yes	No
c.	No	Yes
d.	No	No

(11/89, Law, #5, 0670)

34. Which of the following statements is correct with respect to a limited partnership?
a. A limited partner may **not** be an unsecured creditor of the limited partnership.
b. A general partner may **not** also be a limited partner at the same time.
c. A general partner may be a secured creditor of the limited partnership.
d. A limited partnership can be formed with limited liability for all partners.   (5/92, Law, #11, 2824)

35. Cavendish is a limited partner of Custer Venture Capital. He is extremely dissatisfied with the performance of the general partners in making investments and managing the portfolio. He is contemplating taking whatever legal action may be appropriate against the general partners. Which of the following rights would Cavendish **not** be entitled to assert as a limited partner?
a. To have a formal accounting of partnership affairs whenever the circumstances render it just and reasonable
b. To have the same rights as a general partner to a dissolution and winding up of the partnership
c. To have reasonable access to the partnership books and to inspect and copy them
d. To have himself elected as a general partner by a majority vote of the limited partners in number and amount   (5/82, Law, #4, 7133)

36. Unless otherwise provided in the limited partnership agreement, which of the following statements is correct?
a. A general partner's capital contribution may **not** consist of services rendered to the partnership.
b. Upon the death of a limited partner, the partnership will be dissolved.
c. A person may own a limited partnership interest in the same partnership in which s/he is a general partner.
d. Upon the assignment of a limited partner's interest, the assignee will become a substituted limited partner if the consent of two-thirds of all partners is obtained.
(11/84, Law, #11, amended, 0689)

Items 37 and 38 are based on the following:

White, Grey, and Fox formed a limited partnership. White is the general partner and Grey and Fox are the limited partners. Each agreed to contribute $200,000. Grey and Fox each contributed $200,000 in cash while White contributed $150,000 in cash and $50,000 worth of services already rendered. After two years, the partnership is insolvent. The fair market value of the assets of the partnership is $150,000, and the liabilities total $275,000. The partners have made no withdrawals.

37. Unless otherwise provided in the certificate of limited partnership, which of the following is correct if Grey dies?
a. Grey's executor will automatically become a substituted limited partner.
b. Grey's executor will have all the rights of a limited partner for the purpose of settling the estate.
c. The partnership will automatically be dissolved.
d. Grey's estate will be free from any liabilities which may have been incurred by Grey as a limited partner. (5/87, Law, #9, 0680)

38. Unless otherwise provided in the certificate of limited partnership, which of the following is correct if Fox assigns her interest in the partnership to Barr and only White consents to Barr's admission as a limited partner?
a. Barr will **not** become a substituted limited partner unless Grey also consents.
b. Barr will have the right to inspect the partnership's books.
c. The partnership will be dissolved.
d. Barr will become a substituted limited partner because White, as general partner, consented. (5/87, Law, #8, 0679)

39. What generally is not required in a limited liability company's articles of organization?
a. The character of the business
b. Each member's name and address
c. The location of the business
d. An outline of how the members will conduct the business and the rights each member will have in the event that a member leaves the company
e. The term for which the company is to exist (Editors, 7721)

40. Spartan is a limited liability company undergoing dissolution. In what order are Spartan's liabilities paid in settling accounts after dissolution?

I. To creditors, except claims by members on account of capital contributions.
II. To creditors, except claims by members on account of capital contributions or loans to the company.
III. To members, with respect to loans to the company.
IV. To members with respect to their share of undistributed profits.
V. To members in respect to their capital contributions.

a. I, IV, and V
b. I, V, and IV
c. II, III, IV, and V
d. II, III, V, and IV (Editors, 7722)

Problem 48-2 ADDITIONAL MULTIPLE CHOICE QUESTIONS (32 to 40 minutes)

41. Generally, under the Revised Uniform Partnership Act, a partnership has which of the following characteristics?

	Unlimited duration	*Obligation for payment of federal income tax*
a.	Yes	Yes
b.	Yes	No
c.	No	Yes
d.	No	No

(11/95, Law, #16, amended, 5885)

42. Which of the following best describes a silent partner?
a. A partner with limited liability and who does not participate in the partnership's management
b. A partner with unlimited liability, but who is undisclosed and does not participate in the management of the partnership
c. A partner with unlimited liability who participates in the management of the partnership, but is undisclosed
d. One who is not a partner, but appears to be a partner (Editors, 7711)

43. Which of the following associations of two individuals most likely is a partnership?
a. A pair that owns land through a tenancy in common, with the co-owners sharing all profits made though use of the property
b. A pair that intended, together as partners, to carry on a business for profit, although only one contributed capital
c. An employee shares in gross revenues, with the profits received in payment of wages
d. An agent shares in the profits of the principal, but not the losses   (Editors, 7712)

44. Which of the following is true with regard to a partner's fiduciary duties?
a. The partnership agreement may eliminate a partner's fiduciary duties.
b. The partnership agreement may eliminate the right of a court to expel a partner.
c. The partnership agreement may establish standards for measuring performance of fiduciary duties.
d. The partnership agreement may reduce a partner's fiduciary duty of care below gross negligence.   (Editors, 7713)

45. A partnership agreement may
a. Eliminate the rule that every partner has the power to withdraw from the partnership at any time
b. Eliminate the rule that every partner has the right to withdraw from the partnership at any time
c. Eliminate former partners' rights to access books and records
d. Vary the requirement to wind up the partnership business in all cases   (Editors, 7714)

46. Which is the least likely situation for a court to permit an action at law by a partner?
a. A dispute that arose at the outset of a partnership
b. A dispute between partners independent of the partnership's business
c. A suit by one partner against another for fraud
d. A suit that necessitates a complex accounting of assets   (Editors, 7715)

47. Many states require partnerships to file the partnership name under laws which are generally known as fictitious name statutes. These statutes
a. Require a proper filing as a condition precedent to the valid creation of a partnership
b. Are designed primarily to provide registration for tax purposes
c. Are designed to clarify the rights and duties of the members of the partnership
d. Have little effect on the creation or operation of a partnership other than the imposition of a fine for noncompliance   (11/83, Law, #15, 0690)

48. The apparent authority of a partner to bind the partnership in dealing with third parties
a. Will be effectively limited by a formal resolution of the partners of which third parties are aware
b. Will be effectively limited by a formal resolution of the partners of which third parties are unaware
c. Would permit a partner to submit a claim against the partnership to arbitration
d. Must be derived from the express powers and purposes contained in the partnership agreement   (11/93, Law, #12, 4309)

49. A parent and child currently own and operate a farm as equal partners. Under the Revised Uniform Partnership Act, what effect would the death of the parent have on the partnership?
a. The estate of the deceased partner automatically becomes a partner.
b. The surviving partner could continue the partnership.
c. The partnership would be dissolved and wound up.
d. A partnership agreement could **not** have governed the continuation of the partnership.   (R/03, BEC, #17, 7679)

50. On dissolution of a general partnership, distributions will be made on account of:

  I.   Partners' capital accounts.
 II.   Amounts owed partners with respect to profits.
III.   Amounts owed partners for loans to the partnership.

in the following order:
a. III, I, II
b. I, II, III
c. II, III, I
d. III, II, I   (11/91, Law, #17, 2345)

51. Xavier, Young, and Zebra form the Xavier, Young & Zebra Partnership. Xavier dies. There is no dissolution and winding up of Xavier, Young & Zebra's business. Which of the following is true?
a. Claims of partnership creditors have priority over those of Xavier's individual creditors against non-partnership property.
b. The executor of Xavier's estate automatically becomes a partner of Xavier, Young & Zebra Partnership.
c. Xavier's estate gets the value of Xavier's interest in the partnership at Xavier's death and either any interest accruing or profits attributable to that interest until the date of discharge.
d. Xavier's estate is responsible for debts incurred in the ordinary course of business for as long as Xavier's name appears in the partnership name.
(Editors, 7716)

52. Hilda, Irene, and Jackie formed the HIJ Partnership. Hilda dissociates in accordance with the partnership agreement. There is a dissolution and winding up of the partnership. Which of the following is true?
a. After 90 days, a statement of dissolution gives constructive notice to creditors that the apparent authority of the partnership is ended for all purposes except winding up.
b. All partners must file the statement of dissolution for it to be effective against creditors.
c. Irene and Jackie have the right to continue the business after the dissolution, regardless of whether Hilda waives the right to have the business wound up.
d. Only Irene and Jackie may participate in winding up the partnership business. (Editors, 7717)

53. Lana, Mike, and Neal formed the LMN Partnership. Lana dissociates, but not in accordance with the partnership agreement. Which of the following is true?
a. Lana has no right to the value of her partnership interest.
b. Lana is liable for damages caused by her breach even if she dissociates because it is now unlawful to carry on the partnership business.
c. Mike and Neal have no right to damages from Lana if they continue the business after the dissociation.
d. Mike and Neal have the right to continue the business in the same name after the dissociation. (Editors, 7718)

54. If anyone who suffers a loss through reliance on a limited partnership certificate containing a false statement, who may be held liable?

	General partners	Limited partners
a.	Yes	Yes
b.	Yes	No
c.	No	Yes
d.	No	No
		(Editors, 7719)

55. Under the Revised Uniform Limited Partnership Act, what is not required in a limited partnership certificate?
a. The address of the partnership's registered office and the name and business address of its agent for service of process
b. The general partners' names and business addresses
c. The latest date on which the limited partnership is to dissolve
d. The limited partners' names and business addresses
e. The partnership's name (Editors, 7720)

56. Jones, Smith, and Bay wanted to form a company called JSB Co. but were unsure about which type of entity would be most beneficial based on their concerns. They all desired the opportunity to make tax-free contributions and distributions where appropriate. They wanted earnings to accumulate tax-free. They did not want to be subject to personal holding tax and did not want double taxation of income. Bay was going to be the only individual giving management advice to the company and wanted to be a member of JSB through his current company, Channel, Inc. Which of the following would be the most appropriate business structure to meet all of their concerns?
a. Proprietorship
b. S corporation
c. C corporation
d. Limited liability partnership
(R/03, BEC, #18, 7680)

SIMULATIONS

FYI: The editors encourage candidates to answer simulations as part of their review because such studying provides for content reinforcement, regardless of question format. Simulations currently are not part of the BEC exam; Bisk Education updating supplements will notify readers when this situation changes.

Problem 48-3 (25 to 35 minutes)

On March 1, 2001, Grove, Plane, and Range formed Techno Associates, a general partnership. They made capital contributions to the partnership as follows: Grove contributed $125,000; Plane contributed $250,000; and Range contributed $500,000. They prepared and executed a written partnership agreement that provided that profits would be shared equally, that the partnership would last for five years, and that the partnership use a calendar year for accounting purposes. There was no provision as to how losses would be allocated nor was there any provision regarding the continued use of the partnership name in the event of dissolution. The Revised Uniform Partnership Act applies.

On April 1, 2002, Range assigned Range's partnership interest to Blank. Blank notified Grove and Plane that Blank wanted to participate in the partnership business and vote on partnership issues.

On June 10, 2002, a judgment was entered against Techno in suit for breach of contract.

On December 31, 2002, Grove resigned from the partnership.

During the year-end closing, it was established that Techno had incurred an operating loss in 2002 as a result of the judgment. It was also established that Techno, being unable to pay its debts as they became due, was insolvent.

Select one answer for each item based on Scenario #1.

1. What would be Range's liability for Techno's 2002 operating loss?
   A. No personal liability.
   B. Liability limited to the amount contributed to the partnership.
   C. Liability limited to the amount in the capital account.
   D. Full personal liability for up to one-third of the total amount of the partnership debt.
   E. Full personal liability for up to the total amount of the partnership debt.

2. What would be Blank's liability for Techno's 2002 operating loss?
   A. No personal liability.
   B. Liability limited to the amount contributed to the partnership.
   C. Liability limited to the amount in the capital account.
   D. Full personal liability for up to one-third of the total amount of the partnership debt.
   E. Full personal liability for up to the total amount of the partnership debt.

3. What would be Grove's liability for Techno's 2002 operating loss?
   A. No personal liability.
   B. Liability limited to the amount contributed to the partnership.
   C. Liability limited to the amount in the capital account.
   D. Full personal liability for up to one-third of the total amount of the partnership debt.
   E. Full personal liability for up to the total amount of the partnership debt.

4. As of January 1, 2003, who were the partners in Techno?
    A. Blank and Plane.
    B. Plane and Range.
    C. Blank, Plane, and Grove.
    D. Grove, Plane, and Range.
    E. Blank, Grove, Plane, and Range.

5. On May 1, 2003, what was the status of Techno?
    A. Dissolved.
    B. Liquidated.
    C. Terminated.

(11/97, Law, #1, amended, 6514-6518)

Prime Cars Partnership is a general partnership engaged in the business of buying, selling, and servicing used cars. Prime's original partners were Baker and Mathews, who formed the partnership three years ago under a written partnership agreement, which provided that:

*   Profits and losses would be allocated 60% to Baker and 40% to Mathews.
*   Baker would be responsible for supervising Prime's salespeople and for purchasing used cars for inventory. Baker could not, without Mathews' consent, enter into a contract to purchase more than $15,000 worth of used cars at any one time.
*   Mathews would be responsible for supervising Prime's service department.

On May 1, 2002, Baker entered into a contract on Prime's behalf with Jaco Auto Wholesalers, Inc., to purchase 11 used cars from Jaco for a total purchase price of $40,000. Baker's agreement with Jaco provided that the cars would be delivered to Prime on September 1. Baker did not advise Mathews of the terms and conditions of the contract with Jaco. Baker had regularly done business with Jaco on behalf of Prime in the past, and on several occasions had purchased $12,000 to $15,000 of used cars from Jaco. Jaco was unaware of the limitation on Baker's authority.

Baker also frequently purchased used cars for Prime from Top Auto Auctions, Ltd., a corporation owned by Baker's friend. Whenever Prime purchased cars from Top, Baker would personally receive up to 5% of the total purchase price from Top as an incentive to do more business with Top. Baker did not tell Mathews about these payments.

On August 1, 2002, Baker and Mathews agreed to admit KYA Auto Restorers, Inc., as a partner in Prime to start up and supervise a body shop facility. KYA made a $25,000 capital contribution and Prime's partnership agreement was amended to provide that Prime's profits and losses would be shared equally by the partners.

On September 1, 2002, Mathews learned of the Jaco contract and refused to accept delivery of the cars. Mathews advised Jaco that Baker had entered into the contract without Mathews' consent as required by their agreement. Jaco has demanded a payment of $10,000 from Prime for Jaco's lost profits under the contract. Mathews has also learned about the incentive payments made to Baker by Top.

Mathews has taken the following positions:
*   Prime is not liable to Jaco because Baker entered into the contract without Mathews' consent.
*   In any event, Mathews is not liable to Jaco for more than 40% of Jaco's lost profits because of the original partnership provisions concerning the sharing of profits and losses.
*   Baker is liable to Mathews for any liability incurred by Mathews under the Jaco contract.
*   Baker is liable to Prime for accepting the incentive payments from Top.

KYA contends that none of its $25,000 capital contributions should be applied to the Jaco liability and that, in any event, KYA does not have any responsibility for the obligation.

a.   State whether Mathews' positions are correct and give the reasons for your conclusions.

b.   State whether KYA's contentions are correct and give the reasons for your conclusions.

(5/91, Law, #2, amended, 9649)

Problem 48-4 (25 to 35 minutes)

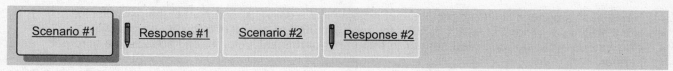

In 2002, Anchor, Chain, and Hook created ACH Associates, a general partnership. The partners orally agreed that they would work full time for the partnership and would distribute profits based on their capital contributions. Anchor contributed $5,000; Chain $10,000, and Hook $15,000.

For the year ended December 31, 2003, ACH Associates had profits of $60,000 that were distributed to the partners. During 2004, ACH Associates was operating at a loss. In September 2004, the partnership dissolved.

In October 2004, Hook contracted in writing with Ace Automobile Co. to purchase a car for the partnership. Hook had previously purchased cars from Ace Automobile Co. for use by ACH Associates partners. ACH Associates did not honor the contract with Ace Automobile Co., and Ace Automobile Co. sued the partnership and the individual partners.

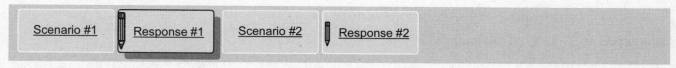

For each item, select one answer based on Scenario #1.

1.
   A.   The ACH Associates oral partnership agreement was valid.
   B.   The ACH Associates oral partnership agreement was invalid because the partnership lasted for more than one year.

2.
   A.   Anchor, Chain, and Hook jointly owning and conducting a business for profit establishes a partnership relationship.
   B.   Anchor, Chain, and Hook jointly owning income producing property establishes a partnership relationship.

3.
   A.   Anchor's share of ACH Associates' 2003 profits was $20,000.
   B.   Hook's share of ACH Associates' 2003 profits was $30,000.

4.
   A.   Anchor's capital account would be reduced by 1/3 of any 2004 losses.
   B.   Hook's capital account would be reduced by 1/2 of any 2004 losses.

5.
   A.   Ace Automobile Co. would lose a suit brought against ACH Associates because Hook, as a general partner, has no authority to bind the partnership.
   B.   Ace Automobile Co. would win a suit brought against ACH Associates because Hook's authority continues during dissolution.

6.

A. ACH Associates and Hook would be the only parties liable to pay any judgment recovered by Ace Automobile Co.

B. Anchor, Chain, and Hook would be jointly and severally liable to pay any judgment recovered by Ace Automobile Co.

(5/95, Law, #2a, amended, 5395-5400)

Edna Slavin intends to enter into a limited partnership with three of her business associates. Slavin wishes to know the advantages and disadvantages of being a general partner as opposed to a limited partner in a limited partnership. The issues of most concern to Slavin are:

- Her right as a general or limited partner to participate in the daily management of the partnership.
- Her liability as a general or limited partner for debts incurred on behalf of or by the partnership.
- Her right as a general or limited partner to assign her partnership interest and substitute a third party as a partner.
- The effect of a clause in the certificate of limited partnership which permits the partnership to continue after the death of one of the general or limited partners.

Answer the following, setting forth reasons for any conclusions stated.

What are the essential differences in the formation of a general partnership and a limited partnership? Discuss in separate paragraphs the issues raised by Slavin.

(11/86, Law, #2, 9651)

Simulation 48-5 (15 to 20 minutes)

Best Aviation Associates is a general partnership engaged in the business of buying, selling and servicing used airplanes. Best's original partners were Martin and Kent. They formed the partnership on January 1, 2002, under an oral partnership agreement which provided that the partners would share profits equally. There was no agreement as to how the partners would share losses. At the time the partnership was formed, Martin contributed $320,000 and Kent contributed $80,000.

On December 1, 2003, Best hired Baker to be a salesperson and to assist in purchasing used aircraft for Best's inventory. On December 15, 2003, Martin instructed Baker to negotiate the purchase of a used airplane without disclosing that Baker was acting on Best's behalf. Martin thought that a better price could be negotiated by Baker if Jackson was not aware that the aircraft was being acquired for Best. The agreement provided that Jackson would deliver the airplane to Baker on January 2, 2004, at which time the purchase price was to be paid. On January 2, 2004, Jackson attempted to deliver the used airplane purchased for Best by Baker. Baker, acting on Martin's instructions, refused to accept delivery or pay the purchase price.

On December 20, 2003, Kent assigned Kent's partnership interest in Best to Green. On December 31, 2003, Kent advised Martin of the assignment to Green. On January 11, 2004, Green contacted Martin and demanded to inspect the partnership books and to participate in the management of partnership affairs, including voting on partnership decisions.

On January 13, 2004, it was determined that Best had incurred an operating loss of $160,000 in 2003. Martin demanded that Kent contribute $80,000 to the partnership to account for Kent's share of the loss. Kent refused to contribute.

On January 28, 2004, Laco Supplies, Inc., a creditor of Best, sued Best and Martin for unpaid bills totaling $92,000. Best had not paid the bills because of a cash shortfall caused by the 2003 operating loss.

Jackson has taken the following position:

*   Baker is responsible for any damages incurred by Jackson as a result of Best's refusal to accept delivery or pay the purchase price.

Martin has taken the following positions:

*   Green is not entitled to inspect the partnership books or participate in the management of the partnership.
*   Only the partnership is liable for the amounts owed to Laco, or, in the alternative, Martin's personal liability is limited to 50% of the total of the unpaid bills.

Kent has taken the following positions:

*   Only Martin is liable for the 2003 operating loss because of the assignment to Green of Kent's partnership interest.
*   Any personal liability of the partners for the 2003 operating loss should be allocated between them on the basis of their original capital contributions.

a. Determine whether Jackson's position is correct and state the reasons for your conclusions.
b. Determine whether Martin's positions are correct and state the reasons for your conclusions.
c. Determine whether Kent's positions are correct and state the reasons for your conclusions.

(5/94, Law, #4, amended, 4976)

Simulation 48-6 (15 to 20 minutes)

Smith, Edwards, and Weil formed Sterling Properties Limited Partnership to engage in the business of buying, selling and managing real estate. Smith and Edwards were general partners. Weil was a limited partner entitled to 50% of all profits.

Within a few months of Sterling's formation, it became apparent to Weil that Smith and Edwards' inexperience was likely to result in financial disaster for the partnership. Therefore, Weil became more involved in day-to-day management decisions. Weil met with prospective buyers and sellers of properties; assisted in negotiating partnership loans with its various lenders; and took an active role in dealing with personnel problems. Things continued to deteriorate for Sterling, and the partners began blaming each other for the partnership's problems.

Finally, Smith could no longer deal with the situation, and withdrew from the partnership. Edwards reminded Smith that the Sterling partnership agreement specifically prohibited withdrawal by a general partner without the consent of all the other partners. Smith advised Edwards and Weil that she would take no part in any further partnership undertaking and would not be responsible for partnership debts incurred after this withdrawal.

With Sterling on the verge of collapse, the following situations have occurred:

Weil demanded the right to inspect and copy the partnership's books and records and Edwards refused to allow Weil to do so, claiming that Weil's status as a limited partner precludes that right.

Anchor Bank, which made a loan to the partnership prior to Smith's withdrawal, is suing Sterling and each partner individually, including Smith, because the loan is in default. Weil denied any liability based on his limited partner status. Smith denies liability based on her withdrawal.

Edwards sued Smith for withdrawing from the partnership and is uncertain about the effect of her withdrawal on the partnership.

Weil wants to assign his partnership interest to Fred Alberts, who wants to become a substitute limited partner. Weil is uncertain about his right to assign this interest to Alberts and, further, the right of Alberts to become a substitute limited partner. Edwards contends that Edwards' consent is necessary for the assignment or the substitution of Alberts as a limited partner and that without this consent any such assignment would cause a dissolution of the partnership. The Sterling partnership agreement and certificate are silent in this regard.

Answer the following questions, setting forth reasons for the conclusions stated.

a. Is Weil entitled to inspect and copy the books and records of the partnership?

b. Are Weil and/or Smith liable to Anchor Bank?

c. Will Edwards prevail in the lawsuit against Smith for withdrawing from the partnership?

d. What is the legal implication to the partnership of Smith's withdrawal?

e. Can Weil assign his partnership interest to Alberts?

f. Can Edwards prevent the assignment to Alberts or the substitution of Alberts as a limited partner?

g. What rights does Alberts have as assignee of Weil's partnership interest?

h. What effect does an assignment have on the partnership?   (5/90, Law, #4, 3200)

Simulation 48-7 (15 to 20 minutes)

On January 5, Stein, Rey, and Lusk entered into a written general partnership agreement by which they agreed to operate a stock brokerage firm. The agreement stated that the partnership would continue upon the death or withdrawal of a partner. The agreement also provided that no partner could reduce the firm's commission below 2% without the consent of all of the other partners. On March 10, Rey, without the consent of Stein and Lusk, agreed with King Corp. to reduce the commission to 1-1/2% on a large transaction by King. Rey believed this would entice King to become a regular customer of the firm. King was unaware of any of the terms of the partnership agreement.

On May 15, Stein entered into a contract conveying Stein's partnership interest to Park and withdrew from the partnership. That same day, all of the partners agreed to admit Park as a general partner. Notice of Stein's withdrawal and Park's admission as a partner was properly published in two newspapers. In addition, third parties who had conducted business with the partnership prior to May 15 received written notice of Stein's withdrawal.

a. In separate paragraphs, discuss whether:
1. The partnership could recover the 1/2% commission from King.
2. The partnership could recover the 1/2% commission from Rey.

b. In separate paragraphs, discuss:
1. Park's liability for partnership obligations arising both before and after being admitted to the partnership.
2. Stein's liability for partnership obligations arising both before and after withdrawing from the partnership.

(11/88, Law, #4, amended, 9650)

Solution 48-1 MULTIPLE CHOICE ANSWERS

Nature

1. (b)   Under the Revised Uniform Partnership Act (RUPA), a partnership must be carried on for a profit, and the persons engaged in a partnership must be co-owners. Partners are not required to share gross receipts from a business.

2. (b)   Under the Revised Uniform Partnership Act, a partnership is by definition "an association of *two or more persons* to carry on a business for profit as co-owners." In general, a partnership does not pay federal income tax. Instead it passes through, to the individual partners, separately stated items of income and deductions for inclusion on the partners' personal returns. A partnership does not have to be evidenced by a writing. There is no requirement that a partnership must provide for the apportionment of liability for partnership debts.

3. (d)   For most employment purposes, a partnership is regarded as a separate legal entity; it must withhold a portion of its nonpartner employees' incomes for FICA contributions. Similarly, the partnership must make deductible contributions to FUTA and state unemployment plans for its nonpartner employees. Additionally, premiums paid by the partnership for workers' compensation are deductible if for nonpartner employees but are *nondeductible if for partner employees.* The partnership does not make FICA, FUTA, or FIT payments for employee-partners; however, as stated above, the partnership will make nondeductible contributions to state workers' compensation plans for its employee-partners. With the exception of these workers' compensation payments, the partnership is not an entity vis-à-vis the partners; rather, the partnership is a conduit through which items of revenue, loss, and credit are passed through to the individual partners. The partners themselves are responsible for FICA payments through the self-employment tax and FIT through estimated tax payments.

4. (c)   The Revised Uniform Partnership Act (RUPA) defines a partnership as an association of two or more persons to carry on a business for profit. In order to achieve its business purposes, a partnership may own property. Partners are not considered employees, but are co-owners of the partnership. General partners are always personally liable for the acts of the partnership. It is only the corporate form of ownership that insulates owners from personal liability. The death of one partner will cause a dissociation of the deceased partner from the partnership.

5. (d)   A joint venture resembles a partnership except that it is formed for only one transaction (or in some cases, a *limited* number of transactions). It is possible to have more than two persons as part of the joint venture. A joint venture is for a profit undertaking *not* a nonprofit undertaking. A joint venture is treated as a partnership and not as a corporate enterprise.

6. (b)   Both a limited partnership and a corporation can only be created pursuant to state statute, and each must file a copy of its certificate with the proper state authorities. Furthermore, both a corporation's stock and a limited partnership interest are subject to the federal securities laws registration

requirements if they are "securities" under the federal securities laws. A limited partner is not an agent of the partnership as a general partner is, and so would not occupy a fiduciary relationship with the partnership. A limited partner is not prohibited from voting on *any* partnership matter. S/he must, however, take care to prevent becoming involved in the management or operation of the partnership so as not to lose her/his status as a limited partner.

7. (b) All partners are agents of each other; thus, each must consent to the relationship. Under RUPA, every partner has the power to dissociate from the partnership whether or not the partner has that right under the partnership agreement. Barring a specific agreement to the contrary, all partners have equal rights in the management and control of the partnership's business; thus they each may authorize expenditures and conveyances.

8. (c) Both a general partnership and a corporation may declare bankruptcy. General partners have unlimited personal liability. A partnership is of limited duration (for example, a partner's death results in dissociation from the partnership and the death of one of two partners results in dissolution). Partnerships generally are tax-reporting, but not tax-paying, entities.

Formation & Existence

9. (d) A general partner's interest in the partnership refers to that partner's right to participate in profit distributions and a return of capital upon dissolution. Thus, a general partner may transfer this interest without dissolving the partnership. The assignee receives nothing more that the assignor's interest in partnership profits and surplus. The assignee does not become a partner and, thus, incurs no liability for partnership debts.

10. (d) The partners of Owen Associates have entered into an enforceable agreement providing that a partner's distributive share of profits would represent each partner's percentage of capital contribution. The Revised Uniform Partnership Act (RUPA) provides that a partner's liability for losses is the same percentage as their right to profits unless otherwise specified by the partnership agreement. Kale contributed 5/9 [$50,000 / ($10,000 + 30,000 + 50,000)] of all capital, thus receives 5/9 of all profits and 5/9 of all losses. $180,000 × 5/9 = $100,000.

11. (b) The Revised Uniform Partnership Act (RUPA) provides that the only element necessary to confer partnership status is mutual consent by all partners. Since all the partners in DSJ agreed to admit Ward, Ward is a partner in DSJ with all the rights and duties which accompany partnership status, including the right to participate in management. Since DSJ has agreed to admit Ward as a substitute partner, there has been a transfer from Lark to Ward of more than a mere assignment of Lark's interest in the partnership. RUPA provides that a partner entering a partnership has only limited liability for partnership liabilities arising before being admitted as a partner. In this instance, it was the other partners of DSJ, not Ward, who promised to hold Lark harmless for past liabilities of DSJ. RUPA does not require an incoming partner to contribute cash or property to the partnership.

12. (d) Since a partnership is viewed as an aggregate of the partners, there is an automatic dissociation whenever there is a change in partners. A deceased partner's executor would not automatically become a partner, since no person can become a partner without the express consent of all other partners. Since a decedent's estate continues to be liable for the debts of the decedent, the estate would not be free from any partnership liabilities that were incurred while the decedent was still a partner.

13. (c) A partner may assign her/his partnership interest and thus the partnership distributions. Each partner also has a right to possess and use the partnership property for partnership purposes, but this right is not assignable except in connection with the assignment of rights of all the partners in the same property. Therefore, only the distributions can be assigned by a partner.

14. (a) A partnership agreement may be either expressed or implied depending on the activities and conduct of the parties. A partnership agreement can be oral unless the agreement falls within the Statute of Frauds, e.g., partnership that cannot be completed within one year.

15. (b) Unless otherwise agreed, a partner's interest is freely assignable. The assignee is entitled to receive only profits and capital to which the partner would have been entitled. S/he does not become a partner and is not entitled to exercise control over the partnership.

16. (c) The Revised Uniform Partnership Act provides that where a partnership agreement is silent as to the division of profits, then profits are divided equally among the partners, regardless of their capital contributions or degree of participation in management. Liability for partnership losses is allocated according to the same ratio as distribution of profits.

17. (b) The Revised Uniform Partnership Act (RUPA) provides that a partner's liability for losses is

the same percentage as their right to profits unless otherwise specified by the partnership agreement. Since Grant has a 10 percent profit share percentage, s/he is also attributed with 10 percent of the losses. In this case, Grant's losses total $20,000 ($200,000 × 0.10). The capital balances play no part in calculating the loss attributable to the partners.

18. (a) When a partnership agreement is silent regarding the allocation of partnership losses, losses are allocated in the same manner as partnership profits. Accordingly, Elgar is saddled with 30% of the $200,000 loss or $60,000. Elgar also is responsible for one-third of the deficit capital balance of Grant. Grant, who began with an $11,000 contribution to capital, sustained 10% of the loss, or $20,000, and as a result, has a negative capital balance of $9,000. It is Grant's responsibility to eliminate the deficit; however, Grant refuses to make any further contribution to the partnership. Therefore, the other partners must make up the difference, but then are free to go after Grant for the additional amount each contributes. Thus, Elgar's [30 / (40 + 30 + 20)] share of Grant's deficit is $3,000 leaving Elgar's capital account at $37,000 ($100,000 − $60,000 − $3,000).

	D(40%)	E(30%)	F(20%)	G(10%)	T
Beg. capital	120	100	75	11	306
Allocate loss	<80>	<60>	<40>	<20>	<200>
Subtotal	40	40	35	<9>	106
Allocate deficit	<4>	<3>	<2>	9	-0-
Total	36	37	33	0	106

19. (b) Unless agreed otherwise, partnership profits and losses are shared equally regardless of unequal capital contributions or services.

Partner's Authority & Liability

20. (b) If a third party knows that a partner's dealings exceed the partner's authority or is outside of the scope of the partner's apparent authority, the other partners are not liable; however, if the other partners ratify the contract, the partnership would be bound by the contract. Amending the partnership agreement has no effect on contract enforceability.

21. (c) Apparent authority arises in situations where a third party could reasonably believe the principal (partnership) has authorized the actions of the agent (partner). The actions of a partner which are apparently for the carrying on of the partnership's business in the usual way, such as the sale of goods, even though not actually authorized, will still bind the partnership if the third party does not know of the partner's lack of actual authority. Apparent authority is not necessarily derived from the express powers and purposes contained in the partnership agreement, and is not effectively limited by a formal resolution of the partners when the third parties are unaware of such resolution. The Revised Uniform Partnership Act imposes limitations on a partner's authority, including that no partner may submit a partnership claim or liability to arbitration without authorization to do so.

22. (c) Generally, the rules of agency apply in determining whether or not the partnership is bound by the dealings of one of its members with a third party. For the purpose of conducting partnership business, every partner is an authorized agent for the partnership and for every other partner in addition to being a principal. Partners are jointly and severally liable for all debts and contract obligations as well as torts of the partnership.

23. (c) The Revised Uniform Partnership Act provides several limitations on the ability of an individual partner to bind the partnership, in addition to any limitations spelled out in the written partnership agreement. One such limitation indicates that, without authorization to the contrary, no partner may dispose of the goodwill of the business or do any other act that would make it impossible to carry on the ordinary business of the partnership. Answers (a), (b), and (d) are examples of transactions frequently performed by individual partners, in carrying on partnership business, that will bind the partnership.

24. (a) All general partners in a partnership are jointly and severally liable for partnership torts. However, a general partner may be liable for the unauthorized acts of partnership employees and other partners.

25. (c) Partnership creditors have first claim on partnership assets before proceeding against individual partners' personal assets. In this problem, Trent, a partnership creditor, must go after partnership assets first and, once partnership assets are exhausted, proceed after the individual assets of Eller. Partners have unlimited liability for partnership debts, and Trent can proceed against those individual partners the creditor has sued individually.

Dissociation

26. (d) Under RUPA, every partner has the power to withdraw from the partnership whether or not the partner has that right under the partnership agreement. When the withdrawing partner acts in violation of the agreement, the partner may be held liable for any losses caused by the dissociation.

27. (c) The Revised Uniform Partnership Act (RUPA) provides that all partners have personal liability for partnership liabilities incurred while they

were partners. Their liability would continue even after dissociation. RUPA also provides that unless a partnership dissolves by operation of law, the partnership, to terminate the partners' apparent authority, must give actual notice to all third parties who have had dealings with the partners and constructive notice to all others. Since College Assoc. has not provided any notice, the partners continue to have apparent authority.

28. (c) A partner's bankruptcy results in that partner's dissociation from the partnership. As long as it does not violate the partnership agreement, a partner may also be a partner in another partnership. The attachment of a partner's interest by a court does not dissolve the partnership, although it may dissociate that partner from the partnership. One or more partners suing another partner for an accounting does not of itself dissolve the partnership.

29. (a) If the partnership agreement is silent as to duration, then the partnership is at-will, and any partner may terminate at any time without incurring liability. A partner's dissociation from a partnership-at-will does not require the consent of other partners, creditors, or the courts. In a partnership with only two partners, one partner's dissociation from the partnership effectively dissolves the partnership; a partnership must have a minimum of two partners.

30. (a) By operation of law, a partner's death results in the dissociation of the deceased partner from the partnership. Even if the agreement provides for the continuation of the business, it does not prevent dissociation. Dissociation is a change in the relation of partners; either the partnership will "wind up" and terminate, or the partnership will purchase the interest of the dissociated partner and continue.

31. (c) When a partnership agreement is silent regarding the allocation of partnership losses, the losses are allocated in the same manner as partnership profits. Vick's share of the undistributed losses would be 30% of $30,000 or $9,000.

32. (d) Under RUPA, the deceased partner automatically dissociates from the partnership, but the partnership doesn't dissolve necessarily, unless the original partnership had only two partners, leaving only one remaining partner. Under RUPA, if the original partnership had more than two partners, the partnership would either dissolve or the remaining partners could continue the partnership if the partnership purchases the deceased partner's interest.

Limited Partnerships

33. (d) A limited partner is not subject to personal liability for partnership debts, because a limited partner's liability is limited to the amount of her/his capital contribution. In addition, generally, a limited partner has no right to control (manage) the partnership (there are a few limited exceptions).

34. (c) It is permissible for a general partner to be a secured creditor of the limited partnership. A limited partner may loan money to and transact other business with a partnership. A general partner may be a limited partner at the same time. Only limited partners have limited liability; the general partners are personally liable for the partnership debts.

35. (d) A limited partnership is a statutorily created association for the purpose of conducting a business for profit. It is composed of one or more general partners who manage the affairs of the business and one or more limited partners who remain passive investors in the partnership. Limited partners have essentially the same rights as general partners: to inspect the books, to receive profits, and to cause an accounting and dissolution. Limited partners are not personally liable for partnership debts beyond their capital contributions. However, this shield lasts only as long as the limited partners do not participate in the management of the enterprise or allow their names to be used in the firm name. General partners ordinarily are not selected by election.

36. (c) A person may be a general partner and a limited partner in the same partnership at the same time, although the liability shield will be moot. Under RULPA, both limited and general partners may contribute services for a capital contribution. A limited partner's death will not dissolve a partnership. A limited partner's interest is freely assignable. However, unless otherwise provided in the partnership agreement, an assignee can become a substitute limited partner only if all members of the limited partnership consent.

37. (b) Under §20 of the Revised Uniform Limited Partnership Act, the executor of an estate of a deceased limited partner is provided with all the rights of a limited partner for the purpose of settling the partner's estate, although s/he does not automatically become a substituted limited partner. Furthermore, the estate is liable for all of the deceased partner's liabilities as a limited partner. The death of a limited partner does not dissolve the partnership.

38. (a) The assignment of a limited partnership interest, unless otherwise agreed, entitles the assignee only to receive the profits and capital to which the assigning partner would have been entitled. To become a substituted limited partner, *all* of the partners must agree to Barr's admission as a limited partner and the certificate of limited partnership must be amended to reflect the substitution of limited partners. Since Barr is not a partner, he is not entitled to all of a partner's rights. Furthermore, assignment of a partnership interest does not dissolve the partnership.

Limited Liability Companies

39. (d) LLC members commonly enter into what is known as an operating agreement, company agreement, or regulations. This is a private contract between the members which generally outlines how they will conduct the business and what rights each

member in the company may have in the event a member leaves the company. The LLC members or organizers must file what commonly is referred to as articles of organization, including the name of the company, the character of the business, the location of the business, the term for which the company is to exist, and the name and address of each member. The articles or certificate normally is filed with the Secretary of State and clerk of the court in the county of the principal place of business.

40. (b) In settling accounts after dissolution, LLC liabilities are paid in the following order: (1) to creditors, except claims by members on account of capital contributions; (2) to members in respect to their capital contributions and (3) to members with respect to their share of undistributed profits. No distinction is made between debts owed to third-party creditors and debts owed to members.

Solution 48-2 ADDITIONAL MULTIPLE CHOICE ANSWERS

Nature

41. (d) Under the Revised Uniform Partnership Act, a partnership has neither unlimited duration nor an obligation for the payment of federal income tax (FIT). A partnership, unlike a corporation, may dissolve every time its ownership changes, limiting its duration. For FIT purposes, a partnership is considered a conduit in that the individual owners are obligated for the payment of federal taxes.

42. (b) A silent partner has unlimited liability, but does not share in the management of the partnership. A limited partner contributes capital to the partnership, but does not have any authority in the partnership's management and has liability limited to the amount of capital contributed. A secret partner participates in the partnership's management, but is undisclosed. An ostensible or nominal partner is one who is not actually a partner, but who may become a partner by estoppel insofar as she or he is held out to appear to be a partner.

Formation & Existence

43. (b) The determining test of partnership existence is whether or not the parties intended to carry on together, as partners, a business for profit; it must appear that the parties intended joint responsibility in the management and operation of the business and intended to share in its profits and losses. It is not essential to the existence of a partnership that all the partners contribute capital. Tenancy in common or any other type of joint ownership of property does not in itself establish a

partnership, regardless of whether the co-owners share any profits made through use of the property. Inference of a partnership shall not be drawn if the profits were received in payment of wages of an employee.

44. (c) Fiduciary duties may not be waived or eliminated in a partnership agreement, but the agreement may identify activities and determine standards for measuring performance of the duties, if not manifestly unreasonable. The partnership agreement may not vary the right of a court to expel a partner nor unreasonably reduce the partners' duty of care below the statutory standard, that is, to refrain from engaging in grossly negligent or reckless conduct, intentional misconduct, or a knowing violation of law. The standard may be increased by agreement to a higher standard of care.

45. (b) A partnership agreement may require partners not to dissociate from the partnership; in this case, a dissociating partner has the power, but not the right, to dissociate, and thus bears any losses caused by the dissociation. A partnership agreement may not eliminate the traditional rule that every partner has the power to withdraw from the partnership at any time. A partnership agreement may not unreasonably restrict partners' or former partners' access rights to books and records nor vary the requirement to wind up the partnership business in certain cases.

46. (d) Actions at law seldom are permitted by partners, except in situations involving controversies in which no complex accounting is necessary or in

which the partner's activity is outside the scope of the partnership business. Thus, the courts will allow an action at law involving a dispute which arose at the outset of the partnership, a suit between partners not related to partnership business, or a suit for fraud or conversion of partnership assets.

47. (d) Fictitious name statutes have no operational effect on partnerships. Partnership operations and the rights and duties of partners are affected by the partnership agreement, state statutes codifying the Revised Uniform Partnership Act (RUPA), and the Revised Uniform Limited Partnership Act (RULPA). A general partnership comes into existence when the partners intend its creation to begin. Such intent can be found in the partnership agreement or from the circumstances surrounding the firm's operation. Partnership existence for federal tax purposes is determined under the Internal Revenue Code, not state statute.

Partner's Authority & Liability

48. (a) Apparent authority depends upon what third parties believe about the authority of an agent. Answer (a) is correct because it addresses what third parties are "aware of." The partnership can effectively limit partner's apparent authority if it makes the third parties "aware" of the limitation. A resolution which third parties are unaware of will have an effect on the partner's actual authority, but will not affect the partner's apparent authority since third parties are not informed of the change. A partner's authority is limited to preclude any partner from submitting a claim or liability to arbitration without all partners' concurrence.

Dissociation

49. (c) Under RUPA, a deceased partner automatically dissociates from the partnership, but the partnership doesn't necessarily dissolve. When dissociation occurs, either the continuing partners purchase the dissociating partner's interest and continue the partnership or the partnership dissolves. In this case, as there were only two partners in the partnership, when one partner dissociated from the partnership, the partnership dissolved because there was only one former partner remaining.

50. (a) On dissolution of a general partnership, there is a specific order of distributions to be made to the partners. Of the alternatives listed in this question, the first distribution to be made would be on account of amounts owed partners for loans to the partnership. Although not given as one of the answer choices, amounts owed to creditors, other than the partners, is the first distribution made when

applicable. Following the payments of amounts owed to partners for loans to the partnership is payment of the partner's capital accounts and amounts owed partners with respect to profits, respectively.

51. (c) When a partner dies and the business is continued without any settlement of accounts, the partner's estate has the option of taking the value of the partner's partnership interest as of the date of dissolution and either any interest accruing or profits attributable to that interest until the date of discharge. One can become a partner only with the consent of all the other partners; no one can become a partner automatically. The claims of a decedent's individual creditors have priority over those of any partnership creditors as against the nonpartnership property. RUPA provides that a dissociated partner is not liable for the debts of the continuing business simply because of continued use of the dissociated partner's name as a part of the partnership name.

52. (a) After 90 days, a statement of dissolution gives constructive notice to creditors that the apparent authority of the partnership is ended for all purposes except winding up. RUPA makes explicit the right of the remaining partners to continue the business after an event of dissolution, if all of the partners [including the dissociating partner(s)] waive the right to have the business wound up and the partnership terminated. After dissolution, any partner who has not dissociated wrongfully may file a statement of dissolution on behalf of the partnership. After dissolution, all nonbreaching partners have authority for the purpose of winding up the business.

53. (d) Partners who have not dissociated wrongfully from the partnership have all their ordinary rights, and the right to damages from breaching partner or partners. If all nonbreaching partners desire to continue the business in the same name, they may do so. They are entitled to possess the partnership property, but must pay the value of that partner's interest to any partner who dissociated from the partnership wrongfully. Dissolution of a partnership results automatically upon the occurrence of any event that makes it unlawful for the partnership business to be conducted.

Limited Partnerships

54. (a) If a limited partnership certificate contains a false statement, anyone who suffers a loss through reliance thereon may hold all the partners liable. If the partnership is organized improperly and the limited partner fails to renunciate on discovery of the defect, that partner can be held personally liability by the firm's creditors. Liability for false statements in a partnership certificate favors people relying on

the false statements and against anyone who signed the certificate knowing of the falsity. (Note that limited partners rarely sign the certificate.) Upon discovery of a defect in a limited partnership's formation, a limited partner can shelter from future liability by causing a filing of an appropriate amendment or renouncing an interest in the partnership's profits. Remember that the examiners instruct candidates to select the best answer.

55. (d) The certificate must include (1) the limited partnership's name, (2) the address of the partnership's registered office and the name and business address of its agent for service of process, (3) the name and business address of each general partner, (4) its mailing address, and (5) the latest date on which the limited partnership is to dissolve.

Limited Liability Companies

56. (d) A limited liability partnership (LLP) can accept contributions, make distributions, and accumulate earnings without incurring taxes or penalties. A LLP is not subject to personal holding tax or double taxation of income. A corporation has no implied power to enter into a partnership; however, it may enter into a partnership if authorized to do so by its corporate charter or state corporation statute. By definition, a proprietorship has only one owner. Corporations may not be shareholders of S corporations. Before 2003, corporations typically incurred double taxation and could not accumulate earnings without penalty. Note: Recent tax changes make similar questions less likely to be asked on future exams.

PERFORMANCE BY SUBTOPICS

Each category below parallels a subtopic covered in Chapter 48. Record the number and percentage of questions you correctly answered in each subtopic area.

Nature

Question #	Correct	√
1		
2		
3		
4		
5		
6		
7		
8		
# Questions	8	
# Correct		
% Correct		

Formation & Existence

Question #	Correct	√
9		
10		
11		
12		
13		
14		
15		
16		
17		
18		
19		
# Questions	11	
# Correct		
% Correct		

Partner's Authority & Liability

Question #	Correct	√
20		
21		
22		
23		
24		
25		
# Questions	6	
# Correct		
% Correct		

Dissociation

Question #	Correct	√
26		
27		
28		
29		
30		
31		
32		
# Questions	7	
# Correct		
% Correct		

Limited Partnerships

Question #	Correct	√
33		
34		
35		
36		
37		
38		
# Questions	6	
# Correct		
% Correct		

Limited Liability Companies

Question #	Correct	√
39		
40		
# Questions	2	
# Correct		
% Correct		

SIMULATION SOLUTIONS

Solution 48-3

Response #1: Liability (5 points)

1. E

Under the Revised Uniform Partnership Act, Range is jointly and severally liable (full personal liability) for up to the total amount of the partnership debt to third parties, even though Range assigned Range's partnership interest to Blank. An assignor remains liable on all partnership debts. Among the partners themselves, partnership losses are shared in the same proportion as profits, unless otherwise agreed in the partnership agreement. Therefore, among the partners, each would owe 1/3.

2. A

Blank has no personal liability for Techno's 2002 operating loss. As the assignee, Blank is entitled to receive the profits and capital to which Range would have been entitled, but Blank does not become a partner. Range remains fully liable on all partnership debts.

3. E

Grove has full personal liability to third parties for up to the total amount of the partnership debt. Under RUPA, all general partners are jointly and severally liable for all debts and contract obligations of the partnership. Among the partners themselves, partnership losses are shared in the same proportion as profits, unless otherwise agreed in the partnership agreement. Therefore, among the partners, each would owe 1/3.

4. B

The partners, as of January 1, 2003, were Plane and Range. Grove resigned as of December 31, 2002, and thus was no longer a partner. Even though Range assigned Range's interest to Blank, Blank did not become a partner. Blank, as the assignee, is entitled to receive the profits and capital to which Range would have been entitled; however, Blank does not become a partner and is not entitled to exercise control in the partnership. Range remains a partner and is fully liable.

5. A

Bankruptcy of the partnership normally results in dissolution of the partnership.

Response #2: Liability & Authority (5 points)

a. 1. Mathews' first position is incorrect. A **partner is considered an agent** of the partnership in carrying out its **usual business.** In this case, Baker **lacked actual authority to bind** Prime to the Jaco contract; however, Baker did have, from Jaco's perspective, **apparent authority** to do so because of the **general character** of Prime's business and, more important, because Baker had previously purchased cars from Jaco on Prime's behalf. Jaco was **not bound by the limitation** on Baker's authority unless Jaco was aware of it.

2. Mathews' second position is also incorrect. As a general rule, a **partner is liable for the debts of the partnership, and a third party is not bound by the profit and loss sharing agreements** between partners because the third party is **not a party to** the partnership agreement. Therefore, Jaco can look to Prime's assets and Mathews' personal assets to satisfy the obligation.

3. Mathews' third position is correct. A **partner is liable to other partners for any liability associated** with contracts entered into ostensibly on **behalf of the partnership but outside the partner's actual authority.** In this case, because Baker **violated the agreement** with Mathews concerning the $15,000 limitation on used car purchases, Baker will be liable to Mathews for any liability that Mathews may have to Jaco.

4. Mathews' fourth position is also correct. A **partner owes a fiduciary duty** (that is, a duty of loyalty) to the partnership and every other partner. A **partner may not benefit** directly or indirectly at the expense of the partnership. A partner must account to the partnership for any benefits derived from the partnership's business without the consent or knowledge of the other partners. In this case, Baker was **not entitled to accept and retain the incentive payments** made by Top. Doing so violated Baker's fiduciary duty to Prime and Mathews. Baker must account to Prime for all the incentive payments received.

b. KYA's contention that its $25,000 capital contribution cannot be used to satisfy Prime's obligation to Jaco is incorrect. A **new partner is liable for partnership liabilities that arose prior** to the new partner's **admission,** but the liability is **limited to the partner's capital contribution** and **interest** in partnership property. Therefore, KYA's liability is limited to its capital contribution and its interest as a partner in Prime's assets.

Solution 48-4

Response #1: Liability (5 points)

1. A

The Statute of Frauds requires that contracts which are not performable within one year of execution be in writing. ACH Associates partnership agreement could be performed within one year; thus, the Statute of Frauds is not applicable and the oral agreement is valid.

2. A

RUPA defines a partnership as an association of two or more persons who jointly carry on a business for profit. Merely owning property jointly, without active involvement in management of the business, does not create a partnership.

3. B

RUPA specifies that partnership profits are shared equally unless the partnership agreement specifies otherwise. The ACH Associates partnership agreement specifies that partners will share in profit distributions based on their capital contributions. As a result, Hook's share of ACH Associates' 2003 profits was $30,000. Anchor's share of ACH Associates' 2003 profits was $10,000.

4. B

RUPA provides that if partners agree on unequal profit percentages, but are silent as to loss-sharing percentages, losses are to be shared using the profit sharing proportions. Since Hook's share of partnership profits is 50%, Hook's capital account would be reduced by one-half of any 2004 losses.

5. B

RUPA provides that upon the dissociation of a partnership for any reason other than by operation of law, the partnership must provide actual notice to third parties with whom the partners have dealt in order to sever the apparent authority of partners or other agents. Since ACH Associates failed to provide Ace Automobile Company with notice of the partnership's dissociation and since Ace was not aware of the dissociation, Hook's apparent authority to conduct partnership business will continue, and ACH will be bound.

6. B

Since all partners are agents of one another, Anchor, Chain, and Hook will all be liable to pay any judgment recovered by Ace Automobile Company.

_____

Response #2: General vs. Limited Partnership (5 points)

Typically, a **general partnership** is formed by an **agreement between** or **among two or more persons,** whether the agreement is written, oral, or implied. **No filing of a partnership agreement is necessary** in order to legally create the general partnership. In contrast, a **limited partnership** can be **formed only where a state statute permits** such formation. In addition, a duly signed **certificate of limited partnership** must be completed and **filed** with the appropriate state or local agency. A limited partnership, like a general partnership, is formed by two or more persons. However, unlike a general partnership, the **limited partnership must have** as members **one or more general partners** and **one or more limited partners.**

As a limited partner, Slavin would not be able to participate in the **daily management** of the partnership's business if she wishes to **limit her liability** to her investment in the partnership. Thus, if Slavin intends to be involved in the daily operations of the partnership and to participate in the **control** of the partnership, she should consider becoming a **general partner** since general partners have rights in the **management** and **conduct** of the partnership's business.

In her capacity as a limited partner, Slavin's **liability** would be **limited** to her investment in the partnership for partnership debts if her interest is fully paid and nonassessable. However, if Slavin were to become a **general partner,** she would have **unlimited liability** which would allow partnership creditors to satisfy the debts of the partnership out of Slavin's **personal** assets.

Unless otherwise provided in the partnership agreement, Slavin has the **right to assign** her limited partnership interest and may also **substitute** the third party as a limited partner if **all** the members (except the assignor) **consent** thereto. Similarly, as a general partner, Slavin may **assign** her interest in the partnership and the **third party** may become a **general partner** if **all** of the partners consent.

A clause providing for the partnership to continue **after the death** of a general partner is **valid** and the partnership will continue. The clause has relatively **little** if any **effect** where a limited partner dies since the limited partnership continues upon the death of one of the limited partners, whether or not the clause is contained in the certificate.

Solution 48-5

Response: Assignment (10 points)

a. Jackson is correct. Baker, as an **agent** acting on behalf of an **undisclosed principal** (Best), is **personally liable** for any contracts entered into in that capacity.

b. Martin's first position that Green is not entitled to inspect the partnership books or participate in partnership management is correct. Green, as an **assignee** of Kent's **partnership interest,** is entitled to receive Kent's share of partnership profits only. Green is not entitled, as an assignee of Kent's partnership interest, to **inspect** the partnership **records** or to **participate in the management** of the partnership.

Martin's second position that only the partnership is responsible for the debt owed Laco is incorrect. Although the partnership is **primarily liable** for the unpaid bills, both Martin and Kent, as Best's partners, are personally liable for the **unpaid** amount of the debt. Laco will be entitled to seek recovery against Martin or Kent for the full amount owed.

c. Kent's first position that only Martin is liable for the 2003 operating loss because of the **assignment** of Kent's partnership interest to Green is incorrect. A partner's assignment of a partnership interest does **not terminate** that partner's **liability** for the partnership's losses and debts.

Kent's second position that any personal liability of the partners for the 2003 operating loss should be allocated on the basis of their original capital contributions is incorrect. The 2003 loss will be **allocated in the same way** that **profits were to be allocated** between the parties, that is, equally, because Martin and Kent had not agreed on the method for allocating losses between themselves.

Solution 48-6

Response: Limited Partnership (10 points)

a. Weil is entitled to **inspect and copy** Sterling's books and records. A limited partner such as Weil has the right to have the **partnership books kept at the principal place of business** of the partnership and to inspect and copy them at all times.

b. Generally, limited partners are **not liable to partnership creditors except to the extent of their capital contribution.** In Weil's case, however, he will probably be **liable to Anchor Bank** in the same manner as Sterling's general partners because he has **taken part in the control** of the business of the partnership and, therefore, has lost his limited liability. Smith, as a general partner, would also be personally liable to Anchor because liability was incurred prior to withdrawal.

c. Edwards **will likely prevail in** his lawsuit against Smith for withdrawing because the partnership agreement specifically prohibits a withdrawal by a general partner without the consent of the other partners. Therefore, Smith has **breached the partnership agreement** and will be **liable** to Edwards **for any damages** resulting from Smith's withdrawal.

d. The withdrawal (retirement) of a general partner **dissolves the partnership** unless the remaining general partners continue the business of the partnership under a right to do so provided in the limited partnership certificate, or unless all partners consent. Therefore, it is possible that Smith's withdrawal will result in Sterling's dissolution.

e. Weil is **free to assign** his limited partnership interests to Alberts in the absence of any prohibitions in the Sterling partnership agreement or certificate.

f. Alberts, however, **cannot be a substitute limited partner without the consent** of the remaining general partner, Edwards.

g. Therefore, Alberts, as an assignee of Weil's limited partnership interest, **may not exercise any rights of a partner.** Alberts is **entitled only** to any **distributions** from Sterling to which Weil would have been entitled.

h. Finally, the assignment by Weil of his partnership interest **does not cause a dissolution** of the partnership.

Solution 48-7

Response: Liability (10 points)

a.　1.　The partnership cannot recover the 1/2% commission from King because Rey had the **apparent authority** to reduce the commission to 1-1/2%. The Revised Uniform Partnership Act states that **every partner is an agent** of the partnership for the purpose of its business, and the act of every partner for apparently carrying on in the usual way the business of the partnership, **binds the partnership,** unless the partner so acting has in fact no authority to act for the partnership in the particular matter, and the person with whom the partner is dealing has **knowledge of the fact that the partner has no such authority.** In determining whether Rey had the apparent authority to bind the partnership, one must examine the circumstances and conduct of the parties and whether King **reasonably believed such authority to exist.** Because brokerage commissions are generally not uniform, it would be reasonable for King to believe that Rey had the authority to perform the transaction at 1-1/2% commission. Furthermore, King **lacked knowledge** of the restriction in the partnership agreement that prohibited Rey from reducing a commission below 2% without the other partners' consent. Therefore, King will not be liable for the 1/2% commission.

　　2.　The partnership can recover the 1/2% commission from Rey because Rey **violated the partnership agreement** by reducing the commission to 1-1/2% without the partners' consent. Rey **owes a duty to act in accordance with the partnership agreement.**

b.　1.　Under the Revised Uniform Partnership Act, a person admitted as a partner into an existing partnership is liable for all the obligations of the partnership arising before being admitted as though that person had been a partner when such obligations were incurred, except that this liability may be satisfied **only out of partnership property.** Thus, Park **will not be personally liable** for the partnership obligations arising prior to being admitted as a partner but would be liable based upon the extent of partnership interests held. Park **will be personally liable for partnership obligations arising after being admitted to the partnership.**

　　2.　Stein will continue to be personally liable for partnership obligations arising prior to withdrawing from the partnership, unless Stein obtains a release from the existing creditors. Stein will have **no liability** for partnership obligations arising **after actual and constructive notice of withdrawing** was properly given. However, Stein may be personally liable for partnership obligations arising after withdrawing but prior to notice being given. **Actual notice** of Stein's withdrawal was **given by written notification** to partnership creditors that had conducted business with the partnership prior to May 15. **Constructive notice** of Stein's withdrawal was given by **proper publication** in two newspapers to those third parties who had not dealt with the partnership, but may have known of its existence.

The CPA Examination

The CPA exam is designed as a licensing requirement to measure the technical competence of CPA candidates. Although licensing occurs at the state level, the exam is uniform at all sites and has national acceptance. In other words, passing the CPA exam in one jurisdiction generally allows candidates to obtain a reciprocal certificate or license, if they meet all the requirements imposed by the jurisdiction from which reciprocity is sought.

State boards also rely upon other means to ensure that candidates possess the necessary technical and character attributes, including interviews, letters of reference, affidavits of employment, ethics examinations, and educational requirements. Addresses of state boards are listed in the **Practical Advice** appendix or (along with applicable links) on the web site of the National Association of the State Boards of Accountancy (http://www.nasba.org).

Generally speaking, the CPA exam is essentially an academic examination that tests the breadth of material covered by good accounting curricula. It also emphasizes the body of knowledge required for the practice of public accounting. It is to your advantage to take the exam as soon as possible after completing the formal education requirements.

We also recommend that most candidates study for two examination sections at once, since there is a **synergistic** learning effect to be derived through preparing for more than one part. That is, all sections of the exam share some common subjects (particularly Financial Accounting & Reporting and Auditing & Attestation); so as you study for one section, you are also studying for the others. This advice will be different for different candidates. Candidates studying full-time may find that studying for all four sections at once is most beneficial. Some candidates with full-time jobs and family responsibilities may find that studying for a single exam section at once is best for them.

More helpful exam information is included in the **Practical Advice** appendix in this volume.

CHANGE ALERT

American Jobs Creation Act of 2004 (AJCA '04)

The American Jobs Creation Act of 2004 increased the maximum number of shareholders of an S corporation from 75 to 100. To determine the number of shareholders for S corporation status, AJCA '04 allows family members to be counted as one shareholder. Formerly, only a husband and wife were treated as one shareholder for this purpose.

STUDY TIP

Agency topics are tested explicitly in the REG exam section. As partners each are agents of each other and the partnership and corporate officers are agents of the corporation, a basic understanding of agency topics promotes an understanding of some partnership and corporation topics. Accordingly, a brief discussion and limited number of questions on agency topics are included in this chapter.

CHAPTER 49

CORPORATIONS

EXAM COVERAGE: The *Business Structure* portion of the BEC section of the CPA exam is designated by the examiners to be about 20 percent of the section's point value. Historically, exam coverage of corporations was slightly greater than partnerships. That relationship may not hold true under the new CSO. More information about the point value of various topics is included in the Practical Advice section of this volume.

CHAPTER 49

CORPORATIONS

I. Overview

A. Definitions

1. **Domestic Corporation** A corporation that does business in the state in which it is incorporated.

2. **Foreign Corporation** A corporation doing business in any state except the one in which it is incorporated. This type of corporation is subject to the requirements and administrative controls of the states in which it is doing business.

3. **Professional Corporation** A corporation under state law that allows professionals such as doctors, attorneys, and accountants to incorporate. Usually shares are owned only by the professionals who retain personal liability for their professional acts.

4. **Shareholder & Stockholder** These terms typically are used interchangeably to refer to an owner of an equity interest in a corporation.

5. **Insiders** Under common law, corporate directors and officers had no fiduciary duty directly to shareholders. While insiders were liable for fraud and deceit, they generally had no duty to disclose inside information concerning the sale and purchase of stock. An exception to this rule existed when an insider was dealing face to face with a buyer or seller of stock. Under these circumstances, an insider was required to disclose any known facts of an unusual nature. Today, insider trading is subject to regulation under federal securities law, primarily under the Securities Exchange Act of 1934.

   a. **SEC Rule 10b-5** This rule makes it unlawful to (a) employ any device, scheme, or artifice to defraud; (b) make any untrue statement of a material fact or to omit a material fact necessary in order to make the statement made not misleading; or (c) engage in any act, practice, or course of business that operates as fraud or deceit upon any person in connection with the purchase or sale of any security in interstate commerce.

   b. **Rule 16b., Insider Trading** This rule applies to officers, directors, and holders of more than 10% of the company's stock. It makes it unlawful for these individuals to buy and sell stock for a profit within any 6-month period.

B. Attributes
A corporation is an artificial person or legal entity created by, or under the authority of, a state statute. It may be owned by one or more persons, but is considered to be a single, separate legal entity. It is vested with the capacity of continuous succession, irrespective of changes in its ownership or operating management. In carrying out its purpose, a corporation is limited by the provisions of its charter as well as state and federal regulating statutes. The Revised Model Business Corporation Act (RMBCA) governs the formation, activities, and termination of corporations in many, but not all, states.

1. **Centralization** The corporation's management is centralized in the board of directors, elected by the shareholders.

2. **Limited Liability** Generally, a shareholder is not personally liable for the debts and obligations of the corporation. Risk of loss extends only to the shareholder's actual investment in the corporation.

3. **Continuous Life** A corporation customarily is regarded as having a perpetual life. Although it may be terminated by such acts as merger or dissolution, it continues independent of changes in ownership and management.

4. **Transferability of Interest** A shareholder's interest in the corporation may be bought or sold with little effect on the operation of the corporate business.

5. **Taxation** Absent an election to be taxed as an S corporation, corporation potentially suffers double taxation on its profits. Taxation occurs once on the corporate level and again when profits pass into the hands of the shareholders. This is mitigated somewhat by recent tax law changes.

6. **Costs** Initially, a corporation must incur the cost of formally incorporating. Subsequent to formation and throughout its life, a corporation must remain cognizant of and responsive to a variety of procedural and administrative regulations.

C. **Corporate Powers**
A corporation has the **express** power to perform any act authorized by state law, the articles of incorporation, or the bylaws.

1. **Implied Powers** A corporation also possesses those powers that are reasonably necessary to promote and carry out the express corporate powers. These powers may be **implied** if the transaction undertaken is in furtherance of the objectives and purposes for which the corporation was formed. Examples of implied powers are as follows.

   a. Power to sue and be sued in the corporate name.

   b. Power to make or amend corporate bylaws.

   c. Power to acquire, mortgage, and transfer property for corporate purposes.

   d. Power to issue corporate bonds.

2. **Particular Powers** Certain powers may **not** be implied to exist in a corporation due to public policy considerations.

   a. **Gifts** As a general rule, a corporation has no implied power to give away its money or other assets at the expense of the shareholders. However, in certain situations, such as when a gift promotes the purpose for which the corporation was formed, the courts may recognize an implied power to make such a gift.

   b. **Partnerships** A corporation has no implied power to enter into a partnership with a person or another entity. The rationale is that the corporation should not be bound by the acts of partners who are not its duly appointed agents and officers. However, a corporation may enter into a partnership if authorized to do so by the corporate charter or state corporation statute.

   c. **Surety** Generally, a corporation may not lend money unless specifically authorized to do so by charter or statute. However, a corporation may become a surety on a particular customer's debt if this action promotes the corporate business. A corporation may not pledge its credit or assets as an accommodation.

   d. **Acquiring & Reacquiring Shares** Most courts hold that a corporation may purchase its own shares and the shares of other corporations, provided such action promotes the corporate business. Such purchases normally must be made from accumulated profits, or surplus.

D. Directors

The right to manage the affairs of the corporation is vested in the board of directors. Although the directors are elected by the shareholders, they have a statutory right to manage the corporation independent of any direct shareholder influence. Directors need **not** be shareholders.

1. **Appointment** The original board of directors is named in the articles of incorporation. Subsequently, directors are elected at shareholder meetings, with the board having the power to fill vacancies that occur during the term. Traditionally, the minimum number of directors prescribed by various statutes was three; however, the modern trend is to allow as few as one.

    a. **Inside Director** An employee, officer or stockholder of a corporation elected to the corporation's board of directors. If part of the company's management team, they are also referred to as executive directors.

    b. **Outside Director** A person elected to a corporation's board of directors who is not an employee, officer or stockholder of the corporation. Outside directors have very little conflict of interest and generally offer an impartial or unbiased outlook.

    c. **Audit Committee** An operating committee of the board of directors.

        (1) Should contain at least one financial expert

        (2) Members may serve on the board of directors or any other board committee

        (3) Under Sarbanes-Oxley, each member of the audit committee of a listed company must be independent, meaning that the person cannot accept any consulting, advisory or other compensatory fees from the company, and cannot be an affiliated person of the company or any of its subsidiaries

        (4) Responsibilities typically include

            (a) Overseeing the financial reporting process

            (b) Monitoring choice of accounting policies and principles

            (c) Monitoring internal control process

            (d) Appointment, compensation, and oversight of the external auditors

            (e) Receipt of communications and audit reports directly from the external auditors

2. **Elections** Directors usually hold office for a given statutory period, unless a shorter term is specified by the articles. Board members are elected by a plurality or through cumulative voting. The articles also may provide that the terms of various directors be staggered.

3. **Removal** Under common law, directors could be removed only for cause, e.g., fraud or incompetency. However, under many modern statutes a director may be removed at any time during her/his term, with or without cause, with the consent of the shareholders.

4. **Meetings** Corporate board powers usually are exercised at a properly noticed board meeting attended by the necessary number of directors.

    a. **Notice** The general rule is that a director must receive notice of an impending meeting within a reasonable time before each meeting. However, notice of a meeting may be waived before or after the meeting. Many jurisdictions have modified these requirements by prescribing specific board meeting procedures.

b. Quorum In order for board action to be binding, a simple majority of the directors must be present at the meeting. Furthermore, a simple majority of those present is sufficient to bind the corporation legally, unless the articles call for a higher percentage.

c. Without Meeting Some state statutes allow the board of directors to act without a meeting if all of the directors consent in writing to the proposed action and such consent is filed in the minutes book of the corporation.

d. Delegation of Authority It is a common practice in many jurisdictions for the board of directors to appoint an "executive committee" to handle specific matters or the day-to-day affairs of the corporation. This committee must be composed of directors. However, it is important to note that there are certain statutory duties that the directors may not delegate to such a committee, e.g., declaring dividends or amending bylaws.

5. Powers Generally, the board of directors has the power to manage the business of the corporation, initiate fundamental changes subject to final approval by the shareholders, fill vacancies on the board, adopt and amend the bylaws, elect and fix the compensation of officers, remove officers, and declare dividends. Directors are personally liable for dividends that are wrongfully or unlawfully paid, unless they acted with due care in accordance with the information upon which they reasonably relied.

6. Rights Directors have the right to be reimbursed for their expenses, to inspect the corporate books, and to rely on reports and statements made by management and personnel. Normally, a director does not have the right to compensation for services unless specifically stated in the bylaws.

7. Duties Directors are fiduciaries of the corporation and have the duty to act with reasonable care and loyalty.

a. Due Care Directors must exercise the care and skill that an ordinarily prudent person would exercise under similar circumstances. While a director may not delegate duties by appointing another to act in her/his place, a director may rely on information given to her/him by others associated with the corporation. A director who fails to act with due care may be negligent and liable to the corporation in damages for losses or injuries suffered as a result of her/his breach.

- **Business Judgment Rule** Finding directors guilty of negligence for their breach of duty of due care discouraged many qualified people from serving as directors. In order to mitigate this result, courts adopted the rule that when the acts or omissions involve a question of policy or business judgment, a director who acted in good faith will not be held personally liable for "mere errors of judgment or want of prudence, short of clear and gross negligence."

b. Loyalty A director often has a personal stake in some aspect of the corporation's business. Common law generally prohibited a director from having any personal dealings with her/his corporation. Today, most jurisdictions allow individual dealings with the corporation, if full disclosure is made to the other board members and they approve of the action. In addition, the courts may examine such transactions to determine their fundamental fairness. If any contract is determined not to be in the corporation's best interest, it may be rescinded. The breaching director also may be liable for any losses or damages resulting to the corporation from the transaction.

c. Corporate Opportunity Doctrine A director may not divert to her/himself a business opportunity belonging to the corporation (i.e., one in which the corporation has a right, interest, or expectancy) without first giving the corporation a chance to act. Failure to give the corporation this opportunity will result in the director's being liable in damages for any profit made on the venture.

d. **Sarbanes-Oxley Act** The audit committee of an issuer of publicly traded securities must approve all auditing and nonauditing services provided to the issuer by its auditor. The Sarbanes-Oxley Act specifies that the audit committee, not management, is responsible for appointment and oversight of any audit work performed by the audit firm. The audit committee is a committee of board members who are independent of the corporation.

E. Officers

In most jurisdictions, the major officers are elected by the board of directors and serve at the board's pleasure. The same individuals may be both officers and directors. A person can hold more than one office. Officers need **not** be shareholders in the corporation.

1. **Authority to Contract** Officers are granted the express authority to contract by virtue of statute, articles, and bylaws. They also possess that degree of implied authority that is reasonably necessary to carry out their duties. As with other corporate agents, officers may bind the corporation by apparent authority, even though they are acting beyond their actual authority.

2. **Tort Liability** The usual rules of agency apply to officers. The corporation is liable for the torts of its officers if they are committed within the course and scope of the employment relationship, even if the act itself is unauthorized.

3. **Fiduciary Duties** Officers are held to the same fiduciary standards as directors.

4. **Sarbanes-Oxley Act** The Sarbanes-Oxley Act requires the principal executive officer or officers (CEO) and the principal financial officer or officers (CFO), or persons performing similar functions, to certify annual and quarterly Securities and Exchange Commission (SEC) reports. The Act prohibits an issuer of publicly traded securities from providing false or misleading information about the financial condition of the issuer to an accounting firm conducting an audit for the issuer. The Act requires executives of an issuer to forfeit any bonus or incentive-based pay or profits from the sale of stock received in the twelve months prior to an earnings restatement.

F. Corporate Liability

A corporation is liable on the contracts of its employees and, in particular situations, for torts committed by employees.

1. *Respondeat Superior* Under the *respondeat superior* doctrine, a corporation is liable for the tortious acts of its employees, provided that the acts were committed within the course and scope of employment.

2. *Ultra Vires* *Ultra vires* acts are acts by the corporation or its management that are beyond the scope of corporate authority as granted by its charter, bylaws, and state law. A corporation may not act or contract in any way that is not authorized either expressly or impliedly by state statute, the articles of incorporation, or the bylaws. Such acts or contracts are termed "*ultra vires*," and while they are not illegal, they are void or unenforceable under common law. In most jurisdictions today, the *ultra vires* doctrine may **not** be asserted by either the corporation or a third party to nullify an action or contract. However, it can be asserted by the **shareholders** of the *ultra vires* corporation. These shareholders, as well as the state, can sue the corporation to enjoin it from acting in violation of its charter or state statute.

G. Corporate Veil

Under certain circumstances individual shareholders may be held personally liable for the debts of the corporation. Piercing the corporate veil is the act of disregarding the shareholders' general shield from liability for corporate debts. This occurs when the court finds corporate fraud and desires to hold shareholders liable. Occasionally, a corporation is formed by its owners for the purpose of committing frauds, circumventing the law, or for pursuing, in some other way, illegal objectives. If a court determines that such is the case, it will pierce the corporate veil and hold the shareholders personally liable for a loss suffered by a third party. Some of the factors examined by the courts in making their determination are whether there is a bona fide corporate purpose, whether the corporate funds are segregated carefully from the shareholders' funds, and whether the formalities of corporate existence have been followed (such as shareholders and directors meetings). Other common situations that may cause a court to pierce the corporate veil are as follows.

1. **Undercapitalization** The courts will examine the amount of capital present at the formation of the corporation. If that amount is inadequate to meet the reasonably foreseeable financial needs of the corporation, it is undercapitalized and shareholders may be held personally liable upon the insolvency of the corporation.

2. **Subsidiary Corporations** Normally, a subsidiary is treated as a unique entity distinct from the parent corporation. However, if the subsidiary is inadequately capitalized, its activities are substantially intermingled with the parent's, or if it exists solely for the benefit of the parent, the courts will treat the two entities as one and hold the parent liable for the debts of the subsidiary.

3. **Loans** Shareholders often will contribute money at the inception of the corporation in the form of loans. Contributors do this in hopes of elevating their position to that of creditors, with rights superior to those of other shareholders in the event of corporate liquidation. Such shareholder loans are suspect. In cases of undercapitalization and bankruptcy, courts will subordinate insider loans to loans of outside creditors or transform insider "loans" into capital contributions (stock).

II. Formation

A. Promoter
The individual who is primarily responsible for forming, arranging for capitalization, and initiating the general business of the corporation. The promoter's duties also include drawing up the corporate charter and promoting stock subscriptions.

1. **Fiduciary Duty** A promoter is said to be a fiduciary of the not-yet-formed corporation. This special relationship imposes a duty on the promoter to act in good faith and in the corporation's best interest. The promoter is barred from making secret profits (self-dealing) at the expense of either the corporation or those subscribing to the shares of the corporation. The promoter must make full disclosure of her/his dealings with the corporation to anyone with an interest in the corporation who is in a position to legally consent to her/his activities. In the event of any self-dealing, the promoter is required to turn her/his secret profits over to the corporation.

2. **Promoter's Contracts** The general rule is that a corporation is not liable on pre-incorporation contracts entered into on behalf of the corporation by the promoter. The rationale is that there can be no ratification of the promoter's contract by a nonexistent entity. However, a corporation may become liable on such contracts by **adoption.**

   a. **Adoption** To circumvent the harsh results of placing the complete financial burden on the promoter for pre-incorporation contracts, the courts formulated the theory of adoption. Adoption is the act of corporate acceptance of the promoter's pre-incorporation contract. It may occur in three ways.

      (1) **Statute** The corporation may be forced by state statute to adopt the contracts made by the promoter.

      (2) **Agreement** Adoption may occur by an express agreement, entered into after incorporation, between the promoter and the corporation.

      (3) **Implied** The corporation implicitly may adopt a pre-incorporation contract by accepting the benefits of the contract.

b. **Continuing Promoter Liability** Even if the corporation adopts the contract, the promoter remains personally liable unless one of the following occurs.

(1) The promoter states in the contract that s/he is not personally liable.

(2) A novation occurs when a third party creditor agrees to look to the corporation for satisfaction of the contract, thereby releasing the promoter from liability.

3. **Securities Act of 1933** A promoter has a duty to comply with the Securities Act of 1933. The Act requires the filing of a registration statement with the Securities and Exchange Commission (SEC) if securities are to be offered through the mail or through some other means of interstate commerce. In addition, the Act requires the promoter to provide each potential purchaser with a prospectus containing detailed information about the corporation. The registration statement must include information relating to such matters as corporate management, control, capitalization, and financial condition.

B. **Incorporation**
Corporations are regulated by state laws that usually allow their formation for the purpose of carrying on lawful activity. The primary statutory requirement is the execution and filing of articles of incorporation.

1. **Incorporators** Incorporators sign the articles of incorporation. Frequently, the incorporators and promoters are the same persons.

2. **Articles of Incorporation** Under state law, the articles of incorporation (sometimes referred to as a certificate of incorporation or a corporate charter) must contain certain mandatory provisions. Thus, the articles normally include the name of the corporation, corporate purpose, capital stock authorized, location of the principal office, number of directors, the name and address of the registered agent for service of process, capital structure, and a duration. Additionally, some states require that a minimum amount of capital be paid into the corporation and that the board of directors elect officials and adopt bylaws before the certificate of incorporation is valid.

3. **Procedure** After the articles of incorporation are signed and acknowledged by the persons named as directors, the document, accompanied by the appropriate fee, must be filed with the designated state office. Under common law, the corporation does not come into existence until that office issues a certificate of incorporation. Under the modern trend, corporate existence begins at the time of filing and before the certificate is issued.

4. **Bylaws** The bylaws are the rules and regulations that govern the internal management of a corporation. Adoption of the bylaws is one of the first items of business after incorporation. Under the Revised Model Business Corporation Act, either the incorporators or the board of directors may adopt the bylaws. In contrast to the articles of incorporation, the bylaws do not have to be publicly filed. The shareholders or the board of directors may amend or repeal the bylaws, unless the articles of incorporation or other sections of the Revised Model Business Corporation Act reserve that power exclusively to the shareholders. The Statutory Close Corporation Supplement permits close corporations to operate without bylaws as long as the required bylaw information is included in a shareholder agreement or in the articles of incorporation.

C. **Defects in Formation**
Under former common law, a corporation that did not follow the above procedure for formation might not achieve corporate status. This allowed third persons an alternative to performing contracts entered into with the corporation; that is, if there were no corporation, then there would be no duty to perform. Also, without corporate status, a third party could hold the shareholders directly liable for any contract entered into in the corporate name. To avoid this result, the courts adopted several doctrines to deal with defects in the incorporation process.

1. ***De Jure* Corporation** Under current common law, any corporation that substantially complies with the mandatory statutory requirements of incorporation is deemed a *de jure* corporation. Such corporate status cannot be attacked by anyone, including the state.

2. ***De Facto* Corporation** If the corporation fails to comply substantially with mandatory requirements, the courts might, nevertheless, recognize its existence as *de facto*. This status forces third parties to perform on corporate contracts and shields shareholders from direct liability. However, the state still may bring a suit challenging the corporate existence through a "*quo warranto*" proceeding. The essential elements of a *de facto* corporation are as follows.

   a. A valid statute under which the business could have been incorporated legally.

   b. Existence of a corporate charter.

   c. A good faith effort to incorporate.

   d. Some good faith business dealings in the corporate name.

3. **Corporation by Estoppel** In the absence of even a *de facto* corporation, many courts have protected shareholders from third-party suits. If the third party entered into a contract believing s/he was dealing with a corporation, the courts will not allow the third party to hold shareholders liable on the contract.

4. **Noncorporation** If a corporation fails to obtain any status mentioned above, it may be attacked by anyone. Generally, in such cases the shareholders are liable for the debts of the corporation in the same manner as partners if they have participated actively in the venture.

III. Financing

A. Subscription Agreements

A subscription agreement is a contract by which the subscriber agrees to purchase a number of shares of corporate stock at a subscription price specified in the agreement.

1. **Pre-Incorporation Subscribers** The major problem with pre-incorporation subscribers is determining at what point the subscriber becomes bound by her/his commitment to buy stock. Generally, the courts have held that a subscription for shares in a corporation not yet formed is an unenforceable contract, due to the lack of parties. Therefore, some act of acceptance by the corporation, after incorporation, is required before pre-incorporation subscription agreements will become binding.

   a. **Enforceable Pre-Incorporation Subscriptions** If individuals agreed to subscribe to corporate stock, and it appears that each party's promise was dependent on the other parties also subscribing, then an enforceable contract exists. The subscription is enforceable not between the corporation and each subscriber, but rather among the subscribers themselves.

   b. **Model Business Corporation Act (MBCA)** Under this Act, pre-incorporation stock subscriptions are deemed to be continuing offers that are irrevocable for purposes of administrative convenience for a period of six months.

2. **Post-Incorporation Subscribers** Any agreement to subscribe that comes into existence after the corporation is formed constitutes a binding obligation to sell or purchase stock.

3. **Conditional Subscription** Normally, a subscriber may condition a purchase on any event or occurrence s/he chooses. Generally, any such condition must appear in writing on the face of the subscription agreement. However, courts have long held that the stock subscription contract contains both of the following implied conditions.

      a.   The corporation has achieved a *de jure* status.

      b.   The corporation has complied with all applicable securities laws.

B.   **Authorized Capital**
The articles of incorporation must specify the types and number of shares that a corporation may issue. Although fewer shares may be issued than specified, it is unlawful to issue a greater number than is authorized in the articles. Capital is the consideration or other property received by a corporation in exchange for issued and outstanding stock. The original capital may be contributed in the form of money, property, or services. In a state with a minimum capitalization requirement, the fair market value of the property or services contributed will determine whether the corporation has met its requirement.

1.   **Authorized Stock** The stock that is authorized to be issued in the articles of incorporation.

2.   **Issued Stock** That portion of authorized stock that has been issued to shareholders.

3.   **Outstanding Stock** That portion of authorized stock that has been issued to, and still is owned by, shareholders.

4.   **Treasury Stock** Stock that has been issued, but that is no longer outstanding because the corporation has redeemed it (reacquired it). Treasury stock may be purchased only with surplus. Additionally, it carries no right to vote or receive dividends, it may be resold without regard to par value. It may be distributed as a stock dividend. If treasury stock is canceled, the effect is to reduce stated capital by the amount represented by the shares, and such canceled shares are restored to the status of authorized, but unissued, shares.

5.   **Watered Stock** Stock that is issued for less than its par or stated value.

6.   **Common Stock** Stock that entitles its owner to share in any dividends declared by the board of directors. Additionally, common stock is entitled to share in liquidating distributions of corporate assets. Common stock may be either voting or nonvoting.

7.   **Preferred Stock** Preferred stock has certain rights and preferences, which are defined in the articles of incorporation, the bylaws, or the share contract itself. The shares may be either voting or nonvoting. At liquidation, holders of preferred stock receive the par value of their stock before the common stock holders are entitled to any value. Other rights and preferences of preferred stock vary depending on the class of preferred held.

      a.   **Unspecified** Shareholders are entitled to be paid a fixed dividend before any dividends are paid to holders of common stock. This class of stock does not include the rights to any other profits.

      b.   **Cumulative** The holders of cumulative preferred have the right to receive fixed yearly dividends. If the corporation fails in its payment for year one, the stockholder's rights cumulate to year two. Additionally, preferred shareholders must receive full payment of all arrearages before common shareholders receive their dividends.

      c.   **Participating** Participating preferred shareholders share ratably with common shareholders in any profit distribution beyond the prescribed preferred rate. Fully participating preferred holders share equally with common holders in excess profit distribution, while partially participating preferred holders share in a more limited manner in such excess.

      d.   **Convertible** Holders of this stock may convert into common stock after a stipulated time.

8.   **Voting Stock** Any class of stock may be designated as voting or nonvoting. A shareholder is entitled to one vote for each voting share that s/he owns.

9.   **Contributed Capital** The total amount paid for stock when issued; i.e., stated capital plus paid-in surplus.

10.   **Par Value** Par value is the nominal value assigned to the stock, which is established by the corporation. However, the corporation may sell the stock at par value or any price above par value. The par value is allocated to the capital account; all value received in excess of par value is allocated to capital surplus accounts. Corporations may issue no-par stock, i.e., a stock that has no established par value. State statutes usually require that a certain portion of the value received for no-par stock be allocated to the capital account.

11.   **Paid-In Surplus** Any amount paid for stock above the par (stated) value.

12.   **Earned Surplus (Retained Earnings)** The total net profits of a corporation minus any dividends paid out in past years plus, or minus any prior period adjustments.

13.   **Legal Capital (Stated Capital)** The number of shares issued times their par value or stated value. This fund primarily is reserved, for the payment of creditors in the event of a liquidation. Dividends may not come from this source.

14.   **Surplus** Earned surplus combined with paid-in surplus, also stated as net assets minus stated, or legal, capital.

C.   **Stock Issuance**
The Uniform Commercial Code sets forth the measure of liability to be borne by a corporation with regard to its issued securities. Furthermore, a corporation is liable to good faith purchasers for damages caused by its employees or agents who have forged or signed corporate securities without corporate authority.

1.   **Consideration** A corporation may receive only certain types and quantities of consideration for its shares.

   a.   **Types** A corporation may issue its stock in return for cash or property, including promissory notes. It also may accept past services and contracts for future services as consideration for the issuance of stock.

   b.   **Quantity** A corporation may issue its no-par stock at a price determined by the board of directors. Par value shares may not be issued for less than par value.

2.   **Transfer** Stock may be transferred by endorsement and delivery. If a stock certificate is endorsed in blank, it may be transferred by delivery alone. A transfer becomes legally effective against the corporation only when the security is presented to the corporation, or a duly appointed agent, for registration. The corporation is bound to accept such stock for registration as long as the stock was endorsed properly and all other formalities of transfer were complied with. The corporation may place certain restrictions on the transfer of stock. For example, it may require the holder to offer the corporation the right of first refusal on a repurchase of the stock before any sale is permitted to anyone else. However, in order to be enforceable, such restrictions must be reasonable and must be noted conspicuously on the face of the certificate.

3.   **Shareholder** If one or more shareholders own 80% of the stock immediately after contribution of property (including money) to the corporation, solely in exchange for stock, the shareholder(s) generally recognize no gain or loss in the transaction. The basis of the stock equals the basis of property contributed to the corporation. If a shareholder is not in control immediately after the exchange, gain or loss is recognized to the extent of fair market value minus the basis of property exchanged for the stock. The basis of stock in the shareholder's hands is its fair market value.

4.   **Corporation** No gain or loss is recognized by the corporation for contribution of property by shareholders. If the contribution was tax-free to the shareholder, the corporation carries over

the shareholder's basis in property transferred for stock. If the contribution creates a recognized gain, the corporation's basis in property received is the stockholder's basis plus the gain recognized on the exchange of property for stock.

IV. Stockholders

A. Rights

Although a stockholder may not exercise any direct control over corporate management, there are several ways a stockholder may affect the corporation indirectly through the exercise of stock ownership rights.

Exhibit 1 ▶ Basic Stockholder Rights Mnemonic

D	**D**erivative action
A	**A**sset share on dissolution
V	Right to **V**ote
I	**I**nspect books
P	**P**reemptive right to subscribe to newly authorized stock in proportion to existing holdings (not to treasury stock)

1. **Derivative Action** Stockholders have the right to sue for the benefit of the corporation in an action called a derivative suit. In a derivative action, proof must be shown that the corporation suffered harm, such as in the case of a director stealing from the corporation. Any recovery goes to the corporation.

2. **Direct Action** A shareholder has the right to sue for her/his own benefit (direct action suit).

3. **Asset Share on Dissolution** Upon liquidation of a corporation, the stockholders have the right to their proportionate shares of any remaining assets, or proceeds from those assets, after the creditors are paid.

4. **Voting Rights** The right to vote is held by shareholders of record. The articles or bylaws may designate some classes of stock as nonvoting, but at least one class of stock at all times must have the right to vote.

    a. **Straight Voting** Under this method of voting, a shareholder is entitled to one vote for every share held. When there are several classes of shares, one class may be given multiple votes (weighted voting). A simple majority determines the outcome.

    b. **Cumulative Voting for Directors** This type of voting is designed to give minority shareholders a greater say on the board of directors. Cumulative voting means that each shareholder receives votes equal to the number of her/his shares times the number of directors to be elected.

    Example 1 ▶ Cumulative Voting for Directors

    > S holds 100 shares. There are 5 directors to be elected. S holds 500 votes. S's chances for electing a board member are increased because all 500 votes may be cast for one candidate if S so desires.

5. **Right to Inspect Books & Records** Corporations are required to keep records pertaining to such things as shareholder names and addresses and minutes of corporate-related meetings. Under the common law, a shareholder had a right to inspect these records provided s/he could prove to the court that the inspection was for a proper purpose. In most jurisdictions today, shareholders have statutory rights to inspect the corporate books or records.

However, in most states the right is qualified, and the shareholder must demonstrate that the purpose for inspecting the materials is related reasonably to her/his interest as a shareholder.

6. **Preemptive Right** In a newly authorized issue of stock, existing stockholders have the right of first refusal to subscribe to the new issue in proportion to their existing holdings. This does not apply to treasury stock or previously authorized, but unissued, stock.

7. **Dividends** A shareholder has the right to share in dividends, if and when declared by the board of directors. The board of directors has the discretionary right to declare dividends. Stockholders generally have no inherent right to force a dividend declaration. One important exception to this rule is when there is a surplus and stockholders can convince a court of equity that the directors have acted fraudulently, oppressively, or arbitrarily in refusing to declare a dividend. Dividends always may be paid out of a corporation's unrestricted and unreserved earned surplus (retained earnings) and, depending on the state, also may be paid out of its paid-in surplus. However, legal capital (stated capital) is never an appropriate source for the payment of dividends.

8. **Meetings** A shareholder has the right to receive notice of, and attend, meetings. Some state statutes allow actions without a meeting if the shareholders consent in writing to the proposed actions.

9. **Fundamental Changes** Certain types of changes, such as amendments to the articles, merger, consolidation, dissolution, or sale of a substantial part of the corporate assets, require approval by an absolute majority of the shareholders, unless a greater proportion is required by the articles. In addition, if the rights of one particular class of shareholders are to be affected, an absolute majority of that class must also approve.

10. **Shareholder Control Devices** Shareholders may agree to vote their stock in a particular way in order to maximize their effect on corporate policy.

    a. **Voting Trust** One effective means of controlling votes is through the use of a voting trust. Under such a trust, shareholders turn over their voting rights to a trustee for a period not exceeding 10 years. The trustee has a copy of the trust agreement that also is filed with the corporation, and s/he becomes the record holder, entitled to vote the shares. The shareholder receives a voting trust certificate from the trustee, and all dividends received on the stock are paid to the shareholder. Upon termination of the trust, the shares are transferred back to the certificate holder.

    b. **Pooling Agreements** Any two or more shareholders may agree to vote their shares in a given way. Such agreements must be in writing and signed by the shareholders. At common law, many courts refused to recognize pooling agreements, but today most jurisdictions recognize them if instituted for a proper purpose. A primary difference between pooling agreements and voting trusts is that in a pooling agreement, title to the shares pooled remains with the individual shareholders, while in a voting trust, title to the shares in trust is transferred to the trustee.

    c. **Proxy** A proxy is authorization to vote for another. A shareholder may appoint an agent to vote or take other action. A general proxy allows the agent to vote the shares only as directed by the shareholder. State statutes generally provide that the appointment may be revocable or irrevocable if the proxy is coupled with an interest. Proxies generally expire after a certain amount of time, but may be valid for a longer period of time if expressly provided in the appointment form.

11. **Fiduciary Duty** Generally, a shareholder owes no fiduciary duty to the corporation; the shareholder's primary concern is her/his own self-interest. An exception to this rule is the duty of the majority or controlling shareholders to the minority shareholders. The courts have held that a group in *de facto* control of a corporation may not use that control to injure, oppress, or defraud the minority shareholders.

B.   Liabilities

The liability of a shareholder generally is limited to her/his capital investment. However, a shareholder may be liable for so called "watered stock" that was issued for less than lawful consideration. The liability here is the difference between what actually was paid and what lawfully should have been paid. Also, a shareholder is liable to the corporation or its creditors for any unpaid portion of her/his stock subscription contract. A shareholder, knowingly or unknowingly, who receives illegally-declared dividends is liable for repayment of the dividend amount to an insolvent corporation.

V.   Fundamental Changes

A.   Reorganization

As a general rule, reorganizations effected under the tax-free reorganization provisions (e.g., stock for stock mergers and consolidations effected under state statutes) of the Internal Revenue Code (§§354-374) will be tax free to the corporations and shareholders involved.

1. **Merger**   A merger is a process by which two (or more) companies join together, with one company losing its identity, while the other company retains its corporate identity. (A + B = A)

2. **Consolidation**   Consolidation is a process by which two or more companies join together. All the old companies disappear and are absorbed by a completely new corporation. (A + B = C)

3. **Procedure**   Although procedures vary somewhat among jurisdictions, the basic reorganization requirements are specified in the Revised Model Business Corporations Act.

    a.   **Boards of Director Approvals**   A merger or consolidation plan must be approved by the board of directors of each corporation involved.

    b.   **Shareholder Approvals**   The plan must be approved by the shareholders of each corporation involved. Most state statutes require the approval of two-thirds of the outstanding shares of voting stock.

    c.   **State Filing**   The approved plan then is filed with the state.

    d.   **Certificate Issued**   The state issues a certificate of merger or a certificate of consolidation when all requirements are met.

    e.   **Appraisal Rights**   A shareholder of any of the corporations involved has the right to dissent and may be entitled to payment of the fair value for the number of shares held on the date of the merger or consolidation. Dissenting shareholders must follow elaborate procedures prescribed by statute, that generally include filing a written notice of dissent prior to the shareholder vote on the proposed combination.

    f.   **Short-Form Mergers**   The Revised Model Business Corporation Act (RMBCA) provides a simplified procedure for the merger of a substantially owned subsidiary corporation into its parent corporation, referred to as a "short-form merger" or a "parent-subsidiary merger." This form of merger can be used only when the parent corporation owns at least 90% of the outstanding shares of each class of stock of the subsidiary corporation. The plan only need be approved by the board of directors of the parent corporation, not the board of directors of the subsidiary corporation or the shareholders of either corporation, before it is filed with the state. A copy of the merger plan must be sent to each shareholder of record of the subsidiary corporation and the subsidiary corporation's dissenting stockholders must be given an appraisal remedy.

B.   Quasi-Reorganization

A quasi-reorganization is a reorganization or revision of the capital structure, which is permitted in some states. This procedure eliminates an accumulated deficit as if the company had been reorganized legally without much of the cost and difficulty of a legal reorganization. Thus, the corporation will be able to pay dividends again. It involves the following steps.

1. Assets are revalued at net realizable value, but there is no net asset increase. (Any loss on revaluation increases the deficit.)

2. A minimum of the amount of the adjusted deficit must be available in paid-in capital (PIC). This might be created by donation of stock from shareholders or reduction of the par value.

3. The deficit is charged against PIC and thus is eliminated.

C. Dissolution

Dissolution involves the termination of a corporation's status as a legal entity. After dissolution, the affairs of the corporation must "wind up" or be liquidated. This process entails paying creditors and distributing any remaining assets or proceeds from those assets to the shareholders.

1. **Voluntary** For voluntary dissolution to occur, most jurisdictions require a vote by the board of directors recommending dissolution. This must be followed with approval of at least an absolute majority of the shareholders and filing of a certificate of dissolution with the appropriate state court.

2. **Involuntary** Involuntary dissolution may be brought about by an individual shareholder or the state.

   a. *Quo Warranto* **Action** If a corporation exceeds the authority conferred on it under statutory law, the state may bring an action for dissolution.

   b. **Shareholder Action** A shareholder may bring an action for dissolution if the board of directors has committed fraud, waste, oppression, or misapplication of corporate funds. Also, dissolution may be sought by shareholders if the board of directors is deadlocked and the corporate business may no longer be conducted in a manner advantageous to the shareholders.

   c. **Miscellaneous Grounds** Dissolution of a corporation may arise by expiration of the time period set out in the charter, consolidation, or merger.

VI. Federal Income Tax Ramifications

A. C Corporations

Corporations formed under state corporate law generally are taxed as corporations for federal tax purposes. Unless a corporation properly elects S corporation status, it is a C corporation.

1. **Cash & Other Property Dividend Distributions** Cash and other ordinary dividends generally are income to shareholder to the extent of the corporation's current and accumulated earnings and profits. The corporation generally will recognize gain or loss on any nonliquidating or liquidating distribution of property.

2. **Stock Dividend Distributions** Stock dividends are additional shares issued to shareholders in proportion to their existing holdings. They neither reduce total assets nor affect stockholder's equity. The effect of a stock dividend is to reduce retained earnings and increase legal capital. Distributions by a corporation of its common stock to its common shareholders is tax free to the shareholders. The distributing corporation may also use unissued or treasury stock for this common-on-common dividend. Generally, dividends of any other type of property (money, preferred stock) on common stock will be taxable to the shareholder. A tax-free stock dividend also will have no effect on earnings and profits of the corporation for federal income tax purposes. The corporation making the distribution generally does not recognize gain on stock dividend distributions.

   - In contrast to a stock dividend, a stock split simply increases the number of shares outstanding and proportionately decreases the par or stated value of the stock. There is no change in the dollar amount of capital stock, retained earnings, or total stockholders' equity.

3. **Constructive Dividends** Corporations and other business entities are entitled to a deduction from gross income for reasonable salaries paid to employees. If the IRS finds that a salary is unreasonable in amount, it will disallow the deduction for the portion of salary found to be unreasonable. In closely-held corporations, such disallowance may have the effect of recharacterizing the salary into ordinary dividend income to the extent of current and accumulated earnings and profits.

B. S Corporations

An S corporation has the advantage of being classified as a corporation while generally being taxed at the shareholder level instead of the corporate level. S corporation status is relevant only with regard to federal income tax considerations. Eligibility requirements for S corporation status include the following.

1. The American Jobs Creation Act of 2004 (AJCA '04) allows a maximum of 100 shareholders for an S corporation. To determine the number of shareholders for S corporation status, AJCA '04 allows family members to be counted as one shareholder. Each beneficiary of a voting trust is considered a separate shareholder.

2. Only one class of stock is allowed. A corporation with shares of stock that differ solely in voting rights will not be treated as having more than one class of stock.

3. Shareholders may be individuals, estates (testamentary and bankruptcy), trusts and tax-exempt entities.

4. Nonresident aliens, corporations, and foreign trusts may **not** be shareholders. One exception is that certain S corporations may have qualified S corporation subsidiaries (referred to as Q subs).

5. Ineligible corporations generally include members of affiliated groups, corporations owning 80% subsidiaries, certain financial institutions, insurance companies, companies electing the possessions tax credit, and Domestic International Sales Corporations (DISCs).

6. All current shareholders, plus any shareholders who held stock during the taxable year before the date of the election, must consent to the election.

Exhibit 2 ▶ Comparison of Various Business Entities

	General Partnership	Limited Liability Partnership	Limited Partnership	Limited Liability Company	Corporation
State Filing Required	No	Yes	Yes	Yes	Yes
Designation of Owners	Partners	Partners	General Partners and Limited Partners	Members	Shareholders
Persons With Authority to Bind	Partners	Partners	General Partners	Members or Managers	Officers
Governing Documents	Partnership Agreement	Partnership Agreement and Application for LLP	Certificate and Partnership Agreement	Articles of Organization and Operating Agreement	Articles of Incorporation and Bylaws, Shareholder Agreements
Limited Liability	No	Yes, if election made	No for General Partners, Yes for Limited Partners, provided they do not participate in management	Yes	Yes
Ownership Interest Treated as a Security	Generally No	Generally No	Generally No for General Partnership Interests; Generally Yes for Limited Partnership Interests	Generally depends on management form—if all members do not have management authority, interest is similar to Limited Partnership Interest	Generally Yes

VII. Appendix: Agency

A. Nature
Agency is a consensual, fiduciary relationship whereby one person, the agent, agrees to act on behalf and under the control of another, the principal.

1. **Business Organizations** Partners are general agents of the partnership and each other. Corporate officers typically are general agents of the corporation. General agents have broad authority to act for the principal in a variety of transactions. Corporations must act through agents; on the other hand, partnerships may act through partners or through outside agents.

Unincorporated associations are not legal entities and, thus, generally cannot appoint agents; only their individual members, as principals, may appoint agents.

2. **Notice** Notice by a third person to an agent is considered notice to the principal if the agent has actual or apparent authority to receive the notice. However, if the third person has knowledge that the agent's personal interest is adverse to the principal's interest, then notice to the agent is not notice to the principal.

3. **Knowledge** Similarly, the agent's knowledge is imputed to the principal if the agent has the authority to represent the principal in the matter, unless the agent's personal interest is adverse to the principal's interest.

4. **Admissions** Out-of-court statements by an agent to a third person, which are within the scope of her/his employment, may be treated as admissions of the principal and introduced into evidence against the principal.

5. **Principal's Duties to Agent** The principal owes the agent the following duties.

    a. **Compensation for Services** To compensate the agent for services rendered, either according to their agreement or, if there is no agreement, in an amount that reasonably reflects the value of the services.

    b. **Reimbursement of Expenses** To reimburse the agent for reasonable expenses incurred in the course of the agency.

    c. **Indemnification** To indemnify the agent against loss or liability for acts performed at the principal's direction, unless they are unlawful.

    d. **Compensation for Injury** To compensate the agent for physical injury (for example, workers' compensation).

6. **Agent's Duties to Principal**

    a. **Loyalty** An agent has a fiduciary duty to be loyal to her/his principal.

        (1) The agent cannot act for two principals with conflicting interests unless both principals consent.

        (2) The agent cannot deal for her/his own interest (for example, to make a profit at the principal's expense), and if the agent does, s/he is a constructive trustee for the principal of whatever should have been acquired for the principal.

        (3) The agent cannot compete with her/his principal without the principal's consent.

        (4) The agent cannot disclose to others any confidential information learned during the agency relationship.

        (5) An agent who violates the duty of loyalty is subject to liability for any losses caused thereby and is not entitled to compensation, reimbursement, or indemnification.

    b. **Follow Instructions** An agent must follow the principal's lawful instructions, using reasonable care and skill.

        (1) The agent cannot delegate duties involving discretion, except with the principal's permission.

        (2) The agent is liable to the principal for losses resulting from her/his own negligence.

    c.   **Communicate Material Facts** An agent has the duty to communicate notice of any material facts that come to the agent's attention while s/he is acting in her/his agency capacity.

    d.   **Account for Property** An agent must account for any property (including money) s/he receives through the agency. The agent may not commingle her/his own funds with those of the principal. If the agent does, s/he is liable for any resulting loss.

B.   **Agent's Authority**

An agent has the authority to represent the principal in contractual matters so as to affect the legal relationships between the principal and third parties. When an agency arises from a contractual arrangement, the law of contracts applies. An agency also may arise solely from the consent of the principal to have the agent represent her/him.

1.   **Actual** An agent's actual authority is that power consented to by the principal that affects the principal's legal relations.

2.   **Express or Implied** This authority may be express or implied from the principal's conduct. Implied authority includes the authority to do acts reasonably necessary to accomplish an authorized act. Implied authority may also arise from customary practices in the business community.

3.   **Apparent or Ostensible** If the conduct of the principal leads a third party to believe that an agent has authority beyond that to which the principal has actually consented, the agent is said to have apparent authority. For example, if a principal places an agent with limited authority in a position usually held by an agent with greater authority, the principal may lead others to believe the agent has greater authority than is actually the case.

    a.   Between the principal and the third party, it is as if the agent's authority were actual and neither can deny it.

    b.   If losses to the principal result, the principal can hold the agent liable for exceeding her/his actual authority.

C.   **Creation**

An agency relationship may be created by appointment, ratification, or operation of law.

1.   **Appointment** A principal may appoint an agent. Consideration is not necessary. An express agency is created by written or oral agreement between the parties that one shall act for and be subject to the control of the other. An implied agency is created by conduct of the principal that manifests the intention that the agency relationship should exist. Most agency relationships need not be in writing to be valid; however, some are required by statute to be evidenced by a written memorandum. For instance, if the agent's duties involve the making of a contract governed by the Statute of Frauds, such as a sale of real property, the agent's authority usually must be in writing. Also, the agreement must be in writing if the agency contract cannot be completed within one year. The principal may create an agency by a written instrument called a **power of attorney,** authorizing another, the "attorney in fact," to act as her/his agent. One may **not** appoint an agent to perform certain duties.

    a.   Those that the principal is bound to perform personally (nondelegable duties).

    b.   Those precluded by statute. For example, the execution of a will.

    c.   Those that the principal cannot perform. For example, a minor cannot appoint an agent to convey real estate since the minor can void the conveyance.

2.   **Ratification (Approval)** Acts performed by one who is not an agent, or unauthorized acts performed by an agent, may be ratified by the principal. A single transaction must be ratified in its entirety or not at all. Ratification may be either express or implied, depending on the circumstances.

    a.   **Requirements** Ratification requires the following.

        (1)   An act capable of ratification (for example, a tort may be ratified, but a crime may not be ratified) that is performed on behalf of the principal.

        (2)   A principal who (a) has the capacity to appoint the agent; (b) has knowledge of the material facts of the transaction; (c) was either a fully or partially disclosed principal; a fully undisclosed principal cannot ratify; and (d) was in existence at the time the act was done. For example, a corporation cannot ratify the acts of its promoters done before it came into existence; however, it may later adopt those acts.

        (3)   Any formalities that would be required for an appointment.

    b.   **Timing** If the purported agent contracts with a third party on the principal's behalf, the third party can withdraw at any time prior to ratification. The third party's withdrawal ends the principal's power to ratify. Alternatively, if the principal impairs the third party's rights by waiting too long, the principal also may lose her/his power to ratify.

    c.   **Effect** After ratification, the parties stand in the same position as if the agent had authority to do the act at the time it was done. The ratification "relates back" to the time the act was performed; thus, it is as if the act were authorized when performed.

        (1)   The principal cannot charge the agent with exceeding her/his authority nor can the third party hold her/him liable for breach of warranty of authority.

        (2)   The principal cannot retract her/his ratification.

  3.   **Operation of Law** The law may operate so as to create an agency relationship.

    a.   **Estoppel** Where no actual agency relationship in fact exists, but because the acts of the principal cause a third party to reasonably believe in the existence of the agency, and to reasonably rely on the existence of the agency, the principal is estopped from denying its existence.

    b.   **Representation, Appearance, or Apparent Authority** A person who represents to a third party that another is her/his agent may be bound to that party by her/his "agent's" actions, whether or not the third party acted in reliance.

    c.   **Necessity** The law implies an agency in certain situations, such as emergencies.

D.   **Termination**
An agency relationship may be terminated by agreement, renunciation, or operation of law.

  1.   **Notice** No notice of termination is required if the agency terminates by operation of law. In all other cases, notice must be given. If the principal or agent revokes or the agent renounces, each must notify the other.

    a.   **Actual** Third parties who have dealt with the agent must be given actual notice; otherwise, if they have no knowledge of the termination, their transactions with the agent will still bind the principal.

    b.   **Constructive** Third parties who have not previously dealt with the agent may be given constructive notice (for example, by publication).

2. **Agreement** An agency can terminate by agreement. The agency agreement may specify that it will terminate at a particular date, that it will end when an objective is accomplished, or that either party may terminate the relationship at will. The parties mutually may consent to terminate their relationship at any time.

3. **Renunciation** An agency can terminate by renunciation. The agent always has the power to renounce the agency; however, the agent may be liable to the principal for breach, unless the principal violated her/his duties or the agency was gratuitous. In most cases, the principal has the power to revoke the agency.

   a. **Coupled With Interest** If the principal has given an "agency coupled with an interest," it is irrevocable, (i.e., s/he has neither the right nor the power to revoke).

   b. **Right & Power** If the agent violates her/his duties to the principal, the principal has the right to revoke the agency.

   c. **Power** In all other cases, the principal has the power to revoke, but if the principal has no right to revoke (for example, the principal has contracted not to revoke) the principal will be subject to liability for breach of the agency contract.

4. **Operation of Law** On the occurrence of certain events, most agencies will terminate by operation of law. These events includes: (a) death or insanity of either party; (b) bankruptcy or insolvency of the principal; (c) bankruptcy of the agent if it affects the agency relationship; and (d) illegality or impossibility.

E. Respondeat Superior
A maxim that means that a master is liable in certain cases for the wrongful acts of her/his servant, and a principal is liable for the wrongs of her/his agent. Under this doctrine, the master is responsible for want of care on the servant's part toward those to whom the master owes a duty of care, provided the servant's failure to exercise due care occurred during the course of that servant's employment. In other words, the principal is vicariously liable (i.e., liable regardless of whether s/he is at fault) for the torts of an employee agent if they are committed within the scope (actual or apparent) of the agent's employment.

1. **Scope of Agent's Employment** The act falls within the scope of the agent's employment if it is the type of act the agent is authorized to perform, if it takes place substantially within the time and place that is authorized, and if it is intended to serve the principal in some way.

   a. Even if the agent violated the principal's instructions in committing the tort, the rule of *respondeat superior* applies.

   b. If the agent or servant departs from the performance of her/his duties and acts on her/his own ("independent journey," "frolic and detour"), the principal is not liable. Note: An intentionally tortious act is unlikely to be performed within the scope of employment. It usually is for the agent's own benefit.

2. **Recovery** An injured third person can choose to hold either the agent or the agent's principal liable.

3. **Agent's Crimes** Ordinarily, a principal is not liable for her/his agent's crimes even when they are committed in the course of the agent's employment. A principal cannot ratify crimes of an agent after their commission. A principal is liable if either: (a) the principal participated in the crime in some way (i.e., the principal planned, directed, ordered, or acquiesced in its commission) or (b) a statute makes the principal liable (e.g., the sale of liquor to minors).

F. Contracts
A material misrepresentation of the facts inducing the third party to enter into the contract may be grounds for her/his rescission.

1. **Disclosed** If the third party dealing with the agent knows of the existence of the agency and the identity of the principal, then contracts made by the agent in the exercise of her/his actual or apparent authority will bind the **principal** only.

2. **Partially Disclosed** If the third party dealing with the agent knows of the existence of the agency but **not** the identity of the principal, then contracts made by the agent bind both the agent **and** the principal.

3. **Undisclosed** If the third party dealing with the agent has no knowledge of either the existence of the agency or the identity of the principal, then contracts made by the agent bind the **agent** only. The undisclosed principal has the right to enforce the contract against the third party, so long as it does not involve personal service, trust, or confidence. Defenses the agent has against the third party that arose from the transaction and are not personal to the agent are available to the principal. The principal takes the contract subject to the following: (a) any defenses the third party has arising from the transaction; (b) any personal defenses or set-offs the third party has against the principal; and (c) in cases where it is impliedly authorized, any set-offs the third party has against the agent.

4. **Discovery of Principal** After discovering the identity of the principal, the third party may choose to hold her/him liable for acts either actually or apparently authorized unless: (a) the contract is a negotiable or sealed instrument; (b) the agent has performed already; (c) the third party already has elected to hold the agent liable after discovering the principal's identity; or (d) the contract provides that no undisclosed principal shall be liable.

G. **Agent's Liability to Third Parties**
An agent is liable to third parties for her/his own torts, even if the agent's principal is also vicariously liable for them. However, the third party is entitled to only one recovery. **Note:** Unless varied by statute, the agent is solely liable for her/his own crimes.

1. **Act for Disclosed Principal** An agent who is authorized to act by a disclosed principal is personally liable to third parties if the agent either: (a) contracts in her/his own name (for example, by carelessly signing her/his name to a written contract without indicating her/his representative capacity); (b) makes her/himself a party to the contract between the principal and the third party; (c) personally guarantees the principal's performance and the principal does not perform; or (d) signs a negotiable or sealed instrument on which the principal's name does not appear.

2. **Act for Partially Disclosed Principal** When an agent is representing a partially disclosed principal, the agent is liable on contracts for that principal unless both (a) the agent and third party agree that the agent is not to be bound; and (b) the identity of the principal is indicated so that it can become known.

3. **Unauthorized Acts** An agent who fails to bind her/his principal because her/his act is unauthorized generally is liable on the contract unless the third party knew of the purported agent's lack of authority.

   a. The agent is liable to a third party for breaching her/his implied warranty of authority. Damages are limited to those that the third party could have recovered from the principal had the agent been authorized. For example, if the principal is insolvent, damages obtainable from the agent are nominal.

   b. The agent also may be liable in tort for fraud and deceit.

4. **Act for Nonexistent Principal** A person who purports to contract as an agent for a principal the person knows to be nonexistent or incompetent is liable on the contract so long as the person either: (a) knows the third party is ignorant of the nonexistence or incompetence; or (b) represents to the third party that the principal exists or is competent

State Boards of Accountancy

Certified Public Accountants are licensed to practice by individual State Boards of Accountancy. Application forms and requirements to sit for the CPA Exam should be requested from your individual State Board. IT IS EXTREMELY IMPORTANT THAT YOU COMPLETE THE APPLICATION FORM CORRECTLY AND RETURN IT TO YOUR STATE BOARD BEFORE THE SPECIFIED DEADLINE. Errors and/or delays may result in the rejection of your application. Be extremely careful in filling out the application and be sure to enclose all required materials. In many states, applications must be received by the State Board at least **ninety** days before the examination date. Requirements as to education, experience, internship, and other matters vary. If you have not already done so, take a moment to contact the appropriate State Board for specific and current requirements. Complete the application in a timely manner.

It may be possible to sit for the exam in another state as an out-of-state candidate. Candidates wishing to do so should contact the Board of Accountancy in their home state as well as the other jurisdiction.

Approximately one month before the exam, check to see that your application to sit for the exam has been processed. DON'T ASSUME THAT YOU ARE PROPERLY REGISTERED UNLESS YOU HAVE RECEIVED YOUR NOTICE TO SCHEDULE.

The AICPA publishes a booklet entitled *The Uniform CPA Examination Candidate Bulletin: Information for Applicants,* usually distributed by Boards of Accountancy to candidates upon receipt of their applications. To request a complimentary copy, write your State Board or the AICPA, Examination Division, 1211 Avenue of the Americas, New York, NY 10036 (or download it from www.cpa-exam.org). Addresses of State Boards of Accountancy are provided in the **Practical Advice** section of this volume and on the site of the National Association of the State Boards of Accountancy (http://www.nasba.org).

Using Audio Tutor to Study

Actively listen to the audio lectures, taking notes if convenient. If you are strong in a topic, your audio review and question drill may be sufficient. If your strength is moderate in a topic, you might find that reading the related text before listening to the audio lectures is helpful. If you are weak in a topic, one successful strategy is to listen to the audio lectures, read the book, and then listen to the audio lectures again.

FYI: The Audio Tutor lectures have similar content as the Hot•Spot, Intensive, and online video lectures, but they are not exactly the same. Audio Tutor and this book have topics arranged in essentially the same chapters, although material might be organized differently within the chapters.

Call a customer service representative for more details about Audio Tutor.

———————————

CHAPTER 49—CORPORATIONS

Problem 49-1 MULTIPLE CHOICE QUESTIONS (80 to 100 minutes)

1. Under the Revised Model Business Corporation Act, which of the following statements regarding a corporation's bylaws is(are) correct?

  I. A corporation's initial bylaws shall be adopted by either the incorporators or the board of directors.
  II. A corporation's bylaws are contained in the articles of incorporation.

a. I only
b. II only
c. Both I and II
d. Neither I nor II   (5/98, Law, #3, 7582)

2. Under the Revised Model Business Corporation Act, which of the following must be contained in a corporation's articles of incorporation?
a. Quorum voting requirements
b. Names of stockholders
c. Provisions for issuance of par and nonpar shares
d. The number of shares the corporation is authorized to issue   (5/94, Law, #11, 4766)

3. Which of the following facts is(are) generally included in a corporation's articles of incorporation?

	Name of registered agent	Number of authorized shares
a.	Yes	Yes
b.	Yes	No
c.	No	Yes
d.	No	No

    (11/95, Law, #21, 5890)

4. Which of the following statements is (are) correct regarding the methods a target corporation may use to ward off a takeover attempt?

  I. The target corporation may make an offer ("self-tender") to acquire stock from its own shareholders.
  II. The target corporation may seek an injunction against the acquiring corporation on the grounds that the attempted takeover violates federal antitrust law.

a. I only
b. II only
c. Both I and II
d. Neither I nor II   (R/01, Law, #10, 7045)

5. Furl Corp., a corporation organized under the laws of State X, sued Row, a customer residing in State Y, for nonpayment for goods sold. Row attempted to dismiss a suit brought by Furl in State Y, on the grounds that Furl was conducting business in State Y but had not obtained a certificate of authority from State Y to transact business therein. Which of the following actions by Furl would generally result in the court ruling that Furl was conducting business in State Y?
a. Maintaining bank accounts in State Y
b. Shipping goods across state lines into State Y
c. Owning and operating a small manufacturing plant in State Y
d. Holding board of directors meetings in State Y
    (R/03, BEC, #22, 7685)

6. Which of the following statements best describes an advantage of the corporate form of doing business?
a. Day to day management is strictly the responsibility of the directors.
b. Ownership is contractually restricted and is **not** transferable.
c. The operation of the business may continue indefinitely.
d. The business is free from state regulation.
    (11/95, Law, #22, 5891)

7. Assuming all other requirements are met, a corporation may elect to be treated as an S corporation under the Internal Revenue Code if it has
a. Both common and preferred stockholders
b. A corporation as a stockholder
c. One-hundred or fewer stockholders
d. The consent of a majority of the stockholders
    (5/92, Law, #15, amended, 2828)

8. Which of the following statements is correct concerning the similarities between a limited partnership and a corporation?
a. Each is created under a statute and must file a copy of its certificate with the proper state authorities.
b. All corporate stockholders and all partners in a limited partnership have limited liability.
c. Both are recognized for federal income tax purposes as taxable entities.
d. Both are allowed statutorily to have perpetual existence.   (11/92, Law, #1, 3083)

9. Which of the following securities are corporate debt securities?

	Convertible bonds	Debenture bonds	Warrants
a.	Yes	Yes	Yes
b.	Yes	No	Yes
c.	Yes	Yes	No
d.	No	Yes	Yes

(11/93, Law, #17, 4314)

10. Price owns 2,000 shares of Universal Corp.'s $10 cumulative preferred stock. During its first year of operations, cash dividends of $5 per share were declared on the preferred stock but were never paid. In the second year, dividends on the preferred stock were neither declared nor paid. If Universal is dissolved, which of the following statements is correct?
a. Universal will be liable to Price as an unsecured creditor for $10,000.
b. Universal will be liable to Price as a secured creditor for $20,000.
c. Price will have priority over the claims of Universal's bond owners.
d. Price will have priority over the claims of Universal's unsecured judgment creditors.

(5/92, Law, #19, 7134)

11. Which of the following statements concerning treasury stock is correct?
a. Cash dividends paid on treasury stock are transferred to stated capital.
b. A corporation may **not** purchase its own stock unless specifically authorized by its articles of incorporation.
c. A duly appointed trustee may vote treasury stock at a properly called shareholders' meeting.
d. Treasury stock may be resold at a price less than par value.

(5/84, Law, #9, 0715)

12. Golden Enterprises, Inc. entered into a contract with Hidalgo Corporation for the sale of its mineral holdings. The transaction proved to be ultra vires. Which of the following parties, for the reason stated, may properly assert the ultra vires doctrine?
a. Golden Enterprises to avoid performance
b. A shareholder of Golden Enterprises to enjoin the sale
c. Hidalgo Corporation to avoid performance
d. Golden Enterprises to rescind the consummated sale

(5/80, Law, #12, 7135)

13. The limited liability of a stockholder in a closely held corporation may be challenged successfully if the stockholder
a. Undercapitalized the corporation when it was formed
b. Formed the corporation solely to have limited personal liability
c. Sold property to the corporation
d. Was a corporate officer, director, or employee

(5/91, Law, #6, 0697)

14. The corporate veil is most likely to be pierced and the shareholders held personally liable if
a. The corporation has elected S corporation status under the Internal Revenue Code.
b. The shareholders have commingled their personal funds with those of the corporation.
c. An ultra vires act has been committed.
d. A partnership incorporates its business solely to limit the liability of its partners.

(11/93, Law, #20, 4317)

15. Ambrose purchased 400 shares of $100 par value original issue common stock from Minor Corporation for $25 a share. Ambrose subsequently sold 200 of the shares to Harris at $25 a share. Harris did not have knowledge or notice that Ambrose had not paid par. Ambrose also sold 100 shares of this stock to Gable for $25 a share. At the time of this sale, Gable knew that Ambrose had not paid par for the stock. Minor Corporation became insolvent and the creditors sought to hold all the above parties liable for the $75 unpaid on each of the 400 shares. Under these circumstances
a. The creditors can hold Ambrose liable for $30,000.
b. If $25 a share was a fair value for the stock at the time of issuance, Ambrose will have no liability to the creditors.
c. Since Harris acquired the shares by purchase, he is not liable to the creditors and his lack of knowledge or notice that Ambrose paid less than par is immaterial.
d. Since Gable acquired the shares by purchase, he is not liable to the creditors, and the fact that he knew Ambrose paid less than par is immaterial.

(11/83, Law, #24, 7136)

16. Under the Revised Model Business Corporation Act, a corporate director is authorized to
a. Rely on information provided by the appropriate corporate officer
b. Serve on the board of directors of a competing business
c. Sell control of the corporation
d. Profit from insider information

(11/96, Law, #12, 6423)

17. Which of the following actions may be taken by a corporation's board of directors without stockholder approval?
a. Purchasing substantially all of the assets of another corporation
b. Selling substantially all of the corporation's assets
c. Dissolving the corporation
d. Amending the articles of incorporation
(5/97, Law, #3, 6444)

18. Acorn Corp. wants to acquire the entire business of Trend Corp. Which of the following methods of business combination will best satisfy Acorn's objectives without requiring the approval of the shareholders of either corporation?
a. A merger of Trend into Acorn, whereby Trend shareholders receive cash or Acorn shares
b. A sale of all the assets of Trend, outside the regular course of business, to Acorn, for cash
c. An acquisition of all the shares of Trend through a compulsory share exchange for Acorn shares
d. A cash tender offer, whereby Acorn acquires at least 90% of Trend's shares, followed by a short-form merger of Trend into Acorn
(R/01, Law, #11, 7046)

19. Under the Revised Model Business Corporation Act, which of the following statements is correct regarding corporate officers of a public corporation?
a. An officer may **not** simultaneously serve as a director.
b. A corporation may be authorized to indemnify its officers for liability incurred in a suit by stockholders.
c. Stockholders always have the right to elect a corporation's officers.
d. An officer of a corporation is required to own at least one share of the corporation's stock.
(5/94, Law, #12, 4767)

20. Knox, president of Quick Corp., contracted with Tine Office Supplies, Inc. to supply Quick's stationery on customary terms and at a cost less than that charged by any other supplier. Knox later informed Quick's board of directors that Knox was a majority stockholder in Tine. Quick's contract with Tine is
a. Void, because of Knox's self-dealing
b. Void, because the disclosure was made after execution of the contract
c. Valid, because of Knox's full disclosure
d. Valid, because the contract is fair to Quick
(11/90, Law, #15, 0699)

21. Absent a specific provision in its articles of incorporation, a corporation's board of directors has the power to do all of the following, **except**
a. Repeal the bylaws
b. Declare dividends
c. Fix compensation of directors
d. Amend the articles of incorporation
(5/90, Law, #7, 0704)

22. Jane Cox, a shareholder of Mix Corp., has properly commenced a derivative action against Mix's Board of Directors. Cox alleges that the Board breached its fiduciary duty and was negligent by failing to independently verify the financial statements prepared by management upon which Smart & Co., CPAs, issued an unqualified opinion. The financial statements contained inaccurate information which the Board relied upon in committing large sums of money to capital expansion. This resulted in Mix having to borrow money at extremely high interest rates to meet current cash needs. Within a short period of time, the price of Mix Corp. stock declined drastically. Which of the following statements is correct?
a. The Board is strictly liable, regardless of fault, since it owes a fiduciary duty to both the corporation and the shareholders.
b. The Board is liable since any negligence of Smart is automatically imputed to the Board.
c. The Board may avoid liability if it acted in good faith and in a reasonable manner.
d. The Board may avoid liability in all cases where it can show that it lacked scienter.
(11/85, Law, #3, 7138)

23. Fairwell is executive vice president and treasurer of Wonder Corporation. He was named as a party in a shareholder derivative action in connection with certain activities he engaged in as a corporate officer. In the lawsuit, it was determined that he was liable for negligence in performance of his duties. Fairwell seeks indemnity from the corporation for his liability. The board would like to indemnify him. The articles of incorporation do not contain any provisions regarding indemnification of officers and directors. Indemnification
a. Is **not** permitted since the articles of incorporation do **not** so provide
b. Is permitted only if he is found **not** to have been grossly negligent
c. **Cannot** include attorney's fees since he was found to have been negligent
d. May be permitted by court order despite the fact that Fairwell was found to be negligent
(5/82, Law, #10, 7137)

24. Bixler obtained an option on a building he believed was suitable for use by a corporation he and two other individuals were organizing. After the corporation was successfully promoted, Bixler met with the Board of Directors who agreed to acquire the property for $200,000. Bixler deeded the building to the corporation and the corporation began business in it. Bixler's option contract called for the payment of only $155,000 for the building and he purchased it for that price. When the directors later learned that Bixler paid only $155,000, they demanded the return of Bixler's $45,000 profit. Bixler refused, claiming the building was worth far more than $200,000 both when he secured the option and when he deeded it to the corporation. Which of the following statements correctly applies to Bixler's conduct?
a. It was improper for Bixler to contract for the option without first having secured the assent of the Board of Directors.
b. If, as Bixler claimed, the building was fairly worth more than $200,000, Bixler is entitled to retain the entire price.
c. Even if, as Bixler claimed, the building was fairly worth more than $200,000, Bixler nevertheless must return the $45,000 to the corporation.
d. In order for Bixler to be obligated to return any amount to the corporation, the Board of Directors must establish that the building was worth less than $200,000. (5/81, Law, #23, 7139)

25. Under the Revised Model Business Corporation Act, when a corporation's bylaws grant stockholders preemptive rights, which of the following rights is(are) included in that grant?

	The right to purchase a proportionate share of newly-issued stock	The right to a proportionate share of corporate assets remaining on corporate dissolution
a.	Yes	Yes
b.	Yes	No
c.	No	Yes
d.	No	No

(11/98, Law, #7, 6752)

26. To which of the following rights is a stockholder of a public corporation entitled?
a. The right to have annual dividends declared and paid
b. The right to vote for the election of officers
c. The right to a reasonable inspection of corporate records
d. The right to have the corporation issue a new class of stock (11/95, Law, #23, 5892)

27. A corporate stockholder is entitled to which of the following rights?
a. Elect officers
b. Receive annual dividends
c. Approve dissolution
d. Prevent corporate borrowing
(5/92, Law, #18, 2831)

28. Which of the following rights is a holder of a public corporation's cumulative preferred stock always entitled to?
a. Conversion of the preferred stock into common stock
b. Voting rights
c. Dividend carryovers from years in which dividends were **not** paid, to future years
d. Guaranteed dividends (5/94, Law, #13, 4768)

29. A stockholder's right to inspect books and records of a corporation will be properly denied if the stockholder
a. Wants to use corporate stockholder records for a personal business.
b. Employs an agent to inspect the books and records.
c. Intends to commence a stockholder's derivative suit.
d. Is investigating management misconduct.
(11/92, Law, #2, 3084)

30. Under the Revised Model Business Corporation Act, a dissenting stockholder's appraisal right generally applies to which of the following corporate actions?

	Consolidations	Short-form mergers
a.	Yes	Yes
b.	Yes	No
c.	No	Yes
d.	No	No

(R/99, Law, #6, 6857)

31. Which of the following would be grounds for the judicial dissolution of a corporation on the petition of a shareholder?
a. Refusal of the board of directors to declare a dividend
b. Waste of corporate assets by the board of directors
c. Loss operations of the corporation for three years
d. Failure by the corporation to file its federal income tax returns (5/84, Law, #6, 0714)

32. Under the Revised Model Business Corporation Act, which of the following actions by a corporation would entitle a stockholder to dissent from the action and obtain payment of the fair value of her/his shares?

   I.   An amendment to the articles of incorporation that materially and adversely affects rights in respect of a dissenter's shares because it alters or abolishes a preferential right of the shares.

   II.   Consummation of a plan of share exchange to which the corporation is a party as the corporation whose shares will be acquired, if the stockholder is entitled to vote on the plan.

a. I only
b. II only
c. Both I and II
d. Neither I nor II   (11/98, Law, #8, 6753)

33. All of the following distributions to stockholders are considered asset or capital distributions, **except**
a. Liquidating dividends
b. Stock splits
c. Property distributions
d. Cash dividends   (11/90, Law, #17, 0701)

34. For what purpose will a stockholder of a publicly held corporation be permitted to file a stockholders' derivative suit in the name of the corporation?
a. To compel payment of a properly declared dividend
b. To enforce a right to inspect corporate records
c. To compel dissolution of the corporation
d. To recover damages from corporate management for an *ultra vires* management act
      (5/98, Law, #4, 7583)

35. Which of the following statements is a general requirement for the merger of two corporations?
a. The merger plan must be approved unanimously by the stockholders of both corporations.
b. The merger plan must be approved unanimously by the boards of both corporations.
c. The absorbed corporation must amend its articles of incorporation.
d. The stockholders of both corporations must be given due notice of a special meeting, including a copy or summary of the merger plan.
      (11/95, Law, #25, 5894)

36. Under the Revised Model Business Corporation Act, a merger of two public corporations usually requires all of the following **except**
a. A formal plan of merger
b. An affirmative vote by the holders of a majority of each corporation's voting shares
c. Receipt of voting stock by all stockholders of the original corporations
d. Approval by the board of directors of each corporation   (5/94, Law, #14, 4769)

37. A parent corporation owned more than 90% of each class of the outstanding stock issued by a subsidiary corporation and decided to merge that subsidiary into itself. Under the Revised Model Business Corporation Act, which of the following actions must be taken?
a. The subsidiary corporation's board of directors must pass a merger resolution.
b. The subsidiary corporation's dissenting stockholders must be given an appraisal remedy.
c. The parent corporation's stockholders must approve the merger.
d. The parent corporation's dissenting stockholders must be given an appraisal remedy.
      (11/94, Law, #25, 5202)

38. Under the Revised Model Business Corporation Act, which of the following conditions is necessary for a corporation to achieve a successful voluntary dissolution?
a. Successful application to the secretary of state in which the corporation holds its primary place of business
b. A recommendation of dissolution by the board of directors and approval by a majority of all shareholders entitled to vote
c. Approval by the board of directors of an amendment to the certificate of incorporation calling for the dissolution of the corporation
d. Unanimous approval of the board of directors and two-thirds vote of all shareholders entitled to vote on a resolution of voluntary dissolution
      (R/03, BEC, #16, 7678)

39. Carr Corp. declared a 7% stock dividend on its common stock. The dividend
a. Must be registered with the SEC pursuant to the Securities Act of 1933
b. Is includable in the gross income of the recipient taxpayers in the year of receipt
c. Has **no** effect on Carr's earnings and profits for federal income tax purposes
d. Requires a vote of Carr's stockholders
      (11/95, Law, #24, 5893)

40. The stock of Crandall Corporation is regularly traded over the counter. However, 75% is owned by the founding family and a few of the key executive officers. It has had a cash dividend record of paying out annually less than 5% of its earnings and profits over the past 10 years. It has, however, declared a 10% stock dividend during each of these years. Its accumulated earnings and profits are beyond the reasonable current and anticipated needs of the business. Which of the following is correct?

a. The shareholders can compel the declaration of a dividend only if the directors' dividend policy is fraudulent.

b. The Internal Revenue Service **cannot** attack the accumulation of earnings and profits since the Code exempts publicly held corporations from the accumulations provisions.

c. The fact that the corporation was paying a 10% stock dividend, apparently in lieu of a cash distribution, is irrelevant insofar as the ability of the Internal Revenue Service to successfully attack the accumulation.

d. Either the Internal Revenue Service or the shareholders could successfully obtain a court order to compel the distribution of earnings and profits unreasonably accumulated.

(5/81, Law, #25, 7696)

Problem 49-2 ADDITIONAL MULTIPLE CHOICE QUESTIONS (24 to 30 minutes)

41. The owners of Elsie Components made a good faith effort to incorporate. Not realizing that all of the prescribed procedures were not followed, the entity established a corporate charter and entered into good faith business dealings in the corporate name with Miner Company. A valid statute exists under which the business could have been incorporated legally. Despite the defects in the incorporation process, an appropriate court held that Elsie Components was a corporation. What type of entity is Elsie Components?

a. A corporation by estoppel
b. A *de facto* corporation
c. A *de jure* corporation
d. Not a corporation   (Editors, 7723)

42. In which of the following situations is a subscription contract least likely to be enforceable?

a. A group of investors each agree to subscribe to corporate stock before the corporation exists, if the other investors also subscribe.

b. An investor agreed to subscribe to corporate stock before the corporation existed and the corporation accepted the contract after incorporation.

c. An investor agrees to subscribe to a corporation's stock without any explicit conditions, but the corporation has not complied with all applicable securities laws.

d. An investor agrees to subscribe to an existing corporation's stock.   (Editors, 7724)

43. A corporation may not
a. Accept contracts for future services as consideration for the issuance of stock
b. Accept past services as consideration for the issuance of stock
c. Issue par shares for any price determined by the board of directors
d. Require a holder to offer the corporation the right of first refusal on a repurchase of its stock before any sale is permitted to anyone else
(Editors, 7725)

44. Plating Corp. hired Armor as a sales representative for six months at a salary of $5,000 per month plus 6% of sales. Which of the following statements is correct?
a. Plating does **not** have the power to dismiss Armor during the six-month period without cause.
b. Armor is obligated to act solely in Plating's interest in matters concerning Plating's business.
c. The agreement between Plating and Armor formed an agency coupled with an interest.
d. The agreement between Plating and Armor is not enforceable unless it is in writing and signed by Armor. (Editors, 7958)

45. Port, Inc. hired Ajax as a purchasing agent. Port gave Ajax written authorization to purchase, without limit, electronic appliances. Later, Ajax was told not to purchase more than 300 of each appliance. Ajax contracted with Sorrel Corp. to purchase 500 tape recorders. Sorrel had been shown Ajax's written authorization. Which of the following statements is correct?
a. Ajax will be liable to Sorrel because Ajax's actual authority was exceeded.
b. Ajax will **not** be liable to reimburse Port if Port is liable to Sorrel.
c. Port will be liable to Sorrel because of Ajax's actual and apparent authority.
d. Port will not be liable to Sorrel because Ajax's actual authority was exceeded. (Editors, 7959)

46. Prime Corporation's accountant and business manager has the authority to
a. Mortgage Prime's real estate
b. Obtain bank loans for Prime
c. Insure Prime's property against fire loss
d. Sell Prime's business (Editors, 7960)

47. Which of the following actions requires an agent for a corporation to have a written agency agreement?
a. Purchasing office supplies for the principal's business
b. Purchasing an interest in undeveloped land for the principal
c. Hiring an independent general contractor to renovate the principal's office building
d. Retaining an attorney to collect a business debt owed the principal (11/94, Law, #16, 7961)

48. Pole Corp. dismissed Alan as its general sales agent and notified all of Alan's known customers by letter. Tripp Corp., a retail outlet located outside of Alan's previously assigned sales territory, had never dealt with Alan. Tripp knew of Alan as a result of various business contacts. After his dismissal, Alan sold Tripp goods, to be delivered by Pole, and received from Tripp a cash deposit for 20% of the purchase price. It was not unusual for an agent in Alan's previous position to receive cash deposits. In an action by Tripp against Pole on the sales contract, Tripp will
a. Lose, because Alan lacked any implied authority to make the contract
b. Lose, because Alan lacked any express authority to make the contract
c. Win, because Pole's notice was inadequate to terminate Alan's apparent authority
d. Win, because a principal is an insurer of an agent's acts (Editors, 7962)

49. A corporation will **not** be liable to a third party for a tort committed by corporate officer
a. Unless the board of directors instructed the officer to commit the tort
b. Unless the tort was committed within the scope of the agency relationship
c. If the agency agreement limits the corporation's liability for the officer's tort
d. If the tort is also regarded as a criminal act
(Editors, 7963)

50. Elm, an employee of National Courier Corp., was hired to deliver electronic files containing personal financial information for National's clients. Unknown to National, Elm carried a concealed pistol. While Elm was making a delivery, he suspected an attempt was being made to steal the package, drew his gun and shot Clark, an innocent passerby. Clark will **not** recover damages from National if
a. Elm's weapon was unlicensed and illegal.
b. Elm was correct and an attempt was being made to steal the package.
c. National instructed its messengers **not** to carry weapons.
d. National discovered that Elm carried a weapon and did nothing about it. (Editors, 7964)

51. When a valid contract is entered into by an agent on a corporate principal's behalf, in a non-disclosed principal situation, which of the following statements concerning the principal's liability is correct?

	The principal may be held liable once disclosed	The principal must ratify the contract to be held liable
a.	Yes	Yes
b.	Yes	No
c.	No	Yes
d.	No	No

(Editors, 7965)

52. An agent usually will be liable under a contract made with a third party when the agent is acting on behalf of a(an)

	Disclosed principal	Undisclosed principal
a.	Yes	Yes
b.	Yes	No
c.	No	Yes
d.	No	No

(Editors, 7966)

SIMULATIONS

FYI: The editors encourage candidates to answer simulations as part of their review because such studying provides for content reinforcement, regardless of question format. Simulations currently are not part of the BEC exam; Bisk Education updating supplements will notify readers when this situation changes.

Problem 49-3 (10 to 25 minutes)

Drain Corp. has two classes of stock: 100,000 shares of authorized, issued, and outstanding voting common stock; and 10,000 shares of authorized, issued, and outstanding nonvoting 5% cumulative, nonparticipating preferred stock with a face value of $100 per share. In 2004, Drain's officers and directors intentionally allowed pollutants to be discharged by Drain's processing plant. These actions resulted in Drain having to pay penalties. Solely as a result of the penalties, no dividends were declared for the years ended December 31, 2004 and December 31, 2005. The total amount Drain paid in penalties was $1,000,000. In 2005, Drain was able to recover the full amount of the penalties from an insurance company that had issued Drain a business liability policy. Drain's directors refused to use this money to declare a dividend and decided to hold the $1,000,000 in a special fund to pay future bonuses to officers and directors.

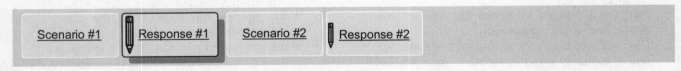

1. The actions by Drain's officers and directors in allowing pollutants to be discharged generally would be considered a violation of the
2. A stockholder's derivative suit, if successful, probably would result in the officers and directors being
3. A stockholder's derivative suit, if successful, probably would result in the $1,000,000 being considered
4. If the $1,000,000 was distributed to the shareholders in 2005, the distribution would be characterized as a

Responses

A. Available for distribution as a dividend.
B. Fiduciary duty to prevent losses.
C. Cash dividend.
D. Fiduciary duty of care.
E. Fiduciary duty of loyalty.
F. Illegal dividend.
G. Immune from liability.
H. Liable for abuse of discretion.
I. Liable to the corporation for $1,000,000.
J. Property dividend.
K. Stock dividend.
L. Surplus or earnings held for expansion.

(5/96, Law, #2 (1-4), amended, 6267-6270)

Major formed the Dix Corp. for the purpose of operating a business to repair, install, and sell used refrigerators. Major is the sole shareholder and president of Dix. Major owns 2,000 shares of $10 par value common stock. He paid for 1,000 of these shares by transferring to Dix property with a fair market value of $3,500 and his promissory note for $2,500 due and payable on June 1, 2003. He also received at a later date 1,000 shares in consideration of services rendered to Dix fairly valued at $7,000 and his agreement to render specific additional services starting with January 1, 2002 which are fairly valued at $1,000. The promissory note has not been paid nor have the additional services been rendered.

Fox, a customer of Dix, was seriously injured when a refrigerator negligently repaired by Major on behalf of Dix caught fire. Dix has $500,000 of liability insurance covering itself and its employees for such occurrences. Fox wishes to hold Major personally liable since Dix has insufficient assets and insurance to pay Fox's claim.

Pine, one of Dix's largest creditors, has asserted claims against Major, individually, claiming that Major is:

- Personally liable to the extent of $6,000 for the common shares issued to him.
- Personally liable for all of the debts of Dix because he instructed several of Dix's customers to make checks payable to the order of Major which were deposited in his individual account and not recorded on the corporate books.

Discuss Major's liability and the liability of Dix for the injuries sustained by Fox. What effect does the insurance carried by Dix have on Major's and Dix's liability to Fox? Set forth reasons for any conclusions stated.

(5/86, Law, #4a, amended, 9662)

Problem 49-4 (10 to 25 minutes)

In 2000, Amber Corp., a closely-held corporation, was formed by Adams, Frank, and Berg as incorporators and stockholders. Adams, Frank, and Berg executed a written voting agreement which provided that they would vote for each other as directors and officers. In 2004, stock in the corporation was offered to the public. This resulted in an additional 300 stockholders. After the offering, Adams holds 25%, Frank holds 15%, and Berg holds 15% of all issued and outstanding stock. Adams, Frank, and Berg have been directors and officers of the corporation since the corporation was formed. Regular meetings of the board of directors and annual stockholders meetings have been held.

1. Amber Corp. must
A. Be formed under a state's general corporation statute.
B. Include the names of all stockholders in its Articles of Incorporation.
C. Include its corporate bylaws in the incorporation documents filed with the state.

(5/95, Law, #67, amended, 5401)

2. Amber Corp.'s initial bylaws ordinarily would be adopted by its
A. Stockholders.
B. Officers.
C. Directors.

(5/95, Law, #68, 5402)

3. Amber Corp.'s directors are elected by its
A. Officers.
B. Outgoing directors.
C. Stockholders.

(5/95, Law, #69, 5403)

Major formed the Dix Corp. for the purpose of operating a business to repair, install, and sell used refrigerators. Major is the sole shareholder and president of Dix. Major owns 2,000 shares of $10 par value common stock. He paid for 1,000 of these shares by transferring to Dix property with a fair market value of $3,500 and his promissory note for $2,500 due and payable on June 1, 2003. He also received at a later date 1,000 shares in consideration of services rendered to Dix fairly valued at $7,000 and his agreement to render specific additional services starting with January 1, 2002 which are fairly valued at $1,000. The promissory note has not been paid nor have the additional services been rendered.

Fox, a customer of Dix, was seriously injured when a refrigerator negligently repaired by Major on behalf of Dix caught fire. Dix has $500,000 of liability insurance covering itself and its employees for such occurrences. Fox wishes to hold Major personally liable since Dix has insufficient assets and insurance to pay Fox's claim.

Pine, one of Dix's largest creditors, has asserted claims against Major, individually, claiming that Major is:

- Personally liable to the extent of $6,000 for the common shares issued to him.
- Personally liable for all of the debts of Dix because he instructed several of Dix's customers to make checks payable to the order of Major which were deposited in his individual account and not recorded on the corporate books.

Discuss the assertions of Pine and reach a conclusion for each. Set forth reasons for any conclusions stated.

(5/86, Law, #4b, amended, 9662)

Problem 49-5 (15 to 25 minutes)

Edwards, a director and a 10% stockholder in National Corp., is dissatisfied with the way National's officers, particularly Olsen, the president, have been operating the corporation.

Edwards has made many suggestions that have been rejected by the board of directors, and has made several unsuccessful attempts to have Olsen removed as president.

National and Grand Corp. had been negotiating a merger that Edwards has adamantly opposed. Edwards has blamed Olsen for initiating the negotiation and has urged the board to fire Olsen. National's board refused to fire Olsen. In an attempt to defeat the merger, Edwards approached Jenkins, the president of Queen Corp., and contracted for Queen to purchase several of National's assets. Jenkins knew Edwards was a National director, but had never done business with National. When National learned of the contract, it notified Queen that the contract was invalid.

Edwards filed an objection to the merger before the stockholders' meeting called to consider the merger proposal was held. At the meeting, Edwards voted against the merger proposal.

Despite Edward's efforts, the merger was approved by both corporations. Edwards then orally demanded that National purchase Edwards' stock, citing the dissenters rights provision of the corporation's by-laws, which reflects the Model Business Corporation Act.

National's board has claimed National does not have to purchase Edward's stock.

As a result of the above:

- Edwards initiated a minority stockholder's action to have Olsen removed as president and to force National to purchase Edward's stock.
- Queen sued National to enforce the contract and/or collect damages.
- Queen sued Edwards to collect damages.

Answer the following questions and give the reasons for your answers.

a. Will Edwards be successful in a lawsuit to have Olsen removed as president?

b. Will Edwards be successful in a lawsuit to have National purchase the stock?

c. 1. Will Queen be successful in a lawsuit against National?
   2. Will Queen be successful in a lawsuit against Edwards?

(5/93, Law, #3, 9659)

Problem 49-6 (15 to 25 minutes)

Frost, Glen, and Bradley own 50%, 40%, and 10%, respectively, of the authorized and issued voting common stock of Xeon Corp. They had a written stockholders' agreement that provided they would vote for each other as directors of the corporation.

At the initial stockholders' meeting, Frost, Glen, Bradley, and three others were elected to a six-person board of directors. The board elected Frost as president of the corporation, Glen as secretary, and Bradley as vice president. Frost and Glen were given two-year contracts with annual salaries of $50,000. Bradley was given a two-year contract for $10,000 per year.

At the end of its first year of operation, Xeon was in financial difficulty. Bradley disagreed with the way Frost and Glen were running the business.

At the annual stockholders' meeting, a new board of directors was elected. Bradley was excluded because Frost and Glen did not vote for Bradley. Without cause, the new board fired Bradley as vice president even though 12 months remained on Bradley's contract.

Despite the corporation's financial difficulties, the new board, relying on the assurances of Frost and Glen and based on fraudulent documentation provided by Frost and Glen, declared and paid a $200,000 dividend. Payment of the dividend caused the corporation to become insolvent.

- Bradley sued Frost and Glen to compel them to follow the written stockholders' agreement and reelect Bradley to the board.
- Bradley sued the corporation to be reinstated as an officer of the corporation, and for breach of the employment contract.
- Bradley sued each member of the board for declaring and paying an unlawful dividend, and demanded its repayment to the corporation.

State whether Bradley would be successful in each of these suits and give the reasons for your conclusions.

(11/91, Law, #2, 3209)

Problem 49-7 (15 to 25 minutes)

On May 1, 2002, Cray's board of directors unanimously voted to have Cray reacquire 100,000 shares of its common stock. On May 25, 2002, Cray did so, paying current market price. In determining whether to reacquire the shares, the board of directors relied on reports and financial statements that were negligently prepared by Cray's internal accounting department under the supervision of the treasurer and reviewed by its independent accountants. The reports and financial statements indicated that, as of April 30, 2002, Cray was solvent and there were sufficient funds to reacquire the shares. Subsequently, it was discovered that Cray had become insolvent in March 2002 and continued to be insolvent after the reacquisition of the shares. As a result of the foregoing, Cray experienced liquidity problems and losses during 2002 and 2003.

The board of directors immediately fired the treasurer because of the treasurer's negligence in supervising the preparation of the reports and financial statements. The treasurer had three years remaining on a binding five-year employment agreement which, among other things, prohibited the termination of the treasurer's employment for mere negligence.

Discuss the following assertions, indicating whether such assertions are correct and the reasons therefor.

- It was improper for Cray's board of directors to authorize the reacquisition of Cray's common stock while Cray was insolvent.
- The members of Cray's board of directors are personally liable because they voted to reacquire shares while Cray was insolvent.
- Cray will be liable to the treasurer as a result of his termination by the board of directors.

(5/89, Law, #4, amended, 9660)

Drain Corp. has two classes of stock: 100,000 shares of authorized, issued, and outstanding voting common stock; and 10,000 shares of authorized, issued, and outstanding nonvoting 5% cumulative, nonparticipating preferred stock with a face value of $100 per share. In 2004, Drain's officers and directors intentionally allowed pollutants to be discharged by Drain's processing plant. These actions resulted in Drain having to pay penalties. Solely as a result of the penalties, no dividends were declared for the years ended December 31, 2004 and December 31, 2005. The total amount Drain paid in penalties was $1,000,000. In 2005, Drain was able to recover the full amount of the penalties from an insurance company that had issued Drain a business liability policy. Drain's directors refused to use this money to declare a dividend and decided to hold the $1,000,000 in a special fund to pay future bonuses to officers and directors.

The $1,000,000 was distributed in 2005.

Scenario #1   Response #1   Scenario #2   Response #2

1. What amount would each share of Drain Corp. 5% cumulative preferred stock receive?
2. What amount would each share of Drain Corp. voting common stock receive?

(5/96, Law, #2 (5-6), amended, 6271-6272)

Solution 49-1 MULTIPLE CHOICE ANSWERS

Characteristics

1. (a) Under the Revised Model Business Corporation Act, either the incorporators or the board of directors may adopt the bylaws. The bylaws are not contained in the articles of incorporation. The bylaws are the rules and regulations that govern a corporation's internal management, and are contained in a separate document from the articles of incorporation. In contrast to the articles of incorporation, the bylaws do not have to be publicly filed.

2. (d) The Revised Model Business Corporation Act (RMBCA) requires that the articles of incorporation set forth a corporate name, the street address of the corporation and its registered agent, the name and address of each incorporator, and the number of shares the corporation is authorized to issue (MBCA 2.02). It is not necessary to list shareholder names, provide for the issuance of par and non-par shares, or list state quorum voting requirements. Inclusion of this information in the articles of incorporation is optional.

3. (a) Most state enabling acts (incorporation statutes) require both the name of the registered agent and the number of authorized shares.

4. (c) Most courts hold that a corporation may purchase its own shares, provided such action promotes the corporate business. A corporation has express power to perform any act authorized by state law, its articles of incorporation, or its bylaws. The existence of a takeover attempt doesn't restrict these actions.

5. (c) The operation of a plant in a state is strong evidence that a corporation is doing business there. The location of bank accounts, shipments, or board of directors meetings is incidental to business operations.

6. (c) A primary advantage of the corporate form of doing business is that ownership is freely and easily transferable and does not result in a dissolution, thus permitting the business to continue indefinitely. Day to day management is the responsibility of the officers, not the directors. A corporation is subject to state regulation.

7. (c) An S corporation is allowed to have no more than 100 stockholders, is allowed only one class of stock, and is not allowed to have a corporation as a stockholder. All stockholders, not just the majority, must consent to the election to be treated as an S corporation.

8. (a) Both a limited partnership and a corporation may be created only under a state statute, and each must file a copy of its certificate with the proper state authorities. Further, both a corporation's stock and a limited partnership interest are subject to the federal securities laws registration requirements if they are "securities" under the federal securities laws. General partners in a limited partnership do not have limited liability. Partnerships are not recognized for federal income tax purposes as taxable entities. Instead, the income flows through to the partners and is taxed on their individual returns. Partnerships do not have perpetual existence. Their existence can be affected by the death of a partner.

Financing & Liability

9. (c) Convertible bonds are classified as debt securities as long as they are not converted into stock shares (equity). Debenture bonds are debt securities by definition. Warrants, however, represent the right to buy a given number of shares of stock, usually within a set time period, and are classified as equity instruments.

10. (a) A cash dividend on preferred stock becomes a legal debt of the corporation when the dividend is declared, and the preferred shareholder becomes an unsecured creditor of the corporation. However, dividends not paid in any year concerning cumulative preferred stock are not a liability of the corporation until they are declared. Therefore, Universal will be liable to Price as an unsecured creditor for $10,000, which is the amount of the declared dividends. Price has become a general

unsecured creditor for the declared dividends and will have the same priority as the bond owners and the unsecured judgment creditors.

11. (d)   Newly issued stock must be issued at par or above, but treasury stock may be sold below par. No dividends are paid on treasury stock. A corporation has the right to purchase its own stock unless specifically denied by statute or by specific provision in the articles of incorporation. Treasury stock does not have any voting rights. (Otherwise, management could take control of the corporation away from its owners simply by purchasing enough treasury stock and then voting it according to management's wishes.)

12. (b)   The doctrine of ultra vires states that a corporation may not act or contract in any way that is not authorized either expressly or implied by state statute, the articles of incorporation, or the bylaws. If an action or contract is ultra vires, it is void or unenforceable under common law. However, in most jurisdictions today, the doctrine may be raised by a shareholder, but it may not be raised by either the corporation or a third party to nullify an action or contract.

13. (a)   Courts may "pierce the corporate veil" and hold a shareholder personally liable under the following circumstances: the corporation was undercapitalized when formed, the shareholders commingle personal assets/transactions with business assets/transactions, or the corporation is used to perpetrate a fraud on others. There is nothing wrong with forming a corporation to limit personal liability or with selling property to a corporation. A shareholder does not lose her/his limited liability just by being an officer, director, or employee of the corporation.

14. (b)   Four factors that frequently cause the courts to pierce the corporate veil are listed below:

1. Fraudulently inducing someone into dealing with the corporation rather than the individual.
2. "Thinly capitalized" corporations.
3. Failure to act as a corporation.
4. Commingling personal and corporate assets to the extent that the corporation has no identity of its own.

Answer (b) falls within the description of Factor #4; thus, it would be most likely to cause the courts to pierce the corporate veil.

15. (a)   Under the general rule, a subscriber who pays less than par or stated value for stock ("watered stock") as well as a transferee with knowledge of the deficiency are liable jointly and/or

severally for the deficiency to creditors of the corporation.

Directors & Officers

16. (a)   The Revised Model Business Corporation Act authorizes corporate directors to rely on information provided by the appropriate corporate officer. Directors have the duty of loyalty to the corporation, which would prevent them from serving on the board of directors of a competing business and from selling control of the corporation. Profiting from insider information would also be a breach of the fiduciary duty of loyalty, and is prohibited by the federal securities laws.

17. (a)   Generally, the board of directors has the power to manage the business of the corporation. This would include purchasing substantially all of the assets of another corporation and does not require the approval of the acquiring company's stockholders. The board of directors may initiate fundamental changes, such as selling substantially all of the corporation's assets, dissolving the corporation, or amending the articles of incorporation, but these changes require approval by the shareholders.

18. (d)   Most fundamental changes must be approved by shareholders of each involved corporation. An action that exchanges cash or Acorn shares for Trend shares is such a fundamental change. A sale of all assets is a de facto dissolution. A plan to acquire 90% of Trend in the stock market doesn't require formal shareholder approval, but risks not achieving its objective.

19. (b)   Under the Revised Model Business Corporations Act (RMBCA 8.50 and 8.56), a corporation may be authorized to indemnify its officers and directors for liability incurred in a suit by shareholders. The RMBCA does not prohibit a person from serving as both an officer and director in a corporation. Corporate officers are chosen by the corporation's directors. The RMBCA does not require that an officer also be a shareholder.

20. (d)   Corporate officers are fiduciaries and are ordinarily prohibited from engaging in self-dealing or making a secret profit from contracts with the corporation. However, most states make an exception where the self-interest is disclosed and fair to the corporation.

21. (d)   The amendment of the articles of incorporation is a task ultimately left to the shareholders, via a majority or perhaps even greater (e.g., two-thirds) vote.

22. (c) The business judgment rule, as used to explain the board of director's duty of due care, means that directors will not be held liable for acts or omissions involving a question of policy or business judgment, so long as they acted in good faith and without gross negligence. A director may reasonably rely on information given her/him by others associated with the organization. Scienter is an element of knowing, reckless behavior, and directors can be held liable in cases where they were sufficiently negligent, but lacked scienter. Smart and Co. is an independent contractor performing specialized services, and its negligence cannot be imputed to the directors.

23. (d) There are two types of shareholder suits: representative suits (direct suits against the corporation by shareholders to prevent a corporate act) and derivative suits (indirect suits brought by shareholders as representatives of the corporation against directors, officers, or outside partners). In the absence of any contrary provision in the articles, indemnification of officers and directors found to be negligent will be made only by court order.

24. (c) In this situation, Bixler is a promoter. As a promoter, he has a fiduciary duty to the not-yet-formed corporation and is, thereby, barred from making secret profits in his dealings with the corporation. Bixler should have made a full disclosure of his private dealings; however, because he did not divulge the details and obtain approval of the directors, he must return the $45,000 profit to the corporation.

Stockholders

25. (b) Preemptive rights, under the Revised Model Business Corporation Act, grant the stockholders the right to purchase a proportionate share of newly-issued stock. Although stockholders generally have the right to a proportionate share of corporate assets remaining on dissolution after the creditors are paid, this right is not part of the definition of preemptive rights.

26. (c) A stockholder of a public corporation is entitled to a reasonable inspection of corporate records for a proper purpose. A stockholder does not have the right to an annual payment of dividends or to have the corporation issue a new class of stock. A stockholder has the right to vote for corporate directors, not officers.

27. (c) Certain types of changes, such as amendments to the articles, merger, consolidation, *dissolution,* or sale of a substantial part of the corporate assets, require approval by an absolute majority of the shareholders, unless a greater proportion is required by the articles of incorporation. The board of directors is responsible for electing officers. Stockholders do not have a right to receive *annual* dividends nor to prevent corporate borrowing.

28. (c) Cumulative preferred stock is stock that entitles its holders to future year dividend carryovers from years in which dividends were not paid. The right to convert preferred stock to common stock is a matter of contract, and, thus, is not always present. Preferred stock may be either voting or non-voting. A corporation cannot declare a dividend distribution if such would render the corporation insolvent. Thus, there is no guarantee that dividends will be declared or paid.

29. (a) Corporations are required to keep books and records pertaining to such things as stockholder names and addresses and minutes of corporate-related meetings. Under common law, a stockholder has the right to inspect these books and records, in person or by her/his attorney, agent, or accountant, if there is a proper purpose, such as gathering information to commence a stockholder's derivative suit, to solicit stockholders to vote for a change in the board of directors, or to investigate possible management misconduct. The use of stockholder records for a personal business is not a proper purpose.

30. (a) Under the Revised Model Business Corporation Act, the dissenting stockholders of the subsidiary corporation have appraisal rights for consolidations as well as short-form mergers.

31. (b) A shareholder may bring an action for dissolution if the board of directors has committed fraud, *waste,* oppression, or misapplication of corporate funds. Dissolution may also be sought by the shareholders if the board of directors is deadlocked and the corporate business may no longer be conducted in a manner advantageous to the shareholders.

32. (c) Under the Revised Model Business Corporation Act, fundamental changes that alter the corporation's basic structure require shareholder approval. Minority shareholders have the right of appraisal remedy, which allows them to dissent and to recover the fair value of their shares if they follow the prescribed procedure for doing so. Fundamental changes that alter the corporation's basic structure include an amendment to the articles of incorporation that alters or abolishes a preferential right of certain shares, the consummation of a plan of share exchange such as in a merger or consolidation, and also the sale of substantially all of corporate assets.

The right of appraisal remedy is only available to shareholders that are entitled to vote.

33. (b) A stock split does not represent an asset or capital distribution to shareholders. A stock split simply increases the number of shares outstanding and proportionately decreases the par or stated value of the stock. There is no change in the dollar amount of capital stock, retained earnings, or total stockholders' equity.

34. (d) Stockholders have the right to sue for the benefit of the corporation in an action called a derivative suit. A derivative suit may be filed to recover damages from corporate management for an *ultra vires* management act; that is, an act that is beyond the express or implied powers of corporate management. Although a stockholder has the right to receive payment of a properly declared dividend and the right to inspect corporate records, a suit to enforce such rights or to compel dissolution of the corporation is not a derivative suit.

Fundamental Changes

35. (d) The Model Business Corporations Act provides that a merger requires that the stockholders of both corporations be given a copy of the merger plan as well as proper notice of a special meeting at which the merger plan will be presented. Although the merger plan must be approved by the stockholders and directors of both corporations, it is not necessary that the vote be unanimous. The articles of incorporation of the absorbing corporation may be amended, but the articles of the absorbed corporation cease to exist.

36. (c) The Revised Model Business Corporations Act requires a formal plan of merger (RMBCA 11.01) and requires that the board of directors and the shareholders of each corporation approve the merger (RMBCA 11.03). The RMBCA does not require that all stockholders of the original corporations be issued voting stock.

37. (b) The Revised Model Business Corporation Act (RMBCA) 11.04 provides a simplified procedure for the merger of a substantially owned subsidiary corporation into its parent corporation, referred to as a "short-form merger" or a "parent-subsidiary merger." This form of merger can be used only when the parent corporation owns at least 90% of the outstanding shares of each class of stock of the subsidiary corporation. The plan need only be approved by the board of directors of the parent corporation, not the board of directors of the subsidiary corporation, before it is filed with the state. A copy of the merger plan must be sent to each shareholder of record of the subsidiary corporation and the subsidiary corporation's dissenting stockholders must be given an appraisal remedy. The dissenting stockholders, upon fulfilling the proper procedures, have the right to obtain payment for the fair market value of their shares. This form of merger can be accomplished without the approval of the shareholders of either corporation.

Note that this simplified procedure differs from mergers and consolidations where the parent owns less than 90% of the subsidiary corporation. When the parent owns less than substantially all of the subsidiary, the board of directors and the shareholders of each corporation involved must approve a merger or consolidation plan before the plan can be filed with the state, and dissenting shareholders of each corporation may have appraisal rights.

38. (b) For voluntary dissolution, most jurisdictions require a vote by the BOD recommending dissolution, approval of at least a majority of the shareholders, and the filing of a certificate of dissolution with the appropriate state agency. The certificate of incorporation generally is not amended. Involuntary dissolution involves action by shareholders or the state.

FIT Ramifications

39. (c) The declaration of a stock dividend has no impact on the earnings and profits of the corporation for federal income tax purposes. Stock dividends are exempt securities under the Securities Act of 1933. A stock dividend, unlike a cash dividend, is not includable in the gross income of recipient taxpayers; rather it results in an adjustment to stock basis. Declaration of a stock dividend requires a vote of the board of directors, not of the stockholders.

40. (c) Corporations (except S corporations, personal holding companies, tax exempt organizations, and passive foreign investment companies) are liable for the accumulated earnings tax on sums of accumulated taxable income in excess of $250,000. The board of directors controls the timing, amount, and character of lawful dividends as long as it does not abuse its discretion. The IRS cannot compel distribution by court order; however, the mere presence of the accumulated earnings tax has some influence on frequency of cash dividend distributions. Stock dividends will not reduce amounts subject to the tax.

Solution 49-2 ADDITIONAL MULTIPLE CHOICE ANSWERS

Financing & Liability

41. (b) The essential elements of a *de facto* corporation are: (1) a valid statute under which the business could have been incorporated legally; (2) existence of a corporate charter; (3) a good faith effort to incorporate; and, (4) some good faith business dealings in the corporate name. If a third party entered into a contract believing s/he was dealing with a corporation, the courts will not allow the third party to hold shareholders liable on the contract; this is called corporation by estoppel. Under current common law, any corporation that substantially complies with the mandatory statutory requirements of incorporation is deemed a *de jure* corporation; it is indeterminate whether Elsie Components meets the "substantially compliance" requirement.

42. (c) Any agreement to subscribe that comes into existence after the corporation is formed constitutes a binding obligation to sell or purchase stock. Explicit conditions must appear on the face of the subscription agreement; however, courts have long held that the stock subscription contract is conditioned implicitly on the corporation's compliance with applicable securities laws. If individuals agree to subscribe to corporate stock, and each party's promise is dependent on the other parties also subscribing, then the subscription is enforceable—not between the corporation and each subscriber, but rather among the subscribers. Generally, the courts have held that a subscription for shares in a corporation not yet formed is an unenforceable contract, due to the lack of parties; however, some act of acceptance by the corporation after incorporation, allows pre-incorporation subscription agreements to become binding.

43. (c) Par value shares may not be issued for less than par value. A corporation may accept contracts for future services as consideration for the issuance of stock; accept past services as consideration for the issuance of stock; and require a holder to offer the corporation the right of first refusal on a repurchase of its stock before any sale is permitted to anyone else; in order to be enforceable, such restrictions must be reasonable and must be noted conspicuously on the face of the certificate.

Appendix: Agency

44. (b) An agent's duties to a principal include an obligation to act solely in the principal's interest in matters concerning the principal's business. Unless there is an agency coupled with an interest, the principal has the power to terminate the agency relationship, although the principal may not have the right to do so. The Statute of Frauds does not apply to the agreement between Plating and Armor, since the contract was for less than one year. Thus, their oral agreement is enforceable. An agency coupled with an interest results when the principal gives the agent a property or security interest in the subject matter of the agency. The paying of a commission does not create a property or security interest.

45. (c) Ajax had actual authority to purchase 300 of the tape recorders. Ajax also had apparent authority due to the fact that the third party, Sorrel, was aware of the written authorization giving Ajax unlimited power to purchase electronic appliances, but not of its revocation. Therefore, the apparent authority of Ajax existed with respect to Sorrel. This combination of actual and apparent authority effectively bound Port to the contract and makes Port liable to Sorrel. Ajax is liable for breaching the implied warranty of authority. An agent with apparent authority can bind a principal and third party to a contract even though s/he has exceeded her/his actual authority. Therefore, both Port and Ajax would be liable to the third party on the contract, but the best answer is (c) because the third party would be more likely to pursue the party with more assets, usually the principal. If losses to the principal result, the principal can hold the agent liable for exceeding her/his actual authority. Port will be held liable to Sorrel due to the fact that Ajax's apparent authority does bind Port to contract.

46. (c) The accountant and business manager has authority to do "normal" or "reasonable" business activities. Insuring property against fire loss is the activity that would be the most reasonable for a business manager to perform. The others all involve activities that would not generally happen within normal business activities. An agent would not have the apparent authority to mortgage the business property, obtain bank loans, or sell the business. In those situations, s/he would need specific authorization.

47. (b) It is generally not necessary for an agent to have a written agency agreement. An exception to the general rule exists if the agent's duties will involve the buying and selling of real property, or if the agency agreement is to last more than one year.

48. (c) Where an agency relationship terminates for any reason other than by operation of law, the principal must give actual notice of the termination to all third parties who have previously dealt with the agent and constructive notice to all other parties to

terminate the agent's apparent authority. Since Pole did not give constructive notice, and since Tripp had no knowledge of the termination, Tripp will be able to hold Pole liable for the Alan contract. It is irrelevant that Alan lacked any express or implied authority since apparent authority to act was still present.

49. (b)   The general rule is that the principal is vicariously liable for the torts of her/his agent if the tort is committed within the scope of the employment (the doctrine of *respondeat superior*). The principal is generally liable whether the principal instructed the agent to commit the tort or not. A limitation of liability in an agency agreement has no bearing on the right of the third party to sue the principal. It is possible for a principal to be liable for a tort that is also a criminal act (for example, where the principal instructs the agent to injure a customer if the customer does not pay).

50. (a)   Tort liability under *respondeat superior* arises when the agent is acting within the scope of her/his employment. Conduct was motivated by service to the principal. Thus, only if Elm's weapon was unlicensed and illegal is National not liable.

51. (b)   When an agent enters into a contract on behalf of a nondisclosed principal, the agent may be held liable on the contract. If the agent acted with authority, the principal may also be held liable upon disclosure. It is not necessary for a principal to ratify a contract in order to be held liable.

52. (c)   An agent usually will not be liable under a contract made with a third party if the principal is disclosed and if the agent acts within the scope of her/his agency. Agents for undisclosed principals always have contract liability.

PERFORMANCE BY SUBTOPICS

Each category below parallels a subtopic covered in Chapter 49. Record the number and percentage of questions you correctly answered in each subtopic area.

Characteristics

Question #	Correct	√
1		
2		
3		
4		
5		
6		
7		
8		
# Questions	8	
# Correct		
% Correct		

Financing & Liability

Question #	Correct	√
9		
10		
11		
12		
13		
14		
15		
# Questions	7	
# Correct		
% Correct		

Directors & Officers

Question #	Correct	√
16		
17		
18		
19		
20		
21		
22		
23		
24		
# Questions	9	
# Correct		
% Correct		

Stockholders

Question #	Correct	√
25		
26		
27		
28		
29		
30		
31		
32		
33		
34		
# Questions	10	
# Correct		
% Correct		

Fundamental Changes

Question #	Correct	√
35		
36		
37		
38		
# Questions	4	
# Correct		
% Correct		

FIT Ramifications

Question #	Correct	√
39		
40		
# Questions	2	
# Correct		
% Correct		

SIMULATION SOLUTIONS

Solution 49-3

Response #1: Distributions (4 points)

1. E

Drain's officers and directors violated their fiduciary duty of loyalty by intentionally allowing pollutants to be discharged and, thereby, exposing the corporation to a financial detriment.

2. H

A successful stockholder's derivative suit would most likely result in the officers and directors being held liable for abuse of discretion.

3. A

A successful stockholder's derivative suit would most likely result in the $1,000,000 being made available for distribution as a dividend.

4. C

A distribution of the $1,000,000 in 2005 to the stockholders would be characterized as a cash dividend.

Response #2: Stockholder Liability (6 points)

Although officers are **generally insulated** from personal liability for the negligence of the corporation or its employees, they are subject to personal liability **in tort** for their **own negligent conduct** or **participation,** even while engaged in corporate business activities. **Shareholders** generally **will not be held liable** for the negligence of the corporation unless they have in some way **participated in the negligent act.** Based on the facts presented, Major is **personally liable** to Fox for his **own negligence** even though the negligent acts were committed **while engaged in corporate business activities.** Major **may also be liable** because of his status as a shareholder if the **corporate veil is pierced.**

A corporation is **liable** under the doctrine of **respondeat superior** for the **torts committed by its agents and employees** (officers) **in the course of their employment.** Thus, Dix will also be liable to Fox for the negligence of Major.

The liability insurance carried by Dix will provide **coverage of Dix and Major up to $500,000 of liability to Fox.** If Fox were to obtain a judgment in excess of $500,000, Major and Dix would be **liable for the uninsured balance.**

Solution 49-4

Response #1: Formation (3 points)

1. A

Corporations are regulated by state laws which allow their formation. Thus, a corporation must be formed in accordance with a state's general corporation statute. It is not necessary that Articles of Incorporation include the names of all stockholders, nor is it necessary that corporate bylaws be included with the incorporation documents.

2. C

The Model Business Corporation Act (MBCA) provides that a corporation's initial bylaws will be adopted by the initial Board of Directors.

3. C

The Model Business Corporation Act (MBCA) specifies that a corporation's directors are elected by its shareholders.

Response #2: Stockholder Liability (7 points)

Pine's assertion that Major is personally liable to the extent of $6,000 for the common shares issued to Major is incorrect as to the dollar amount of his potential liability. Where a corporation issues par value stock in return for property or services rendered having a fair market value less than the par value, the **shareholder purchasing the stock at the discounted price** will remain **potentially liable to the creditors of the corporation.** The **potential liability** is the **difference between** the **fair market value** of the consideration given and the **total par value** of the stock. Stock issued at such a discounted price is commonly referred to as **"watered stock."** In this case, Major's part payment by a promissory note and future services is **insufficient consideration.** Therefore, Major is **potentially liable** to Pine and the other corporate creditors for **$9,500,** calculated as follows:

First Acquisition

Total par value	
(1,000 shares × $10 par value)	$10,000
Less: Consideration given (fair market value of property)	(3,500)
Potential liability on first acquisition	$ 6,500

Second Acquisition

Total par value	
(1,000 shares × $10 par value)	$10,000
Less: Consideration given (services rendered)	(7,000)
Potential liability on second acquisition	3,000
Total Potential Liability	$ 9,500

Pine's assertion that Major may be personally liable as a result of his directing customers to make checks payable to him in his individual capacity and depositing the checks in his individual account without recording the checks on the corporation's books is correct. Although a corporation may be established to limit the liability of the shareholders, the courts will **pierce the corporate veil** (disregard the corporate entity) and hold the shareholders personally liable when the corporation is **used to perpetuate a fraud** or in a closely held corporation when the shareholders fail to treat the corporation as a separate business entity. The **commingling** of the corporation's funds with Major's own funds amounts to a disregard of the corporate entity and will likely **subject Major to personal liability for the debts of Dix.**

Solution 49-5

Response: Stockholder Rights (10 points)

a. Edwards will not win the suit to have Olsen removed as president. The **right to hire and fire** officers is held by the **board of directors. Individual stockholders,** regardless of the size of their holding, **have no vote in the selection of officers.** Individual stockholders may exert influence in this area by voting for directors at the annual stockholders' meeting.

b. Edwards will lose the suit to have National purchase the stock. A stockholder who **dissents from a merger** may require the corporation to purchase her/his shares if the statutory requirements are met and would be entitled to the fair value of the stock **(appraisal remedy).** To **compel the purchase,** Edwards would have had to **file an objection** to the merger before the stockholders meeting at which the merger proposal was considered, **vote against** the merger proposal, and make a **written demand** that the corporation purchase the stock at an appraised price. Edwards will lose because the first two requirements were met but Edwards failed to make a written demand that the corporation purchase the stock.

c. 1. Queen will lose its suit against National to enforce the contract, even though Edwards was a National director. Jenkins may have assumed that Edwards was **acting as National's agent,** but Edwards had **no authority** to contract with Queen. A director has a **fiduciary duty** to the stockholders of a corporation but, unless **expressly authorized** by the board of directors or the officers of the corporation, has **no authority to contract on behalf of the corporation.** There is **no implied agency authority** merely **by being a director.**

2. Queen will win its suit against Edwards because Edwards had **no authority to act** for National. Edwards will be **personally liable** for Queen's damages.

Solution 49-6

Response: Board of Directors & Officers (10 points)

Bradley would be **successful** in the suit against Frost and Glen for failing to vote Bradley to the board of directors. The stockholders have the **right to elect the directors** of a corporation. The stockholders have **the right to agree among themselves on how they will vote.** Therefore, the voting provision of the stockholders' agreement between Bradley, Frost, and Glen is **enforceable.**

Bradley would be **unsuccessful** in attempting to be reinstated as vice president. A corporation's board oversees the operations of the business, which includes **hiring officers and, at its discretion, dismissing officers with or without cause.** Bradley would be **successful in collecting some damages** for the breach of the employment contract because there was no demonstrated cause for Bradley's dismissal.

Bradley would be successful in having Frost and Glen held **personally liable to** the corporation for declaring and paying the dividend because **payment of a dividend that threatens a corporation's solvency is unlawful.** Ordinarily, **directors who approve such a dividend would be personally liable** for its repayment to the corporation. However, the directors, other than Frost and Glen, in relying on the assurances and information supplied by Frost and Glen, as corporate officers, are protected by the **business judgment rule.** Therefore, only Frost and Glen would be held personally liable.

Solution 49-7

Response #1: Board of Directors (8 points)

The assertion that it was improper for the board of directors to authorize the reacquisition of Cray's common stock while Cray was insolvent is correct. A board of directors may authorize and the corporation may reacquire its shares of stock subject to any restriction in the articles of incorporation, except that **no reacquisition may be made if,** after giving effect thereto, **either the corporation would be unable to pay its debts as they become due** in the usual course of business **or the corporation's total assets would be less than its total liabilities.** Because Cray was **insolvent** before and after the reacquisition of Cray's common stock, it was improper for the board of directors to authorize the reacquisition.

The assertion that the members of Cray's board of directors are personally liable because Cray reacquired its own shares of Cray stock while Cray was insolvent is incorrect. In general, directors who vote or assent to a reacquisition by the corporation of its own shares while the corporation is insolvent will be **jointly** and **severally liable** to the corporation. However, the directors will not be liable if they **acted in good faith,** in a manner they reasonably believed to be in the best interests of the corporation, and with such care as an **ordinarily prudent person** in a like position would use under similar circumstances. In performing their duties, **directors are entitled to rely on information, opinions, reports, or statements,** including financial statements and other financial data prepared or **presented by one or more officers or employees of the corporation** whom the directors reasonably believe to be reliable and competent in the matters presented. The directors may rely on the same information prepared or presented by independent accountants that the directors reasonably believe to be within such person's professional competence. Based on the facts of this case, the directors' reliance on the reports and financial statements prepared by Cray's internal accounting department under the supervision of the treasurer and reviewed by its independent accountants was proper so long as the directors **exercised due care, acted in good faith,** and **acted without knowledge** that would cause such reliance to be unwarranted. In addition, the courts are precluded from substituting their business judgment for that of the board of directors if the directors have acted with due care and in good faith.

The assertion that Cray will be liable to the treasurer as a result of his termination by the board of directors is correct. **An officer may be removed** by the board of directors **with or without cause** whenever in its judgment the best interests of the corporation will be served by the removal. However, such removal is **without prejudice to the contract rights** of the person so removed. Thus, the board of directors had the power to remove the treasurer. The treasurer will prevail in a breach of contract action for damages against Cray because **the firing violated the employment agreement.**

Response #2: Distributions (2 points)

1. $10.00

Each share would receive $5.00 ($100 face value × 5%) for each year. Because the preferred stock is cumulative, the preferred shareholders would be entitled to a dividend for both 2004 and 2005.

2. $9.00

Total distribution	$1,000,000
Distribution to preferred	
$10 × 10,000 shares	(100,000)
Distribution to common	900,000
Number of common shares	/ 100,000
Dividend per common share	$ 9.00

BEC Hot•Spot™ Video Descriptions
(Subject to change without notice.)

CPA 3460 Corporations & Partnerships
Coverage of corporations includes derivative action, preemptive rights, watered stock, foreign corporations, mergers, consolidations, and dissenting stockholders. When discussing partnership topics, the presentation assumes candidates have a solid understanding of agency topics (tested in the *Regulation* exam section). Review assignment of partner's interest, joint ventures, and rights and liabilities of general partners, limited partners, stockholders...and more! Ivan Fox discusses 27 multiple choice questions during this lecture. Approximate time is one hour.

CPA 3420 Economics
Kevin Kemerer provides coverage of microeconomics, macroeconomics, and international trade including the topics of demand, supply, elasticity, market structures, the business cycle, classical and Keynesian models of economic analysis, money supply, price indexes, absolute and comparative advantage, foreign exchange, and balance of payments. Kevin covers several valuable study tips and 49 multiple choice questions during this program. Approximate time is 3:25.

CPA 3430 Financial Management
Includes coverage of working capital management, capital structure, interest rates, security valuation, and capital budgeting. The discussion of working capital management includes cash, cash equivalents, accounts receivable, inventory, and short-term debt. Kevin Kemerer provides several valuable study tips and guides viewers through 45 multiple choice questions during this program. Approximate time is three hours.

CPA 3470 Cost & Managerial Accounting
Robert Monette thoroughly discusses managerial topics such as break-even analysis, with examples worked throughout the lecture. An in-depth examination of direct vs. absorption costing is provided, as well as coverage of incremental analysis, budgeting, and strategic management. Recurring exam topics are highlighted in the lecture and 37 multiple choice questions. Approximate time is 3:20.

CPA 3410 Information Technology
Russell Jacques discusses exam study techniques as well as covering software, networks, files, databases, systems development, transaction processing modes, business information systems, controls, business continuity, and eCommerce. Russ highlights probable exam topics in the lecture and his discussion of 42 objective questions. Approximate time is three hours.

Call a customer representative toll-free at 1 (800) 874-7877 for more details about videos.

Other Videos
(Subject to change without notice.)

CPA 1565 How to Pass the CPA Exam

While watching this video, CPA candidates will gain insight about the CPA exam in general and computer-based testing in particular. Robert Monette discusses when to take the exam and the new content specifications. Bob delineates the different question types and explores exam-taking, exam-scheduling, and study strategies. Approximately 30 minutes.

Complimentary copies of this valuable video are available for a limited time to qualified candidates.

CPA 4150 Intensive: Business Environment & Concepts

Robert Monette provides a thorough review of business environment and concepts. Corporations and partnerships are distilled to the essentials needed for the exam. After watching this video, any gray areas you might have had concerning cost accounting will evaporate, including standard cost. Financial management and economics are discussed. Information technology is reviewed using actual AICPA questions previously used in the Auditing & Attestation exam section. As well as answering and explaining 115 multiple choice questions, Robert Monette explains exam-taking techniques and helps you mentally prepare for the uncertainty surrounding this new exam section. Approximate time is 4:45.

In order to ensure current materials, Bisk Education leases (rather than sells) videos to candidates. At lease completion (after your exam), contact your customer service representative (either info@cpaexam.com or customerservice@cpaexam.com) regarding the return of videos. If needed, extensions on leases are available—but with material this effective, it's a rare occurrence. Call a customer representative toll-free at 1 (800) 874-7877 for more details about videos.

CHAPTER 50

ECONOMIC THEORY

EXAM COVERAGE: The *Economic Concepts* portion of the Business Environment & Concepts (BEC) section of the CPA exam is designated by the examiners to be 8 to 12 percent of the BEC section's point value. Candidates should plan their use of study time accordingly. More information about the point value of various topics is included in the **Practical Advice** section of this volume.

CHAPTER 50

ECONOMIC THEORY

I. Microeconomics

A. Overview

Economics is the study of the allocation of scarce resources among alternative uses. Microeconomics is the study of the decisions that individual units (such as firms and households) make when using limited resources to maximize satisfaction. By comparison, macroeconomics is the study of community (aggregate) decisions about allocating resources (labor and capital) to maximize social welfare. Microeconomics focuses on individuals (typically, as purchasers of production and suppliers of labor and capital) and firms (typically, as sellers of production and purchasers of labor and capital).

1. **Assumptions** Economics assumes unlimited human wants and limited resources to satisfy those wants. Throughout this chapter, *goods* implicitly includes both goods and services, unless noted otherwise.

2. **Economic Systems** Labels attached to economic systems are useful for describing them relative to each other. The existence of pure capitalistic and socialistic societies on a large scale are not as common as at first might appear. Each economic system answers the following questions. What is produced? How much is produced? How is it produced? Who uses production?

   a. **Capitalism** Capitalism also is called the free-enterprise system. Every economic unit (firm, investor, consumer, etc) is free to act in its own interests. Resources are owned privately and decisions made individually. Economic questions are answered by the pricing mechanism of free markets.

   b. **Communism** Resources are owned by the state and most decisions are made by the state. Individuals make limited choices. Economic questions are answered by government planning.

   c. **Socialism** Socialism is something of a mixture of capitalism and communism, with varying degrees of governmental intervention and private ownership. Some industries may be exclusive to state ownership. Economic questions are answered by government planning as well as the market system.

B. Demand

Demand is the amount a good that consumers as a group will (are willing and able to) purchase at a given price during a given period of time. Demand analysis concentrates on consumer behavior.

1. **Law of Demand** The price and quantity demanded for a good are related inversely; that is, the lower the price, the higher the demand. The classic list of demand determinants assume a pure capitalist system: all consumers acting in their individual interests. Group actions, such as boycotts and price controls, also influence demand.

   a. **Cross-Elasticity of Demand** Closely-related goods influence demand. The degree to which two goods are related to each other influences the degree to which demand will change.

   (1) **Substitutes** If good A has a substitute, B, relatively lower in price, buyers leave the market for A and purchase the substitute B. For instance, a price increase for wool clothing may increase demand for acrylic clothing.

(2) **Complements** If good A has a complement, B, price changes for either have a corresponding change in the demand for the other. For instance, a price increase for breakfast cereal will decrease demand for milk.

b. **Income** The amount of consumers' income relative to prices influences demand.

(1) **Normal Goods** Demand for normal goods has a positive relationship to income. In other words, as income increases, the demand for normal goods increases; as income decreases, the demand for normal goods decreases. Generally, silk clothing is a normal good and nylon clothing is an inferior good.

(2) **Inferior Goods** Demand for inferior goods has a negative relationship to income. In other words, as income decreases, the demand for inferior goods increases; as income increases, the demand for inferior goods decreases.

c. **Expectations** Consumer expectations as to price changes influence demand positively. If consumers expect prices to increase, or inflation, they increase current demand. If consumers expect prices to decrease, or deflation, they decrease current demand.

d. **Preference** Consumer taste or preference influences demand. Consumer preference is perhaps the least predictable determinant. For instance, in colonial times, oysters often were an inferior good, but are now a normal good.

e. **Market Size** The number of consumers (also called the population) tends to have a positive relationship to demand.

2. **Graphic Illustration** Typically, price is shown on the y-axis and quantity demanded is shown on the x-axis. Demand often is represented as a curve or line to illustrate consumers' smaller demand at a higher price, all other factors remaining the same. With the *price* and *quantity demanded* as the axes, there is no means to show changes, such as income changes, except by labeling different demand curves for such changes. An increase in demand is represented by a shift to the right.

Exhibit 1 ▶ Positive Demand Curve Shift

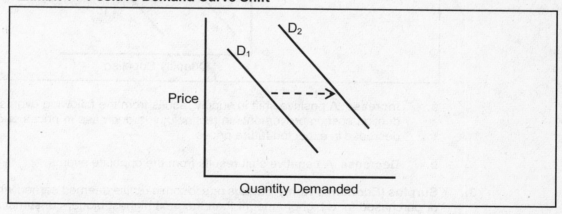

a. **Increase** A positive shift in demand results from the following events: increase of substitute's price; decrease in complement's price; for normal goods, an increase in consumer income; for inferior goods, a decrease in consumer income; expected future price increases, a favorable change in preferences (due, for instance, to an advertising campaign), an increase in the number of consumers, and the end of a boycott.

b. **Decrease** A negative shift results from the opposite events.

C. **Supply**

Supply (or market supply) is the amount a good that producers as a group will (are willing and able to) supply at a given price during a given period of time. Supply analysis focuses on producers' behavior.

1. **Law of Supply** The price and quantity supplied for a good are related directly; that is, the higher the price, the higher the supply.

   a. **Production Costs** Taxes are effective increases in production costs. Subsidies act as effective decreases in production costs.

   b. **Technology** Technological improvements in production of a good increase the supply of that good.

   c. **Prices of Other Goods** An increase in price for another good encourages firms to use resources for the production of that other good.

   d. **Price Expectations** An increase in the expected future price for a good encourages firms to supply less currently.

2. **Graphic Illustration** Typically, price is shown on the y-axis and quantity supplied is shown on the x-axis. Supply often is represented as a curve or line to illustrate producers' larger supply at a higher price, all other factors remaining the same. An increase in supply is represented by a shift to the right.

   Exhibit 2 ▶ Positive Supply Curve Shift

   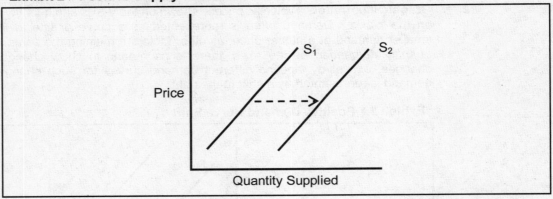

   a. **Increase** A positive shift in supply results from the following events: decrease of production cost; improvements in technology; a decrease in prices of other goods; and a decrease in expected future prices.

   b. **Decrease** A negative shift results from the opposite events.

3. **Surplus (Economic Rent)** Surplus or economic rent is deemed earned when an input is paid or purchased for a higher amount than the next highest bidder-consumer of that input would pay. For resources with perfect inelasticity (such as land and other limited natural resources), all of the price is deemed economic rent; a higher price will not increase the supply.

   Example 1 ▶ Economic Rent

   A musician earns $500,000 as a rock star. The musician's alternative employment is a sales clerk for $20,000. The economic rent is $480,000.

D. Elasticity

Elasticity is a measure of how responsive the market is to change in a determinant.

1. **Price Elasticity of Demand** Price elasticity of demand (E_d) measures responsiveness of demand to changes in price. If demand is elastic, demand will fluctuate as the price changes; if demand is inelastic, demand will not change as the price changes. Algebraically, E_d is the percentage change in quantity demanded divided by the percentage change in price; thus, it is represented graphically as the slope of the demand line. Increases in production costs are passed readily to buyers when demand is inelastic, but must be absorbed by sellers when demand is elastic.

   Exhibit 3 ▸ Price Elasticity of Demand (Elasticity Coefficient) Formula

   $$E_d = \frac{\text{Percentage change in quantity demanded}}{\text{Percentage change in price}}$$

   a. **Factors** The following factors increase demand elasticity: classification as a luxury, rather than a necessity; longer length of time period analyzed; greater number of substitutes; and percent of income spent on that good.

   b. **Elasticity Coefficient** If the absolute value of E_d is greater than one, demand is classified as elastic; if less than one, demand is classified as inelastic; if equal to one, demand is classified as having unitary elasticity.

   Exhibit 4 ▸ Elasticity Coefficient & Total Revenue Relationship

	$|E_d| > 1$	$|E_d| = 1$	$|E_d| < 1$
Price increase	total revenue down	same	total revenue up
Price decrease	total revenue up	same	total revenue down

2. **Price Elasticity of Supply** Price elasticity of supply (E_s) measures responsiveness of supply to changes in price. If supply is elastic, supply will fluctuate as the price changes; if supply is inelastic, supply will not change much as the price changes. Algebraically, E_s is the percentage change in quantity supplied divided by the percentage change in price; thus, it is represented graphically as the slope of the supply line. A high cost and low feasibility of storage decreases supply elasticity. Attributes of the production process influence elasticity: a by-product's elasticity is influenced strongly by the elasticity of the main product. The ability to supply goods becomes more elastic with time.

   Exhibit 5 ▸ Price Elasticity of Supply (Elasticity Coefficient) Formula

   $$E_s = \frac{\text{Percentage change in quantity supplied}}{\text{Percentage change in price}}$$

3. **Cross-Elasticity of Demand** Cross-elasticity of demand (E_{xy}) measures responsiveness of demand to changes in price of another good. If E_{xy} is positive, the goods are substitutes; if negative, the goods are complements; if equal to zero, the goods are unrelated.

   Exhibit 6 ▸ Cross-Elasticity of Demand (Elasticity Coefficient) Formula

   $$E_{xy} = \frac{\text{Percentage change in quantity demanded of good X}}{\text{Percentage change in price of good Y}}$$

4. **Income Elasticity of Demand** Income elasticity of demand (E_i) measures responsiveness of demand to changes in income. If E_i is positive, the good is normal; if negative, the good is inferior.

Exhibit 7 ▶ Income Elasticity of Demand (Elasticity Coefficient) Formula

$$E_i = \frac{\text{Percentage change in quantity demanded}}{\text{Percentage change in income}}$$

E. **Market**
The market is the interaction of buyers and sellers of a good for exchange purposes. The point where supply and demand curves meet is the market, or equilibrium, price. Anyone may purchase or sell the good at the market price. The market forces of supply and demand create an automatic rationing system. The system acts to allocate goods to consumers willing to pay for them. When a shortage exists, the market price will rise and quantity demanded will decrease, eliminating the shortage. When surplus exists, the market price will decrease and quantity demanded will increase, eliminating the surplus.

1. **Graphic Illustration** As price is shown on the y-axis and quantity is shown on the x-axis for both the supply and demand graphs, the two graphs can be superimposed to show the market as a whole. The point where the two curves intersect is market equilibrium. P_e is the equilibrium price and Q_e is the equilibrium quantity.

Exhibit 8 ▶ Market

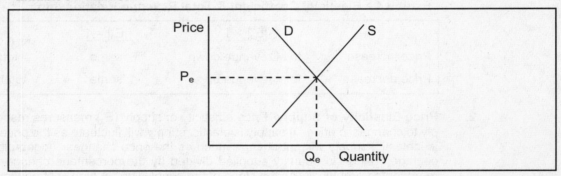

2. **Price Fixing** Governments may set mandatory or artificial prices, interfering with the market's automatic allocation system often with unintended results (although the results are not unpredictable as far as broad direction).

    a. **Floor** When a price is set above the market (equilibrium) price, surpluses develop. This usually causes non-price competition among sellers (for example, advertising and "gifts" for customers) and reduced demand by buyers. The price set for airfare before airline industry deregulation is an example of a price floor. In Exhibit 9, the surplus is the difference between Q_d and Q_s in the graph illustrating a floor set above market price.

    b. **Ceiling** When a price is set below the market (equilibrium) price, shortages develop. This usually causes non-price competition among buyers (for example, waiting lines) and reduced production by suppliers. In Exhibit 9, the shortage is the difference between Q_d and Q_s in the graph illustrating a ceiling set below market price.

Exhibit 9 ▶ Price Ceiling & Floor Graphs

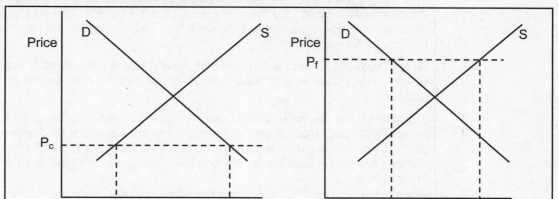

P_c = Ceiling price
Q_s = Quantity supplied

P_f = Floor price
Q_d = Quantity demanded

Example 2 ▶ Price Ceiling

There are 10,000 two-bedroom apartments for rent for $1,100 a month in Big City. Big City's council decides that the high rent for a two-bedroom apartment is the reason that the population is decreasing, so it initiates rent controls. The two-bedroom apartments now have a ceiling of $800 a month. Because the rent is lower, 1,500 more families want to live in Big City; however, landlords decide to change the buildings to retail and office space because it is more profitable, so only 9,000 two-bedroom apartments are available for the 11,500 families that want to rent them.

Even if the council prohibits conversion of existing property when the rent controls are enacted, there probably will be fewer residences available for rent, eventually. Any grand-fathered changes from residential rental to commercial use will still be made. Planned changes from commercial to residential use will halt. Existing rental residential stock will age and be condemned as unfit for residential use, but there is little incentive for use-lengthening maintenance or new rental residential construction.

3. **The Common (Externalities)** Assets used in common may suffer poor maintenance. The damage to common assets are called externalities as the cost is external to the abuser's cost (or once is divided among the whole community, the cost is insignificant to the abuser). Some common assets gaining prominence in the public eye are air, landfill, and water resources. Some corporations are taking voluntary steps to curb abuse of these commons to engender goodwill with consumers as well as to delay the advent of mandatory rationing or to mimimalize its disruption to their operations. The transformation of externalities borne by the community as a whole to internal cost borne by individuals is called full cost accounting.

Example 3 ▶ The Common & Externalities

Small Township has a common field where all the township residents' livestock may graze, but it is insufficient to supply food for all the livestock. While some grazing has no long-term impact, there is a limit to the grazing that the common can endure without damage (lower yield in the future). Additional food must be purchased by the livestock owners. If each of the residents uses the common indiscriminately, the common will be overgrazed; therefore, it is in each resident's interest to use the common carefully; however, Slippery Sam's livestock grazes more than an equal share.

The cost of the overgrazing is carried by all residents (either damage to the common or the purchase of more food than otherwise), but the benefits (the purchase of less food) are received disproportionately by Slippery Sam. The damage to the common is an externality to Slippery Sam.

Small Township Council is worried that, having borne the results of Slippery Sam's abuse of the common, fewer and fewer residents will restrain their use of the common as time passes.

To maintain the common, Small Township Council rations grazing, allowing grazing rights to be bought and sold. After this change, it is not beneficial for Slippery Sam for his live-stock to graze more than his share, because he will have to purchase grazing rights from another resident. Damage to the common has been changed from an externality to an internal cost.

4. **Impact of Shifts in Demand & Supply**

   a. **Demand** An increase in demand, when supply doesn't change, will increase the market price. A decrease in demand, when supply doesn't change, will decrease the market price.

   b. **Supply** An increase in supply, when demand doesn't change, will decrease the market price. A decrease in supply, when demand doesn't change, will increase the market price.

   c. **Simultaneous & Similar** An increase in supply and demand will increase the output quantity with an indeterminate effect on market price. A decrease in supply and demand will decrease the output quantity with an indeterminate effect on market price.

   d. **Simultaneous & Different** An increase in demand and decrease in supply will increase the market price with an indeterminate effect on output quantity. A decrease in demand and increase in supply will decrease the market price with an indeterminate effect on output quantity.

F. **Utility Theory**
An assumption of utility theory is that an individual's objective is to maximize the total utility from available income. Total utility is maximized when the last dollar spent on each of several different goods provides the same utility; in other words, for a fixed amount of income, a higher level of utility can not be achieved.

Example 4 ▶ Utility Theory

Owning two pairs of pants and two pairs of shoes, the consumer decides that another pair of pants will provide more utility than another pair of shoes, so the consumer buys another pair of pants. Knowing that s/he has a limited amount to spend, the consumer will buy pants until buying shoes will provide more utility.

Exhibit 10 ▶ Utility Maximization Formula

$$\frac{\text{Marginal utility of A}}{\text{Price of A}} = \frac{\text{Marginal utility of B}}{\text{Price of B}}$$

1. **Measurement** Cardinal measurements assign numerical values to benefits received from each good. Ordinal measurements establish a rank to each good, without assigning a specific unit of worth.

2. **Diminishing Marginal Utility Principle** Equal increments of additional consumption of a good provide smaller and smaller additional units of utility. For instance, the first pair of shoes provides more utility than the 101st.

3. **Indifference Curve** The various combinations of commodities × and Y that give equal utility to a consumer form an indifference curve. In other words, a consumer is indifferent to, or has no preference for, one combination over another along the curve. Because of diminishing marginal utility, indifference curves are nonlinear: if consumers obtained equal utility from the first unit as the last, the relationship would be linear. Indifference curves cannot intersect, are sloped negatively, and are convex to the origin.

4. **Budget Constraints** All the combinations of two commodities an individual can purchase with a given income at given prices for the two commodities form budget constraints. A change in income causes a parallel shift in the budget constraint line. A change in either or both goods' prices changes the slope of the budget constraint line. If relative prices of both goods change proportionately, a parallel shift in the budget constraint line results.

5. **Graphic Illustration** The x-axis is the quantity of one good and the y-axis is the quantity of the other good. The point of maximum utility is where the budget constraint line is tangent to the highest possible indifference curve.

Exhibit 11 ▶ Indifference Curves & Budget Constraint Lines

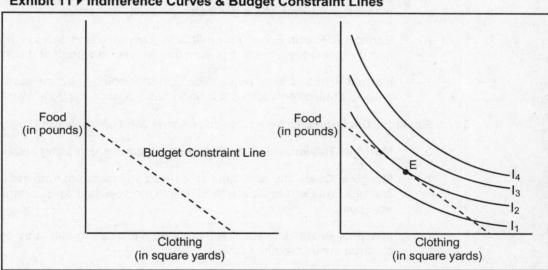

G. **Production & Costs**
Production factors also are called inputs. They can be classified by the type of return that they generate. Capital and land sometimes are combined in one category, as interest is merely the rent paid for the use of capital. Governmental services, capital goods, entrepreneurial services, and research and development can be considered special instances of the basic four factors.

Exhibit 12 ▶ Production Factors & Returns

Factor	Return
Labor	Wages
Capital	Interest
Land	Rent
Management	Profit

1. **Short vs. Long** The short run is a time period in which an entity cannot vary the amounts of all inputs. In other words, the quantity of at least one input is fixed. The long run is a time period in which an entity can change all inputs (including plant capacity).

2. **Cost Classification** These classifications assume a short-run time period. In the long-run, all costs are variable.

   a. **Fixed Costs** Fixed costs are those costs that do not change with the level of output. Average fixed costs are total fixed costs divided by output quantity.

   b. **Variable Costs** Variable costs are those costs that vary with the level of output. Average variable costs are total variable costs divided by output quantity.

   c. **Total Costs** Total costs are the sum of fixed and variable costs. Average total costs are total costs divided by output quantity.

   d. **Historical (Explicit) Costs** Historical costs are actual expenditures made in producing a product.

   e. **Implicit Costs** Implicit costs are amounts that would have been received if resources had been used for other purposes.

   f. **Opportunity (Alternative) Costs** Opportunity costs are the costs of not engaging in an alternative activity.

   g. **Economic Cost** Economic cost is the income that an entity must provide in order to attract resource suppliers (for instance, equity investors).

   h. **Economic Profit** Economic profit is total revenue less all economic costs. When economic profit is zero, the firm is earning just a normal profit or a normal rate of return.

   i. **Normal Profit** Normal profit is the cost of keeping entrepreneurial skills in the organization. Another definition is the opportunity cost of using the owner's own resources.

3. **Basis for Decisions** Economic decisions are based on analysis of marginal factors.

   a. **Marginal Revenue** The additional revenue from increasing output by one unit.

   b. **Marginal Cost** The additional cost (fixed and variable) from increasing production by one unit. As fixed costs are fixed, within the specified limits, marginal cost equals variable cost.

   c. **Marginal Profit** The additional profit from increasing output by one unit; the marginal revenue minus marginal cost.

   d. **Marginal Product** The additional output from increasing input by one unit.

   e. **Marginal Revenue Product** The marginal revenue times marginal product. Alternatively, the marginal revenue product is that additional unit of output at which the marginal revenue from an input is equal to its marginal physical product quantity times the marginal revenue from the sale of an additional unit of output.

4. **Principle of Diminishing Returns** There is a point beyond which additional units of variable input will contribute less and less to total production; in other words, the marginal production will decline. Optimal use occurs when a variable input is used up to the point at which the marginal increase in revenue from use of that input is equal to the marginal cost from use of that input. In other words, an entity will profit from use of additional resources up to the point at which marginal revenue product equals marginal resource cost.

Exhibit 13 ▶ Returns on Input

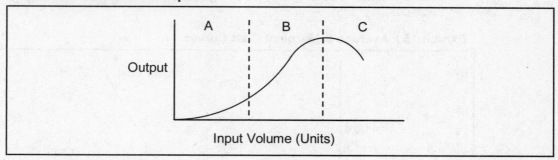

a. **Marginal Revenue Product** The marginal revenue product is that additional unit of output at which the marginal revenue from an input is equal to its marginal physical product quantity times the marginal revenue from the sale of an additional unit of output.

b. **Marginal Resource Cost** The marginal resource cost of an input is equal to its market price.

5. **Average Cost Curve** The average cost curve is u-shaped because of economies and diseconomies of scale.

Exhibit 14 ▶ Average Cost Curve

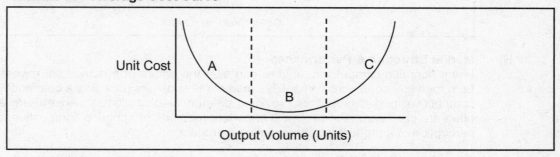

a. **Increasing Returns to Scale** If all outputs are changed by a factor greater than the factor that changes inputs, returns to scale increase. For instance, there are increasing returns to scale, or economies of scale, when inputs triple, but outputs more than triple. As most entities expand output, average costs of production decline due to better use, including specialization, of resources: management, labor, and equipment. This is shown graphically by the part of the input-return (Exhibit 13) and the average-cost (Exhibit 14) curves labeled "A."

b. **Constant Returns to Scale** If all outputs are changed by a factor that is the same as the factor that changes inputs, returns to scale remain constant. This is shown graphically by the part of the input-return (Exhibit 13) and the average-cost (Exhibit 14) curves labeled "B."

c. **Decreasing Returns to Scale** If all outputs are changed by a factor less than the factor that changes inputs, returns to scale decrease. For instance, there are decreasing returns to scale, or diseconomies of scale, when inputs triple, but outputs merely double. Eventually, as entities continue to expand output, the marginal cost of production tends to increase. The common explanation is the difficulty of managing a large-scale organization. This is shown graphically by the part of the input-return (Exhibit 13) and the average-cost (Exhibit 14) curves labeled "C."

6. **Marginal & Average Cost Curves** Marginal cost is equal to average cost whenever average cost is at a minimum. If average cost is falling (economies of scale), marginal cost is below

average cost. If average cost is rising (diseconomies of scale), marginal cost is above average cost.

Exhibit 15 ▶ Average & Marginal Cost Curves

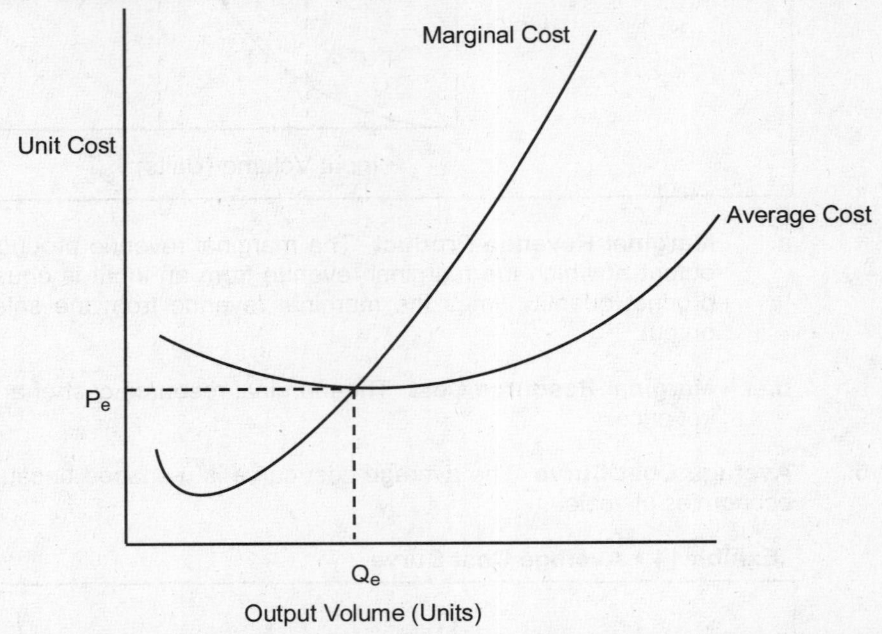

H. Market Structure & Performance

Using nonprice competition, entities can alter the nature of a market somewhat, moving a product from for instance, a pure competitive market (all suppliers providing a commodity) to a monopolistic competitive market (suppliers providing differentiated products). Advertising and product quality often are considered the two most important methods of nonprice competition, either changing the perception of a product or differentiating a product.

1. **Pure (Perfect) Competition** The classic example of a competitive market is any commodity, for example, iron ore, lumber, or wheat. These are not perfect examples of competitive markets; for instance, environmental and food-handling laws may restrict free entry into or exit from these markets.

    a. **Characteristics** When discussing a purely competitive market, the following are assumed: a large number of buyers and sellers acting independently; a homogeneous or standardized product; free entry into and exit from the market for firms; perfect information; no price controls; and no non-price competition.

    b. **Short-Run** A producing entity must sell at the market prices. In other words, a producing entity is a price taker. Thus, the demand curve is perfectly elastic (or horizontal). For profit maximization, the producing entity equates price to marginal cost. If the price is less than average variable cost (lower than P_a in Exhibit 16), the entity would stop producing to reduce loss. If the price is above marginal cost (such as P_b in Exhibit 16), more producers eventually will enter the market, but in the short-run, economic profit is earned. Between P_e and P_a (in Exhibit 16) in the short-run, the producer will continue production to cover some of the fixed costs.

Exhibit 16 ▶ Short-Run Competition

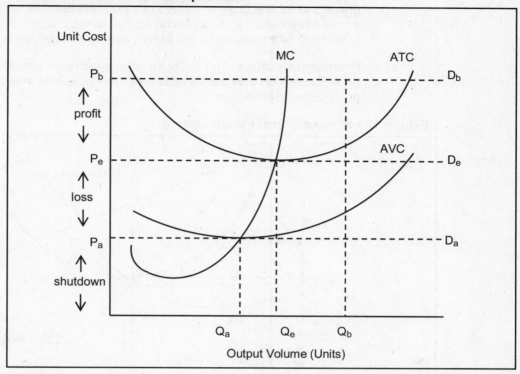

c. **Long-Run** This analysis assumes that all firms are equally efficient. As economic profits are available, more entities will enter the market, eventually driving the price down to a point where no economic profits occur. If too many entities enter the market, eventually driving the price down to a point where economic losses occur, some entities will leave the market, eventually driving the price back up to a point where no economic profits occur. Because price equals marginal cost, allocation of resources is optimal: entities produce the ideal output (the output at which average cost is lowest). The price is lower and output greater than in any other market structure. An entity in a competitive market in long-run equilibrium earns no economic profit. Exhibit 15 shows the long-run equilibrium at P_e and Q_e. At equilibrium, market price equals marginal revenue, which also equals average revenue.

2. **Pure Monopoly** The term *monopoly* comes from the word *monarch;* this connection is due to governments granting exclusive rights to deal in goods or services. Telephone service in the United States used to be an example of a monopolistic market.

a. **Characteristics** When discussing a monopoly, the following are assumed: a single seller; a unique product without close substitutes; blocked entry for other firms; perfect information; significant price controls; and goodwill advertising.

b. **Short-Run** The demand schedule is sloped negatively. Marginal revenue lies below demand and is sloped negatively.

c. **Long-Run** Blocked entry in a monopoly market allows the entity to earn an economic profit, similar to the economic profit earned in a competitive market in the short run. Price exceeds marginal cost, so there is an under-allocation of resources. The entity produces less than the ideal output. Price is higher and output lower than in a competitive market.

d. **Natural Monopoly** A natural monopoly exists when economic or technical conditions permit only one efficient supplier. For example, within a geographic area, a gravel supplier is likely to have a monopoly because the increased cost of shipping (due to gravel's weight) is likely to exceed any price difference that consumers are able to get from a more distant source. Technological conditions include large economies of scale (extremely large operations are prerequisite to achieve low unit costs).

e. **Profit Maximization** The entity equates marginal revenue with marginal cost unless price is less than average variable cost. If price is less than average variable cost, the entity ceases production.

Exhibit 17 ▶ Monopoly Profit Maximization

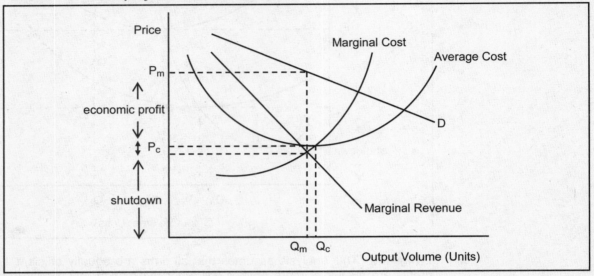

f. **Legislation** Monopoly power is discouraged by the U.S. government because prices are higher and output lower than in a competitive market.

(1) **Sherman Act (1890)** Prohibits trade restraint in interstate and foreign trade, including price fixing, boycotts, agreements to divide markets, and resale restrictions.

(2) **Clayton Act (1914)** Prohibits mergers (acquiring competitors' **stock**) if the resulting corporation would tend to lessen competition. Prohibits price discrimination. Prohibits directors in common between two competing corporations.

(3) **Robinson-Patman Act (1936)** Prohibits discounts that are not based on cost differences to large purchasers.

(4) **Celler-Kefauver Anti-Merger Act (1950)** Prohibits acquiring competitors' **assets** if the result would tend to lessen competition.

g. **Antitrust Policy** Although a pure monopoly is rare, markets are judged as monopolistic based on how closely they approach the characteristics of a monopoly, either from a performance or market structure perspective. Performance factors include market performance, technological growth rate, efficiency, and profit. Structure factors include the number and size of competitors, ease of market entry, product differentiation, and buyer and seller distribution.

3. **Monopolistic Competition** Wireless telephone service in the United States is an example of a monopolistic competitive market.

a. **Characteristics** When discussing a monopolistic competition, the following are assumed: a large number of sellers; differentiated products; relatively easy entry into and exit from the market for firms; some price controls; considerable non-price competition (advertising, brands, etc).

b. **Profit Maximization** Each producing entity equates marginal revenue with marginal cost unless price is less than average variable cost. If price is less than average variable cost, an entity ceases production.

c. **Short-Run** The demand schedule is sloped negatively. Marginal revenue lies below demand and is sloped negatively.

d. **Long-Run** Limited entry in a monopolistic competition market allows the entity to earn a normal profit. Price exceeds marginal cost, so there is an under-allocation of resources. Price is higher and output lower than in a competitive market, but generally price is lower and output higher than in a monopoly.

   (1) **Waste** Entities produce less than the ideal output. The market has too many entities that are too small.

   (2) **Foreign Competition** Foreign competition tends to offset monopolistic behavior.

4. **Oligopoly** An example of an oligopoly is the airplane manufacturing market.

   a. **Characteristics** When discussing a oligopoly, the following are assumed: a very few sellers; barriers to entry into the market (either natural, such as an absolute cost advantage, or created, such as ongoing advertising). The oligopoly has so few firms that the actions of rivals are noticed, usually both by the firms and their customers. Products may be differentiated or standardized. Price leadership is typical in oligopolistic markets.

   b. **Analysis** The high degree of interaction between oligopolistic competitors makes an oligopoly difficult to analyze. Some economists ague that the nature of oligopolies (rival's expected reactions) causes "sticky" prices or price rigidity in these markets. The hypothesis is that if one oligopolist increases its price, competing oligopolists will maintain their prices and gain market share while the first entity loses sales; if one oligopolist decreases its price, competing oligopolists will lower their prices to match it. There is some empirical evidence contradicting this explanation of market behavior.

   c. **Price Leadership** Price leadership occurs when a major firm in an oligopoly announces a price change and other market members match it. Within a geographical area, newspapers often form a oligopolistic market, evidenced by price leadership.

   d. **Cartel** A cartel is a group of oligopolistic firms intentionally joining to fix prices. This practice is illegal within the United States. OPEC (Organization of Petroleum Exporting Countries) is an example of a cartel, although it has varying success at enforcing its minimum prices.

5. **Regulation** As monopoly markets produce less goods at higher prices than competitive markets, federal antitrust policy attempts to promote competition and curtail monopolies. The influence of any one entity (and therefore the monopoly power) tends to diminish as the number of entities in a market increases.

   a. **Arguments** Arguments for large entities include: (1) facilitation of innovation by having resources for research and development (R&D); and (2) economies of scale. Arguments against large entities include: (1) market power facilitates an unfair flow of wealth to large entities; (2) restrictions on expansion of output; and (3) little incentive for innovation, and hence for using resources for R&D.

    b.   **Measurements** Several factors are used as a measure of monopolistic tendencies in a market. As these factors become more characteristic of a monopoly, the more that the market is assumed to be a monopoly. Performance measures include market performance, the rate of technological growth, efficiency, and profit. Market structure measures include the number and size of competitors, distribution of buyers and sells, ease of entry, and product differentiation. The **concentration ratio** is the percentage of a market's output quantity from its four largest entities.

    c.   **Taxes**

        (1)   **Profit** A tax on profits doesn't change the relationship between revenue and cost, so optimal output is not affected on an entity basis or market level basis (assuming all markets have the same profit tax).

        (2)   **License Fee (Lump-Sum Tax)** The fixed and average costs increase, but variable (marginal) costs remain the same. In the short-run, an entity's output remains the same. In the long-run, the increased fixed costs of a competitive market (no economic profit) will drive entities into a loss situation, so some entities will leave the market. Thus, the market price is higher and the output quantity is lower than without the license fee.

        (3)   **Per Unit Tax (Sales Tax, Excise Tax, Value-Added Tax)** A per unit tax changes the price that consumers are willing to pay and the price that suppliers are paid. This disconnection decreases marginal revenue, and hence, the output quantity entities are willing to produce. Thus, the output quantity is lower than without the per unit tax.

    d.   **Monopoly Encouragement** Several government actions are anticompetitive. For instance, large, well-established entities tend to benefit by government spending because those entities are familiar with, and have resources to bid on, proposals for government contracts as well as the size to handle large orders. Other anticompetitive actions include: patent, copyright, trademark, and similar protection; price supports (such as for agricultural commodities); price ceilings (utility rates); minimum quality standards (such as for food transport); restrictions on foreign entities' access to domestic markets (tariffs or import quotas); costs of compliance with regulations (in effect, a tax); and licensing (radio stations or food handling).

  6.   **Merger Types** A merger is the union of two entities, generally leading to an increase in size of the resulting entity.

    a.   **Vertical** A vertical merger describes mergers along a supply chain, for example, an iron mine and a steel manufacturer.

    b.   **Horizontal** A horizontal merger describes the merger of two entities that are competitors or near-competitors, for example, two steel manufacturers or a steel manufacturer and a copper refining entity.

    c.   **Conglomerate** A conglomerate merger is the merger of two entities in different markets, for example, a steel manufacturer and a computer manufacturer.

II. Macroeconomics

  A.   **Measures**
These measures are for a specified time period; if unspecified, the assumption is that these are annual measures. Sales tax is an example of indirect business taxes as used in these formulas.

  1.   **Gross Domestic Product (GDP)** The total market value of all final goods and services produced within a specified country. There are two roughly equivalent approaches to measuring GDP. To avoid multiple counting of the same production, either only the value added to goods

at each production stage is counted or only the final goods are counted. An aircraft engine, for instance, typically would not be a final good.

    a.   **Output (Income & Cost) Approach** The sum of wages, interest, rent, profits, depreciation, and indirect business taxes.

    b.   **Input (Expenditure) Approach** The sum of consumption, investment, government expenditures, and net exports.

2.   **Gross National Product (GNP)** The total market value of all final goods and services produced with resources from a specified country, not necessarily within its borders. Recently, this measure is less used than GDP.

3.   **Net Domestic Product (NDP)** GDP less depreciation.

4.   **National Income** NDP plus a country's net income earned abroad less indirect business taxes. In other words, it is the sum of wages, interest, rent, and profits plus a country's net income earned abroad.

5.   **Personal Income** National income plus transfer payments (such as corporate profit distributions and social security benefits) less both corporate income taxes and undistributed profits and less social security contributions.

6.   **Disposable Income** Personal income less personal income taxes. Disposable income is divided between consumption, interest payments, and savings.

7.   **Real Per-Capita Output** Real per-capita output is GDP divided by population, adjusted for inflation. It is used as a measure of the standard of living.

B.   **Business Cycles**

Business activity waxes and wanes. These fluctuations commonly are referred to as cycles. Economists commonly include investment expenditures in explanations of business cycle occurrence. Businesses or industries that perform much better than average during expansions and much worse than average during recessions are called cyclical; businesses or industry that that perform better than average during recessionary phases and worse than average during expansionary phases are called counter-cyclical or defensive.

Exhibit 18 ▶ Business Cycle

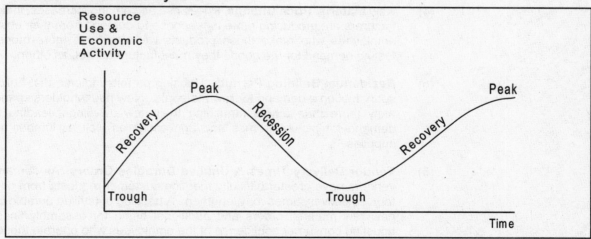

1.   **Phases** A business cycle has four commonly recognized phases. Alternatively, a recovery-recession pair can be considered a cycle, with the trough marking the end of the recession and a peak marking the end of the recovery.

a. **Trough** A trough is characterized by low levels of economic activity and resource under-use.

b. **Recovery** Recovery (expansion) is characterized by increasing levels of economic activity.

c. **Peak** A peak is characterized by high levels of economic activity and full use of resources.

d. **Recession** Recession (contraction) is characterized by decreasing levels of economic activity. During the recession stage, employment levels contract and inventories frequently build.

2. **Indicators** Business cycles usually vary in intensity and length. Also, the long-term trend of business activity may be increasing or decreasing; a trough or peak in one cycle may be higher or lower than the same point in the previous cycle. These factors make it difficult to determine changes in phases. Economists attempt to forecast phases changes using several economic indicators. Indicators are selected because historically they had a high correlation with aggregate economic activity. In one way or another, many indicators are related to investment expenditures. Coinciding indicators change at the same time as the activity that they indicate.

a. **Leading** Indicators that occur before the phase change in the cycle are classified as leading indicators. These include consumer confidence survey results as well as somewhat more objective measures.

(1) **Average Hours Worked per Week by Manufacturing Workers** As employers foresee increased demand, they often have current employees work a few additional hours rather than recruit, hire, and train additional employees.

(2) **Initial Unemployment Claims** A decrease in initial claims indicates that employers foresee increased demand and, thus, are retaining employees.

(3) **Stock Prices** An increase in stock prices indicates that investors are willing to pay more for the higher returns that they expect, so this indicator often is based on the same factors as consumer confidence.

(4) **Raw Material Price Change** Prices rise as demand increases, indicating manufacturers are producing more in response to demand from their customers. The employees who make these products will also have more money to spend, fueling demand for the goods they manufacture as well as others.

(5) **Residential Building Permits** Housing permits indicate that building will start soon, fueling a demand for raw materials. New householders spend proportionately more than others furnishing their new dwellings, leading to increased demand for picture frames and appliances as well as lumber and plumbing supplies.

(6) **Vendor Delivery Times & Unfilled Durables Orders** As demand increases, vendors have greater difficulty meeting customer requests from on-hand inventory, so delivery times may lengthen. A backlog of unfilled durable orders inspire new raw material orders and additional hiring for assembly lines as well as boosting consumer confidence of the employees who operate those lines.

(7) **Money Supply Changes** An increase in bond prices indicates that investors are willing to pay more for the higher returns that they expect, so this indicator often is based on the same factors as consumer confidence. An increase in bond prices is equivalent to a decrease in effective interest rates. With lower

interest rates, additional investment in fixed assets and inventories is cheaper for producers and retailers.

b. **Trailing** Indicators that occur after the phase change in the cycle are classified as trailing or lagging indicators. These include the average prime rate charged by banks; the unit labor costs in the private business sector; and the average duration of employment, in weeks.

3. **Accelerator Theory** The accelerator theory states that capital investment is related to the rate of change in national income. It assumes a given level of capital equipment corresponds to a given level of output.

    a. Given an economy producing at capacity and a subsequent increase in demand, an increase in capital investment is the only way to meet any increased demand. The demand for capital goods creates a secondary increase in demand, which can only be met with another increase in capital investment. This secondary increase in demand produces a tertiary increase in demand, and so on.

    b. The process of investing to meet demand continues to accelerate. Once a recovery is started, it creates a momentum that continues for some time.

C. **Classical Economics**
Classical economic theory holds that an economy is in equilibrium at full employment; the economy generates and maintains full employment over the long run without artificial (government) intervention due to price and wage flexibility.

1. **Assumptions** If people are unemployed, wages experience downward pressure until all people who want to work at the prevailing rates are employed. Therefore, unemployment doesn't exist in the long run. Similarly, if investors have capital that is not invested, returns on capital experience downward pressure until all people who want to invest at the prevailing rates are invested.

    a. Flexible prices (and wages) allow self-correcting of shortages and surpluses in product (or labor) markets.

    b. Flexible interest rates allow self-correcting equilibrium of savings vs. investments.

    c. An increase in money leads to an increase in aggregate demand.

2. **Demand for Money** The impact of money on the level of national income (aggregate demand) usually is stated as MV = GDP or MV = PQ, where M = money supply; V = income velocity of money; GDP = gross domestic product; P = aggregate price index; and Q = aggregate output index. Velocity is the average turnover of the money supply in transactions that comprise national income.

3. **Fiscal Policy Implications** A debt-financed increase in government spending has little effect on demand because it is offset by diminished spending in the private sector. An increase in government spending, if financed by printing money, will impact demand. First, the larger quantity of money will increase demand. Secondarily, the increase in government spending will lead to an velocity increase, leading to increased demand.

D. **Keynesian Economics**
Keynesian economic theory holds that an economy can be in equilibrium at less than full employment. Keynesian economics focuses on spending and fiscal policy (governmental expenditures, taxes, etc.) as determinates of economic activity.

1. **Assumptions**

   a. **Downward Price Inflexibility** Price flexibility doesn't ensure full employment because prices are not lowered readily.

   b. **Savings vs. Investment** Understanding changes in levels of income is dependent on distinguishing between savings and investment functions.

   c. **Equilibrium** Full employment is not necessarily an attribute of equilibrium.

2. **Production Possibility Frontier (PPF)** The PPF is all the possible combinations of output, with all other factors held constant. In the short run, national income is limited by the amount of resources. Production at the PPF implies full employment and optimal resource use. If production is at the PPF, no additional output can be produced in the short run, because all the resources are being used. Different combinations of goods can be produced, but these combinations will be at or below the PPF.

   Exhibit 19 ▶ PPF for Two-Good Economy

   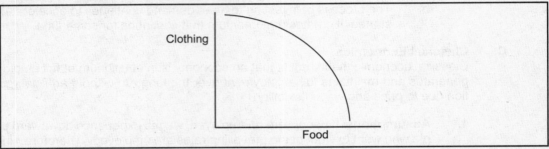

   a. **Shift** With an outward shift in the PPF, commonly called economic growth, a nation can have more output. Change in the PPF are caused by changes in resources (land, labor, capital, etc.) or technology.

   b. **Inflation** If production is at the PPF boundary and demand increases, consumers will bid up prices of goods.

3. **Savings** Loosely speaking, savings are income that is not consumed. Income typically is regarded as the major determinant of savings, but other factors play a role. A low savings rate causes a scarcity of capital for businesses. Propensities to consume and save commonly are compared among different groups or time periods. Because income can either be spent or saved, the total equals 100% (MPC + MPS = 100% and APC + APS = 100%).

   Exhibit 20 ▶ Propensities to Consume & Save

Propensity	=	Numerator	/	Denominator
Average propensity to consume (APC)	=	consumption	/	income
Average propensity to save (APS)	=	savings	/	income
Marginal propensity to consume (MPC)	=	change in consumption	/	change in income
Marginal propensity to save (MPS)	=	change in savings	/	change in income

   a. **Price Expectations** Consumer expectations about price increases or future shortages cause an increase in current purchases to avoid higher prices or to guarantee access. Inflation impairs the future purchasing power of money saved today.

   b. **Interest Rates** Rising interest rates tend to cause increased savings and decreased consumption. Income taxes act as decreases in interest rates.

c.   **Liquid Assets Quantity** People with many liquid assets tend to increase consumption at every level of disposable income.

d.   **Credit** People with large debt loads tend to reduce their consumption.

e.   **Attitude/Incentive** People with a belief in the virtues of saving for tomorrow tend to have lower consumption than those who "spend for today." Social safety nets (such as Medicare, social security, unemployment insurance, and disaster assistance) may reduce incentive to save for retirement or contingent emergencies. Estate and property taxes also may reduce incentives to save rather than consume. Note that the attitude attribute used to explain savings behavior is comparable to the role of the preference attribute used to explain demand.

f.   **Durable Goods Quantity** With a large amount of durables, consumption at a high level doesn't translate into spending. For instance, once having bought a washing machine, the consumer doesn't spend any more income (cash outflow) on washing machines for the 20-year life of the machine and yet still uses it to clean clothes (consumes the washing machine) for that period.

4.   **Investment** Investment commonly is divided into three components: residential construction, inventories, and plant and equipment. Depreciation (sometimes called **capital consumption allowance**) is a negative component of plant and equipment investment.

a.   **Expected Profitability** A high technology growth rate tends to increase investment, because innovations often are profitable. Real (nominal less inflation factor) interest rate declines tend to increase investment, as new projects have a lower interest cost. A high capital goods (equipment to make goods) stock quantity tends to decrease investment, as entities have no need to spend more to make product. Higher acquisition and maintenance costs decrease investment, as they lower the investment's expected profitability. Several government actions can change investment: effectively changing the acquisition costs (changing depreciation allowed in determining taxable income); changing tax rates; changing consumers' purchasing preferences or propensity to spend through tax code changes; or increasing government purchases of specific goods or overall quantity.

b.   **Categories** Autonomous investments are made due to expected profitability without regard for national income levels. By definition, autonomous investments are constant regardless of expansion or contraction of economic activity. Induced investments increase or decrease to correspond to expansion or contraction of economic activity.

c.   **Volatility** Investment holds central importance in income determination theory because it tends to be more volatile than other elements of private spending. This volatility is due to capital durability, technology states, expectations, and the acceleration principle. Repairs can increase the lifespan of capital equipment; this allows flexibility in the replacement schedule. Technological breakthroughs are infrequent and erratic, plus they usually promote large amounts of investment. Changes in expectations radically alter expected profits. The acceleration principle refers to the disproportionate fluctuation in inventory and capital equipment investments due to changes in sales volume.

5.   **Multiplier Coefficient** Any increase in autonomous investment, consumption, or government spending results in a multiplied increase in national income. The same income is spent several times. The impact of this effect is determined by the marginal propensity to save (MPS).

Example 5 ▶ Multiplier Effect

The marginal propensity to save is 30%. Clark Company increases its autonomous investment by $100,000.

Required: What is the increase in national income?

Discussion: The $100,000 that Clark spends is income to other entities. These entities (on average) spend $100,000 × 70% = $70,000 and save $30,000. This $70,000 is income to still other entities that spend $70,000 × 70% = $49,000 and so on.

Solution: Increase in national income = $100,000 + $70,000 + $49,000 + ... = 1 / 0.3 × $100,000 = $333,333 (rounded).

a. **Formula** The multiplier coefficient equals 1 / MPS. The change in national income (NI) due to a change in spending (SP) is the multiplier coefficient times the change in spending. Algebraically, change in NI = (1 / MPS) × change in SP.

b. **Direction** As the change in spending can be either positive or negative, the effect can be positive or negative. In other words, a negative change in spending can result in a multiplied negative effect on national income.

6. **Model of Closed Economy** In a simple economy without a government, a money market, or international trade, equilibrium income occurs when aggregate savings equals aggregate investment. In other words, equilibrium income occurs when aggregate demand (consumption and investment) equals aggregate supply (equated with production).

Exhibit 21 ▶ Simple Economy Model

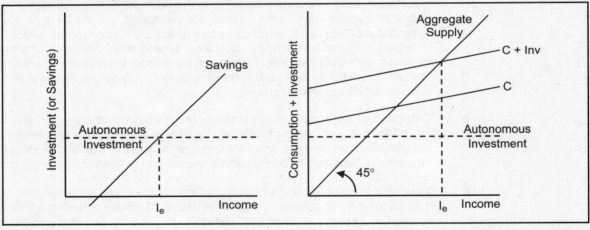

7. **Model of Closed Economy With Government** Adding government actions to a simple economy, equilibrium income occurs when aggregate savings plus taxes equals aggregate investment plus government expenditures (assuming a balanced budget). In other words, equilibrium income occurs when aggregate demand (consumption, investment, and government expenditures) equals aggregate supply (production plus taxes).

Exhibit 22 ▶ Economy Model With Government & Without Money Market

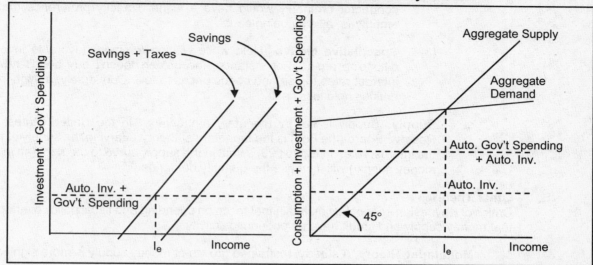

a. **Tax Multiplier** Changes in taxes affect the economy through consumption changes. The tax multiplier coefficient equals –MPC / MPS. The change in national income (NI) due to a change in taxes (T) is the multiplier coefficient times the change in taxes. Algebraically, change in NI = (–MPC / MPS) × change in T.

b. **Budget Surplus (Deficit)** A balanced budget means that taxes equal government expenditures. When there is a surplus or deficit, this assumption no longer holds true.

8. **International Trade** In a model with international trade, net exports add to aggregate demand and net imports reduce aggregate demand.

9. **Money Market** The supply of, and demand for, money determine the interest rate. The nominal interest rate is the real rate plus an inflation premium or deflation discount. Historically, the real rate ranges from approximately 2% to 4%.

Exhibit 23 ▶ Money Market (Supply & Demand for Money)

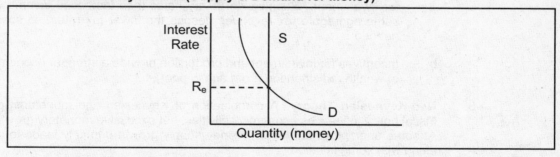

a. **Inflation Premium/Deflation Discount** Any expected inflation (or deflation) rate determines the size of the inflation premium (or deflation discount) and hence influences the nominal interest rate.

b. **Liquidity Preference** Demand for money is influenced heavily by liquidity preference, which depends on motives for holding money. In the illustration in Exhibit 23, supply (S) is fixed in the short-run (set by monetary authorities); income is assumed to be fixed; and the equilibrium interest rate (R_e) is where the supply and demand curves intersect.

(1) **Transaction Motive** Held to facilitate day-to-day business transactions.

(2) **Precaution Motive** Held for contingencies. For instance, an independent contractor ordinarily would have a higher liquidity preference than a salaried employee, all else being equal.

(3) **Speculative Motive** Held while waiting for more favorable investment conditions to arise. For instance, the holder doesn't buy bonds now, expecting interest rates to rise and bonds prices to fall. Conversely, at high interest rates, entities hold less cash.

c. **Supply** Supply is set by monetary authorities. In the United States, the Federal Reserve Board (the Fed) is the monetary authority. Varying the supply of money alters the interest rate. In Exhibit 23, a shift in the supply curve to the right (an increase in the money supply) will increase the quantity demanded.

E. **Other Theories**
Critics of Keynesian economics maintain that focus on spending and fiscal policy overlook the impact that money supply and credit have on economic activity.

1. **Monetarist Theory** A steady, restrained growth of money supply is more significant than fiscal policy on economic activity, inflation, and employment.

a. **Inflation** In the long run, excessive increases in the money supply cause inflation. Inflation can be controlled only by restricting money supply growth.

b. **Multiplier Effect** Fiscal policy is too blunt an instrument to tinker with most (small) economic fluctuations. Due to imperfections in measuring business cycle changes, fiscal policy actions to ameliorate business cycle changes are initiated too late to have the desired impact. Fiscal policy impacts an economy already finding its own equilibrium, swinging the pendulum too far in the other direction, acting as a magnifier rather than a dampener.

2. **Supply-Side Theory** Cutting taxes stimulates work, savings, and investments and restores incentive to the economy.

a. A progressive tax structure is a disincentive to increased investment. Cuts in taxes will produce a recovery due to an increase in aggregate demand and increased motivation for investment. Supply-side theory holds than increased income would result in the same aggregate tax revenues despite the lower tax rates, so spending cuts are not needed.

b. Incentives for investment and production provide a stronger economy than fiscal policy of wealth redistribution (from rich to poor).

3. **Neo-Keynesian Theory** A combination of Keynesian and monetarist economic theories. Fiscal policy influences economic activities, but excessive monetary growth leads to inflation. At some unemployment levels, money supply growth primarily leads to increases in output along with some inflation.

F. **Money**
Money is a medium of exchange, a standard of value, and a store of value. A broad definition of money is anything accepted as an exchange medium, i.e., parties accept it in trade who would not purchase the medium for their own use, but because it is recognized as a common medium of exchange. For instance, in American colonial times, some schoolteachers were paid in tobacco. Immediately after World War II, potatoes were a medium of exchange in some parts of Europe.

1. **Definitions** Narrow money is abbreviated as M_1. The Fed's monetary growth targets focus on M_2. M_1 and M_2 are the most commonly referenced measures. Near money includes items such as short-term government securities, nonchecking savings deposits, and time deposits.

Exhibit 24 ▶ Components of Various Definitions of Money

Money Components	M₁	M₂	M₃
Currency (coins and bills)	√	√	√
Checking deposits	√	√	√
Nonchecking savings		√	√
Small (less than $100,000) time deposits		√	√
Other time deposits			√

2. **Federal Reserve Board** The Federal Reserve Board (the Fed) controls the money supply, supervises the banking system, facilitates check clearing, serves as the federal government's fiscal agent, and holds deposits for member institutions (banks). Each bank must have minimum reserves, calculated on a daily basis. Banks with excess reserves lend money overnight to banks with shortfalls. These overnight loans are called **federal funds** and the interest rate on these loans is called the federal funds rate.

3. **Monetary Policy** Monetary policy is policy intended to control the money supply. Control of money supply growth is deemed essential to control inflation, spending, and credit availability. Stable interest rates and monetary control are mutually exclusive goals. The Fed focuses sometimes on interest rates and sometimes on money supply.

   a. **Open-Market Operations** The primary means of monetary control is the purchase and sale of government debt.

      (1) **Sale** Sales decrease the money supply by removing money from circulation.

      (2) **Purchase** Purchases increase the money supply by adding money to circulation.

   b. **Discount Rate** Member banks may borrow from the Fed at a rate known as the discount rate. Lowering the discount rate encourages borrowing and increases the money supply. Conversely, raising the rate decreases the money supply.

   c. **Reserves** The legal reserve is the percentage of customers' deposits that banks must keep. The mechanism of changing the reserve requirement is used rarely because it is so powerful.

   d. **Credit Controls** The Fed may require a minimum down payment on certain purchases. When this minimum applies to securities, it is called a margin requirement. Raising the down payment percentage decreases the money supply.

4. **Lag** Effective monetary policy is complicated by inherent delays. The time that it takes a change in the business cycle to be recognized is recognition lag. Administrative lag is the time for the Fed to implement a change (for example, to buy or sell government debt). The time that it takes the economy to react to the Fed's changes is called operational lag. By the time these lags pass, the economy already may have exited of the phase that initiated the Fed's action. Thus, instead of mitigating the effects of one phase of the business cycle, careless Fed action could magnify the effects of the next phase inadvertently.

G. **Inflation & Deflation**
   Inflation is an increase in the general level of prices. The general price level is related inversely to the purchasing power of money. Deflation is a decrease in the general level of prices.

1. **Impact** Because holding money during an inflationary period results in an economic loss, inflation discourages saving behavior.

   a. **Restricts Lending** Usury laws prohibit charging interest over a stated rate. When the inflation rate is high, the stated rate less the inflation premium may be less than the real interest rate. In this circumstance, credit becomes tight.

      b.   **Relationships Strained** The uncertainty of inflation is a further complication in nego-tiating long-term contracts. Contracts that were reasonable when signed may become onerous for some of the contracting parties, encouraging breaches.

      c.   **Wealth Redistribution** Inflation arbitrarily redistributes wealth without regard for market operations or social goals. Debtors repay loans in less valuable dollars, reducing the value of the creditors' assets. Pension plans pay pensioners defined benefit pensions in less valuable dollars, making pensions worth less.

  2.   **Measurement**

      a.   **Consumer Price Index (CPI)** A comparison of the price of items in a "typical" shopping cart to a base value.

      b.   **Wholesale Price Index (WPI)** A comparison of the price of items in a "typical" shopping cart at wholesale quantities to a base value.

      c.   **GDP Deflator** A factor that includes all production of an economy at the price used for the GDP calculation.

  3.   **Cost-Push Theory** Inflation is caused when increased product costs are passed on to consumers in the form of higher prices. Labor unions are considered the primary source of these costs. This theory is of decreased significance with less powerful unions because of fewer manufacturing workers (proportionate to service industry workers) and membership declines.

  4.   **Demand-Pull Theory** Inflation is caused by excess aggregate demand for goods and services. Usually excess aggregate demand is deemed to be due to expansionary fiscal policy (additional government expenditures).

H.   **Employment**
Full employment theoretically exists when all individuals **willing to work** at **market wages** are employed at tasks that **use their skills.** Unemployment results in forgone output; its economic costs can be measured in terms of the gap between potential and actual GDP. Less measurable are other costs, including degradation associated with the loss of meaningful occupation and income on both an individual and societal level.

  1.   **Unemployment**

      a.   **Frictional** Frictional unemployment is due to labor market mechanics. From a policy standpoint, job turnover results in some unemployment in a "fully" employed condition; a 3% unemployment rate may be "full" employment for an economy. In other words, some individual will be unemployed between being laid off by employer A and learning about and being hired by employer B, even if employer B has a job opening when the individual is laid off by employer A.

      b.   **Structural** Aggregate demand is equal to aggregate labor supply, but the nature of the supply doesn't match the nature of the demand. For example, unemployed individuals have machinist skills when employers have unfilled engineering jobs. Mismatches can occur in skills, occupation, industries, or geographic location.

      c.   **Cyclical** Aggregate demand is less than aggregate labor supply during low points in the economic cycle.

  2.   **Inflation vs. Unemployment** The Phillips curve attempts to illustrate the relationship between inflation and unemployment.

Exhibit 25 ▸ Phillips Curve

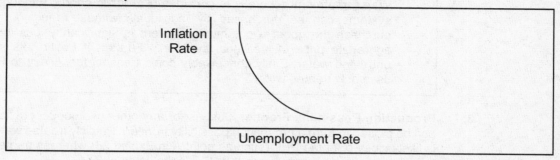

a. **Historical** Historically, economic theory holds inflation and unemployment are related inversely.

b. **Modern** Modern economic theory holds there is little relationship between inflation and unemployment; in the long run, frictional rate regardless of the inflation rate and the Phillips curve is applicable only to the short run. (In this context, *short run* may last for years).

I. **Government**
With the Full Employment Act of 1946, the U.S. federal government justified entering a market in which market forces do not allocate resources efficiently.

1. **Fiscal Policy** Government actions (taxes, tax credits, expenditures, etc.) intended to result in economic goals (such as a certain national income level, certain income distribution, acceptable unemployment levels, etc.) are referred to as fiscal policy. Other government actions may have an impact on the economy unintended by legislators that is nonetheless foreseeable by economists.

2. **Consumer Goods Spectrum** Private goods are goods for which consumption is able to be traced to one entity. Consumers of private goods purchase as much of a good as they want, with different people in the same community able to purchase differing quantities and levels of quality. Public goods are goods for which benefits can not be excluded readily from part of a community. Also, the good itself is not divisible for practical purposes. The decision of quantity and quality for public goods must be decided at a community-wide level.

Example 6 ▸ Public vs. Private Goods

Discuss the public vs. private nature of (a) a sweater; (b) law enforcement; and (c) treatment of the water supply.

a. A sweater is a private good. If half a community decides to buy sweaters, benefits are gained by the ones who buy sweaters, but not by the ones that do not buy the good. Only one person can wear a sweater at a time. If Arnold wears a sweater, Betty derives little benefit from it.

b. Law enforcement is a public good. If half a community decides to purchase law enforcement, benefits are gained by the ones that do not buy the good, plus either the ones who pay for the system either pay proportionately more than they would if the whole community purchased the system or they have a less expensive system (presumably not as large or as well-equipped). The arrest of a thief stealing from Chris benefits Dave because the thief will not be able to steal from Dave while imprisoned.

c. Water treatment generally is considered a public good. Although small treatment systems can be purchased by individuals without requiring the community to purchase the good, a community system is significantly less expensive than the aggregate price of individual systems. Further, if Emily gets sick from drinking untreated water, Emily conceivably could transmit the illness to Fred, even if Fred uses only treated water.

3. **Production Possibility Frontier** Just as for any other two goods, public and private goods can be plotted to form a production possibility frontier. Publicly treated water (see Example 6) is likely close or at the PPF (such as point A in Exhibit 26) whereas treated water from small private systems would not be on the PPF (such as point B).

Exhibit 26 ▸ PPF for Private & Public Goods

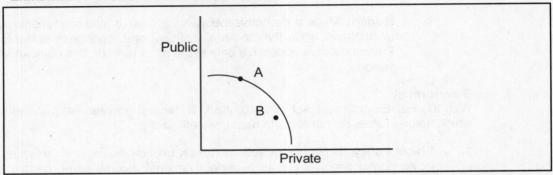

4. **Allocation** Due to the nature of public goods, there may be inefficiencies with regard to consumption. Because a public good cannot be excluded from certain individuals, people may receive the benefit of the good without paying for it. In other words, some may just get a "free ride."

Example 7 ▸ Consumption Inefficiencies

a. Gerald, an out-of-town visitor, doesn't pay taxes that purchase park land or maintenance although he uses the municipal park.

b. Harriet doesn't want chloride and fluoride in the water she drinks, but the municipal water contains these additives to kill bacteria and prevent tooth decay.

Required: Discuss the consumption inefficiencies associated with these two situations.

a. There may be no reasonable way to charge Gerald for use of the community park. Purchasing a system to charge admission to the park may generate less revenue than total park receipts (leaving nothing to use for park maintenance) and either further burden residents with carrying proof of residency or require residents to pay admission.

b. Harriet either must filter chloride and fluoride out of the municipal water or purchase untreated water from a different source. Both of these options involve additional cost to Harriet.

5. **Taxation** Taxes often are imposed based on two principles: the ability to pay (a progressive tax structure) and the derived benefit (fee-for-service, such as property taxes paying for trash removal). Unlike customers paying fees to a private entity, taxpayers might not get direct benefits from their expenditures and taxes are not optional.

a.   **Classification** Taxes may be classified in several ways, including the focus on ability to pay or the manner of payment.

    (1)   **Direct** Direct taxes include sales taxes, income taxes, and the property taxes that property owners pay. For example, income taxes are paid by (or withheld from) an entity directly.

    (2)   **Indirect** Indirect taxes are hidden in forgone income or compliance costs. Although the employer's share of Social Security and unemployment taxes are paid by employers, this is an indirect tax on employees; employers base the decision to hire employees on the whole compensation cost, including what is required to be paid in Social Security taxes.

    (3)   **Proportional** Entities pay the same proportion regardless of income (or wealth).

    (4)   **Progressive** Entities with higher income (or wealth) pay more tax as a proportion of income (or wealth) than entities with low income (or wealth).

    (5)   **Regressive** Entities with higher income (or wealth) pay less tax as a proportion of income (or wealth) than entities with low income (or wealth).

b.   **Incidence** Taxes may be paid by one entity, but borne by another. For example, landlords may increase rents to cover property taxes. Corporations may pass corporate income and property taxes and excise taxes to consumers with the higher prices they charge for goods. Social Security, unemployment, and other taxes paid by employers are indirectly borne by the employees; presumably wages would be higher if the employer didn't have to pay the taxes.

c.   **Types**

    (1)   **Income** Income taxes are levied against taxable income. In the U.S., the rate structure is progressive, but due to various exclusions, credits, and deductions in calculating taxable income from economic income, the end result (tax paid as a percentage of economic income) is not necessarily progressive.

    (2)   **Property** Property taxes are levied against wealth, not income. Because entities that rent typically pay property taxes indirectly, taxes on real property may not be as progressive as they first appear. Taxes on property often have exclusions (such as homestead value up to a specified amount or retirement funds) and progressive rates.

    (3)   **Sales** Because sales taxes are levied against income that is spent, rather than saved, sales taxes fall proportionately heavier on entities that spend most of their income. While this may be said to encourage saving, entities with low levels of income may have enough only for essentials and little left for savings. Thus, sales taxes generally are regarded as regressive.

    (4)   **Wage** Social Security taxes are a common example of wage taxes. Social Security taxes are regressive, because after a threshold amount is reached, the whole tax is not levied for the remainder of the year. Indirect taxes such as unemployment taxes also may be considered wage taxes.

    (5)   **Value-Added** A value-added tax (VAT) is common in other industrial nations and considered occasionally in the U.S. Each entity in a production and distribution chain pays tax on the difference between its sales and purchases. Consumers ultimately bear the incidence of a VAT. Under a VAT structure, all entities pay taxes, regardless of income. A VAT tax is held to encourage savings because only consumption is taxed (not consumption and savings, as is the case with an income tax).

6. **Debt Financing** When taxes do not cover expenditures, governments borrow. Debt holders differ from taxpayers in that their participation cannot be mandated.

    a. **Timing** Taxes result in contemporaneous payment for expenditures. Debt financing extends payment for expenditures over time. If debt-financed expenditures have no future benefit, intergenerational inequity results.

    b. **Market Effect** Government bonds compete with corporate bonds (and to a lesser extent stock) changing the quantity supplied. When there is already robust economic activity, this may increase interest rates and reduce corporate borrowing and investment. When there is little economic activity, additional spending shifts aggregate demand which increases national income and encourages investment.

7. **Governmental Transfer Payments** Transfer payments (such as welfare, unemployment compensation, and Social Security) alter the distribution of income of the population.

III. International Economics

A. Direction of Trade

Countries vary in the efficiency with which they produce certain goods, due to immobility of many resources. Just as individuals specialize to produce more goods at lower cost, so can nations. When countries specialize in the goods that they produce most efficiently and exchange with other countries, assuming free trade, pure competition, and minimal shipping costs, more is produced than if each country tries to be self-sufficient. Total output is maximized when each country specializes in the product in which it has the greatest comparative advantage.

1. **Absolute Advantage** Absolute advantage for a good exists when the cost of producing that good in one country is less than the cost of producing that good in another country.

Example 8 ▶ Absolute Advantage

The Untied Kingdom and Neverland each produce only food and cloth. They have no other trading partners, no trade restrictions, and no transportation costs. In the Untied Kingdom, 1,000 units of input (labor, land, and capital) produces 100 bushels of food or 20 bolts of cloth; this comes to 10/bushel or 50/bolt. In Neverland, 1,000 units of input produces 125 bushels of food or 16 bolts of cloth; this comes to 8/bushel or 62.5/bolt.

Required: Which country has an absolute advantage for producing cloth and which for producing food?

Solution: Neverland has an absolute advantage in producing food and the Untied Kingdom has an absolute advantage in producing cloth; it is cheaper to produce food in Neverland than it is in the Untied Kingdom and it is cheaper to produce cloth in the Untied Kingdom than in Neverland.

Observation: If each country produced half of these goods, with 1,000 units of input, Neverland would produce 62.5 bushels of food and 8 bolts of cloth and the Untied Kingdom, would produce 50 bushels of food and 10 bolts of cloth; this totals 112.5 bushels of food and 18 bolts of cloth. If each country specializes in the good in which it has a comparative (and an absolute) advantage, Neverland produces 125 bushels of food and the Untied Kingdom produces 20 bolts of cloth. No other combination results in more goods produced.

2. **Comparative Advantage** Comparative advantage for a good exists when the opportunity cost of producing that good is less than the cost of producing other goods in the same country, compared to another country.

Example 9 ▶ Comparative Advantage

The Untied Kingdom and Neverland each produce only food and cloth. They have no other trading partners, no trade restrictions, and no transportation costs. In the Untied Kingdom, 1,000 units of input (labor, land, and capital) produces 100 bushels of food or 20 bolts of cloth; this comes to 10/bushel or 50/bolt. In Neverland, 1,000 units of input produces 125 bushels of food or 40 bolts of cloth; this comes to 8/bushel or 25/bolt.

Required: Which country has an absolute advantage for producing cloth and which for producing food? Which country has the comparative advantage for producing cloth and which for producing food?

Solution: Neverland has an absolute advantage in producing both food and cloth; it is cheaper to produce both food and cloth in Neverland than it is in the Untied Kingdom.

In the Untied Kingdom, the opportunity cost to produce a bushel of food is 1/5 of a bolt of cloth and the opportunity cost to produce a bolt of cloth is 5 bushels of food. In Neverland, the opportunity cost to produce a bushel of food is 2/5 of a bolt of cloth and the opportunity cost to produce a bolt of cloth is 3 1/8 bushels of food. Therefore, Neverland has a comparative advantage in cloth production: its opportunity cost is 3 1/8 bushels of food compared to Untied Kingdom's 5 bushels. The Untied Kingdom has a comparative advantage in food production: its opportunity cost is 1/5 of a bolt of cloth compared to Neverland's 2/5 of a bolt.

Observation: If each country produced half of these goods, each with 1,000 units of input, Neverland would produce 61.25 bushels of food and 20 bolts of cloth and the Untied Kingdom, would produce 50 bushels of food and 10 bolts of cloth; this totals 111.25 bushels of food and 30 bolts of cloth. If each country specializes in the good in which it has a comparative advantage, Neverland produces 40 bolts of cloth and the Untied Kingdom produces 100 bushels of food. Because there one country has an absolute advantage in production of both goods, there are multiple high production solutions. The optimal solution will depend on demand; in other words, if there is greater total demand for food than 100 bushels, Neverland would produce some food and less than 40 bolts of cloth.

3. **Factor Endowment** The Heckscher-Ohlin theory states that regional differences in efficiency occur because of difference in supply of production factors: land, labor, and capital. For instance, farming is favored by a slowly moving river as a reliable irrigation source, but manufacturing is favored by a swiftly moving river as a power source. The labor, land, and capital model used in Examples 8 and 9 is relatively simple. Factors generally are classified in the following categories: climatic (weather) and geographical (land) conditions; human capacities (labor); supply and nature of capital accumulation; and proportions of resources. Some economists also include political and social environment (legislated minimum wages and tax credits) and technological environment as factors; these factors were ignored or assumed constant in earlier models. The Heckscher-Ohlin theory assumes the following.

   a. **Product Classification** The theory assumes a given product always uses the same proportion of inputs. This may not be the case. For instance, cows can be milked by hand (a labor-intensive process) or by machine (a capital-intensive process).

   b. **Technology** The theory assumes a given technology is globally available or present. The **Leontief paradox** notes that technology intensive goods produced by skilled labor may be exported by a labor-poor region to a labor-intensive region at a lower price than the same good produced locally by a labor-intensive process.

   c. **Transportation Cost** The theory assumes transportation costs are minimal. This assumption obviously is contradicted by some products that have prohibitively high shipping charges, such as slate, gravel, and other stone for building construction.

      d.   **Consumer Taste** The theory assumes the impact of consumer taste is minimal. Consumer taste plays a considerable role in trade, often resulting in the reverse of factor endowment theory. For example, wine is imported to the United States from France, although land for vineyards is more plentiful in the United States than France.

4.   **Specialization** Production factors and efficiency determine which goods countries will export and import. Countries tend to export goods in which they have comparative advantages and import goods in which they have comparative disadvantages. For instance, in a model with only labor, land, and capital as production factors, countries with a relative abundance of labor will import capital-intensive and land-intensive goods and export labor-intensive goods.

      a.   Capital-intensive goods are those requiring a relatively high level of investment, for example, a construction plant to produce aircraft.

      b.   Labor-intensive goods are those requiring a relatively high level of labor, for example, the labor involved in making computer programs.

      c.   Land-intensive goods are those requiring a relatively high level of land, for example, the land involved in beef production.

5.   **First Mover Theory** The first mover theory is that entities that first enter a market will dominate it, as latecomers will not be able to capture market share away from the standard-setting pioneers who are able to achieve economies of scale most readily. Subsequent studies indicate that the original research, based on surveys of surviving firms, did not consider the true pioneers of some markets: entities no longer in business when the survey was performed.

6.   **Overlapping Demand** The Linder theory of overlapping demand contends that while factor endowment (focusing on supply) explains raw materials trade, it doesn't adequately explain manufactured goods trade. The Linder theory (attending to demand) states that as consumers' tastes depend heavily on their income, per-capita income of a country will influence demand, but doesn't predict the direction of trade. Because local entities will produce goods for local demand, the nature of local manufacturing will depend on local per-capita income. Local entities also will make their goods available for export. The theory also states that countries with similar per-capita income will have greater trade than between countries with dissimilar per-capita incomes, due to consumers' different tastes. Thus, the United States and Germany both import cars from each other, with consumers perceiving differences between Ford Mustangs and Volkswagen New Beetles.

B.   **Trade Barriers**
Usually, the effect of trade barriers is to keep resources (land, labor, capital, etc) in less efficient protected industries rather than move its use to relatively efficient industries. Real wages and total world output do not reach full potential. General Agreement on Tariffs & Trade (GATT) is an international agreement to reduce trade barriers.

1.   **Purpose** Trade restrictions exist due to many factors. An exporting country may allow conditions that are not permitted in a country that would otherwise import goods from that exporting country. For instance, the exporting country may have no health care, minimum safety standards, minimum wage, or minimum age requirements for workers or permit pollution or other practices banned in a country that has a trade barrier.

    Example 10 ▶ Trade Barrier

> Two decades ago, International Chemicals Company developed DeadBugs, a highly effective agricultural insecticide. While food grown in fields where DeadBugs was used was apparently safe for most of the population to consume, this food made infants and other susceptible people sick. DeadBugs is highly stable; after it was approved for use on food crops, researchers discovered that prolonged consumption of food grown with DeadBugs resulted in people formerly considered unsusceptible to it accumulating toxic amounts in

their bodies. Further, once DeadBugs gets into the food chain, it takes a long time to be eliminated. As a result, the nation of Greenacres has banned the production, sale, and use of DeadBugs within its borders for the last decade. Additionally, Greenacres restricts the importation of food from Strapped, a country that allows the production, sale, and use of DeadBugs.

Discussion: Greenacres can not mandate laws for another sovereign nation, but a trade barrier allows it to restrict circumvention of its protective policies.

a. **Barrier Support** Competition costs are obvious (direct and concentrated). For instance, it is noticeable when people lose jobs or plants are closed. Special interest groups are established readily with a concentration of publicly known stakeholders, resulting in groups that are strong, well organized, and effective at lobbying for protection.

b. **Free Trade Support** Competition benefits are less obvious (marginal and scattered) and often delayed (lower prices, better products, more export industry jobs). For instance, several dispersed entities may each export a little more product, leading to widespread, but individually small, increases in hiring or orders of components from several different suppliers.

2. **Self Sufficiency** Countries may avoid free trade for crucial goods due to reasons such as economic security (possible labor strikes in supplying countries) and national defense (possible political upheaval in other countries or tensions between countries) as well as national pride and supply disruption avoidance (possible transportation disruptions due to weather). For instance, an island nation may grow some food on a long-run basis, even though it would be cheaper to import it. The economies of countries exporting primarily raw materials are particularly sensitive to fluctuations in the business cycle; these countries may have some local production that evens out employment.

a. **Incubate Infant Industry** One argument against free trade is that a country has a comparative advantage in the long run, but a temporary disadvantage. Infant industries may seek temporary protection from imports until labor is trained, production techniques are perfected, and economies of scale obtained. In practice, an industry will be slow to admit its maturity. While protected from foreign competition, an industry has little reason to improve efficiency.

b. **Protect Local Jobs From Cheap Foreign Labor** One argument against free trade is that a country with legislated high wages and benefits will be flooded by goods from countries with low wages, unhealthy or unsafe working conditions and no benefits, putting local workers out of work. In countries with high hourly wages, worker productivity tends to be higher because of superior employee training, management, and technology. These factors tend to make the labor cost per unit lower. Further, if imports are stopped or restricted domestically, exports will be stopped or restricted by other countries seeking the same sorts of protection; the local jobs involved in manufacturing those exported goods would then be eliminated.

c. **Fair Competition Tariff** Proponents of the fair competition or scientific tariff argument hold that an import tariff that brings the cost of imported goods up to the domestic price levels the playing field for imports, eliminating an "unfair" advantage foreign producers have due to lower raw material costs, labor costs, etc. Given that some domestic entities have lower costs than others, the import tariff would likely be set to align foreign prices with the prices of the domestic producer with the highest domestic cost. This practice is similar to incubation, except it is permanent. The least efficient local producer has little incentive to increase efficiency, other local entities have exceptional profits, and efficient foreign entities are penalized; this could result in import tariffs (also called countervailing tariffs) by the foreign countries.

3. **Control Strategies** Some control strategies may backfire. For instance, imposing import quotas and tariffs may either reduce domestic imports or encourage the foreign country to institute quotas of its own. Import quotas and tariffs also may encourage smuggling or incite the foreign country in question to adopt additional import quotas in retaliation. International unions of trading nations (for instance, the European Union) or national government barriers to free trade include the following.

   a. **Import Quota** An import quota is a limit on the quantity of specific products that may be imported. In the short run, the balance of payments becomes more favorable, domestic employment increases, and prices on the specified products increase.

   b. **Tariff** Tariffs, or taxes on imports, allow any quantity to be imported, but make it more expensive to do so. Tariffs may be a flat amount per item or a percentage of price.

   c. **Export Incentives** Subsidies are government payments to producers, typically in a protected industry. Indirect subsidies, or incentives, include favorable tax treatment on export-related income. This practice might have similar effects on the foreign country as import quotas or tariffs.

   d. **Substitution** Develop substitutes for imported products, for instance, photovoltaic-generated (solar) electricity replacing electricity generated from imported oil.

   e. **Shift Customer Preferences** Encourage consumers to buy domestic products as a patriotic activity, for instance, saving local jobs or national self-sufficiency. An American business that attempts a "Buy American" campaign for domestic marketing may have it backfire in foreign markets or America if it uses imported components or raw materials. If a government sponsors this campaign, the potential for backlash might be minimized.

   f. **Domestic Content Quotas** Requiring, or encouraging through favorable tariff treatment, a portion of imported products in protected industries be constructed, at least partially, in the importing nation. Such a requirement typically is used by capital-intensive nations. Thus, parts produced utilizing idle capacity in capital-intensive countries are assembled in labor-intensive countries.

4. **European Union (EU)** The European Union is a federation of nations with four primary objectives: (1) establish European citizenship; (2) ensure freedom, security, and justice; (3) promote economic and social progress; (4) assert Europe's role in the world. The European Union's member nations delegate sovereignty to common institutions representing the interests of the EU as a whole on questions of joint interest.

   a. **European Monetary Union** The European Monetary Union shares one currency, the euro (€). It has 12 member nations: Austria, Belgium, Finland, France, Germany, Greece, Ireland, Italy, Luxemburg, the Netherlands, Portugal, and Spain.

   b. **Other** Denmark, Sweden, and the United Kingdom, while part of the EU, are not yet part of the EMU. The EU envisions adding other European countries as members.

5. **North American Free Trade Agreement (NAFTA)** Partly in response to the EU, NAFTA is an agreement among Mexico, the United States, and Canada to reduce trade barriers among the three countries. The phase-out of tariffs on goods covered by the agreement is staggered over a lengthy period to allow producers to adapt gradually. NAFTA is considerably smaller in scope, concentrating on economic policies and not attempting integration on the scale of the EU.

6. **Central American – Dominican Republic Free Trade Agreement (CAFTA-DR)** Approved by the U.S. Congress in July 2005 and signed it into law by the President on August 2, 2005, the agreement will come into force on a date to be agreed upon among the members. Once implemented, CAFTA will reduce barriers to U.S. trade with El Salvador, Guatemala, Honduras, Costa Rica, Nicaragua and the Dominican Republic. In addition, it also requires

important reforms of the domestic legal and business environment that are key to encouraging business development and investment in those five Central American countries and the Dominican Republic. CAFTA will make certain U.S. exports duty-free immediately, while most other tariffs will be phased out over a number of years.

C.   Foreign Exchange
Exchange between entities in different countries requires either a common medium of exchange (such as the European market's Euro) or a ready means of converting currencies (such as a foreign currency exchange market).

1.   Exchange Rate An exchange rate is the price of one country's currency in terms of another currency. Currency appreciates when it can buy more units of another currency and depreciates when it buys fewer units of another currency.

a.   Market Equilibrium (Floating Exchange Rate) Prices are set by market forces (supply and demand) just as for other goods. This can lead to occasional extreme short-run fluctuations. In the long run, assuming a free trade situation with perfect information, market interactions will set exchange rates such that relative prices will be equivalent worldwide. For practical purposes, relative price levels have merely significant influence on exchange rates.

Exhibit 27 ▶ Floating Exchange Rate

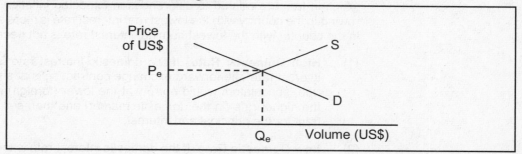

b.   Government Policy (Fixed Exchange Rate) A government may set a fixed exchange rate. This has only limited success; to eliminate a surplus or deficit of payments between countries, the rate eventually must be returned to the equilibrium price.

Exhibit 28 ▶ Fixed Exchange Rate

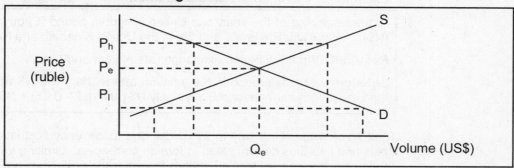

(1)   High Exchange Rate If the price is set above the market equilibrium price, shown in Exhibit 28 as P_h, there is a surplus; more people are willing to supply than there is demand and a deficit of payments results. In the short-run, deficits may be met by using foreign reserves (previous payment surpluses) or by borrowing from the foreign country's central bank. Usually a country devalues its currency to improve its balance of payments; in other words, it lowers the price of its currency, reversing the effect of the fixed exchange rate set above market equilibrium.

        (2)   **Low Exchange Rate** If the price is set below the market equilibrium price, shown in Exhibit 28 as P_l, there is a shortage; not enough entities are willing to supply to meet the demand and a surplus of payments results. Eventually, the country will have greater foreign reserves than it wants and will have to raise the price of its currency to avoid further increases to its surplus.

    c.   **Managed Float** Market forces primarily guide exchange rates. Governments (or central banks, etc.) intervene to maintain stability during periods of extreme fluctuations.

2.   **Foreign Exchange Market Operation**

    a.   **Spot Rate** The spot rate is the rate paid for currency now (on the spot).

    b.   **Forward Exchange Rate** The forward exchange rate is the rate agreed to be paid in the future. The difference between the spot rate and the forward exchange rate is called a discount or premium. If the forward rate is greater than the spot rate, speculators expect the currency to increase in value and, thus, are willing to buy at a premium. If the forward rate is less than the spot rate, speculators expect the currency to decrease in value and, thus, will buy only at a discount.

    c.   **Interest Rates** The discount or premium is related to differences between true interest rates (nominal interest rates adjusted for inflation) paid by foreign and domestic banks, which in turn are related to differences in expected inflation between countries. Borrowing in the country with the lowest real interest rate is more advantageous. Borrowing in the country with the lowest nominal interest rate is not necessarily advantageous.

        (1)   **High Domestic Rate** If the domestic interest rate is higher than the foreign interest rate, the forward exchange contract sells at a premium. If this were not true, speculators would borrow at the lower (foreign) interest rate and invest at the higher rate (in the domestic market) and then sell a forward exchange contract for the principal and interest.

        (2)   **Low Domestic Rate** If the domestic interest rate is lower than the foreign interest rate, the forward exchange contract sells at a discount.

3.   **Exchange Rate Influences** One currency will depreciate relative to another at a rate equivalent to the difference in their inflation rates.

Example 11 ▶ Exchange Rates & Inflation

> At the beginning of the year, one Untied Kingdom pound (£) buys 2.00 Neverland dollars (N$). Annual inflation is 8% and 5% in the Untied Kingdom and Neverland, respectively.
>
> **Required:** What will be the exchange rate at year end?
>
> **Solution:** The difference in the inflation rate is 3%. The N$ will depreciate by 3% less than the £. At year end, one £ buys only N$1.94. [(1 − 0.97) × N$2.00]

4.   **Risk Avoidance** One way to avoid risk due to currency fluctuations is to minimize receivables and liabilities denominated in foreign currencies. Limiting transactions denominated in foreign currencies may limit an entity's foreign trade unduly, as not all customers or suppliers will be willing to trade in that entity's local currency.

    a.   **Hedge** Hedging involves offsetting a gain or loss on receivables or payables denominated in foreign currencies by purchasing or selling forward exchange contracts. Buying these contracts covers liabilities in the foreign currency; selling covers receivables.

b. **Balance** Entities with large amounts of foreign business establish centers to attempt to achieve balance between foreign receivables and payables.

c. **Barter** If an entity barters (meaning that transactions are nonmonetary) currency fluctuations don't affect the transaction.

> ### Example 12 ▶ Barter
>
> Gold, Inc., an American company that makes Sugar Rush Cola, estimates that the cola market in Shiver, a former soviet bloc country, will be highly profitable in a decade, when Shiver's vast resources are put to efficient use. Gold wants its product to become the cola market leader in Shiver now, in preparation for that period. Shiver placed restrictions on the exchange of currency to stop the drastic devaluation of rubles shortly after the conversion to a capitalistic market. If Gold imports cola to Shiver now, it will be paid in Shiver rubles. Shiver rubles currently are difficult to exchange into American dollars.
>
> Gold predicts that there is a high probability that, in accordance with its new economic discipline policy, Shiver will replace its rubles with euros at highly unfavorable rates before the decade is finished.
>
> **Discussion:** Gold's potential customers (wholesalers in Shiver) cannot covert rubles into dollars any more readily than Gold can. However, these customers can swap cola for vodka, which Gold can sell in America. Gold insulates itself from exchange risk by arranging a nonmonetary trade.

5. **Foreign Investment Analysis** Foreign operations are more difficult to manage and control than domestic operations. As with any investment, relevant cash flows are the dividends and the potential future sales price. These cash flows must be adjusted for risks generally not considered with domestic investments. Further, both the host and home country may have tax structures that result in paying taxes on the same income to both countries. Also, there may be risk of loss of trade secrets or copyright risk issues.

a. **Exchange Risk** Exchange risk is the risk that exchange rates will change.

b. **Sovereignty Risk** Sovereignty risk is risk of significant restrictions on removal of the investment, either as dividends or sale of the operations, including nationalization. Nationalization is government ownership of business. A foreign government could appropriate assets or purchase them through a forced sale. Alternatively, a foreign government could establish a monopoly.

6. **Foreign Presence** Entities can expand into foreign markets in several ways.

a. **Sales Representative** By contracting with an independent local representative, an entity can sell its goods with a minimum investment (typically, inventory in the host country is the only tangible asset that would be at risk). This arrangement also can result in a minimum of control.

b. **Sales (or Production) Branch** By establishing a sales branch or plant staffed by employees, an entity would gain more control and also increased risk exposure to control by the host country's government. For instance, the host government's labor standards and income taxes would apply to the branch employees and income, respectively. Aside from the additional complexity of managing from a distance across cultural lines, attitudes to imported goods in the host country with only a sales branch may make this approach awkward.

c. **Division** By establishing a stand-alone subsidiary (with production, sales, and perhaps financing) in a foreign country, an entity minimizes upsetting local stakeholders with imported goods. The total investment is larger, with production facilities as well as inventory involved. The host country may limit foreign ownership, compromising the entity's control. Also, duplication of facilities (domestic and foreign) may result.

7. **Multinational Operations** Proponents of multinational operations claim that they tend to support international trade, free trade policies, a more robust international monetary system, and improved cultural tolerance. Large multinational entities' size, complexity, and sophistication may make them difficult for countries to police or shareholders to have an effective say in corporate policies, leading to activities (such as cartels, questionable labor practices, etc.) that are the opposite of those positive characteristics.

a. **Home Advantages** Royalties, dividends, and profits promote a favorable balance of payments. Local charities and cultural institutions may be supported at a disproportionately higher degree than foreign ones. A multinational entity may be better able to obtain scarce resources than a domestic one.

b. **Home Disadvantages** Disadvantages include potential reduced domestic investment, training, output, and tax revenues. Jobs may be lost to foreign subsidiaries and unions weakened. There is a greater risk of technology appropriation.

c. **Host Advantages** Advantages include additional investment of capital and technology, training for local labor, increased output and efficiency, stimulation of competition, increased tax revenues, and increased living standards.

d. **Host Disadvantages** Royalties, dividends, and profits may result in an unfavorable balance of payments. A multinational company may establish transfer pricing among subsidiaries so that profits are reported in the country of lowest taxes or least profit-exporting restrictions. Multinational competition may overwhelm struggling local competition. As multinational entities are willing to move into a country when the economic climate is favorable, they may be quick to leave as well. There also is an absent landlord effect: local management may have considerable autonomy as long as it meets profitability standards; if the same management had local shareholders, it might concern itself more with local goodwill. In this instance, if foreign shareholders were aware of the entity's actions in the context of host country's business climate, they might demand more such concern from local management.

Example 13 ▶ Absent Landlord

EvaporMilk Corporation had a thriving business in America with dehydrated milk and milk formula for infants. Consumer preferences changed and more infants are now breast fed, so the infant milk formula business diminished considerably.

EvaporMilk establishes a subsidiary in Farwestern, an underdeveloped country. Farwestern is just entering a growth period, so modernity, education, health, and sanitation are popular in Farwestern. EvaporMilk establishes a campaign promoting the health aspects of its infant formula and extorting mothers to question whether they have "weak" or "thin" milk. In a country not accustomed to scrutinizing advertiser's claims, repeated messages delivered by responsible-appearing spokespeople are convincing. Mothers who want only the best for their children feed their infants only EvaporMilk's infant formula. These children don't receive the natural immunity-granting elements in breast milk and consequently have higher instances of infant disease. Given the still sporadic inoculation system in Farwestern, this is of even greater significance than it would be in America.

If the American public knew of this situation, it would put pressure on EvaporMilk to halt such practices. The general Farwestern public is slow to notice this trend and respond to it.

D. **Balance of Payments**
International payments—imports, exports, debt or equity investments—rarely net to zero. The balance of payments (the deficit or surplus) typically is tracked in two principal accounts: current and capital; i.e., the balance of payments is the total of these two accounts. The following references to debits and credits refer to treating these accounts as if they were revenue or expense accounts. A debit is similar to an expense in that it increases a deficit or reduces a surplus; a credit has the opposite effect.

1. **Current Account** The current account includes the balance of goods and services, net interest and dividends, and net unilateral transfers.

   a. **Balance of Trade** The difference between total imports (debit) and total exports (credit) of goods, excluding services, is the balance of trade.

   b. **Balance of Goods & Services** The difference between total imports and total exports of goods, including services, is the balance of goods and services.

   c. **Interest & Dividends** Total interest and dividends received (debit) within a country on investments outside of a country, offset by total interest and dividends paid (credit) outside a country on investments by foreign entities within a country.

   d. **Unilateral Transfers** Net unilateral transfers effect the deficit or surplus depending on whether the transfer is out (debit) or in (credit). Unilateral transfers include foreign aid and payments to relatives. Pension payments often are counted as unilateral transfers.

2. **Capital Account** The capital account tracks capital flows resulting from the exchange of fixed or financial assets (i.e., equipment and securities). A capital account surplus (inflows exceed outflows) indicates that foreign entities buy more domestic equipment and securities than domestic entities buy foreign equipment and securities.

   a. **Security Sales** Purchases of domestic stocks and bonds by foreign entities, or inflows of investment (credits), increase foreign reserves.

   b. **Security Purchases** Purchases of foreign stocks and bonds by domestic entities, or outflows of investment (debits), consume foreign reserves.

3. **Deficit & Surplus** A deficit, also called an unfavorable balance of payments, is equalized by additional exports or reductions in reserves. A surplus is equalized by additional imports or increases in reserves. A surplus or deficit may impact the domestic economy.

   ### Example 14 ▶ Unfavorable Balance of Payments

   > More imports than exports cause a deficit balance of payments. If consumers are replacing purchases of domestic products with imported products, domestic demand is reduced, resulting in domestic production reduction and layoffs.
   >
   > With domestic production reduced, less profit is available for investments. With reduced domestic demand, there is also less investment opportunity. So domestic investors seek foreign investment opportunity, essentially importing foreign securities, increasing the deficit of balance of payments.
   >
   > As domestic demand decreases, prices for domestic goods fall. These goods will find buyers among local entities that were importing goods as well as foreign entities, reducing the balance of payments. This automatic correcting process may result in unemployment and deflation.

4. **Control Strategies** Attempts at control usually focus on eliminating deficits in the balance of payments. Since one country's deficit balance is another's surplus balance, these attempts may encounter considerable resistance. See the information on trade barriers in this chapter.

5. **Debtor Nation Consequences**

   a. **Debt Service** Part of the GDP is used for debt service.

   b. **Reserves** A reserves reduction may lead to devaluation of money, inflation, and increased exports. There may be increased political pressure for trade protectionism.

   c. **Deficit** A decline in net imports and shrinking of the deficit in balance of payments.

   d. **Savings** Interest rates kept high to curb inflation and encourage foreign investment. Increased savings may occur as a result of economic uncertainty or high interest rates.

6. **International Monetary System** In the post-World War II period, the international monetary system was based on fixed exchange rates based on a modified gold standard. The U.S. dollar became the key world currency for transactions and reserves. As war-damaged economies improved, the U.S. dollar remained a key currency, so the U.S. departure from the gold standard in the early 1970s radically changed the international monetary system. Initial agreements to allow currencies to float were disregarded as countries intervened frequently to support their currencies. The 1976 Jamaica Agreement established a system of managed floating exchanges, with each country having some autonomy in managing its exchange rate.

   a. **International Monetary Fund (IMF)** IMF resources are a currency pool available to cover member countries' short-term deficits in balance of payments.

   b. **World Bank** The World Bank lends money to underdeveloped countries for development.

   c. **Euro** The European Common Market combines most member countries' monetary system s into one system with the use of the Euro instead of individual currencies.

   d. **Dollars** Even transactions not involving any U.S. entities frequently are denominated in U.S. dollars, so there is a relatively high liquidity.

E. **Transfer Pricing**
   Transfer pricing is the process of establishing prices used between related parties (typically divisions of the same company) for loans, sales or leases of tangible personal property, licensing of intangibles, and the sale of services. It is done to facilitate the determination of income for these divisions. Typically, international transfer pricing receives the most attention because of the tax implications; however, it can be used by an entity in a single location to measure performance by divisions or departments.

   1. **Considerations** Multidivisional and multinational firms use transfer pricing for coordination of divisional objectives, allocating internal resources, and maximizing after-tax profits, among other goals. Interdependencies of profit centers make the method and application of transfer pricing an important subject. Currently, most companies set transfer prices primarily to minimize overall corporate taxes. This approach ignores other important areas: management incentives among various divisions, allocation of production capacities, and guidance for future capital investment. It's legal to maintain two sets of transfer prices. Most people think of transfer pricing as a tax optimization issue, yet transfer prices also are management tools. They have important decision-making functions, valuing intermediate product so that regional managers may maximize the profit of the company as a whole.

Example 15 ▸ Transfer Pricing

Grand Prix Motors, Inc., is an multinational corporation with an engine plant in Germany and assembly plants in Sweden and Mexico. Only one set of transfer prices is used for both tax and financial reporting purposes. Of the three countries, corporate income taxes are highest in Sweden and lowest in Mexico. Accordingly, Grand Prix sets a low transfer price on engines sent to Mexico and a high transfer price on engines sent to Sweden in order to produce the lowest taxable profits in Sweden, low taxable profits in Germany, and highest taxable profits in Mexico. The managers of the German engine plant have bonuses that fluctuate with profits for the German plant, so they reduce the emphasis on producing engines for export to Mexico.

a. **Tax** Because governments base firms' tax liability on transfer prices, their taxing authorities operate to ensure transfer prices adequately reflect the value of goods and services, challenging firms' established transfer pricing if it is deemed necessary. For income tax purposes, a company may want to shift income from, or deductions into, a high-tax country. To reduce the amount of customs duties or property taxes, a company may want to reduce inbound price for imports.

b. **Decision Making** A company may want to reduce amount of income of a particular subsidiary where employees participate in profits. Alternatively, a company may seek to generate information that provides a clear basis for internal decision making. For managerial purposes, when deciding what metric should be selected to evaluate a unit's performance, the following should be is considered: controllability of costs, the effect by random shocks, and possible dysfunctional behavior induced by the evaluation system (discussed in greater detail in Chapter 54).

2. **Types** Transfer pricing determines how companies price goods or services that they transfer between their own divisions or related companies.

a. **Market-Based Prices** When a product has an established market, the market price may be used. By definition, these transactions aren't arms-length deals in an open marketplace, and, unless the involved divisions are at liberty to purchase or sell the goods from any source (a rare occurrence), these prices may not reflect economic reality or be appropriate bases for decision making.

b. **Variable Cost Prices** In 1956, economist Jack Hirshleifer showed that the best economic result occurred when transfer prices were set either at a market price for the product being shipped or, failing that, the marginal cost of the item to the division making it; however, Hirshleifer's approach does not consider differences in corporate income taxes.

c. **Full Cost Prices** Full cost prices tend to reduce incentives for the producing division to eliminate unnecessary costs.

d. **Negotiated Transfer Prices** Prices may be set by the corporate entity, with various degrees of input from regional managers and considerations of market prices, costs, and other factors.

Time Management

Approximately 20 percent of the multiple choice questions in every section of every exam given after November 2003 are questions that are being pre-tested. These questions are **not** included in candidates' final grades; they are presented only so that the Board of Examiners may evaluate them for effectiveness and possible ambiguity.

The Scholastic Achievement Test and the Graduate Record Exam both employ similar but not identical strategies. Those tests include an extra section, which is being pre-tested, and test-takers do not know which section is the one that will not be graded. On the Uniform CPA Examination, however, the extra questions are mixed in among the graded questions.

This makes time management crucial. Candidates who are deciding how much time to spend on a difficult multiple choice question must keep in mind that there is a 20 percent chance that the answer to the question will not affect them either way. Also, candidates should not allow a question that seems particularly difficult or confusing to shake their confidence or affect their attitude towards the rest of the test; it may not even count.

This experimental 20 percent works against candidates who are not sure whether they have answered enough questions to earn 75 points. Candidates should try for a safety margin, so that they will have accumulated enough correct answers to pass, even though some of their correctly answered questions will not be scored.

See the **Practical Advice** appendix for more information regarding the exam.

CHAPTER 50—ECONOMIC THEORY

Problem 50-1 MULTIPLE CHOICE QUESTIONS (120 to 150 minutes)

1. What is characteristic of the free-enterprise system?
a. Public ownership of resources and most economic decisions made by private individuals
b. Public ownership of resources and most economic decisions made by government planning
c. Public and private ownership of resources and decisions made by resource owners
d. Private ownership of resources and decisions made by government planning
e. Private ownership of resources and decisions made by resource owners　(Editors, 7141)

2. The demand curve for an inferior good is
a. Downward sloping because of income and substitution effects of price changes
b. Downward sloping because of increasing marginal utility
c. Horizontal
d. Upward sloping because higher prices indicate higher quality
e. Upward sloping because entities produce more at higher prices　(Editors, 7142)

3. The price of good X increases, causing the demand for good Y to decrease. Goods X and Y most likely are

	Complements	*Substitutes*
a.	No	No
b.	No	Yes
c.	Yes	Yes
d.	Yes	No　(Editors, 7143)

4. Two goods, Alpha and Beta, are substitutes. What will an increase in the price of Beta cause?
a. The demand curve for Alpha to shift left
b. The demand curve for Alpha to shift right
c. The supply curve for Alpha to shift left
d. The supply curve for Alpha to shift right
e. No change in the demand or supply curve for Alpha　(Editors, 7144)

5. When income in Payor City increases, the residents buy more fish and less chicken. Which of the following is an attribute of chicken in Payor?
a. Inferior good
b. Normal good
c. Perfectly inelastic demand
d. Relatively elastic demand
e. Relatively inelastic demand　(Editors, 7145)

6. Demand for peanut oil formerly rose and fell directly with changes in income, but now varies inversely with income, despite price increases. What change is the most likely explanation for this shift?
a. Boycott by consumers protesting industry practices
b. Expectation of deflation
c. Increase in income
d. Change in preferences　(Editors, 7146)

7. How do the quantity supplied and demanded relate to price changes?

	Supplied	*Demanded*
a.	Inversely	Directly
b.	Inversely	Inversely
c.	Directly	Inversely
d.	Directly	Directly　(Editors, 7147)

8. The supply curve for a normal good is
a. Downward sloping because of income and substitution effects of price changes
b. Downward sloping because of increasing marginal utility
c. Horizontal
d. Upward sloping because higher prices indicate higher quality
e. Upward sloping because entities produce more at higher prices　(Editors, 7148)

9. Young and Zeta are substitute goods. What would cause a shift in the supply curve to the right for Young, a normal good?
a. Cost-saving technological improvements in the production process for Young
b. Cost-saving technological improvements in the production process for Zeta
c. An expected increase in the future price of Young
d. An increase in the price paid for Zeta
　(Editors, 7149)

10. Bob Bounce has two job offers: one as an accountant and one as a basketball player. He would accept either job for $50,000 annually. Due to his basketball skills, he is offered $500,000 as a basketball player. The $450,000 difference is called
a. Cross elasticity of demand
b. Economic rent
c. Equilibrium price
d. Marginal cost
e. Price elasticity of supply　(Editors, 7150)

11. In which of the following situations would there be inelastic demand?
a. A 5 percent price increase results in a 3 percent decrease in the quantity demanded.
b. A 4 percent price increase results in a 6 percent decrease in the quantity demanded.
c. A 4 percent price increase results in a 4 percent decrease in the quantity demanded.
d. A 3 percent price decrease results in a 5 percent increase in the quantity demanded.
(R/03, BEC, #23, 7686)

12. Which of the following factors decrease demand elasticity?
a. Classification as a luxury, rather than a necessity
b. Greater number of substitutes
c. Large percentage of income spent on that good
d. Shorter length of time period analyzed
(Editors, 7152)

13. The widgets market is elastic and purely competitive. Barring Company supplies only widgets. The market price of widgets increases. What is the effect on Barring's total revenue?
a. Decreases
b. Increases
c. Indeterminate from the given information
d. Remains the same   (Editors, 7153)

14. Fairfield Co. graphed the quantity demanded against price for its three products, X, Y, and Z.

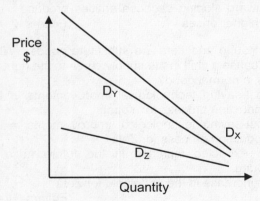

Which product has the most price elasticity of demand?
a. Indeterminate from the given information
b. X
c. Y
d. Z   (Editors, 7154)

15. What effect on output quantity and market price will simultaneous increases in supply and demand have?

	Output quantity	Market price
a.	Increase	Increase
b.	Increase	Indeterminate
c.	Indeterminate	Increase
d.	Indeterminate	Indeterminate

(Editors, 7155)

16. A competitive market model of supply and demand predicts a long-run shortage only when
a. Maximum price is set above the equilibrium price
b. Maximum price is set below the equilibrium price
c. Minimum price is set above the equilibrium price
d. Minimum price is set below the equilibrium price
e. Increase in emission control standards requiring a more expensive production technology
(Editors, 7156)

17. Kingston Company is considering replacing its factory's existing equipment with robotic equipment. What is an irrelevant factor in this decision?
a. The capital-to-labor ratio
b. Economies of scale
c. The existing equipment's cost
d. Opportunity cost
e. Technological efficiency   (Editors, 7157)

18. What generally is the result of government price ceilings in competitive markets?
a. Prices less than equilibrium prices
b. Prices greater than equilibrium prices
c. Persistent surpluses
d. No impact on market prices   (Editors, 7158)

19. In competitive markets, what generally is the short-term result of a government price ceiling set below the equilibrium market price?
a. Decreased demand
b. Shortage
c. Surplus
d. No effect   (Editors, 7159)

20. Coffee and tea are substitutes. What are the **two** most likely results of a widespread coffee boycott?
a. Decreased demand for coffee
b. Higher economic profits for coffee producers
c. Increased demand for tea
d. Increased inelasticity in demand for coffee
e. Increased supply of coffee   (Editors, 7160)

21. Which of the following is **not** characteristic of indifference curves for a two-good economy?
a. They are plotted on a graph with the quantities of one good on the x-axis and another good on the y-axis
b. They are sloped convex to the origin
c. They are sloped negatively
d. They do not intersect
e. They shift to the right with an increase in income
(Editors, 7161)

22. Which of the following examples illustrates the principle of diminishing returns?
a. Bill's Mowing takes 30 minutes to mow and trim a 5,000 square foot lawn and 45 minutes to mow and trim a 10,000 square foot lawn.
b. In the Maher Inn's kitchen, three cooks can prepare 150 meals in one evening; four cooks can prepare 180 meals.
c. A single copy of a 5,000-copy printing of a 120-page paperback and a single copy of a 10-copy printing a 30-page presentation have the same unit cost.
d. A small furnace is less efficient than a large one.
(Editors, 7162)

23. What is normal profit?
a. The cost of resources from an economic perspective
b. Equal to economic profit
c. Equal to net income prepared in conforming with generally accepted accounting principles
d. Profit calculated using only explicit costs
(Editors, 7163)

24. What is the sum of average variable costs and average fixed costs for a given output?
a. Average total cost
b. Economic cost
c. Explicit costs
d. Implicit costs
e. Total costs
(Editors, 7164)

25. Clegg Company's average cost is decreasing over a range of increased output. What is Clegg experiencing?
a. Decreasing fixed costs
b. Decreasing returns
c. Economies of scale
d. Technological efficiency
(Editors, 7165)

26. The costs of the use of a resource for the production of one good rather than another are
a. Economic costs
b. Fixed costs
c. Historical costs
d. Opportunity costs
e. Variable costs
(Editors, 7166)

27. The sprocket market is purely competitive. Searing, a sprocket producer, is considering strategies. Which is the least likely business strategy for Searing to select?
a. Cost leadership
b. Cost differentiation
c. Differentiation
d. Process reengineering
e. Value-chain partnership
(Editors, 7697)

28. What is an example of an oligopoly market?
a. Automobile industry
b. Medical transcription service industry
c. Pea market
d. Retail clothing industry
(Editors, 7168)

29. The marginal cost curve is the supply curve for a business in what type of market?
a. Monopolistic competition
b. A monopoly
c. A natural monopoly
d. An oligopoly
e. Pure competition
(Editors, 7169)

30. How do monopolists typically compare to producers in perfectly competitive markets?
a. Monopolists produce larger quantities.
b. Monopolists produce smaller quantities.
c. Monopolists use more capital and less labor.
d. Monopolists use more economies of scale.
(Editors, 7171)

31. How do cartels maintain prices above the competitive market price?
a. Advertise to increase market demand
b. Encourage high prices on substitute goods
c. Increase costs to force prices to increase
d. Require members to limit output (Editors, 7172)

32. How does a company maintain a natural monopoly?
a. The company owns patents.
b. The company owns natural resources.
c. Economic or technological conditions permit only one efficient supplier.
d. Entry and exit barriers to the market exist.
e. The government limits entry into the market by competitors. (Editors, 7173)

33. What volume provides the most profitable results for companies in monopolist and monopolist competitive markets?
a. Where average costs are minimized
b. Where marginal costs equals marginal revenue
c. Where price equals marginal cost
d. Where price equals average cost
e. Where total revenue is maximized
(Editors, 7174)

34. Which of the following concepts compares the price of goods in a given year to a base year?
a. Consumer price index
b. Consumer confidence index
c. Gross national product
d. Net national product   (R/03, BEC, #4, 7666)

35. Fluctuations in business activity commonly are referred to as cycles. Which of the following industries is best described as counter cyclical?
a. Washing machine industry
b. Replacement auto part industry
c. New home construction
d. Cruise industry   (Editors, 7698)

36. What is characteristic of the recession of a business cycle?
a. Low unemployment
b. Excessive productive capacity
c. Increasing capital investments
d. Increasing price levels   (Editors, 7176)

37. What factor would explain a low propensity for savings?
a. Ownership of a high proportion of liquid assets
b. Increasing real interest rates
c. High debt loads
d. Consumer expectations of future price decreases   (Editors, 7177)

Items 38 and 39 are based on the following information about countries Cleo and Elin.

Disposable Income Level	Cleo Consumption	Elin Consumption
$52,000	$40,000	$39,000
28,000	24,000	27,000

38. What is Cleo's marginal propensity to save?
a. 0.14
b. 0.23
c. 0.33
d. 1.30
e. 1.50   (Editors, 7180)

39. Which country has a higher average propensity to save at each income level?

	$52,000	*$28,000*
a.	Cleo	Cleo
b.	Cleo	Elin
c.	Elin	Elin
d.	Elin	Cleo (Editors, 7181)

40. What factor tends to increase investment?
a. A high capital goods stock quantity
b. A increase in acquisition costs
c. A low technology growth rate
d. A real interest rate decrease   (Editors, 7178)

41. The multiplier effect explains
a. Increases in autonomous investment
b. Increases in induced investments
c. Multiplied increases in national income due to increases in autonomous investment
d. Multiplied increases in national income due to increases in induced investment   (Editors, 7179)

42. What increases when U.S. commercial banks increase net deposits?
a. Purchasing power of the U.S. dollar
b. Real U.S. national income
c. Real wealth of the U.S.
d. U.S. money supply
e. U.S. national debt   (Editors, 7182)

43. What is the discount rate set by the Federal Reserve?
a. The rate that the central bank charges commercial banks for loans
b. The rate that commercial banks charge their best customers for loans
c. The rate that commercial banks charge each other for loans
d. The ratio of a bank's reserves to its demand deposits
e. The percentage of reserves mandated to be on deposit at the central bank   (Editors, 7183)

44. Carlton Bank has an increase in reserves of $1,000,000. If the reserve ratio is 10%, by what amount may Carlton increase its demand deposits?
a. $ 100,000
b. $ 900,000
c. $ 1,000,000
d. $10,000,000   (Editors, 7184)

45. What action would the Federal Reserve most likely take to implement an expansionary monetary policy?
a. Decrease the discount rate and increase the reserve requirement
b. Decrease the discount rate and purchase U.S. government debt securities
c. Increase the discount rate and decrease the reserve requirement
d. Increase the discount rate and sell U.S. government debt securities
e. Increase the discount rate and the reserve requirement   (Editors, 7185)

46. Deflation arbitrarily redistributes wealth away from
a. Creditors only and to debtors
b. Debtors and to creditors
c. Pensioners only and to pension trustees
d. Pensioners and creditors   (Editors, 7186)

47. Keynesian economic theory holds that during the peak of the business cycle, the normal workings of the labor market result in
a. Cyclical unemployment
b. Frictional unemployment
c. Phillips unemployment
d. No unemployment   (Editors, 7187)

48. Which classification best applies to the employer's portion of Social Security taxes, from the employee's perspective?
a. Direct
b. Proportional
c. Progressive
d. Regressive   (Editors, 7188)

49. What is the most likely impact of government borrowing to finance deficits that increases the demand for loan funds?
a. Decrease in the supply of loan funds
b. Decrease interest rates
c. Increase the ease with which businesses can borrow funds
d. Increase interest rates   (Editors, 7189)

50. What is the federal budget deficit?
a. The excess of imports over exports in one year
b. The excess of federal government spending over revenues in one year
c. The excess of the federal government's liabilities over assets on its balance sheet
d. The cumulative excess of federal government spending over revenues   (Editors, 7190)

51. What is a consequence of trade between nations?
a. Possibility of an increase in total world output
b. Less variety in consumer products
c. Tendency for imports to exceed exports
d. Higher consumer prices   (Editors, 7191)

52. Which statements regarding absolute and comparative advantage are valid?
I. Absolute advantage is the ability of one nation to produce goods at relatively lower opportunity costs than another nation.
II. International trade allows a nation to specialize in goods that it produces efficiently, while still obtaining goods it doesn't produce.
III. Total global output is maximized if each nation specializes in goods in which it has a comparative advantage.
a. I only
b. II only
c. III only
d. I and II
e. II and III   (Editors, 7192)

53. What group would an import tariff on cars benefit most?
a. Consumers of domestic cars
b. Consumers of imported cars
c. Producers of domestic cars
d. Producers of imported cars   (Editors, 7200)

54. What is the effect on prices of U.S. imports and exports when the dollar depreciates?
a. Import prices and export prices will decrease.
b. Import prices will decrease and export prices will increase.
c. Import prices will increase and export prices will decrease.
d. Import prices and export prices will increase.
            (R/03, BEC, #20, 7682)

55. What is an investor who intentionally assumes risk in the foreign exchange market called?
a. Arbitrageur
b. Exporter
c. Importer
d. Speculator   (Editors, 7194)

56. Toil, a U.S. company, is submitting bids for a shipment to Japan. The Japanese purchaser wants the bids in Japanese yen for delivery in six months. Toil estimates that the inflation rate in the U.S. is at an annual rate of 4% and that the yen will depreciate at about an annual rate of 6% compared to the dollar during the next six months. Toil's price for a current shipment is ¥3 million. What approximate price will Toil quote for shipment in six months?
a. ¥2.94 million
b. ¥3.03 million
c. ¥3.06 million
d. ¥3.15 million
e. ¥3.31 million   (Editors, 7195)

57. What factor would tend to cause a nation's currency to appreciate in a foreign exchange market with freely fluctuating exchange rates?
a. Relatively high domestic real interest rates
b. Relatively high domestic inflation
c. Increased environmental protection measures resulting in higher prices on goods for export
d. Increased demand for imports   (Editors, 7196)

58. When considering the international balance of payments, where are transactions involving the exchange of physical products among entities in foreign and domestic markets classified?
a. The balance in the current account
b. The balance in the capital account
c. The capital account surplus
d. Reserves held by central banks   (Editors, 7198)

59. India's central bank sharply raised interest rates. What is the likely effect on the value of India's currency?
a. Decrease in relative value
b. Fluctuate widely initially and then return to its value before the interest rate change
c. Increase in relative value
d. Remain the same   (Editors, 7199)

60. When deciding on transfer pricing used in compiling internal financial statements used to evaluate a division's performance for managerial purposes, what factor should receive the least consideration?
a. Controllability of costs
b. Effect of random shocks
c. Minimize world-wide corporate taxes
d. Possible dysfunctional behavior induced by the evaluation system   (Editors, 7728)

Problem 50-2 ADDITIONAL MULTIPLE CHOICE QUESTIONS (156 to 195 minutes)

61. Which of the following products are **not** complementary goods?
a. Cars and tires
b. Chips and dip
c. Lamps and light bulbs
d. Video tapes and DVDs   (Editors, 7201)

62. Tea and sugar cubes are complementary goods. Tea and coffee are substitute goods. What effect does a decrease in the price of tea have?
a. Increase the price of coffee
b. Shift the supply curve for sugar cubes to the left
c. Shift the demand curve for sugar cubes to the left
d. Shift the demand curve for sugar cubes to the right   (Editors, 7202)

63. Ice skates and skis are substitute goods. What causes the demand curve for ice skates to shift to the right?
a. A decrease in average household income
b. A decrease in the popularity of skating
c. A decrease in the price of ski equipment
d. An increase in the price of ice rink admissions
e. An increase in the population   (Editors, 7203)

64. Baseball bats and baseballs are most likely
a. Complementary goods
b. Independent goods
c. Inferior goods
d. Substitute goods   (Editors, 7204)

65. What is the most likely result of increased safety regulations for bicycles?
a. Decreased bicycle prices
b. Increased bicycle consumption levels
c. Increased bicycle prices
d. Increased supply of bicycles   (Editors, 7205)

66. Over the past three years, widget manufacturing companies have established Internet sites for routine customer inquires about orders. Consequently, each customer service representative now handles five times as many customers. The costs of site maintenance are substantially less than one representative's wages. What is the most likely result of this change?
a. Lower wages for representatives
b. A widget supply curve shift to the left and increased widget prices
c. A widget supply curve shift to the left and decreased widget prices
d. A widget supply curve shift to the right and decreased widget prices   (Editors, 7206)

67. What does a supply curve illustrate?
a. The relationship between costs and quantity supplied
b. The relationship between demand and supply
c. The relationship between income and price
d. The relationship between price and quantity supplied   (Editors, 7207)

68. Under what circumstances is the complete purchase price of natural resources deemed economic rent?
a. Completely elastic supply
b. Fixed and limited supply
c. Legislated ceiling price
d. Legislated floor price   (Editors, 7208)

69. Essex Co. graphed the quantity supplied against price for its three products: E, F, and G.

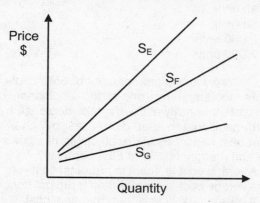

Which product has the least price elasticity of supply?
a. Indeterminate from the given information
b. E
c. F
d. G   (Editors, 7209)

70. The total quantity of merle demanded changes when its price changes according to this schedule.

Quantity demanded	Unit price
1,500 units	$50
1,600 units	$40
1,700 units	$35
1,800 units	$32

Which is the price elasticity of demand for merle when the price decreases from $40 to $35?
a. 2.0
b. 0.5
c. 0.05
d. 0.025   (Editors, 7210)

71. Noodles have a 0.7 price elasticity of demand. What is the best description of the state of demand for noodles?
a. Elastic
b. Inelastic
c. Perfectly elastic
d. Perfectly inelastic   (Editors, 7211)

72. When does demand for a product tend to be price inelastic?
a. Consumers spend a large proportion of income on the product.
b. Few good complements to the product exist.
c. Few good substitutes for the product exist.
d. The product is a luxury item.   (Editors, 7212)

73. What is the effect on the market price when both the supply and demand for a good increase?
a. Decrease only with inelastic demand
b. Decrease only with inelastic supply
c. Increase only with inelastic demand
d. Indeterminate from the given information
          (Editors, 7213)

74. What is the predictable effect when both the supply and demand for a good increase equally?
a. Decrease both market-clearing quantity and price
b. Decrease market-clearing quantity only
c. Decrease price only
d. Increase market-clearing quantity only
e. Increase price only   (Editors, 7214)

75. Broccoli and peas are substitutes. What is the most likely effect of an increase in the market supply of broccoli?
a. Decrease in the quantity of broccoli demanded
b. Decrease in the price of broccoli
c. Increase in the quantity of peas demanded
d. Increase in the price of peas   (Editors, 7215)

76. Marginal utility
a. Decreases when consumption expands
b. Increases when consumption expands
c. Indicates that a high consumption quantity is preferred to a low consumption quantity
d. Indicates that consumption decreases over time
          (Editors, 7216)

77. What does the principle of diminishing marginal utility state?
a. Total utility declines as consumption of additional units of a specific product increases.
b. The price of a specific product decreases proportionately with its decrease in marginal utility.
c. Marginal utility declines when short-term supply curves are upward sloping.
d. Marginal utility declines as consumption of additional units of a specific product increases.
          (Editors, 7217)

78. The net income presented on an income statement prepared in conforming with generally accepted accounting principles generally is
a. Equal to economic profit
b. Greater than economic profits because interest is not considered in calculating economic profits
c. Greater than economic profits because opportunity costs are not considered in calculating net income
d. Less than economic profits because economic profits don't include fixed costs
e. Less than economic profits because economic profits don't include depreciation (Editors, 7218)

79. What is marginal revenue?
a. Equal to price in a monopoly market
b. The change in total revenue related to selling an additional unit
c. The change in total revenue related to increased prices
d. The change in cost associated with increasing returns of scale (Editors, 7219)

80. Which of the following examples illustrates economies of scale?
a. Doubling the capacity of a day care facility requires compliance with more stringent regulations, resulting in more than double the costs.
b. Each additional labor hour input to production is less efficient than the previous one.
c. Increasing a factory's size results in lower average costs.
d. Increasing a factory's size results in lower total costs. (Editors, 7220)

81. What is economic cost?
a. The opportunity cost less the explicit costs
b. The same as opportunity cost
c. The total of all explicit and implicit costs
d. The total revenue less total costs (Editors, 7221)

Items 82 through 84 are based on the following daily information about Dane Company.

Number of Employees	Total Units Produced	Average Selling Price
100	2,000	$50
101	2,030	$46
102	2,080	$45

82. What is Dane's marginal revenue per unit when the 102nd additional employee is added?
a. $ 4.40
b. $ 45.00
c. $ 50.00
d. $220.00 (Editors, 7222)

83. What is Dane's marginal revenue product when the 102nd additional employee is added?
a. $ 45
b. $ 50
c. $ 220
d. $93,380
e. $93,600 (Editors, 7223)

84. What is Dane's marginal physical product when the 101st additional employee is added?
a. 30 units
b. 50 units
c. 2,000 units
d. 2,030 units (Editors, 7224)

85. Cook Co.'s plant operates at 85% capacity. If inputs increase by one-sixth, additional output increases by one-twelfth. If inputs decrease by one-sixth, additional output decreases by one-twelfth. What best describes the relationship of Cook's average and marginal costs at 85% capacity?
a. Average cost is equal to marginal cost
b. Average cost is greater than marginal cost
c. Average cost is less than marginal cost
d. The relationship is indeterminate with the given information (Editors, 7151)

86. What is the effect of economic profit in a pure monopoly market?
a. Decrease in the number of producers
b. Decrease in prices for substitutes
c. Increase in the number of producers
d. No influence on the number of producers (Editors, 7225)

87. What is an example of a monopolistic competitive market?
a. Lawn care service industry
b. Pharmaceutical industry
c. Restaurant industry
d. Wheat market (Editors, 7226)

88. Which of the following is the best example of a purely competitive market?
a. Automobile industry
b. Lawn care service industry
c. Pharmaceutical industry
d. Ice cream industry (Editors, 7227)

89. Under what short-term circumstances will a manufacturer exit a market?
a. Prices fall below average economic costs.
b. Prices fall below average fixed costs.
c. Prices fall below average total costs.
d. Prices fall below average variable costs. (Editors, 7228)

90. Which of the following is **not** characteristic of monopolistic competitive markets?
a. Advertising
b. Economics of scale
c. Heterogeneous products
d. One seller of the product   (Editors, 7229)

91. Which of the following is characteristic of a perfectly competitive market?
a. Consumers avoid diminishing returns.
b. Consumers exhibit high brand loyalty.
c. Consumers purchase goods at the lowest price.
d. Producers often will produce goods at below average cost due to high exit barriers.
          (Editors, 7230)

92. The labor market for masons is competitive and stable. What is the likely short-term result of an attempt to increase masons' wages?
a. Decreased employment levels
b. Decreased employer size
c. Increased employer size
d. Increased labor supplied   (Editors, 7231)

93. Which of the following is characteristic of an oligopoly market?
a. Mutual influence among industry firms on each others' prices
b. No entry or exit barriers
c. No promotional or informational advertising
d. One seller of a product with no close substitutes
e. Technological conditions permit only one efficient supplier   (Editors, 7232)

94. What is the classification of a market with low entry barriers, product differentiation, and many independent producers?
a. Monopolistic competition
b. A monopoly
c. A natural monopoly
d. An oligopoly
e. Pure competition   (Editors, 7233)

95. What is **not** characteristic of perfect competition?
a. Few entry or exit barriers
b. High customer loyalty
c. Many independent producers
d. Perfect information
e. Standardized products   (Editors, 7234)

96. What is the classification of a market with homogeneous products, few entry or exit barriers, many independent producers, and low customer loyalty?
a. Monopolistic competition
b. A monopoly
c. A natural monopoly
d. An oligopoly
e. Pure competition   (Editors, 7167)

97. What does a high concentration ratio indicate?
a. Monopolistic competition
b. A monopoly
c. An oligopoly
d. Pure competition   (Editors, 7170)

98. Neal City requires taxicabs to display a medallion. Neal issued a limited number of these medallions; those wishing to become taxi operators must purchase medallions from current holders, although no one may own more than 30% of the medallions. Taxi fares must be in accordance with a maximum price schedule set by the city; no medallion holder sets fares lower than the municipal schedule. To taxi operators, what term best describes these medallions?
a. Cartel
b. Collusion
c. Entry barrier
d. Exit barrier
e. Monopoly
f. Non-price competition   (Editors, 7699)

99. What is disposable income?
a. The sum of consumption spending, interest payments, and savings
b. Gross domestic product divided by population, adjusted for inflation
c. Net domestic product plus a country's net income earned abroad less indirect business taxes
d. The total market value of all final goods and service produced within a specified country, less depreciation   (Editors, 7175)

Items 100 through 103 are based on the following information about Tamar, a nation with a population of 100,000. Tamar had the following financial transactions for the year.

Gross domestic product	£5,000,000
Transfer payments	625,000
Corporate income taxes	60,000
National retirement plan contributions	250,000
National retirement plan disbursements	220,000
Indirect business taxes	210,000
Personal taxes	300,000
Undistributed corporate profits	25,000
Depreciation	600,000
Net income earned abroad	50,000

100. What is Tamar's net domestic product?
a. £4,425,000
b. £4,400,000
c. £4,370,000
d. £4,315,000 (Editors, 7235)

101. What is Tamar's national income?
a. £4,450,000
b. £4,370,000
c. £4,240,000
d. £4,190,000
e. £4,180,000 (Editors, 7236)

102. What is Tamar's personal income?
a. £4,780,000
b. £3,530,000
c. £3,500,000
d. £3,230,000
e. £3,200,000 (Editors, 7237)

103. What is Tamar's real per-capita output?
a. £50.50
b. £50.00
c. £44.00
d. £35.30 (Editors, 7238)

104. What is characteristic of a business cycle trough?
a. Decreasing purchasing power
b. Increasing capital investments
c. Rising costs
d. Shortages of essential raw materials
e. Unused productive capacity (Editors, 7239)

105. Which of the following are not assumptions of classical economic theory?
a. Flexible interest rates allow self-correcting equilibrium of savings and investing.
b. Flexible prices allow self-correcting of shortages and surpluses in product markets.
c. Full employment is not necessarily an attribute of equilibrium.
d. An increase in money leads to an increase in aggregate demand. (Editors, 7726)

106. What condition exists when the addition of capital goods exceeds the capital consumption allowance?
a. Equilibrium investment
b. Negative gross investment
c. Negative net investment
d. Positive net investment (Editors, 7240)

107. Which of the following are not assumptions of the supply-side theory of economics?
a. Cuts in taxes will produce a recovery due to an increase in aggregate demand and increased motivation for investment.
b. Excessive monetary growth leads to inflation.
c. Increased income would result in the same aggregate tax revenues despite lower tax rates, so spending cuts are not needed.
d. A progressive tax structure is a disincentive to increased investment. (Editors, 7727)

108. The federal government measures inflation with which of the following indicators?
a. Dow Jones index
b. Consumer price index
c. Consumer confidence index
d. Corporate profits (R/03, BEC, #2, 7664)

109. What is characteristic of a period of rising inflation?
a. Increases the purchasing power of money
b. Increases the price level and decreases the purchasing power of money
c. Increases the price level, which benefits anyone who is owed a specific amount of money
d. Benefits anyone who is owed a specific amount of money and harms anyone who owes a specific amount (Editors, 7241)

110. Which of the following circumstances is **not** characteristic of structural unemployment?
a. All labor is employed, although some people are working at jobs for which they are overqualified
b. The economic cycle is in recessionary phase
c. The labor shortage in Calgary is equal to the labor surplus in Atlanta
d. A placement agency has unfilled programming positions and resumes from airline pilots, but no unfilled pilot positions   (Editors, 7242)

111. What is an example of indirect taxes?
a. Social Security taxes paid by employees
b. Real property taxes paid by landlords
c. Real property taxes paid by homeowners
d. Intangible property taxes paid by businesses
e. Income taxes paid by individuals (Editors, 7243)

112. What is the most likely impact of government transfer payments?
a. Decrease aggregate demand for goods provided by the private sector
b. Increase aggregate demand for goods provided by the private sector
c. Increase aggregate demand for goods provided by the public sector
d. Reallocate the consumption of goods within the private sector
e. Reallocate the consumption of goods to the public sector from the private sector (Editors, 7244)

Items 113 through 115 are based on the following assumptions of the production potential of one unit of resources:

	Beef	Chips
Argentina	15 tons	1,800 units
Taiwan	6 tons	1,500 units

113. In trade between Argentina and Taiwan, Taiwan has
a. An absolute advantage in producing beef
b. An absolute advantage in producing chips
c. A comparative advantage in producing beef
d. A comparative advantage in producing both beef and chips
e. A comparative advantage in producing chips   (Editors, 7245)

114. If free trade exists between Argentina and Taiwan,
a. Argentina would export chips to Taiwan.
b. Argentina would specialize in both chip and beef production.
c. Taiwan would not gain any advantage from Argentine imports.
d. Taiwan would specialize in chip production.   (Editors, 7246)

115. If free trade exists between Argentina and Taiwan, the relative price of beef and chips would be
a. Exactly 120 chips for one ton of beef.
b. Exactly 250 chips for one ton of beef.
c. Within 0.008 and 0.009 tons of beef for one chip.
d. Within 120 and 250 chips for one ton of beef.   (Editors, 7247)

116. What effect does the existence of an economic bloc of nations, such as the European Union, have?
a. Discourages foreign investment by multinational companies based in nonmember nations
b. Discriminates against nonmember nations economically
c. Encourages trade among member and nonmember nations
d. Necessitates a common currency (Editors, 7264)

117. What is a consequence of tariffs on imports of a product?
a. Lower profits on rival domestic products
b. Lower cost for the consumer on rival domestic products
c. Higher consumption of the product
d. Higher cost for the consumer of the imported product   (Editors, 7266)

118. Which statements regarding international trade are valid?

I. The U.S. cannot compete with nations that have lower labor costs.
II. Imports raise U.S. living standards.
III. The U.S. can achieve full employment only if it limits imports.

a. I only
b. II only
c. III only
d. I and II
e. I and III   (Editors, 7265)

119. Rice production in Japan is protected partially by import tariffs and quotas. What is a consequence of this protection?
a. Decreased domestic price for rice
b. Decreased short-run employment in domestic rice production
c. Increased domestic price for rice
d. Increased volume of international rice trade   (Editors, 7267)

120. What is the result of purchasing power parity?
a. Holds the relative price levels constant between nations when measured in a common currency
b. Fixes the exchange rate
c. Causes net importer nations to devalue their currencies
d. Causes net exporter nations to devalue their currencies (Editors, 7248)

121. Tog, a Canadian importer of British clothing, contractually must pay an invoice fixed in British pounds in three months. Tog is concerned about the Canadian dollar depreciating against the British pound before that date. How can Tog remove the uncertainty of the cost of the transaction due to depreciating dollars?
a. Buy dollars in the forward exchange market
b. Buy pounds in the forward exchange market
c. Sell dollars in the forward exchange market
d. Sell pounds in the forward exchange market (Editors, 7249)

122. A single U.S. dollar is quoted at 1.32 British pounds on the spot market and 1.353 pounds on the 60-day forward market. What is the approximate annual effect of the forward market?
a. The U.S. dollar is at a discount of 15%.
b. The U.S. dollar is at a discount of 2.5%.
c. The U.S. dollar is at a premium of 2.5%.
d. The U.S. dollar is at a premium of 15%. (Editors, 7250)

123. Ole, an Argentina company, imports goods from the U.S., paying in pesos. For the next year, the annual U.S. inflation rate is expected to be 5% and the U.S. dollar is expected to appreciate against the peso by 20%. What approximate change should Ole expect in the amount of pesos that it pays for imports compared to the current amount?
a. Increase by 25%
b. Increase by 20%
c. Increase by 15%
d. Increase by 5%
e. Decrease by 5%
f. Decrease by 15%
g. Decrease by 20%
h. Decrease by 25% (Editors, 7251)

124. The value of the United States dollar was $1 for 2.5 Brazilian reals. What result will a change in the exchange rate to $1 for 2.3 reals have?
a. The Brazilian real depreciated against the U.S. dollar.
b. Brazilian products will be more expensive for U.S. importers.
c. Visitors will be able to purchase more products in Brazil with their U.S. dollars.
d. U.S. exports to Brazil will tend to decrease. (Editors, 7252)

125. What will be the likely result of a decline in the value of the U.S. dollar relative to the currencies of the United States' trading partners?
a. The U.S. trade deficit will increase.
b. U.S. imports will increase.
c. U.S. exports will increase.
d. Foreign currencies will depreciate compared to the U.S. dollar. (Editors, 7253)

126. The Japanese yen has a floating exchange rate and has fallen compared to other currencies in the last year. What effect does this circumstance have?
a. The cheaper yen helps Japanese exporters.
b. The cheaper yen helps Japanese importers.
c. The fall in the yen's value has no effect on the Japanese trade balance.
d. The fall in the yen's value eliminates any surplus or deficit in the trade account in the balance of payments. (Editors, 7254)

127. What is the impact of an overvalued exchange rate?
a. Affects capital flows, but not trade flows
b. Affects trade flows, but not capital flows
c. Effectively imposes a tax on exports and provides a subsidy to imports
d. Effectively imposes a tax on imports and provides a subsidy to exports (Editors, 7255)

128. Generally, what sets exchange rates?
a. Commercial exporters and importers
b. Each country's central bank
c. Supply and demand in the foreign exchange market
d. The International Monetary Fund (Editors, 7256)

129. To what does the term "managed float" refer in foreign exchange markets?
a. Commercial activity between businesses of different nations that sets exchange rates
b. Discretionary currency trading by central banks
c. The International Monetary Fund's role in covering short-term deficits in balance of payments
d. The tendency of currencies of nation's experiencing inflation to depreciate (Editors, 7257)

130. A company manufactures goods in Esland for sale to consumers in Woostland. Currently, the economy of Esland is booming and imports are rising rapidly. Woostland is experiencing an economic recession, and its imports are declining. How will the Esland currency, $E, react with respect to the Woostland currency, $W?
a. The $E will remain constant with respect to the $W.
b. The $E will increase with respect to the $W.
c. The $E will decline with respect to the $W.
d. Changes in imports and exports will not affect currency changes.
e. Indeterminate from the given information
(R/03, BEC, #5, amended, 7667)

131. Consumers in the United States increase purchases of products made in Japan. What will tend to be the reaction in foreign exchange markets?
a. Demand for Japanese yen increases.
b. Supply for Japanese yen decreases.
c. Supply for Japanese yen increases.
d. The U.S. dollar appreciates compared to the Japanese yen. (Editors, 7193)

132. What situation would ease the debt servicing burdens of debtor nations that primarily sell raw materials to the United States?
a. Increases in U.S. food exports
b. Increases in U.S. import tariffs
c. A U.S. economy in expansion with stable money supply growth
d. A U.S. economy in recession with stable money supply contraction (Editors, 7197)

133. What is the primary reason for nations to devalue their currencies?
a. Discourage exports without using quotas
b. Encourage citizens to make foreign investments
c. Improve the balance of trade
d. Slow inflation by increasing imports
(Editors, 7258)

134. Which of the following would **not** contribute to a high currency value?
a. Relatively high real interest rates
b. Relatively high demand for foreign goods
c. Relatively low inflation
d. Relatively stable government (Editors, 7259)

135. Generally, how are balance-of-payment deficits and surpluses eliminated?
a. By adopting a common monetary unit
b. By adopting tight monetary policies
c. By the market mechanism of flexible exchange rates
d. By taxing imports as necessary for import and export quantities to match (Editors, 7260)

136. Which statements regarding balance of payments are valid?

I. Only transactions involving the exchange of merchandise are included in the current account.
II. The current account and trade balance are equivalent.
III. Only transactions involving the international transfer of financial capital are included in the capital account.

a. I only
b. II only
c. III only
d. I and II
e. I and III (Editors, 7261)

137. What item would increase a surplus in the Canadian balance of payment accounts?
a. Spending by Canadians vacationing abroad
b. Loans to Canadians by foreigners
c. Dividends paid to foreigners that own stock in Canadian corporations
d. Bananas imported to Canada (Editors, 7262)

138. Jamaica had the following summary transactions.

Imports of goods	$203,000
Exports of goods	157,000
Investment in foreign nations	14,000
Foreign investment within Jamaica	63,000
Interest payments on foreign loans	37,000
Gifts received from abroad	13,000

Jamaica's balance of payments has a
a. $49,000 deficit in the capital account
b. $70,000 deficit in the current account
c. $12,000 surplus in the capital account
d. $22,000 deficit in the current account
(Editors, 7263)

Solution 50-1 MULTIPLE CHOICE ANSWERS

Overview

1. (e) The free-enterprise system, also called capitalism, involves private ownership of resources and economic decision made by those owners. Economic questions are answered by the free market pricing mechanism. Communism has state ownership and decision-making. Socialism involves both state and private ownership and state and private decision making.

Demand

2. (a) A downward sloping demand curve is appropriate for both inferior and normal goods. The demand curve shows the effects on quantity demanded of an increase in price. As the price of the good increases or substitutes are available relatively cheaper, the quantity demanded is less. Income effect: Price changes cause changes in consumers' purchasing power; as prices rise, consumers can buy less with their incomes (consumers' real income decreases). Substitute effect: Price changes cause changes in the price of substitutes relative to the price of the good. As substitutes for a good become relatively cheaper, quantity demanded of that good decreases. Marginal utility is relevant when discussing purchases of multiple goods within budget constraints. A horizontal curve would indicate that a difference in price has no effect on quantity demanded. A upward sloping curve would indicate that as the price increases, all other things held constant, quantity demanded increases.

3. (d) Goods cannot be both substitutes and complements of each other. If good A has a substitute, B, relatively lower in price, buyers leave the market for A and purchase the substitute. If good A has a complement, B, then when the price of A increases, buyers demand less of both A and B. Since demand for Y decreases when the price of X increases, the two goods demonstrate the attributes of complements.

4. (b) If a good has a substitute relatively lower in price, buyers leave the market for one good and purchase the substitute, increasing demand for the substitute. The supply curve for the alternative remains the same.

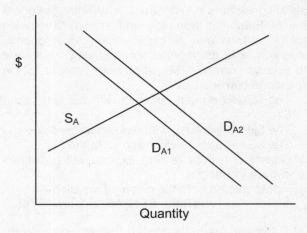

5. (a) Demand for an inferior good decreases as income increases (consumers substitute the inferior good with a normal good). Demand for a normal good increases as income increases. Elasticity deals with the degree of substitution.

6. (d) Of the options given, an increase in demand despite price increases would mostly likely be due to a change in consumer preferences; a preference shift would cause the category of the good to change from inferior to normal. A boycott would tend to reduce demand. The expectation of deflation would cause consumers to delay purchases as much as possible, as deflation is the decrease of prices. An increase in income would not change an inferior good to a normal good.

Supply

7. (c) The price and quantity demanded for a good are related inversely; the lower the price, the higher the quantity demanded. The price and quantity supplied for a good are related directly; the higher the price, the higher the quantity supplied.

8. (e) Entities supply more quantity at higher prices. For goods of differing quality, separate supply curves would be needed to plot the goods on the price-quantity graph; basically, different quality goods would count as different goods. A horizontal curve would indicate that a difference in price has no effect on quantity supplied. A downward sloping curve would indicate that as the price increases, all other things held constant, quantity supplied decreases.

9. (a) A shift in the supply curve to the right indicates suppliers are willing to supply greater quantities than previously supplied at every price. A decrease in the costs for producing a good tend to increase supply of that good; this is not influenced by whether the good is normal or inferior. Cost

savings in producing Zeta would tend to increase the supply of Zeta, rather than Young; if anything, supply of Young would tend to decrease. An expected increase in the future price of a good would tend to decrease the current supply of the good. An increase in the price paid for Zeta encourages firms to supply Zeta rather than Young, decreasing the supply of Young.

10. (b) Economic rent, or surplus, occurs when the input (salary) is purchased for a higher amount than the next highest bidder (typically in a different market) of that input would pay. Elasticity is a measure of how responsive the market is to a change in a determinant. Cross elasticity of demand relates to the influence of the demand of one good on another. Price elasticity of supply measures responsiveness of supply to changes in price. The equilibrium, or market, price is the price set by the market; it is the intersection of the demand and supply curves for a market. Marginal cost is the additional cost to supply one more unit.

Elasticity

11. (a) Price elasticity of demand measures responsiveness of demand to changes in price. If demand is relatively inelastic, demand will not change much as the price changes. A five percent price increase with a three percent decrease in quantity demanded is an example of relatively inelastic demand (quantity demanded changes *less* than the price change). Both a four percent price increase with a six percent decrease in quantity demanded and a three percent price decrease with a five percent increase in quantity demanded are examples of elastic demand (quantity demanded changes *more* than the price change). A four percent price increase with a four percent decrease in quantity demanded is an example of unitary elasticity (quantity demanded changes by the *same* amount as the price change).

12. (d) Demand elasticity is the percentage change in quantity demanded divided by the percentage change in price. When a good is a luxury, it can be done without entirely, so demand is very sensitive to price. When a good has a large number of substitutes, chances are that a cheap alternative will be found and used in response to a price increase. When a large percentage of income is spent on a good, consumers are willing to spend more time finding substitutes. In the long run, more substitutes can be found than in the short run.

13. (a) If demand is elastic, demand will be very sensitive to price changes. Demand elasticity (E_d) is the percentage change in quantity demanded divided by the percentage change in price. When

demand is classified as elastic, E_d is greater than one; in other words, the percentage change in quantity demanded will be more than the percentage change in price. When the price of widgets increases, the demand will drop so much that total revenue will be less than before the price increase.

14. (d) Price elasticity of demand (E_d) measures responsiveness of demand to changes in price. Algebraically, E_d is the percentage change in quantity demanded divided by the percentage change in price; thus, it is represented graphically as the slope of the demand line. The most elasticity is represented by the line with the mildest slope, the one for product Z. In other words, the line with the mildest slope has the most change in quantity demanded for the same change in price.

Market

15. (b) An increase in supply and demand will increase the output quantity with an indeterminate effect on market price. An increase in demand and a decrease in supply will increase the market price with an indeterminate effect on output quantity.

16. (b) A price ceiling, or maximum, set below the market, or equilibrium, price causes a shortage, as consumers demand more at that price than producers are wiling to supply at that price. A price ceiling set above the market price has no effect, as the market will seek the market price unhindered. A price floor set above the market price causes a surplus. A price floor set below the market price has no effect, as the market will seek the market price unhindered. Production cost increases will cause a shift in supply, resulting in a new equilibrium price, but not a shortage.

17. (c) The original cost of the factory will not change regardless of the action selected; it is irrelevant. The capital-labor ratio affects the fixed cost structure of operations. Economies of scale are present when average costs diminish with higher production volumes. Opportunity cost is the cost of not taking an alternative course of action. Technological efficiency compares actual and achievable physical units of output, as compared to financial efficiency, which is measured in monetary terms.

18. (a) A price ceiling sets the maximum price below the market equilibrium price, reducing the quantity that suppliers are willing to supply and increasing the quantity demanded. Governments typically have no incentive to set price ceilings above the market equilibrium price.

19. (b) A price ceiling sets the maximum price below the market equilibrium price, reducing the quantity that suppliers are willing to supply and increasing the quantity demanded. This rapidly creates a shortage.

20. (a, c) Two responses are required for full credit. Assuming a competitive market, a boycott reduces demand for a product and tends to increase demand for substitutes. Economic profit is total revenue less all economic costs: coffee suppliers would sell less coffee and would not be able to raise prices, resulting in lower total revenues, with no change in fixed costs. Inelasticity in demand for coffee would mean that consumers would continue buying a product regardless of price; inelasticity doesn't exist if those consumers are willing to boycott the product. In other words, elasticity might affect the decision to boycott, but a boycott doesn't affect elasticity directly. The coffee supply would not be increased by a boycott.

Utility

21. (e) Budget constraints lines, not indifference curves, shift with income change. Indifference curves for a two-good economy are plotted on a graph with the quantities of one good on the x-axis and another good on the y-axis. They are sloped convex to the origin. They are sloped negatively. They do not intersect.

22. (b) The principle of diminishing returns holds that there is a point at which equal additional units of input add less to the output than previous units of input. In other words, instances of diminished returns are instances of decreasing efficiency with larger inputs. This point is reached in the Maher Inn's kitchen: with three cooks, each cook prepares an average of 50 meals; the fourth cook only adds an incremental 30 units of output. The other situations are instances of increasing returns. Bill's Mowing takes only half again as much time to mow and trim twice the area. The volume print job has an additional 90 pages for the same unit cost.

Production & Costs

23. (a) Normal profit is the profit necessary to motivate investors to enter and remain in an industry; in other words, the cost of resources (total return on investment) from an economic perspective. Economic profit is total revenue less total costs. Normal profit is an implicit cost used to calculate economic profit; economic profit is the excess return after normal profit is considered. Net income determined in conformity with generally accepted accounting principles doesn't consider implicit costs.

24. (a) Average total cost are total costs divided by output quantity, or in other words, the sum of average variable costs and average fixed costs. Economic cost is the income that an entity must provide in order to attract resource suppliers (investors). Explicit costs are actual expenditures made in operations. Implicit costs are amounts that would have been received if resources had been used for other purposes. The sum of two average costs will not produce total costs.

25. (c) Economies of scale result in decreasing average cost over a range of increased output. Decreasing average costs could be due to other factors than decreasing fixed costs or technological efficiency; for instance, decreasing variable costs. Decreasing returns don't affect decreasing average costs; instead, decreasing average costs are likely to cause increasing returns.

26. (d) Opportunity costs are the costs of not engaging in another activity. Economic cost is the income that is provided to investors to attract resources (investment). Fixed costs are costs that do not change with the level of output. Historical costs are actual expenditures made in producing a product. Variable costs are costs that vary with the level of output.

Market Structure & Performance

27. (c) Differentiation strategy involves competing in a broad market on the basis of superior value in terms of quality, special features, or service. Buyer loyalty serves as an entry barrier and allows cost increases to be passed on to customers. Purely competitive markets are characterized by low customer loyalty, making competing on the basis of superior quality an unlikely strategy; low cost strategies are more likely. Cost leadership involves competing on the basis of low cost in a broad market. Cost focus involves competing on the basis of low cost in a narrow market. Process reengineering involves examining current processes and either improving them or designing replacement processes, which tends to lower costs. A strategic alliance, such as a value-chain partnership, is a partnership of entities to achieve strategic and mutually beneficial objectives. For further strategic management coverage, see the *Planning & Control* chapter.

28. (a) The automobile industry has the oligopoly characteristics of few sellers; entry barriers, and price leadership. The retail clothing industry has monopolistic competition characteristics: large number of sellers, differentiated products, relatively easy entry and exit, considerable non-price competition, and some price controls. The pea market and

medical transcription service industry have characteristics of pure competition: homogeneous products, few entry or exit barriers, many independent producers, and low customer loyalty.

29. (e) Individual businesses in a purely competitive market have no effective means of influencing price; they are price takers. For profit maximization, producers in a purely competitive market equate price to marginal cost. If the price is less than average variable cost, the producers stop producing; if the price is above marginal costs, more producers enter the market, eventually lowering the price. In a purely competitive market, economic profit is earned only in the short term.

30. (b) Firms maximize profits when marginal revenue equals marginal costs. For monopolists to increase sales they must lower prices, so marginal revenues will decrease as volume increases. A competitive producer is a price taker, so increased sales have not effect on marginal revenues. Given the same costs, the monopolist's marginal revenue curve intersects the cost curve at a lower level than the competitive producer. Therefore the monopolist's volume will be lower than the competitive producers' volume. Economies of scale and the ratio of capital to labor are based on decisions that impact costs, not revenues, and are not linked closely to market structure.

31. (d) A cartel is a group of oligopolist companies formed to fix prices. Cartel member voluntarily restrict their output to limit the total supply, and thus, increase prices. While cartels may advertise to increase demand, limiting output is their definitive characteristic. Cartels don't encourage use of substitutes; except for encouraging such use, they have little influence on substitutes' prices. Increased costs do not cause increased prices automatically.

32. (c) A natural monopoly exists when economic or technological conditions permit only one efficient supplier. A company could own patents or natural resources and yet still not have a natural monopoly; a natural monopoly does not require ownership of patents or natural resources. Entry and exit barriers are not exclusive to a natural monopoly. A government limits market entry by competitors for a regular, not a natural, monopoly.

33. (b) The most profit is earned (by companies in any market) at the volume where marginal costs equals marginal revenue. Below this volume greater marginal revenue may be earned for less marginal costs, so the company will sell more. At greater volumes, the company will have marginal costs that are more than the marginal revenue that it

will earn from one more sale. For monopolies, maximum profit may occur at a volume where average cost is not minimized. Price equals marginal revenue for purely competitive markets, so profits are maximized when price equals marginal cost only in these markets. If price equals average cost, there is no profit. Maximization of total revenue ignores the impact of costs on profits.

Measures

34. (a) The consumer price index is a comparison of the price of items in a "typical" shopping cart to a base value. The consumer confidence index is a comparison of a consumer assurance survey to a base consumer assurance survey. Gross national product (GNP) is the total market value of all financial goods and service produced with resources from a specified country. Net national product is GNP less depreciation.

Business Cycle

35. (b) Businesses or industries that perform much better than average during expansions and much worse than average during recessions are called cyclical; businesses or industry that that perform better during recessionary phases and worse during expansionary phases are called counter-cyclical or defensive. During an economic downturn, car owners are more likely to repair cars and other durables than to buy new ones; the retail market for auto parts tends to be counter-cyclical. During recessions, consumers tend to delay large purchases such as washing machines and homes as well as choosing less expensive alternatives such as camping instead of a cruise.

36. (b) Recession is characterized by decreasing levels of economic activity. Employment levels contract (unemployment increases) and inventories build, which tends to have a depressing effect on price levels. Capital investment slows as returns dwindle. Because inventories accumulate, entities decrease production, resulting in excessive productive capacity.

Keynesian Economics

37. (a) People with many liquid assets tend to increase consumption at every level of disposable income. Savings results from income not spent on consumption. People with high debt loads tend to consume less, resulting in increased savings. Increasing real interest rates and consumer expectations of future price decreases tend to increase the propensity for savings.

38. (c) Marginal propensity to save is the change in savings divided by the change in income. Savings equals income less consumption. For Cleo, savings at $52,000 and $28,000 is $12,000 and $4,000, respectively. ($12,000 – $4,000) / ($52,000 – $28,000) = 0.33

39. (d) Average propensity to save (APS) is savings divided by income. Savings equals income less consumption. For Cleo, savings at $52,000 and $28,000 is $12,000 and $4,000, respectively. Cleo's APS at $52,000 and $28,000 is $12,000 / $52,000 = 0.23 and $4,000 / $28,000 = 0.14, respectively. For Elin, savings at $52,000 and $28,000 is $13,000 and $1,000, respectively. Elin's APS at $52,000 and $28,000 is $13,000 / $52,000 = 0.25 and $1,000 / $28,000 = 0.04, respectively. At the $52,000 income level, Elin's 0.25 rate is higher than Cleo's 0.23 rate. At the $28,000 income level, Cleo's 0.14 rate is higher than Elin's 0.04 rate.

40. (d) Investment tends to increase based on expected profitability. Real (nominal less inflation factor) interest rate declines tend to increase investment, as new projects have a lower interest cost. A high technology growth rate tends to increase investment, because innovations often are profitable. A high capital goods (equipment to make goods) stock quantity tends to decrease investment, as entities have little need to spend more to make product. Higher acquisition costs lower the investment's expected profitability.

41. (c) The multiplier effect is that any increase in autonomous investment, consumption, or government spending results in a multiplied increase in national income. The original autonomous investment is spent several times. Increases in induced investment include spending subsequent to the autonomous investment. Autonomous investments are made without regard for national income levels.

Money

42. (d) Banks only retain a specified percentage of funds due to reserve requirements. The more funds banks hold, the more they may lend to qualified customers. As the amount of deposits increase, the amount of loans increases, directly increasing the money supply. Purchasing power of the U.S. dollar may be decreased by a money supply expansion. Real national income and wealth are not changed directly by increases in money supply. National debt is government debt; governmental debt is not changed by private deposits.

43. (a) The discount rate is the rate that the central bank (the Fed) charges commercial banks for loans. A bank's prime rate is the rate that it charges its best customers. The legal reserve requirement is the percentage of reserves mandated to be on deposit; the actual ratio of a bank's reserves to its demand deposits typically is close to the legal reserve requirement. Banks with excess funds lend money overnight to banks with shortfalls. The rate that these commercial banks charge each other is called the federal funds rate.

44. (d) Reserves are that portion of demand deposits that may not be lent ($1 million / 0.10 = $10 million). Alternatively, with additional demand deposits of $10 million, there must be an increase of $1 million in reserves ($10 million × 10% = $1 million).

45. (b) Decreasing the discount rate decreases banks' cost of money, so they charge their customers lower interest rates, increasing loans. Purchasing U.S. government debt securities reduces the number of outstanding securities, increasing the price, and hence, reducing the effective interest rate on the debt. Decreasing the reserve requirement makes more money available for banks to lend, increasing the amount supplied, and hence, the interest rate.

Inflation & Deflation

46. (b) Holding money or rights to money payments during a deflationary period results in an economic gain. Pensioners and creditors have rights to such payments. Debtors, on the other hand, must make such payments in money that is worth more now than when the money was borrowed.

Employment

47. (b) Frictional unemployment is due to labor market mechanics, including that resulting from time lost in changing jobs. Cyclical unemployment occurs during low points in the economic cycle, when aggregate demand is less than aggregate labor supply. Phillips unemployment is not a term in common use. The Phillips curve purports to illustrate the relationship between inflation and unemployment; modern economics theory holds there is little relationship between inflation and unemployment. Keynesian economic theory holds that an economy can be in equilibrium at less than full employment.

Government

48. (d) When entities with higher income pay less tax as a proportion of income than entities with low income, the tax is classified as regressive. When entities with higher income pay more tax as a proportion of income than entities with low income, the tax

is progressive. When entities with higher income pay the same tax as a proportion of income as entities with low income, the tax is proportional. Although the employer's share of Social Security is paid by the employer, this is an indirect tax for the employee, as employers base the decision to hire employees on total compensation cost. If the employer were not paying Social Security taxes, the employer would increase the employee's wages accordingly. After reaching a threshold amount, for each employee, the tax is no longer applied.

49. (d) An increase in the demand for loan funds tends to increase interest rates. An increase in the demand for loan funds has no direct effect on the supply of loan funds. With increased interest rates and more competition for available loan funds, businesses most likely have increased difficulty borrowing.

50. (b) The federal budget deficit is the excess of federal government spending over revenues in one year; it is not an international trade concept, a balance sheet concept, nor a cumulative amount.

Direction of Trade

51. (a) The comparative advantage theory posits that when each nation specialized in products for which it has the greatest comparative advantages, total world output is maximized. Variety in products and lower prices are expected with free trade. One nation's import is another's export; imports equal exports on a global basis. A single nation's exports are as likely to exceed imports as the reverse.

52. (e) Comparative advantage is the ability of one nation to produce goods at relatively lower opportunity costs than another nation. Absolute advantage exists when the actual costs are lower in one nation than in another. Comparative, not absolute, advantage determines which goods each nation should produce to achieve maximum global output. International trade reduces the necessity for individual nations' self-sufficiency.

Trade Barriers

53. (c) Import tariffs result in higher costs for the consumer of the imported product. As domestic producers have little incentive to lower prices, it also tends to result in higher profits for domestic producers and higher costs for the domestic product consumer.

Foreign Exchange

54. (c) A decline in the value of a currency relative to the currencies of that nation's trading partners is called depreciation. When depreciation occurs, generally export prices decrease, as the nation's goods are cheaper to foreign purchasers than before the decline. When depreciation occurs, generally import prices increase, as foreign sellers want more of the devalued currency in exchange for their goods.

55. (d) A speculator purposely assumes risk in the foreign exchange market. The second-best answer to this question is an arbitrageur; an arbitrageur buys in one market and sells in another at a slightly higher price, and thus, has significantly less risk than a speculator. Exporters and importers are interested primarily in movement of products among nations and often hedge their purchases to avoid risk.

56. (d) Both the U.S. inflation and the increase in the dollar's comparative value cause the cost of imports, measured in yen, to increase. For a domestic shipment in six months, Toil would submit a bid 2% higher (4% × 6 months/12 months) than what it would bid currently. For a shipment denominated in a foreign currency, Toil also would adjust for the anticipated change in the comparative value of the yen; since the yen is expected to depreciate, the factor for the change in comparative value also increases the price in yen. ¥3 million × (1 + 0.04 × 6/12) × (1 + 0.06 × 6/12) = ¥3.15 million.

57. (a) Relatively high real interest rates and low inflation make investment in a nation attractive, fueling demand for its currency. A price increase on export goods would reduce demand for those goods, and hence, the nation's currency. High demand for foreign goods (imports) drives demand for foreign, not domestic, currency.

Balance of Payments

58. (a) The balance of payments (or trade) represents payments made between nations; transactions usually are classified into the capital account and the current account. The current account involves the net trade of goods and services, net unilateral transfers (pensions and gifts), and investment receipts and payments (dividends and interest). The capital account involves capital transfers, not physical products. Reserves are central bank assets. A capital account surplus is an excess of inflows over outflows of capital.

59. (c) Comparative values of currencies change based on relative demand for each currency.

When real interest rates are high, investment within a nation is attractive, and demand for that currency is high.

Transfer Pricing

60. (c) Currently, most companies set transfer prices primarily to minimize overall corporate taxes. This approach ignores other important areas: management incentives among various divisions, allocation of production capacities, and guidance for future capital investment. It's legal to maintain two sets of transfer prices. Most people think of transfer pricing as a tax optimization issue, yet transfer prices also are management tools. They have important decision-making functions, valuing intermediate product so that regional managers may maximize the profit of the company as a whole. A company may seek to generate information that provides a clear basis for internal decision making. For managerial purposes, when deciding what metric should be selected to evaluate a unit's performance, the following should be considered: controllability of costs, the effect by random shocks, and possible dysfunctional behavior induced by the evaluation system.

Solution 50-2 ADDITIONAL MULTIPLE CHOICE ANSWERS

Demand

61. (d) Video tapes and DVDs are substitute goods. Complementary goods experience a corresponding change in demand with a change in the price of the other good: as the price of one increases, the demand for the other decreases.

62. (d) A decrease in the price of tea shifts the demand curve to the right (an increase) for its compliment, sugar cubes. The sugar cube supply curve will not change. A decrease in the price of tea shifts the demand curve to the left (a decrease) for its substitute, coffee.

63. (e) A shift to the right indicates increased demand at all price levels. An increased population increases demand. A decrease in average household income, consumer preferences, and the price of substitute goods would decrease demand at all price levels, resulting in a shift to the left. An increase in the price of ice rink admissions (a complementary good) also would decrease demand for ice skates.

64. (a) Complementary goods experience a corresponding change in demand with a change in the price of the other good: as the price of one increases, the demand for the other decreases. Independent goods have no relationship. Inferior goods are goods that are purchased in diminishing quantity as income rises. Substitute goods are goods that replace each other: as the price of one increases, the demand for the other increases.

Supply

65. (c) Compliance with new bicycle safety regulations most likely causes increased costs for suppliers. Depending on price elasticity, suppliers will either pass these costs along to consumers in the form of higher prices or supply less at the same price level. Consumers will demand (consume) less at a higher price.

66. (d) Producers' abilities to lower costs and produce more at a given market price shift the supply curve to the right, indicating an increased supply at all price levels. The shifted supply curve intersects the demand curve at a lower price level than before the change. The effect on wages cannot be determined from the given information: there will be less demand for customer service representatives, but there probably will be less supply also, as many representatives will seek other types of work or similar work in other industries.

67. (d) The points on a supply curve are the quantity that sellers are willing to supply for a range of price levels. Costs influence the supply curve, but are not shown on a single curve; a change in costs is represented by drawing a second curve. The relationship between demand and supply is illustrated by plotting the demand and supply curves on the same graph. Income levels influence the demand curve.

68. (b) When there is a completely inelastic (or fixed) supply of a resource, no increase in price will increase supply and all of the purchase price is deemed economic rent or surplus. In other words, no part of the price provides incentive to increase supply.

Elasticity

69. (b) Price elasticity of supply (E_s) measures responsiveness of supply to changes is price. Algebraically, E_s is the percentage change in quantity supplied divided by the percentage change in price; thus, it is represented graphically as the slope of the demand line. The least elasticity is represented by the line with the greatest slope, the one for

product E. In other words, the line with the greatest slope has the least change in quantity supplied for the same change in price.

70. (b)   Price elasticity of demand (E_d) measures responsiveness of demand to changes in price. Algebraically, E_d is the percentage change in quantity demanded, 6.25% [(1,600 units − 1,700 units) / 1,600 units] divided by the percentage change in price, 12.5% [($40 − $35) / 40]. 6.25% / 12.5% = 0.5.

71. (b)   Price elasticity of demand (E_d) measures responsiveness of quantity demanded to changes in price. A product with an absolute elasticity coefficient value less than 1 is defined as inelastic. Perfect inelasticity results when a change in price causes no change in quantity demanded.

72. (c)   Price elasticity of demand (E_d) measures responsiveness of demand to price changes. Demand tends to be inelastic (little response to price changes) when there are few good substitutes for a product. Demand tends to be inelastic when consumers don't spend much of their income on a product, as it is not as worthwhile to seek a substitute. Demand tends to be inelastic when the product is a necessity, rather than a luxury. The number of complements for a product has little effect on its elasticity.

Market

73. (d)   With the same demand, an increase in supply will lower the price. With the same supply, an increase in demand will raise the price. When both change concurrently, the effect on the market price depends on the size of the changes and the slopes of the supply and demand curves.

74. (d)   With the same demand, an increase in supply will lower the price. With the same supply, an increase in demand will raise the price. When both change concurrently, the effect on the market price depends on the size of the changes and the slopes of the supply and demand curves (in other words, elasticity). The only reliable prediction is that the market-clearing quantity, or volume of goods traded, will increase.

75. (b)   With the same demand for broccoli, an increase in broccoli supply will lower the price of broccoli, which in turn will increase the quantity demanded. The quantity demanded of substitutes, such as peas, most likely would decrease. It is extremely unlikely that the price of substitutes would rise in that circumstance.

Utility

76. (a)   The principle of diminishing marginal utility states that equal additional quantities of consumption result in less than equal additional amounts of consumer utility. In other words, utility decreases as consumption increases. The benefit, or utility, from a tenth glass of water is less than the benefit from the fifth glass; the benefit from each of those is less than the benefit from the first glass. A high consumption quantity typically is preferred to a low consumption quantity; marginal utility is a means of comparing alternatives in the allocation of limited resources. Marginal utility does not predict total consumption will decrease over time.

77. (d)   The principle of diminishing marginal utility states that equal additional quantities of consumption result in less than equal additional amounts of consumer utility. A rational consumer maximizes total utility from income, or in other words, obtains the same utility from the last dollar spent on each different product purchased. Not all consumption of additional units of a specific product decreases total utility, although there may be a point at which total utility declines. (For instance, 1 aspirin may be good and 2 aspirin better, but 20 aspirin probably would have decreased total utility.) The price of a specific product is set by market supply and demand; marginal utility is determined by individual consumers. The principle of diminishing marginal utility explains demand, not supply, behavior.

Production & Costs

78. (c)   Economic profit is total revenue less total costs. GAAP net income is greater than economic profits because opportunity costs are not considered in calculating net income. The calculation of economic profit includes all of the costs that are included in determining net income in conformity with GAAP.

79. (b)   Marginal revenue is the change in total revenue, not cost, related to selling an additional unit, not from a change in prices. In a purely competitive market, marginal revenue is equal to price; in a monopoly, the seller generally may set prices and will maximize profits by setting prices such that marginal revenue equals marginal cost, unless price is less than average variable cost.

80. (c)   Economies of scale refers to reduced average, not total, costs as production volume increases. An increase in costs greater than the increase in capacity is the opposite. Less efficient labor results in more costs.

81. (c) Economic cost is the income that an entity must provide in order to attract resource suppliers (investors); it is the sum of explicit and implicit costs. Opportunity cost is a type of implicit cost; it is the cost of not taking an alternative course of action. Economic profit is total revenue less total costs.

82. (a) Marginal revenue per unit is the change in revenue per unit when an additional unit of input (in this case, labor) is added. The total revenue with 101 employees is $93,380 ($46 × 2,030 units). The total revenue with 102 employees is $93,600 ($45 × 2,080 units). The marginal revenue per unit is ($93,600 − $93,380) / (2,080 units − 2,030 units) = $4.40.

83. (c) Marginal revenue product is the change in revenue when an additional unit of input (in this case, labor) is added. The total revenue with 101 employees is $93,380 ($46 × 2,030 units). The total revenue with 102 employees is $93,600 ($45 × 2,080 units). $93,600 − $93,380 = $220.

84. (a) Marginal physical product is the additional units produced with the addition of another unit of input (labor). 2,030 units − 2,000 units = 30 units.

85. (c) At 85% capacity, Cook is experiencing deceasing returns to scale. Outputs are changed by a factor that is less than the change in inputs. In other words, marginal costs exceed average costs. This situation is illustrated by part C of the marginal and average cost curves (see graph). The meeting point of the marginal and average cost curves (Point B) is where marginal and average costs are equal. Part A of the marginal and average cost curves is where marginal cost is less than average cost.

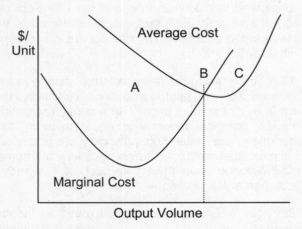

Market Structure

86. (d) A pure monopoly market, by definition, has only one producer. The same forces that exist to exclude additional producers operate when there is an economic profit as when there is not. Economic profit is revenues less explicit and implicit costs, including a normal profit. Economic profit is normal for a monopoly. If a producer is earning an economic profit, it would be unlikely to go out of business. The existence of an economic profit would not tend to decrease the prices of any substitutes; if anything, it would tend to increase them.

87. (c) The restaurant industry has monopolistic competition characteristics: large number of sellers, differentiated products, relatively easy entry and exit, considerable non-price competition, and some price controls. The lawn care service industry and wheat market have characteristics of pure competition: homogeneous products, few entry or exit barriers, many independent producers, and low customer loyalty. The pharmaceutical industry has the oligopoly characteristics of few sellers; entry barriers, and price leadership.

88. (b) The lawn care service industry has characteristics of pure competition: homogeneous products, few entry or exit barriers, many independent producers, and low customer loyalty. The automobile and pharmaceutical industries have the oligopoly characteristics of few sellers; entry barriers, and price leadership. The ice cream industry has monopolistic competition characteristics: many sellers, differentiated products, relatively easy entry and exit, considerable non-price competition, and some price controls.

89. (d) In the short run, while prices cover average variable costs, the producer will continue to supply product and cover at least some fixed costs. Economic cost is the income that an entity must provide in order to attract resource suppliers; when total revenue matches economic cost, the producer is earning a normal profit.

90. (d) Defining characteristics of a monopolistic competitive market include many sellers, differentiated (heterogeneous) products, relatively easy entry and exit, and considerable non-price competition (brand names and advertising). Economies of scale can exist with any market structure.

91. (c) Perfect competition results in the highest output at the lowest price compared to monopolies, oligopolies, and monopolistic competition. Diminishing returns can exist with any market structure. Characteristics of pure competition include low customer loyalty, perfect information, and few entry barriers.

92. (a) Masons likely will be able to increase their wages (prices) only by reducing supply (employment). Rather than changing size, employers may shift the capital-labor ratio. If the market starts in equilibrium, the only way that labor supplied will increase is if the wages decrease so that employers will hire more masons.

93. (a) An oligopoly is characterized by price leadership (mutual influence among industry firms on each others' prices) and interdependence on output decisions. Oligopolies typically have entry barriers as well as advertising. A monopoly has one seller of a product with no close substitutes. A natural monopoly exists when economic or technological conditions permit only one efficient supplier.

94. (a) Monopolistic competition characteristics include many sellers, differentiated products, relatively easy entry and exit, considerable non-price competition, and some price controls. Monopolies, natural monopolies, and oligopolies have substantial entry or exit barriers. Pure competition markets have homogeneous products.

95. (b) Characteristics of pure competition include low customer loyalty, few entry or exit barriers, many independent producers, perfect information, and homogeneous (standardized) products.

96. (e) A purely competitive market has the following characteristics: homogeneous products, few entry or exit barriers, many independent producers, and low customer loyalty (customers seek the lowest price without regard to the seller). A monopoly is characterized by one seller, a unique product without close substitutes, goodwill advertising, significant price control, and blocked entry. A natural monopoly is a monopoly due to economic or technical conditions permit only one efficient supplier. Monopolistic competition is characterized by a large number of sellers of differentiated products, relatively easy entry and exit, considerable non-price competition, and some price controls. An oligopoly is characterized by few sellers; entry barriers, and price leadership.

97. (b) A concentration ratio is the percentage of total market sales due to the four largest producers. The U.S. government uses (along with other tools) the concentration ratio to estimate the degree of monopoly power in a market. A high ratio indicates that few entities account for most sales, which is characteristic of a monopoly.

98. (c) An entry barrier is a prerequisite to entering a market. Entry barriers can include an absolute cost advantage, economies of scale, and customer loyalty. An example of an exit barrier is when a building owner must bring a restaurant up to current code before selling it or leasing to another party, but may continue to operate the restaurant in the building as it currently exists without renovation. A cartel is an illegal entity whose members collude. Collusion is the action of voluntarily limiting output to raise the market price. The taxi fare structure is set by government regulation and is not voluntary. A monopoly is a market structure with one seller of a unique product without close substitutes and blocked entry for other firms. While price controls are common in a monopoly, the taxi market doesn't have a single seller. Non-price competition has little to do with the costs that an entity must cover.

Measures

99. (a) Disposable income is personal income less personal income taxes and is divided among consumption spending, interest payments, and savings. Per-capita income is GDP divided by population, adjusted for inflation. Net domestic product (NDP) is GNP less depreciation. National income is NDP plus a country's net income earned abroad less indirect business taxes.

100. (b) Net domestic product is gross domestic product less depreciation. £5,000 − £600 = £4,400.

101. (c) National income is net domestic product plus a country's net income earned abroad less indirect business taxes. In other words, the sum of wages, interest, rent, and profits plus a country's net income earned abroad. £5,000 − £600 + £50 − £210 = £4,240.

102. (a) A nation's personal income is national income plus transfer payments (such as corporate profit distributions and social security benefits) less both corporate income taxes and undistributed profits and less social security contributions. While "national retirement plan" could describe the U.S. Social Security system, it also could describe the assorted defined benefit or deferred compensation arrangements that exist in the U.S. tax code: 401(k), etc. The editors advise candidates to assume that the examiners will make it clear if a plan is to be deemed the equivalent of social security in an exam question. £4,240 + £625 − (£60 + £25) − £0 = £4,780.

103. (b) Real per-capita output is gross domestic product divided by population, adjusted for inflation. £5,000,000 / 100,000 people = £50 / person.

Business Cycle

104. (e)   The business cycle trough is characterized by low levels of economic activity, underuse of resources (productive capacity), and investors unwilling to risk new investments in productive capacity. In the absence of inflation or deflation, purchasing power remains stable during a trough. Costs generally don't rise and shortages rarely occur during a trough because of the excess capacity.

Classical Economics

105. (c)   Under classical economic theory, full employment is an attribute of equilibrium; flexible wages allow self-correcting of shortages and surpluses in labor markets. Classical economic theory also assumes that flexible interest rates allow self-correcting equilibrium of savings vs. investments; flexible prices allow self-correcting of shortages and surpluses in product markets; and an increase in money leads to an increase in aggregate demand.

Keynesian Economics

106. (d)   Investment commonly is divided into three components: residential construction, inventories, and plant and equipment. The capital consumption allowance (or depreciation) is a negative component of plant and equipment investment.

Other Theories

107. (b)   Neo-Keynesian theory holds that fiscal policy influences economic activities, but excessive monetary growth leads to inflation. Supply-side theory holds that a progressive tax structure is a disincentive to increased investment. Cuts in taxes will produce a recovery due to an increase in aggregate demand and increased motivation for investment. Supply-side theory holds than increased income would result in the same aggregate tax revenues despite the lower tax rates, so spending cuts are not needed.

Inflation and Deflation

108. (b)   Inflation is an increase in the general level of prices. The consumer price index is a comparison of the price of items in a "typical" shopping cart to a base value. A Dow Jones index is a comparison of prices of various lists of stocks; the stocks are selected and the indices are complied by Dow Jones Indexes, an independent company that develops, maintains, and licenses market indices for investment products. The consumer confidence index is a comparison of a consumer assurance survey to a base consumer assurance survey.

Corporations, not the federal government, report corporate profits.

109. (b)   Inflation is an increase in price levels. Rising inflation is inflation increasing at a faster rate than previous increases. Price levels are related inversely to the purchasing power of money. Debtors benefit from inflation, as they pay debts with money that is worth less than it was when they received the loan. Those who are owed a specific amount of money (such as creditors, pensioners, and landlords) are harmed by inflation, as they receive repayment in money that is worth less than what they previously expected.

Employment

110. (b)   Cyclical unemployment occurs during low points in the economic cycle, when aggregate demand is less than aggregate labor supply. Structural unemployment is when aggregate labor demanded is equal to aggregate labor supplied, but the nature of the supply doesn't match the nature of the demand. Mismatches can occur in terms of skills, occupations, industries, or geographic locations.

Government

111. (b)   Real property taxes paid by landlords are indirect taxes to the residents; without the tax, residents would have lower rents. Social Security taxes paid by employees, real property taxes paid by homeowners, intangible property taxes paid by businesses, and income taxes paid by individuals are direct taxes.

112. (d)   Government transfer payments (such as welfare, Social Security benefits, unemployment compensation, etc.) redistribute income, thus they reallocate the consumption of goods in the private sector. Aggregate demand doesn't change; an aggregate shift of demand between the private and public sectors is possible, but less likely than the reallocation of consumption within the private sector. Reallocation is not to the public sector; private individuals still decide how the money is spent.

Direction of Trade

113. (e)   Comparative advantage is the lowest opportunity cost for production of a good. For one chip, opportunity costs are 0.0083 (15/1,800) and 0.004 (6/1,500) tons of beef for Argentina and Taiwan, respectively. In other words, Taiwan has the lowest opportunity cost for chips. For one ton of beef, opportunity costs are 120 (1,800/15) and 250 (1,500/6) chips for Argentina and Taiwan, respectively. By definition, comparative advantage cannot be held by the same country for all goods. Argentina has an absolute advantage in both beef and chip production; it produces both more beef (15 vs. 6 tons) and more chips (1,800 vs. 1,600 units) for each unit of resources.

114. (d)   In a free trade situation, a country tends to export those goods for which it has a comparative advantage. For one chip, opportunity costs are 0.0083 and 0.004 tons of beef for Argentina and Taiwan, respectively. Taiwan would specialize in chip production and import beef. Both countries benefit from free trade as specialization results in maximum total output.

115. (d)   For one ton of beef, opportunity costs are 120 (1,800/15) and 250 (1,500/6) chips for Argentina and Taiwan, respectively. The lowest price Argentina would accept for beef is 120 chips; if the price is lower, Argentina would make its own chips. The highest price Taiwan would pay for a ton of beef is 250 chips, because Taiwan can produce beef itself for that price. For one chip, opportunity costs are 0.0083 and 0.004 tons of beef for Argentina and Taiwan, respectively, so the price per chip would fall somewhere within this range.

Trade Barriers

116. (b)   An economic trading bloc such as the European Union, provides incentives for member nations to trade among themselves and, hence, discourages trade between member and nonmember nations. The European Union lifted tariffs and import quotas among its member nations, but imposed common tariffs on nonmember nations' goods. Foreign investment may be either encouraged or discouraged by a trading bloc. NAFTA is a trading bloc without a common currency.

117. (d)   Import tariffs on a product result in higher costs for the consumer of the imported product. As domestic producers have little incentive to lower prices, it also tends to result in higher profits for domestic producers and higher costs for the domestic product consumer. Hence, lower consumption of both domestic and imported versions of the product generally results from tariffs.

118. (b)   The comparative advantage theory holds that when each nation specialized in products for which it has the greatest comparative advantages, total world output is maximized. This specialization requires imports; specialization raises living standards as more goods are available. The U.S. can compete with nations that have lower labor costs because it has advantages in other production factors. Inefficiencies caused by trade barriers generally lead to greater unemployment eventually.

119. (c)   Import tariffs result in higher costs for consumers of the imported product. Quotas indirectly raise the price by decreasing the supply. As domestic producers have little incentive to lower prices, it also tends to result in higher profits for domestic producers and higher costs for the domestic product consumer. Short-run employment is likely to increase. The volume of international trade decreases as demand is supplied by domestic production.

Foreign Exchange

120. (a)   Purchasing power relates to measurements of inflation and deflation; parity relates to equivalence. The purchasing power parity theorem holds that the real price of the same good eventually will be the same, in different nations' currencies, as expressed in a common currency (converted at the current exchange rates), after adjustments for tariffs, transportation costs, etc. Purchasing power parity is dependent on floating exchange rates. Purchasing power parity doesn't affect currency valuation.

121. (b)   By buying pounds in the forward exchange market, any gain on the forward exchange contract offsets any loss from paying more dollars than expected to settle the debt. The second best answer is to sell dollars in the forward exchange market; this is not as good an answer, as it doesn't specify that pounds are purchased for the sale of dollars. Selling pounds (or buying dollars for pounds) in the forward exchange market would offset future exchange losses if Tog had a future receivable denominated in pounds.

122. (d)   Because the forward price is higher in the future, the dollar is at a premium in the forward market. (£135.3 − £132) / £132 / 60 days × 360 days = 15%.

123. (a)   Both the U.S. inflation and the increase in the dollar's comparative value cause the cost of imports, measured in pesos, to increase. Assume an original trade rate of 200 pesos for $1. After 5% U.S. inflation, the costs for what once cost $1 will be 210 pesos (200 × 1.05). As the dollar appreciates against the peso, more pesos will be needed to purchase dollars: the exchange rate will be 240 pesos (200 × 20%) to $1. Both factors combined result in 252 pesos (240 pesos × 1.05) to purchase what originally purchased $1 of goods. 252 pesos / 200 pesos = 126%, or an increase of about 25%.

124. (b) Each U.S. dollar now buys less Brazilian reals (BRL); Brazilian products will be more expensive for U.S. importers. The BRL appreciated against the U.S. dollar. Visitors will be able to purchase fewer products in Brazil with their U.S. dollars. U.S. exports to Brazil will tend to increase as they are cheaper in BRL than previously.

125. (c) A decline in the value of a currency relative to the currencies of a nation's trading partners generally causes an increase in exports, as the nation's goods are cheaper than before the decline. Exports, and hence, any trade deficit will tend to decrease. Foreign currencies would appreciate compared to the U.S. dollar.

126. (a) The cheaper yen makes Japanese exports relatively cheaper to foreign purchasers. The fall in the yen's value tends to reduce any deficit in the trade account in the balance of payments; it may not be eliminated entirely within a single year, as consumption habits are slow to change. Any surplus would tend to be increased.

127. (c) An overvalued exchange rate effectively imposes a tax on exports, as exports are higher priced to foreign purchasers. For instance, if the exchange rate is £1 for $5, although the true value is £1 for $4, American purchasers of British pottery will pay a 25% premium ($5/$4) and British purchasers of American lumber will get a 25% discount. An overvalued exchange rate affects both capital and trade flows: few purchasers of goods or investments will be willing to pay a premium and few sellers will be willing to accept a discount.

128. (c) Under current international agreements, foreign exchange rates are allowed to float; supply and demand for currencies set the exchange rates. Exporters and importers influence exchange rates only insofar as they affect supply and demand. Central banks may manage exchange rates temporarily, to maintain market stability, but such efforts rapidly become prohibitively expensive. The IMF resources are a currency pool available to cover member countries' short-term deficits in balance of payments.

129. (b) Under current international agreements, foreign exchange rates are allowed to float; supply and demand for currencies set the exchange rates. "Managed float" refers to central banks temporary management of exchange rates to maintain market stability; such efforts rapidly become prohibitively expensive. Exporters and importers influence exchange rates only insofar as they affect supply and demand. While the IMF's role is to cover short-term deficits in balance of payments and currencies

of nation's experiencing inflation tend to depreciate, neither of these are managed float.

130. (e) The AICPA's unofficial solution was answer (c); this was before answer (e) was added by Bisk Education editors. The editors believe all responses to the original question are incorrect, but that answer (a) was least incorrect. Generally, one currency will depreciate relative to another at a rate equivalent to the difference in their inflation rates. While inflation often is associated with expansion and deflation with recession, few economic theories correlate these events. No mention of inflation or deflation is made in this question. Assuming that inflation rates between the countries already is accounted for in their current exchange rates and the inflation rates do not change, generally no change is expected in the currency exchange rates. A deficit or surplus in the balance of payments is equalized with additional imports, exports, or reserve changes. Woostland's economy is in a recession, which is characterized by decreasing levels of economic activity, with contracting employment levels and building inventories. With Woostland's imports declining, Woostland consumers will have less need for Esland's currency ($E) to pay for those imports. If Woostland and Esland are exclusive trading partners, Esland's additional imports will come from Woostland. Esland will pay for those imports in $E (which is less desirable for Woostland suppliers) or Woostland's currency ($W). Thus, consumers will increase the demand for $W and decrease the demand for $E. Offsetting these forces, investment in Esland will appear attractive to holders of capital in Woostland. Capital holders will decrease the demand for $W and increase the demand for $E. Whether these conflicting forces will net to zero is indeterminable from the given information. Note: Due to the ambiguity with regard to inflation, the editors do not expect similar questions to appear on future exams. If you encounter a question during your exam that you believe is in error, notify the AICPA in accordance with the AICPA's publication, *Uniform CPA Examination Candidate Bulletin: Information for Applicants*. Bear in mind, approximately 20% of multiple choice questions are not scored.

131. (a) Purchases of products made in Japan will tend to create additional demand for Japanese yen to pay for purchases. The supply for yen will remain unaffected. The U.S. dollar will tend to depreciate compared to the yen, as there will be less demand for dollars.

Balance of Payments

132. (c)   In an expanding U.S. economy, there is increased demand for raw materials, so a nation exporting raw materials to the U.S. would benefit. Stable money supply increases during growth periods also tend to lower interest rates. Increases in U.S. food exports to a debtor nation would increase its debt. Increases in U.S. import tariffs and a U.S. economy in recession both would reduce exports to the U.S., leaving less money for debt service for a nation exporting to the U.S.

133. (c)   Currency devaluation makes a nation's exports cheaper in foreign markets, increasing exports and improving the balance of trade. Currency devaluation also may increase domestic inflation (money is worth less than it was before devaluation) and reduce foreign investment, as prices for foreign goods and investments higher priced (in terms of local currency).

134. (b)   High demand for foreign goods drives demand for foreign currency. High real interest rates, low inflation, and stable government make investment in a country attractive, fueling demand for its currency.

135. (c)   Flexible exchange rates automatically eliminate balance-of-payment deficits and surpluses. If U.S. exports to Japan exceed imports, the dollar is in greater demand to pay for exports; thus, the dollar becomes expensive relative to the yen, and demand for U.S. exports in Japan diminishes, eliminating the surplus. Adopting a common monetary unit or tight monetary policies are unusual measures. Taxing imports often strains international relations and leads to other nations imposing taxes on the taxing nation's exports; the end result may be increased deficits or surpluses.

136. (c)   The balance of payments (or trade balance) represents payments made between nations; transactions usually are classified into capital and current accounts. The current account involves the net trade of goods and services, net unilateral transfers (such as pensions and gifts), and investment payments and receipts (such as interest). The capital account involves capital transfers.

137. (b)   An increase in a balance of payments surplus or deficit reduction occurs when more money enters a nation than leaves it. Loans to Canadians by foreigners result in money entering Canada. Purchases by Canadians of foreign goods and dividends paid to foreigners are outflows of money.

138. (b)   The current account reflects goods and services, unilateral transfers, and investment payments and receipts (interest and dividends). $157K − $203K − $37K + $13K = $70,000. As more money for current account items left the nation than entered, there is a current account deficit. The capital account reflects domestic investments by foreigners and foreign investments by residents. $63K − $14K = $49,000. As less capital left the nation than entered, there is a capital account surplus.

PERFORMANCE BY SUBTOPICS

Each category below parallels a subtopic covered in Chapter 50. Record the number and percentage of questions you correctly answered in each subtopic area.

Overview

Question #	Correct	√
1		
# Questions	1	

Correct _____
% Correct _____

Demand

Question #	Correct	√
2		
3		
4		
5		
6		
# Questions	5	

Correct _____
% Correct _____

Supply

Question #	Correct	√
7		
8		
9		
10		
# Questions	4	

Correct _____
% Correct _____

Elasticity

Question #	Correct	√
11		
12		
13		
14		
# Questions	4	

Correct _____
% Correct _____

Market

Question #	Correct	√
15		
16		
17		
18		
19		
20		
# Questions	6	

Correct _____
% Correct _____

Utility

Question #	Correct	√
21		
22		
# Questions	2	

Correct _____
% Correct _____

Production & Costs

Question #	Correct	√
23		
24		
25		
26		
# Questions	4	

Correct _____
% Correct _____

Market Structure & Performance

Question #	Correct	√
27		
28		
29		
30		
31		
32		
33		
# Questions	7	

Correct _____
% Correct _____

Measures

Question #	Correct	√
34		
# Questions	1	

Correct _____
% Correct _____

Business Cycle

Question #	Correct	√
35		
36		
# Questions	2	

Correct _____
% Correct _____

Keynesian Economics

Question #	Correct	√
37		
38		
39		
40		
41		
# Questions	5	

Correct _____
% Correct _____

Money

Question #	Correct	√
42		
43		
44		
45		
# Questions	4	

Correct _____
% Correct _____

Inflation & Deflation

Question #	Correct	√
46		
# Questions	1	

Correct _____
% Correct _____

Employment

Question #	Correct	√
47		
# Questions	1	

Correct _____
% Correct _____

Government

Question #	Correct	√
48		
49		
50		
# Questions	3	

Correct _____
% Correct _____

Direction of Trade

Question #	Correct	√
51		
52		
# Questions	2	

Correct _____
% Correct _____

Trade Barriers

Question #	Correct	√
53		
# Questions	1	

Correct _____
% Correct _____

Foreign Exchange

Question #	Correct	√
54		
55		
56		
57		
# Questions	4	

Correct _____
% Correct _____

Balance of Payments

Question #	Correct	√
58		
59		
# Questions	2	

Correct _____
% Correct _____

Transfer Pricing

Question #	Correct	√
60		
# Questions	1	

Correct _____
% Correct _____

CHAPTER 51

FINANCIAL MANAGEMENT

EXAM COVERAGE: The *Financial Management* portion of the BEC section of the CPA exam is designated by the examiners to be 17 to 23 percent of the section's point value. Candidates should plan their use of study time accordingly. More information about the point value of various topics is included in the **Practical Advice** section of this volume.

CHAPTER 51

FINANCIAL MANAGEMENT

I. Overview

A. Business Objectives
A business' objectives is to maximize the wealth of its owners within the applicable legal and societal boundaries. This chapter mentions corporations for the sake of convenience; these principles apply to other entities as well.

1. **Managers' Objectives** Management is supposed to operate the business in the owners' best interests. There is the potential for divergence of goals between management and owners. In an effort to align management objectives with owners' interests, many corporations link managers' compensation to stock performance.

   a. **Diversification** Entrenched managers might view a risky venture in a different light than shareholders. Presumably, shareholders' portfolios are diversified, so that the risk of a venture at one corporation would be offset by a opposing risk at another corporation. Managers are not diversified, having planned on a high percentage of income from one business. In an effort to avoid risk to their jobs, managers conceivably would avoid ventures with a risk-reward ratio acceptable to shareholders. The potential for this situation is offset by the potential for replacement of entrenched management by mergers and acquisition, i.e., shareholders effectively replacing underperforming management (no matter how seemingly entrenched) through stock disposition.

   b. **Autonomy** In the case of a widely held corporation, management has considerable autonomy. This autonomy could translate into actions that, rather than maximizing shareholder wealth, merely keep shareholders satisfied while other goals were pursued: public service, employee benefits, high executive salaries, social change, etc. The long-term and indirect return on some actions may make it difficult to distinguish between these different action types.

   c. **Incentives** Linking management compensation to stock price performance can backfire, as management then has incentive to achieve merely the appearance of performance, i.e., deceptive or fraudulent financial reporting.

2. **Social Responsibility** Businesses with above-normal profit levels can devote resources to social projects; however, capital markets constrain such activities. Conventional wisdom dictates that an investor considering two otherwise equivalent businesses would choose the business with the shareholder-wealth focus rather than the social orientation. An alternative view is that by behaving in a socially responsible manner now, whether or not legal, businesses reduce their exposure to future liability; first, by producing a corporate culture where integrity is stressed; and, second, by avoiding the consequences of irresponsible actions (for instance, avoiding claims by consumers who were injured using a business' unsafe products). Two arguments against a corporation taking cost-increasing socially responsible actions are as follows.

   a. **Mandates Increase Effectiveness** Social responsibility actions, especially those that increase costs, are likely to be most effective if mandated. Mandated and enforced standards level the playing field, so that the cost of socially responsible behavior is spread relatively evenly among businesses. If not universally mandated, the actions are likely not to prove as effective.

b. **Owners' Benefit Equals Social Benefit** Within the constraints of legal activity, the same actions that maximize owners' wealth generally also benefit society. Insofar as ethical or socially approved activity may be more narrow than legal activity, this argument is questionable. This argument assumes that all socially detrimental behavior is illegal and businesses follow both the letter and spirit of the law.

    (1) **Efficiency** Stock price maximization requires efficient, low-cost operations (efficient service, adequate inventory, well-placed locations, etc.).

    (2) **Innovation** Stock price maximization requires development and production of products that consumers want so concern for owners' interests leads to new technology, new products, and new jobs.

3. **Performance Measures** To maximize shareholder wealth, management should concentrate on total return per share, rather than other measures. Thus, total return per share includes earnings per share (EPS) and stock value changes. If dividends and EPS are different, part of the stock value change is due to untransferred earnings, rather than performance. If dividends and EPS are the same, all of the stock value change is due to performance. Thus, total return usually is calculated in terms of the sum of dividends paid plus capital gains (or losses) to eliminate the effect of the transfer of assets.

a. **Profit Maximization** Maximization of earnings ignores the potential dilution of widespread ownership.

Example 1 ▶ Profit Maximization

> In year 1, Quest Company has 1 million shares outstanding and earned $2 million, or $2/share. In year 2, Quest issued another 2 million shares and earned $3 million, or $1/share.
>
> **Discussion:** Although profits increased, earning per share decreased. The original shareholders suffered earnings dilution.

b. **EPS Maximization** EPS maximization ignores the potential change in share value. Temporary EPS increases that cripple future earning potential might not be taken into account when comparing current performance.

Example 2 ▶ Total Return per Share

> In year 1, Pacific Company had 1 million shares outstanding and earned $2 million, or $2/share, manufacturing and selling widgets. Pacific's stock was $30/share at year-end. In year 2, Pacific earned $2 million after taxes and issued dividends for that amount. Although competitors invested in equipment to make gizmos, a substitute for widgets, Pacific didn't invest in any new equipment, preferring not to incur debt or issue new stock. At the end of year 2, it becomes apparent that demand for widgets is reduced sharply. Pacific's stock was $15/share at the end of year 2.
>
> **Required:** What is Pacific's total return per share in year 2?
>
> **Solution:**
>
>   Earnings per share = $2,000,000 / 1,000,000 shares = $2.00/share
>
>   Stock value change per share = $15.00/share – $30.00/share = ($15.00/share)
>
>   Total return per share = $2.00/share + ($15.00/share) = ($13.00/share)
>
> **Discussion:** Shareholder wealth (total return per share) declined over the year, despite positive earnings per share.

    c.   **Stock Value Factors** Maximization of earnings per share ignores the potential decrease in share value. Investors and potential investors value shares based on expected profitability, timing of cash flows, and degree of risk (or uncertainty). These attributes can be affected by several types of factors. Value depends on the expected usable (after-tax) income available to investors. As all important corporate decisions should be analyzed in terms of how a course of action will affect shareholder wealth, (in other words, earnings per share and stock price), it is important for management to know what determines stock prices.

Example 3 ▶ Leverage

> In year 1, Pacific Company had 1 million shares outstanding and earned $2.5 million before taxes, $1,750,000 after taxes, or $1.75/share. In year 2, Pacific earned $3 million before taxes and had a 30% marginal tax rate. At the beginning of year 2, Pacific issued 6% bonds with a $1 million face value, with no premium or discount. Pacific had a 30% marginal tax rate for both years.
>
> **Required:** What is Pacific's earnings per share in year 2?
>
> **Solution:** Earnings before taxes = $3,000,000 – ($1,000,000 × 6%) = $2,940,000
>
>   Earnings after taxes = $2,940,000 × (1 – 0.30) = $2,058,000
>
>   Earnings per share = $2,058,000 / 1,000,000 shares = $2.058
>
> **Discussion:** Profits increased and the number of shares remained the same, increasing the earnings per share. The difference in the interest rate paid on the debt and the return generated with the financed assets increased shareholders' return. If the interest rate paid on the debt was greater than the return generated with the financed assets, shareholders' returns would have decreased.

    (1)   **External Constraints** Societies make antitrust, employment, environmental, product safety, workplace safety, and other laws, regulations, and practices.

    (2)   **Strategic Policy Decisions** Management makes strategic policy decisions, or policies, such as those regarding dividends, degree of debt leverage, production methods, and types of goods produced.

    (3)   **Economic Activity** The level and nature of economic activity and corporate taxes.

    (4)   **Stock Market Conditions** To some extent, stock prices tend to move up and down collectively.

B.   Life Cycle
The life cycle of a product, industry, or entity can be described by four phases or stages: infancy, growth, maturity, and decline. Some models also include a fifth stage. The product life cycle stage influences whether a product should be harvested for cash or receive additional funding.

    1.   **Infancy** When a product is introduced initially, it has little direct competition, but also may have limited consumer acceptance, prompting promotional expenses (such as extensive advertising or free samples) to gain widespread acceptance. New products with the potential for success typically require substantial resources to establish the new product and the new market. This stage is also called the experimentation stage.

    2.   **Growth** In the growth or exploitation stage, sales increase dramatically. Above-normal profits attract direct competitors, who may be able to produce similar products without incurring the heavy R&D or promotional expenses that the first movers incurred. Profitable products in the growth cycle typically are able to generate cash, but significant resources might need to be reinvested to maintain the products' profitability.

3. **Maturity** In the maturity stage, sales may increase, but the rate of increase slows from the growth phase. Profits shrink as direct competition increases. Profitable products typically bring in more money than needed to maintain market share; this excess can be used to fund the next generation of products or pay dividend to investors. Unprofitable or low-margin products at this stage probably will never become particularly profitable; rather than generating excess cash, they tend to generate losses as the market size contracts and margins shrink.

4. **Decline** In the decline stage, sales decrease and losses occur as replacement products evolve.

C. **Financial Markets**
    Entities that want to borrow money connect with entities that want to invest money in financial markets. Corporations raise capital in two essential forms: debt and equity. Businesses typically raise capital to expand without raising the money from earnings. Expansion activities include building a new factory or increasing inventory. Some entities have income greater than current expenditures (expenditures used in this sense include expenses, capital investments, and dividend payments). Markets may be defined by type of security, customer, or location. Efficient financial markets allow rapid, low-cost transactions between borrowers and lenders; financial markets are as much a part of a developed country's infrastructure as roads and communication systems.

    1. **Physical Asset vs. Financial Asset Markets** Physical (or tangible or real) assets include real estate, grains, computers, etc. Financial assets are claims on assets; examples include stocks, bonds, warrants, options, notes, and mortgages.

    2. **Spot vs. Futures Markets** Spot markets are characterized by delivery within days; futures markets are for delivery at a future date.

    3. **Money vs. Capital Markets** Money markets are exchanges for short-term debt securities (less than 1 year). Capital markets exchange long-term debt and equity.

    4. **Debt vs. Equity Markets** Debt markets exchange bonds, notes, and loans. Equity markets exchange stock and other ownership interests.

    5. **Mortgage vs. Consumer Credit Markets** Loans secured by real estate (whether residential, commercial, industrial, or agricultural) comprise the mortgage markets. Consumer credit markets include loans on consumer goods, including education, vacations, and durables (such as cars or stereo systems). Typically, these debts are not secured by real estate.

    6. **World, National, Regional, or Local Markets** Markets may be categorized by location and scope, for instance, the European market.

    7. **Primary vs. Secondary Markets** Primary markets exchange newly issued securities. Secondary markets exchange securities that were issued previously.

D. **Financial Institutions**
    There are different means of transferring financial assets; the use of financial institutions is a common one. The entity seeking capital could be a business, a government, or a home purchaser. The entity providing capital could be a business, a government, or an individual saving for retirement, vacation, home, or education. For simplicity, the following paragraphs assume the capital-seeking entity is a corporation and the supplier (or saver) is a private individual.

    1. **Direct Transfers** Direct transfers or exchanges between two entities, such as a corporation and an individual. These transfers are typical of a closely held corporation's stock, employee stock purchase or stock bonus plan, or a dividend reinvestment plan (DRIP). A DRIP involves the corporation providing more shares of its stock (usually treasury stock) to shareholders, rather than cash, at the shareholder's option.

    2. **Facilitated Transfers** Indirect transfers of a corporation's securities and an individual's money through a middleman. A mortgage broker is such a middleman for mortgage

exchanges. An investment bank commonly serves as a middleman for the exchange of corporate securities. Investment banks commonly: (1) help corporations design securities with features that will attract investors; (2) buy these securities; (3) re-sell these securities to investors.

3. **Repackaged Transfers** Indirect transfers also can involve the exchange of corporations' securities and a financial intermediary's money and the financial intermediary's securities and individuals' money. This helps borrowers and savers (or investors) with amounts too small to otherwise buy or sell large issues, spread risk through diversification, and gain ancillary financial services (checking accounts and life insurance).

    a. **Banks** Banks capitalize large, diverse portfolios of loans and other assets with pooled deposits. The pooling function promotes liquidity; checking accounts usually have a high guarantee of liquidity, savings accounts less so. Banks have more experience in analyzing credit risk, establishing loans, and collection activity than most savers. Bank savers benefit by investing savings in accounts that are overall more liquid, better managed, and less risky than they would reasonably be able to get on individual loans to individual debtors. Bank borrowers benefit by obtaining more capital with less transaction costs than otherwise. The distinction between bank types are blurred from those prevalent in the past.

        (1) **Commercial Bank** Commercial banks historically provided checking services tailored to businesses.

        (2) **Savings & Loan (S&L)** Savings and loan associations (S&Ls) traditionally served individual savers and residential mortgage borrowers.

        (3) **Mutual Savings Bank** Historically, mutual saving banks were similar to S&Ls, except that they also lent to corporations.

        (4) **Credit Union** Traditionally, credit unions are cooperative associations with members (usually with some other commonality) instead of customers; deposits are accepted from and loans are made to members only.

        (5) **Pension Funds** Pension funds primarily are funded by employers and administered by trustees, historically the trust departments of commercial banks or insurance companies. Common pension investments include stocks, bonds, mortgages, and real estate.

    b. **Mutual Funds** Mutual funds are corporations that pool dollars from stockholders (savers) to invest, typically in debt and equity securities. Mutual funds attempt to reduce risk through professional management and diversification as well as lower costs through economies of scale. There are hundreds of funds with different goals, often characterized in terms of risk, return type, capital preservation or appreciation goals, type of investment, and liquidity. At one end of the scale are money market funds, which emphasize liquidity and capital preservation. At the other end of the scale, funds tend to focus on capital appreciation.

    c. **Insurance Companies** Insurance companies invest premiums and make payments to beneficiaries in the event of specified events: the insured's death, the insured's property's destruction, etc.

    d. **Financial Service Corporations** Deregulation has diminished the distinction between types of financial institutions, resulting in financial service corporations such as Merrill Lynch.

4. **Securities Markets** The price of each stock, and correspondingly, the value of a corporation is set in the stock market. Generally, corporate bonds are traded less frequently than stocks.

a. **Organized Exchanges** Organized exchanges, such as the New York Stock Exchange (NYSE), have members and governing bodies. Membership commonly is referred to as a **seat** on the exchange. **Listed stocks** are those stocks traded on an organized exchange. Originally, brokers verbally auctioned shares while located in the same physical marketplace. Now, exchanges have specialist members who keep an inventory of shares of stocks in which they specialize. If buy orders arrive when no sell orders arrive, some shares are sold from this inventory; if sell orders arrive when no buy orders arrive, some shares are bought for this inventory. The specialists set bid prices (the price at which the specialist will buy) and asked prices (the price at which the specialist will sell) at levels that will keep the inventory in balance. If large number of orders arrive without offsetting orders, the specialist will raise or lower these prices to balance the inventory. Refinements allow the market to absorb large blocks of securities (new issues or mutual fund re-allocation) with a minimum of stress.

b. **Over-the-Counter (OTC) Markets** The OTC markets deal with less frequently traded stock or bonds. Matching the few buy and sell orders within a reasonable time is difficult, so inventories are essential. Relatively few dealers who hold OTC securities are said to **make a market** in those securities. Brokers act as agents in bringing investors together with these dealers. Corporate bonds tend to be traded in large lots among relatively few holders (large financial institutions) facilitating their trade in the OTC market.

E. Interest Rates

The price for borrowed capital is interest. The price for equity capital is dividends and capital gains. Economists usually define the real interest rate as the interest rate on a default-free U.S. Treasury security with zero inflation present.

1. **Time Preferences for Consumption** Consumers' time preferences establish the quantity of consumption they are willing to defer (save) at different levels of interest offered by borrowers. Borrowers' expected rate of return sets the upper limit on the rate they can pay for savings. Savers will save more if borrowers offer higher interest rates; borrowers will borrow more if savers will accept a lower return.

2. **Default Risk** The default risk, or risk that a borrower will not pay the interest or principal, affects the interest rate. U.S. Treasury bonds have no default risk; thus, on an after-tax basis, they have the lowest interest rates in the United States. The default risk premium for a given security is the difference between the security rate and the U.S. Treasury bond rate.

3. **Inflation** To offset the impact of inflation, investors require an inflation premium added to the rate they would have charged in the absence of inflation. The inflation rate used to determine the premium is the expected average future inflation rate over the life of the security, not past rates. Expectations for future inflation are influenced by rates in the recent past. Although inflation rates might be low currently, memories of recent high inflation might keep interest rates high.

4. **Liquidity** A security that can be converted to cash on short notice is highly *liquid*. Investors add a liquidity premium to bonds without an active secondary market.

5. **Term Structure of Interest Rates** The inflation rate rarely remains constant. If the inflation rate is expected to decrease, for instance, over a three-year period, the interest rate on a one-year bond is expected to be greater than the interest rate on a three-year bond; in other words, the yield-to-maturity curve points down. This is illustrated by Y_d in Exhibit 1. If the inflation rate is expected to increase, for instance, over a three-year period, the interest rate on a one-year bond is expected to be less than the interest rate on a three-year bond; in other words, the yield curve points up. This is illustrated by Y_i in Exhibit 1.

Exhibit 1 ▶ Yield-to-Maturity Curves With Different Inflation Expectations

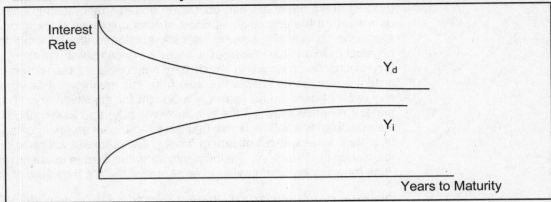

6. **Maturity Risk Premium** If investors expected the inflation rate to remain constant in the future, a horizontal yield curve initially might seem reasonable. All long-term bonds have an element of risk called interest rate risk, or the risk that a better rate of interest will be available in the future. The longer the term of the bond, the greater this risk, and thus, the greater the maturity risk premium. The effect of a maturity risk premium is to have higher interest rates on long-term bonds as opposed to comparable short-term bonds.

7. **Risk Premium** The risk premium generally is considered to be the sum of the default risk premium and the maturity risk premium. Generally it is easier to predict that a corporation will be able to repay short-term debt than long-term debt; thus, default premiums increase, along with maturity premiums, as the bond maturity lengthens.

8. **Federal Reserve Policy** If the Fed wants to stimulate economic activity, it frequently increases the money supply growth rate. This initially may lower interest rates, but also may lead to an increase in the expected inflation rates, causing nominal interest rates to increase. During periods of active Fed intervention, the yield curve tends to be distorted.

9. **Normal Yield** In a stable economy (where inflation fluctuates in a low narrow range, expected future inflation rates are roughly equal to current rates, and no active invention by the Fed occurs), the yield curve is relatively low and generally has a slight upward slope reflecting maturity effects. This yield curve is called normal. Downward sloping yield curves commonly are called inverted or abnormal, despite frequent occurrence.

10. **Recession** During recessions, demand for money falls while the Fed tends to increase the money supply in order to stimulate the economy, resulting in the tendency of interest rates to decline. Short-term rates fall more rapidly than long-term rates because (a) the Fed mainly operates in short-term markets and (b) long-term rates reflect the expected average inflation over decades and expectations regarding future inflation rates don't shift dramatically during a relatively short recession.

11. **Business Decisions** Even given the difficulty of predicting interest rate levels, it is easy to predict that interest rates will fluctuate. Given this probable fluctuation, prudent financial management dictates a mixture of long- and short-term debt as well as equity financing, such that a business can survive in most interest rate environments. Optimal financial management depends, in part, on a business's assets. The more liquid the assets (the more likely that assets could be converted into cash for debt repayment at minimal loss), the more feasible it is to use large amounts of short-term debt.

12. **Stock Prices** Interest rates directly affect profits of corporations that borrow, thus affecting stock prices. Because of competition in the securities markets between stocks and bonds, higher return rates mean that bonds may be more attractive to investors than stocks, so rising interest rates tend to depress stock prices.

II. Time Value of Money

A. Future Value of an Amount

Due to the time value of money, a dollar a year from now is worth less than a dollar today. The future value of a lump-sum amount (and other time values) may be determined by using factors from pre-calculated tables. The CPA exam historically provided an assortment of time value factors, rather than complete tables, and requires candidates to determine the correct factor to use in a given situation. The formula (used to develop the factors) is itself not tested on the CPA exam. Selection, manipulation, and use of the correct factor is tested. (See Appendix D for present value and future value tables as well as additional examples.)

Example 4 ▶ Future Value of an Amount (Lump-Sum)

Sam deposits $1,000 in a CD at the bank for two years at 5%. The future value interest factor for 2 years at 5% (FVIF 2, 5%) is 1.1025.

Required: What will be the total of the CD at maturity?

Solution: FV = PV × FVIF (2, 5%) = $1,000 × 1.1025 = $1,102.50

Proof: Value at end of first year   = principal + interest = $1,000 + $1,000 × .05 = $1,050.00
Value at end of second year = principal + interest = $1,050 + $1,050 × .05 = $1,102.50

B. Present Value of a Future Amount

This looks at the future value of money from a slightly different perspective. Note that present value factors may be derived from future value factors by simple algebraic manipulation. Manipulation of the figures from a present value table will provide future values and vice versa. A similar manipulation is also possible with annuity factors.

Example 5 ▶ Present Value of an Amount

Patricia wants to deposit enough money in a CD at the bank at 5% to have $5,000 in 2 years. The future value interest factor for 2 years at 5% (FVIF 2, 5%) is 1.1025. The present value interest factor for 2 years at 5% (PVIF 2, 5%) is 1 / 1.1025 = 0.907029.

Required: What amount will Patricia need to deposit now?

Solution: PV = FV × PVIF (2, 5%) = $5,000 × 0.907029 = $4,535 (rounded)

Proof: Value at end of first year   = principal + interest = $4,535 + $4,535 × .05 = $4,761.75
Value at end of second year = principal + interest = $4,762 + $4,762 × .05 = $5,000.10

C. Annuities

An annuity is a series of payments of a fixed amount for a specified number of years. With an **ordinary** annuity (an annuity in **arrears**) the payment occurs at the **end** of the year. With an annuity **due** (an annuity in **advance**) the payment is made at the **beginning** of the year.

1. **Ordinary Annuities** The present and future value factors for ordinary annuities are applied in a manner similar to the factors for lump-sum payments.

2. **Annuities Due** The factors used for ordinary annuities can be used for annuities in advance, with a slight modification.

   a. **Future Value of an Annuity Due** Value of annuity in advance of amount A at the end of n periods = Value of ordinary annuity for (n + 1) periods A.

   b. **Present Value of an Annuity Due** Present value of annuity in advance of amount A for n periods = Present value of ordinary annuity for (n − 1) periods + A.

3. **Perpetuity** A perpetuity, a special instance of annuity, continues infinitely. The effect of each additional payment far in the future decreases to a point were the impact of individual future

payments approaches zero, or in other words, is imperceptible. Therefore, the present value of a perpetuity is the payment divided by the discount rate.

D.   Non-Annual Compounding Periods
For compounding periods other than a year, the interest rate and the number of periods to get a factor are modified appropriately. In the case of quarterly compounding, the present value factor for 4 times the number of periods and one-quarter of the interest rate is used. In the case of monthly compounding, the present value factor for 12 times the number of periods and one-twelfth of the interest rate is used.

Example 6 ▶ Present Value of an Annuity & a Single Sum Combined

Rick won $160,000 in a state lottery. He will receive an immediate payment of $30,000, three annual payments of $30,000 (at the end of each year), and a payment of $40,000 at the end of the fourth year. Rick only has the following time value factors.

Ordinary annuities: PVIFA (3 years, 8%) = 2.577097   PVIFA (4 years, 8%) = 3.312127
Annuities due: PVIFAA (4 years, 8%) = 3.577097   PVIFAA (5 years, 8%) = 4.312127

Required: Determine the present value of Rick's payments, discounted at a rate of 8%, using only: (A) the ordinary annuity factors, and (B) the annuity due factors.

Solution A: Add together the value of the immediate payment, the present value of an annuity of $30,000 for three years, and the present value of one $40,000 payment at the end of four years. (The present value of the immediate payment is its face value.)

PV = $30,000 + $30,000 × PVIFA (3, 8%) + $40,000 × [PVIFA (4, 8%) − PVIFA (3, 8%)]
   = $30,000 + $30,000 × 2.577097 + $40,000 × (3.312127 − 2.577097)
   = $30,000 + $30,000 × 2.577097 + $40,000 × 0.735030
   = $30,000 + $77,313 + $29,401 = $136,714

Solution B: Add together the present value of an annuity due of $30,000 for five years and the present value of one $10,000 payment at the beginning of the fifth year. (The end of the fourth year is the same as the beginning of the fifth year.)

PV = $30,000 × PVIFAA (5, 8%) + $10,000 × [PVIFAA (5, 8%) − PVIFAA (4, 8%)]
   = $30,000 × 4.312127 + $10,000 × 0.735030 = $129,364 + $7,350 = $136,714

Note: PVIF (4 years, 8%) = 0.735030. This is shown in Appendix D, Table 2, *Present Value of $1*. This is calculated here from the difference between the annuity factors of different lengths of time. (See Solution A.)

III.   Security Valuation

A.   Bond Valuation
Bonds represent the right to receive any interest payments specified in the bond and the return of principal upon maturity.

1.   **Definitions** The bond's stated face value or **par value** is to be repaid at a specified future date, called the **maturity date.** Typically, par value is $1,000. The **coupon interest rate,** or stated interest rate, is the rate the issuer uses to calculate the interest payments (interest payments equal the par value times the coupon interest rate). Bonds are called new issues for about two weeks after they have been issued. After that, the bond is called an **outstanding** or **seasoned** issue.

2.   **Basic Bond Valuation Model** Bonds promise the payment of a specified amount of interest for a stated number of years and for the repayment of the par value at the maturity date. In other words, a bond is an annuity plus a lump sum; barring default, its value is the present value of the specified payment stream. Bondholders have capital losses or gains when interest rates change.

Exhibit 2 ▶ Model of Bond Value

$$\text{Bond Value} = \text{Present value of principal payment (lump sum)} + \text{Present value of interest payments (annuity)}$$

Example 7 ▶ Bond Value

Master Corporation owns a $1,000 par value bond issued by Dimity Corporation that pays interest annually based on a 12% coupon interest rate. The bond is due in 4 years. Currently, after factoring in liquidity, risk, and maturity premiums, Master estimates the effective interest rate on the bond at 10%.

Required: What is the bond's current value (BV_4), rounded to the nearest whole dollar?

Solution: BV_4 = Present value of principal payment + Present value of interest payments

Future value of principal payment = FV(principal) = $1,000

Future value of interest payments = FV(interest) = $1,000 × 12% = $120

BV_4 = FV(principal) × PVIF(4 years, 10%) + FV(interest) × PVIFA(4 years, 10%)

BV_4 = ($1,000 × 0.6830) + ($120 × 3.1699) = $683 + $380 = $1,063

Discussion: Because the stated interest rate is higher than the effective interest rate, the value of the bond is higher than its par value. If Master were to sell the bond now, it could command a premium over its par value of $63, assuming Master's evaluation of the effective interest rate corresponds to the bond purchaser's evaluation.

Note: PVIF(4 years, 10%) = 0.6830; PVIFA(4 years, 10%) = 3.1699

a. **Premiums & Discounts** As potential bond purchasers will not buy bonds at below market rates and bond issuers will not issue bonds at more than market rates, all bonds are discounted or awarded a premium until effective interest rates match market rates. If a 12% bond is available when the market rate is 10%, a premium will be awarded to the 12% bond, such that the effective interest rate is 10%.

Example 8 ▶ Interest Rate Change & Discount

Master Corporation bought, for $1,000, a $1,000 par value bond issued by Dimity Corporation that pays interest annually based on a 12% coupon interest rate. The bond then was due in 5 years. The next day, market interest rates rose to 15%.

Required: What are the bond's new value (BV_5) and discount or premium, rounded to the nearest whole dollar?

Solution: BV_5 = Present value of principal + Present value of interest payments

Future value of principal payment = FV(principal) = $1,000

Future value of interest payments = FV(interest) = $1,000 × 12% = $120

BV_5 = FV(principal) × PVIF(5 years, 15%) + FV(interest) × PVIFA(5 years, 15%)

BV_5 = ($1,000 × 0.497177) + ($120 × 3.352155) = $497 + $402 = $899

Discussion: Because the stated interest rate (12%) is lower than the market (effective interest) rate, the value of the bond is lower than its par value; in other words, there is a discount. If Master were to sell the bond now, it would have to accept a discount of $1,000 − $899 = $101.

Note: PVIF(5 years, 15%) = 0.497177; PVIFA(5 years, 15%) = 3.352155

b. **Maturity Date** As the maturity date approaches, the present value factor for the principal approaches 1. After the next-to-last interest payment is made, the interest payment stream turns into a single sum, with a present value approaching 1. In other words, as the maturity date draws near, the value of the bond approaches the par value plus the final interest payment, barring default by the issuer.

Example 9 ▶ Total Return on Bond Investment

One year ago, Master Corporation bought a $1,000 par value five-year bond issued by Dimity Corporation that pays interest annually based on a 12% coupon interest rate. Master paid $1,075 for the bond. The bond matures in four more years. The market interest rate was 10% when the bond was purchased as well as currently.

Required: What is the total rate of return on this investment?

Solution: BV_4 = Present value of principal + Present value of interest payments

BV_4 = FV(principal) × PVIF(4 years, 10%) + FV(interest) × PVIFA(4 years, 10%)

BV_4 = ($1,000 × 0.6830) + ($120 × 3.1699) = $683 + $380 = $1,063

Return from interest (current yield) = $120/$1,075	11.2%
Return from capital gain/loss = ($12)/$1,075	(1.1)
Total rate of return on investment	10.1%

Discussion: The value of the bond has decreased by ($1,075 − $1,063 =) $12, bringing the total return (approximately 10%) on the bond in line with the prevailing market interest rate.

Note: PVIF(4 years, 10%) = 0.6830; PVIFA(4 years, 10%) = 3.1699

3. **Yield to Maturity (YTM)** The yield to maturity or rate of return on a bond is the effective, or real, rate of interest the bondholder earns, as opposed to the stated rate.

Example 10 ▶ Yield to Maturity

Gnome Corporation bought, for $1,092, a $1,000 par value bond issued by Elf Corporation that pays interest annually based on a coupon interest rate of 10%. The bond will mature in 6 years.

Required: What is the yield to maturity, rounded to the nearest whole percentage?

Solution: The yield to maturity, or effective interest rate, is the total return earned if the bond is purchased and held to maturity. Let k be the unknown interest rate. Find the present value factors (by trial and error) that result in the future value of the lump sum payment and annuity stream equaling the current price ($1,092). As the purchase price includes a premium, the effective interest rate must be below 10%.

$1,092 = Present value of principal payment + Present value of interest payments

$1,092 = FV(principal) × PVIF(6 years, k) + FV(interest) × PVIFA(6 years, k)

$1,092 = [$1,000 × PVIF(6 years, k)] + [$100 × PVIFA(6 years, k)]

Trial of 6%: ($1,000 × 0.7050) + ($100 × 4.9173) = $705 + $492 = $1,197 (k > 6%)

Trial of 9%: ($1,000 × 0.5963) + ($100 × 4.4859) = $596 + $449 = $1,045 (k < 9%)

Trial of 8%: ($1,000 × 0.6302) + ($100 × 4.6229) = $630 + $462 = $1,092 (k = 8%)

Discussion: When the present value of the bond is greater than the trial amount, the rate used for a trial is too low; when the present value of the bond is less than the trial amount, the rate used for a trial is too high. When the present value of the bond is the same as the trial amount, the rate used is the yield to maturity; in this case, 8%.

Note: PVIF(6, 6%) = 0.7050; PVIFA(6, 6%) = 4.9173   PVIF(6, 8%) = 0.6302; PVIFA(6, 8%) = 4.6229

PVIF(6, 7%) = 0.6663; PVIFA(6, 7%) = 4.7665   PVIF(6, 9%) = 0.5963; PVIFA(6, 9%) = 4.4859

4. **Yield to Call (YTC)** If current market rates are below an outstanding callable bond's stated rate, the bond is likely to be called. For a callable bond, the yield to maturity is not as significant as the yield to call. Instead of the maturity date, the yield to call calculation uses the first date the corporation could call the bond.

5. **Interest Rate Risk** As interest rates change, the values of outstanding bonds also fluctuate. Bondholder's exposure to interest rate risk is higher on bonds with long maturities than those with comparatively short maturities. All else being equal, the longer the bond maturity, the greater the price change in response to a given change in interest rates.

6. **Semiannual Compounding** Most bonds pay interest semiannually, rather than annually. The same tables can be used as for annual payments, after adjusting. Bear in mind that the present value tables have factors for specified interest rates for specified periods, not necessarily years. For a 10-year bond that pays interest semiannually, figuring a present value for the interest payments at 10% effective interest rate uses the factor for 20 periods at 5% interest.

7. **Interest Rate Changes** The value of bonds (what buyers would pay) increases as interest rates fall and decreases as interest rates rise.

B. **Stock Valuation**

Common stock represents a right to receive a corporation's dividends (if declared) and any residual assets upon dissolution. While most stock is not purchased in expectation of dissolution, shareholders can sell the stock to other investors, resulting in a comparable event from the former shareholder's viewpoint. If stock is sold at a price higher than was paid for it, the result is a capital gain; the opposite is a capital loss. If the current stock valuation is different from the purchase price, but the shareholder hasn't sold the stock, the capital gain or loss is unrealized.

1. **Expected Total Return** The expected total return is the expected dividend yield plus the expected capital gain (or loss) yield. Like bonds, stock values are determined as the present value of a stream of cash flows; the basic equation is the same for stock valuation as for bond valuation.

a. **Buy & Hold Infinitely** If the shareholder doesn't expect ever to sell the stock, the value would be the present value of an infinite stream of cash flows (dividend payments).

b. **Buy & Resell** If the shareholder plans to sell the stock, the value still would be the present value of an infinite stream of cash flows (dividend payments), because the value that the subsequent purchaser would place on the stock would be the present value of an infinite stream of cash flows. The price at any sale date would be the then-current present value of the remaining infinite stream of cash flows.

c. **Bigger Fool Theory** After analyzing a stock's value and concluding that the stock's market price exceeds the present value of expected dividends (a reasonable value), a purchaser may buy the stock anyway. This purchaser may reason that while s/he is a fool to buy the stock at an excessive price, there will be a bigger fool who subsequently will buy it at a more excessive price.

2. **Constant Growth Stock** The present value of a constant growth stock is the next annual dividend divided by the difference between the discount rate and the growth rate. For a stock with a constant rate of growth, the current stock value (PV_0) is the payment stream that starts with a dividend (d_1) a year from now (the current date being year 0) and increasing the dividend amount by a growth factor (g), discounted at a minimum acceptable rate of return (k). Unless the discount rate (k) is greater than the growth factor (g), this formula is meaningless. This model is named after Myron J. Gordon, who contributed to its development and dissemination.

Exhibit 3 ▶ Gordon Model of Present Value of a Constant Growth Stock

$$PV_0 = d_1 / (k - g)$$

3. **Zero Growth Stock** The term **zero growth stock** describes a stock with constant dividends. In this case, the formula is simplified, as one of the elements is zero. Such a stock has the characteristics of a perpetuity. The present value of a perpetuity is the dividends (d) divided by the discount rate (k).

Example 11 ▶ Infinity Assumption

R. Son, CPA, is trying to explain stock valuation based on the present value of an infinite stream of dividends to her client, Ed Mote. Mote is uncomfortable with the notion of a valuation based on an infinite payment stream. Under consideration is a stock with a market price of $50 and a zero growth rate. The stock is expected to pay annual dividends at $2.00. Ed Mote expects a 3% rate of return on investment. Inflation is expected to remain at zero.

Required: Calculate the payment stream present value at 30, 40, 50, and 100 years. Determine if the stock's market price is a bargain when compared to the present value of the expected dividend payments, in light of the assumptions about the expected dividends and rate of return.

Solution: Let d_1 stand for dividends in the upcoming year (assuming year-end payment), n = the number of years, PV_n stand for the present value calculated using n periods; and k stand for the discount rate (or minimum acceptable rate of return on the stock).

Time Period	Dividend Stream Valuation Using Different Limits
PV formula (n = ∞)	$PV_\infty = d_1 / k = \$2 / 0.03 = \$66.67$
PV formula (n = other)	$PV_n = d_1 \times$ PVIFA (n years, 3%)
30 years	$PV_{30} = \$2 \times$ PVIFA (30 years, 3%) = $2 × 19.60044 = $39.20
40 years	$PV_{40} = \$2 \times$ PVIFA (40 years, 3%) = $2 × 23.1477 = $46.30
50 years	$PV_{50} = \$2 \times$ PVIFA (50 years, 3%) = $2 × 25.72976 = $51.46
100 years	$PV_{100} = \$2 \times$ PVIFA (100 years, 3%) = $2 × 31.59891 = $63.20

Discussion: The difference between the 30-year and 40-year valuation is $7.10; difference between the 40-year and 50-year valuation is smaller, $5.16. The difference between the 50-year and 100-year valuation ($11.74) is quite small, considering the doubled time period (and hence doubled amount of payments). The payments in the far future have little impact on the present value. The present value of the expected dividend payment is in excess of the market price, making this stock a bargain.

Note: PVIFA(30 years, 3%) = 19.60044; PVIFA(40 years, 3%) = 23.11477

4. **Uneven Growth Stock** While the value of a zero or constant growth stock is calculated readily, uneven growth is more realistic. The present value of an uneven growth stock is the sum of a collection of present values of the uneven dividend payments. A present value formula must be tailored specifically to cope with a given situation.

Example 12 ▸ Uneven Growth Stock Valuation

In January, year 1, Nile Corporation's dividend forecast is as follows: year 1 and year 2, 0; year 3, $5/share; year 4 and year 5, 15% growth; year 6 and year 7, 30% growth; thereafter, 7% growth. Dividends are expected to be paid at year end.

Required: Determine the stock's value (rounded to the nearest dollar) as the present value of the expected dividend payments using a 10% rate of return on investment in January, year 1.

Solution: Let d_1, d_2, d_3,...d_n stand for dividends in years 1, 2, 3,...n; n = the number of years; g_1, g_2, g_3,...g_n stand for growth in years 1, 2, 3,...n; k stand for the discount rate (or minimum acceptable rate of return on the stock); PV_0, = the present value of the dividend stream in January, year 1 (or year 0); $PV(d_n)$ = the present value of the nth dividend; and s_7 = the stock value at year 7.

Dividend Calculation

$d_1 = d_2 = \$0$; $d_3 = \$5$; $d_4 = \$5 \times 1.15 = \$5.75$; $d_5 = \$5.75 \times 1.15 = \$6.61$

$d_6 = \$6.61 \times 1.30 = \$8.59$; $d_7 = \$8.59 \times 1.30 = \$11.17$; $d_8 = \$11.17 \times 1.07 = \$11.95$

Present Value of Expected Dividends

$PV(d_1) = PV(d_2) = \$0$

$PV(d_3) = d_3 \times PVIF$ (3 years, 10%) = $\$5 \times 0.751315 = \$3.76$

$PV(d_4) = d_4 \times PVIF$ (4 years, 10%) = $\$5.75 \times 0.683013 = \$3.93$

$PV(d_5) = d_5 \times PVIF$ (5 years, 10%) = $\$6.61 \times 0.620921 = \$4.10$

$PV(d_6) = d_6 \times PVIF$ (6 years, 10%) = $\$8.59 \times 0.564474 = \$4.85$

$PV(d_7) = d_7 \times PVIF$ (7 years, 10%) = $\$11.17 \times 0.513158 = \$5.73$

$s_7 = (d_8) / (k - g) = \$11.95 / (10\% - 7\%) = \$398.33$; $s_7 = d_{8+}$

$PV(d_{8+}) = PV(d_{8+})$ at year 7 $\times$ PVIF (7 years, 10%) = $\$398.33 \times 0.513158 = \$204.41$

$PV_0 = PV(d_1) + PV(d_2) + PV(d_3) + PV(d_4) + PV(d_5) + PV(d_6) + PV(d_7) + PV(d_{8+})$

$PV_0 = \$0 + \$0 + \$3.76 + \$3.93 + \$4.10 + \$4.85 + \$5.73 + \$204.41 = \$226.78$

Discussion: Differing payments of the expected stream are separated. Present values are determined for different groups and added together. The stock's value is $227.

Note: PVIF(3 years, 10%) = 0.751315; PVIF(4 years, 10%) = 0.683013

5. **Actual Prices & Returns** The actual total return is the actual dividend yield plus the actual capital gain (or loss) yield. Differences between expected and realized prices and returns can be significant.

C. **Risk & Rates of Return**
Risk is related to variability of expected future returns. Given that rational investors usually hold portfolios of assets, they generally are concerned primarily with portfolio risk rather than any one asset's risk. Beta coefficients measure the tendency of stock prices to change with the market changes. A high-beta stock is more volatile than the market average; a low-beta stock is less volatile than the market average. By definition, an average stock has a beta coefficient equal to 1.0. The required rate of return on a stock consists of the rate for a "riskless" bond plus a risk premium based on the stock's beta coefficient. Stocks typically are in equilibrium, meaning their expected and required rate of returns are equal. Stock prices may change due to several factors, including: a riskless rate change due to changes in anticipated inflation, a stock's beta coefficient changing, or expected growth rate fluctuations.

Example 13 ▶ Probability Distribution & Expected Rate of Return

The following rates of return relate to an Internet advertising provider and a local electric company. Gotchya.com has cyclical sales and wide swings in profitability. Flatbush Power operates in a relatively stable and predictable environment.

State of Economy	Probability of State Occurrence	Rate of Return Under State	
		Gotchya.com	Flatbush Power
Boom	0.3	90%	20%
Typical (moderate growth)	0.4	15	15
Recession	0.3	–60	10

Required: Determine the stocks' expected rate of return.

Solution: While the average return for both stocks is 15%, there is a wider range of probable returns for Gotchya than for Flatbush.

State (Probability)	Rate of Return Under State		Product	
	Gotchya.com	Flatbush Power	Gotchya.com	Flatbush Power
Boom (0.3)	90%	20%	27%	6%
Typical (0.4)	15	15	6	6
Recession (0.3)	–60	10	–18	3
Sum (1.0)			15%	15%

Discussion: Graphing the possible outcomes provides a picture of their variability. The height of each bar signifies the probability of the occurrence of a given outcome.

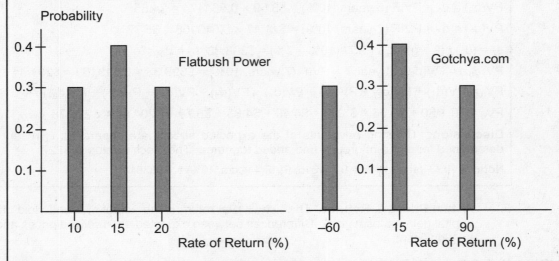

Note: In this example, the economy only has three states: boom, typical, and recession. A continuous range of activity, with more refined expectations about rates of return, is more realistic.

1. **Expected Rate of Return** The expected rate of return is the weighted average of outcomes; in other words, the sum of each possible outcome multiplied by its probability. An event's probability is the chance of its occurrence. A probability distribution is a listing of all possible events and their probabilities, or chances of occurrence. By definition, the probabilities in a probability distribution must total 100%; if not: (1) the listing is not a probability distribution; and (2) either all possible events are not listed or their probabilities are incorrect.

2. **Risk Definition** Risk is exposure to some unfavorable event. There are two broad categories of risk connected with stocks: market risk and company-specific risk. Since rational investors diversify, minimizing company-specific risk, the relevant risk for stock investment decisions is market risk, which is measured by the beta coefficient (commonly abbreviated as beta). In this chapter, whenever risk is unspecified, it means market risk.

a. **Market Risk** Market risk cannot be eliminated by diversification; it can be eliminated only by remaining out of the market. Market risk is caused by change in the stock market at large. For instance, market risk includes the risk that interest rates will rise, lowering all stock prices. Market risk also is called nondiversifiable risk or systematic risk.

b. **Company-Specific Risk** Company-specific risk is the risk that any one company will suffer losses. For instance, a computer chip manufacturer may have risk that its competitors will find a significantly cheaper production technology, that its major customers will declare bankruptcy, that its plant will be destroyed by a hurricane, or that its officers will embezzle. Company-specific risk can be eliminated by holding a diversified portfolio. Company-specific risk also is called diversifiable risk or unsystematic risk.

3. **Risk Measurement** The standard deviation of a continuous probability distribution is used as a measure of a stock's risk. The tighter that the probability distribution is for an investment, the more likely that the actual outcome will be close to the expected value, and thus, the less risky the investment is.

Exhibit 4 ▶ Continuous Probability Distribution

Graphing the possible outcomes of a continuous range of activity provides a more realistic picture of variability. Instead of graphing a distribution with only three possible outcomes, a graph of 1,000 outcomes, for instance, would provide a picture that approaches that of a continuous range. In this graph, the assumptions are changed from those in Example 13 to increased number of outcomes and more refined expectations.

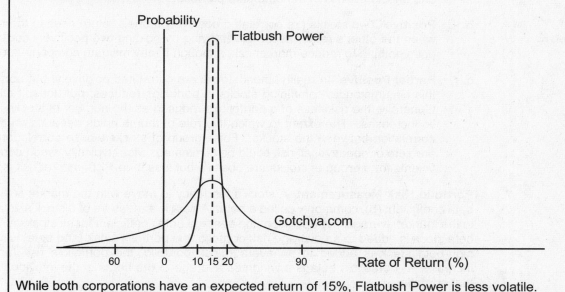

While both corporations have an expected return of 15%, Flatbush Power is less volatile.

4. **Risk Aversion** Most investors are risk averse; given the same expected rate of return from two investments, they will choose the least risky investment. All other things held constant, the higher an investment's risk, the lower its price and the higher its expected return. The difference in returns is called a risk premium, or the additional compensation investors require for assuming the additional risk of the high-risk investment.

Exhibit 5 ▶ Risk & Return

> Two stocks with equal return are selling for the same price. Southern Power becomes a high-risk investment with energy deregulation, but Tri-State Cable remains a low-risk investment. Investors, preferring the low-risk investment, bid up the price of Tri-State Cable, increasing Tri-State Cable's price and decreasing its expected return.
>
> Further, investors holding Southern Power sell it to purchase Tri-State Cable, depressing Southern Power's price and increasing its expected return.

5. **Portfolio Risk** A stock held as part of a portfolio can be less risky than the same stock held in isolation. The expected portfolio return is the weighted average of the expected returns of the securities in the portfolio. Unlike return, portfolio risk is not the weighted average of the standard deviations of individual portfolio securities. From an investor's perspective, the fluctuations of a particular stock's return and risk is less important than the return and risk of the portfolio as a whole.

6. **Correlation** Correlation is the tendency of two variables to move jointly. The correlation coefficient (r) ranges from +1.0 to −1.0. A correlation coefficient equal to +1.0 indicates perfect positive correlation. A correlation coefficient equal to −1.0 indicates perfect negative correlation.

   a. **Negative** Two stocks are correlated negatively if one's return falls when the other's return rises. These two stocks are said to have countercyclical movement; the risk of one offsets the risk of the other in a portfolio.

   b. **Positive** Two stocks are correlated positively if one's return rises to the same degree when the other's return rises. Diversifying by holding two positively correlated stocks does nothing to reduce market risk, although it may mitigate company-specific risk.

   c. **Partial Positive** In reality, most stocks are correlated positively, but not perfectly. In this circumstance, combining stocks in portfolios reduces, but doesn't eliminate, risk. Generally, the riskiness of a portfolio is reduced as the number of stocks in the portfolio increases. The extent to which this rule of thumb holds depends on the degree of correlation between the stocks. For a group of stocks whose correlation coefficients are zero or negative, all risk could be eliminated. More typically, when correlation coefficients for a group of stocks are positive but less than +1.0, market risk is mitigated.

7. **Portfolio Risk Measurement** A stock's tendency to move with the market is indicated by a beta coefficient (b), commonly called a beta. A beta is a measure of a stock's volatility relative to the market average. By definition, the average beta coefficient for all stocks is 1.0. If a low-beta stock is added to an average risk portfolio, the portfolio's risk (and beta) will decline. If a high-beta stock is added to an average risk portfolio, the portfolio's risk (and beta) will increase. A portfolio's beta is a weighted average of the betas of the individual elements of that portfolio.

Exhibit 6 ▶ Beta Coefficients

> Alpha's, Hillcrest's, and Landale's stocks have beta coefficients of 1.0, 2.0, and 0.5, respectively.
>
> **Required:** Determine the stocks' change in value if the market moves up by 10%.
>
> **Solution:**
>
> | | |
> |---|---|
> | Alpha | 10% market increase × 1.0 = 10% market increase |
> | Hillcrest | 10% market increase × 2.0 = 20% market increase |
> | Landale | 10% market increase × 0.5 = 5% market increase |

Example 14 ▶ Portfolio Beta Coefficient

Morgan held the following nine stocks, with percentage of portfolio and beta coefficients as indicated. On February 1, Morgan sold St Elmo Recovery's stock and purchased Westend Brewing's stock. Westend Brewing's stock is 15% of the new portfolio and has a beta coefficient of 0.80.

Campbell Paper (10% of portfolio)	1.21	Olympia Foods (20%)	0.88
Caterpillar Retail (10%)	0.70	Polar Outfitters (10%)	1.24
Data 1000 Archival Service (5%)	2.02	Safeway Soup (5%)	0.74
Dean Drilling & Exploration (15%)	1.96	St Elmo Recovery (15%)	1.70
General Tractor (10%)	1.13		

Required: Calculate the portfolio's beta coefficients in January (b_j) and February (b_f).

Solution: A portfolio's beta coefficient is the weighted average of the component items' beta coefficients. The portfolio's beta coefficient drops after the exchange of a high-beta stock for a low-beta stock.

$b_j = (0.10 \times 1.21) + (0.10 \times 0.70) + (0.05 \times 2.02) + (0.15 \times 1.96) + (0.10 \times 1.13) + (0.20 \times 0.88) + (0.10 \times 1.24) + (0.05 \times 0.74) + (0.15 \times 1.70)$

$b_j = 0.121 + 0.070 + 0.101 + 0.294 + 0.113 + 0.176 + 0.124 + 0.037 + 0.255$

$b_j = 1.291$, in January

$b_f = 0.121 + 0.070 + 0.101 + 0.294 + 0.113 + 0.176 + 0.124 + 0.037 + (0.15 \times 0.80)$

$b_f = 1.156$, in February

8. **Capital Asset Pricing Model (CAPM)** The capital asset pricing model, also called the security market line (SML), attempts to specify relationships between risk and rates of return. Beta coefficients are determined based on past volatility, yet investors often attempt to use them to predict future results without full regard for changing conditions.

Exhibit 7 ▶ Security Market Line Shift Caused by Inflation Expectations

The required rates of return are plotted on the vertical axis, and risk, as measured by beta, is plotted on the horizontal axis. The SML slope represents the average investor's aversion to risk (the extent of risk aversion in the economy). Since default-free securities have b = 0, the SML intercepts the vertical axis at the default-free rate of return.

Two stocks, S and H, have betas of $b_s = 0.5$ and $b_h = 2.0$, and required rates of return R_s and R_h, respectively. The rate of return (R_{f1}) on long-term U.S. Treasury bonds is 4% at time 1. The average rate of return on stocks is 7% at time 1.

The line labeled SML_0 indicates no risk aversion by investors; this line indicates that investors are equally as likely to buy risky investments as riskless investments, an unlikely circumstance. At time 1, indicated by the line labeled SML_1, investors have a relatively low expectation of inflation. At time 2, indicated by the line labeled SML_2, investors have a relatively high expectation of inflation. The increase in anticipated inflation is 4%.

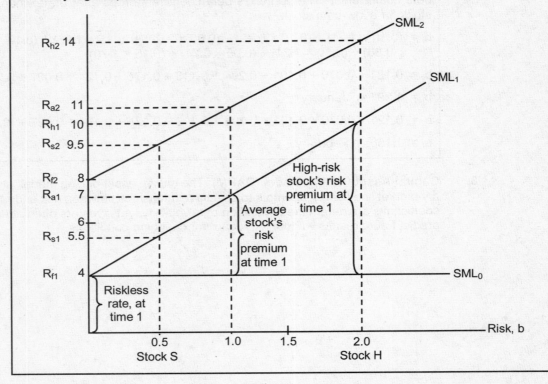

a. **Assumed Rates of Return** A default-free rate of return (R_F) typically is estimated as the rate of return on long-term U.S. Treasury bonds. The required rate of return on an average stock (R_M) by definition, is one with a beta of 1.0.

b. **Market Risk Premium** The market risk premium (RP_M) is the additional return over the default-free rate required for the average stock ($RP_M = R_M - R_F$). The risk premium (RP_n) and beta coefficient (b_n) for stock n can be used to calculate market risk premium ($RP_n = b_n \times RP_M$) for stock n. If stock h is twice as risky as the market average ($b_h = 2$), its risk premium is estimated at twice that of an average stock.

c. **Rate of Return Estimates** The rate of return required for stock n is the default-free rate of return plus the beta for stock n times the market risk premium. [$R_n = R_F + b_n (R_M - R_F) = R_F + b_n (RP_M)$]

d. **Changes in Beta Coefficients** As a corporation's assets or operating environment changes, so will its stock's beta coefficient.

Exhibit 8 ▶ Increased Risk Aversion & Changing Beta Coefficient

Two stocks, S and H, have betas of $b_s = 0.5$ and $b_h = 2.0$, and required rates of return R_s and R_h, respectively. The rate of return on long-term U.S. Treasury bonds is 4%. The average rate of return on stocks is 7%.

At time 1, indicated by the line labeled SML_1, investors have a relatively low risk aversion. At time 2, indicated by the line labeled SML_2, investors have a relatively high risk aversion. Stock J has a changing beta; $b_j = 1.0$ at one point and $b_j = 1.5$ at another, resulting in a changed required rate of return regardless of the risk aversion level.

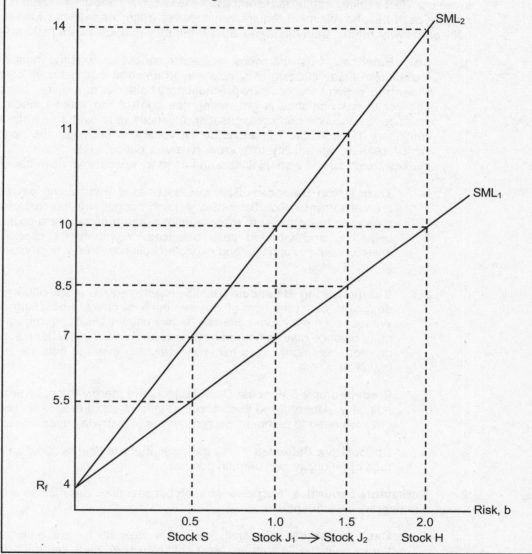

9. **Rational Investor Behavior** A rational investor will buy a stock if its expected rate of return exceed its required rate of return; sell a stock if its expected returns are less than its required returns, and hold a stock if its expected returns equal its required returns. If a stock's expected returns are less than its required returns, many investors will seek to sell the stock, but few will buy until the stock price drops to the point where the expected returns equal the required returns (the equilibrium price). The stock market, particularly for widely traded stocks, reacts quickly to disequilibrium situations. These stock price changes reflect changing expectations.

10. **Efficient Markets Hypothesis (EMH)** Many different events cause change in the equilibrium price of a stock. EMH holds that stock prices quickly reach and remain in equilibrium,

making it impossible for an investor to beat the market for widely traded stocks with any consistency, given the large numbers of full-time analysts. In other words, information about all widely held stocks is reflected in stock prices almost all the time. EMH does not apply to situations with insider trading or closely held stocks.

IV. Working Capital

A. Cash & Marketable Securities

Working capital is a entity's current assets: cash, marketable securities, accounts receivable, and inventory. Net working capital is current assets less current liabilities. Cash is a low-earning asset; holding cash beyond minimum requirements lowers a firm's earnings. Marketable securities typically earn lower returns than operating assets, but they generally earn higher returns than cash.

1. **Cash Balances** Cash balances facilitate business operations; most often, payments and receipts are made in cash. A simple way to arrive at a target cash balance is the larger of either transaction balances plus precautionary balances or required compensating balances. The actual cash balance is not merely the sum of the various kinds of balances as, for instance, transaction and compensating balances may overlap. Both transaction and precautionary balances are influenced by the volume of business, the degree of uncertainty in cash forecasts, and ability to borrow on short notice. Ready access to credit or holding marketable securities also minimizes the need for speculative cash balances.

    a. **Transaction Balances** Balances associated with routine payments and collections are called transaction balances. A cash budget is a forecast of required transaction balances, being the sum of cash inflows and outflows for a given period, considering beginning and targeted cash balances, payments for capital asset acquisitions, inventory, and expenses, and expected collections from customers, debtors, and capital asset sales.

    b. **Compensating Balances** Banks usually require a specified minimum balance on deposit to offset the cost of services such as check processing or lockbox collection. Without such minimum balances, banks usually would charge an explicit fee. A minimum balance may be figured as the actual balance in the bank account at any one time or, more commonly, as a minimum weighted average balance throughout the period, usually a month.

    c. **Precautionary Balances** Cash budgets are merely forecasts with varying degrees of reliability. Unpredicted fluctuations in inflows could reduce an account just as normal outflows need to be made, causing havoc in everyday operations.

    d. **Speculative Balances** Cash balances that are held to allow an entity to take advantage of an unplanned bargain purchase.

2. **Marketable Securities' Purpose** Marketable securities are held as a cash substitute or as a temporary investment.

    a. **Cash Substitute** Generally securities are held for precautionary reasons, in case bank credit should tighten. Most entities rely on bank credit for temporary transaction shortages or speculative needs.

    b. **Temporary Investment** Securities generally are held as a temporary investment when an entity needs to finance seasonal or cyclical operations, plans an unusual financial requirement (such as construction progress or tax payments), or recently has sold long-term securities and not yet reinvested or distributed the funds.

3. **Cash Management Efficiencies** The better that an entity's cash flow forecast is, the lower its need for transaction and precautionary balances.

a. **Synchronization** By arranging collections and payments so that receipts coincide with outflows, entities can minimize transaction balances. For instance, an apartment complex with a mortgage payment due just after tenants have made rent payments will need a relatively low balance.

b. **Speeding Collections & Slowing Payments** Quickly processing checks received from customers makes the funds available for use quickly. Funds are not immediately available for use by the depositing entity; the check must clear first. Checks spend time in both the mail and a bank clearinghouse. Cash inflow speed can be increased by the use of lockboxes or electronic transfers. A lockbox arrangement involves payment checks addressed to an entity to be physically mailed to a nearby bank, which clears the check nearby and then wires funds to the entity's main bank. Electronic transfers eliminate the need for the physical movement of a paper check as well as typically reducing the labor cost in processing payments significantly. Delaying payments generally has limited application. Several schemes to "legitimately" delay payment times, including slow payment procedures and cutting checks on accounts in banks distant from the check recipient now are recognized and, in some cases, outlawed.

c. **Float** Float is the difference between the amount on the depositor's books and the balance according to the bank. If an entity's own collection and clearing process is more efficient than that of its check recipients, the entity can reduce considerably its precautionary balance. With accurate forecasting and careful monitoring, an entity may decide even to have a negative balance on its records and a positive balance on its bank statements. The Check Clearing for the 21st Century Act, or Check 21, is a federal law intended to improve the efficiency and safety of the nation's check payment system. While implementation of Check 21 does not ensure that checks will be processed more quickly or that funds will be available sooner, it may result in reduced float.

Exhibit 9 ▶ Float

Justin Company both writes and collects $5,000 of checks daily from its operating account, in which it must keep an average minimum balance of $5,000. Justin has a credit arrangement with its bank and marketable securities that eliminate the need for precautionary or speculative balances in its checking account.

Justin's suppliers take 3 days to clear Justin's checks, so Justin has $5,000 × 3 = $15,000 of float on checks that it writes. Justin clears its customers' checks in 1 day, so Justin has $5,000 × 1 = $5,000 of negative float on checks that it receives. The net float is $10,000.

As Justin can predict its float accurately, it could reduce the transaction balance that it otherwise would keep in its checking account. Conceivably, the $5,000 compensating balance plus as a $5,000 transaction balance could be offset by the float, resulting in a zero balance per books and a $10,000 balance per the bank. A more aggressive plan would be to maintain a negative $5,000 balance per books and a $5,000 balance per the bank.

d. **Overdraft System** An overdraft system is one where a bank issues loan proceeds to depositors contingent on the existence of shortages (overdrafts). Checks are cleared with the funds from the overdraft loans.

4. **Temporary Investment Strategies** The temporary investment goals to holding marketable securities also may be served by short-term borrowing. Compare the advantages and disadvantages of three alternative strategies for meeting seasonal cash needs. The considerations discussed for meeting seasonal cash needs also apply to other temporary investments goals.

In practice, whether one strategy is better than another depends on several factors, including external factors difficult to predict, such as interest rate changes.

    a.   **Marketable Securities** By holding marketable securities during slack periods and selling them during peak periods, an entity ties up resources in low-yielding assets, contributing to an overall lower return on assets; however, the entity's current ratio is favorable and there is no risk that the entity will not be able to obtain essential financing.

    b.   **Short-Term Borrowing** By borrowing during peak periods, an entity frees resources for high-yielding uses, contributing to an overall higher return on assets; however, the entity's current ratio is lower than other strategies and there is risk that the entity will not be able to obtain essential financing.

    c.   **Combination** By holding and selling some marketable securities, but less than necessary to meet completely the peak period requirements, and borrowing the remaining required cash during peak periods, an entity keeps only some resources in low-yielding assets and mitigates the risk that it will not be able to obtain essential financing. While returns are not as high as with the short-term borrowing strategy, neither is the risk.

5.   **Security Selection Factors** An entity's selection of securities depends on several factors: default risk, interest rate risk, purchasing power risk, liquidity risk, and expected return. Since short-term investments generally are held for a specific known need or emergency use, liquidity and value preservation usually are the primary considerations. Consequently, a marketable securities portfolio generally is restricted to highly liquid, safe, short-term securities such as those issued by the U.S. government or highly rated corporations.

6.   **Target Cash Balance** The Baumol model uses the similarities between cash and inventories to apply the economic order quantity (EOQ) model to determine an optimal cash balance, in a manner similar to the way the EOQ model is used to determine an optimal inventory balance. The fixed costs of security trades or borrowing replaces the fixed costs of placing an order. The total net additional cash needed for a period replaces the total sales per period. The opportunity cost of holding cash (rate of return on securities or interest rate on loans) replaces the per unit inventory carrying costs. Just as with inventory, a safety stock (precautionary balance) can be added to this model, although for a entity with the ability to sell securities or borrow on short notice, the safety stock may be very small. The Baumol model assumes stable, predictable cash flows and doesn't allow for seasonal or cyclical trends. More sophisticated models allow for these factors to some extent, but all models have limitations.

B.   **Accounts Receivable**
Outstanding accounts receivable (A/R) is determined by credit sales volume and the length of time between sales and collections. Specifically, outstanding accounts receivable (A/R) is calculated multiplying credit sales volume by the average length of time between sales and collections. This asset must be financed like any other asset. Credit policy variables include credit standards; credit period; cash discounts designed to expedite payment; and collection policies.

1.   **Credit Standards** Credit standards are financial attributes of customers to which an entity chooses to given credit. The costs of extending credit to customers with marginal quality financial condition include (a) bad debt (default) losses; (b) higher investigation and collection costs; and (c) higher investment in A/R resulting when less creditworthy customers pay accounts slowly, increasing the average collection period. As it is illegal to offer more favorable credit terms to one customer than to another, unless there are cost-justifiable differences, having a set of standards based on credit quality can be important.

2.   **Credit Quality** Credit quality usually is described in terms of probability of default. While determining whether individual debtors will pay or default usually is difficult, the behavior of different classes of customers may be predicted reasonably accurately. Previous experience with customers and credit-reporting agencies provide information on several factors significant for classifying customers. Character refers to the probability that the customer will attempt to honor a debt. Capacity refers to a subjective judgment about a customer's ability to pay. Capital refers to the customer's general financial condition, typically measured by ratios such as the current ratio. Customers may offer assets (collateral) as security to obtain credit. Credit managers also consider general economic trends and relevant geographic region or industry sector trends.

3. **Credit Period** Credit period is the duration, or length of time, an entity elects to extend credit. Lengthening the credit period generally stimulates sales, but increases the receivable investment. First, current customers likely will increase the time they take to pay. Second, increased credit sales will increase the overall volume of receivables. Thus, the change in profit associated with a proposed credit period increase is equal to the incremental sales times the contribution margin less the sum of the cost of carrying new receivables, the incremental bad debts losses, incremental fixed cost increases. The cost of carrying new receivables (or the incremental investment in receivables) is the increased investment in receivables related to original sales (the change in average collection period times the current sales per day) plus the investment related to new sales (the variable costs as a percentage of sales times the new average collection period times the incremental sales per day).

4. **Cash Discounts** Frequently a discount for payment within a specified time is allowed (for example, "2/10, net 30" refers to a discount of 2 percent if payment is received in ten days, otherwise the payment, without the discount, is due within 30 days). Some potential customers consider discounts a price reduction. Discounts also often decrease the average collection period. The downside to discounts is the reduced margin on sales.

5. **Collection Policy** The procedures that an entity takes to collect past due accounts generally are referred to as a collection policy. Collections can be expensive in terms of lost goodwill as well as more readily measurable expenditures.

6. **Incremental Analysis** Credit policy impacts sales volume. An optimal credit policy matches credit costs with profits from the related sales volume. In other words, easing credit policies stimulates sales, but also increases costs. Ideally, additional sales increase profits; however, if a looser credit policy results in new customers of lower creditworthiness and existing customers paying more slowly than before the change, it may lead to reduced profits. Incremental analysis commonly is used to predict the profitability of a change in credit policy. Incremental profit is the difference between incremental sales and incremental costs. Generally credit policy changes affect sales, production costs related to a different sales volume, bad debt losses, discount expenses, the cost of capital in financing A/R, credit department administration costs, and collection expenses. To estimate the impact to sales requires insight on how competitors as well as customers will react to an entity's credit policy change.

7. **Interest Income** If the terms of the loan allow an entity to assess a carrying change on outstanding receivables, credit sales may be more profitable than cash sales.

8. **Aging Schedule** An entity could have an average outstanding A/R time matching its credit terms while still including amounts for customers with receivables outstanding far longer than its credit terms. Long overdue accounts are more prone to default than current accounts. An aging schedule highlights overdue accounts, providing a simple means of evaluating the quality of A/R.

C. **Inventory**
Inventory differs from accounts receivable in that it is acquired before sales occur. This increases the complexities of inventory estimates. In addition to forecasting aggregate demand, entities must forecast distribution (style, color, and size of products). Good inventory management is characterized by high inventory turnover, low obsolescence or deterioration write-offs, and infrequent work stoppages or lost sales due to stock-outs.

1. **Economic Order Quantity (EOQ)** The economic order quantity is the purchase order size that minimizes the total of inventory order cost and inventory carrying costs. It is important to note: (1) this formula can be used by a manufacturer to determine the optimum size for a production run by replacing "order cost" with the "set-up costs" necessary for a production run, (2) the formula assumes that periodic demand for the good is known, (3) inventory cost flow assumptions, such as LIFO and FIFO, do **not** affect the computation, and (4) neither the actual cost per inventory unit, the cost of carrying safety stock, nor the cost of a stock-out are used in the formula.

Exhibit 10 ▶ Economic Order Quantity

$$\text{Economic order quantity} = \sqrt{\frac{2 \times \text{Order cost} \times \text{Annual demand}}{\text{inventory carrying cost per unit}}}$$

Example 15 ▶ Economic Order Quantity

Pierce plans to manufacture 10,000 blades for its electric lawn mower division. The blades will be used evenly throughout the year. The setup cost every time a production run is made is $80, and the cost to carry a blade in inventory for the year is $.40. Pierce's objective is to produce the blades at the lowest cost possible.

Required: Determine the number of production runs Pierce should make.

Solution:

$$\text{Optimal production run} = \sqrt{\frac{2 \times 80 \times 10,000}{0.40}} = 2,000 \text{ units}$$

Annual demand	10,000
Divided by: Optimal production run	/ 2,000
Number of production runs	5

2. **Lead Time & Reorder Point** Lead time is the time lag between placing an order and the receipt of the goods. If safety stock is ignored, the reorder point is computed as the anticipated demand during the lead time. If safety stock is considered, the reorder point is computed as the anticipated demand during the lead time plus the level of safety stock.

3. **Safety Stock** If the demand during the lead time is not known with certainty, it may be important to keep extra inventory (known as safety stock) on hand so as to avoid the possibility of a stock-out in case the lead time demand was higher than average. Its level is determined by balancing the cost of a stock-out (i.e., lost business and customer goodwill) against the cost of carrying extra inventory.

Example 16 ▶ Reorder Point & Safety Stock

Eagle Company's material A will be required evenly throughout the year.

Annual usage in units	7,200	Normal lead time in working days	20
Working days per year	240	Maximum lead time in working days	45

Required: Determine reorder point and the level of safety stock.

Solution:

Average usage of units per work day (7,200 / 240)	30
Times: Maximum lead time in working days	45
Maximum demand during lead time = Reorder point with safety stock	1,350
Maximum demand during lead time	1,350
Less: Expected demand during lead time [(7,200 / 240) × 20]	600
Safety stock	750

D.   **Short-Term Credit**
Comparisons of the cost of credit should examine the effective interest rates, not merely the stated interest rates.

1.   **Nature** Historically, entities financed current assets with short-term credit and capital assets with long-term credit.

   a.   **Flexibility** Cyclical or seasonal debt needs are well matched by short-term debt. Costs to float long-term debt are usually material, but minor for short-term credit. While long-term debt may be repaid early, expensive pre-payment penalties usually result.

   b.   **Cost** Interest rates typically are lower on short-term debt than on long-term debt.

   c.   **Risk** Short-term credit involves fluctuating interest rates, whereas long-term debt has relatively stable and predictable interest rates. If an entity is in a weak financial position when short-term loans are due, the lenders may not extend the loan, forcing the entity into bankruptcy.

2.   **Accruals** Accruals (such as for wages and taxes) are part of short-term liabilities and technically finance part of assets. While no interest is paid on most accruals, entities have little control over the amount.

3.   **Accounts Payable** Accounts payable (A/P) or trade credit arises from ordinary business transactions, typically the purchase of inventory and supplies. Trade credit commonly is divided into two components: a free component and a "costly" component.

   a.   **Free Component** The credit received during the discount periods commonly is called free. A supplier has the cost of carrying receivables during that discount period and must pass that cost to the customer. Thus, the costs of the discount period credit is included in the form of higher base prices. However, unless a suppler will lower the base price for cash purchases, the discount period credit is free for practical purposes.

   b.   **Costly Component** "Costly" trade credit's cost is an implicit cost equal to foregone discounts. Entities should use the costly component only after determining that the cost of this credit is less than the cost of funds from other sources.

   c.   **Stretching Terms** Sometimes customers will stretch terms. For instance, customers will pay a 2/10, net 30 invoice either after 15 days (taking the discount) or after 40 days (without the discount). During periods when suppliers are under capacity, they may tolerate this stretching by customers because they are hard up for business. This leads to A/P sometimes being called **spontaneous** credit. While this increases the amount and reduces the cost of credit for customers in the short term, these customers will impair their goodwill with those suppliers. These least-favored customers likely will get little leeway when they need extra support or the suppliers' situations improve. Extra support could include additional credit or quickly fulfilled orders on scarce products.

Example 17 ▶ Accounts Payable Implicit Cost

Unified Manufacturing buys $365,000 worth of raw materials from its only supplier, Harvester, Inc. Harvester has terms of 2/10, net 30.

Required: Determine whether Unified should take Harvester's discount and pay within 10 days or forgo the discount and take 30 days to pay.

Solution: Unified should take the 2% discount unless it can earn 36.5% or more with the additional credit, or alternatively, cannot borrow at less than 36.5% from other sources.

If Unified takes the discount and pays at the end of the tenth day, its payables will average (10 days × $365,000/365 days) $10,000. In other words, Unified will receive $10,000 of credit from Harvester.

If Unified doesn't take the discount and pays at the end of the 30th day, its payables will average (30 days × $365,000 / 365 days) $30,000. In other words, Unified will receive $30,000 of credit from Harvester.

The difference in the cost of purchases is $7,300 (2% × $365,000 – 0% × $365,000). The difference in credit is $20,000 ($30,000 – $10,000). The percentage cost (interest rate) of the additional credit is 36.5% ($7,300 / $20,000).

4. **Notes Payable (Short-Term Bank Loans)** A bank's influence on an entity is disproportionate to the amount of the credit it extends because it provides **non-spontaneous** funds. As an entity's financing needs increase, it must request additional funds. A bank has no incentive to extend credit at less than favorable terms to sell its inventory, as an ordinary supplier does. If banks deny the entity's request, the entity may have to scale back its growth. Notes payable are often short-term, often as short as 90 days. If a borrower's financial position deteriorates at renewal time, the bank may refuse to renew a loan. A promissory note is contract for a loan specifying: the amount borrowed, the interest rate, the repayment schedule, and any collateral or other terms and conditions.

   a. **Compensating Balances** A bank may require a borrower to maintain an average checking account balance of, for instance, 10 percent of the loan face amount. Thus, to pay a $90,000 tax payment, an entity must borrow $100,000 and keep $10,000 in its checking account in order to have enough for the tax payment. The stated interest rate on the loan may be 8%, but the actual interest rate is about 8.9% ($8,000 / $90,000).

   b. **Line of Credit** An understanding between a bank and borrower indicating the maximum outstanding debt the bank will extend is called a line of credit. The borrower may take and pay interest on a portion of the maximum amount, but still have the assurance that more funds are available.

   c. **Revolving Credit Agreement** A formal line of credit usually involves a commitment fee as a percentage of the unused balance as well as interest on the borrowed amount.

5. **Commercial Paper** Commercial paper is unsecured promissory notes of established entities. It is sold primarily to insurance companies, pension funds, mutual funds, banks, and other sophisticated investors, so as to avoid SEC registration requirements. Commercial paper dealings generally are less personal than bank relationships; dealers prefer to handle paper for entities with large net worth and strong financial position. This is a disadvantage for a debtor in temporary financial difficulty. One advantage is the ability to utilize a wide range of lenders, including non-financial institutions seeking a short-term use for cash and banks with which the debtor has a minimal relationship.

6. **Collateral** The use of collateral often enables financial weak entities to (a) get any loan at all or (b) borrow at lower interest rates than otherwise available. Secured transactions are tested in the REG section of the CPA exam.

7. **Long-Term Assets** Occasionally, entities finance their long-term assets with short-term credit to take advantage of short-term rates that are lower than long-term rates. As long as short-term rates are stable and the entity continually is strong enough to obtain financing, this policy works well. If rates suddenly rise during even a temporary period of economic distress, this policy can result in bankruptcy, if lenders will not renew loans.

E. Derivatives

As their name implies, derivatives are financial contracts that are derived from an underlying asset, reference rate, or index. The current extensive use of derivatives is due primarily to volatile markets, deregulation, and emerging technologies. These types of situations generate uncertainty and, hence, risk. The primary purpose of derivatives is to manage risk. Using derivatives divides financial risk into pieces that can be exchanged with other entities. Entities may retain the risks they find acceptable and transfer those they find unacceptable to entities that are willing to accept them. An entity's decision to use derivatives should be driven by a risk-management strategy that is based on its overall objectives.

1. **Nature** Most derivatives are designed to hedge risks in an effort to reduce uncertainties. With few exceptions, the risks associated with derivatives are man-made, but inherent in the financial system. For instance, when a homeowner negotiates a fixed-rate mortgage with a lender, the potential for interest rate fluctuation creates risk for both the homeowner and the lender. Derivatives improve market efficiencies because risks can be divided, packaged, and sold to those who are willing to accept them.

2. **Categories** Most derivatives can be classified as one, or as a combination of more than one, of the following types: forward contracts, future contracts, swap contracts, and option contracts based on interest rates or currencies. New derivative products generally are variations and combinations of these basic derivative types.

    a. **Forward Contract** Foreign-exchange forward contracts obligate one party to buy, and a counterparty to sell, a fixed amount of currency at an agreed-upon future date. By entering into a foreign-exchange forward contract, entities can offset the risk that large movements in foreign-exchange rates will destroy the economic viability of overseas projects. These derivatives initially were intended to hedge specific risks.

    b. **Future Contract** Future contracts were developed from forward agreements. Future contracts differ from forward contracts in that exchange clearinghouses standardize future contracts and mark them to market daily. Thus, these clearinghouses facilitate a competitive and liquid market. The daily **mark to market** decreases counterparty risk. **Counterparty risk** is the risk that the other party to a contract will be unable to meet its obligations on the maturity date.

    c. **Swap Contract** A swap contract is a forward-based derivative that obligates two parties to trade a series of cash flows at specified future settlement dates. Swaps are negotiated privately to meet each party's specific risk-management needs. The primary types of swaps are interest-rate swaps and currency swaps. Interest-rate swaps tend to account for the majority of swap activity. The **fixed-for-floating-rate swap** is the most common interest-rate swap. In a fixed-for-floating-rate swap, one party agrees to make fixed-rate interest payments in return for floating-rate interest payments from a counterparty, with the payment calculations based on a hypothetical amount of principal called the *notional* amount.

    d. **Option Contract** An option represents a right for one party to purchase something at a specified price during a specified period of time.

3. **Risk-Management Strategy** Risk management does not eliminate risk; it is about selectively choosing those risks that an entity finds acceptable and minimizing those that it finds unacceptable. Derivative use should integrate with an entity's overall risk-management strategy and harmonize with its broad philosophy and objectives.

a. **Considerations** An entity's risk-management strategy should address the following questions. Which risks should be hedged? What kinds of instruments and trading strategies are appropriate? How will appropriate instruments perform when there are large fluctuations in interest rates, exchange rates, and other significant factors?

b. **Tool** Derivatives are tools that can help entities to meet risk-management goals. As with all tools, the user must understand this tool's characteristics, operations, and hazards. Derivatives can fulfill risk-management objectives and, thus, should be considered for risk-control plans.

c. **Selection** Entities should use only those instruments that they understand and that fit with their risk-management philosophy. Evaluation of derivatives requires a solid understanding of the tradeoff of risks and rewards. Entities that use derivatives should establish policies to provide a framework for effectively managing and controlling financial derivative activities. Those policies should outline the role of senior management, valuation policies, market risk management, credit risk management, enforcement, operating systems, internal controls, accounting practices, and adequate disclosure of risk-management positions.

d. **Risk** The types of risks relating to derivatives are no different from those relating to traditional instruments, although they may be more complex. Without a well defined risk-management strategy, derivative use can result in unsound practices that rapidly could lead to insolvency. When used appropriately, derivatives can increase stakeholder value by providing a means to control a entity's risk exposures and cash flows. Used correctly, derivatives can save costs and increase returns. When used inappropriately, derivatives can cause extensive losses or propel an entity in a poor direction given its overall objectives. Businesses should develop proper safeguards within trading protocols and appropriate incentives so that traders do not assume unwarranted risks.

V. Capital Budgeting

A. Overview
Capital budgeting pertains to the allocation of capital among alternative investment opportunities. An important aspect of the capital budgeting process is the application of various investment criteria to proposed projects in order to determine which one would be the most profitable for the firm to implement. Another important concept in this context is that of the firm's cost of capital.

1. **Classification** Projects may be classified by type of project. Some classifications (such as mandated investments) get less analysis than others (such as expansion into new products or markets). Common classifications are: (a) maintenance-of-business replacements; (b) cost reduction replacements; (c) expansion of existing products or markets; (d) expansion into new products or markets; (e) safety and environmental projects (also called mandated investments); and (f) other (small, mixed use or generic facilities for which a breakdown in project classification probably will outweigh the benefit, such as parking lots or buildings).

2. **Category** Projects also may be classified based on whether they are independent or mutually exclusive. A project is independent if its projected cash flows are unaffected by another project's existence. For independent projects, NPV and IRR criteria lead to the same accept or reject decisions. When considering mutually exclusive projects, an entity may choose only one project. It is possible for the NPV and IRR criteria to assign different rankings to mutually exclusive projects; when such conflicts exist, the NPV ranking generally is more reliable.

3. **Post-Project Audit** A post-project evaluation or audit involves a comparison of actual and predicted results and an explanation of observed differences. Post-project audit results must be used with discretion or potentially profitable, but risky, projects will not be recommended.

a. **Purpose** A post-project audit both: (1) supports refinements in future predictions; and (2) improves the project implementation as an implementation team has incentive to make the project happen, for their reputations if nothing else, just because the team is aware of the post-project audit.

b.   **Considerations** A reasonably venturesome entity should expect some percentage of all projects to fail to meet expectations. Projects may fail to meet expectations for reasons: (1) beyond a implementation team's control; and (2) that are not reasonably predictable. Expectations are based on cash flow (and other) forecasts that are subject to uncertainty at every step. It is often difficult to separate the results of one project from those of the larger environment. Project designers or implementation team members may have left the project by the time the results of their decisions are known.

4.   **Depreciation & Tax Shield** Before considering investment criteria and the cost of capital, consider depreciation and the tax shield. Incremental earnings from a project have a related incremental tax liability. Since depreciation is deductible as a regular business expense, it reduces taxable incremental earnings, and therefore reduces incremental tax liability. Thus, depreciation "shields" part of the cash inflow from taxation when income taxes are a factor.

Example 18 ▶ Depreciation

A company buys a new machine for $10,000 that increases its annual earnings by $5,000. The tax rate is 30% and the machine has a 10-year life and no salvage value. Using straight-line depreciation, the annual depreciation provision would be $1,000. The yearly incremental tax liability would be $1,200 [($5,000 – $1,000) × 0.30]. Depreciation reduces the tax liability by $300 ($1,000 × 0.30).

a.   **Excluded** When income tax considerations are ignored, depreciation expense is excluded from the calculations for the (a) net present value, (b) internal rate of return, and (c) payback methods. These methods focus on cash flow, and depreciation expense is not a cash flow, but an allocation of past cost. Deduction of depreciation would constitute a double counting of a cost, because the initial cost of the project has already been considered as a lump-sum cash outflow.

b.   **Included** Even when income taxes are ignored, depreciation expense is included when calculating the accounting rate of return.

B.   **Investment Evaluation Methods**
Both the net present value and the internal rate of return methods (1) can be used regardless of whether cash flows from period to period are uniform or uneven, (2) do not use depreciation expense when income tax considerations are ignored, and (3) can both easily accommodate a requirement that projects with longer lives must earn a higher specified rate of return. For instance, projects with less than a five-year life must earn a return of 10%, while those with a life of five years or more must earn a return of 12%.

1.   **Accounting Rate of Return on Average Investment** This is the average annual net income from the project divided by the average investment in the project. The numerator is the average annual increase in **net income,** not **cash flow,** so depreciation and incremental income taxes are subtracted. The denominator also takes account of depreciation in the carrying amount of the asset.

a.   **Advantage** An advantage of the accounting rate of return method is that it is understood easily because its terms and computation are based upon financial accounting income, and since it is based upon the average annual financial accounting income the project generates, revenue over the entire life of the project is used.

b.   **Disadvantage** Disadvantages of the method are that it is based upon financial accounting income that uses the accrual basis (capital budgeting decisions generally should rely on estimates of cash flows) and it ignores the time value of money.

2. **Payback Period** This is the length of time required to recover the initial cash outflow from the incremental cash benefits after tax. Thus, if we have an investment of $10,000 that yields $4,500 each year after tax, it would take us 2.22 years (i.e., $10,000 / $4,500) to recover the original investment from the cumulative net cash inflows. (We assume here that the $4,500 cash inflow during any given year is spread uniformly over the year.) Depreciation expense is excluded from the calculation when income taxes are ignored.

    a. **Advantage** Advantages of the payback method are (1) it is based upon cash flows, (2) it serves as a rough screening device to determine the time it will take to recoup the original investment, and (3) it is simple to understand and easy to compute.

    b. **Disadvantage** Disadvantages of the method are (1) the time value of money is ignored, (2) not all of the cash flow over the life of the project is used—all cash flow beyond the payback period for the investment is ignored, and (3) it does not measure profitability.

3. **Internal Rate of Return** This is the rate of interest that would make the present value of the future cash flows from the project equal to the cost of the initial investment. Projects with a rate less than a minimum rate (or hurdle rate) set by the company are eliminated from consideration.

    a. **Advantage** Advantages of the internal rate of return method are (1) all of the cash flow over the life of the project is used, including the estimated residual sales value of the project, (2) the time value of money is explicitly recognized, and (3) the project's rate of return is estimated.

    b. **Disadvantage** Disadvantages of the internal rate of return method are (1) cash flows are assumed to be reinvested at the rate earned by the project, and (2) it is more difficult to use than other less sophisticated capital budgeting techniques.

4. **Net Present Value** Net present value (NPV) is the present value of the future cash inflows from the project **minus** the cost of the initial investment. Unlike the internal rate of return method where the rate of interest is an unknown to be determined, a certain rate at which to compute the present value of the cash inflows is given. This rate is called the cost of capital, a concept that will be explained later in this section. A project that will earn exactly the desired rate of return will have a NPV of zero. A positive net present value identifies projects that will earn in excess of the minimum rate of return.

    a. **Advantage** Advantages of the net present value method are (1) all of the cash flow over the life of the project is used, including the estimated residual sales value of the project, (2) the time value of money is explicitly recognized, and (3) cash flows are assumed to be reinvested at the enterprise's cost of capital.

    b. **Disadvantage** Disadvantages of the method are (1) it does not estimate the project's rate of return but merely tests the rate against a minimum rate (i.e., the enterprise's cost of capital), (2) it is more difficult to use than other less sophisticated capital budgeting techniques, and (3) it is difficult to apply to strategic investments that do not generate identifiable cash flows. However, such investments can be more critical to an entity's success than those with more readily identifiable cash flows.

5. **Profitability Index** Because projects can differ greatly in size, it would not be meaningful to compare the NPVs of different projects directly. Instead, a **profitability index** is used.

    Exhibit 11 ▶ Profitability Index

$$\text{Profitability index} = \frac{\textit{Present value of cash flow}}{\textit{Initial investment}}$$

Example 19 ▶ Profitability Index

A machine, purchased for $10,000, yields cash inflows of $5,000, $4,000, and $4,000. The cost of capital is 10%.

Required: Determine the profitability index.

Solution:

Year	Cash flow	PV factor at 10%	PV of cash flow
1	$5,000	0.909	$ 4,545
2	4,000	0.826	3,304
3	4,000	0.751	3,004
		Total	$10,853

Net present value = $10,853 – $10,000 = $853

Profitability index = $10,853 / $10,000 = <u>1.0853</u>

C. Cost of Capital

The firm's cost of capital is a weighted average of the costs of debt and equity funds. Equity funds here include both capital stock and retained earnings. These costs are expressed in terms of a percentage per annum. An entity's **cost of capital** is equal to the weighted average of the cost of debt, preferred and common stock, and retained earnings, with their market values as weights. (The tax rate adjustment is made to the cost of debt because interest payments are deductible for income tax purposes.)

Example 20 ▶ Cost of Capital Calculation

Required: Given the following facts, determine a firm's cost of capital.

Total interest payments	$10,000	Bonds	$200,000
Common dividends	14,560	Common stock	150,000
Annual common dividend growth	3%	Preferred stock	100,000
Preferred dividends	6,000	Retained earnings	50,000
Company tax rate	40%	Total market values	$500,000
Stockholders' marginal tax rate	30%		

Solution: Firm's cost of capital = 0.4(3%) + 0.3(12.7%) + 0.2(6%) + 0.1(8.9%) = 7.1%

	Cost			Weight	
Debt	$10,000 (1 – 0.4) / $200,000	=	3%	$200,000 / $500,000	= 0.4
Preferred stock	$6,000 / $100,000	=	6%	$100,000 / $500,000	= 0.2
Common stock	$14,560 / $150,000 + 3%	=	12.7%	$150,000 / $500,000	= 0.3
Retained earnings	(1 – 0.3) × 12.7%	=	8.9%	$ 50,000 / $500,000	= 0.1

Exhibit 12 ▶ Cost of Debt

$$\text{Cost of debt} = \frac{\text{Interest payments} \times (1 - \text{tax rate})}{\text{Average market value of debt (e.g., bonds)}}$$

Exhibit 13 ▶ Cost of Preferred Stock

Cost of preferred stock = Preferred dividends / Average market value of preferred stock.

Exhibit 14 ▶ Cost of Common Stock

$$\text{Cost of common stock} = \frac{\text{Dividends on common stock}}{\text{Average market value of common stock}} + \frac{\text{Expected growth}}{\text{rate in dividends}}$$

Exhibit 15 ▶ Cost of Retained Earnings

Cost of retained earnings = $(1 - t_s)$ × Cost of common stock
Where t_s is the marginal tax rate per dollar for the firm's stockholders

D. Return on Investment

The return on investment measures the relationship of profit to invested capital for a unit of account-ability. The return on investment is **increased** when operating income increases or when average invested capital decreases. Return on investment **decreases** when operating income decreases or when average invested capital increases. Operating income increases when costs decrease, and decreases when costs increase.

Exhibit 16 ▶ Return on Investment

$$\text{Return on investment} = \frac{\text{Percentage of profit to sales}} \times \text{Capital-employed turnover rate}$$

$$= \frac{\text{Operating income}}{\text{Sales}} \times \frac{\text{Sales}}{\text{Average invested capital}}$$

$$= \frac{\text{Operating income}}{\text{Average invested capital}}$$

E. Residual Income

The objective of maximizing residual income assumes that as long as the accounting unit earns a rate of return in excess of the imputed interest charge for invested capital, the unit should expand. Residual income is a unit's operating income less an imputed interest charge on its average invested capital.

Exhibit 17 ▶ Residual Income

$$\text{Residual income} = \text{Operating income} - \left(\begin{array}{c} \text{Imputed} \\ \text{interest rate} \\ \text{(cost of capital)} \end{array} \times \begin{array}{c} \text{Average} \\ \text{invested} \\ \text{capital} \end{array} \right)$$

F. Economic Value Added

Economic value added is the net operating profit after tax less the opportunity cost of capital. A focus on economic value added attempts to emphasize the creation of shareholder wealth over time. Managers' attention is focused on managing assets as well as income, helping them properly assess the tradeoffs between the two. Companies using an array of measures to express financial goals and objectives may find their efforts resulting in inconsistent standards, goals, and terminology as well as incohesive planning, operating strategy, and decision making among different levels of management and across divisional and departmental lines. Economic value added is a single financial measure that attempts to eliminate this confusion by providing all decision makers with a common and readily understood focus.

Exhibit 18 ▶ Simple Economic Value Added Formula

$$\text{Economic value added} = \text{Operating profit} \times (1 - \text{Tax rate}) - \begin{array}{c} \text{Opportunity cost} \\ \text{interest rate for} \\ \text{equity capital} \\ \times \\ \text{Employed} \\ \text{equity capital} \end{array} - \begin{array}{c} \text{Opportunity cost} \\ \text{interest rate for} \\ \text{debt} \\ \times \\ \text{Employed} \\ \text{debt} \end{array}$$

VI. Long-Term Financing

A. Investment Banking

Investment banks assist entities in issuing securities in primary markets and often function as brokers in secondary markets. They typically help entities (issuers) design securities with attractive features, buy the securities, and resell securities in the primary market. Investment banks frequently are divisions of large corporations involved in a range of financial services.

1. **New Security Issue** An investment bank evaluates the size and nature of an issue and advises the issuer on how to maximize the offering. As investment banks often sell issues largely to their brokerage customers, the nature of those customers has an impact on the type of issuers that are suitable clients for that bank. As a percentage of proceeds, costs tend to be higher for stocks than for bonds as well as higher for small issues than for large issues, primarily due to fixed costs. Many entities build up short-term debt to a certain amount, sell one stock or bond issue, use the proceeds to retire the short-term debt, and start the cycle again.

   a. **Best Effort vs. Underwritten Issues** When working on a **best effort** basis, an investment bank doesn't guarantee that securities will be sold or that the target amount of capital will be raised. For an **underwritten** issue, an investment bank buys the issue at a discount from the price at which they are offered to the public and resells them, effectively guaranteeing that the issue will sell. The discount, or spread, is designed to cover the investment bank's costs and profit.

   b. **Setting Offering Price** If the offering price is set relatively low, the investment bank will be able to sell it readily, but the issuer will raise less capital, so a conflict of interest on price is almost inevitable between the issuer and bank. If the stock already is owned publicly, the offering price usually is based on the existing market price of stock or yield on bonds. If pressure from the new shares drives down the stock (or bond) price, all outstanding shares (or bonds) are affected, not just the new issue. To avoid having the large supply of shares (or bonds) pull the market price down, **promoting** or advertising the entity may cause the demand curve for the stock to shift to the right. For a corporation going public, the investment bank must estimate the equilibrium price, a difficult and significant task: too high and new shareholders see a distressing drop in value shortly after they buy the issue, too low and original shareholders will have exchanged too much stock or bonds for capital.

2. **Selling Procedures** Issuers and investment banks prepare and file an SEC registration statement and prospectus. After receiving SEC approval, securities may be offered to the public. On an underwritten offering, the issuer receives the agreed-upon price and the investment bank absorbs any losses. If the issue is large and substantial price fluctuation is possible, an investment bank is exposed to considerable risk. Investment banks typically do not handle large issues singled-handedly; they form underwriting syndicates to minimize the risk each bank carries, with the underwriter who arranges the issue as the lead underwriter.

3. **Secondary Market** If a stock is traded in the over-the-counter market, the lead underwriter generally agrees to make a market in the stock to keep it liquid. This is done to further relations with the issuer, keep brokerage customers who bought the issue happy, and to encourage future referral business.

B. Common Stock

Corporations with common stock held by a few people are called **privately owned** or **closely held.** Corporations with common stock held by a large number of investors are called **publicly owned.** Publicly owned corporations must meet additional regulations and disclosure requirements.

1. **Transactions** The stock market is divided into the primary and secondary markets. New shares, whether offered by established, publicly owned companies or public offerings by previously closely held firms, are called the primary market. The secondary market involves exchanges of outstanding shares of established, publicly owned companies. **Going public**

is the process of offering stock to the public by previously closely held corporations for the first time; it may involve the issue of new stock or a current shareholder may sell closely held stock to a number of investors. In other words, a corporation goes public if an owner of closely held stock sells it to the general public, even though the corporation itself raises no capital in the process.

2. **Advantages & Disadvantages** Businesses often begin as proprietorships or partnerships and then incorporate as they grow. Typically, new corporations' stock generally is owned by key employees and a few investors. Going public has advantages and disadvantages.

    a. **Simplifies Diversification** Founders often have a significant part of their wealth in one company. By going public, founders can diversify their holdings, reducing risk in their personal portfolios.

    b. **Financing** It is awkward to get outsiders to invest in a closely held company because it is easy for those with voting control to run roughshod over those without control. Reliable disclosure may not occur; insiders may arrange private deals with the corporation or lavish compensation. Insiders may keep outsiders from knowing the corporation's true earnings or worth. The SEC requires disclosure and regulates public corporations, so these problems are reduced significantly. Both debt and equity financing may be easier with disclosure.

    c. **Self Dealings** Owner-managers of a closely held company have opportunities for legal self dealings: high compensation, favorable leasing arrangements, nepotism, lavish travel policies, etc. While these self dealings may be legal, they may not be tolerable to shareholders. Going public requires disclosure of details. Managers of publicly owned corporations are accountable to stockholders and subject to stockholder suits.

    d. **Liquidity** Often, no ready market exists for the stock of a closely held entity. It is difficult to find potential buyers. A stock technically can be public and yet not trade often, so the liquidity advantages are not present. The market may value illiquid stocks lower than their true value, discounting the stock (called an illiquidity discount).

    e. **Establishes Corporation's Value vs. Disclosure** Valuation by the market is convenient for several purposes. It facilitates appraisal for estate tax purposes. A publicly determined value (and liquidity) makes it far easier for a shareholder to use the stock for collateral for other financing and make stock or stock options more attractive to employees. Corporations dislike reporting because information is available to competitors. Owners may dislike disclosure of their net worth; publicly held corporations must disclose the number of shares owned by officers, directors, and major shareholders.

    f. **Reporting Cost** Publicly owned corporations file occasional, quarterly, and annual reports with the SEC and state officials, necessitating annual audits and an understanding of events that require reporting.

3. **Listing Stock** Listing requirements usually include a minimum net income and a minimum number of shares held by outside investors. Stock is listed on an exchange when the corporation meets the exchange's requirements, applies for a listing, and pays a listing fee. Listed corporations receive some free publicity. A listing often enhances a corporation's reputation, increasing its product sales as well as lowering the required rate of return on stock. By contrast, unlisted stock is said to be traded over-the-counter (OTC). A listed corporation discloses information to the exchange in an effort to detect stock price manipulation. Investors trade listed shares *through* a stockbroker acting as an agent rather than *to or from* a stockbroker acting as a dealer.

C.   Fixed-Income Securities

Term loans, bonds, and preferred stock are the three main types of long-term fixed-income securities. When an entity is planning to "fund its floating debt," it plans to replace short-term debt with long-term securities.

1.   **Term Loan**   A term loan is a contract involving a borrower who agrees to make principal and interest payments to a lender on specified dates. It usually involves one borrowing entity and one financial institution (bank, insurance company, or pension fund). Its chief advantages are speed, low issue costs, and flexibility. With only two parties to a contract, key loan provisions can be negotiated readily as well as tailored to circumstances. SEC filing is not needed. Possible future modifications need involve only two parties. Most term loans are amortized or, in other words, repaid in equal installments during the loan life. This avoids having a large lump sum fall due all at once, lessening the possibility that the borrower will fail to make adequate provision for debt repayment.

2.   **Bonds**   Otherwise similar to term loans, a bond issue typically is advertised publicly as well as offered and sold to many investors.

   a.   **Indenture & Trustee**   An indenture defines the rights and obligations of bondholders and the issuer. Indentures may specify a times-interest-earned ratio that the issue must maintain to sell additional bonds, restrictions against dividend payments unless earnings meet minimums, and similar provisions. A trustee represents the bondholders in ensuring the indenture terms are fulfilled. The SEC approves indentures and ensures indenture provisions are met initially (before bonds are ever sold). Many issues of bonds for the same corporation may be covered by the same indenture; a current bond issue might be covered by a decades-old indenture.

   b.   **Restrictive Covenant Ratio**   A restrictive covenant is a provision in an indenture or term loan contract that requires the debtor to meet certain financial standards. Typical provisions include debt as a certain maximum percentage of total capital, a specified current ratio, and dividend payments only in the presence of specified earnings levels.

   c.   **Debenture vs. Mortgage Bond**   A debenture bond is unsecured, in other words, the bondholders are general creditors. Debentures are issued by financially strong entities or entities with assets inappropriate as collateral for long-term debt, such as inventory, receivables, and computers. In the case of liquidation, **subordinated debentures** are paid only after all specified debts are settled; subordinated debentures are designed to strengthen the position of other debt holders. Mortgage bonds are bonds with specified real assets as collateral or security for the bond issue. Second, or **junior** mortgages are subordinated to first, **senior,** or **primary** mortgages.

   d.   **Zero or Low-Coupon Bond**   A zero or low-coupon bond is offered at a substantial discount below the par value. Although zero coupon bonds pay no annual interest, the bondholder is paid face value upon maturity. The issuer doesn't have to outlay cash until the bond matures, yet may take a tax deduction for interest expense. The effective interest rate generally is slightly lower than regular bonds, but zero coupon bonds typically are not callable. Financial institutions that make actuarial contracts based on assumed reinvestment rates (pension funds and life insurance companies) tend to be the primary purchasers of zero coupon bonds because they needn't worry about reinvesting the interest and principal payments. As these financial institutions are the largest purchasers of corporate bonds, issuing zero coupon bonds doesn't tend to restrict the market for a corporation's bonds.

   e.   **Callable, Convertible & Redeemable Bond**   A callable bond contains a call provision that makes it callable at a specified price at the bond issuer's option. Usually the issuer pays an additional amount over par to call a bond, called a call premium. A convertible bond is convertible into common stock at a specified price at the bondholder's option. A redeemable bond is redeemable at a specified price at the bondholder's option.

f. **Coverage Ratio** Coverage is a measure of an issuer's ability to meet interest and principal. The times-interest-earned ratio (earnings before interest and taxes, or EBIT / interest payments) and the fixed charge coverage ratio [(EBIT + lease payments) / {interest payments + lease payments + (sinking fund payment / (1 – tax rate))}] are common coverage ratios.

g. **Repayment Provisions** A typical sinking fund provision requires an issue to retire a portion of a bond issue each year. A rare alterative provision is for the issuer to deposit money with a trust, who invest the money and retires all the bonds at their maturity. A failure to meet sinking fund provisions can throw the entire bond issue into default. The provision may specify that a number of bonds be retired annually. Bonds may be called for redemption by lottery (based on the bonds' serial numbers); a call for sinking fund purposes typically has no call premium. Alternatively, bonds for redemption may be purchased on the open market and retired.

h. **Bond Ratings** Analysts rate bonds based on quantitative information plus subjective judgment. Bond ratings, or grades, are an indication of risk, significantly influencing the issuer's interest rate and cost of debt. Most institutions have policies that restrict bond purchases to certain grades. Institutions purchase far more bonds than individual investors. If an issuer's rating falls below what typically is called investment grade, the pool of potential bond purchasers will be small. Entities at the bottom level of investment grade could suffer rating downgrading. Downgrading a bond with a marginal rating would force restricted bondholders to sell the bonds (to meet the policy requirements) at a loss; thus, some financial managers will not purchase bonds that just meet minimal rating requirements. The lower an issuer's bond rating, the smaller the group of available purchasers for its new issues becomes. Rating entities usually review outstanding bonds periodically and on the announcement of a new bond issue. If a debtor is experiencing temporary financial deterioration, it may delay a bond issue, financing with short term bank loans, until its situation improves, in order to delay review by rating entities.

3. **Preferred Stock** Preferred stock combines some characteristics of common stocks and bonds. It provides financial leverage like bonds; however, if earnings fall, the non-payment of dividends will not force the issuer into bankruptcy. Preferred stock has a dividend set at issue; yields change as the price of the stock fluctuates. Typically, preferred stock also has a par (or liquidating) value. Preferred dividends need not be paid, but common stock dividends may not be paid unless the preferred dividends are paid.

a. **Cumulative** Usually, preferred stock is cumulative; unpaid dividends from one year become **dividends in arrears,** or arrearages, in subsequent years; all dividends in arrears must be paid before common stock dividends may be paid. Dividends in arrears are not debts, nor do they accrue interest. As an indication of financial difficulty, dividends in arrears may make it difficult for an entity to raise additional capital using either bonds or more stock.

b. **Risk** From an issuer's perspective, preferred stock is less risky than bonds; in a period of financial strain, no payment need be made to shareholders. From investors' perspective, preferred stock is more risky than bonds. In liquidation, bondholders' claims have priority over preferred shareholders. Bondholders are more likely to receive interest payments than preferred shareholders are to receive dividends. The after-tax yield on preferred stock typically is higher than similarly graded bonds.

c. **Callable & Convertible** Callable preferred stock may be recalled at the issuer's option. Some preferred stock is subject to a sinking fund provision, such as 1% of the original issue is retired each year; these issues effectively mature. Convertible preferred stock may be exchanged for common stock at the shareholder's option.

d.   Participating In addition to the "regular" dividend, participating preferred stock receives part of dividends over the amount assigned to the common stock dividend. For instance, 4% fully participating preferred stock will earn a 4% return on par value, plus if amounts paid on common stock exceed 4%, then dividends above that limit will be shared ratably with common stockholders. Alternatively, 4% preferred stock participating in distributions in excess of 10%, will earn a 4% return on par value, plus if amounts paid on common stock exceed 10%, then dividends above that limit will be shared ratably with common stockholders.

4.   Differentiation Considerations Different securities enable an issuer to take advantage of current market conditions, resulting in an overall lower cost of capital. Investors have different risk-return trade-off preferences. Entities issue different classes of securities to appeal to the broadest group of investors possible within cost-benefit restraints.

a.   Limited Income & Cost Bondholders and preferred stockholders receive a limited income, regardless of profit. This preserves the issuer's capital, but also limits the amount that the holders may gain.

b.   Control Bondholders and preferred stockholders typically do not vote for directors; control remains in the hands of common stockholders.

c.   Taxes Bond interest is tax deductible by the issuer; dividends are not.

d.   Risk Unpaid bond interest could force an issuer into bankruptcy; undeclared dividends will not. Bond interest continues to accrue regardless of whether the entity generates profits or cash to pay interest, potentially magnifying losses or cash shortfalls.

e.   Restrictions Bond indentures may be more restrictive and enforced more stringently than short-term loan covenants. Indentures typically don't apply to stock.

f.   Flexibility An entity that has a debt-to-asset ratio at the upper limits during good economic conditions may not be able to obtain financing during unfavorable economic conditions. By maintaining some **reserve borrowing capacity,** entities ensure some flexibility.

D.   Capital Structure Decisions
There is no model to determine unequivocally what a proper debt-to-equity mix is for an entity. Debt leverage can magnify an entity's performance dramatically. In other words, when things are good, they are very, very good; and when things are bad, they are awful. A capital structure that propels one corporation to stellar profits during moderately favorable economic times can drive a similar entity into bankruptcy during a moderate downturn. Changes to capital structure weights can change the cost of capital and consequently the set of acceptable projects and the riskiness of ownership of an entity and hence, the required rate of return.

1.   Risk When evaluating an individual entity, risk typically is categorized as business risk or financial risk.

a.   Business Business risk is the riskiness of the entity's operations without any debt; in other words, risk inherent in operations. Business risk is defined as the uncertainty inherent in projections of earnings before interest and taxes (EBIT). Business risk usually is the single most significant factor in determining an appropriate capital structure. Fluctuations in EBIT commonly are caused by business cycle changes, new products brought to market by an entity or its competitors, labor or transportation strikes, raw material shortages, price controls, political or social upheaval in supplier or customer locations, extreme weather, disasters, accidents, dramatic customer preference changes, etc. While these factors are influenced heavily by an entity's industry, they also are influenced by an entity's operating characteristics. The following determinants commonly are considered most significant.

(1) **Demand Variability** Other factors held constant, the more that demand for an entity's products is stable, the lower the entity's risk.

(2) **Sales Price Volatility** The degree to which sales prices change. Other factors held constant, the more sales prices for an entity's products change, the higher the entity's risk.

(3) **Input Price Volatility** Other factors held constant, the more input prices for an entity's products are uncertain, the higher the entity's risk.

(4) **Sales Price Influence** Other factors held constant, the more a producer can charge higher sales prices when input prices change, the lower the entity's risk, as the producer passes the price changes along to the consumer.

(5) **Operating Leverage** Other factors held constant, the higher fixed costs are for an entity, the higher the entity's risk.

b. **Financial** Financial risk is the **additional** risk that the owners' bear due to the entity's decision to carry debt.

2. **Operating Leverage** When a relatively small change in sales results in a large change in operating income (or EBIT), a high degree of operating leverage exists. This results when a high percentage of the entity's total costs are fixed. Generally, the greater the operating leverage that exists, the greater business risk will be. Operating leverage choices influence capital structure; the amount of fixed assets directly relates to the amount of capital.

Exhibt 19 ▶ Degree of Operating Leverage (DOL)

$$DOL = \text{Contribution Margin} / EBIT$$

3. **Financial Leverage** When a relatively small change in EBIT results in a large change common shareholders' return, a high degree of financial leverage exists. This results when a high percentage of the entity's financing is through fixed income securities: debt and preferred stock. Generally, the greater the financial leverage that exists, the greater business risk will be.

Exhibit 20 ▶ Degree of Financial Leverage (DFL)

$$DFL = EBIT / (EBIT - \text{Interest})$$

a. **Operating Income Impact** Traditionally, EBIT often is treated as if it is affected by operating leverage only, and not financial leverage. Financial policy (or financial leverage) does have an indirect effect on operating income. A weak financial situation caused by excessive debt could result in lost contracts (potential customers worry about supply interruption), difficulty hiring employees, (potential employees worry about job security), weak negotiating positions with unions (unable to weather negotiation periods), and an inability to finance during periods of high interest rates (resulting in passing up good investment opportunities).

b. **Capital Structure** An entity establishes and modifies its **target capital structure** based on its analysis of several factors and then makes individual financing decisions consistent with its target. An **optimal capital structure** maximizes the price of the stock by balancing risks and returns.

4. **Stock Valuation Factors** Expected stock prices first rise as a corporation begins to borrow, peaks, and then declines as debt becomes excessive. Since interest is tax deductible, a corporation has a greater proportion of operating income flowing through to investors as debt increases, increasing stock prices. The risk of bankruptcy is related directly to debt levels.

Eventually, an entity could borrow so much that the bankruptcy risk is so great that the stock price declines. The optimal capital structure is where the marginal tax shelter benefits of the interest are equal to the marginal bankruptcy costs.

5. **Analysis Factors** Difficulties with optimal capital structure analysis are significant. Difficulty in calculating the impact of different degrees of financial leverage on P/E ratios and equity capitalization rates introduces additional uncertainty into the analysis. Management may have a different degree of conservatism than the average stockholder and may set a different target structure than the one that would maximize stock prices. Short-run stock price maximization may conflict with long-run viability; entities may have obligations to provide continuous service (particularly utilities) or meet the terms of long-term contracts. These considerations tend to increase the weight given to bankruptcy risk.

a. **Stability** An entity with predictable, stable sales can assume greater debt with greater safety than one with unpredictable sales. Utilities typically carry proportionately more debt than drug manufacturers. Utilities have a stable customer base and monthly billing; drug manufacturers have considerable uncertainties connected with research and lawsuits related to adverse drug reactions.

b. **Asset Structure** An entity with appropriate collateral can convince investors that default risk is low, and thus will tend to issue more debt. An entity with significant real estate holdings will be able to float more debt than a retailer with accounts receivable as collateral.

c. **Operating Leverage** An entity with less operating leverage tends to be a better candidate for use of financial leverage than one with more operating leverage, due to the decreased business risk with less operating leverage.

d. **Growth Rate** Costs involved in common stock issues tend to be greater than debt issues. A quickly growing entity tends to have more frequent needs for additional capital than a slowly growing entity.

e. **Profitability** High cash flows are related to profitability. Entities who can finance with retained earnings often do not borrow.

f. **Taxes** The higher a corporation's tax rate, the greater the advantage of using debt and deducting the interest payments.

g. **Control** Management's control position may influence its capital structure decision. Issuing additional common stock may shift the voting control away from current management. Too little debt may make a corporation a takeover target. Too much debt may drive a corporation to bankruptcy.

h. **Attitudes** Conservative managers may use less debt than industry averages. Management seeking leverage beyond industry averages may find rating agency attitudes increase the cost of debt.

i. **Market Conditions** During periods of high interest rates, corporations with low ratings may have to issue stock instead of debt. During periods of low investor confidence in equity securities, in general or of a particular industry, a planned stock issue might have to be delayed.

E. **Dividend Policy**
Dividend policy relates to deciding how much earnings to distribute to shareholders (payout) and how much earnings to retain for future investment (plowback). Dividend policy has two contrary effects. To some extent, paying dividends tends to increase the stock price; a cash payment decreases the uncertainties involved with stock ownership. Offsetting that effect, paying dividends also makes less money available for reinvestment, lowering expected growth, which will have a

depressing effect on stock prices. Optimal dividend policy balances current dividends and future growth to maximize the stock price.

1. **Residual Theory** The residual theory of dividends states that a corporation should (a) determine the optimal capital budget, (b) calculate the equity necessary to finance that capital budget, (c) supply that equity from retained earnings insofar as possible, and (d) pay dividends to the extent retained earnings exceed the equity needed (in other words, leftover or residual earnings). Despite considerable research, there is no widely accepted optimal dividend policy model, but the residual theory is a common starting point for determining dividend policy.

    a. **Assumptions** This theory assumes that (1) the corporation can reinvest earnings at a higher rate of return than investors can find though another investment with comparable risk, (2) investors prefer to have the corporation re-invest the earnings, and (3) the rate of return that investors require is not affected by dividend policy.

    b. **Other Equity** To maintain its target capital structure, a corporation's increases in debt financing must be balanced with increases in equity. Once retained earnings (internally generated equity) are exhausted, the only alternative to increase equity is to issue additional common stock, an expensive undertaking. Stock issue costs increase the marginal cost of capital.

2. **Influences** The following factors are used to explain dividend policies differing from the residual theory.

    a. **Constraints** Debt contracts (including bond indentures) often limit dividends to earnings generated after the contract date and require specified ratios be met before dividends are declared. Legally, ordinary dividends may not exceed retained earnings. Cash dividends are limited by the amount of cash available to pay dividends. The accumulated earnings tax is a penalty tax designed to discourage accumulation of retained earnings to enable shareholders to avoid paying personal income taxes on dividends, which are taxed at a higher rate than capital gains.

    b. **Investment Opportunities** The greater the internal rate of return on investments, the more favorable it will be to retain earnings for reinvestment. The potential for accelerating or delaying projects permits flexibility in dividend policy.

    c. **Alternative Capital Sources** If stock issue costs are low, retained earnings are less important as a source of financing. If management is concerned about control, it will be hesitant to issue new common stock. If the average cost of capital is stable over a relatively wide range, dividend policy becomes less significant to financing decisions.

    d. **Effects on Required Rate of Return** Shareholders can shift investments among corporations; investors displeased with a corporation's dividend policy (or other policies) will exchange shares with investors who like it. This **clientele effect** results because individual corporations tend to attract certain types of investors. Corporations that frequently change their dividend policy may not attract many investors because investors incur costs to switch investments: brokerage costs, capital gains taxes, and potential capital loss if the new policy is attractive to fewer investors.

        (1) **Capital Gains** Capital gains are taxed a lower rate than dividends. The extent to which this is important to shareholders depends on their tax situation.

        (2) **Shareholder Nature & Timing Preference** Some shareholders prefer current income; these shareholders must sell stock, incurring brokerage costs, if dividends are not paid. Some shareholders prefer capital gains; these shareholders must seek a new investment for dividends after paying taxes on them, incurring brokerage costs.

    (3)   **Dividend vs. Capital Gain Risk** Corporations with capital gains but no dividends tend to be perceived as more risky than corporations that pay dividends.

    (4)   **Legal List** States regulate fiduciary institutions. Certain fiduciary institutions legally may purchase stocks of certain companies only; the list of these solid companies is called the legal list. (There are several legal lists, although the lists tend to be similar.) Other investors exempt from legal lists choose to restrict investments to a legal list. Thus, demand for stocks on the list is greater than for stocks off the list; corporations like to be on the list. A frequent requirement for legal list inclusion is the absence of dividend reductions; thus, corporations are reluctant to decrease dividends.

    (5)   **Signal Value** Corporations are reluctant to decrease dividends, so they tend to be hesitant to raise dividends unless they anticipate earnings in the future that can maintain dividends at or above those levels. Thus, a dividend increase tends to be read as a signal of a positive management forecast.

3.   **Payment Policies** Most corporations avoid changing their dividend policy.

    a.   **Stable Dividend** Many corporations maintain a set dividend amount, increasing it only when future earnings seem sufficient to support an increased dividend amount. In other words, they avoid ever reducing annual dividends. The related **stable growth rate policy** strives to increase dividends annually by a set or indexed percentage; this variation is popular during inflationary periods.

    b.   **Constant Payout Ratio** A very few corporations pay dividends as a constant percentage of earnings.

    c.   **Regular Plus Extra Dividends** Corporations with volatile earnings may pay a relatively stable "regular" dividend plus, when cash flow is favorable, extra dividends paid after profits and investment requirements are known. This compromise provides some stability to investors and leaves the corporation with some flexibility.

    d.   **Residual Dividend** High growth, start-up corporations requiring capital for expansion may plan to reinvest all their profits and not pay dividends, or only pay dividends when no suitable investment is available for retained earnings.

4.   **Payment Procedures** Regular dividends commonly are paid quarterly. If a corporation pays a *regular quarterly dividend* of $1.25, its *regular annual dividend* commonly is said to be $5.00.

    a.   **Declaration Date** The declaration date is when the board of directors declare a dividend and it becomes a corporate liability.

    b.   **Holder-of-Record Date** The notifications of ownership that a corporation receives before the close of business on the holder-of-record date determine who gets the dividend payments.

    c.   ***Ex Dividend* Date** To avoid conflict because of a delay between an exchange and corporate receipt of notification of an exchange, the *ex dividend* date is the date after which the right to the dividend is not transferred with the sale of stock. After eliminating market fluctuations, the stock price is expected to drop by the dividend amount on the *ex dividend* date.

    d.   **Payment Date** The payment date is when the corporation pays the dividend (mails checks or releases electronic transfers).

5.   **Dividend Reinvestment Plan (DRIP)** A DRIP allows stockholders to reinvest dividends automatically in the corporation's stock. These corporations can pay a stable dividend, with or without extra dividends, and yet mimimalize shareholder brokerage costs if the shareholder

wants to reinvest dividends. DRIP plans also may provide feedback to corporations about their dividend policies; a high degree of DRIP participation may indicate that shareholders may preferred lower dividends.

a. **Outstanding Stock DRIP** A trustee purchases the corporation's stock on the open market and allocates the shares to participating shareholders. Brokerage and trustee costs are lower than the brokerage costs each small shareholder would pay buying a few shares independently, so this is particularly advantageous for small shareholders.

b. **New Stock Issue DRIP** A corporation may raise new capital through a DRIP by issuing new stock. Often these plans have a discount on the stock as well as no brokerage fees for shareholders. The savings in investment bank fees offsets, for the corporation, the program costs and discounts.

6. **Stock Repurchase** Stock repurchases are a dividend alternative that allow a corporation to distribute income to those stockholders who want cash. Those shareholders who want cash may acquire it by selling shares to the corporation; those shareholders who do not want cash simply hold shares and benefit by the higher future earnings per share and stock price. Repurchases also avoid the high personal tax rate on cash dividends. However, the irregular nature of repurchases make them an unreliable source of cash for investors. Further, regular or frequent repurchases might prompt scrutiny by the IRS; tax avoidance schemes are subject to penalty taxes.

7. **Stock Dividends & Splits** Stock dividends and splits may be beneficial if the stock price is relatively high, but otherwise they have little effect on aggregate stock value. A relatively high stock price excludes some investors as minimum investment amounts become unwieldy for small portfolios.

F. **Options**

Warrants and convertible instruments are options that can make a corporation's securities attractive to a broader range of investors, increasing the supply and decreasing the cost of capital. In liquidation, bonds and preferred stock are satisfied before common stock and yet the possibility of participating in a stock price increase still remains. Thus, options are considered particularly appropriate to volatile economic environments. Options may enable financially marginal corporations to sell debt or preferred stock that otherwise would not sell. Options may enable financially strong corporations to issue debt or preferred stock at lower rates than otherwise.

1. **Warrant** A warrant is an option to buy a specific amount of common stock at a stated price (the exercise price), usually within a specific time period. A detachable warrant may be traded separately from the bond or preferred stock; a non-detachable warrant remains with the underlying security when the security is traded. The market assigns a value to warrants (even if the market value of the stock is under the exercise value) because warrants represent capital gain potential combined with a loss limitation. The exercise of warrants provides new capital, although it still leaves the corporation with any related debt or preferred stock. As growth fuels the rise of the stock price, investors are more likely to exercise options, so the corporation gets additional capital during growth periods, when it is needed. If expected growth doesn't occur, the stock price probably will not increase enough to trigger investors to exercise options, and additional capital is not raised.

Exhibit 21 ▶ Warrants & Premium Declines

Upside Company warrants allow holders to purchase one share of stock at $25/share. On January 1, the stock price is $20/share and the warrants' exercise value is a negative $5/warrant, the warrants' market price is $1/share, or at a $6 premium over the exercise value. On July 1, the stock price is $40/share and the warrants' market price is $19/share, or at a $4 premium over the exercise value. On December 31, the stock price is $80/share and the warrants' market price is $56/share, or at a $1 premium over the exercise value.

In both six month periods, the stock price doubles. In other words, the percentage gain on the sale of stock for both six month periods would be 100% [($40 − $20)/$20] with an annualized of 200%. The potential loss and return on a warrant investment is different at the two stock price levels.

If Faith purchases the stock on January 1, her potential loss would be $20/share. Faith purchases warrants on January 1, so her potential loss is merely $1/share. Faith converts the warrants to stock on July 1. Faith pays a total of $26/share for a stock valued at $40/share, resulting in a 400% annualized return in 6 months [($40 − $20)/$1 × 100% × (12 months/6 months)] on her $1/share warrant investment. On January 1, the market values the capital gain potential combined with the loss limitation to be worth $6/warrant.

If Hope purchased the stock on July 1, her potential loss would be $40/share. Hope purchases warrants on July 1, so her potential loss is $19/share, less than if she bought the stock, but higher than buying warrants when they had a negative exercise value. Hope converts the warrants to stock on December 31. Hope pays a total of $44/share for a stock valued at $80/share, resulting in a 210% annualized return in 6 months [($80 − $40)/$19 × 100% × (12 months/6 months)] on her $19 warrant investment. On July 1, the market values the capital gain potential combined with the loss limitation to be worth $4/share, or $2/share less than in January, when the stock price was lower.

As the stock price increased, the potential loss on an investment in warrants increased (from $1/warrant to $19/warrant) and the leverage decreased (the return on the warrant investment decreased from 400% to 210% although the return on the stock investment remained the same). This is why the premium declines as the stock price increases.

a. **Exercise Value** An option's exercise, or formula, value is the value of the warrant if exercised currently. In other words, the exercise value is the difference in the market price and the exercise price times the number of shares that each warrant allows the warrant holder to purchase at the exercise price. This formula results in a negative value when the stock price is below the exercise price.

b. **Actual Value** An option's actual value is the market price. Often, warrants' market prices are above exercise values, yet the premium of market price over exercise value tends to diminish with stock price increases. In other words, while the market price of the option increases as the stock price increases, the premium over exercise value decreases. This is because (1) the declining impact of leverage, and (2) at a higher warrant price, the investor has an increased risk of loss.

2. **Convertible Instrument** A convertible instrument or security is an option to exchange a specific amount of bonds or preferred stock into a specific amount of common stock under specified conditions. The conversion itself results in no new capital, although the corporation's debt and equity change, which may allow a corporation to borrow more in the future. Selling convertible securities is a means essentially to sell common stock at higher than the currently prevalent price. Corporations interested in selling common stock, but with temporarily depressed stock prices, instead may issue convertible bonds or preferred stock with a conversion price higher than the current common stock price. This way, the corporation doesn't have to relinquish as many shares for the same amount of capital. If the stock price doesn't increase as anticipated, however, the corporation still has the debt burden. Also, if

the common stock price increases significantly more than anticipated, the corporation forgoes the additional capital that might have been raised if it had waited until after the stock price increase.

3. **Independent Options** An option is merely a contract allowing one contracting party to purchase an asset under certain conditions at specified terms from the other contracting party. Options may be created by independent investors, rather than by the corporations whose securities are involved. These options don't raise capital for the corporations whose securities are involved. A **call option** is an option to buy stock. A **put option** is an option to sell stock.

4. **Employee Options** Corporations may include options unconnected with any security as part of employee compensation. They seek to align employee goals with investor goals; this can backfire, particularly in the case of employees who are also responsible for financial reporting. Also, employee options and the related compensation expense can be problematic to value.

Wondering how to allocate your study time?

In your excitement to answer multiple choice questions, don't forget that you can learn valuable content from questions in simulation format as well!

The first pass through a chapter:

1. Strive to answer **all** the multiple choice questions and the objective elements of the simulations.

2. Choose one or more of the simulations to answer completely. Read the questions and responses for the simulation elements that you don't answer.

3. At the very beginning of your review, don't worry about whether you finish questions within the time allocated. As you become more familiar with the content and the way the examiners ask questions, your speed will increase. Start concerning yourself about time when you are on the first pass through your fourth or fifth chapter.

When you review the chapter later:

1. Answer **at least** those objective questions that you did not understand the first time. (If you had a lucky guess, did you really understand?)

2. Select a new simulation to answer completely. Read the questions and responses for the simulation elements that you don't answer.

When you review the chapter for the final time (for some chapters, the second time may **be** the final time):

1. Answer the questions "cold turkey" (without reviewing the text materials just before answering questions). Before answering questions, only review the notes you would review just before the exam. For a whole exam section, this should take less than five minutes.

2. Answer **at least** those objective questions that you did not understand the first time.

3. Select a new simulation, if available, to answer completely. Read the questions and responses for the simulation elements that you don't answer.

Remember, with the techniques and information in your material,

A passing score is well within reach!

Examination Registration

CPA Examination Services, a division of the National Association of State Boards of Accountancy (NASBA) administers the examination for the following states. Contact CPA Examination Services at (800) CPA-EXAM (272-3926), (615) 880-4250, or www.nasba.org.

Colorado	Louisiana	New Hampshire	South Carolina
Connecticut	Maine	New Jersey	Tennessee
Delaware	Massachusetts	New Mexico	Utah
Florida	Michigan	New York	Vermont
Georgia	Minnesota	Ohio	Virginia
Hawaii	Missouri	Pennsylvania	Wisconsin
Iowa	Montana	Puerto Rico	Indiana
Kansas	Nebraska	Rhode Island	

Castle Worldwide at (800) 655-4845 administers the examination for Washington.

The following boards of accountancy administer the examination themselves. The Bisk Education web site **(www.cpaexam.com)** has a link to NASBA's site, which has links or addresses for all of the U. S. boards of accountancy.

Alabama	Guam	Nevada	Texas
Alaska	Idaho	North Carolina	U. S. Virgin
Arizona	Illinois	North Dakota	Islands
Arkansas	Kentucky	Oklahoma	West Virginia
California	Maryland	Oregon	Wyoming
District of	Mississippi	South Dakota	
Columbia			

See the **Practical Advice** appendix for more information.

CHAPTER 51—FINANCIAL MANAGEMENT

Problem 51-1 MULTIPLE CHOICE QUESTIONS (210 to 263 minutes)

1. Pole Co. is investing in a machine with a 3-year life. The machine is expected to reduce annual cash operating costs by $30,000 in each of the first 2 years and by $20,000 in year 3. Present values of an annuity of $1 at 14% are:

Period	1	0.88
	2	1.65
	3	2.32

Using a 14% cost of capital, what is the present value of these future savings?
a. $59,600
b. $60,800
c. $62,900
d. $69,500 (5/95, AR, #38, 5456)

2. On March 15, Year 1, Ashe Corp. adopted a plan to accumulate $1,000,000 by September 1, Year 5. Ashe plans to make four equal annual deposits to a fund that will earn interest at 10% compounded annually. Ashe made the first deposit on September 1, Year 1. Future value and future amount factors are as follows.

Future value cf 1 at 10% for 4 periods	1.46
Future amount of ordinary annuity of 1 at 10% for 4 periods	4.64
Future amount of annuity in advance of 1 at 10% for 4 periods	5.11

Ashe should make four annual deposits (rounded) of
a. $250,000
b. $215,500
c. $195,700
d. $146,000 (11/91, PI, #9, amended, 2397)

3. Yates Company sold $1,000, 7% bonds for $1,250 each. Which **two** of the following statements are correct?
a. The market rate of interest is less than 7%.
b. The market rate of interest is greater than 7%.
c. The market rate of interest equals the coupon rate of interest.
d. The bond sells at a premium.
e. The bond sells at a discount. (Editors, 7273)

4. What is the effect of a stock dividend?
a. Decreases future earnings per share
b. Decreases the debt-to-equity ratio
c. Increases the size of the entity
d. Increases some shareholders' ownership percentages (Editors, 7274)

5. What could a corporation do to decrease the market value per share of common stock?
a. Bond retirement as scheduled
b. Treasury stock purchase
c. Reverse stock split
d. Stock dividend (Editors, 7275)

6. Tremor Company has a stock price of $40, an estimated dividend at the end of the year of $2, and an expected growth rate of 10%. What is the approximate estimated cost of equity capital using the dividend growth model?
a. 15%
b. 12%
c. 10%
d. 5% (Editors, 7276)

Items 7 and 8 are based on the following:

Velocity Company estimates the following for the next year, when common stock is expected to trade at a price-earnings ratio of seven.

Earnings before interest and taxes	$45 million
Interest expense	$5 million
Effective income tax rate	30%
Preferred stock dividends	$10 million
Common shares outstanding	2 million
Common stock payout ratio	25%

7. What is Velocity's expected common stock dividend for the next year?
a. $2.25
b. $3.50
c. $8.75
d. $9.00 (Editors, 7277)

8. What is Velocity's approximate expected common stock market price per share next year?
a. $ 63
b. $ 75
c. $ 98
d. $105 (Editors, 7278)

9. Which of the following would a rational investor consider when purchasing an entity for cash?

I. The cash paid to the entity's current shareholders
II. The after-tax cash flow from operations
III. The present value of the entity's liabilities

a. I only
b. I and II only
c. I and III only
d. I, II, and III   (Editors, 7279)

10. Beam Company currently has 100,000 shares of common stock outstanding and a price-earnings ratio of seven. Net income for the recently ended year is $375,000. Beam's board of directors declared a 15-for-2 stock split. Sunshine owned 100 shares of Beam before the split. What is the approximate value of Sunshine's investment in Beam immediately after the split?
a. $ 26
b. $ 350
c. $2,625
d. $5,250   (Editors, 7280)

11. Why is equity capital generally more expensive than debt financing?
a. Dividends fluctuate more than interest rates.
b. Interest on bonds is a legal obligation.
c. Investors expect to be paid more for exposure to higher risk.
d. Investors have a greater demand for equity investments than for debt investments.
                                     (Editors, 7281)

12. What ratios are characteristic of an entity with high financial risk?

	Debt-to-equity	Interest coverage
a.	High	High
b.	Low	High
c.	High	Low
d.	Low	Low	(Editors, 7282)

13. An appropriate level of working capital is determined by
a. Balancing the probability of insolvency against the profitability of current assets and liabilities
b. Evaluating the capital structure and dividend policy
c. Evaluating the capital leases used to finance fixed assets
d. Minimizing long-term debt because it is more expensive than short-term debt   (Editors, 7283)

14. Overreach Company is implementing a more conservative working capital policy. Which of the following is Overreach likely to have?
a. An increase in the quick ratio
b. An increase in risk due to interest rate fluctuations
c. An increase in the ratio of current assets to noncurrent assets
d. An increase in the ratio of current liabilities to noncurrent liabilities   (Editors, 7284)

15. Fluid Company's current assets increased by $120 and current liabilities decreased by $200. Fluid's net working capital
a. Decreased by $320
b. Decreased by $80
c. Did not change
d. Increased by $80
e. Increased by $320   (Editors, 7285)

16. Which of the following ratios provides the most appropriate liquidity measure?
a. Current assets to current liabilities
b. Current liabilities to long-term liabilities
c. Net income to current liabilities
d. Total assets to total liabilities   (Editors, 7286)

17. Which **three** of the following ratios are most appropriate for evaluating the effectiveness of working capital management?
a. Average collection period ratio
b. Debt-to-equity ratio
c. Inventory turnover ratio
d. Quick ratio
e. Return on assets   (Editors, 7287)

18. Vie Company is evaluating a plan to expand capacity that will affect the following financial statement amounts.

	Current	Plan
Cash	$ 7,000	$13,000
Marketable securities	$20,000	$11,000
Accounts receivable	$40,000	$55,000
Inventory	$38,000	$48,000
Fixed assets	$70,000	$90,000
Accounts payable	$35,000	$44,000
Mortgage payable (current)	$17,000	$33,000
Mortgage payable (long-term)	$60,000	$85,000
Retained earnings	$50,000	$75,000

What is the estimated effect of the expansion on Vie's working capital?
a. Decrease of $3,000
b. Increase of $13,000
c. Increase of $19,000
d. Increase of $22,000   (Editors, 7288)

19. Which of the following would decrease working capital?
a. Acquiring airplanes using a capital lease with semi-annual payments
b. Collection of accounts receivable
c. Payment of payroll taxes payable
d. Refinancing commercial paper with a 10-year bond issue (Editors, 7289)

20. Griswold Corporation has average ages of inventory, accounts payable, and accounts receivable of 65, 30, and 40, respectively. What is the number of days in the cash flow cycle?
a. 135
b. 105
c. 75
d. 70 (Editors, 7290)

21. The economic order quantity model may be used for cash management to determine appropriate
a. Ratio of current assets to current liabilities
b. Mix of cash and marketable securities
c. Long-term capitalization
d. Credit and collection policies (Editors, 7291)

22. A compensating balance is
a. A quantity of inventory above the economic order quantity held to cover use variation
b. Maintained in an account at a financial institution to cover the cost of services to the account holder
c. The prepaid interest on a loan
d. Used to compensate for potential losses on marketable securities used as collateral (Editors, 7292)

23. Which of the following is least likely to be used to prepare a cash budget for a manufacturing firm?
a. Estimated net income
b. Estimated purchases
c. Estimated sales and collections
d. Payment terms (Editors, 7293)

24. Which of the following cash management techniques focuses on cash disbursements?
a. Lockbox system
b. Zero-balance account
c. Preauthorized checks
d. Depository transfer checks
(R/03, BEC, #25, 7688)

25. A financial manager seeking to delay cash outflows would be most likely to consider using
a. Compensating balances
b. Drafts
c. Electronic funds transfers
d. A lockbox system (Editors, 7295)

26. Advantage Company writes and receives checks totaling $1,000 daily. It takes five days for Advantage's checks to clear its account, but only three days for Advantage's deposits to be available for use. What is the amount of Advantage's float?
a. $ 500
b. $1,000
c. $2,000
d. $3,000 (Editors, 7296)

27. Burrell Company is preparing its cash budget for November. Burrell expects 50% of credit sales to be paid in the month of sale, 30% in the month following the sale, and the remainder paid two months after the month of sale. Burrell expects the following cash and credit sales.

	Cash	Credit
November	$25,000	$100,000
October	$20,000	90,000
September	$15,000	80,000
August	$10,000	95,000

Without any bad debts, what is Burrell's expected October cash inflow?
a. $100,000
b. $108,000
c. $109,500
d. $110,000 (Editors, 7297)

28. What of the following is the primary concern of a treasurer managing cash and short-term investments?
a. Liquidity
b. Maximizing return on working capital
c. Minimizing taxes
d. Minimizing transaction fees (Editors, 7298)

29. Of the following, the marketable security with the least risk is
a. Commercial paper of an AAA-rated company
b. Common stock of an AAA-rated company
c. Gold
d. Stock options of an AAA-rated company
(Editors, 7299)

30. Short-term unsecured notes issued by large corporations are called
a. Agency securities
b. Bankers' acceptances
c. Certificates of deposit
d. Commercial paper
e. Treasury bills (Editors, 7300)

31. Short-term notes issued by Federal National Mortgage Association (Fannie Mae) are called
a. Agency securities
b. Bankers' acceptances
c. Municipal bonds
d. Repurchase agreements
e. Treasury bills   (Editors, 7301)

32. Which of the following is most often used as a cash substitute?
a. Bankers' acceptances
b. Certificates of deposit
c. Gold
d. Municipal bonds
e. Treasury bills   (Editors, 7302)

33. Commercial paper's advantages include that it
a. Can be purchased without commission costs
b. Is readily available as a financing source to most businesses
c. Provides a line of credit at a preset fixed rate that can be used as needed
d. Typically is cheaper than a commercial bank loan   (Editors, 7303)

34. Of the following, the marketable security with the least default risk is
a. Agency securities
b. Bankers' acceptances
c. Certificates of deposit
d. Commercial paper
e. Treasury bills   (Editors, 7304)

35. Using a 360-day year, what is the current price of a $100 U.S. Treasury bill due in 90 days discounted at a 8% rate?
a. $102
b. $100
c. $ 98
d. $ 92   (Editors, 7305)

36. What is short selling?
a. Selling securities financed by money from a loan that is still outstanding
b. Selling securities based on inside information
c. Selling securities that are not owned by the seller
d. Speculating that securities will have a dramatic price increase   (Editors, 7306)

37. Innovate Corporation changed its credit policy. The result is increased sales, increased discounts taken, reduced accounts receivable, and reduced doubtful accounts. Which of the following is also true?
a. The average collection period is reduced.
b. The bad debt loss percentage increased.
c. The discount offered decreased.
d. Gross profit decreased.
e. Net profit increased.   (Editors, 7307)

38. Stellar Company is considering a change in collection procedures that would result in an increase of the average collection period from 28 to 36 days. Stellar estimates next year's sales to be $9 million and that 80% of sales will be on credit. Stellar estimates short-term interest rates at 6% and uses a 360 day year for decision making. What minimum savings in collection costs would the procedure change have to generate to offset the increased investment in accounts receivables?
a. $ 1,200
b. $ 9,600
c. $12,000
d. $33,600   (Editors, 7308)

39. Dawn Company is considering a new group of customers that would increase annual sales by $100,000. Dawn expects uncollectible debt expense and collection costs for this group to be 15% and 5% of sales, respectively. Aside from those expenses, Dawn's combined cost of goods sold and selling expenses are 65% of sales. Dawn will incur no additional fixed costs. What is Dawn's estimated change to income before taxes?
a. $ 5,000 decrease
b. $15,000 increase
c. $20,000 increase
d. $80,000 increase   (Editors, 7309)

40. When would a business most likely offer credit terms of 2/10, net 30?
a. The business can borrow funds only at a rate higher than the effective annual interest rate of these terms.
b. The business can borrow funds at a rate lower than the effective annual interest rate of these terms.
c. Competitors are offering the same terms and the business has a cash shortage.
d. Competitors are not offering terms and the business has a cash surplus.   (Editors, 7310)

41. Raking Company is basing next year's budget on sales of $36 million. Raking offers credit terms of 1/10, n/30 and expects that 80% of sales will be on credit, with discounts taken on 50% of the credit sales. What are estimated discounts taken by customers for next year?
a. $144,000
b. $180,000
c. $288,000
d. $360,000 (Editors, 7311)

42. An accounts receivables aging indicates
a. The percentage of credit sales that are collected in a given period
b. An entity's ability to meet short-term debts
c. The average length of time that receivables are outstanding
d. Amounts of receivables outstanding for given lengths of time (Editors, 7312)

43. Revel Company has average daily sales of $5,000, 90% of which are on credit. Receivables are collected 28 days after sales, on average. What is Revel's average accounts receivable balance?
a. $ 4,500
b. $ 5,000
c. $126,000
d. $140,000 (Editors, 7313)

44. What is the average collection period?
a. The average number of days before a receivable account becomes delinquent
b. The average number of days from a credit sale to payment receipt
c. The average number of days from inventory purchase to sale
d. The average number of days from the time a customer issues a check to the time the vendor receives use of the funds (Editors, 7314)

45. Jones Wholesaling has average daily sales of $50,000, based on a 360-day year. All of Jones's sales are on credit with terms of 2/10, net 45. Customers representing 30% of sales pay on day 45 and the remaining customers take the discount and pay on day 10. What are Jones' average daily collections from customers?
a. $34,300
b. $45,000
c. $49,300
d. $50,000 (Editors, 7315)

46. In Belk Co.'s "just-in-time" production system, costs per setup were reduced from $28 to $2. In the process of reducing inventory levels, Belk found that there were fixed facility and administrative costs that previously had not been included in the carrying cost calculation. The result was an increase from $8 to $32 per unit per year. What were the effects of these changes on Belk's economic lot size and relevant costs?

Lot size	Relevant costs
a. Decrease	Increase
b. Increase	Decrease
c. Increase	Increase
d. Decrease	Decrease

(11/92, PII, #26, 3360)

47. What **two** costs are included in ordering costs in the economic order quantity model?
a. Handling
b. Insurance
c. Interest on invested capital
d. Quantity discounts lost
e. Shipping (Editors, 7272)

48. The economic order quantity model indicates the
a. Annual inventory quantity ordered
b. Annual inventory quantity used
c. Average inventory held
d. Inventory quantity ordered at once (Editors, 7268)

49. What costs are **not** included in carrying costs in the economic order quantity model?
a. Handling
b. Insurance
c. Interest on invested capital
d. Shipping
e. Spoilage (Editors, 7269)

50. Unity Company has made changes in its inventory handling policies that are expected to increase turnover from 7 to 8 times per year. Unity's budgeted sales and costs of sales for the next year are $42 million and $28 million, respectively. At a 6% interest rate, what are Unity's expected savings from the lower inventory level?
a. $15,000
b. $30,000
c. $45,000
d. $60,000 (Editors, 7270)

51. Mystery Company uses the economic order quantity model to determine order size. Mystery's order quantity for Product XYZ is 150 units. Mystery has a safety stock of 50 units for Product XYZ. What is Mystery's average inventory level for Product XYZ?
a. 200
b. 150
c. 125
d. 50   (Editors, 7271)

52. In computing the reorder point for an item of inventory, which of the following is used?

I. Cost
II. Usage per day
III. Lead time

a. I and II
b. II and III
c. I and III
d. I, II, and III   (R/00, AR, #14, 6919)

53. As a consequence of finding a more dependable supplier, Dee Co. reduced its safety stock of raw materials by 80%. What is the effect of this safety stock reduction on Dee's economic order quantity?
a. 80% decrease
b. 64% decrease
c. 20% increase
d. No effect   (5/94, AR, #46, 4651)

54. The following information pertains to material X which is used by Harbor Co.:

Annual usage in units	40,000
Working days per year	250
Safety stock in units	800
Normal lead time in working days	30

Units of material X will be required evenly throughout the year. The order point is
a. 1,600
b. 3,200
c. 4,800
d. 5,600   (Editors, 1548)

55. Green Co. has an inventory conversion period of 80 days and annual revenue of $4,200,000. How many times per year (360 days) does Green turn over its inventory?
a. 2.25
b. 4.30
c. 4.50
d. 9.00   (R/03, BEC, #11, 7673)

56. When would a retailer tend to decrease the safety stock of inventory?
a. Cost of carrying inventory increases
b. Sales variability increases
c. Sales volume permanently increases
d. Transportation time increases   (Editors, 7356)

57. Pickle Pharmacy wants to determine the optimum safety stock level for drug Alpha. The annual carrying cost of Alpha is 25% of the inventory investment. The inventory investment averages $10 per unit. The stock out cost is estimated at $2 per unit. Pickle Pharmacy orders Alpha 20 times annually. Pickle Pharmacy defines the total costs of safety stock as carrying costs plus expected stock out costs. With 100 units of safety stock, there is a 15% probability of a 30-unit stock out per order cycle. What is the total annual cost of the 100 units of Alpha safety stock?
a. $250
b. $259
c. $277
d. $430   (Editors, 7347)

58. What is called a spontaneous financing source?
a. Chattel mortgage
b. Debentures
c. Notes payable
d. Preferred stock
e. Trade credit   (Editors, 7348)

59. Quail Company's suppliers offer terms of 2/10, net 35. Using a 360-day year, what is the approximate cost of foregoing the discount?
a. 36%
b. 29%
c. 21%
d. 19%   (Editors, 7349)

60. Which **two** of the following are secured debt?
a. Commercial paper
b. Factored receivables
c. Floating lien
d. Line of credit
e. Revolving credit   (Editors, 7350)

61. What is the prime rate?
a. The rate on commercial paper
b. The rate that banks charge their strongest commercial customers
c. The rate that banks are charged for overnight loans for funds to meet minimal reserve requirements
d. The rate that the Federal Reserve charges banks for funds   (Editors, 7351)

62. A small retail business most likely would finance merchandise inventory with
a. A chattel mortgage
b. Commercial paper
c. Factored accounts receivable
d. A line of credit   (Editors, 7352)

63. Hardy Company must maintain a compensating balance of $50,000 in its checking account as one of the conditions of its short-term 6% bank loan of $500,000. Hardy's checking account earns 2% interest. Ordinarily, Hardy would maintain a $20,000 balance in the account for transaction purposes. What is the loan's approximate effective interest rate?
a. 5.88%
b. 6.00%
c. 6.17%
d. 6.25%
e. 6.38%   (Editors, 7353)

64. Level Company's current ratio is 2.5 to 1. Level's current liabilities are $252,000. Loan provisions require that Level's current ratio not drop below 1.5 to 1. What is the maximum additional short-term debt that Level may incur?
a. $168,000
b. $378,000
c. $420,000
d. $630,000   (Editors, 7354)

65. Nor Corporation borrowed $400,000 using a discounted note with a stated 6% interest rate. What is the effective rate of interest on the debt?
a. 5.62%
b. 6.00%
c. 6.38%
d. 6.76%   (Editors, 7355)

66. Major Corp. is considering the purchase of a new machine for $5,000 that will have an estimated useful life of five years and no salvage value. The machine will increase Major's after-tax cash flow by $2,000 annually for five years. Major uses the straight-line method of depreciation and has an incremental borrowing rate of 10%. The present value factors for 10% are as follows:

Ordinary annuity with five payments   3.79
Annuity due for five payments   4.17

Using the payback method, how many years will it take to pay back Major's initial investment in the machine?
a. 2.50
b. 5.00
c. 7.58
d. 8.34   (11/92, PII, #38, 3372)

67. Neu Co. is considering the purchase of an investment that has a positive net present value based on Neu's 12% hurdle rate. The internal rate of return would be
a.   0%
b.   12%
c.   > 12%
d.   < 12%   (11/92, PII, #37, 3371)

68. A project should be accepted if the present value of cash flows from the project is
a. Equal to the initial investment
b. Less than the initial investment
c. Greater than the initial investment
d. Equal to zero   (R/03, BEC, #24, 7687)

69. A project's net present value, ignoring income tax considerations, is normally affected by the
a. Proceeds from the sale of the asset to be replaced
b. Carrying amount of the asset to be replaced by the project
c. Amount of annual depreciation on the asset to be replaced
d. Amount of annual depreciation on fixed assets used directly on the project
                    (5/93, Theory, #47, 4234)

70. Oak Company bought a machine which they will depreciate on the straight-line basis over an estimated useful life of seven years. The machine has no salvage value. They expect the machine to generate after-tax net cash inflows from operations of $110,000 in each of the seven years. Oak's minimum rate of return is 12%. Information on present value factors is as follows:

- Present value of $1 at 12% at the end of seven periods   0.0452
- Present value of an ordinary annuity of $1 at 12% for seven periods   4.564

Assuming a positive net present value of $12,000, what was the cost of the machine?
a. $480,000
b. $490,040
c. $502,040
d. $514,040   (R/00, AR, #18, 6923)

71. The following selected data pertain to the Darwin Division of Beagle Co. for Year 1.

Sales	$400,000
Operating income	40,000
Capital turnover	4
Imputed interest rate	10%

What was Darwin's Year 1 residual income?
a. $0
b. $ 4,000
c. $10,000
d. $30,000   (11/95, AR, #50, amended, 5793)

72. Residual income of an investment center is the center's
a. Income plus the imputed interest on its invested capital
b. Income less the imputed interest on its invested capital
c. Contribution margin plus the imputed interest on its invested capital
d. Contribution margin less the imputed interest on its invested capital   (11/92, Theory, #48, 3481)

73. Zig Corp. provides the following information:

Pretax operating profit	$ 300,000,000
Tax rate	40%
Capital used to generate profits 50%, 50% equity	$1,200,000,000
Cost of equity	15%
Cost of debt	5%

What of the following represents Zig's year-end economic value-added amount?
a. $0
b. $ 60,000,000
c. $120,000,000
d. $180,000,000   (R/03, BEC, #8, 7670)

74. Select Co. had the following financial statement relationships:

Asset turnover	5
Profit margin on sales	0.02

What was Select's percentage return on assets?
a. 0.1%
b. 0.4%
c. 2.5%
d. 10.0%   (5/95, AR, #45, amended, 5463)

75. The following information pertains to Bala Co. for the year ended December 31, Year 1:

Sales	$600,000
Net income	100,000
Capital investment	400,000

Which of the following equations should be used to compute Bala's return on investment?
a. (4 / 6) × (6 / 1) = ROI
b. (6 / 4) × (1 / 6) = ROI
c. (4 / 6) × (1 / 6) = ROI
d. (6 / 4) × (6 / 1) = ROI
        (5/92, PII, #53, amended, 2685)

76. The following information pertains to Quest Co.'s Gold Division:

Sales	$311,000
Variable cost	250,000
Traceable fixed costs	50,000
Average invested capital	40,000
Imputed interest rate	10%

Quest's return on investment was
a. 10.00%
b. 13.33%
c. 27.50%
d. 30.00%   (5/94, AR, #43, amended, 4648)

77. How do short-term interest rates compare to long-term interest rates?
a. Generally, short-term rates are higher
b. Generally, short-term rates are lower
c. Short-term rates are lower than long-term rates during periods of high inflation
d. Similar to long-term rates   (Editors, 7317)

78. What is an underwriting spread?
a. Commission that an investment banker earns for underwriting a security issue
b. Difference between the price that an investment banker pays for a security and the price that a subsequent investor pays for the security
c. Discount that an investment banker receives on a security issue
d. Fee that an investment banker receives to prepare, print, and distribute a security issue
        (Editors, 7318)

Items 79 and 80 are based on the following:

Carmen Company has the following equity amounts and no dividends in arrears.

Preferred stock, $1,000 par	$24 million
Common stock, $100 par	$20 million
Paid-in capital in excess of par	$36 million
Retained earnings	$18 million

79. What is the book value of Carmen's common stock?
a. $100
b. $190
c. $280
d. $370 (Editors, 7319)

80. Diego owns 1,000 shares of Carmen. If Carmen Company issues an additional 100,000 shares of common stock, how many additional shares does Diego have the opportunity to buy?
a. 500
b. 1,000
c. 2,000
d. 3,000 (Editors, 7320)

81. What is the primary advantage of zero coupon bonds for an issuer?
a. Low issue costs
b. No annual cash outflow
c. No interest expense recognized by issuer until bond maturity
d. No interest income recognized by purchaser until bond maturity (Editors, 7321)

82. What is the primary advantage of serial bonds for an purchaser?
a. All bonds in an issue mature at the same time.
b. Purchasers may select the maturity that matches their financial goals.
c. The bonds are retired by lottery based on serial numbers.
d. The coupon rate is adjusted based on the maturity date. (Editors, 7322)

83. What is the primary disadvantage of convertible bonds for an issuer?
a. Convertible bonds have higher interest rates than bonds that are not convertible.
b. Dilution of financial leverage.
c. Holders of nonconvertible bonds typically accept less restrictive covenants in bond indentures.
d. Investors may choose not to convert the bonds. (Editors, 7323)

84. What is characteristic of debentures?
a. Require interest payments only when earnings are sufficient
b. Secured by the full faith and credit of the issuer
c. Secured by a lien on specified collateral
d. A set of covenants that typically restricts the amount of debt than a bond issuer may carry and the dividends it may pay (Editors, 7324)

85. What is characteristic of junk bonds?
a. No collateral
b. Bonds rated at less than investment grade
c. Bonds whose ratings have been downgraded
d. Worthless bonds (Editors, 7325)

86. What is characteristic of income bonds?
a. Pay interest only if the issuer has earned it
b. Junior to subordinated debt in the event of liquidation
c. Junior to preferred and common stock in the event of liquidation
d. Guaranteed income over the security life (Editors, 7326)

87. Which of the following statements is true?
a. A call premium is a premium that investors are required to pay when the bond is purchased.
b. A call provision generally is deemed unfavorable to investors.
c. Convertible bonds must be converted to common stock either prior to, or at, maturity.
d. A sinking fund provision prohibits the issuer from redeeming a bond issue before maturity. (Editors, 7327)

88. Balsam Company's issued nonparticipating, 8%, cumulative preferred stock. Which of the following characteristics is not true of this stock?
a. Dividend payments are not tax deductible by Balsam
b. Fixed dividend amount
c. Higher claim than common stock in the event of liquidation
d. Voting rights (Editors, 7328)

89. Which of the following items represents a business risk in capital structure decisions?
a. Contractual obligations
b. Management preferences
c. Cash flow
d. Timing of information (R/03, BEC, #10, 7672)

90. Quiche Corporation has preferred stock with a market value of $107 per share, a face value of $100 per share, underwriting costs of $5 per share, and annual dividends of $10. Quiche's tax rate is 30%. What is Quiche's approximate cost of capital for preferred stock?
a. 6.9%
b. 9.3%
c. 9.8%
d. 10.5% (Editors, 7330)

91. Which of the following involves an imputed cost?
a. Depreciation
b. Interest portion of a capital lease
c. Interest paid on a bank loan
d. Interest on internally generated cash used to purchase fixed assets (Editors, 7331)

92. Which of the following objectives is consistent with an optimal capital structure?
a. Maximize earnings per share
b. Maximize the total value of the entity
c. Minimize the cost of debt
d. Minimize the cost of equity (Editors, 7332)

93. Karma Company finances each asset with financial instruments with maturities with lengths similar to asset life. What is this policy called?
a. Financial leverage
b. Hedging approach
c. Operating leverage
d. Return maximization (Editors, 7333)

Items 94 and 95 are based on the following:

Owens Company sells 500,000 bottles of condiments annually at $3 per bottle. Variable costs are $0.60 per bottle and fixed costs are $110,000 annually. Owens has annual interest expense of $60,000 and a 30% income tax rate.

94. What is Owens' approximate degree of operating leverage?
a. 1.01
b. 1.06
c. 1.08
d. 1.10
e. 1.51 (Editors, 7334)

95. What is Owens' approximate degree of financial leverage?
a. 1.01
b. 1.06
c. 1.08
d. 1.10
e. 1.51 (Editors, 7335)

96. Which of the following factors would influence an entity to increase its proportion of debt financing?
a. A decrease in the times-interest-earned ratio
b. An increase in economic uncertainty
c. An increase in the effective income tax rate
d. An increase in the federal funds rate (Editors, 7336)

97. What is the overall cost of capital?
a. Average rate of return that an entity earns on its assets
b. Cost of an entity's equity capital
c. Expected rate of return for the risk level that an entity represents
d. Rate of return on assets that meets the costs connected with employed funds (Editors, 7337)

Items 98 and 99 are based on the following:

Reinhold Company is considering a $50 million project in the upcoming year. Reinhold plans to use both debt and equity to finance the project. Reinhold's beta coefficient is estimated at 0.95. Reinhold has a 30% effective income tax rate. The equity market is expected to have average earnings of 12%. U.S. Treasury bonds currently yield 4%.

- Funds generated from earnings, $35 million.
- Additional funds from $15 million 20-year, 6% bonds at a price of 102, with flotation costs of 3% of par.

98. For the first year of the project, what is the approximate estimated before-tax cost of Reinhold's debt financing, net of flotation costs?
a. 5.88%
b. 6.00%
c. 6.06%
d. 7.00% (Editors, 7338)

99. The capital asset pricing model (CAPM) computes a security's expected return by adding the risk-free rate of return to the incremental yield of the expected market return, adjusted by the issuer's beta. What is Reinhold's expected rate of return using this model?
a. 12.4%
b. 12.0%
c. 11.6%
d. 11.4% (Editors, 7339)

100. Snaps Company will start a $30 million project in the upcoming year. Snaps will use $22.5 million of debt and $7.5 million of equity to finance the project. Snaps has a 30% effective income tax rate. The after-tax cost of debt is 6% and the cost of equity is 12%. What is Snaps' approximate weighted average cost of capital for this project?
a. 6.00%
b. 6.15%
c. 7.50%
d. 9.00%
e. 9.43% (Editors, 7340)

101. Unity Company has a higher degree of operating leverage than the industry average. Compared to the industry average,
a. Unity has higher variable costs.
b. Unity is less risky.
c. Unity's profits are more sensitive to changes in sales volume.
d. Unity uses more debt financing. (Editors, 7341)

102. Deep Company has 5,000 shares of 7% cumulative, $1,000 par value preferred stock and 50,000 shares of $100 par value common stock outstanding. Deep last declared and paid dividends on April 30, Year 1, for the year ending March 31, Year 1. There are no dividends in arrears for fiscal years ending March 31, Year 1, or earlier. For the year ending March 31, Year 4, Deep's net income is $1,500,000. Deep declared a common stock dividend that is 25% of net income for the fiscal year ending March 31, Year 4, to be paid on April 30, Year 4. What is the total amount of dividends to be paid on April 30, Year 4?
a. $ 375,000
b. $ 625,000
c. $1,425,000
d. $1,450,000 (Editors, 7343)

103. Egret Company expects next year's net income to be $2 million. Egret's current capital structure is 30% debt, 30% preferred equity, and 40% common equity. Next year, Egret's plans to issue debt and common stock as needed to maintain their 30:40 ratio, not to issue more preferred stock. Interest payments on Egret's 10,000 4%, $1,000 par value bonds are current. Egret can issue up to $1 million more 4% bonds at face value. Egret's marginal tax rate is 30%. There are no dividends in arrears on Egret's 10,000 shares of 6%, $1,000 par value cumulative preferred stock. Optimal capital spending for next year is estimated at $1.4 million. Using a strict residual dividend policy, what is the approximate estimated common stock dividend payout ratio for the next year?
a. 0%
b. 16%
c. 30%
d. 35%
e. 70% (Editors, 7342)

104. Which of the following is an assumption of an active policy strategy for dividends?
a. The rate of return that investors require is not affected by dividend policy.
b. Dividends are irrelevant to investor decisions.
c. Dividends provide information to the market.
d. Stock dividends are preferable to cash dividends when management is concerned about control. (Editors, 7344)

105. What is the typical reason for a corporation to use warrants?
a. To avoid dilution of earnings per share
b. To improve the current cash flow
c. To lower the cost of debt
d. To permit the early buy-back of bonds (Editors, 7345)

Problem 51-2 ADDITIONAL MULTIPLE CHOICE QUESTIONS (116 to 145 minutes)

106. To maximize shareholder wealth, which of the following measures is most appropriate for management focus?
a. Earnings per share
b. Profits
c. Stock value
d. Total return per share (Editors, 7729)

107. Which of the following are characteristic of the growth or exploitation phase of a product life cycle?
a. High promotional expenses as a percentage of sales
b. Little direct competition
c. Profits shrink as direct competition increases.
d. Sales increase dramatically. (Editors, 7730)

108. Amalgamated Corporation is a public company that is not issuing new stock currently. Bill Charge wants to invest in Amalgamated. In which market would Bill Charge purchase Amalgamated's stock?
a. Debt market
b. Real estate market
c. Mortgage market
d. Secondary market (Editors, 7731)

109. Which of the following most likely is said to "make a market" in a particular security?
a. A commercial bank
b. A dealer in an over-the-counter market
c. A mutual fund
d. A pension fund (Editors, 7732)

110. Two different companies of approximately similar financial strength and with similar management teams both have 30-year bonds that trade in active secondary markets. Nile Company is located in a country with relatively small increases in overall price levels; its bonds have a 4% return. Amazon Company is located in a country with relatively large increases in overall price levels each year; its bonds have a 14% return. What is the difference in the interest rate between Nile Company's bonds and Amazon Company's bonds called?
a. Default risk premium
b. Inflation premium
c. Liquidity premium
d. Maturity risk premium   (Editors, 7733)

111. Mott Company has a $100 ten-year, 6% certificate of deposit that receives interest annually. Present and future value factors are as follows:

Present value of 1 at 6% for 10 periods   0.614
Future value of 1 at 6% for 10 periods   1.791
Present value of ordinary annuity of
  1 at 6% for 10 periods   7.360
Future value of ordinary annuity of
  1 at 6% for 10 periods   13.181

How much will Mott Co. receive in ten years?
a. $ 61
b. $ 179
c. $ 736
d. $1,381   (Editors, 7734)

112. For the next 2 years, a lease is estimated to have an operating net cash inflow of $7,500 per annum, before adjusting for $5,000 per annum tax basis lease amortization, and a 40% tax rate. The present value of an ordinary annuity of $1 per year at 10% for 2 years is $1.74. What is the lease's after-tax present value using a 10% discount factor?
a. $ 2,610
b. $ 4,350
c. $ 9,570
d. $11,310   (11/95, AR, #42, 5785)

113. Mutt Company has a $100 ten-year, 8% certificate of deposit that receives interest quarterly. Future value factors are as follows:

Future value of 1 at 2% for 10 periods   1.219
Future value of 1 at 8% for 10 periods   2.159
Future value of 1 at 2% for 40 periods   2.208
Future value of 1 at 8% for 40 periods   21.725

How much will Mutt Co. receive in ten years?
a. $122
b. $216
c. $221
d. $2,173   (Editors, 7735)

114. Which working capital policy has the greatest likelihood that a firm will be unable to meet obligations as they become due?
a. Financing all current assets with long-term debt
b. Financing all current assets with short-term debt
c. Financing fluctuating current assets with short-term debt and permanent current assets with equity
d. Financing fluctuating current assets with short-term debt and permanent current assets with long-term debt   (Editors, 7357)

115. Net working capital is the difference between
a. Capital assets and long-term liabilities
b. Current assets and current liabilities
c. Current assets, except for inventories, and current liabilities
d. Fixed assets and long-term liabilities
e. Total equity and stock par value   (Editors, 7358)

116. Yeats Company issued common stock for cash. What was the impact on the current ratio and working capital?

	Current ratio	Working capital
a.	Increase	Decrease
b.	Increase	Increase
c.	Decrease	Increase
d.	Decrease	Decrease

(Editors, 7359)

117. Which of the following is the **least** likely reason for an entity to hold cash and marketable securities?
a. Maintain sufficient cash to meet transaction requirements
b. Maintain a reserve for unexpected events
c. Fulfill compensating balance requirements
d. Earn maximum returns on assets (Editors, 7360)

118. Brooks Company has daily cash receipts of $400,000. Brooks' bank offers a lockbox service that will reduce collection time by two days for a $2,000 monthly fee. Brooks can earn 8% annually with any additional funds. What will be the annual increase to income before taxes from using the lockbox service?
a. $24,000
b. $32,000
c. $40,000
d. $64,000   (Editors, 7361)

119. An automated clearing house electronic funds transfer is
a. A check-like instrument drawn against the payor and rather than a bank
b. A computer-generated deposit ticket
c. An electronic payment to a company's bank account
d. A transfer charge generated by an automated clearing house   (Editors, 7362)

120. Windfall Company has daily cash receipts of $300,000. Windfall's bank offers a lockbox service that will reduce collection time by four days for a $2,500 monthly fee. If money market rates average 3% for the year, what will be the annual impact on income before taxes from using the lockbox service?
a. $30,000 decrease
b. $ 9,000 decrease
c. $ 6,000 increase
d. $33,500 increase   (Editors, 7294)

121. Commercial paper
a. Generally has interest rates lower than treasury bills
b. Has maturities of greater than 1 year
c. Is a secured promissory note
d. Typically does not have an active secondary market   (Editors, 7363)

122. Which of the following is **least** appropriate for use as a cash substitute?
a. Banker's acceptances
b. Commercial paper
c. Convertible bonds
d. U.S. Treasury bills   (Editors, 7364)

123. Tough Company is basing next year's budget on sales of $27 million. Tough expects that 80% of sales will be on credit, with n/30 terms. Tough estimates that relaxing the credit policy will increase credit sales by 30% and increase the average collection period from 28 to 40 days. Based on a 360-day year, what is the expected increase in Tough's average accounts receivable balance?
a. $ 504,000
b. $ 720,000
c. $1,440,000
d. $1,800,000   (Editors, 7365)

124. Stiffening Company is evaluating a proposed credit policy change. The proposed policy would change the average number of days for collection from 60 to 27 days and would reduce total sales by 25%, all of the decrease due to credit sales. Under the current policy, next year's sales are estimated at $128 million, with 75% of them being credit sales. Based on a 360-day year, what is the decrease in Stiffening's average accounts receivable balance of implementing the proposed credit policy change?
a. $16 million
b. $11.2 million
c. $10 million
d. $ 4.8 million   (Editors, 7366)

125. Evermore Company has average daily cash collections of $3 million, based on a 360-day year. A new system is estimated to reduce the average collection period by two days without affecting sales. The new system's annual cost is $100,000 plus 0.01% of collections. Evermore estimates that it would earn 6% on additional funds. What is the estimated annual net benefit from the new system?
a. $152,000
b. $180,000
c. $260,000
d. $360,000   (Editors, 7367)

126. To determine the inventory reorder point, calculations normally include the
a. Ordering cost
b. Carrying cost
c. Average daily usage
d. Economic order quantity   (R/01, AR, #16, 7001)

127. Stewpot Company uses the economic order model to determine the size of its purchase orders. What would cause an increase in the economic order quantity?
a. Annual demand decrease
b. Carrying cost decrease
c. Ordering cost decrease
d. Safety stock level decrease   (Editors, 7369)

128. Baker manufacturers small appliances. Baker uses the economic order quantity model to determine the appropriate size of production runs or batches. What does Baker use as the order costs in the economic order quantity formula?
a. Assembly line reconfiguration costs
b. Handling
c. Insurance and taxes
d. Storage   (Editors, 7370)

129. Which of the following is least likely to affect the optimal inventory level?
a. Cost per unit
b. Current inventory level
c. Inventory usage rate
d. Order placement cost
e. Time from order placement to receipt
                                    (Editors, 7371)

130. Which of the following is least likely to affect the inventory safety stock level?
a. Degree of customer intolerance for backorders
b. Degree of sales forecast uncertainty
c. Degree of shipment lead time uncertainty
d. Order placement cost
e. Stock out cost   (Editors, 7346)

131. When would a retailer tend to increase the safety stock of inventory?
a. Cost of carrying inventory increases
b. Cost of running out of stock decreases
c. Lead time variability increases
d. Sales variability decreases   (Editors, 7372)

132. What is the largest source of short-term credit for small businesses?
a. Commercial paper
b. Debentures
c. Mortgages
d. Notes payables
e. Trade credit   (Editors, 7373)

133. Mason has a $400,000 loan with a stated 6% interest rate. Mason must maintain a 20% compensating balance in its checking account. Without the loan provisions, Mason otherwise would keep a zero balance in its checking account. What is the effective rate of interest on the loan?
a. 4.5%
b. 6.0%
c. 7.5%
d. 26%   (Editors, 7374)

134. Which of the following statement is true with regard to financial derivatives?
a. A forward contract is a forward-based derivative that obligates two parties to trade a series of cash flows at specified future settlement dates.
b. Due to their extreme risk, extensive purchase of derivatives are more likely to occur when markets are stable.
c. Use of derivatives should eliminate risk.
d. Using derivatives divides financial risk into separate elements that can be exchanged between entities.   (Editors, 7967)

135. How do exchange clearinghouses promote liquidity in futures markets?

I.   The daily mark to market decreases the risk that the other party to a futures contract will be unable to meet its obligations on the maturity date.
II. Exchanges develop appropriate incentives so that traders do not assume unwarranted risks.
III. Exchanges use standardized contracts.

a. I and II only
b. I and III only
c. II and III only
d. I, II, and III   (Editors, 7968)

136. Capital projects may be classified by type of project. Which classification generally would be assigned to a project to retrofit equipment to meet new safety regulations?
a. Cost-reduction replacements
b. Expansion of existing products or markets
c. Expansion into new products or markets
d. Mandated investments   (Editors, 7736)

137. Lin Co. is buying machinery it expects will increase average annual operating income by $40,000. The initial increase in the required investment is $60,000, and the average increase in required investment is $30,000. To compute the accrual accounting rate of return, what amount should be used as the numerator in the ratio?
a. $20,000
b. $30,000
c. $40,000
d. $60,000   (11/92, PII, #39, 3373)

138. The capital budgeting technique known as accounting rate of return uses

	Revenue over life of project	Depreciation expense	Time value of money
a.	No	Yes	No
b.	No	No	Yes
c.	Yes	No	Yes
d.	Yes	Yes	No

                                    (Editors, 2247)

139. Which of the following characteristics represent an advantage of the internal rate of return technique over the accounting rate of return technique in evaluating a project?

   I.   Recognition of the project's salvage value
   II. Emphasis on cash flows
   III. Recognition of the time value of money

a. I only
b. I and II
c. II and III
d. I, II, and III   (11/92, Theory, #49, 3482)

140. Which of the following is a strength of the payback method?
a. It considers cash flows for all years of the project.
b. It distinguishes the sources of cash inflows.
c. It considers the time value of money.
d. It is easy to understand.   (R/01, AR, #14, 6999)

141. Para Co. is reviewing the following data relating to an energy saving investment proposal:

Cost	$50,000
Residual value at the end of 5 years	10,000
Present value of an annuity of 1 at 12% for 5 years	3.60
Present value of 1 due in 5 years at 12%	0.57

What would be the annual savings needed to make the investment realize a 12% yield?
a. $ 8,189
b. $11,111
c. $12,306
d. $13,889   (5/94, AR, #38, 4643)

142. How are the following used in the calculation of the internal rate of return of a proposed project? Ignore income tax considerations.

	Residual sales value of project	Depreciation expense
a.	Exclude	Include
b.	Include	Include
c.	Exclude	Exclude
d.	Include	Exclude

(11/91, Theory, #49, 2556)

143. Mudd Co. is planning to buy a coin-operated machine costing $20,000. For tax purposes, this machine will be depreciated over a five-year period using the straight-line method and no salvage value. Mudd estimates that this machine will yield an annual cash inflow, net of depreciation and income taxes, of $6,000. At the following discount rates, the net present values of the investment in this machine are:

Discount rate	Net present value
12%	+ $1,629
14%	+ 599
16%	– 354
18%	– 1,237

Mudd's expected internal rate of return on its investment in this machine is
a. 3.3%
b. 10.0%
c. 12.0%
d. 15.3%   (Editors, 1540)

144. Which of the following capital budgeting techniques implicitly assumes that the cash flows are reinvested at the company's minimum required rate of return?

	Net present value	Internal rate of return
a.	Yes	Yes
b.	Yes	No
c.	No	Yes
d.	No	No

(11/90, Theory, #47, 2244)

145. Polo Co. requires higher rates of return for projects with a life span greater than five years. Projects extending beyond five years must earn a higher specified rate of return. Which of the following capital budgeting techniques can readily accommodate this requirement?

	Internal rate of return	Net present value
a.	Yes	No
b.	No	Yes
c.	No	No
d.	Yes	Yes

(5/90, Theory, #48, 2248)

146. A proposed project has an expected economic life of eight years. In the calculation of the net present value of the proposed project, salvage value would be
a. Excluded from the calculation of the net present value
b. Included as a cash inflow at the future amount of the estimated salvage value
c. Included as a cash inflow at the estimated salvage value
d. Included as a cash inflow at the present value of the estimated salvage value   (Editors, 2258)

147. The discount rate (hurdle rate of return) must be determined in advance for the
a. Payback period method
b. Time adjusted rate of return method
c. Net present value method
d. Internal rate of return method

(5/91, Theory, #48, 2241)

148. The invested capital-employed turnover rate would include
a. Invested capital in the numerator
b. Invested capital in the denominator
c. Net income in the numerator
d. Sales in the denominator (Editors, 2260)

149. Division A is considering a project that will earn a rate of return which is greater than the imputed interest charge for invested capital, but less than the division's historical return on invested capital. Division B is considering a project that will earn a rate of return which is greater than the division's historical return on invested capital, but less than the imputed interest charge for invested capital. If the objective is to maximize residual income, should these divisions accept or reject their projects?

	Project A	Project B
a.	Accept	Accept
b.	Reject	Accept
c.	Reject	Reject
d.	Accept	Reject

(11/90, Theory, #48, 2245)

150. Kim Co.'s profit center Zee had Year 1 operating income of $200,000 before a $50,000 imputed interest charge for using Kim's assets. Kim's aggregate net income from all of its profit centers was $2,000,000. During Year 1, Kim declared and paid dividends of $30,000 and $70,000 on its preferred and common stock, respectively. Zee's Year 1 residual income was
a. $140,000
b. $143,000
c. $147,000
d. $150,000 (11/92, PII, #28, amended, 3362)

151. Following is information relating to Kew Co.'s Vale Division for Year 1:

Sales	$500,000
Variable costs	300,000
Traceable fixed costs	50,000
Average invested capital	100,000
Imputed interest rate	6%

Vale's residual income was
a. $144,000
b. $150,000
c. $156,000
d. $200,000 (5/92, PII, #52, amended, 2684)

152. Which of the following is characteristic of primary capital markets?
a. Exchanges of existing debt and equity securities
b. Exchanges of future commodity contracts
c. Exchanges of future commodity contracts and new issues of debt and equity securities
d. New issues of debt and equity securities

(Editors, 7368)

153. Which of the following is not characteristic of venture capital?
a. Initial private placement
b. Lack of liquidity for some time period
c. Common stock issue
d. Minimum 5-year holding period (Editors, 7379)

154. What is the par value of common stock?
a. The value of the stock that must be entered as equity in the issuer's financial statements
b. The value of the stock that must be entered as paid-in-capital in the issuer's financial statements
c. A shareholder's liability ceiling if the issuer goes bankrupt
d. Estimated market value of the stock when it was issued (Editors, 7380)

155. Pan Company's bonds are yielding 6% currently. Why is Pan's cost of debt lower than 6%?
a. Additional debt is issued less expensively than initial debt.
b. Interest is deductible in calculating taxable income.
c. Interest rates decreased since Pan issued these bonds.
d. Interest rates increased since Pan issued these bonds. (Editors, 7381)

Items 156 through 159 are based on the following:

Lemur Company's $10 par value common stock currently sells at $100 per share. Lemur has retained earnings of $100,000; once this is exhausted, Lemur will raise any more necessary equity capital through a stock issue. Lemur can raise cash by selling common stock at a $2 per share discount with a $3 per share floatation cost. Annual cash dividends are $7 per share and are not expected to change.

The estimated after-tax cost of funds raised by long-term bonds is 5%. The estimated cost of funds raised by preferred stock is 6%. Lemur's preferred capital structure is 30% long-term debt, 20% preferred stock, and 50% common stock. Not counting the $100,000 of retained earnings, the current capital structure is Lemur's preferred structure.

156. What would be Lemur's cost of funds from a common stock sale?
a. 7.00%
b. 7.14%
c. 7.22%
d. 7.37% (Editors, 7375)

157. What would be Lemur's cost of funds on retained earnings?
a. 7.00%
b. 7.14%
c. 7.22%
d. 7.37% (Editors, 7376)

158. If Lemur raises funds for projects requiring capital of $200,000 and keeps its preferred capital structure, what would be the approximate weighted-average cost of capital?
a. 6.63%
b. 6.39%
c. 6.35%
d. 6.20%
e. 6.00% (Editors, 7377)

159. If Lemur raises funds for projects requiring capital of $1,000,000 and keeps its preferred capital structure, what would be the weighted-average cost of capital?
a. 6.63%
b. 6.39%
c. 6.35%
d. 6.20%
e. 6.00% (Editors, 7378)

160. Aardvark Company's beta coefficient is 1.2. The current rates for U.S. treasury bonds and expected corporate returns are 7% and 12%, respectively. What is Aardvark's approximate expected rate of return using the capital asset pricing model (CAPM)?
a. 8.4%
b. 10.6%
c. 13.0%
d. 14.4% (Editors, 7382)

161. Which of the following objectives is consistent with an optimal capital structure?
a. Maximum earnings per share
b. Minimum cost of debt
c. Minimum risk
d. Minimum weighted average cost of capital (Editors, 7383)

162. What is the impact of a purchase of treasury stock with surplus cash from operations?
a. Decreases earnings per share
b. Increases assets
c. Increases equity
d. Increases financial leverage (Editors, 7329)

163. Which of the following is an assumption of the residual theory of dividends?
a. The rate of return that investors require is not affected by dividend policy.
b. Dividend payments should be a percentage of earnings.
c. Dividend payments should be stable.
d. The number of dividend distributions should be minimized. (Editors, 7316)

SIMULATIONS

FYI: The editors encourage candidates to answer simulations as part of their review because such studying provides for content reinforcement, regardless of question format. Simulations currently are not part of the BEC exam; Bisk Education updating supplements will notify readers when this situation changes.

Problem 51-3 (10 to 20 minutes)

Tam Co. is negotiating for the purchase of equipment that would cost $100,000, with the expectation that $20,000 per year could be saved in after-tax cash costs if the equipment were acquired. The equipment's estimated useful life is 10 years, with no residual value, and would be depreciated by the straight-line method. Tam's predetermined minimum desired rate of return is 12%. Present value of an annuity of 1 at 12% for 10 periods is 5.65. Present value of 1 due in 10 periods at 12% is .322.

1. Rounded to the nearest $10, what is the net present value?   (5/92, PII, #57, 2689)

2. Rounded to the nearest tenth of a year, what is the payback period?   (5/92, PII, #58, 2690)

3. What is the accrual accounting rate of return based on initial investment?   (5/92, PII, #59, 2691)

4. In estimating the internal rate of return, the factors in the table of present values of an annuity should be taken from the columns closest to what amount?   (5/92, PII, #60, 2692)

Helm invested $400,000 in a five-year project at the beginning of Year 1. Helm estimates that the annual cash savings from this project will amount to $130,000. The $400,000 of assets will be depreciated over their five-year life on the straight-line basis. On investments of this type, Helm's desired rate of return is 12%. Information on present value factors is as follows:

	At 12%	At 14%	At 16%
Present value of 1 for 5 periods	0.57	0.52	0.48
Present value of an annuity of 1 for 5 periods	3.60	3.40	3.30

1. What is the net present value of the project?   (Editors, 1535)

2. Helm's internal rate of return on this project is
   A. Less than 12%
   B. Less than 14%, but more than 12%
   C. Less than 16%, but more than 14%
   D. More than 16%   (Editors, 1536)

3. For the project's first year, what would be Helm's accounting rate of return, based on the project's average book value for Year 1?   (Editors, 1537)

Problem 51-4 (10 to 15 minutes)

A company has two mutually exclusive projects, A and B, which have the same initial investment requirements and lives. Project B has a decrease in estimated cash inflows each year, and project A has an increase in estimated net cash inflows each year. Project A has a greater total net cash inflow. Diagram I below depicts the net cash inflows of each project by year. Diagram II depicts the net present value (NPV) of each project assuming various discount rates.

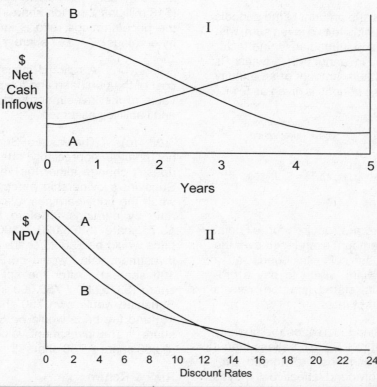

Select your answer from the following list:

A. Project A
B. Project B
C. Both projects equal
D. Indeterminate from information given

1. Which project would be likely to have the shorter payback period?

2. Which project would have the greater average accounting rate of return?

3. Which project would have the greater internal rate of return?

4. Assume, due to innovation, the projects were to terminate at the end of year 4 with cash flows remaining as projected for the first 4 years and no cash flows in year 5. Which project would have the greater internal rate of return?   (11/93, Theory, #66-69, amended, 7478)

Solution 51-1 MULTIPLE CHOICE ANSWERS

Time Value of Money

1. (c) The present value for a single sum in 3 years is the difference between the present value of an annuity for 3 years and the present value of an annuity for 2 years. (2.32 – 1.65 = 0.67)

Reduction in costs for the first 2 years ($30,000 × 1.65)	$49,500
Reduction in costs for Year 3 ($20,000 × 0.67)	13,400
Present value of future cost savings	$62,900

2. (c) To determine the amount of the periodic payments required to accumulate to a given sum, with the first payment to be made immediately, the factor for the future amount of an annuity in advance is used. The factor for the future amount of an annuity in advance of 1 at 10% for 4 periods is given as 5.11.

Annual deposit amount	×	Applicable factor for future amount of annuity in advance	=	Future annuity in advance

Annual deposit × 5.11 = $1,000,000
Annual deposit = $1,000,000 / 5.11 = $195,700

Valuation

3. (a, d) Both answers are required for full point value. A premium is any amount exchanged over the par (face) amount; Yates sold its bonds at a $250 premium. Investors are willing to pay a premium for a bond when its stated (coupon) rate is higher than prevailing market rates.

4. (a) A stock dividend increases the quantity of outstanding stock. Future EPS will be less than it would otherwise be, as earnings are spread over more shares. A stock dividend effectively moves equity from retained earnings to paid in capital. Debt, total equity, entity size, and shareholders' ownership percentages remain the same.

5. (d) A stock dividend increases the number of shares without any difference to the underlying assets they represent; typically, this decreases the market value per share. The retirement of bonds as scheduled likely would have no effect on the market value of stock. A treasury stock purchase would reduce the number of shares, which would tend to increase the market value per share. A reverse stock split would reduce the number of shares without any difference to the underlying assets they represent, which would increase the market value per share.

6. (a) The dividend growth model predicts the cost of equity equal to the sum of next year's dividend divided by the current market price plus the expected growth rate. $2 / $40 + 0.10 = 0.15.

7. (a) Estimated net income is $28 million [($45 million – $5 million) × (1 – 0.30)]. After paying preferred stock dividends, there is $18 million available to common shareholders, or EPS of $9 ($18 million / 2 million shares). 25% × $9 = $2.25.

8. (a) Estimated earnings are $28 million [($45 million – $5 million) × (1 – 0.30)]. After paying preferred stock dividends, there is $18 million available to common shareholders, or EPS of $9 ($18 million / 2 million shares). To figure price when the price/earnings ratio is known, multiply the ratio by earnings. 7 × $9 / share = $63 / share.

9. (d) A rational investor would consider the cost of the purchase and the value of the asset. The value of the investment is influenced by cash flows and liabilities assumed.

10. (c) The value of Sunshine's investment will not change appreciably due to the split; the split doesn't change either the value of the company or Sunshine's ownership percentage. To figure price when the price/earnings ratio is known, multiply the ratio by earnings. Before the split, earnings are $3.75/share ($375,000 / 100,000 shares) and the price would be $26.25/share (7 × $3.75/share). The investment value would be $2,625 ($26.25/share × 100 shares). After the split, earnings are $0.50/share ($375,000 / 750,000 shares). After the split, Sunshine would own 750 shares (100 shares / 2 × 15) and the price would be $3.50/share (7 × $0.50/share). The investment value still would be $2,625 ($3.50/share × 750 shares).

Risk & Return

11. (c) Shareholders are exposed to more risk than creditors: dividend payments are not required and, in the event of liquidation, debts are repaid before shareholders' claims. Dividends are set by the board of directors, which may set a constant dividend; interest rates fluctuate on a daily basis, as they are determined by the market. The legal nature of bond interest obligations is a less complete explanation for the expensive nature of equity capital than the premium for higher risk. The demand for equity investments vs. debt investments has to do with risk tolerance; if equity capital didn't provide potentially higher returns, demand would not be so high.

12. (c) A high debt-to-equity ratio puts an entity at a high risk of insolvency; debt payments legally must be made in recessive periods as well as boom periods, while dividends never are required to be declared. A low interest coverage ratio signifies that

earnings before interest and taxes with which to pay interest are small in proportion to required interest payments. A small earnings drop for an entity with high interest coverage would have minimal impact on financial condition. A drop of the same dollar amount could throw an entity with low interest coverage into insolvency.

Working Capital Overview

13. (a) Holding current assets generally is not profitable because of the low rate of return, yet insufficient working capital could cause, for example, a failure to pay bills as they become due, resulting in involuntary bankruptcy. Working capital management requires balancing profitability with liquidity. Working capital management generally doesn't involve capital structure issues, dividend policy, or financing long-term assets. Minimal long-term debt may not be the best policy in a given situation.

14. (a) A conservative working capital policy is characterized by a high net working capital; some policies try to keep inventory relatively low, to mitigate the impact of obsolescence. Increases in current assets and decreases in current liabilities increase net working capital. The same factors that increase net working capital tend to increase the quick ratio [(cash + marketable securities + net receivables) / current liabilities]. A reduced inventory level, while keeping a high net working capital, would tend to increase the quick ratio. A conservative policy insulates an entity from interest rate fluctuations. All other things equal, an increase in net working capital would increase the ratio of current assets to noncurrent assets or decrease the ratio of current liabilities to noncurrent liabilities. While implementing a more conservative working capital policy does not increase the quick ratio invariably, the other three options are unlikely ever to occur in connection with the implementation of a more conservative working capital policy.

15. (e) Net working capital is the difference between current assets and current liabilities. An increase in current assets increases net working capital. A decrease in current liabilities increases net working capital. $120 + $200 = $320.

16. (a) Liquidity is the ability to use assets to meet maturing debts (i.e., short-term liabilities). The current ratio (current assets to current liabilities) and the quick ratio (current assets less inventory to current liabilities) provide measures of the amount of assets to settle short-term liabilities. Comparing short-term and long-term debt ignores the impact of current assets. Net income typically includes non-cash items (such as depreciation) that cannot be

used to settle debts. Comparing total assets to total liabilities introduces irrelevant considerations: assets that are not converted into cash readily and debts that need not be retired shortly.

17. (a, c, d) Three responses are required for full credit. Working capital is current assets less current liabilities; ratios used to evaluate working capital management concentrate on working capital components. The average collection period ratio is the number of days' sales in accounts receivable. The inventory turnover ratio is the number of times in a year that the inventory is sold (computed by dividing cost of goods sold by average inventory). The quick (or acid-test) ratio is current assets, except for inventory, divided by current liabilities. The current ratio, not mentioned in this question, is current assets divided by current liabilities. The debt-to-equity ratio is total debt divided by total equity; this ratio is used when evaluating capital structure. The return on assets ratio is net income after taxes divided by average total assets; this ratio is used when evaluating total asset management.

18. (a) Working capital is the difference between current assets and current liabilities. Working capital before the expansion is $53,000 (7 + 20 + 40 + 38 – 35 – 17). Working capital after the expansion would be $50,000 (13 + 11 + 55 + 48 – 44 – 33). $53,000 – $50,000 = $3,000 decrease. The current portion of the mortgage payable is part of current liabilities, and hence, working capital.

19. (a) Acquiring an airplane with a capital lease increases long-term assets and long-term liabilities; however, the part of the obligation that is short-term debt decreases working capital. A/R collection and payment of payroll taxes have no effect on net working capital; these transactions merely exchange short-term items. Refinancing commercial paper with long-term debt decreases current liabilities without affecting current assets and, thus, increases net working capital; the short-term portion of the bond interest would be less than the commercial paper retired.

Cash

20. (c) The cash flow cycle is measured as the length of time that an entity pays for inventory to the time it receives cash from inventory sales. If inventory is held for 65 days and accounts payables have an average age of 30 days, cash is disbursed 35 days after inventory is received. Receivables are collected 40 days after sale. 35 + 40 = 75 days.

21. (b) As cash is merely an inventory of money; the economic order quantity (EOQ) model

may be used to determine when to "order" cash, or in other words, when to convert marketable securities into cash. Determination of an appropriate current ratio (current assets to current liabilities) and credit and collection policy is based in part on factors other than what the EOQ model encompasses: bond indentures, customer reactions, etc. Cash management is not concerned with long-term capitalization.

22. (b) A compensating balance is held in an account at a financial institution to cover the cost of services to the account holder, typically including check processing. Compensating balances also may apply in a loan contract, effectively raising the interest rate. Safety stock is a quantity of inventory above the economic order quantity held to cover use variation. Prepaid interest on a loan is called discount interest. Secondary collateral might be used to cover potential losses on marketable securities used as collateral in a loan contract.

23. (a) Net income has many non-cash elements. Sales, purchases, and collections, as well as payment terms all directly influence cash flows.

24. (b) A zero-balance account is a subsidiary account that is maintained at a specified balance (usually zero) and is linked electronically to a master account; when funds are needed to pay checks drawn on the zero-balance account, they are transferred from the master account. Lockbox systems and preauthorized checks are associated with reducing float connected with customer payments. A **lockbox system** is an arrangement whereby an entity instructs its customers to send payments to a lockbox that bonded bank employees open; the bank employees deposit the enclosed checks, forwarding the accompanying remittance advices to the account-holder. **Preauthorized** checks are checks that a company writes on behalf of its customers to pay the amount owed to the company, by previous arrangement; no further customer action is required. Preauthorized checks appear on customers' bank statements like other checks; they often are used by businesses that receive regular monthly payments from customers for the same amount (for example, financing payments). **Depository transfer** checks are made out directly by a local bank to a particular firm or person, typically used by a company to transfer funds from one of its outlying depository locations to its concentration account.

25. (b) Drafts are negotiable instruments with which one person orders a second person to pay a third person. Drafts may be dated on the due date of an invoice and may not be processed until that date, requiring a delay in processing and thus, delaying cash outflows. A compensating balance is held in an account at a financial institution to cover the cost of services to the account holder, typically including check processing. Electronic funds transfers (EFT) and lockbox systems speed cash inflows; correspondingly, they speed outflows for senders.

26. (c) Float is the difference between the time when a check is written and the time that the money is removed from the account. Float effectively is a zero interest loan to the check writer. If checks written take one more day to clear than checks deposited and checks written equal the same amount as deposits, the net float equals one day's deposits. $1,000 × 2 days = $2,000.

27. (b) October cash inflows are composed of October cash sales, 50% of October credit sales, 30% of September credit sales, and 20% of August credit sales. $20K + (50% × $90K) + (30% × $80K) + (20% × $95K) = $108K.

28. (a) Holding current assets generally is not profitable because of the low rate of return, yet insufficient working capital could cause, for example, a failure to pay bills as they become due, resulting in involuntary bankruptcy. Working capital management requires balancing profitability with liquidity. Maximum returns on working capital are secondary to having sufficient working capital to pay bills as they become due. Minimizing taxes and transaction fees are secondary considerations.

Short-Term Investments

29. (a) Commercial paper is short-term debt; in liquidation, debt has a higher priority than equity claims. Gold is not a security; also it is subject to price fluctuations due to causes that don't impact commercial paper.

30. (d) Short-term unsecured notes issued by large, financially strong commercial enterprises to institutional investors are called commercial paper. Commercial paper's short-term nature exempts it from SEC registration requirements. Agency securities are short-term securities issued by federal government agencies or corporations. Bankers' acceptances are drafts drawn on bank deposits for which the bank guarantees payment. Certificates of deposit are issued by banks. Treasury bills are short-term securities issued by the U.S. Treasury.

31. (a) Agency securities are short-term securities issued by federal government agencies or corporations, such as Fannie Mae. Bankers' acceptances are drafts drawn on bank deposits on which the bank guarantees payment. Municipal bonds are issued by states and cities. Repurchase agreements

are contracts involving a loan secured by a securities portfolio; typically, they involve state or local governments. Treasury bills are short-term securities issued by the U.S. Treasury.

32.   (e)   A Treasury bill is a highly liquid short-term U.S. government obligation that is considered practically risk-free; it frequently is held as a cash substitute. Bankers' acceptances are drafts for which the bank guarantees payment; they are designed to facilitate transfers; thus, they must be low risk and highly liquid. Certificates of deposit (CDs) are issued by banks; while relatively safe, bankers' acceptances and CDs are not considered as safe as treasury bills. Gold is subject to price fluctuations and it is not particularly liquid. Municipal bonds are issued in varying maturities by states and cities with varying creditworthiness.

33.   (d)   Commercial paper is short-term unsecured notes issued by large, financially strong commercial enterprises to institutional investors. Typically, it has lower rates than bank loans because it draws from a wide pool of lenders compared to the banks that have a close relationship with the issuer. Only entities with high credit ratings can issue commercial paper at a reasonable rate; for other entities, there is no incentive to issue it. Investors usually pay commissions to purchase commercial paper. Banks typically issue lines of credit, or commit to lending up to a maximum amount for a period; businesses tap a line of credit when they need funds. A commercial paper issuer gets funds when the paper is issued. Although the effective rate on any one issue is determined when it is issued, commercial paper rates fluctuate, typically on a daily basis.

34.   (e)   Treasury bills are backed by the U.S. government. Agency securities are backed primarily by the issuing federal government agencies or corporations and only secondarily by the U.S. government. Bankers' acceptances and certificates of deposit are backed by the issuing banks. Commercial paper is backed by the issuing entity, which is why only financially strong entities are able to find purchasers for them.

35.   (c)   The interest rate times time times the face amount determines the interest income. $100 × 0.08 × 90 days / 360 days = $2. The price is the face amount less the interest. $100 – $2 = $98. The price is less than the face amount when a security is sold at a discount.

36.   (c)   Short selling involves borrowing shares from a broker, selling them, and repaying the loan with securities bought on the open market; it is done by investors that speculate that the securities will

have a dramatic price decrease. Insider trading is selling securities based on inside information.

Accounts Receivable

37.   (a)   The rate of collections increases (i.e., when the average collection period is reduced) when an increase in sales and discounts taken with simultaneous reductions in A/R balances and doubtful accounts occurs. The average collection period is calculated by dividing the number of days in a year by A/R turnover. A/R turnover is net sales divided by average A/R. As sales have increased while doubtful accounts declined, the bad debt loss percentage apparently has decreased. As discounts taken have increased, it is more likely that the discount offered increased, rather than decreased. Without information about costs, conclusions cannot be drawn regarding profits.

38.   (b)   Estimated annual credit sales are $7.2 million (80% × $9 million), so estimated average daily credit sales are $20,000 ($7,200,000 / 360). The increase in the average collection period is 8 days (36 days – 28 days), so the estimated increase in A/R is $160,000 ($20,000 × 8 days). Annual interest expense will increase by $9,600 ($160,000 × 6%) with the changed collection procedures.

39.   (b)   Aside from uncollectible debt expense and collection costs, sales less both cost of goods sold and selling expenses is $35,000 [(100% – 65%) × $100,000]. Estimated uncollectible debt expense and collection costs are $15,000 and $5,000, respectively, resulting in $15,000 increase to income before taxes.

40.   (c)   Credit terms are often fairly standard within industries; businesses often must match these standard terms, regardless of their cash flow situations, or lose market share. If a business doesn't have a cash shortage, it would only offer terms to match competition. If a business does have a cash shortage, offering terms would be less attractive than borrowing funds elsewhere at a lower rate. If a business does have a cash shortage, it might offer terms rather than borrowing funds elsewhere at a higher rate, but this situation is less likely than offering terms to match competition.

41.   (a)   Estimated credit sales are $28.8 million (80% × $36 million). The estimated discount taken is based on credit sales of $14.4 million (50% × $28.8 million). The estimated discount is $144,000 (1% × $14,400,000).

42. (d)   An accounts receivables (A/R) aging groups receivables by due dates; typical categories are: current, less than 30 days past due, 30 to 59 days past due, 60 to 89 days past due, and 90 or more days past due. Uncollectible amounts commonly are estimated by applying a separate estimated bad debt percentage to the various categories; the oldest accounts are assumed to be the least collectible. An A/R aging doesn't show information on collected amounts or averages. An A/R aging relates to receivables, not debts.

43. (c)   Average daily credit sales are $4,500 ($5,000 × 0.9) and are in A/R for an average of 28 days. $4,500 × 28 = $126,000. Cash sales have no impact on the A/R balance.

44. (b)   The average collection period is the average number of days from a credit sale to payment receipt. It is a measure of the promptness of customer payments when compared to the credit terms. The average number of days before a receivable account becomes delinquent is the normal credit period; this is established by entity policy, not customer behavior. The average number of days from inventory purchase to sale is the number of days of inventory. The average number of days from the time a customer issues a check to the time that the vendor receives use of the funds is the average float.

45. (c)   After 45 days, average daily undiscounted collections are $15,000 ($50,000 × 30%) and discounted collections are $34,300 ($50,000 × 70% × 98%). $15,000 + $34,300 = $49,300.

Inventory

46. (d)   The economic lot size formula is as follows.

$$\text{Economic lot size} = \sqrt{\frac{2 \times \text{Setup costs} \times \text{Annual demand}}{\text{Inventory carrying cost per unit}}}$$

Since setup costs are in the numerator of the formula, a decrease in setup costs will *decrease* the economic lot size. Since inventory carrying cost per unit is the denominator of the formula, an increase in this amount will also *decrease* the economic lot size. Since both the decrease in setup costs and the increase in the inventory carrying amount decrease the economic lot size, the economic lot size *decreases.* Relevant costs can be defined as expected future costs that differ in amount between alternative courses of action. Since the costs per setup are a variable cost and they were reduced, relevant costs *decrease.* Since the increase in inventory carrying cost is due to *fixed costs* that have been

incurred, but not included in the carrying cost calculation, their inclusion does not increase relevant costs.

47. (d, e) Both responses are required for full point value. Ordering costs include quantity discounts lost, shipping costs, purchasing costs, and, in a manufacturing facility, set-up costs for production runs. Carrying costs include handling, interest on invested capital, storage costs, and obsolescence.

48. (d)   The economic order quantity (EOQ) model determines the ideal order quantity (or production size) based on demand, order costs, and carrying costs. The annual inventory quantity ordered and used reflects demand, which is a model input, not a result.

49. (d)   Carrying costs include handling, insurance, interest on invested capital, storage costs, spoilage, and obsolescence. Ordering costs include quantity discounts lost, shipping costs, purchasing costs, and, in a manufacturing facility, set-up costs for production runs.

50. (b)   Inventory turnover is cost of sales divided by average inventory; average inventory is (the cost of sales divided by inventory turnover). Estimated average inventory before the policy change is $4 million ($28 million / 7); after the policy change, it is $3.5 million ($28 million / 8). $500,000 × 6% = $30,000.

51. (c)   Typically, the quantity of safety stock on hand will be 50 units prior to receipt of an order. When an order for 150 units is received, there will then be 200 units on hand. Without information to the contrary, assume even use. Average inventory is 125 units [(50 units + 200 units) / 2].

52. (b)   The EOQ formula doesn't include the cost of inventory. It is as follows.

$$\text{Economic order quantity} = \sqrt{\frac{2 \times \text{Purchase order cost} \times \text{Annual demand}}{\text{Inventory carrying cost}}}$$

53. (d)   The economic order quantity (EOQ) minimizes the sum of carrying costs and ordering costs. The EOQ is the square root of the following: two times the annual demand in units times the order cost for one order with the resulting product divided by the annual cost to carry one unit. Safety stock is important in determining when to place an order. However, changing the safety stock has no effect on the EOQ.

54.   (d)

Annual usage, in units	40,000
Working days per year	/ 250
Daily usage, in units	160
Normal lead time, working days	× 30
Units required for lead time	4,800
Safety stock, in units	800
Order point, in units	5,600

55.   (c)   An inventory conversion period is the amount of time that an average item is held. 360 / 80 = 4.5 times that inventory is turned over in a 360-day year.

56.   (a)   A business holds safety stock to minimize losses caused by stock outs (loss sales or production time). As the variability in lead time or usages rates (sales) decreases, the safety stock tends to decrease. As the stock-out cost decreases, there is less need to protect against stock outs. As the cost of carrying inventory increases, the cost of a stock out becomes relatively less expensive. As sales volume increases, higher demand increases the likelihood of a stock out. As transportation time increases, the lead time lengthens, increasing the likelihood of a stock out.

57.   (d)   Carrying costs are $250 annually ($10 / unit × 0.25 / unit × 100 units). Stock-outs are expected 3 times (15% × 20 order cycles) annually. Stock-out costs are $60 (30 units × $2 / unit) per occurrence, or $180 ($60 × 3) annually. $250 + $180 = $430.

Short-Term Debt

58.   (e)   Trade credit (accounts payable) is called a spontaneous financing source because it originates automatically from purchasing transactions. Chattel mortgages, debentures, notes payable, and preferred stock are arranged explicitly; a purchase transaction could be completed without them easily. A chattel mortgage typically is a loan with equipment as collateral. A debenture is an unsecured bond.

59.   (b)   One means of answering this question is to assume a $100 gross invoice balance. On a $100 invoice, Quail could pay $98 [$100 × (1.0 − 0.02)] after 10 days or $100 after 35 days. In other words, Quail would pay $2 for borrowing $98 for 25 days (35 days − 10 days). The annualized percentage rate is approximately 0.29 [$2 / $98 × (360 days / 25 days)].

60.   (b, c) Two responses are required for full credit. Collateral is absent for an unsecured debt contract. Factoring involves using receivables as collateral. A floating lien is secured by property, typically inventory, of which the particular components may change. Commercial paper, lines of credit, and revolving credit typically are debts without collateral.

61.   (b)   Each bank sets its own prime rate, or rate that it charges its financially strongest customers. A single bank doesn't determine the effective rate on commercial paper; the market does. The federal fund rate is the rate that banks charge each other for overnight loans for funds to meet minimal reserve requirements. The discount rate is the rate that the Federal Reserve charges banks for funds.

62.   (d)   Because of its lack of access to major capital markets, a small business usually is restricted to owner financing, bank loans, and lines of credit. A line of credit typically is a contract for a bank to lend up to a specified amount during a specified period. A chattel mortgage typically is a loan with equipment, not inventory, as collateral. Commercial paper typically is issued by large, financially strong commercial enterprises to institutional investors; it is unlikely that a small business would be able to issue commercial paper at reasonable rates. Factoring accounts receivable typically is done by manufacturers or wholesalers who sell to a few repeat customers on account, rather than retail enterprises who have mostly cash sales.

63.   (d)   The compensating balance condition requires a minimum balance that is $30,000 ($50,000 − $20,000) greater than usually maintained, so Hardy effectively has a $470,000 ($500,000 − $30,000) loan. Annually, Hardy will pay $30,000 ($500,000 × 6%) in interest for the loan and will earn only $600 ($30,000 × 2%) in interest on the excessive compensating balance. Effectively, Hardy pays $29,400 for a $470,000 loan, resulting in a 6.25% ($29,400 / $470,000) effective interest rate.

64.   (a)   Current assets are $630,000 ($252,000 × 2.5). Maximum current liabilities may be $420,000 [$630,000 / (1.5 / 1)]. Maximum additional current liabilities are $168,000 ($420,000 − $252,000).

65.   (c)   With a discounted note, Nor effectively has borrowed $376K [$400K − (6% × $400K)]. The interest for the loan is $24K (6% × $400K). $24K / $376K = 6.38%.

Investment Evaluation

66.   (a)   The payback period is the period of time it takes for the cumulative sum of annual net cash inflows from a project to equal the initial cash outlay. Since the net cash inflows from the project in question are a constant amount, the payback period is = $5,000 / $2,000 = 2.5.

$$\text{Payback period} = \frac{\text{Initial cash outlay}}{\text{Annual net cash inflows}}$$

67. (c) The internal rate of return (IRR) is the discount rate which would make the net present value of the project equal to zero. Since the investment has a positive net present value at a discount rate of 12%, the IRR of the investment is greater than 12%.

68. (c) Net present value (NPV) is the present value of future cash inflows from the project minus the cost of the initial investments. A positive NPV identifies projects that will earn in excess of the minimum rate of return; a zero NPV identifies projects that will earn merely the minimum required rate of return. Remember, the examiners' instructions are to select the **best** answer. While answer (d) is correct, answer (c) is better; a project that has a positive NPV is preferable to a project that has a zero NPV.

69. (a) Under the net present value (NPV) method of capital budgeting, the present value of all cash inflows associated with an investment project are compared to the present value of all cash outflows. Ignoring income taxes, a project's NPV is increased by the amount of proceeds received from the sale of the asset to be replaced. The carrying amount of the asset to be replaced, the amount of annual depreciation on the asset to be replaced, and the amount of annual depreciation on fixed assets used directly on the project do not affect the NPV of the project because they do not represent inflows or outflows of cash.

70. (b) The net present value (NPV) of $12,000 is the present value of the ordinary annuity of $110,000 less the unknown cash outflow (X).

$110,000 × 4.564 − X = $12,000
X = $502,040 − $12,000 = $490,040

Residual Income

71. (d) Residual income is equal to operating income less imputed interest (the product of a required rate of return and operating assets). The operating assets are equal to the sales divided by the capital turnover ratio. Thus, the operating assets are $100,000 ($400,000 / 4).

Operating income	$ 40,000
Less: Imputed interest (10% × $100,000)	(10,000)
Residual income	$ 30,000

72. (b) Residual income is the income of an investment center less an imputed interest charge on the invested capital used by the center.

$$\text{Residual Income} = \text{Operating income} - \left(\text{Imputed interest rate} \times \text{Average invested capital} \right)$$

Economic Value Added

73. (b) Economic value added is the net operating profit after tax less the opportunity cost of capital. The post-tax operating profit is $180,000,000 [$300,000,000 × (1 − 0.40)] The equity capital is $600M (50% of $1,200M) so the cost of equity capital is $90M ($600M × 15%). The cost of debt capital is $30M ($600M × 5%). $180M − ($90M + $30M) = $60M. Editor's Note: Candidates should note that the word "debt" seems to be missing from this question in the fourth line; if something similar occurs during your exam, answer as best you can and bring the potential error to the examiners' attention. To answer this question, we must assume that 50% of the capital is debt and that the cost of equity and debt is the same as the opportunity cost of that capital. This assumption is warranted because a cost of debt is provided and no other explanation for the source of 50% of the capital is provided.

Percentage Return on Assets

74. (d) Return on Assets = Profit Margin on Sales (0.02) × Asset Turnover (5) = 0.10 = 10.0%

Return on Investment

75. (b)

Return on investment	=	Profit margin on sales	×	Capital-employed turnover rate
	=	$\dfrac{\text{Net income}}{\text{Sales}}$	×	$\dfrac{\text{Sales}}{\text{Capital investment}}$
	=	$\dfrac{\$100,000}{\$600,000}$	×	$\dfrac{\$600,000}{\$400,000}$

76. (c) A division's return on investment (ROI) is its segment margin divided by the average invested capital. There is no deduction for imputed interest on invested capital. The ROI is compared to the target ROI to evaluate the performance of the division manager. Imputed interest on capital invested is also used in the calculation of residual income. $11,000 / $40,000 = 0.275 = 27.50%

Segment sales	$ 311,000
Less: Segment variable costs	(250,000)
Segment contribution margin	61,000
Less: Segment traceable fixed costs	(50,000)
Segment margin	$ 11,000

Investment Banking

77. (b) Generally, short-term rates are lower than long-term rates. This is due to several factors, including lower risk in the short run and liquidity preference. Short-term rates are higher than long-term rates when future interest rates are expected to be lower than current rates, i.e., during inflationary periods.

78. (b) Underwriting involves an investment banker purchasing a new security issue from the issuer and then reselling that issue to subsequent investors. The underwriting spread is the difference between the price that the investment banker pays and the price that a subsequent investor pays, rather than a commission or discount. Any price fluctuations while the investment banker holds the security are gains or losses to the banker; a drop in the security price could eliminate any spread. Typically, the issuer bears the costs of preparing, printing, and distributing a security.

Common Stock

79. (d) Common stock's book value is the equity attributable to common stock divided by the number of common shares. With no dividends in arrears, all retained earnings are attributable to common stock. $20 million + $36 million + $18 million = $74 million. $20 million total par value / $100 par value / share = 200,000 shares. $74 million / 200,000 shares = $370 book value / share.

80. (a) Shareholders have preemptive rights; they must get the first chance to purchase any new issues of stock, as necessary, to maintain their pre-issue ownership percentages. $20,000,000 total pre-issue par value / $10 par value/share = 200,000 pre-issue shares. The proposed issue quantity is half (100,000 / 200,000) of the pre-issue shares; owners would be able to purchase half of the quantity of their pre-issue shares. 1,000 × ½ = 500.

Fixed Income Securities

81. (b) A zero coupon bond is issued below its face amount. The issuer pays the holder the face amount at maturity, but has no interest payments until then. Issue costs are not appreciably different from other bond types. The issuer and purchaser must recognize interest expense and income, respectively, throughout the bond term.

82. (b) Serial bonds have maturities staggered over a period of years. To lessen the default risk for a large bond issue, sinking fund provisions may require that portions of a bond issue be retired at random, which might be inconvenient for investors who planned on holding the bonds for longer. With serial bonds, investors can select a maturity appropriate for their purposes. Typically, the coupon rate is the same for all bonds in an issue, the bond selling price determines the effective interest rate.

83. (d) A convertible bond generally gives the purchaser the option of converting the bond into common stock at a specified price. This feature gives the bondholder a chance at high returns if the common stock does outstandingly and the safety net of a regular interest payment and priority over shareholders in the event of liquidation. A conversion feature typically attracts investors at a lower rate than nonconvertible bonds. Corporations may issue convertible bonds when the equity market is unattractive; effectively they postpone the stock issue until the stock price is high and yet get immediate financing. If the stock price does not rise to the point where bondholders convert, the issuer must meet regular interest payments and be unable to issue more debt if it is close to the debt ceiling imposed by debt covenants. Financial leverage is when a relatively small change in earnings before interest and taxes (EBIT) results in a large change in common shareholders' return. Generally, the higher the percentage of debt financing, the greater the financial leverage. A bond issue increases the percentage of financing from debt. Convertible bondholders typically accept less restrictive covenants in bond indentures than nonconvertible bondholders.

84. (b) Debentures are bonds that are secured only by the issuer's full faith and credit, as opposed to specified collateral. Income bonds require interest payments only when earnings are sufficient. Bond indentures are a set of covenants that typically restrict the amount of debt that a bond issuer may carry and the dividends it may pay.

85. (b) Junk bonds are securities rated at less than investment grade. Debentures are bonds without collateral. Junk bonds may have had low ratings continually; securities whose ratings have been downgraded may still be within investment grade. Junk bonds are not necessarily worthless, they merely have low ratings and a higher potential than other bonds for becoming worthless.

86. (a) Income bonds pay interest only if the issuer has earned it; no income from them is guaranteed. All non-subordinated debt is senior to subordinated debt. All debt is senior to preferred and common stock.

87. (b) A callable bond may be redeemed by the issuer prior to maturity, usually with the issuer paying the face amount plus a call premium. Typically, bonds are recalled when interest rates decline, and are thus unfavorable to the bondholders, who otherwise would earn the high interest of the bond. Convertible bonds may be converted to common stock before maturity at the bondholders' option; conversion is not required. A sinking fund provision effectively mandates annual retirement of a specified portion of the bond issue; it decreases the likelihood of default, but does not disallow early redemption.

88. (d) Preferred stockholders typically don't have voting rights. Neither preferred nor common stock dividends are tax deductible by the payer. Non-participating signifies that dividend payments are fixed at the face amount of the stock times the rate; participating stock participates with common stock in any excess dividends. In the event of liquidation, preferred stockholders are paid before common stockholders.

Capital Structure Decisions

89. (d) Business risk is the riskiness of operations without any debt; in other words, risk inherent in operations, as opposed to financial risk, or the additional risk that the owners bear due to the decision to carry debt. Of the four options, cash flow is the item most likely to impact capital structure decisions. For instance, a start-up company with risky (uncertain) cash flow and little capital may plan to pay its employees and vendors partially in stock (a capital structure decision). While these arrangements are contracts, if the entity had steady and substantial cash flow, the contractual obligations probably would have little impact on the capital structure decisions. Investor preferences tend to override management preferences in capital structure decisions. Timing of financial information would be a financial risk affecting capital structure decisions; timing of operational information would be a business risk that would tend to have minimal impact on capital structure decisions. Note: The editors believe similar questions are unlikely to appear on future exams.

90. (c) The cost of capital is the annual cost divided by the funds received [$10 / ($107 − $5) = 9.8%].

91. (d) An imputed cost is not recognized by GAAP, but is estimated in order to model economic reality for decision making purposes. Interest is not paid on internally generated cash, although an imputed amount often is determined to recognize the interest that owners otherwise would earn on that money. Depreciation, lease interest, and bank loan interest are all recognized by GAAP.

92. (b) Capital structure is the long-term debt and equity of an entity. Optimal capital structure minimizes the cost of all capital and thus maximizes shareholder wealth, or in other words, the entity's total value. Debt generally is cheaper than equity, until high debt levels increase risk levels, driving up the weighted average cost of capital. Maximum earnings per share (EPS) is not always optimal; steps to increase EPS may cause market value per share to drop. Insofar as an entity can earn more on debt or

equity than it pays in interest, that financing may be appropriate.

93. (b) Selecting a debt instrument maturity based on the life of the asset it finances is a hedging approach. Financial leverage is when a relatively small change in earnings before interest and taxes (EBIT) results in a large change in common share-holders' return; generally, the higher the percentage of debt financing, the greater the financial leverage. Operating leverage relates to the proportion of fixed costs in an entity's cost structure. Return maximization is using the cheapest form of financing, usually short-term debt; this generally is considered more risky than a hedging approach.

94. (d) Operating leverage is present when a small change in sales causes a relatively large change in earnings before interest and taxes (EBIT). The degree of operating leverage is the contribution margin divided by EBIT [{500,000 units × ($3 − $0.60)} / ($1,200,000 − $110,000) = 1.10].

95. (b) Financial leverage is present when a small change in earnings before interest and taxes (EBIT) cause a relatively large change in common shareholders' return. The degree of financial leverage is EBIT divided by EBIT less interest. [(500,000 units × $2.40 − $110,000) / ($1,090,000 − $60,000) = 1.06 (rounded)]

96. (c) An increase in the effective income tax rate would make debt financing more attractive than equity financing because interest payments are tax deductible, reducing taxes, but dividends generally are not. A decrease in the times-interest-earned ratio indicates greater difficulty making future interest payments; an entity with a low times-interest-earned ratio will likely be able to issue debt only at high rates. An increase in economic uncertainty causes greater difficulty in predicting the ability to make future interest payments, which must be made regardless of performance, as opposed to dividends, which need not be declared in unfavorable economic periods. The federal funds rate is the rate that the Federal Reserve charges banks; an increase in the federal funds rate tends to raise all interest rates, making debt more expensive.

97. (d) The overall cost of capital is that rate of return on assets that meets the costs connected with employed funds. It is equal to the weighted average cost of all debt and equity elements present. The cost of capital is the cost incurred, not the return earned or expected to be earned.

98. (c) Bond proceeds, net of flotation costs, are $14,850,000 [($15 million × 1.02) − ($15 million

× 0.03)]. Annual interest payments are $900,000 ($15 million × 0.06). $900,000 / $14,850,000 = 6.06%.

99. (c)   The market risk premium is the difference between the average market rate and the risk-free rate (12% − 4% = 8%). An individual issuer's expected rate of return is the risk-free rate plus the market risk premium, adjusted by the individual issuer's beta coefficient, which is a measure of how closely an individual issuer's return correlates to the market average. 4% + (8% × 0.95) = 11.6%.

100. (c)   The financing will be 25% ($7.5 million / $30 million) equity and 75% debt. (0.25 × 0.12) + (0.75 × 0.06) = 0.03 + 0.045 = 0.075.

101. (c)   Operating leverage is present when a small change in sales causes a relatively large change in earnings before interest and taxes (EBIT); this is possible because of relatively high fixed costs and relatively low variable costs. High leverage is more risky than low, because fixed costs are incurred regardless of sales volume. The proportion of debt and equity financing influences financial leverage, not operating leverage.

Dividend Policy

102. (c)   Preferred stock dividends, both current and in arrears, must be paid before common stock (CS) dividends are paid. Annual preferred dividends are $350,000 (5,000 shares × $1,000 × 7%). Preferred dividends must be paid for three years (fiscal years ending March 31, Year 2, Year 3, and Year 4). The CS dividend is $375,000 ($1,500,000 × 25%). In absence of indication to the contrary, the preferred stock is assumed to be non-participating. $350K × 3 + $375K = $1,425K.

103. (c)   The residual theory of dividends is that earnings should be reinvested to the extent that profitable projects exist, consistent with the target capital structure, and only earnings remaining after profitable projects are funded should be distributed. As no new preferred stock will be issued, capital spending will require an additional $600,000 [$1.4 million × 3/(3 + 4)] of debt financing and $800,000 [$1.4 million × 4/7] of common stock financing. Annual preferred dividends are $600,000 (10,000 × 6% × $1,000). After capital spending and preferred dividends, earnings remaining for common stock dividends are $600,000 ($2,000,000 − $800,000 − $600,000). The common stock dividend payout ratio is the common stock dividend divided by net income. $600,000 / $2,000,000 = 30%. Interest payments are included in the calculation of net income.

104. (c)   A dividend increase tends to be read as a signal of a positive management forecast. This is because many corporations hesitate to raise dividends unless they anticipate future earnings to be sufficient to allow dividends at that level to avoid ever decreasing dividends. Residual dividend theory assumes that the rate of return that investors require is not affected by dividend policy. An active policy strategy assumes that dividends are relevant to investor decisions, hence dividends are not set mechanically. Neither stock nor cash dividends affect control; shareholders have the same proportionate ownership after both dividend types.

Options

105. (c)   Warrants are rights to purchase common stock at a specified price. These options typically are attached to long-term debt or preferred stock to make a corporation's securities attractive to a wider range of investors, increasing the supply and decreasing the cost of capital. Warrants decrease EPS if exercised; if not exercised, warrants may decrease the amount reported for diluted EPS. Warrants generally don't provide cash inflows until exercised. A bond call provision, not a warrant, permits the early redemption of bonds by the issuer.

Solution 51-2 ADDITIONAL MULTIPLE CHOICE ANSWERS

Business Objectives

106. (d)   To maximize shareholder wealth, management should concentrate on total return per share, rather than other measures. Total return per share includes earnings per share (EPS) and stock value changes. Maximization of earnings per share ignores the potential decrease in share value. Maximization of profits ignores the potential dilution of widespread ownership. Maximization of stock value ignores the potential decrease in earnings.

Life Cycle

107. (d)   In the growth or exploitation stage, sales increase dramatically. When a product is introduced initially in the infancy phase, it has little direct competition, but also may have limited consumer acceptance, prompting relatively high promotional expenses to gain widespread acceptance. In the maturity stage, profits shrink as direct competition increases.

Financial Markets

108. (d) Secondary markets exchange securities that were issued previously. Debt markets exchange bonds, notes, and loans. Physical asset markets exchange real estate, grains, computers, etc.; financial asset markets exchange claims on assets, including stocks. Mortgage markets exchange loans secured by real estate.

Financial Institutions

109. (b) The over-the-counter (OTC) markets deal with less frequently traded stock or bonds. Matching the few buy and sell orders within a reasonable time is difficult, so inventories are essential. The relatively few dealers who hold any particular OTC security are said to "make a market" in that security. Commercial banks provide checking and loan services, historically tailored to businesses. Mutual funds are corporations that pool dollars from their shareholders to invest. Pension funds are trusts for the investment and distribution of retirement investments; they operate much like mutual funds.

Interest Rates

110. (b) To offset the impact of inflation, investors require an inflation premium added to the rate they would have charged in the absence of inflation (price level increase). The default risk premium is due to the risk that a borrower will not repay the interest or principal. Investors add a liquidity premium to bonds without an active secondary market. The longer the term of a bond, the greater the risk that a better rate of interest will be available in the future, and thus, the greater the maturity risk premium; the effect of a maturity risk premium is to have higher interest rates on long-term bonds as opposed to comparable short-term bonds.

Time Value of Money

111. (b) To determine how much Mott will receive in ten years in the future, the future value of a single sum is used. $100 × 1.791 = $179 (rounded). A present value factor is used to determine the present value of a future amount. An annuity is a series of payments.

112. (d) The amortization deduction does not require the use of cash. However, the amortization deduction does reduce taxable income. The tax liability reduces cash flow. Thus, the first step is to determine the tax. Next, the tax liability is subtracted from the cash flow before taxes to determine the after-tax cash flow. This amount then is multiplied by the present value of an annuity factor to determine the after-tax present value of the lease.

Cash Flow before amortization and taxes	$ 7,500
Less: Amortization deduction	(5,000)
Taxable income	2,500
Tax rate	40%
Tax liability	$ 1,000
Cash flow before amortization and taxes	$ 7,500
Less: Tax liability	(1,000)
Net cash flow after taxes	6,500
Times: PV factor of a 10% annuity for 2 years	1.74
After tax present value of lease	$11,310

113. (c) To determine how much Mutt will receive in 40 quarterly interest periods (10 years × 4 quarters/year) in the future, the interest must be based on the same duration as the interest periods (8% interest per year / 4 quarters/year = 2% interest per quarter). $100 × 2.208 = $221 (rounded).

Working Capital Overview

114. (b) While current assets are short-term in nature, typically there is some level of ever-present, or permanent, current assets. There often are increases beyond this level due to seasonal or business cycle fluctuations; this variable amount typically is called fluctuating current assets. In an economic downturn or period of temporary financial stress, the fluctuating layer most likely would be unnecessary, but the permanent layer still would be needed, despite the difficulty of obtaining short-term financing in adverse conditions. Failure to obtain financing could require business contraction or even liquidation. A moderately conservative working capital policy is to finance permanent current assets with long-term debt, recognizing that these assets must be financed on an ongoing basis. An even more conservative working capital policy is to finance all current assets with long-term debt; this policy tends to be rare, as short-term rates tend to be lower than long-term rates.

115. (b) Net working capital (also called merely working capital) is the difference between current assets and current liabilities; only current items are components of working capital.

116. (b) The current ratio is current assets to current liabilities. Working capital is the difference between current assets and current liabilities. By issuing common stock for cash, current assets increased without a change in current liabilities.

Cash

117. (d) Cash and marketable securities rarely earn high returns; businesses try to minimize the amount they hold in order to maximize return on assets. Entities must hold enough cash to pay bills as they become due, or face bankruptcy. Entities also hold cash and marketable securities to be able to take advantage of unexpected events or fund occasional projects, such as fixed asset purchases. A compensating balance is held in an account at a financial institution to cover the cost of services to the account holder, typically including check processing.

118. (c)   The annual benefit from interest earned on collections (or savings from avoiding interest paid to finance A/R) for two days is $64,000 ($400,000/ day × 2 days × 8%). The annual cost is $24,000 ($2,000/month × 12 months). The annual net benefit from the lockbox service is $40,000 ($64,000 – $24,000).

119. (c)   An automated clearing house (ACH) electronic funds transfer (EFT) is an electronic payment to a company's bank account. ACHs are electronic networks; no physical checks are involved, allowing quick processing. EFTs are the actual transfer of money, not merely the documentation or fee.

120. (c)   The annual benefit from interest earned on collections (or savings from avoiding interest paid to finance A/R) for four days is $36,000 ($300,000/ day × 4 days × 3%). The annual cost is $30,000 ($2,500/month × 12 months). The annual net benefit from the lockbox service is $6,000 ($36,000 – $30,000).

Short-Term Investments

121. (d)   Although there is no active secondary market, commercial paper dealers typically will repurchase issues that they have sold. Treasury bills generally have lower interest rates than commercial paper, reflecting their lower risk. Commercial paper's short-term nature exempts it from SEC registration requirements. Commercial paper is short-term unsecured notes issued by large, financially strong commercial enterprises, typically to institutional investors.

122. (c)   Convertible bonds are long-term securities issued by entities with varying degrees of creditworthiness. Bankers' acceptances are drafts for which the bank guarantees payment; they are designed to facilitate transfers; thus, they must be low risk and liquid. Commercial paper is short-term unsecured notes issued by large, financially strong commercial enterprises, typically to institutional investors. A U.S. Treasury bill is a highly liquid short-term government obligation that is considered practically risk-free.

Accounts Receivable

123. (c)   Without the policy change, estimated credit sales are $21.6 million (80% × $27 million), so estimated average daily credit sales are $60,000 ($21,600,000 / 360) and the average accounts receivable balance is $1,680,000 ($60,000 × 28 days). With the policy change, estimated credit sales are $28.08 million (130% × $21.6 million), so estimated average daily credit sales are $78,000 ($28,080,000 / 360) and the average accounts receivable balance is $3,120,000 ($78,000 × 40 days). $3,120,000 – $1,680,000 = $1,440,000.

124. (b)   Under the current policy, next year's estimated A/R balance averages $16 million ($128 million × 75% / 360 days × 60 days). Under the proposed policy, next year's estimated credit sales are $64 million ($128 million × 50%) and the A/R balance would average about $4.8 million ($64 million / 360 days × 27 days). $16 million – $4.8 million = $11.2 million decrease.

125. (a)   Additional funds are estimated at $6 million ($3 million/day × 2 days). Interest on the additional funds is $360,000 ($6 million × 6%). The annual cost is $208,000 [$100,000 + 0.0001 × ($3 million × 360)]. $360,000 – $208,000 = $152,000.

Inventory

126. (c)   The inventory reorder point is figured as anticipated demand during lead time, the time lag between ordering and receiving goods. The reorder point can be calculated by multiplying average daily usage by lead time in days.

127. (b)   Ordering costs and annual demand are in the numerator of the economic order quantity (EOQ) formula; an decrease in these factors will decrease the EOQ. Carrying costs are in the denominator of the EOQ formula; an decrease in this factor will increase the EOQ. Alternatively, candidates who have trouble remembering the exact formula probably could answer this question after applying logic to the situation. If carrying costs decrease, it is cheaper to hold inventory; therefore, more inventory will be held, resulting in fewer orders of increased quantity. Conversely, if ordering costs decrease, there is little incentive to minimize orders, resulting in more orders of smaller quantity. The safety stock level has no impact on the EOQ; it is not part of the formula. Safety stock levels usually are determined after an order quantity is decided.

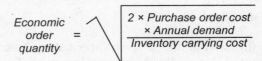

$$\text{Economic order quantity} = \sqrt{\frac{2 \times \textit{Purchase order cost} \times \textit{Annual demand}}{\textit{Inventory carrying cost}}}$$

128. (a) The economic order quantity (EOQ) model determines the ideal order quantity (or production size) based on demand, order (or production set-up) costs, and carrying costs. The costs of assembly line reconfiguration are production set-up costs. Insurance, taxes, obsolescence, storage, and handling are carrying costs.

129. (b) The order quantity and safety stock affects the optimal inventory level. The economic order quantity (EOQ) model determines the ideal order quantity (or production size) based on demand, order costs, and carrying costs. The cost per unit influences the carrying costs. The inventory usage rate determines demand. Safety stock is held to minimize losses caused by stock outs (loss sales or production time). As time from order placement to receipt (lead time) lengthens, the likelihood of a stock out increases.

130. (d) Order placement costs are incorporated into the economic order quantity model, but are irrelevant to determining an appropriate safety stock quantity. Safety stock is held to minimize losses caused by stock outs (loss sales or production time). High customer intolerance for backorders increases the importance of avoiding stock outs. As sales forecast and shipment lead time uncertainty increases, the likelihood of a stock out increases. As the stock-out cost decreases, there is less need to protect against stock outs.

131. (c) A business holds safety stock to minimize losses caused by stock outs (loss sales or production time). As the variability in lead time or usages rates (sales) increases, the safety stock tends to increase. As the stock-out cost decreases, there is less need to protect against stock outs. As the cost of carrying inventory increases, the stock-out cost becomes relatively less expensive.

Short-Term Debt

132. (e) Trade credit (accounts payable) is called a spontaneous financing source because it originates automatically from purchasing transactions. Commercial paper typically is issued by large, financially strong commercial enterprises to institutional investors; it is unlikely that a small business would be able to issue commercial paper at reasonable rates. A debenture is an unsecured bond. Debentures, mortgages, and notes payable tend to be long-term.

Derivatives

133. (c) With the 20% compensating balance provision, Mason effectively has borrowed $320K

(80% × $400K). The interest for the loan is $24K (6% × $400K). $24K / $320K = 7.5%.

Derivatives

134. (d) Using derivatives divides financial risk into elements that can be exchanged between entities. Foreign-exchange forward contracts obligate one party to buy, and a counterparty to sell, a fixed amount of currency at an agreed-upon future date; a swap contract is a forward-based derivative that obligates two parties to trade a series of cash flows at specified future settlement dates. Extensive use of derivatives is due primarily to uncertainties cause by factors such as volatile markets, deregulation, and revolutionary technologies. Risk management does not eliminate risk; it is about selectively choosing those risks that an entity finds acceptable and minimizing those that it finds unacceptable.

135. (b) Future contracts differ from forward contracts in that exchange clearinghouses standardize future contracts and mark them to market daily. Thus, these clearinghouses facilitate a competitive and liquid market. The daily mark to market decreases counterparty risk. Counterparty risk is the risk that the other party to a contract will be unable to meet its obligations on the maturity date. Each entity dealing in derivatives should develop its own safeguards and appropriate incentives so that its traders do not assume unwarranted risks.

Investment Evaluation

136. (d) Common classifications are: (1) maintenance-of-business replacements; (2) cost-reduction replacements; (3) expansion of existing products or markets; (4) expansion into new products or markets; (5) safety and environmental projects (also called mandated investments); and (6) other (small, mixed use or generic facilities for which a breakdown in project classification probably will outweigh the benefit, such as parking lots).

137. (c) The accrual accounting rate of return (ARR) for a project is computed by dividing the average annual income the project generates by the initial (or average) increase in required investment. Thus, the numerator of the ratio is the increase in average annual operating income of $40,000. (To compute the accrual ARR on the initial investment, the denominator is the $60,000 initial increase in the required investment. The $30,000 average increase in the required investment would be used as the denominator to compute the rate of return on the average investment.)

138. (d) Unlike the net present value, internal rate of return, and payback methods of capital budgeting, the accounting rate of return (ARR) method does not focus on cash flows. Rather, it focuses on accounting net income. The ARR is computed by dividing the expected increase in future average annual accounting net income by the initial (or average) increase in required investment. The expected increase in future average accounting net income is determined by subtracting the incremental expenses of the project, including depreciation, from the estimated revenues over the life of the project and dividing this amount by the estimated useful life of the project. The time value of money is *not* considered in computing the ARR.

139. (c) The capital budgeting technique known as internal rate of return (IRR) determines the rate of interest (or discount) that would make the present value of the future cash flows from the project equal to the cost of the initial investment. Therefore, this method uses all of the cash flows over the entire life of the project and the time value of the money. On the other hand, the accounting rate of return (ARR) method of capital budgeting does not recognize the time value of money because it does not focus on cash flows. Rather, it focuses on accounting net income. The ARR is computed by dividing the expected increase in future average annual accounting net income by the initial (or average) increase in the required investment. Both capital budgeting techniques recognize the project's salvage value. The IRR method recognizes the project's salvage value as a future cash inflow. The ARR method subtracts the incremental expenses of the project, including depreciation, from the estimated revenues over the life of the project to determine the expected increase in future average annual accounting income. The ARR method recognizes the project's salvage value in determining the depreciable base of the project.

140. (d) Payback method advantages include its: basis on cash flows, rough determination of the time to recoup the original investment, and simplicity and ease of use.

141. (c) The annual savings needed to realize a 12% yield can be obtained by dividing the $44,300 by the 3.60 present value of an annuity at 12% for 5 years. Thus, the annual savings needed are $12,306 ($44,300 / 3.60), rounded to the nearest dollar.

Cost	$50,000
Less: PV of residual value ($10,000 × 0.57)	(5,700)
Present value of annual savings needed	$44,300

142. (d) The internal rate of return (IRR) capital budgeting method determines the rate of interest which would make the present value of the future cash flows equal to the cost of the initial investment. These cash flows include the net cash generated by the operation of the project plus the cash obtained from its ultimate disposal. Depreciation is a noncash expense, representing merely the allocation of the depreciable base of a plant asset over its estimated useful life. When income taxes are ignored, the IRR method excludes depreciation expense from its computation because no cash flow is involved.

143. (d) The internal rate of return (IRR) of an investment is the discount rate that would yield a net present value (NPV) of $0. The table of net present values included in this problem indicates that a 14% discount rate yields a positive NPV, whereas a 16% rate yields a negative NPV. Therefore, IRR is between 14% and 16%; of the given answers, only 15.3% satisfies this requirement.

144. (b) The net present value method uses a predetermined discount or "hurdle" rate to discount all positive and negative cash flows to their present value. The discounted cash flows are then netted; if the resulting amount is positive, the investment has a rate of return greater than the required rate, and vice versa. The internal rate of return (IRR) method uses the expected cash inflows and outflows (and their timing) to determine the IRR implicit in the investment.

145. (d) The internal rate of return and net present value capital budgeting techniques can both easily accommodate Polo's requirement that projects extending beyond five years must earn a higher specified rate of return. Polo can compare the rate of return of projects with a life of five years or less to one specified rate of return (e.g., 10%) and compare the rate of return of projects with a life of greater than five years to a higher specified rate of return (e.g., 12%). Only projects meeting or exceeding the applicable specified rate of return should be accepted.

146. (d) The net present value of the project is determined by discounting the cash flows generated by the project at the cost of capital. These cash flows include the net cash generated by the operation of the project plus the cash obtained from its ultimate disposal.

147. (c) The net present value method of investment analysis uses a predetermined discount or "hurdle" rate to discount all positive and negative cash flows to their present value. The discounted cash flows are then netted; if the resulting amount is positive, the investment has a rate of return greater

than the required rate, and vice versa. The payback period method ignores return rates—it simply divides the initial investment by the periodic cash inflow to determine the number of periods required to recover the investment. Answers (b) and (d) are incorrect because these two methods (which essentially are the same) use the expected cash inflows and outflows (and their timing) to determine the internal rate of return implicit in the investment.

Residual Income

148. (b)   The capital-employed turnover rate is determined as follows.

$$\frac{\text{Capital-employed}}{\text{turnover rate}} = \frac{\text{Sales}}{\text{Invested capital}}$$

149. (d)   Residual income is the income of an investment center less an imputed interest charge on the invested capital used by the center, and is determined as follows.

$$\frac{\text{Residual}}{\text{Income}} = \frac{\text{Operating}}{\text{income}} - \left(\frac{\text{Imputed}}{\text{interest rate}} \times \frac{\text{Average}}{\text{invested}}{\text{capital}} \right)$$

To maximize residual income, projects earning more than the imputed interest charge would be accepted, while projects earning less than that charge would be rejected. Division A's project should be accepted because it will earn a rate of return greater than the imputed interest rate on invested capital. Division B's project should not be accepted because it will earn a rate of return less than the imputed interest rate on invested capital.

150. (d)   Zee's residual income is $150,000 (i.e., $200,000 − $50,000). The residual income of a profit center is computed by subtracting an imputed interest charge for invested capital from the operating income of the center.

151. (a)   Residual income is the operating income of an investment center less an imputed interest charge on the invested capital used by the center. To compute Kew's residual income, it is first necessary to determine Kew's operating income. Kew's residual income then can be determined.

Sales		$ 500,000
Less: Variable costs	$ 300,000	
Traceable fixed costs	50,000	(350,000)
Operating income		$ 150,000

$$\frac{\text{Residual}}{\text{income}} = \frac{\text{Operating}}{\text{income}} - \frac{\text{Imputed interest on}}{\text{average invested capital}}$$

$$= \$150,000 - (\$100,000 \times 6\%) = \underline{\$144,000}$$

Investment Banking

152. (d)   In primary capital markets, investment bankers buy new debt and equity securities and sell them to investors. The issuers receive the proceeds. Exchanges of existing debt and equity securities occur in secondary capital markets. Future commodity contracts are sold in the futures market.

153. (d)   Venture capital typically describes private security placements for young corporations that cannot obtain financing in common capital markets because of the high risk connected to the securities (usually common stock). Investors risk low liquidity and capital loss for potentially substantial rewards.

Common Stock

154. (c)   Par value is an arbitrary value assigned before the stock is issued that represents a stock's legal capital, or in other words, a shareholder's maximum liability. As long as the par value is paid to the corporation, shareholders obtain limited liability protection. The value all assets received for stock (also called paid-in-capital) must be entered as equity in the issuer's financial statements. Par value rarely is related to market value.

Fixed Income Securities

155. (b)   Because interest is deductible to calculate taxable income, the true cost of debt is the interest payment less the related tax deduction. Additional debt may be issued at a higher or lower rates; such issues have no impact on the current cost of debt. Any change in interest rates after Pan issued the debt will change the yield that bondholders receive if they sell in the secondary markets, but it will not affect Pan's payments to bondholders.

Capital Structure Decisions

156. (d)   The cost of capital is determined by the dividends, the expected dividend growth rate, and the market price of the stock less any discounts or floatation costs. With a zero dividend growth rate, the cost is the dividends divided by the capital received. $7 / ($100 − $2 − $3) = 7.37%.

157. (a)   The cost of capital is determined by the dividends, the expected dividend growth rate, and the market price of the stock. With a zero dividend growth rate, the cost is the dividends divided by the capital received. The market price of the stock is not reduced by the discount or floatation costs as they need not be incurred to obtain these funds. $7 / $100 = 7.00%.

158. (d) $100,000 (50% × $200,000) of the new capital will be common stock; however, the $100,000 retained earnings covers all of the new common equity portion. The remainder will be $60,000 (30% × $200,000) of long-term debt and $40,000 (20% × $200,000) of preferred stock.

Long-term debt [(60 / 200) × 5.00%]	1.50%
Preferred stock [(40 / 200) × 6.00%]	1.20
Retained earnings [(100 / 200) × 7.00%]	3.50
Weighted average cost of capital	6.20%

159. (c) $500,000 (50% × $1,000,000) of the new capital will be common equity; the first $100,000 of the common equity portion will be from retained earnings and $400,000 will be from a new stock issue. The remainder will be $300,000 (30% × $1,000,000) of long-term debt and $200,000 (20% × $1,000,000) of preferred stock. With a zero dividend growth rate, the cost of the new common stock is the annual dividend divided by the capital received: $7 / ($100 − $2 − $3) = 7.37% (rounded).

Long-term debt [(3 / 10) × 5.00%]	1.50%
Preferred stock [(2 / 10) × 6.00%]	1.20
Retained earnings [(1 / 10) × 7.00%]	0.70
Common stock [(4 / 10) × 7.37%]	2.95
Weighted average cost of capital	6.35%

160. (c)   The market risk premium is the difference between the average market rate and the risk-free rate (12% − 7% = 5%). The capital asset pricing model (CAPM) estimates an individual issuer's expected rate of return is the risk-free rate plus the market risk premium, adjusted by the individual issuer's beta coefficient, which is a measure of how closely an individual issuer's return correlates to the market average. 7% + (5% × 1.2) = 13%.

161. (d)   Capital structure is the long-term debt and equity of an entity. Optimal capital structure minimizes the cost of all capital and thus maximizes shareholder wealth, or in other words, the entity's total value. Debt generally is cheaper than equity, until high debt levels increase risk levels, driving up the weighted average cost of capital. Minimal risk is not always optimal; investors are willing to incur risk for the opportunity to achieve high returns. Maximum earnings per share (EPS) is not always optimal; steps to increase EPS may cause market value per share to drop.

162. (d)   Financial leverage occurs when a relatively small change in earnings before interest and taxes (EBIT) results in a large change in common shareholders' return. Generally, the higher the percentage of debt (as opposed to equity) financing, the greater the financial leverage. At some point, the greater risk from the high financial leverage increases the cost of debt financing and this no longer holds true; however, in this circumstance, it is unlikely an entity will purchase treasury stock. The purchase of treasury stock increases the percentage of financing from debt. Earnings per share will increase as there are less outstanding shares; dividends are not paid on treasury stock. A purchase of treasury stock for cash decreases both assets and equity.

Dividend Policy

163. (a)   Residual dividend theory holds that earnings should be reinvested to the extent that profitable projects exist, consistent with the target capital structure, and only earnings remaining after profitable projects are funded should be distributed. This policy assumes (1) the corporation can reinvest earnings at a higher rate of return than investors can find though another investment with comparable risk, (2) investors prefer to have the corporation re-invest the earnings, and (3) the rate of return that investors require is not affected by dividend policy. The constant payout ratio assumes that dividend payments should be a percentage of earnings. A stable dividend policy involves a dividend amount that increases only when future earnings seem sufficient to support the higher dividend indefinitely. Residual dividend theory doesn't address the number of dividend distributions.

PERFORMANCE BY SUBTOPICS

Each category below parallels a subtopic covered in Chapter 51. Record the number and percentage of questions you correctly answered in each subtopic area.

Time Value of Money

Question #	Correct	√
1		
2		
# Questions	2	
# Correct		
% Correct		

Valuation

Question #	Correct	√
3		
4		
5		
6		
7		
8		
9		
10		
# Questions	8	
# Correct		
% Correct		

Risk & Return

Question #	Correct	√
11		
12		
# Questions	2	
# Correct		
% Correct		

Working Capital Overview

Question #	Correct	√
13		
14		
15		
16		
17		
18		
19		
# Questions	7	
# Correct		
% Correct		

Cash

Question #	Correct	√
20		
21		
22		
23		
24		
25		
26		
27		
28		
# Questions	9	
# Correct		
% Correct		

Short-Term Investments

Question #	Correct	√
29		
30		
31		
32		
33		
34		
35		
36		
# Questions	8	
# Correct		
% Correct		

Accounts Receivable

Question #	Correct	√
37		
38		
39		
40		
41		
42		
43		
44		
45		
# Questions	9	
# Correct		
% Correct		

Inventory

Question #	Correct	√
46		
47		
48		
49		
50		
51		
52		
53		
54		
55		
56		
57		
# Questions	12	
# Correct		
% Correct		

Short-Term Debt

Question #	Correct	√
58		
59		
60		
61		
62		
63		
64		
65		
# Questions	8	
# Correct		
% Correct		

Investment Evaluation

Question #	Correct	√
66		
67		
68		
69		
70		
# Questions	5	
# Correct		
% Correct		

Residual Income

Question #	Correct	√
71		
72		
# Questions	2	
# Correct		
% Correct		

Economic Value Added

Question #	Correct	√
73		
# Questions	1	
# Correct		
% Correct		

Percentage Return on Assets

Question #	Correct	√
74		
# Questions	1	
# Correct		
% Correct		

Return on Investment

Question #	Correct	√
75		
76		
# Questions	2	
# Correct		
% Correct		

Investment Banking

Question #	Correct	√
77		
78		
# Questions	2	
# Correct		
% Correct		

Common Stock

Question #	Correct	√
79		
80		
# Questions	2	
# Correct		
% Correct		

Fixed Income Securities

Question #	Correct	√
81		
82		
83		
84		
85		
86		
87		
88		
# Questions	8	
# Correct		
% Correct		

Capital Structure Decisions

Question #	Correct	√
89		
90		
91		
92		
93		
94		
95		
96		
97		
98		
99		
100		
101		
# Questions	13	
# Correct		
% Correct		

Dividend Policy

Question #	Correct	√
102		
103		
104		
# Questions	3	
# Correct		
% Correct		

Options

Question #	Correct	√
105		
# Questions	1	
# Correct		
% Correct		

SIMULATION SOLUTIONS

Solution 51-3

Response #1: Investment Evaluation (4 points)

1. $13,000

Under the net present value method, the present value of all cash inflows associated with an investment project are compared with the present value of all cash outflows. The difference between the present value of these cash flows is the net present value of the project and determines whether or not the project is an acceptable investment.

Annual cash inflows	$ 20,000
Times: Present value annuity factor	× 5.65
Present value of cash inflows	113,000
Less: Initial investment	(100,000)
Net present value of project	$ 13,000

2. 5.0 years

The payback period is the period of time it takes for the cumulative sum of annual net cash inflows from a project to equal the initial cost outlay. When the annual net cash inflows from the project are a constant amount, the payback period for the project is determined as follows.

$$\text{Payback period} = \frac{\text{Initial cash outlay}}{\text{Annual net cash inflows}} = \frac{\$100,000}{\$20,000} = 5.0 \text{ years}$$

3. 10%

The accrual accounting rate of return on initial investment is computed by dividing the average annual accounting income the machine generates by the cost of the machine. The average annual accounting income generated by the machine is the expected annual after-tax cash savings in operating expenses less annual depreciation expense [i.e., $20,000 – ($100,000 / 10) = $10,000].

$$\begin{aligned}
&\text{Accounting rate of} \\
&\text{return on initial} = \frac{\text{Average annual accounting income}}{\text{Initial investment cost}} \\
&\text{investment} \\
&\quad = \frac{\$10,000}{\$100,000}
\end{aligned}$$

4. 5.00

The internal rate of return is the interest rate which would make the present value of the future expected cash flows equal to the initial investment. Since the annual net cash inflows from the project are a constant amount, the internal rate of return of the proposed investment is calculated as follows.

$$\begin{aligned}
&\text{Annual} \quad \text{Present} \quad\quad \text{Cost of} \\
&\text{Cash flows} \times \text{value factor} = \text{initial investment}
\end{aligned}$$

$20,000 × Present value factor	= $100,000
Present value factor	= $100,000 / $20,000
Present value factor	= 5.00

Response #2: Investment Evaluation (3 points)

1. $68,000

The net present value of the project is the amount of the excess of the present value of the cash flows over the cost of the project. As the entity is a tax-exempt organization, the effect of income taxes is irrelevant.

Annual cash flow	$ 130,000
Present value annuity factor	× 3.6
Present value of cash flows	468,000
Less: Cost of project	(400,000)
Net present value of project	$ 68,000

2. D

To determine the internal rate of return (IRR) on this project, the net present value (NPV) of the project is computed at 12%, 14%, and 16%. Since the machine has a positive NPV at a discount rate of 14%, the IRR exceeds 14%. Since the machine has a positive NPV at a discount rate of 16%, the IRR exceeds 16%.

	14%	16%
Annual cash flow	$ 130,000	$ 130,000
PV annuity factor	× 3.4	× 3.3
PV of cash flows	442,000	429,000
Less: Cost of project	(400,000)	(400,000)
Net present value	$ 42,000	$ 29,500

3. 13.9%

To determine the accounting rate of return (ARR), based on the project's average book value for Year 1, annual depreciation expense and the average book value for Year 1 must be computed. Depreciation expense on the straight-line basis is $80,000 [($400,000 – $0) / 5 years]. The book value of the machine at the end of Year 1 is $320,000 ($400,000 – $80,000). The machine's average book value for Year 1 is $360,000 [($400,000 + $320,000) / 2]. The ARR, based on the project's average book value for Year 1, is computed as follows.

$$\begin{aligned}
&\text{Accounting rate of} \\
&\text{return on average} = \frac{\text{Average annual accounting income}}{\text{Average book value}} \\
&\text{book value} \\
&\quad = \frac{\$130,000 - \$80,000}{\$360,000} = 13.9\%
\end{aligned}$$

Solution 51-4

Response: Investment Evaluation (4 points)

1.   B

The payback period is the period of time it takes for the cumulative sum of annual net cash inflows from a project to equal the initial cash outlay. When cash inflows are not uniform, the payback period computation takes a cumulative form. That is, each year's net cash inflows are accumulated until the initial cash outlay is recovered. The question states that Projects A and B have the same initial cash outlay and lives. Per a review of Diagram I, most of the net cash inflows of Project B occur in the first three years of the project's life, and most of the net cash inflows of Project A occur in the last three years of that project's life. Therefore, Project B would be more likely to have the shorter payback period.

2.   A

The average annual accounting income generated by a project is the numerator of the average accounting rate of return (ARR) method of capital budgeting. This amount is computed by subtracting average annual depreciation expense from the average annual net cash inflows generated by the project. Projects A and B have the same initial investment requirements and lives. Therefore, annual average depreciation expense is the same for both projects. Project A has a greater total net cash inflow. Therefore, Project A has greater average annual net cash inflows and thus a greater average ARR.

3.   B

The internal rate of return (IRR) is the discount rate which would make the present value of the project equal to zero. Per a review of Diagram II, projects A and B have a zero present value at discount rates of 16% and 22%, respectively. Hence, projects A and B have internal rates of return of 16% and 22%, respectively. The 22% IRR of project B exceeds the 16% IRR of project A.

4.   B

The internal rate of return (IRR) is the discount rate which would make the present value of a project equal to zero. Per a review of Diagram II, based on 5-year lives, projects A and B have a zero present value at discount rates of 16% and 22%, respectively. Hence, based on 5-year lives, projects A and B have internal rates of return of 16% and 22%, respectively. The 22% internal rate of return of project B based on a 5-year life exceeds the 16% internal rate of return of project A based on a 5-year life. If both projects were to terminate at the end of year 4 with cash flows remaining as projected for the first 4 years and no cash flows in year 5, per a review of Diagram I, the present value of net cash inflows lost by project B is less than that lost by project A. Therefore, although the IRR of both projects would decrease if the projects were to terminate at the end of year 4, the IRR of project B would still exceed that of project A.

_____

CHAPTER 52

DECISION MAKING

EXAM COVERAGE: The *Planning and Measurement* portion of the BEC section of the CPA exam is designated by the examiners to be 22 to 28 percent of the section's point value. Under the former ARE content specification outline, the topics in this chapter were a third or more of the managerial accounting point value. This might not hold true under the new CSO. Candidates should plan their use of study time accordingly. More information about the point value of various topics is included in the **Practical Advice** section of this volume.

CHAPTER 52

DECISION MAKING

I. Managerial Accounting Overview

A.   Cost Definitions

Exhibit 1 ▶ Cost Components in Manufacturing Firms

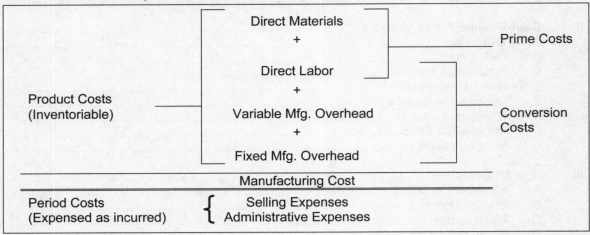

1.   **Conversion Cost** Conversion cost is the sum of the direct labor and manufacturing overhead. It represents the manufacturing costs to convert raw materials into finished products.

2.   **Manufacturing Cost Elements** Manufacturing cost is the sum of all three elements of production.   Collectively these are equivalent to the cost of purchases in a merchandising enterprise.

   a.   Direct materials are the materials that become an integral part of the finished product and are easily traceable to the finished product. Examples include desk tops and legs used in making steel desks.

   b.   Direct labor represents the labor that acts directly on the product and physically transforms or manipulates the product.   Direct labor costs are easily traceable to the product. Examples include the labor costs of workers who assemble desk tops or operate melting equipment.   Direct labor does not include wages paid to a maintenance worker or a supervisor in a factory.

   c.   Manufacturing overhead costs consist of all production costs other than direct material and direct labor costs.   In other words, manufacturing overhead costs are those production costs that cannot be traced to a specific product easily.   Other terms that are synonymous with manufacturing overhead are factory overhead and indirect factory costs.   Examples include indirect labor, indirect materials, repairs and maintenance on factory machinery, factory utilities, factory equipment depreciation, etc.

   •   The overtime premium paid to all factory workers (direct labor as well as indirect labor) usually is considered to be a part of manufacturing overhead.   The overtime premium is considered to be attributable to the heavy overall volume of work; thus, its cost should be borne by all units produced.

3. **Period Costs** Period costs are costs that are not incurred in the production of physical units and are not inventoried. Period costs are charged to expense in the period in which incurred. All selling and administrative costs are period costs.

4. **Prime Cost** Prime cost is the sum of the direct materials and direct labor costs.

5. **Product Costs** Product costs are costs that are inventoriable (i.e., that are directly **or** indirectly related to physical units). These costs become an expense when the goods to which the costs attach are sold. All **manufacturing** cost elements, including depreciation on factory equipment and other manufacturing overhead, are product costs.

B. Cost Classification
Different methods of classification satisfy different needs of various information users. (Also see quality control programs.)

1. **Behavior** Costs are classified as fixed or variable according to their response to changes in levels of activity.

2. **Controllability** Costs also are categorized according to whether they can be influenced by managers of a particular segment of the entity within a specified period of time. (Also see responsibility accounting.)

3. **Function** Under this arrangement, costs are classified according to the function they perform within the business, for example, as manufacturing, selling, or administrative costs.

4. **Object of Expenditure** This involves classifying costs according to the goods or services they purchase, for example, as wages, rent, or advertising.

5. **Traceability** Costs are classified according to whether or not they can be traced to, and directly identified with, a finished unit of production. The distinction may be described as that between direct and indirect manufacturing costs.

C. Cost Behavior
Definitions of fixed and variable costs refer to **total** cost behavior, not **unit** cost behavior.

1. **Fixed Costs** Fixed costs are those costs that tend to remain constant in total within a given period of time and over a wide range of activity. This range of activity is referred to as the relevant range.

    a. **Committed Costs** Represent fixed costs that arise from having property, plant, and equipment, and a functioning organization. These costs remain even when the production volume is zero. Committed costs include depreciation of buildings and long-term lease payments.

    b. **Discretionary Costs** Represent annual budget appropriations. These fixed costs are often unrelated to volume and include, for example, advertising costs and research and development costs.

Exhibit 2 ▶ Behavior of Fixed Costs

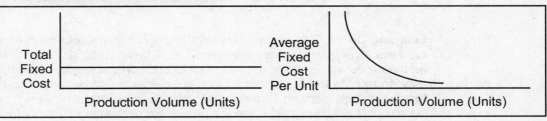

2.   **Variable Costs** Variable costs are those costs that tend to remain constant per unit but that vary in total in direct proportion to changes in the level of activity.

Exhibit 3 ▶ Behavior of Variable Costs

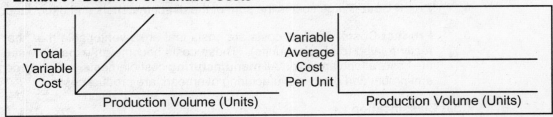

3.   **Mixed (Semivariable) Costs** Are comprised of both variable and fixed cost elements. Due to their variable cost element, mixed costs change in total with a change in volume, but not in direct proportion because of their fixed cost element. Due to their fixed cost element, average mixed cost per unit **decreases** (increases) with an **increase** (decrease) in volume. Mixed costs include electricity, maintenance, etc. Mixed costs typically are split into fixed and variable elements for purposes of cost-volume-profit analysis and budgeting.

   a.   In practice, arbitrary assumptions often are made about the cost behavior patterns of mixed costs. For example, the cost of electric power may be classified entirely as a variable cost, even though it has both fixed and variable elements.

   b.   The fixed and variable elements of mixed costs can be determined through mathematical models such as regression analysis, scatter diagrams, and the high-low estimation method.

4.   **Step-Variable Costs** Costs that are relatively fixed over a small range of output, but are variable over a large range of output. For example, supervision costs may be fixed over a given production volume. However, additional shifts or work crews may be added to increase production. This will require additional supervisors and thus the added cost will go up in a lump sum or "stair step" pattern.

5.   **Comparison**

   a.   **Total Costs** Total fixed cost does not change with a change in volume (within the relevant range). **Total** variable cost has a **direct** relationship with volume. The total variable cost increases or decreases in direct proportion to the change in volume.

   b.   **Average Costs** Average fixed cost per unit has an **inverse** relationship with volume. Average variable cost per unit does not change with volume; it remains constant.

      (1)   The average fixed cost per unit decreases as volume increases. Because total fixed costs remain constant, an increase in volume spreads the fixed costs over more units.

      (2)   The average fixed cost per unit increases as volume decreases. Because total fixed costs remain constant, a decrease in volume spreads the fixed costs over fewer units.

6.   **Learning Curve** The learning curve is the graphic representation of how units per labor hour increase as a person gains experience with a task. It results when time per unit are plotted on the x-axis with cumulative units of production on the y-axis. The phrase *learning curve* is used to refer to the phenomenon that when people first perform a task, they will be slower than when they perform it for the 100th time. Hence, labor hours will be greater (and associated costs will be higher) when the people are performing the work for the first time.

7. **Experience Curve** The experience curve is the graphic representation of time (and costs) for a broad category of tasks decreasing as a group gains experience with a set of tasks. This phrase can refer to several situations. For example, it may refer to the reduced time for a group to train a new member or to reduced time (and costs) for a number of cost areas (perhaps including distribution and customer service) to add their part to the value chain.

Exhibit 4 ▶ Cost Behavior Patterns

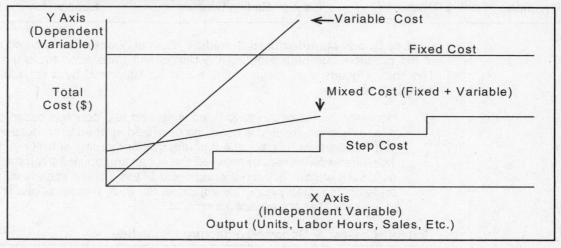

D. **Manufacturing Firm Statements**

1. **Comparison With Merchandising Firms** The income statement of a manufacturing firm is similar to that of a merchandising firm except that the cost of goods sold section will include a "cost of goods manufactured" schedule. Essentially, the difference between the two cost of goods sold sections is that in a manufacturing firm, cost of goods manufactured replaces purchases.

Exhibit 5 ▶ Comparison of Income Statements: Manufacturing vs. Merchandising Firm

Manufacturing Co.			Merchandising Co.		
Sales		$ 500,000	Sales		$ 500,000
Cost of goods sold:			Cost of goods sold:		
Finished goods, Jan. 1	$125,000		Merchandise inventory, Jan. 1	$125,000	
Cost of goods mfd. (see schedule)	300,000		Purchases, net	300,000	
Cost of goods available for sale	425,000		Cost of goods available for sale	425,000	
Finished goods, Dec. 31	120,000		Merchandise inventory, Dec. 31	120,000	
Cost of goods sold		(305,000)	Cost of goods sold		(305,000)
Gross margin		195,000	Gross margin		195,000
Selling & administrative expense		(160,000)	Selling & administrative expense		(160,000)
Net income		$ 35,000	Net income		$ 35,000

Exhibit 6 ▸ Account Activity for a Typical Manufacturing Company

Raw Material Inventory	Work-in-Process Inventory	Finished Goods Inventory
Beginning Balance	Beginning Balance	Beginning Balance
Plus: Purchases	Plus: Raw Material, Labor, OH Used	Plus: Goods Finished (From WIP)
Equals: Available for Use	Equals: Available to Finish	Equals: Available for Sale
Less: Raw Material Used (To WIP)	Less: Goods Finished (To FG)	Less: Cost of Goods Sold
Equals: Ending Balance	Equals: Ending Balance	Equals: Ending Balance

2. **Cost of Goods Manufactured Schedule** Cost of goods manufactured represents the cost of the products **completed** during the period and transferred to finished goods inventory. The cost of goods manufactured figure can be supported by a schedule of cost of goods manufactured.

- Normally, manufacturing overhead is applied to production based on a predetermined rate. When this method is used, the overhead **applied** to production would be reported in this statement (usually one amount), rather than the **actual** overhead cost incurred. The difference (variance) between the actual and applied overhead is usually reported as an adjustment to cost of goods sold in the income statement. Conceptually, it is preferable to ratably apply the adjustment to work-in-process and finished goods inventories as well as the cost of goods sold.

Exhibit 7 ▸ Cost of Goods Manufactured Schedule

Beginning work-in-process			$ 55,000
Beginning inventory	$ 32,000		
Add purchases	116,000		
Materials available for use	148,000		
Less: Ending inventory	(28,000)		
Direct materials used		$120,000	
Direct labor		60,000	
Indirect material	25,000		
Indirect labor	30,000		
Miscellaneous	35,000		
Manufacturing overhead		90,000	
Add: Total current manufacturing costs incurred			270,000
Total manufacturing costs to account for			325,000
Less: Ending work-in-process			(25,000)
Cost of goods manufactured			$300,000

Exhibit 8 ▸ Cost of Goods Manufactured Schedule (Alternative Format)

Direct materials used (same as similar section in Exhibit 7)	$120,000	
Direct labor (same as in Exhibit 7)	60,000	
Manufacturing overhead (same as in Exhibit 7)	90,000	
Total manufacturing cost incurred		$270,000
Add: Beginning work-in-process		55,000
Total manufacturing cost to account for		325,000
Less: Ending work-in-process		(25,000)
Cost of goods manufactured		$300,000

II. Cost-Volume-Profit Analysis

A. Overview

Break-even and cost-volume-profit (CVP) analyses are concerned with the effect upon operating income (or net income) of various decisions regarding sales and costs. CVP analysis is management's study of the relationships among cost, volume, and profit. This study is used in planning, controlling, and evaluating the incremental impact of business decisions. The general assumptions are as follows.

1. The behavior of costs and revenues has been determined reliably and is linear over the relevant range.

2. Costs are classified as fixed or variable.

3. Variable costs change at a linear rate.

4. Fixed costs remain unchanged over relevant range.

5. Selling prices do not change as sales volume changes.

6. For multiple products, the sales mix remains constant.

7. Production efficiency does not change.

8. Inventory levels remain constant, i.e., production equals sales.

9. Volume is the only relevant factor affecting costs.

10. There is a relevant range for which all of the other underlying assumptions and concepts are valid.

B. CVP Charts

1. **Cost-Volume-Profit Chart** The cost-volume-profit (CVP) chart (Exhibit 9) shows the profit or loss potential for the range of volume within the relevant range. At any given level of output, the predicted profit or loss is the vertical difference between the sales line and the total cost line. The **break-even point** is at the intersection of sales and total costs. The **contribution margin** at any level of output is the vertical difference between the sales line and the variable costs line. Note that the total costs and variable costs lines are parallel, with the difference between them equal to fixed costs.

   - All the relationships graphed on the CVP chart are valid only within a band of activity called the **relevant range.** Outside the relevant range, the same relationships are unlikely to hold true. For example, some fixed costs may increase at high levels of output.

Exhibit 9 ▶ Cost-Volume-Profit (CVP) Chart

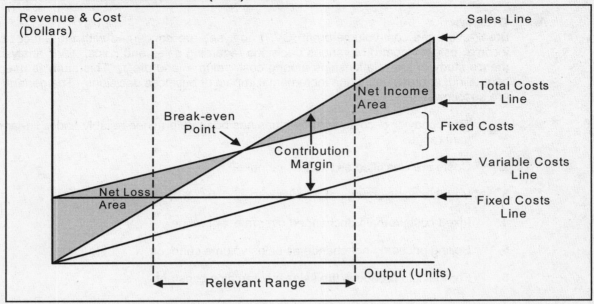

2. **Profit-Volume Chart** The profit-volume chart is a simpler version of the CVP chart which is useful if management is primarily interested in the effect of changes in volume on net income.

Exhibit 10 ▶ Profit-Volume (P/V) Chart

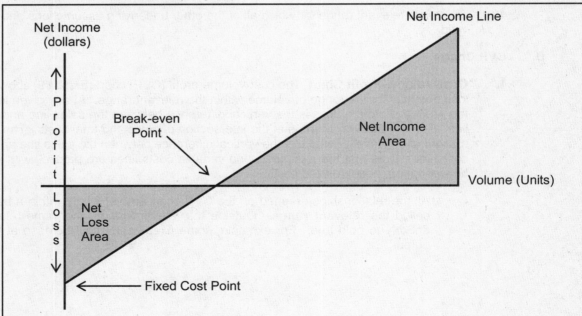

Comments: At **zero** volume, the net loss equals total fixed costs. The sloping net income line moves upward from the fixed costs point at the rate of the **unit contribution margin** and intersects the volume axis at the **break-even** point. Each unit sold beyond the break-even point increases net income by the amount of the unit contribution margin.

C.   **Solutions Approach**

1.   **Define Problem** Determine the objectives of the problem or problem situation. These generally include the following.

    a.   Break-even point in units or dollars.

    b.   Desired sales (units or dollars) to obtain a specified profit level.

    c.   Desired sales in units or dollars to obtain the break-even point or a specified profit level, given that changes will occur in the selling price, fixed cost, and/or variable cost.

    d.   Amount of profit or loss that will result at a specified volume level based on the current or anticipated selling price and cost/volume relationships.

    e.   Selling price to be charged based on anticipated changes in cost, volume, and/or profit level.

2.   **Select Computational Method**

    a.   **Income Equation Method**

Sales = Variable expenses + Fixed expenses + Net income

or

Net income = Sales – Variable expenses – Fixed expenses

    b.   **Contribution Margin Method**

(1) Contribution margin   = Sales – Variable costs

(2) Unit contribution margin = Unit sales price – Unit variable costs

(3) Contribution margin ratio $= \dfrac{\text{Unit contribution margin}}{\text{Unit sales price}}$

or

Contribution margin ratio $= \dfrac{\text{Total contribution margin}}{\text{Total sales}}$

(4) Variable cost ratio $= \dfrac{\text{Variable cost}}{\text{Sales}}$

(5) Break-even point in units $= \dfrac{\text{Fixed expenses}}{\text{Unit contribution margin}}$

(6) Break-even point in dollars $= \dfrac{\text{Fixed expenses}}{\text{Contribution margin ratio}}$

(7) Dollar sales to achieve a desired profit $= \dfrac{\text{Fixed costs \& desired net income*}}{\text{Contribution margin ratio}}$

(8) Unit sales to achieve a desired profit $= \dfrac{\text{Fixed costs \& desired net income*}}{\text{Unit contribution margin}}$

_____

* A predicted operating loss would be subtracted from fixed costs in the numerator.

3. **Classify Costs** Mixed (semi-variable) costs must be split into fixed and variable elements.

4. **Solve For Unknowns** Insert all the given information into the appropriate computational formats and solve for the unknowns.

D. Break-Even Point
The point where sales less fixed and variable costs result in zero profit. Thus, the break-even point is **defined** as the point where net income equals zero. The terms break-even point analysis and cost-volume-profit analysis are sometimes used interchangeably.

Example 1 ▶ Break-Even Point

Bob's Deli specializes in Bob's Bagel Delight. Production and sales data are provided below.

	Per unit	%
Selling price	$0.90	100.00
Variable cost	0.60	(66.67)
Contribution margin	$0.30	33.33

Total fixed costs: $300

Required: Solve for the break-even point in dollars and in units using both the income equation method and the contribution margin method.

Solution:

Income equation method

a. Sales in dollars (S) = Variable costs + Fixed costs + Net income

$$S = 0.6667 S + \$300 + 0$$

$$S = \$300 / 0.3333 = \underline{\$900}$$

b. Sales in units (Su)

$$\$0.90 \, Su = \$0.60 \, Su + \$300 + 0$$

$$\$0.30 \, Su = \$300$$

$$Su = \$300 / \$0.30 = \underline{1,000} \text{ units}$$

Contribution margin method

a. Sales in dollars = $\dfrac{\text{Fixed costs + Net income}}{\text{Contribution margin ratio}}$

$$= (\$300 + 0) / 0.3333 \quad = \underline{\$900}$$

b. Sales in units = $\dfrac{\text{Fixed costs + Net income}}{\text{Unit contribution margin}}$

$$= (\$300 + \$0) / \$0.30 \quad = \underline{1,000} \text{ units}$$

Proof:	Sales (1,000 × $0.90)	$ 900
	Variable costs (1,000 × $0.60)	(600)
	Contribution margin	300
	Fixed costs	(300)
	Net income	$ 0

1. **Composite Break-Even Point** When a company sells more than one product, a break-even point can be determined for each product based on the expected sales mix and the composite or combined contribution margin.

Example 2 ▶ Mixed Sales

Product (sales mix ratio)	A (1/8)	B (3/8)	C (4/8)
Selling price	$ 1.00	$ 2.00	$ 3.00
Variable cost	(0.50)	(1.50)	(2.00)
Contribution margin	$ 0.50	$ 0.50	$ 1.00

Total fixed costs: $60,000

Required: Compute the break-even point in units and dollars for Products A, B, and C.

Solution:

Composite contribution margin

	A	B	C	Composite
Contribution margin	$0.50	$0.50	$1.00	
Sales mix ratio	× 1	× 3	× 4	
Weighted CM	$0.50	$1.50	$4.00	$6.00

Total break-even point

Composite units*   =   Fixed costs / composite contribution margin

10,000 composite units   = $60,000 / $6.00

_____
* A composite unit is the "package" made up of 1 unit of A, 3 units of B, and 4 units of C.

Break-even point for each product

	A	B	C
Composite units	10,000	10,000	10,000
Sales mix ratio	× 1	× 3	× 4
Break-even, units	10,000	30,000	40,000
Selling price	× $1.00	× $2.00	× $3.00
Break-even, dollars	$10,000	$60,000	$120,000

Proof:		
A (10,000 × $0.50)		$ 5,000
B (30,000 × $0.50)		15,000
C (40,000 × $1.00)		40,000
Contribution margin		$ 60,000
Fixed costs		(60,000)
Net income		$ 0

2. **Composite Contribution Margin** The composite contribution margin can be determined from the separate multi-product contribution rates and the forecasted sales mix in dollars.

Exhibit 11 ▶ Composite Contribution Margin Formula

$$\text{Composite Contribution Margin} = \sum \left[\begin{array}{c} \text{Sales mix ratio} \\ \underline{\text{in dollars}}, \text{product}_i \end{array} \times \begin{array}{c} \text{Contribution} \\ \text{margin ratio}_i \end{array} \right]$$

Example 3 ▶ Mixed Sales

Product	X	Y	Z
$ Sales mix ratio	1/19	6/19	12/19
CMR	50%	25%	33.33%

Total fixed costs: $60,000

Required: Compute break-even point in dollars. [Since we are not given the selling price per unit, we can't determine break-even sales in number of units.]

Solution:

Composite CMR
$$= \sum (\text{\$ Sales mix ratio, product}_i \times \text{CMR}_i)$$
$$= 1/19\ (50\%) + 6/19\ (25\%) + 12/19\ (33.33\%)$$
$$= 0.02632 + 0.07895 + 0.21053 = 0.31580$$

Composite sales break-even
$$= \text{Fixed cost / Composite CMR}$$
$$= \$60,000 / 0.31580$$
$$= \underline{\$190,000}\ (\text{rounded})$$

E. Specified Income Level

Example 4 ▶ Sales to Obtain a Specified Net Income Level

Use the same facts from Example 1 plus a desired income level of $100.

Required: Determine the target sales, using the contribution margin method.

Solution:

In units	*In sales dollars*
$\dfrac{\text{Fixed cost + Desired net income}}{\text{Unit contribution margin}}$	$\dfrac{\text{Fixed cost + Desired net income}}{\text{Contribution margin ratio}}$
$= (\$300 + \$100) / \$0.30$	$= (\$300 + \$100) / 0.3333$
$= \underline{1,333}$ units	$= \underline{\$1,200}$

F. Changing Costs

1. **Sales** Desired sales in units or dollars given that the selling price, fixed cost, and/or variable cost will change.

Example 5 ▶ Changing Costs Given in Percentages

Use the facts from Example 1 with the following changes.

Selling price decreased	11.11%
Variable costs decreased	33.33%
Fixed costs increased	33.33%
Desired profit (based on sales)	10%

Required: Determine the target sales in units (Su) and in dollars (S), using the contribution margin method.

Solution:

	Per unit	%
Selling price, $0.90 (1 – 0.1111)	$ 0.80	100%
Variable cost, $0.60 (1 – 0.3333)	(0.40)	(50%)
Revised contribution margin	$ 0.40	50%

In units	*In dollars*
$\dfrac{\text{FC(1 + \% incr.) + NI as \% of sales}}{\text{Unit contribution margin}}$	$\dfrac{\text{FC(1 + \% incr.) + NI as \% of sales}}{\text{Contribution margin ratio}}$

$$Su = \frac{\$300\,(1.3333) + 0.10\,(\$0.80Su)}{\$0.40}$$

$$S = \frac{\$300\,(1.3333) + 0.10\,S}{0.50}$$

$$Su = (\$400 + \$0.08Su) / \$0.40$$

$$0.50S = \$400 + 0.10S$$

$$\$0.40Su = \$400 + \$0.08Su$$

$$0.40S = \$400$$

$$Su = \$400 / \$0.32 = 1{,}250 \text{ units}$$

$$S = \$400 / 0.4 = \$1{,}000$$

2. **Selling Price** Required selling price based on change in cost, volume, and/or profit level.

Example 6 ▶ Changing Costs

Use the facts in Example 1, except that variable cost increased $0.10. The present contribution margin ratio (CMR) is to be maintained.

Required: Determine new unit sale price.

Solution:

CMR	=	Unit contribution margin (CM) / Unit selling price (SP)
SP	=	CM / CMR
SP	=	SP – Revised variable costs / CMR
SP	=	[SP – ($0.60 + $0.10)] / 0.3333
0.3333 SP	=	SP – $0.70
0.6667 SP	=	$0.70
SP	=	$1.05

Note: The break-even point in dollars does not change since the contribution margin ratio remains the same. However, the break-even point in units does change as a result of the revised contribution margin per unit.

	%	*Present Per Unit*	*Revised Per Unit*
Selling price	100.00	$ 0.90	$ 1.05
Variable cost (revised, $0.60 + $0.10)	(66.67)	(0.60)	(0.70)
Contribution margin	33.33	$ 0.30	$ 0.35

Revised break-even point

In units $300 / $0.35 = 857 units (rounded)   In dollars $300 / 0.333 = $900

G. **Income Tax Effect**

Most cost-volume-profit CPA exam problems ignore income taxes. A modified formula is required to include the impact of income taxes.

Exhibit 12 ▶ Income Tax Modification Formula

$$\frac{\text{Fixed cost} + \dfrac{\text{Net income}}{1 - \text{Tax rate}}}{\text{Contribution margin}}$$

Example 7 ▶ Income Tax Considerations

Fixed costs = $300; Desired net income = $100; Tax rate = 40%; Unit contribution margin = $0.30; Contribution margin rate = 33.33%

Required: Compute the sales for net income after tax of $100.

Solution:

<u>In units</u>

$$\frac{\$300 + \dfrac{\$100}{\$1 - 0.40}}{\$0.30}$$

= ($300 + $166.67) / $0.30

= **1,556** units

<u>In dollars</u>

$$\frac{\$300 + \dfrac{\$100}{\$1 - 0.40}}{0.3333\%}$$

= ($300 + $166.67) / $0.30

= **$1,400**

H.   Margin of Safety

The margin of safety (M/S) can be defined as the excess of budgeted (or actual) sales over the break-even volume of sales. It states the amount by which sales can drop before losses begin to be incurred in an organization. The M/S can also be expressed in percentage form. This percentage is obtained by dividing the M/S in dollar terms by total sales.

Exhibit 13 ▶ Margin of Safety in Dollars Formula

Total sales – Break-even sales = Margin of safety (M/S)

Exhibit 14 ▶ Margin of Safety in Percentage Form Formula

$$\frac{\text{M/S in dollars}}{\text{Total Sales}} = \text{M/S percentage}$$

III. Special Decisions

A.   Relevant Costs

Relevant costs are expected future costs that will differ among alternatives. The concept of cost relevance is important in the decision-making process, especially in decisions that are nonroutine. Differential cost analysis is the study of relevant costs that are associated with a decision among possible courses of action so that the most appropriate alternative may be selected.

Example 8 ▶ Relevant Costs

The Sky Company is planning to expand its production capacity. Its plans consist of purchasing a new machine for $100,000 and selling the old machine for $10,000. The new machine has a 5-year life. The old machine has a 5-year remaining life and a carrying amount of $50,000. The new machine will reduce labor costs from $40,000 per year to $20,000 per year. Assume that there are no other related machine costs and that the disposal value at the end of each machine's estimated life is zero.

Required: What are the relevant and differential costs? Ignore present value and income taxes.

Solution:

	Relevant costs		
	Keep	Replace	Differential
Labor costs			
($40,000 × 5)	$200,000		
($20,000 × 5)		$100,000	$100,000
Disposal value of old		(10,000)	10,000
Cost of new machine		100,000	(100,000)
Total relevant costs	$200,000	$190,000	$ 10,000

Comment: The $50,000 carrying amount of the old machine is a sunk cost and is not relevant to the decision.

1. **Avoidable Costs** Costs that will not be incurred if an activity is suspended.

2. **Differential (Incremental) Costs** The difference in cost between two alternatives.

3. **Marginal Costs** The addition to total cost of producing or selling one more unit of output.

4. **Out-of-Pocket Costs** Immediate or near future cash outlays.

5. **Opportunity Costs** The foregone benefits (revenues minus costs) from alternatives not selected. Opportunity costs do not require an actual current or future cash outlay. Although relevant, opportunity costs are generally not incorporated in the accounting system nor included in differential cost analyses, as they are difficult to measure objectively. However, the use of opportunity cost is a practical means of reducing the alternatives under consideration.

Example 9 ▶ Opportunity Costs

	Alternatives considered		Alternatives not considered	
	#1	#2	#3	#4
Relevant revenues	$ 1,000	$ 2,000	$ 3,000	$ 300
Relevant cost	(500)	(1,750)	(2,800)	0
Differential income	$ 500	$ 250	$ 200	$ 300

Required: Prepare an opportunity cost analysis.

Solution:

	Alternatives		
	#1	#2	Differential
Relevant revenues	$1,000	$ 2,000	$ (1,000)
Relevant costs	(500)	(1,750)	1,250
Opportunity costs—contribution foregone from			
next best alternative	(300)	(300)	0
Net advantage	$ 200	$ (50)	$ 250

Note: Notice that the net differential amount between alternative #1 and #2 is still $250. Note also that if all the results of the alternatives formally considered were negative, such a result would indicate that the best **excluded** alternative was in fact optimal.

6. **Irrelevant Costs** Historical costs are always **irrelevant per se,** although they may be helpful in predicting relevant costs. In order to be relevant for decision making, an item must meet both of the following criteria.

    a. It is an expected **future** cost or revenue.

    b. Its amount will **differ** among alternatives.

7. **Sunk Costs** Historical costs incurred as a result of past decisions; they are not relevant in current decision making.

B. **Special Order**
This type of problem usually involves an order at a price lower than the regular selling price, and there are often some cost differences as well. Generally, the requirement is to determine whether the special order should be accepted or rejected, and its effect on pretax income. Only incremental variable costs are relevant, unless additional fixed costs must be incurred because of the special order. If available capacity is not fully utilized, a differential cost analysis may indicate the advisability of accepting a special order at a price lower than the existing unit cost (which includes allocated **fixed** overhead). If the variable cost is covered, any additional revenue can contribute to the recovery of fixed costs.

- When only differential manufacturing costs are taken into account for special order pricing, it is essential to assume that acceptance of the order will not affect regular sales.

Example 10 ▶ Special Order

The Bike Company has enough idle capacity available to accept a special order of 10,000 bicycles at a unit price of $80. There are no additional selling expenses or fixed manufacturing costs associated with the special order. Acceptance of the special order will not affect regular sales. Estimated income for the year without the special order is as follows.

	Per Unit		Total	
Sales		$100		$100,000,000
Variable	$40		$40,000,000	
Fixed	20		20,000,000	
Manufacturing costs		60		60,000,000
Gross margin		40		40,000,000
Variable	20		20,000,000	
Fixed	10		10,000,000	
Selling expenses		30		30,000,000
Operating income		$ 10		$ 10,000,000

Required: Determine the net effect on operating income of the acceptance of the special order.

Solution:

Incremental analysis approach	Differential
Incremental revenues (10,000 × $80)	$800,000
Less: Incremental costs (10,000 × $40)	(400,000)
Increase in operating income	$400,000

Per unit change approach	
Relevant selling price, per unit	$ 80
Less: Relevant variable manufacturing costs, per unit	40
Unit contribution margin	(40)
Times: Number of units	× 10,000
Increase in operating income	$400,000

Contribution margin statement approach

	Without special order	With special order	Special order difference
Sales	$100,000,000	$100,800,000	$800,000
Manufacturing	40,000,000	40,400,000	400,000
Selling & Adm.	20,000,000	20,000,000	0
Variable costs	60,000,000	60,400,000	400,000
Contribution margin	40,000,000	40,400,000	400,000
Fixed costs			
Manufacturing	20,000,000	20,000,000	0
Selling & Adm.	10,000,000	10,000,000	0
Operating income	$ 10,000,000	$ 10,400,000	$400,000

C. Make or Buy

The relevant cost of manufacturing a given product is compared to the cost of purchasing it from an outside supplier. For differential analysis purposes, the relevant cost of production includes variable costs and "fixed" costs that would be **eliminated** if the product were purchased. Any opportunity cost of using production facilities for some other purpose (e.g., manufacturing of a different product, leasing or selling facilities, etc.) is subtracted from the cost of **purchasing** the product from the outside supplier or added to the cost of production.

Example 11 ▶ Make or Buy

The Sun Lamp Company needs 20,000 units of Part 109 used in its production cycle. If Sun Lamp Company buys the required parts rather than producing them, it will eliminate $1 of fixed overhead per unit. The remaining fixed overhead will continue even if the part is purchased from outsiders. The cost to buy the part is $22. The following information is available.

Direct material	$ 4
Direct labor	8
Variable overhead	8
Fixed overhead applied	4
Cost to make the part	$24

Required: Should Sun Lamp manufacture Part 109, or should it buy it from the outside supplier? Determine the relevant unit cost, relevant total costs, and differential costs.

Solution:

	Make	Buy
Direct material	$ 4	
Direct labor	8	
Variable overhead	8	
Fixed overhead which can be eliminated ($4 – $3)	1	
Total relevant unit costs	$ 21	$22

The relevant costs to make Part 109 are $420,000 (20,000 × $21). The relevant costs to buy the part are $440,000 (20,000 × $22). It is to Sun Lamp's advantage ($20,000) to continue to manufacture Part 109.

Example 12 ▶ Make or Buy

The same situation as Example 11, except that the facilities presently used to manufacture Part 109 could be used to manufacture Part 007 for product ABC and generate an operating profit of $30,000. The incremental costs to manufacture Part 109 (i.e., $420,000) must now be compared to the cost of purchasing the part less the operating profit generated in the manufacture of Product ABC (i.e., $440,000 − $30,000). Therefore, it would now be $10,000 ($420,000 − $410,000) cheaper to buy the part.

D. Scrap or Rework

The relevant cost is the added cost of reworking the inventory, compared to the differential revenue from the sale of the refinished goods (i.e., the difference between the scrap value of the inventory and the value of the refinished goods).

Example 13 ▶ Scrap or Rework

The Hippy Company has 1,000 obsolete lava lamps that are carried in inventory at a cost of $20,000. If these parts are reworked for $10,000 they could be sold for $15,000. If they are scrapped, they could be sold for $1,000.

Required: Should these lamps be reworked or scrapped? Determine the relevant and differential costs, sunk costs, and opportunity cost.

Solution: The rework alternative is more attractive since it yields a greater excess of relevant revenues over relevant costs. The $10,000 rework costs are incremental costs; therefore, they are relevant costs. The $20,000 inventory cost represents a sunk cost. It is not relevant to the decision to scrap or rework. The opportunity cost is the <u>$1,000</u> of revenue foregone from not selling the obsolete inventory as scrap.

	Altern	atives	
	Scrap	Rework	Differential
Relevant revenues	$1,000	$ 15,000	$ 14,000
Relevant costs	0	(10,000)	(10,000)
	$1,000	$ 5,000	$ 4,000

E. Sell or Process Further

This is another application of relevant cost and revenue analysis. The additional revenues obtainable from further processing the product are compared to the additional costs that would be incurred. If the additional revenues derived exceed the additional costs, the product should be processed further. The joint costs allocated to the product is **irrelevant** to the decision whether to subject the product to further processing.

Example 14 ▶ Sell or Process Further

The White Company uses a joint process to produce products A, B, and C. Each product may be sold at its split-off point or processed further. Additional processing costs are entirely variable. Joint production costs were $100,000 and are allocated using the relative-sales-value at split-off approach. The following information is available.

Products	Sales value at split-off	Additional processing costs	Final sales value
A	$ 50,000	$20,000	$100,000
B	100,000	20,000	120,000
C	20,000	30,000	40,000
	$170,000	$70,000	$260,000

Required: Should the products be sold at the split-off point or should they be further processed? Determine the net differential income.

Solution: The joint production costs are not relevant (i.e., do not differ between alternatives) and therefore do not affect the decision to process further or sell now. The optimum course of action is to sell product C at the split-off point, further process product A, and either sell at split-off or further process product B, depending on qualitative factors.

	A	B	C
Final sales value	$100,000	$ 120,000	$ 40,000
Sales value at split-off	(50,000)	(100,000)	(20,000)
Incremental revenues	50,000	20,000	20,000
Incremental costs	(20,000)	(20,000)	(30,000)
Differential	$ 30,000	$ 0	$(10,000)

F. Eliminate Product Line or Division

In addition to the differential items relating to the line or division, the effect on sales of related lines or divisions may be relevant. Furthermore, a line may be unprofitable but still contribute to the recovery of total fixed costs. The contribution margin of the line must be compared to its relevant fixed costs (i.e., the fixed costs that would be eliminated if the line were discontinued). If the contribution margin of the line exceeds the fixed costs that would be eliminated, the line should **not** be discontinued. The fixed costs that cannot be eliminated are **irrelevant** to the decision because they will continue regardless of the decision.

Example 15 ▶ Eliminating a Product Line

Management is considering eliminating product line B.

Product line	A	B	C	Total
Revenue	$1,000	$ 2,000	$ 3,000	$ 6,000
Variable costs	(500)	(1,500)	(1,000)	(3,000)
Contribution margin	500	500	2,000	3,000
Avoidable fixed costs	200	100	1,000	1,300
Unavoidable fixed costs	100	500	200	800
Fixed costs	(300)	(600)	(1,200)	(2,100)
Net income	$ 200	$ (100)	$ 800	$ 900

Required: Determine if product line B should be eliminated, based on the given information.

Solution: Product line B should not be eliminated because net income will decrease by $400. The $500 of unavoidable fixed costs allocated to product line B are irrelevant because they will continue regardless of the decision.

	Keep Line B	Eliminate Line B	Difference
Revenues	$ 6,000	$ 4,000	$ 2,000
Variable costs	(3,000)	(1,500)	(1,500)
Contribution margin	3,000	2,500	500
Avoidable	1,300	1,200	100
Unavoidable	800	800	0
Fixed costs	(2,100)	(2,000)	(100)
Net income	$ 900	$ 500	$ 400

G. Product Pricing

Product pricing involves the integration of various disciplines such as economics, statistics, industrial engineering, marketing, and accounting. The objective of product pricing is to maximize profits and thus, shareholders' wealth. Often, costs are the starting point for a pricing decision. Two common approaches to product pricing are the contribution margin approach and cost-plus pricing.

1. **Contribution Margin Approach** Under this approach, product pricing is based upon all relevant variable costs plus any additional fixed costs necessary for the increased production level.

2. **Cost-Plus Pricing** This method takes the product's cost and adds a predetermined markup to compute the targeted selling price. A predetermined markup that is expressed as a percentage of the product's selling price (e.g., a gross margin of 20% is desired) must be converted to a percentage markup on cost.

Exhibit 15 ▶ Conversion Formula

$$\text{Percentage markup on cost} = \frac{\text{Percentage markup on selling price}}{100\% - \text{Percentage markup on selling price}}$$

Example 16 ▶ Cost-Plus Pricing

Pallex Co. wants to sell a product at a gross margin of 20%. The cost of the product is $4.00.

Required: Determine the selling price of the product.

Solution:

Percentage markup on cost $=$ $\dfrac{\text{Percentage markup on selling price}}{100\% - \text{Percentage markup on selling price}}$

$= 20\% / (100\% - 20\%) = 25\%$

Selling price $=$ Cost of product + Gross margin

$= \$4.00 + 25\% (\$4.00) = \underline{\$5.00}$

IV. Direct (Variable) Costing

A. Overview
Direct costing (variable costing) is an inventory costing method whereby direct materials, direct labor, and variable manufacturing overhead are considered to be product costs (inventoriable costs), while fixed manufacturing overhead is considered to be a period cost (cost expensed in the period incurred).

1. **Components of Inventory** Under direct costing, only variable manufacturing costs are included in inventory. No **fixed** manufacturing costs are included in inventory.

2. **Format of Income Statement** Under direct costing, the income statement subtracts all variable expenses from sales to arrive at contribution margin. All fixed expenses are subtracted from contribution margin to arrive at operating income. (There is no gross margin.)

3. **Reporting** Direct costing is used for internal reporting purposes only. Its uses include inventory valuation, income measurement, relevant cost analysis, cost-volume-profit analysis, and other short-run, decision-making situations. Direct costing is not acceptable for external financial reporting (i.e., GAAP) and federal income tax reporting. Companies that use direct costing for internal reporting must convert to absorption costing (GAAP) for external financial reporting.

B. Accounting for Fixed Manufacturing Overhead
No selling or administrative costs are ever part of product costs under either method.

1. **Direct Costing** The costs to be inventoried include only the variable manufacturing costs. Fixed manufacturing overhead is expensed as incurred as a period cost, along with all selling and administrative costs.

2. **Absorption Costing** The costs to be inventoried include **all** manufacturing costs, both variable and fixed.

Exhibit 16 ▶ Comparison of Inventoried Costs

	Direct Costing	Absorption Costing
Direct materials	$XX	$XX
Direct labor	XX	XX
Variable manufacturing overhead	XX	XX
Fixed manufacturing overhead	--	XX
Variable selling and administrative costs	--	--
Fixed selling and administrative costs	--	--
Total product cost	$XX	$XX

C. Effects on Net Income

Under direct costing, income tends to move with sales, whereas under absorption costing, income may be influenced by production levels. Thus, net income can be influenced by inventory changes under absorption costing, but not under direct costing.

Exhibit 17 ▸ Direct & Absorption Costing

DIRECT COSTING	ABSORPTION COSTING
⇨ All VARIABLE product costs are inventoried	⇨ All PRODUCT costs are inventoried
⇨ Direct materials	⇨ Direct materials
⇨ Direct labor	⇨ Direct labor
⇨ Variable factory overhead	⇨ Variable factory overhead
☆ Fixed factory overhead is a period cost	⇨ Fixed factory overhead is an inventoried cost
☆ Selling & administrative costs are period costs	☆ Selling & administrative costs are period costs
☆ Not acceptable for external reporting	☆ Must be used for external reporting

1. **Production Exceeds Sales** When production exceeds sales (that is, when work-in-process and finished goods inventories are increasing), absorption costing shows a **higher** profit than does direct costing. The reason is that in absorption costing, a greater portion of the fixed manufacturing cost of the period is charged to inventory and thereby deferred to future periods. The total fixed cost charged against revenue of the period, therefore, is less than the amount of fixed cost incurred during the period.

2. **Sales Exceed Production** When sales exceed production (that is, when work-in-process and finished goods inventories are decreasing), absorption costing shows a lower profit than does direct costing. Under absorption costing, fixed costs previously deferred in inventory are charged against revenue in the period in which the goods are sold. Total fixed costs charged against revenue, therefore, exceed the amount of fixed cost incurred during the period.

3. **Production Equals Sales** When sales and production are in balance, net income will be the same under direct and absorption costing (assuming that fixed manufacturing costs per unit do not change). Since there is no change in inventories, the fixed manufacturing overhead cost incurred during the period will be charged to expense under both methods. Thus, net income will be the same using either costing method.

4. **Reconciling Net Income Under Absorption Costing & Direct Costing** If the fixed manufacturing overhead per unit cost does not change between periods, the difference between the reported net income under the two costing methods can be reconciled.

Exhibit 18 ▸ Reconciliation With Static Fixed Costs

$$\text{Difference in net income} = \text{Change in inventory level} \times \text{Fixed manufacturing overhead per unit}$$

D. **Advantages**

1. **Focus** All fixed costs (i.e., manufacturing, selling, and administrative) are expensed in the period incurred. This highlights the effect of fixed costs on net income. Net income is not influenced by production and inventory changes. Net income tends to vary with sales.

2. **Simplification** Fixed manufacturing overhead is not accounted for as an inventoriable cost. This simplifies record keeping and provides a more visible basis for controlling the total fixed manufacturing overhead costs.

3. **Internal Reporting** The income statement reporting format (i.e., the contribution margin format) is extremely useful for management purposes, e.g., cost-volume-profit relationships, contribution margin data, etc.

   a. When absorption costing is used, break-even analysis assumes: (1) sales volume equals production volume (i.e., inventory levels remain constant), (2) unit variable costs are unchanged over the relevant range, and (3) a given sales mix is maintained for all volume changes.

   b. If direct costing is used, no fixed manufacturing costs are applied to inventory, and hence it does not matter if sales volume equals production volume. All fixed costs are expensed when incurred.

E. **Disadvantages**

1. **External Reporting** Direct costing is not acceptable for external financial reporting (i.e., GAAP) and federal income tax reporting. Fixed manufacturing overhead is not properly deferred and matched against sales revenue in conformity with GAAP.

2. **Subjectivity** Product costs **and** period costs must be separated into their fixed and variable components. This can be difficult and often is subject to individual judgment.

3. **Focus** Too much attention may be given to variable costs at the expense of disregarding fixed costs. In the long run, fixed costs also must be recovered.

F. **Income Statement Reporting Format**

1. **Direct Costing** Under direct costing a contribution margin format generally is used. One variation is presented in Example 17. In the contribution margin income statement:

   a. All variable expenses (e.g., manufacturing, selling, and administrative) are used in **both** the computation of the contribution margin and the computation of operating income.

   b. All fixed expenses (e.g., manufacturing, selling, and administrative) are used in the computation of operating income but **not** in the computation of the contribution margin.

   c. The term "gross margin" does **not** appear.

2. **Absorption Costing** Under absorption costing, a traditional income statement format is used. One variation is presented in Example 17.

Example 17 ▶ Direct Costing vs. Full Absorption Costing Income Statements

The records of the Nickerson Company reveal the following information.

	20X1	20X2
Beginning inventory balance, in units	0	3,500
Production	10,000	9,000
Available for sale	10,000	12,500
Less units sold	(6,500)	(11,500)
Ending inventory balance, in units	3,500	1,000
Sales ($2/unit)	$13,000	$23,000
Variable manufacturing cost ($0.75/unit)	7,500	6,750
Fixed manufacturing cost	5,000	5,400
Selling and administrative expenses (50% fixed, 50% variable)	4,500	7,500

Required: Prepare Nickerson's partial income statements for 20X1 and 20X2 using both direct costing and absorption costing. Assume a FIFO inventory flow. Ignore income taxes.

Solution:

20X1 Absorption Costing Statement		
Sales (6,500 × $2)		$ 13,000
Var. mfg. costs		
(6,500 × $0.75)	$4,875	
Fixed mfg. costs		
(6,500 × $0.50)	3,250	
CGS		(8,125)
Gross margin		4,875
S&A expense		(4,500)
Operating income		$ 375

20X1 Direct Costing Statement		
Sales		$ 13,000
Var. mfg. costs		
(6,500 × $0.75)	$4,875	
Var. S&A ($4,500 × 0.50)	2,250	
Less: Variable costs		(7,125)
Contribution margin		5,875
Less: Fixed mfg. costs	5,000	
Fixed S&A	2,250	(7,250)
Operating loss		$ (1,375)

Difference in operating income: $375 − ($1,375) = $1,750

Change in inventory level	3,500
Fixed manufacturing OH per unit	$ 0.50
Reconciliation of difference in 20X1 operating income	$1,750

20X2 Absorption Costing Statement		
Sales (11,500 × $2)		$ 23,000
Var. mfg. costs		
(11,500 × $0.75)	$8,625	
Fixed mfg. costs		
(3,500 × $0.50)	1,750	
(8,000 × $0.60)	4,800	
CGS		(15,175)
Gross margin		7,825
S&A expense		(7,500)
Operating income		$ 325

20X2 Direct Costing Statement		
Sales		$ 23,000
Var. mfg. costs		
(11,500 × $0.75)	$8,625	
Var. S&A		
($7,500 × 0.50)	3,750	
Less: Variable costs		(12,375)
Contribution margin		10,625
Less: Fixed mfg. costs		(5,400)
Fixed S&A		(3,750)
Operating income		$ 1,475

Difference in operating income: $325 − $1,475 = $1,150

3,500 units × $5,000 / 10,000 units	$1,750
8,000 units × $5,400 / 9,000 units	4,800
Fixed costs expensed under absorption costing	6,550
Less: Fixed costs expensed under direct costing	5,400
Reconciliation of difference in 20X2 operating income	$1,150

CHAPTER 52—DECISION MAKING

Problem 52-1 MULTIPLE CHOICE QUESTIONS (60 to 75 minutes)

1. Gram Co. develops computer programs to meet customers' special requirements. How should Gram categorize payments to employees who develop these programs?

	Direct costs	Value-adding costs
a.	Yes	Yes
b.	Yes	No
c.	No	No
d.	No	Yes

(11/95, AR, #45, 5788)

2. The following information pertains to the August manufacturing activities of Griss Co.:

Beginning work-in-process	$12,000
Ending work-in-process	10,000
Cost of goods manufactured	97,000
Direct materials issued to production	20,000

Factory overhead is assigned at 150 percent of direct labor. What was the August direct labor?
a. $30,000
b. $30,800
c. $31,600
d. $50,000   (11/98, AR, #22, 6688)

3. When production levels are expected to increase within a relevant range, and a flexible budget is used, what effect would be anticipated with respect to each of the following costs?

	Fixed costs per unit	Variable costs per unit
a.	Decrease	Decrease
b.	No change	No change
c.	No change	Decrease
d.	Decrease	No change

(11/93, Theory, #46, 4551)

4. Day Mail Order Co. applied the high-low method of cost estimation to customer order data for the first 4 months of the year.

Month	Orders	Cost
January	1,200	$ 3,120
February	1,300	3,185
March	1,800	4,320
April	1,700	3,895
	6,000	$14,520

What is the estimated variable order filling cost component per order?
a. $2.00
b. $2.42
c. $2.48
d. $2.50   (5/95, AR, #36, amended, 5454)

5. In the budgeted profit-volume chart below, EG represents a two-product company's profit path. EH and HG represent the profit paths of products #1 and #2, respectively.

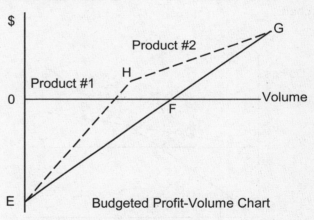

Budgeted Profit-Volume Chart

Sales prices and cost behavior were as budgeted, actual total sales equaled budgeted sales, and there were no inventories. Actual profit was greater than budgeted profit. Which product had actual sales in excess of budget, and what margin does OE divided by OF represent?

	Product with excess sales	OE/OF
a.	#1	Contribution margin
b.	#1	Gross margin
c.	#2	Contribution margin
d.	#2	Gross margin

(11/91, Theory, #47, 7386)

6. Sender Inc. estimates parcel mailing costs using data shown on the chart below.

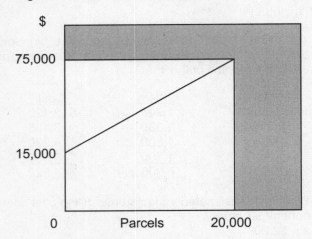

What is Sender's estimated cost for mailing 12,000 parcels?
a. $36,000
b. $45,000
c. $51,000
d. $60,000   (11/95, AR, #39, 7385)

7. The diagram below is a cost-volume-profit chart.

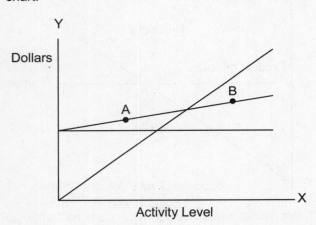

At point A compared to point B, as a percentage of sales revenues

	Variable costs are	Fixed costs are
a.	Greater	Greater
b.	Greater	The same
c.	The same	The same
d.	The same	Greater

(5/90, Theory, #46, 7387)

8. The most likely strategy to reduce the break-even point, would be to
a. Increase both the fixed costs and the contribution margin
b. Decrease both the fixed costs and the contribution margin
c. Decrease the fixed costs and increase the contribution margin
d. Increase the fixed costs and decrease the contribution margin   (11/92, Theory, #46, 3479)

9. Cuff Caterers quotes a price of $60 per person for a dinner party. This price includes the 6% sales tax and the 15% service charge. Sales tax is computed on the food plus the service charge. The service charge is computed on the food only. At what amount does Cuff price the food?
a. $56.40
b. $51.00
c. $49.22
d. $47.40   (5/95, AR, #50, 5468)

Items 10 and 11 are based on the following:

Slick Co. sells radios for $30 each. Fixed expenses total $15,000. Variable expenses are $20 per unit.

10. How many radios must Slick sell to earn an operating income of $35,000?
a. 5,000
b. 3,500
c. 2,500
d. 1,500   (Editors, 1450)

11. What total dollar amount must Slick sell to break even?
a $20,000
b. $37,500
c. $45,000
d $60,000   (Editors, 1451)

12. Product Cott has sales of $200,000, a contribution margin of 20%, and a margin of safety of $80,000. What is Cott's fixed cost?
a. $16,000
b. $24,000
c. $80,000
d. $96,000   (11/95, AR, #43, 5786)

13. Based on potential sales of 500 units per year, a new product has estimated traceable costs of $990,000. What is the target price to obtain a 15% profit margin on sales?
a. $2,329
b. $2,277
c. $1,980
d. $1,935   (11/95, AR, #55, 5798)

14. At annual sales of $900,000, the Ebo product has the following unit sales price and costs:

Sales price	$20
Prime cost	6
Manufacturing overhead	
Variable	1
Fixed	7
Selling & admin. costs	
Variable	1
Fixed	3
	18
Profit	$ 2

What is Ebo's breakeven point in units?
a. 25,000
b. 31,500
c. 37,500
d. 45,000   (R/00, AR, #16, 6921)

15. For 20X1, Abel Co. incurred direct costs of $500,000 based on a particular course of action during the year. If a different course of action had been taken, direct costs would have been $400,000. In addition, Abel's 20X1 fixed costs were $90,000. The incremental cost was
a. $ 10,000
b. $ 90,000
c. $100,000
d. $190,000   (5/92, PII, #56, amended, 2688)

16. Buff Co. is considering replacing an old machine with a new machine. Which of the following items is economically relevant to Buff's decision? (Ignore income tax considerations.)

	Carrying amount of old machine	Disposal value of new machine
a.	Yes	No
b.	No	Yes
c.	No	No
d.	Yes	Yes

(5/92, Theory, #56, 2749)

17. When only differential manufacturing costs are taken into account for special order pricing, an essential assumption is that
a. Manufacturing fixed and variable costs are linear.
b. Selling and administrative fixed and variable costs are linear.
c. Acceptance of the order will **not** affect regular sales.
d. Acceptance of the order will not cause unit selling and administrative variable costs to increase.

(11/90, Theory, #49, 2183)

18. Clay Co. has considerable excess manufacturing capacity. A special job order's cost sheet includes the following applied manufacturing overhead costs:

Fixed costs	$21,000
Variable costs	33,000

The fixed costs include a normal $3,700 allocation for in-house design costs, although no in-house design will be done. Instead the job will require the use of external designers costing $7,750. What is the total amount to be included in the calculation to determine the minimum acceptable price for the job?
a. $36,700
b. $40,750
c. $54,000
d. $58,050   (5/94, AR, #49, 4654)

Items 19 and 20 are based on the following:

Golden, Inc., has been manufacturing 5,000 units of Part 10541 which is used in the manufacture of one of its products. At this level of production, the cost per unit of manufacturing Part 10541 is as follows:

Direct materials	$ 2
Direct labor	8
Variable overhead	4
Fixed overhead applied	6
Total	$20

Brown Company has offered to sell Golden 5,000 units of Part 10541 for $19 a unit. Golden has determined that it could use the facilities presently used to manufacture Part 10541 to manufacture Product RAC and generate an operating profit of $4,000. Golden has also determined that two-thirds of the fixed overhead applied will continue even if Part 10541 is purchased from Brown.

19. In deciding whether to make or buy the part, the total relevant costs to make the part are
a. $70,000
b. $80,000
c. $90,000
d. $95,000   (Editors, 7389)

20. Should Golden accept Brown's offer, and why?
a. No, because it would be $11,000 cheaper to make the part
b. No, because it would be $15,000 cheaper to make the part
c. Yes, because it would be $5,000 cheaper to buy the part
d. Yes, because it would be $9,000 cheaper to buy the part   (Editors, 7390)

21. Gandy Company has 5,000 obsolete desk lamps that are carried in inventory at a manufacturing cost of $50,000. If the lamps are reworked for $20,000, they could be sold for $35,000. Alternatively, the lamps could be sold for $8,000 to a jobber located in a distant city. What alternative is more desirable and what are the total relevant costs for that alternative?
a. Neither, since there is an overall loss under either alternative
b. Rework and $20,000
c. Rework and $70,000
d. Scrap and $50,000 (Editors, 7391)

22. One hundred pounds of raw material W is processed into 60 pounds of X and 40 pounds of Y. Joint costs are $135. X is sold for $2.50 per pound and Y can be sold for $3.00 per pound or processed further into 30 pounds of Z (10 pounds are lost in the second process) at an additional cost of $60. Each pound of Z can then be sold for $6. What is the effect on profits of processing product Y further into product Z?
a. $60 increase
b. $30 increase
c. No change
d. $60 decrease (R/00, AR, #19, 6924)

23. Big Corporation currently operates two divisions that had operating results for the calendar year 20X1, as follows:

	West Division	East Division
Sales	$ 900,000	$ 300,000
Variable costs	(510,000)	(230,000)
Contribution margin	390,000	70,000
Fixed costs for the division	(110,000)	(50,000)
Margin over direct costs	280,000	20,000
Allocated corporate costs	(135,000)	(45,000)
Operating income (loss)	$ 145,000	$ (25,000)

Since the East Division also sustained an operating loss during 20X0, Big's president is considering the elimination of this division. The East Division fixed costs could be avoided if the division was eliminated. If the East Division had been eliminated on January 1, 20X1, Big Corporation's 20X1 operating income would have been
a. $20,000 lower
b. $25,000 higher
c. $45,000 lower
d. $70,000 higher (Editors, 1453)

24. Brent Co. has intracompany service transfers from Division Core, a cost center, to Division Pro, a profit center. Under stable economic conditions, which of the following transfer prices is likely to be most conducive to evaluating whether both divisions have met their responsibilities?
a. Actual cost
b. Standard variable cost
c. Actual cost plus mark-up
d. Negotiated price (5/94, AR, #44, 4649)

25. Vince Inc. has developed and patented a new laser disc reading device that will be marketed internationally. Which of the following factors should Vince consider in pricing the device?

I. Quality of the new device
II. Life of the new device
III. Customers' relative preference for quality compared to price

a. I and II only
b. I and III only
c. II and III only
d. I, II, and III (11/93, Theory, #50, 4555)

26. In calculating the break-even point for a multi-product company, which of the following assumptions are commonly made when variable costing is used?

I. Sales volume equals production volume.
II. Variable costs are constant per unit.
III. A given sales mix is maintained for all volume changes.

a. I and II
b. I and III
c. II and III
d. I, II, and III (5/92, Theory, #52, 7388)

27. Jago Co. has 2 products that use the same manufacturing facilities and cannot be subcontracted. Each product has sufficient orders to utilize the entire manufacturing capacity. For short-run profit maximization, Jago should manufacture the product with the
a. Lower total manufacturing costs for the manufacturing capacity
b. Lower total variable manufacturing costs for the manufacturing capacity
c. Greater gross profit per hour of manufacturing capacity
d. Greater contribution margin per hour of manufacturing capacity (5/95, AR, #49, 5467)

28. Using the variable costing method, which of the following costs are assigned to inventory?

	Variable selling and administrative costs	Variable factory overhead costs
a.	Yes	Yes
b.	Yes	No
c.	No	No
d.	No	Yes

(5/95, AR, #40, 5458)

29. In an income statement prepared as an internal report using the variable costing method, variable selling and administrative expenses would
a. Not be used
b. Be used in the computation of operating income but **not** in the computation of the contribution margin
c. Be treated the same as fixed selling and administrative expenses
d. Be used in the computation of the contribution margin (Editors, 2207)

30. In its first year of operations, Magna Manufacturers had the following costs when it produced 100,000 and sold 80,000 units of its only product:

Manufacturing costs:	
Fixed	$180,000
Variable	160,000

Selling & admin. costs:	
Fixed	90,000
Variable	40,000

How much lower would Magna's net income be if it used variable costing instead of full absorption costing?
a. $36,000
b. $54,000
c. $68,000
d. $94,000 (R/01, AR, #19, 7004)

Problem 52-2 ADDITIONAL MULTIPLE CHOICE QUESTIONS (78 to 98 minutes)

31. A direct labor overtime premium should be charged to a specific job when the overtime is caused by the
a. Increased overall level of activity
b. Customer's requirement for early completion of job
c. Management's failure to include the job in the production schedule
d. Management's requirement that the job be completed before the annual factory vacation closure (11/91, Theory, #43, 2551)

32. Fab Co. manufactures textiles. Among Fab's June manufacturing costs were the following salaries and wages:

Loom operators	$120,000
Factory foremen	45,000
Machine mechanics	30,000

What was the amount of Fab's June direct labor?
a. $195,000
b. $165,000
c. $150,000
d. $120,000 (5/92, PII, #42, amended, 2674)

33. Following are Mill Co.'s production costs for October:

Direct materials	$100,000
Direct labor	90,000
Factory overhead	4,000

What amount of costs should be traced to specific products in the production process?
a. $194,000
b. $190,000
c. $100,000
d. $ 90,000 (11/92, PII, #30, 3364)

34. Given that demand exceeds capacity, that there is no spoilage or waste, and that there is full utilization of a constant number of assembly hours, the number of components needed for an assembly operation with an 80 percent learning curve should

I. Increase for successive periods
II. Decrease per unit of output

a. I only
b. II only
c. Both I and II
d. Neither I nor II (R/01, AR, #17, 7002)

Items 35 through 37 are based on the following information pertaining to Harp Company's manufacturing operations:

Inventories	May 1	May 31
Direct materials	$18,000	$15,000
Work-in-process	9,000	6,000
Finished goods	27,000	36,000

Direct materials purchased in May	$42,000
Direct labor payroll in May	30,000
Direct labor rate per hour in May	7.50
Factory overhead rate per direct labor hour in May	10.00

35. For the month of May, prime cost was
a. $45,000
b. $60,000
c. $72,000
d. $75,000 (Editors, 1459)

36. For the month of May, conversion cost was
a. $45,000
b. $70,000
c. $72,000
d. $85,000 (Editors, 1460)

37. Cost of goods manufactured in May was
a. $109,000
b. $112,000
c. $115,000
d. $118,000 (Editors, 1461)

38. In job cost systems, manufacturing overhead is

	An indirect cost of jobs	A necessary element in production
a.	No	Yes
b.	No	No
c.	Yes	Yes
d.	Yes	No

(11/91, Theory, #41, amended, 2549)

39. Mat Co. estimated its material handling costs at two activity levels as follows:

Kilos handled	Cost
80,000	$160,000
60,000	132,000

What is the estimated cost for handling 75,000 kilos?
a. $150,000
b. $153,000
c. $157,500
d. $165,000 (5/94, AR, #36, amended, 4641)

40. In the profit-volume chart below, EF and GH represent the profit-volume graphs of a single-product company for 20X1 and 20X2, respectively.

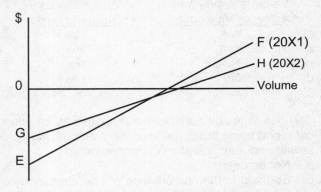

If 20X1 and 20X2 unit sales prices are identical, how did total fixed costs and unit variable costs of 20X2 change compared to 20X1?

	20X2 Total fixed costs	20X2 Unit variable costs
a.	Decreased	Increased
b.	Decreased	Decreased
c.	Increased	Increased
d.	Increased	Decreased

(5/91, Theory, #49, amended, 7384)

41. Briar Co. signed a government construction contract providing for a formula price of actual cost plus 10%. In addition, Briar was to receive one-half of any savings resulting from the formula price being less than the target price of $2,200,000. Briar's actual costs incurred were $1,920,000. How much should Briar receive from the contract?
a. $2,060,000
b. $2,112,000
c. $2,156,000
d. $2,200,000 (5/94, AR, #48, 4653)

42. Del Co. has fixed costs of $100,000 and break-even sales of $800,000. What is its projected profit at $1,200,000 sales?
a. $ 50,000
b. $150,000
c. $200,000
d. $400,000 (5/95, AR, #39, 5457)

43. The contribution margin ratio always increases when the
a. Variable costs as a percentage of net sales increase
b. Variable costs as a percentage of net sales decrease
c. Break-even point decreases
d. Break-even point increases (Editors, 2223)

44. The following information pertains to Casa Co.'s cost-volume-profit relationships:

Break-even point in units sold	1,000
Variable costs per unit	$ 500
Total fixed costs	$300,000

How much will be contributed to profit before income taxes by the 1,001st unit sold?
a. $1,300
b. $1,000
c. $ 300
d. $0 (Editors, 1444)

45. At the break-even point, the contribution margin equals total
a. Variable costs
b. Sales revenues
c. Selling and administrative costs
d. Fixed costs (11/93, Theory, #48, 4553)

46. The following information is taken from Wampler Co.'s contribution income statement:

Sales	$200,000
Contribution margin	120,000
Fixed costs	90,000
Income taxes	12,000

What was Wampler's margin of safety?
a. $ 50,000
b. $150,000
c. $168,000
d. $182,000 (5/98, AR, #8, amended, 6645)

47. The following information pertains to Syl Co.:

Sales	$800,000
Variable costs	160,000
Fixed costs	40,000

What is Syl's break-even point in sales dollars?
a. $200,000
b. $160,000
c. $ 50,000
d. $ 40,000 (11/92, PII, #36, 3370)

48. Break-even analysis assumes that over the relevant range
a. Unit revenues are nonlinear.
b. Unit variable costs are unchanged.
c. Total costs are unchanged.
d. Total fixed costs are nonlinear.
(11/95, AR, #44, 5787)

49. Lake Company increased its direct labor wage rates. All other budgeted costs and revenues were unchanged. How did this increase affect Lake's budgeted break-even point and budgeted margin of safety?

	Budgeted break-even point	Budgeted margin of safety
a.	Increase	Increase
b.	Increase	Decrease
c.	Decrease	Decrease
d.	Decrease	Increase

(5/92, Theory, #54, amended, 2747)

50. The following information pertains to Clove Company:

Budgeted sales	$1,000,000
Break-even sales	700,000
Budgeted contribution margin	600,000
Cashflow break-even	200,000

Clove's margin of safety is
a. $300,000
b. $400,000
c. $500,000
d. $800,000 (5/92, PII, #50, amended, 2682)

51. Bartlett Company is considering a new product, Pear. Bartlett's fixed costs are $200,000. Pear's contribution margin is $200 per unit. Bartlett has a marginal tax rate of 25%. How many units of Pear would Bartlett have to sell to have after-tax net income of $1,000,000?
a. 2,250 units
b. 4,750 units
c. 5,000 units
d. 6,000 units (Editors, 7737)

52. At December 31, Caine Co. had a machine with an original cost of $104,000, accumulated depreciation of $70,000, and an estimated salvage value of zero. On December 31, Caine was considering the purchase of a new machine having a five-year life, costing $130,000, and having an estimated salvage value of $30,000 at the end of five years. In its decision concerning the possible purchase of the new machine, how much should Caine consider as sunk cost at December 31?
a. $130,000
b. $100,000
c. $ 34,000
d. $ 4,000 (Editors, 1448)

53. Rice Co. plans to discontinue a department with a $24,000 contribution to overhead, and allocated overhead of $48,000, of which $21,000 cannot be eliminated. What would be the effect of this discontinuance on Rice's pretax profit?
a. Increase of $24,000
b. Decrease of $24,000
c. Increase of $3,000
d. Decrease of $3,000 (Editors, 7140)

54. Dale Company manufactures products Dee and Eff from a joint process. Product Dee has been allocated $5,000 of total joint costs of $40,000 for the 1,000 units produced. Dee can be sold at the split-off point for $6 per unit, or it can be processed further with additional costs of $2,000 and sold for $10 per unit. If Dee is processed further and sold, the result would be
a. A break-even situation
b. An additional gain of $2,000 from further processing
c. An overall loss of $2,000
d. An additional gain of $4,000 from further processing (Editors, 7393)

55. The manufacturing capacity of Gorb Company's facilities is 30,000 units of product a year. A summary of operating results for the calendar year 20X1 is as follows:

Sales (18,000 units @ $50)	$ 900,000
Variable manufacturing and selling costs	(495,000)
Contribution margin	405,000
Fixed costs	(247,500)
Operating income	$ 157,500

A foreign distributor has offered to buy 15,000 units at $45 per unit during 20X2. Assume that all of Gorb's costs would be at the same levels and rates in 20X2 as in 20X1. If Gorb accepted this offer and rejected some business from regular customers so as not to exceed capacity, what would be the total operating income for 20X2?
a. $195,000
b. $352,500
c. $420,000
d. $427,500 (Editors, 1449)

56. Comel, Inc. has two major product lines: stoves and dryers. Comel's management wants to evaluate whether discontinuing dryers will increase profits. Which of the following is **best** for evaluating the discontinuance of the dryer product line?
a. Absorption cost
b. Variable cost
c. Relevant cost
d. Throughput cost (R/02, AR, #15, 7080)

57. Operating income using direct costing as compared to absorption costing would be higher
a. When the quantity of beginning inventory is less than the quantity of ending inventory
b. When the quantity of beginning inventory is more than the quantity of ending inventory
c. When the quantity of beginning inventory equals the quantity of ending inventory
d. Under no circumstances (Editors, 7392)

58. In an income statement prepared using the variable costing method, fixed factory overhead would
a. Not be used
b. Be treated the same as variable factory overhead
c. Be used in the computation of operating income but **not** in the computation of the contribution margin
d. Be used in the computation of the contribution margin (Editors, 2199)

Items 59 and 60 are based on the following:

Sand Company has a calendar fiscal year and produces a single product that sells for $20 per unit. Sand uses an actual (historical) cost system. In the first year of operations, 100,000 units were produced and 80,000 units were sold. There was no work-in-process inventory at December 31. Manufacturing costs and selling and administrative expenses were as follows:

	Fixed costs	Variable costs
Raw materials	--	$4.00 per unit produced
Direct labor	--	2.50 per unit produced
Factory overhead	$240,000	1.50 per unit produced
Selling and administrative	140,000	2.00 per unit sold

59. What is Sand's operating income under the variable (direct) costing method?
a. $228,000
b. $420,000
c. $468,000
d. $660,000 (Editors, 1478)

60. What is Sand's finished goods inventory at December 31, under the absorption costing method?
a. $160,000
b. $208,000
c. $220,000
d. $248,000 (Editors, 1479)

61. A manufacturing company prepares income statements using both absorption and variable costing methods. At the end of a period actual sales revenues, total gross profit, and total contribution margin approximated budgeted figures, whereas net income was substantially greater than the budgeted amount. There were no beginning or ending inventories. The most likely explanation of the net income increase is that, compared to budget, actual
a. Manufacturing fixed costs had increased.
b. Selling and administrative fixed expenses had decreased.
c. Sales prices and variable costs had increased proportionately.
d. Sales prices had declined proportionately less than variable costs.   (5/93, Theory, #45, 4232)

Items 62 and 63 are based on the following information concerning the operations of Gordon Company for its initial calendar year. There were no work-in-process inventories at year-end.

Units produced	10,000
Units sold	9,000
Direct materials used	$20,000
Direct labor incurred	$10,000
Fixed factory overhead	$12,500
Variable factory overhead	$ 6,000
Fixed selling and administrative expenses	$15,000
Variable selling and administrative expenses	$ 2,250
Finished goods inventory, January 1	None

62. What is Gordon's finished goods inventory cost at December 31, under the variable (direct) costing method?
a. $3,600
b. $3,825
c. $4,000
d. $4,850   (Editors, 1480)

63. Which costing method, absorption or variable costing, would show a higher annual operating income and by what amount?

	Costing method	Amount
a.	Absorption costing	$1,250
b.	Variable costing	$1,250
c.	Absorption costing	$2,750
d.	Variable costing	$2,750

(Editors, 1481)

64. Cay Co.'s fixed manufacturing overhead costs totaled $100,000, and variable selling costs totaled $80,000. Under direct costing, how should these costs be classified?

	Period costs	Product costs
a.	$0	$180,000
b.	$ 80,000	$100,000
c.	$100,000	$ 80,000
d.	$180,000	$0

(11/92, PII, #33, amended, 3367)

65. Dowell Co. manufactures a wooden item. Which of the following is included with the inventoriable cost under absorption costing and excluded from the inventoriable cost under variable costing?
a. Cost of electricity used to operate production machinery
b. Straight-line depreciation on factory equipment
c. Cost of scrap pieces of lumber
d. Wages of assembly line personnel
     (11/98, AR, #23, 6689)

66. During May, Kern Co. produced and sold 10,000 units of a product. Manufacturing and selling costs incurred during May were as follows:

Direct materials and direct labor	$200,000
Variable manufacturing overhead	45,000
Fixed manufacturing overhead	10,000
Variable selling costs	5,000

The product's unit cost under direct (variable) costing was
a. $24.50
b. $25.00
c. $25.50
d. $26.00   (Editors, 1475)

67. Lynn Manufacturing Co. prepares income statements using both standard absorption and standard variable costing methods. For 20X2, unit standard costs were unchanged from 20X1. In 20X2, the only beginning and ending inventories were finished goods of 5,000 units. How would Lynn's ratios using absorption costing compare with those using variable costing?

	Current Ratio	Return on Stockholders' Equity
a.	Same	Same
b.	Same	Smaller
c.	Greater	Same
d.	Greater	Smaller

(11/95, AR, #56, amended, 5799)

68. Of the following, which is the greatest disadvantage of direct (variable) costing?
a. By expensing all fixed costs in the period incurred, the effects of fixed costs on net income are highlighted.
b. By expensing all fixed costs in the period incurred, record keeping is simplified.
c. Net income tends to vary with sales.
d. Product and period costs must be separated into their fixed and variable components.
(Editors, 7738)

69. Waldo Company, which produces only one product, provides its most current monthly data as follows:

Selling price per unit	$ 80
Variable costs per unit:	
Direct materials	21
Direct labor	10
Variable manufacturing overhead	3
Variable selling and administrative	6
Fixed costs:	
Manufacturing overhead	$76,000
Selling and administrative	58,000
Units:	
Beginning inventory	0
Month's production	5,000
Number sold	4,500
Ending inventory	500

Based upon the above information, what is the total contribution margin for the monthly data under the variable costing approach?
a. $ 46,000
b. $180,000
c. $207,000
d. $226,000 (R/03, BEC, #12, 7674)

SIMULATIONS

FYI: The editors encourage candidates to answer simulations as part of their review because such studying provides for content reinforcement, regardless of question format. Simulations currently are not part of the BEC exam; Bisk Education updating supplements will notify readers when this situation changes.

Problem 52-3 (25 to 40 minutes)

| Scenario | Response #1 | Response #2 | Response #3 |

Asta, Inc., is a medical laboratory that performs tests for physicians. Asta anticipates performing between 5,000 and 12,000 tests during the month of April.

Compared to industry averages, at the low range of activity Asta has a lower sales price per test, higher fixed costs, and the same break-even point in number of tests performed. At the high range of activity, Asta's sales price per test and fixed costs are the same as industry averages, and Asta's variable costs are lower. At the low range of activity (0 to 4,999 tests performed) fixed costs are $160,000. At the high range of activity (5,000 to 14,999 tests performed) fixed costs are $200,000.

Sales price per test	$60
Variable costs per test	20

For each item, determine the cost category **and** indicate if the cost is fixed (F) or variable (V).

Categories

A. Direct materials cost
B. Direct labor cost
C. Overhead cost for testing
D. General and administrative cost

1. Office manager's salary
2. Cost of electricity to run laboratory equipment
3. Hourly wages of part-time technicians who perform tests
4. Cost of lubricant used on laboratory equipment
5. Cost of distilled water used in tests
6. Accelerated depreciation on laboratory equipment
7. Straight-line depreciation on laboratory building
8. Cost of expensive binders in which test results are given to physicians

(11/93, PII, #4, amended, 4490-4501)

Calculate the amount.

1. Contribution margin per test
2. Break-even point in number of tests at low activity range
3. Break-even point in number of tests at high activity range
4. Number of units sold to achieve a gross profit of $160,000   (11/93, PII, #4, amended, 4490-4501)

For each item, indicate if Asta's costs are greater than (G), lesser than (L), or the same as (S) the industry average.

1. Variable costs at low activity range
2. Contribution margin at high activity range
3. Break-even point at high activity range   (11/93, PII, #4, amended, 4490-4501)

Problem 52-4 (5 to 10 minutes)

The following information pertains to a product for a 10-week budget period.

- Manufacturing and sales of 70,000 units are expected to occur evenly over the period.
- Materials are paid for in the week following use.
- There are no beginning inventories.

Sales price	$11 per unit
Materials	$3 per unit
Manufacturing conversion costs—Fixed	$210,000
Variable	$2 per unit
Selling and administrative costs—Fixed	$45,000
Variable	$1 per unit
Beginning accounts payable for materials	$40,000

Determine the correct amount using the accompanying information. Any information contained in an item is unique to that item and is **not** to be incorporated in your calculations when answering other items.

1. What amount should be budgeted for cash payments to material suppliers during the period?
2. Using variable costing, what is the budgeted income for the period?
3. Using absorption costing, what is the budgeted income for the period?
4. Actual results are as budgeted, except that 60,000 of the 70,000 units produced were sold Using absorption costing, what is the difference between the reported income and the budgeted net income?
5. If a special order for 4,000 units would cause a loss of 1,000 regular sales, what minimum amount of revenue must be generated from the special order so that net income is not reduced? (All cost relationships are unchanged.)   (11/96, AR, #4, 6329-6333)

Solution 52-1 MULTIPLE CHOICE ANSWERS

Cost Classification

1. (a) Direct costs can be traced easily to a cost object. Value-adding costs are costs for which a customer would be willing to pay. The payments to the employees who develop computer programs can be traced easily to the cost of the computer programs. Costs incurred for employees who work directly on a product desired by a customer are value-adding costs. Therefore, the payments are both direct and value-adding costs.

2. (a) With beginning WIP of $12,000, direct materials added of $20,000, and cost of goods manufactured of $97,000, the only way to have an ending WIP balance of $10,000 is to add $75,000 of direct labor (DL) and factory overhead (FOH) combined. FOH is assigned at 1½ the rate of DL, so 1.5 DL + 1.0 DL = $75,000 and so 2.5 DL = $75,000 and thus DL = $75,000 / 2.5 = $30,000.

3. (d) Since total fixed costs remain constant within the relevant range of activity, an increase in the level of production decreases the fixed costs per unit because the same total fixed costs are allocated over more units. Variable costs do not change on a per unit basis with changes in the level of activity within the relevant range.

Cost Estimation

4. (a) The high month is March with 1,800 orders at a cost of $4,320. The low month is January with 1,200 orders at a cost of $3,120. The estimated variable order filling cost can be obtained by dividing the change in cost by the change in orders, because only variable costs change in total with a change in the order volume.

$$\frac{\$4,320 - \$3,120}{1,800 - 1,200} = \frac{\$1,200}{600} = \$2/\text{order}$$

CVP Charts

5. (a) Total actual sales equaled budgeted sales and sales prices and cost behavior were as budgeted. Thus, the increase in profit cannot be due to additional sales, and neither the contribution margin per unit of either of the products nor total fixed costs changed. The only plausible explanation of the increase in profit is that the sales mix of the two products changed. Total sales must have consisted of a greater percentage of the high contribution margin (CM) product and a lower percentage of the low CM product. Since profit line EH for Product 1 has a steeper slope than profit line HG for Product 2,

Product 1 has a higher CM. Thus, actual sales of Product 1 must have exceeded budgeted sales while actual sales of Product 2 must have been less than budgeted sales. Point E, the point at which the profit line intersects the vertical axis, represents total fixed costs. Point F, the point at which the profit line intersects the horizontal axis, represents the break-even level of sales because there is no profit or loss at this level of activity. At the break-even point, CM equals total fixed costs. Therefore, Line OE represents total CM at the break-even point. Line OF represents the sales volume at the break-even point. Thus, Line OE (total CM at the break-even point) divided by Line OF (sales volume at the break-even point) represents the average contribution margin percentage.

6. (c) The variable cost per parcel is determined using the high-low method by dividing the change in total costs by the change in number of parcels: ($75K – $15K) / (20,000 parcels – 0 parcels) = $60,000 / 20,000 parcels = $3/parcel. The fixed costs are the amount of total cost when no parcels are mailed. The total variable costs are $36K ($3/parcel × 12,000 parcels). The estimated total cost for mailing parcels is equal to the fixed costs plus the total variable costs, or $15K + $36K = $51K.

7. (d) Cost-volume-profit (CVP) analysis assumes that both the selling price and variable cost per unit do not change with volume changes; therefore, variable costs are the same percentage of sales revenues at points A and B. CVP analysis also assumes that fixed costs remain unchanged over the relevant range. Therefore, fixed costs are a greater percentage of revenues at point A than point B because revenues are lower at point A.

Computational Methods

8. (c) The break-even point is computed by dividing fixed costs by the contribution margin. Since fixed costs is the numerator of the formula, a decrease in fixed costs would *decrease* the break-even point. Since contribution margin is the denominator of the formula, an increase in this amount would also *decrease* the break-even point.

9. (c) Let F = sales price of the food only.

Let C = Service charge = 0.15F
    T = Sales tax   = 0.06 (F + 0.15F)
                      = 0.06 (1.15F) = 0.069F

$60 = F + C + T
$60 = F + 0.15F + 0.069F = 1.219F
F = $60 / 1.219 = $49.22

10. (a)   Let X = number of radios sold.

Revenue – (Variable + Fixed expenses) = Operating income
$$\$30X – (\$20X + \$15,000) = \$35,000$$
$$\$10X = \$50,000$$
$$X = 5,000 \text{ radios sold}$$

11. (c)   Let X = dollar amount of sales.

X – Variable expenses – Fixed expenses = Operating income
$$X – (\$20/\$30)X – \$15,000 = \$0$$
$$1/3\ X = \$15,000$$
$$X = \$45,000$$

Break-Even Analysis

12. (b)   Margin of safety (MOS) equals actual sales less break-even (BE) sales; thus, actual sales less MOS equals BE point sales. At BE point, sales are $120,000 ($200,000 – $80,000) and total contribution margin (CM) equals $24,000 ($120,000 × 20%). At BE point, CM equals fixed cost.

13. (a)   Let P = the target price per unit necessary to realize a 15% profit margin on sales.

$$500P – \$990,000 = 0.15(500)P = 75P$$
$$425P = \$990,000$$
$$P = \$2,329.41 \text{ or approx. } \$2,329$$

14. (c)   Dividing the annual sales by the sales price provides the annual budgeted units [$900,000 / $20/unit = 45,000 units] used for determining fixed costs. Thus, annual fixed costs are ($7 + $3) × 45,000 units = $450,000. The breakeven point is that point at which there is zero profit. Sales minus variable and fixed costs equals profit. If X is the number of units at the breakeven point, ($20/unit – $8/unit) × X – $450,000 = 0; or X = $450,000 / 12 = 37,500 units. Candidates also may use trial and error with the responses to determine the answer.

Relevant Costs

15. (c)   Incremental cost is the difference in total cost between the two alternatives. The total amount of fixed costs does not differ between the two alternatives.

16. (b)   The carrying amount of the old machine is irrelevant because it is a sunk (historical) cost. The disposal value of the new machine is relevant because it is an expected future cash inflow that differs between alternatives.

Special Order

17. (c)   When only differential manufacturing costs are taken into account for special order pricing, it is essential to assume that acceptance of the order will not affect regular sales. It is not necessary to assume that costs are linear or unchanging.

18. (b)   The fixed costs are not relevant to the decision as they remain constant in total whether or not Clay Co. accepts the special order. The relevant costs are the variable costs and the additional cost of using the external designers.

Variable costs	$33,000
Plus: Cost of using external designers	7,750
Minimum acceptable price	$40,750

Make or Buy Decisions

19. (b)   The fixed overhead that would continue ($6 × 2/3) even if Part 10541 is purchased is irrelevant to the decision to make or buy.

Direct materials	$ 2
Direct labor	8
Variable overhead	4
Fixed overhead eliminated ($6 × 1/3)	2
Incremental (total relevant) unit cost	16
Times: Units to be manufactured	× 5,000
Incremental cost to manufacture 5,000 units	$80,000

20. (a)   The incremental costs to manufacture Part 10541 must be compared to the net cost of purchasing the part. It is $11,000 (i.e., $91,000 – $80,000) cheaper to manufacture the part.

Incremental manufacturing cost (Question #19)	$80,000
Purchase price of 5,000 units (5,000 × $19)	95,000
Less: Operating profit generated in the manufacture of Product RAC	(4,000)
Net cost of purchasing Part 10541	$91,000

Scrap or Rework

21. (b)   The $27,000 ($35,000 – $8,000) of incremental revenues exceed the $20,000 incremental rework costs.

Sell or Process Further

22. (c)   Product Y can be sold for a revenues of $120 ($3 / lb. × 40 lb.) or used to create 30 lbs. of Z that can be sold for revenues of $180 ($6 / lb. × 30 lb.) less additional costs of $60 = $120. There is no increase or decrease to profits from processing product Y into Z. The cost of raw material W assigned to Y is irrelevant.

Eliminate Line or Division

23. (a)   All amounts relative to East Division through "Margin over direct costs" would be eliminated if the division were eliminated. Therefore, the $20,000 margin would be lost, and income would be

reduced by that amount. Note that the $45,000 allocated corporate costs would *not* be eliminated.

Product Pricing

24. (b) If actual cost or actual cost plus a markup is used, the selling division can pass on inefficiencies to the buying division. Negotiated price may not result in the most efficient transfer pricing, due to inequities in negotiating power. Standard variable cost should be used since the selling division is a cost center and has no incentive to make a profit on the transfer. Furthermore, with standard variable costing, inefficiencies will not be passed on to the buying division, which is concerned with profits.

25. (d) In pricing the new device, the quality and life of the new device should be considered, along with customers' relative preference for quality compared to price.

Direct vs. Absorption Costing

26. (c) Using absorption costing, break-even analysis assumes: (I) sales volume equals production volume (i.e., inventory levels remain constant), (II) unit variable costs are unchanged over the relevant range and (III) a given sales mix is maintained for all volume changes. Using direct costing, no fixed manufacturing costs are applied to inventory because all fixed costs are expensed when incurred. Hence, it does not matter if sales volume equals production volume.

27. (d) When there are products competing for a scarce resource, the company should produce and sell the product that has the greater contribution margin per unit of the scarce resource. In this case, manufacturing capacity is the scarce resource. Manufacturing the product with the greater contribution margin per hour of manufacturing capacity will result in a greater total contribution margin and thus a greater short-run profit.

28. (d) Under variable costing, only variable production costs are treated as inventoriable or product costs. Fixed overhead cost is treated as a period cost. Variable factory overhead costs are assigned to inventory. However, under both variable and absorption costing, selling and administrative costs (whether variable or fixed) are period costs, not product costs assigned to inventory.

29. (d) Variable sales and administration expenses are used in both the computation of the contribution margin and the computation of operating income. The format of an income statement prepared using variable costing is as follows.

Sales		$XXX
Production	$XXX	
Selling and administrative	XXX	
Less: Variable expenses		XXX
Contribution margin		XXX
Production	XXX	
Selling and administrative	XXX	
Less: Fixed expenses		XXX
Operating income		$XXX

30. (a) The only difference between variable and full absorption costing income is the treatment of fixed manufacturing costs. Variable costing expenses the full $180,000. Full absorption costing includes a share of the fixed manufacturing costs in inventory for the 20,000 finished but unsold units. 20,000 units × $180,000 / 100,000 units = $36,000

Solution 52-2 ADDITIONAL MULTIPLE CHOICE ANSWERS

Cost Classification

31. (b) A direct labor overtime premium is generally considered to be attributable to the heavy overall volume of work, and its cost is thus regarded as part of manufacturing overhead, which is borne by all units produced. Sometimes the direct labor overtime premium is not random. For example, a special or rush job may clearly be the sole source of the overtime. In such instances, the premium is regarded as a direct cost of the products made for that job.

32. (d) Direct labor includes all labor that is physically traceable to the finished goods in an economically feasible manner. The labor of a factory machine operator (e.g., a loom operator) and an assembler are common examples of direct labor. Since wages paid to factory foremen and machine mechanics are not physically traceable to the finished goods in an economically feasible manner, they would be included in manufacturing overhead.

33. (b) Direct materials are those materials that are traceable to and an integral part of the finished good. Direct labor is factory labor that is traceable to specific products. Factory overhead is the sum of all indirect product costs (i.e., all product costs except direct materials and direct labor). Therefore, the costs that are traced to specific products in the production process is the sum of the direct materials and direct labor costs.

34. (a) This learning curve pertains to the assembly operation. As workers learn to assemble components faster, they will assemble more components per period in successive time periods. Learning how to assemble components faster has no effect on the number of components needed to produce a unit of output.

35. (d) Prime cost is the sum of direct materials cost and direct labor cost.

Beginning inventory	$ 18,000
Add: Purchases	42,000
Direct materials available for use	60,000
Less: Ending inventory	(15,000)
Direct materials used in production	45,000
Direct labor cost (given)	30,000
Prime cost incurred	$ 75,000

36. (b) Conversion cost is the sum of direct labor cost and manufacturing overhead cost.

Direct labor cost (given)		$30,000
Direct labor cost	$30,000	
Direct labor rate per hour	/ 7.50	
Direct labor hours incurred	4,000	
Factory OH rate per DLH	× 10.00	
Manufacturing OH cost applied		40,000
Conversion cost incurred		$70,000

37. (d)

Beginning work-in-process		$ 9,000
Direct materials cost	$45,000	
Direct labor cost	30,000	
Overhead cost applied	40,000	
Manufacturing costs added		115,000
Manufacturing costs to account for		124,000
Ending work-in-process		(6,000)
Cost of goods manufactured		$118,000

38. (c) Direct materials, direct labor, and manufacturing overhead are the three major elements in the cost of a manufactured product. Manufacturing overhead consists of all manufacturing costs other than direct materials and direct labor.

Cost Estimation

39. (b) The variable cost (VC) per kilo handled can be estimated by dividing the change in cost by the change in kilos handled. Thus, the estimated VC per kilo handled is $1.40 ($28,000 / 20,000 kilos handled). The total VC can be obtained by multiplying the VC per kilo handled times the number of kilos handled. The total cost less the total VC equals the fixed cost. The VC cost for the 75,000 kilos handled can be estimated by multiplying the 75,000 kilos handled by the $1.40 VC per kilo handled. Adding the total VC and the fixed cost gives the total estimated cost for handling 75,000 kilos.

Change in cost: $160,000 – $132,000 = $28,000
Change in kilos handled: 80,000 – 60,000 = 20,000

Total cost	$ 160,000	$132,000
Less: Total variable cost		
80,000 K × $1.40/K	(112,000)	
60,000 K × $1.40/K		(84,000)
Fixed cost	$ 48,000	$ 48,000

Total variable cost (75,000 K × $1.40/K)	$105,000
Fixed cost	48,000
Total estimated cost for 75,000 K	$153,000

CVP Charts

40. (a) Lines EF and GH depict profit lines for 20X1 and 20X2, respectively. Points E and G, the points at which the profit lines intersect the vertical axis, represent the total fixed costs for 20X1 and 20X2, respectively, because there are no variable costs at zero volume. Since Line OG (20X2) is less than Line OE (20X1), total fixed costs decreased in 20X2. The profit lines slope upward from the fixed cost points at the rate of the unit contribution margin. Since the 20X2 profit line (GH) has a less steep slope than the 20X1 profit line (EF), the unit contribution margin decreased in 20X2, meaning that variable costs increased in 20X2.

Computational Methods

41. (c)

Actual costs incurred	$1,920,000
Plus: Markup (10%)	192,000
Formula price	2,112,000

Target price	$ 2,200,000	
Less: Formula price	(2,112,000)	
Savings	88,000	
Additional revenues	× 50%	44,000
Amount Briar should receive		$2,156,000

42. (a) The contribution margin equals fixed costs at the break-even point. Thus, the contribution margin is also $100,000 at the break-even point. The contribution margin ratio is the contribution margin divided by sales. The contribution margin ratio computes to 12.5% ($100,000 / $800,000). Multiplying the sales in dollars by the contribution margin ratio gives the contribution margin in dollars. Because fixed costs remain constant in total when volume changes, the fixed costs can be subtracted from the contribution margin to determine the profit.

Sales	$1,200,000
Times: Contribution margin ratio	× 12.5%
Contribution margin	150,000
Less: Fixed costs	(100,000)
Profit	$ 50,000

43. (b) Questions of this type are usually best answered by setting forth the equation for the required variable (i.e., contribution margin ratio in this case) and then analyzing the effect of changes in the other variables. Based on the equation below, you can easily see that a decrease in variable costs would increase the contribution margin ratio.

$$\text{Contribution margin ration} = \frac{\text{Sales} - \text{Variable costs}}{\text{Sales}}$$

44. (c) For each unit sold above the break-even point, the company will obtain net income equal to the CM / U. Therefore, the 1,001st unit sold will contribute $300 to profits before income taxes.

$$\text{Break-even (units)} = \frac{\text{Fixed costs}}{\text{Contribution margin per unit}}$$

$$1{,}000 \text{ units} = \frac{\$300{,}000}{\text{CM / unit}}$$

CM / unit = $300,000 / 1,000 units = $300 per unit

Break-Even Analysis

45. (d) Contribution margin (CM) less fixed costs equals operating income. At the break-even point, operating income is zero, so CM equals fixed costs.

46. (a) The margin of safety is actual sales less break-even (BE) sales ($200,000 − $150,000 = $50,000). BE sales are sales equal to the sum of variable and fixed costs. The variable manufacturing costs at actual sales (actual sales less the actual contribution margin, or $200,000 − $120,000 = $80,000) are ($80,000 / $200,000 =) 40% of sales. Income taxes generally are not included in calculating the margin of safety. Let SB = break-even sales and F = fixed costs, then 0.4SB = variable costs (at break-even sales), and

$$\begin{aligned} SB &= 0.4SB + F \\ 0.6SB &= F = \$90{,}000 \\ SB &= \$90{,}000 / 0.6 = \$150{,}000 \end{aligned}$$

47. (c) To compute the break-even point in sales dollars, the contribution margin percentage must first be computed. The contribution margin percentage is 80% [i.e., ($800,000 sales − $160,000 variable costs) / $800,000 sales)].

$$\text{Break-even point in dollars} = \frac{\text{Fixed costs}}{\text{Contribution margin percentage}}$$

= $40,000 / 80% = **$50,000**

48. (b) Break-even analysis assumes that costs behave in a linear relationship within the relevant range. Break-even analysis assumes that fixed costs remain constant in total and that variable costs are fixed or unchanged on a per-unit basis.

49. (b) The increase in the direct labor wage rates increased the variable cost per unit, thereby decreasing the contribution margin ratio because the selling price per unit is unchanged. With unchanged budgeted fixed costs and a decreased contribution margin ratio, the budgeted break-even point increases. The margin of safety is the excess of budgeted revenues over the level of revenues at the break-even point. Since budgeted revenues were unchanged and the budgeted break-even point increased, the budgeted margin of safety decreased.

50. (a) The margin of safety is the excess of budgeted revenues over the level of revenues at the break-even point (i.e., $1,000,000 − $700,000).

51. (b) A modified cost-volume-profit formula is required to include the impact of income taxes. Units for a stated after-tax net income = [fixed costs + (after-tax net income) / (1 − tax rate)] / contribution margin per unit = [$200,000 + ($1,000,000) / (1 − 0.25)] / $200 / unit = 4,750 units.

Special Decisions

52. (c) Sunk costs are costs incurred as a result of past decisions and *not* relevant to future decisions. The carrying amount of the machine ($104,000 − $70,000) is a sunk cost with no bearing on the decision to keep or replace the machine.

53. (c) The department contributes $24,000 to overhead. Allocated overhead amounts to $48,000, of which $21,000 cannot be eliminated; thus, $27,000 of overhead can be eliminated by discontinuing the department. This will *increase* Rice's pretax profit by $3,000 (i.e., $27,000 − $24,000).

54. (b) The $5,000 of joint costs allocated to the product is *irrelevant* to the decision whether to subject the product to further processing.

Incremental revenues [1,000 × ($10 − $6)]	$ 4,000
Additional costs	(2,000)
Additional gain from further processing	$ 2,000

55. (b) Variable costs per unit are $27.50 ($495,000 / 18,000 units)

	Regular sales (15,000 units)	Special order (15,000 units)	Total (30,000 units)
Sales	$750,000	$675,000	$1,425,000
Variable costs	(412,500)	(412,500)	(825,000)
CM	$337,500	$262,500	600,000
Fixed costs			(247,500)
Operating income			$ 352,500

56. (c) Relevant costs are those costs that make a difference between alternative courses of action; by definition, they are the best costs to consider for decisions. Variable costs usually are included in relevant costs, but they sometimes are not the only relevant costs. Absorption cost is used in financial accounting to determine amounts in GAAP financial statements, but is often a poor basis for future decisions. Throughput costing includes only direct material costs in inventory; labor and overhead costs can be significant.

Direct vs. Absorption Costing

57. (b) When sales exceed production (i.e., the quantity of beginning inventory is more than ending inventory), the operating income reported using direct costing will generally be higher than operating income reported using absorption costing. When more inventory is sold than is produced, inventories are drawn down, and the amount of fixed manufacturing overhead cost released to expense using absorption costing is greater than the amount that was incurred during the period.

58. (c) Fixed factory overhead is used in the computation of operating income but *not* in the computation of the contribution margin. The format of an income statement using the variable costing method is as follows.

Sales		$ XXX
Manufacturing	$XXX	
Selling and administrative	XXX	
Less: Variable expenses		XXX
Contribution margin		XXX
Manufacturing	XXX	
Selling and administrative	XXX	
Less: Fixed expenses		XXX
Operating income		$XXX

59. (b) Under variable (direct) costing, direct materials, direct labor, and variable manufacturing overhead are product costs, i.e., they are not expensed until the produced item is sold. Fixed manufacturing overhead and all selling and administrative costs are expensed in the period incurred.

Sales (80,000 units @ $20 per unit)		$1,600,000
Less: Var. mfg. costs [80,000 ×		
($4.00 + $2.50 + $1.50)]	$(640,000)	
Var. S & A (80,000 × $2/unit)	(160,000)	(800,000)
Contribution margin		800,000
Less: Fixed manufacturing costs		(240,000)
Fixed selling and administrative		(140,000)
Operating income (variable costing)		$ 420,000

60. (b) Under absorption costing, all manufacturing costs are product costs (and thus inventoriable). The variable manufacturing costs that attach to each produced unit total $8 ($4.00 raw materials + $2.50 direct labor + $1.50 variable overhead). The fixed manufacturing cost that attaches to each produced unit equals $2.40 ($240,000 fixed overhead / 100,000 units). With each unit having $10.40 of costs (variable + fixed) attaching to it, the ending inventory (100,000 units produced – 80,000 units sold) would be carried on the books at $208,000 (20,000 units × $10.40 per unit).

61. (b) The following income statement formats show that operating income is measured under both absorption costing and variable costing.

Absorption Costing Method		
Sales		$ XX
Less: Cost of goods sold		XX
Gross margin		XX
Selling	$XX	
Administrative	XX	
Less: Operating expenses		XX
Operating income		$ XX

Variable Costing Method		
Sales		$XX
Variable production	$XX	
Variable selling	XX	
Variable administrative	XX	
Less: Variable costs		XX
Contribution margin		XX
Fixed production	XX	
Fixed selling	XX	
Fixed administrative	XX	
Less: Fixed costs		XX
Operating income		$XX

With respect to the income statement prepared using the variable costing method, the manufacturing company's sales revenues and total contribution margin approximated budgeted figures; therefore, the company's total variable expenses also approximated budgeted figures. Thus, it is unlikely that the higher net income figure was due to a decrease in variable manufacturing or variable selling and administrative expenses. With respect to the income statement prepared using the absorption costing method, sales revenues and gross profit approximated budgeted figures; therefore, the company's total manufacturing expenses also approximated budgeted figures. Thus, it is also unlikely that the higher net income figure was due to a decrease in fixed manufacturing expenses. Since it is unlikely that the higher net income figure was due to a decrease in either variable manufacturing expenses, variable selling and administrative expenses, or fixed manufacturing expenses, the most likely explanation of the higher net income figure is that fixed selling and administrative expenses had decreased.

62. (a)   Using direct costing, only variable production costs are inventoried. Fixed factory overhead is expensed when incurred as a period cost.

Direct materials	$20,000
Direct labor	10,000
Variable factory overhead	6,000
Total variable production costs	36,000
Portion allocated to ending inventory (1,000 / 10,000)	× 0.10
Cost of ending inventory	$ 3,600

63. (a)   Under variable costing, the entire fixed factory overhead (FOH) is charged to expense as a period cost. Under absorption costing, fixed FOH is a product cost (i.e., an inventoriable cost) and is expensed only to the extent included in cost of goods sold; the portion of fixed FOH allocated to goods not sold during the period becomes part of the ending inventory for the period.

FOH expensed, variable costing	$ 12,500
FOH expensed, absorption costing (9/10 × $12,500)	(11,250)
Excess expense recognized under variable costing	$ 1,250

64. (d)   Under direct costing, both the fixed manufacturing overhead costs and the variable selling costs are classified as period costs. Under direct costing, only variable manufacturing costs (i.e., direct materials, direct labor, and variable manufacturing overhead) are inventoried as product costs. Fixed manufacturing overhead and *all* selling and administrative costs are considered to be period costs, and are therefore expensed when incurred.

65. (b)   Under direct (variable) costing only variable manufacturing costs are inventoried. Fixed manufacturing costs are expensed in the period incurred. Absorption costing includes all manufacturing costs in inventory.

66. (a)   Under direct costing, only variable product costs (i.e., direct materials, direct labor, and variable manufacturing overhead) are inventoried. The fixed manufacturing overhead and variable selling costs are considered to be period costs (rather than product costs) and are expensed when incurred.

Direct materials and direct labor	$200,000
Variable manufacturing overhead	45,000
Total variable product costs	245,000
Units produced during period	/ 10,000
Unit cost under direct costing	$ 24.50

67. (d)   When there is no change in standard costs and inventories, the absorption costing method and variable costing will give the same net income. However, the cost of inventory will be greater under absorption costing because inventory includes fixed overhead cost under absorption costing but not under variable costing. Inventory is a current asset. Costing methods have no effect on other current assets or on the amount of current liabilities. The current ratio is the ratio between current assets and current liabilities. Because inventory is greater under absorption costing, the current ratio will also be greater under absorption costing. Because inventory is greater under absorption costing, stockholders' equity will also be greater under absorption costing. Return on stockholders' equity is net income divided by stockholders' equity. Since the income is the same under both methods, the return on stockholders' equity will be smaller under absorption because of the greater denominator.

68. (d)   Under direct costing, product and period costs must be separated into their fixed and variable components; this can be difficult and often is subject to individual judgment. All fixed costs are expensed in the period incurred, highlighting the effect of fixed costs on net income. Fixed manufacturing overhead is not accounted for as an inventoriable cost. This simplifies record keeping. Net income tends to vary with sales, simplifying decision making.

69. (b)   Variable costs per unit are $40 ($21 + $10 + $3 + $6). Contribution margin per unit is sales per unit less variable costs (including selling and administrative costs) per unit, $80 – $40 = $40. Contribution margin is $40 per unit × 4,500 units = $180,000.

PERFORMANCE BY SUBTOPICS

Each category below parallels a subtopic covered in Chapter 52. Record the number and percentage of questions you correctly answered in each subtopic area.

Cost Classification

Question #	Correct	√
1		
2		
3		
# Questions	3	
# Correct		
% Correct		

Cost Estimation

Question #	Correct	√
4		
# Questions	1	
# Correct		
% Correct		

CVP Charts

Question #	Correct	√
5		
6		
7		
# Questions	3	
# Correct		
% Correct		

Computational Methods

Question #	Correct	√
8		
9		
10		
11		
# Questions	4	
# Correct		
% Correct		

Break-Even Analysis

Question #	Correct	√
12		
13		
14		
# Questions	3	
# Correct		
% Correct		

Relevant Costs

Question #	Correct	√
15		
16		
# Questions	2	
# Correct		
% Correct		

Special Order

Question #	Correct	√
17		
18		
# Questions	2	
# Correct		
% Correct		

Make or Buy Decisions

Question #	Correct	√
19		
20		
# Questions	2	
# Correct		
% Correct		

Scrap or Rework

Question #	Correct	√
21		
# Questions	1	
# Correct		
% Correct		

Sell or Process Further

Question #	Correct	√
22		
# Questions	1	
# Correct		
% Correct		

Eliminate Line or Division

Question #	Correct	√
23		
# Questions	1	
# Correct		
% Correct		

Product Pricing

Question #	Correct	√
24		
25		
# Questions	2	
# Correct		
% Correct		

Direct vs. Absorption Costing

Question #	Correct	√
26		
27		
28		
29		
30		
# Questions	5	
# Correct		
% Correct		

SIMULATION SOLUTIONS

Solution 52-3

Response #1: Cost Categories (7 points)

1. D, F

The office manager's salary is a general and administrative cost. The office manager's salary will not be affected by the number of tests performed.

2. C, V

Overhead cost for testing is the sum of all indirect costs of testing (i.e., all testing costs except direct materials and direct labor). Therefore, the cost of electricity to run laboratory equipment is an overhead cost for testing. The electricity to run laboratory equipment changes in total with a change in the number of tests; therefore, it is variable.

3. B, V

Direct labor cost includes all labor that is physically traceable to the laboratory tests in an economically feasible manner. Therefore, the hourly wages of part-time technicians who perform tests is a direct labor cost. The wages will change in total with a change in the number of tests performed; therefore, it is variable.

4. C, V

Overhead cost for testing is the sum of all indirect costs of testing. The cost of lubricant used on laboratory equipment is an overhead cost for testing. The cost of lubricant used on laboratory equipment changes in total with a change in the number of tests; therefore, it is variable.

5. A, V

The water is physically traceable to the tests; therefore, it is a direct material cost. The water used in tests changes in total with a change in the number of tests; therefore, it is variable.

6. C, F

Overhead cost is the sum of all indirect costs. Therefore, depreciation is an overhead cost. The amount of depreciation will not be affected by the number of tests; therefore, it is fixed.

7. C, F

See the explanation to item #6.

8. A, V

Direct material cost includes all materials that are traceable to the tests in an economically feasible manner. Therefore, the cost of the expensive binders is a direct material cost. The cost of the binders will change in total with a change in the number of tests; therefore, it is variable.

_____

Response #2: Cost Calculations (5 points)

1. $40

Sales price per test	$ 60
Variable costs per test	(20)
Contribution margin per test	$ 40

2. 4,000

$$\text{Break-even point in units at low range of activity} = \frac{\text{Fixed costs for low range of activity}}{\text{Contribution margin per test}}$$

$$= \$160{,}000 \, / \, (\$60 - \$20)$$

$$= 4{,}000 \text{ tests}$$

The break-even point of <u>4,000</u> tests is within the low range of activity of 0 to 4,999 tests.

3. 5,000

$$\text{Break-even point in units at high range of activity} = \frac{\text{Fixed costs for high range of activity}}{\text{Contribution margin per test}}$$

$$= \$200{,}000 \, / \, (\$60 - \$20)$$

$$= 5{,}000 \text{ tests}$$

The break-even point of <u>5,000</u> tests is within the high range of activity of 5,000 to 14,999 tests.

4. 9,000

It first must be determined if Asta can achieve a gross profit of $160,000 at the low range of activity.

$$\text{Unit sales} = \frac{\text{Fixed costs at low range of activity + Desired profit}}{\text{Contribution margin per unit}}$$

$$= (\$160{,}000 + \$160{,}000) \, / \, (\$60 - \$20)$$

$$= 8{,}000 \text{ units}$$

Since 8,000 units exceeds the low range of 0 to 4,999 tests, Asta cannot achieve the desired gross profit at the low range of activity. Next, it must be determined if Asta can achieve the desired gross profit at the high range of activity. The required 9,000 unit sales is within the high range of activity of 5,000 to 14,999 tests.

$$\text{Unit sales} = \frac{\text{Fixed costs at high range of activity + Desired profit}}{\text{Contribution margin per unit}}$$

$$= (\$200{,}000 + \$160{,}000) \, / \, (\$60 - \$20)$$

$$= 9{,}000 \text{ units}$$

_____

Response #3: Cost Comparisons (3 points)

1. L

At the low range of activity, Asta has the same break-even point in number of tests performed as the industry average, despite having higher fixed costs than the industry average. Therefore, Asta's contribution margin per test must be greater than the industry average at the low range of activity. Since Asta has a lower sales price per test and a higher contribution margin per test than the industry average at the low range of activity, Asta's variable cost per test must be *lower* than the industry average at the low range of activity.

2. G

At the high range of activity, Asta has the same sales price per test and lower variable costs per test as compared to the industry average. Therefore, Asta's contribution margin per test is greater than the industry average at the high range of activity. Asta's fixed costs are the same as industry averages at the high range of activity; therefore, since Asta's contribution margin per test is greater than the industry average at the high range of activity, Asta's break-even point in units is lower than the industry average at the high range of activity.

3. L

At the high range of activity, Asta has the same sales price per test as the industry average and lower variable costs per test. Therefore, Asta's contribution margin per test is greater than the industry average at the high range. Asta's fixed costs are the same as industry averages at the high range of activity; therefore, since Asta's contribution margin per test is greater than the industry average at the high range of activity, Asta's break-even point in number of tests performed is lower than the industry average at the high range of activity.

Solution 52-4

Response #1: Direct Costing & Budgets (10 points)

1. $229,000

Beginning accounts payable	$ 40,000
9 payments ($3 × 7,000 units per week)	189,000
Total payments during the 10 weeks	$229,000

2. $95,000

As all units are produced and sold in the same period, direct and absorption costing produces the same income in this circumstance.

Sales per unit	$ 11
Variable costs per unit ($3 + $2 + $1)	6
Contribution margin per unit	5
Times: Units	70,000
Contribution margin	350,000
Fixed expenses ($210,000 + $45,000)	255,000
Budgeted income	$ 95,000

3. $95,000

Also see the explanation to #2.

Sales ($11 × 70)	$770
CGS: Variable ($5 × 70)	350
CGS: Fixed ($210 / 70 × 70)	210
Gross income	210
S&A [($1 × 70) + $45]	115
Budgeted income (in 1,000s)	$ 95

---

4. $20,000

$95,000 − $75,000 = $20,000
Also see the explanation to #3.

Sales ($11 × 60)	$660
CGS: Variable ($5 × 60)	300
CGS: Fixed ($210 / 70 × 60)	180
Gross income	180
S&A [($1 × 60) + $45]	105
Actual income (in 1,000s)	$ 75

5. $29,000

This question is answered by developing an income statement with the known values and "backing in" the unknown values. The fixed amounts will not change regardless of the amount of production or sales, if all production is sold. If the special order must generate net income of $5,000 (to keep total net income the same), then it must generate $9,000 of gross income and $29,000 of sales.

	Total	Regular	Special
Units	73	69	4
Sales (Regular $11/unit)	?	$759	?
CGS: Variable ($5/unit)	365	345	20
CGS: Fixed	210	210	-NA-
Gross income	?	204	?
S&A: Variable ($1/unit)	73	69	4
S&A: Fixed	45	45	-NA-
Actual income	$ 95	$ 90	$ 5

Alternatively, 1,000 units lost of regular sales results in $5,000 lost contribution margin. The revenue from the special order must replace this lost margin, as well as covering variable costs of $6/unit. 4,000 units × $6/unit + $5,000 = $29,000.

CHAPTER 53

COST ACCOUNTING

Some abbreviations used in this chapter:
EU	=	equivalent units	WIP	=	work-in-process
FIFO	=	first in, first out	WA	=	weighted average
AP	=	actual price per unit	AQ	=	actual quantity per unit
SP	=	standard price per unit	SQ	=	standard quantity per unit

EXAM COVERAGE: The *Planning and Measurement* portion of the BEC section of the CPA exam is designated by the examiners to be 22 to 28 percent of the section's point value. Candidates should plan their use of study time accordingly. Under the former ARE content specification outline, the topics in this chapter were less than a third of the managerial accounting point value. This might not hold true under the new CSO. More information about the point value of various topics is in the **Practical Advice** section of this volume.

CHAPTER 53

COST ACCOUNTING

I. Job Order Costing

A. Overview
Job order costing is the accumulation of costs by specific jobs (i.e., physical units, distinct batches, or job lots). This costing method is appropriate when direct costs can be identified with specific units, or groups of units, of production. Job order costing is widely used in industries such as construction, aircraft manufacturing, printing, auto repair, and professional services. (Service organizations frequently use job order costing.)

B. Procedures
Direct materials and direct labor are traced and applied to a particular job. Costs not directly traceable (i.e., manufacturing overhead) are applied to individual jobs using a predetermined overhead application rate.

Exhibit 1 ▶ Job Order Journal Entries

1.	To record the purchase of direct and indirect materials.		
	Stores Control	200	
	Accounts Payable/Cash		200
2.	To record the use of direct and indirect materials previously purchased.		
	WIP Control—Job "X" (direct materials)	75	
	WIP Control—Job "Y" (direct materials)	90	
	Factory Overhead Control (indirect materials)	20	
	Stores Control		185
3.	To record the cost of direct and indirect labor incurred.		
	WIP Control—Job "X" (direct labor)	350	
	WIP Control—Job "Y" (direct labor)	400	
	Factory Overhead Control (indirect labor)	80	
	Accrued Factory Payroll		830
4.	To record the cost of other factory overhead incurred.		
	Factory Overhead Control	270	
	Miscellaneous (utilities payable, accumulated depreciation, etc.)		270
5.	To record the application of factory overhead.		
	WIP Control—Job "X"	545	
	WIP Control—Job "Y"	330	
	Factory Overhead Applied		875
6.	To record the completion of goods (Job "Y" still in process).		
	Finished Goods Control—Job "X"	970	
	WIP Control—Job "X"		270

7.	To record the sale of finished goods.		
	Cash/Accounts Receivable	1,300	
	Sales		1,300
	Cost of Goods Sold	970	
	Finished Goods Control—Job "X"		970

1. **Rate** The overhead rate is a rate that is predetermined yearly using a base that is common to all units produced, such as direct labor hours, machine hours, or direct labor cost.

$$\text{Overhead application rate} = \frac{\textit{Estimated Factory Overhead}}{\textit{Estimated Direct Labor Hours}}$$

2. **Account** The *Factory Overhead Control* account is debited as actual factory overhead costs are incurred. The *Factory Overhead Applied* account is credited as factory overhead is applied to inventory costs at the predetermined rate.

3. **Closing** As a practical matter, the difference between overhead applied and actual overhead incurred often is closed to **cost of goods sold** (CGS) at the end of the period. Theoretically, the difference should be closed to WIP, finished goods, and CGS.

II. Process Costing

A. Overview

Process costing is a cost accumulation method that aggregates production costs by departments or by production phases. Unit cost is determined by dividing the total costs charged to a cost center by the output of that cost center. Process costing is appropriate for enterprises that produce a continuous mass of like units through a series of production steps called operations or processes. Process costing is generally used in the manufacturing of homogeneous products (such as chemicals, petroleum, textiles, paints, and food processing).

1. **Cost of Production Report** Summarizes the total cost charged to a department and the distribution of that total cost between the ending work-in-process inventory and the units completed and transferred to the next department or finished goods inventory.

2. **Equivalent Units** The expression of the physical units of output in terms of doses or units. For example, 600 units that are one-third complete and 400 units that are one-half complete are both 200 equivalent units. Equivalent units are frequently figured on separate inventory components (material, labor, etc.) as product may be complete with respect to material, but only partially complete in regard to conversion costs.

3. **Stage of Completion** The degree, point, or phase in the manufacturing process at which a product currently stands; used in determining the equivalent units of production in beginning and ending work-in-process (WIP) inventory.

4. **Transferred-In Cost** The material, labor, and overhead cost transferred-in from a prior department. By definition, transferred-in costs are always at the 100% stage of completion.

5. **Solutions Approach to Process Costing**

   a. Compute the physical flow of units. (Beginning WIP inventory + Units started = Units transferred out + Ending WIP inventory)

   b. Compute equivalent units of production separately for beginning WIP, materials, and conversion costs.

   c. Determine the total costs, classified by major categories.

d. Calculate the equivalent unit cost, depending on the cost flow assumption used.

e. Allocate total costs between ending work-in-process and finished (i.e., transferred out) goods.

6. **Using Standard Costs With Process Costing** The use of standard costs for inventory valuation simplifies process cost computations. Standard costing eliminates the need to compute the cost per equivalent unit (i.e., Step 4.) because the standard cost **is** the cost per equivalent unit. Standard costs eliminate the complications of WA or FIFO inventory methods, thus simplifying Step 5.

B. Cost Flow Assumptions

Only two flow assumptions are generally used—FIFO and weighted average. Under weighted average, the costs in the **beginning** inventory are averaged with the **current** period's costs to determine one average unit cost for all units passing through the department in a given period. Under FIFO, costs in the beginning inventory are **not** mingled with the current period costs, but are transferred out as a separate batch of goods at a different unit cost than units started and completed during the period.

Example 1 ▶ Cost of Production Report, FIFO

Beginning WIP inventory is 200 units (at 40% completion). Beginning WIP inventory material costs are $200. Beginning WIP inventory conversion costs are $400.

All material for a product is added at the beginning of the production process. Conversion takes place continuously throughout the process. During the period 500 units were started. Material costs for the period are $600. Conversion costs for the period are $5,527.50.

Ending WIP inventory is 100 units (at 30% completion).

Required: Prepare a cost of production report, using a FIFO cost flow assumption.

Solution:

1. *Step One:* Calculate the physical flow in units.

	Physical Flow		Physical Flow
Beginning WIP (40% complete)	200	Units completed	600
Units started	500	Ending WIP (30% complete)	100
Units to account for	700	Units accounted for	700

2. *Step Two:* Compute the equivalent units of production.

	Equivalent Units			
	Materials		Conversion cost	
Units completed	(600 × 100%)	600	(600 × 100%)	600
Ending WIP (30% complete)	(100 × 100%)	100	(100 × 30%)	30
WA EU	(200 × 100%)	700	(200 × 40%)	630
Beginning WIP (40% complete)		(200)		(80)
FIFO EU		500		550

Note: Material is added at the beginning of the process and thus is 100% complete. Conversion costs are incurred evenly throughout the process and thus are 40% and 30% complete.

3. *Step Three:* Determine total costs.

	Beginning WIP	Current costs	Total costs
Materials	$200.00	$ 600.00	$ 800.00
Conversion costs	400.00	5,527.50	5,927.50
Total costs to account for	$600.00	$6,127.50	$6,727.50

4. *Step Four:* Calculate equivalent unit cost.

	Current costs	FIFO EU Divisor	Equivalent unit cost
Materials	$ 600.00	500	$ 1.20
Conversion costs	5,527.50	550	10.05
Total current costs	$ 6,127.50		$11.25

5. *Step Five:* Allocate total costs between work-in-process and finished goods.

		Total Costs
Total costs (from Step 3)		$6,727.50
Ending WIP material costs (100 units × 100% × $1.20/unit)	$120.00	
Ending WIP conversion costs (100 units × 30% × $10.05/unit)	301.50	
Less: Ending WIP		421.50
Cost of finished goods		$6,306.00*

_____

* Proof:
FG = Beginning WIP cost + Cost to complete beginning WIP + Units started and completed
   = $600 + (200 × [1 − 0.4] × $10.05) + (400 × $11.25) = $6,306

6. *Step Six:* Cost of Production Report (complete solution)

	Physical Flow
Beginning WIP (40% complete)	200
Units started	500
Units to account for	700

		Equivalent Units	
		Materials	Conversion cost
Units completed	600	600	600
Ending WIP (30% complete)	100	100	30
Units accounted for	700		
Weighted average EU		700	630
Beginning WIP (40% complete at beginning of period)		(200)	(80)
FIFO EU		500	550

	Allocation of Costs to Product				
	Total costs	Beginning WIP	Current costs	EU Divisor	Current unit cost
Materials	$ 800.00	$200.00	$ 600.00	500	$ 1.20
Conversion costs	5,927.50	400.00	5,527.50	550	10.05
Total costs to account for	$6,727.50	$600.00	$6,127.50		$11.25
Total costs accounted for	$6,727.50				
Ending WIP	421.50				
Goods completed	$6,306.00				

Example 2 ▶ Cost of Production Report, Weighted Average

Required: Prepare a cost of production report under the same conditions as for the FIFO example, using a weighted average cost flow assumption.

Solution:

1. *Step One:* Calculate the physical flow in units. (This is the same as the FIFO example.)

2. *Step Two:* Compute the equivalent units of production. (Note the FIFO example similarities.)

	Equivalent Units			
	Materials		Conversion cost	
Units completed	(600 × 100%)	600	(600 × 100%)	600
Ending WIP (30% complete)	(100 × 100%)	100	(100 × 30%)	30
WA EU		700		630

3. *Step Three:* Determine total costs. (This is the same as the FIFO example.)

4. *Step Four:* Calculate equivalent unit costs.

	Total costs	WA EU Divisor	Equivalent unit cost
Materials	$ 800.00	700	$ 1.14
Conversion costs	5,927.50	630	9.41
Total costs, current period	$6,727.50		$10.55

5. *Step Five:* Allocate total costs between work-in-process and finished goods.

Total costs		$6,727.50
Ending WIP material costs (100 units × 100% × $1.14/unit)	$114.00	
Ending WIP conversion costs (100 units × 30% × $9.41/unit)	282.30	
Less: Ending WIP		396.30
Cost of finished goods		$6,331.20

6. *Step Six:* Cost of Production Report (The physical flow is the same as for FIFO.)

	Physical Units	Equivalent Units	
		Materials	Conversion cost
Units completed	600	600	600
Ending WIP (30% complete)	100	100	30
Units accounted for	700	700	630

	Allocation of Costs to Product				
	Current costs	Beginning WIP	Total costs	EU Divisor	Current unit cost
Materials	$ 600.00	$200.00	$ 800.00	700	$ 1.14
Conversion costs	5,527.50	400.00	5,927.50	630	9.41
Total costs to account for	$6,127.50	$600.00	$6,727.50		$10.55
Goods completed			$6,331.20		
Ending WIP			396.30		
Total costs accounted for			$6,727.50		

III. Spoilage

A. Overview

Spoilage is production that does not result in good finished units.

Exhibit 2 ▶ Spoilage Journal Entry

Finished Goods Control	XX	
WIP Control		XX
To transfer good units completed from WIP to finished goods.		

Loss From Abnormal Spoilage	XX	
WIP Control		XX
To recognize abnormal spoilage.		

1. **Normal Spoilage** Normal spoilage is inherent in the manufacturing process and is uncontrollable in the short run. Management establishes a normal spoilage rate, which is the rate of spoilage that is acceptable under a given combination of production factors. Normal spoilage is a cost of goods produced and, thus, is inventoried as a product cost.

2. **Abnormal Spoilage** Abnormal spoilage is spoilage beyond the normal spoilage rate. It is considered controllable because it is a result of inefficiency. Abnormal spoilage is not a cost of good production, but rather is a **loss** for the period.

3. **Spoiled Goods** Units that do not meet quality or dimensional standards and are junked or sold for salvage (disposal) value.

4. **Defective Units** Units that do not meet quality or dimensional standards and are sold at a reduced price or reworked and sold at the regular or a reduced price.

5. **Scrap** Material residue of the manufacturing process that has measurable but minor recovery value. Scrap may be sold or reused. Examples: Wood or metal shavings in woodworking operations and foundries, bolt-ends of fabric in clothing manufacturing. Generally, the sales value of scrap is regarded as a decrease to factory overhead control. In some job-order situations, the sales value of scrap is credited to the particular job that yielded the scrap.

6. **Waste** Material that is lost in the manufacturing process by evaporation, shrinkage, etc., or material residue that has no measurable recovery value. Disposal of waste may entail additional cost, as in the cost of antipollution devices to clean gaseous wastes. The cost of waste from shrinkage, evaporation, etc., usually is not traced and is not recognized in the accounts. In a standard cost system, an allowance for waste may be included in the determination of standard product cost. Shrinkage in excess of standard is thus revealed as a material usage or quantity variance.

7. **Rework** The cost of reworking defective units is generally charged to manufacturing overhead. The predetermined overhead rate should include a provision for costs of rework.

8. **Innovation** Many enterprises are taking more notice of spoilage and by-products than they once did. Products that were once considered waste or scrap may now be used in producing by-products such as fertilizers, fuel, packaging, or other profitable items. Enterprises are finding innovative ways to use by-products and, in the process, upgrading products formerly classified as waste or by-products to joint products.

Example 3 ▶ Production Innovation

A manufacturer of adult clothing will have some left-over cloth as pieces of clothing are cut from a bolt of cloth. If this cloth is discarded or sold to a recycling facility, it is waste or scrap. Alternatively, pieces of clothing could be cut so that there are relatively large pieces of left-over cloth. These remnants in turn are used to create a line of children's clothing. This results in some of the waste being reclassified as a by-product or joint product.

B. Process Cost System
Both normal spoilage and abnormal spoilage are incorporated into process costing procedure. Additionally, a normal spoilage rate is included in the predetermined overhead application rate.

1. In computing the physical flow in units, the count of spoiled units must take into consideration the stage of production at which the spoilage occurred. Generally, spoilage is deemed to occur at the time of inspection; therefore, the cost of spoiled units generally is allocated to the

manufacturing process from this point forward. If spoiled units are discovered at the end of the process, the entire cost of spoilage should be charged to the completed units.

2. Abnormal spoilage is included in the equivalent unit calculation to the extent of the completion stage where abnormal spoilage occurs.

Example 4 ▶ FIFO, Normal Spoilage

Beginning WIP inventory = 0
Units started = 1,200
Good units completed = 800
Ending WIP inventory = 300 units (1/2 complete)
Material costs are $2,640, added at beginning of process.
Conversion costs are $997.50.
All spoilage is normal spoilage.
Inspection takes place at the end of the process.

Required: *Complete a cost of production report to determine the cost of finished goods and ending WIP.*

Solution:

1. Step One: Calculate the physical flow in units.

	Physical flow
Beginning WIP	0
Units started	1,200
Units to account for	1,200
Normal spoilage	100
Good units completed	800
Ending WIP	300
Units accounted for	1,200

2. Step Two: Compute equivalent units of production.

	Equivalent Units	
	Materials	Conversion
Normal spoilage (100% complete)	100*	100*
Good units completed	800	800
Ending WIP (1/2 complete)	300	150
WA EU	1,200	1,050
Less beginning WIP × % complete	0	0
FIFO EU	1,200	1,050

3. Step Three: Determine the total costs.

	Current costs	Total costs
Materials	$2,640.00	$2,640.00
Conversion costs	997.50	997.50
	$3,637.50	$3,637.50

   * Since spoilage is discovered at the end of the process, it is assumed that all spoiled units are completed units.

4. Step Four: Calculate the equivalent unit costs.

	Current costs	FIFO EU divisor	Current unit cost
Materials	$2,640.00	1,200	$2.20
Conversion costs	997.50	1,050	0.95
	$3,637.50		$3.15

5. **Step Five:** Allocate total costs between ending work-in-process and finished goods.

Goods completed:

Cost before normal spoilage (800 × $2.20) + (800 × $0.95)	$2,520.00
Normal spoilage (100 × $2.20) + (100 × $0.95)	315.00
Total cost of finished goods	2,835.00
Ending WIP (300 × $2.20) + (150 × $0.95)	802.50
Total costs accounted for	$3,637.50

6. Cost of Production Report (complete solution)

Output in Equivalent Units		Equivalent Units	
	Physical flow	Materials	Conversion costs
Beginning WIP	0		
Units started	1,200		
Units to account for	1,200		
Normal spoilage	100	100	100
Good units completed	800	800	800
Ending WIP	300	300	150
Units accounted for	1,200		
Equivalent units		1,200	1,050

Allocation of Costs to Product	Current costs	Total costs	EU divisor	Current unit cost
Materials	$2,640.00	$2,640.00	1,200	$2.20
Conversion costs	997.50	997.50	1,050	0.95
	$3,637.50	$3,637.50		$3.15

Goods completed:	
Costs before normal spoilage	$2,520.00
Normal spoilage	315.00
Total cost of finished goods	2,835.00
Ending WIP	802.50
Total costs accounted for	$3,637.50

Example 5 ▶ FIFO, Abnormal Spoilage

Beginning WIP inventory = 0
Units started = 1,200
Good units completed = 800
Ending WIP inventory = 300 units (1/2 complete)
Material costs are $2,640, added at beginning of process.
Conversion costs are $997.50.
Inspection takes place at the end of the process.
Normal spoilage for a production run of this size is 40 spoiled units.

Required: Determine the cost of finished goods, ending inventory, and abnormal spoilage for the period.

Solution:

Steps 1 through 4 (not illustrated) are similar to the corresponding steps in Example 3, above, except that the 100 spoiled units must be segregated into normal spoilage (40 EU) and abnormal spoilage (60 EU). Step 5 is reproduced below.

Step 5: Allocate total costs between finished goods, work-in-process, and abnormal spoilage loss.

Goods completed:	
Cost before normal spoilage (800 × $2.20) + (800 × $0.95)	$2,520.00
Normal spoilage (40 × $2.20) + (40 × $0.95)	126.00
Total cost of finished goods	2,646.00
Ending WIP (300 × $2.20) + (150 × $0.95)	802.50
Abnormal spoilage loss (60 × $2.20) + (60 × $0.95)	189.00
Total costs accounted for	$3,637.50

C. Job Order Cost System

1. **Abnormal Spoilage** Abnormal spoilage is recognized as a loss when discovered. WIP is credited for the total amount of spoilage, an asset account is debited for the disposal value, and a loss on abnormal spoilage account is debited for the difference.

2. **Normal Spoilage Alternatives** The predetermined overhead application rate may or may not include a provision for normal spoilage.

   a. **Included** When spoilage occurs, WIP is credited for the total amount of spoilage, an asset account is debited for the disposal value, and manufacturing overhead is debited for the difference.

   b. **Not Included** This method is used when spoilage is viewed as directly attributable to the nature of particular jobs. When spoilage occurs, WIP (of a specific job) is credited and an asset account is debited for the disposal value of the spoiled units. Thus, the remaining good units in the specific job bear the cost of net normal spoilage.

IV. Cost Allocation

A. Joint Product & By-Product Definitions
Deciding if a product is a joint-product or a by-product is sometimes a matter of judgment. (CPA exam questions usually give a clear indication of the nature of the product.)

1. **By-Products** By-products are products that (1) have minor sales value as compared with the sales value of the main products and (2) are not identifiable as separate products until their split-off point.

2. **Joint Product Costs** Exist where two or more products are produced from processing the same raw material by a single process. Moreover, the various products are not separately identifiable until a certain stage of production known as the **split-off point.** The cost of the input factors incurred prior to split-off must be allocated to the joint products.

3. **Net Realizable Value** Sales value less estimated cost to complete and sell.

4. **Separable Cost** Additional processing cost after the split-off point.

5. **Split-Off Point** Represents the stage of production where the various products become identifiable as separate individual products. These products can be further processed or sold at the split-off point.

B. Joint Costs

1. **Need for Allocation** By definition, none of the individual products can be produced without its joint products and the related costs.

   a. **Reporting** Allocation of joint costs, however arbitrary, becomes necessary if inventories are carried forward from period to period. In other words, cost allocation is essential for inventory valuation and determining cost of goods sold.

b. **Decisions** Joint product cost allocation should **not** be used in deciding whether to further process or sell the products at the split-off point. Joint costs are **irrelevant** for decision-making purposes.

2. **Relative Market (Sales) Value Method** This method allocates joint costs to products based on their relative sales value at the split-off point. It is considered to be the best allocation method because it allocates the joint cost in proportion to the products' ability to absorb these costs.

3. **Net Realizable Value** Frequently, joint products have no sales value at the split-off point (i.e., separable costs must be incurred before the products become salable). Joint costs are then allocated on the basis of each product's net realizable value. Net realizable value is defined as the difference between sales value and estimated costs to complete and sell. Varying degrees of additional processing often result in increasingly higher sales value. For the purpose of allocating joint costs, net realizable value should be computed on the basis of the **first** sales value obtained as a result of additional processing.

Example 6 ▸ Joint Products

The ABC Company produces two products, Y and Z, from the same raw material. Joint product costs are $900. The process yields 200 units of Y and 400 units of Z. Products Y and Z have no sales value at split-off. Additional processing yields the following results:

Product	Separable Costs	Sales Value
Y	$100	$1,300
Z	200	2,000

Required: Allocate joint costs on the basis of net realizable value (NRV).

Solution:

Product	Sales value	Separable cost	NRV	Ratio	Allocated joint costs	Total Cost
Y	$1,300	$100	$1,200	12/30	$360	$ 460
Z	2,000	200	1,800	18/30	540	740
	$3,300	$300	$3,000		$900	$1,200

4. **Physical Measures Method** The relative sales value method of allocating joint product costs is preferable to an allocation based on physical measures. Under the physical measures method, the percentage weight—for instance—of each kind of product produced would determine the proportion of the joint cost applied to that product. The major disadvantage of the physical measures method is that the allocation of product costs may have no relationship to revenues. For instance, consider a meat-packing company that slaughters cattle. If joint costs were assigned on the basis of weight, steak would be valued at the same unit cost as hamburger, tongue, or tail. Because of this arbitrary allocation of joint costs, some joint products would enjoy hefty profits, while others would experience considerable losses. This is because the allocation base of the joint costs has no relationship to the ability of each joint product to produce revenue.

C. **By-Product Costs**
Deciding if a product is a joint-product or a by-product is sometimes a matter of judgment. If the CPA examiners ask candidates to classify a production element, it generally will not have borderline characteristics. The main product typically is produced in greater quantities than the by-product. Generally, the relative sales value of the by-product(s) should be used to reduce the cost of the main product(s).

1. The net revenue from by-product(s) sold reduces the cost of the main product(s) **sold;** or

2. The net realizable value of by-product(s) produced is deducted from the cost of the main product(s) **produced.** This approach is conceptually superior because it allocates the benefits derived from the by-product(s) between cost of goods sold and ending inventory.

D. SERVICE DEPARTMENT COSTS

1. **Allocation** All manufacturing costs, whether originating in production **or** service departments, must be assigned to the goods produced for proper inventory valuation and cost of goods sold determination. Costs allocated to service departments, as well as costs directly traceable to these departments, must be allocated to production departments. This is necessary for product costing and financial reporting. Ideally, costs incurred by service departments should be allocated on the basis of a **cause and effect** relationship. However, such direct relationships often are not present. This calls for allocation of costs on some other basis, as illustrated by Exhibit 3.

Exhibit 3 ▶ Sample Cost Allocation Bases

Service Department	Bases of Allocation to Other Departments
Factory cafeteria	Number of employees
Factory maintenance	Square footage
Factory storeroom	Material requisitions
General factory administration	Direct labor hours
Power department	Kilowatt hours used

2. **Direct Method** The direct method allocates the costs of each service department directly to producing departments. No consideration is given to services performed by one service department for another service department.

3. **Step Method** The step method involves allocation of service department costs to both service and production departments.

   a. Costs of the most widely used service department (or the department with the greatest total cost) are first allocated to all other departments. The costs of the next most widely used service department are then allocated. These costs will include those previously allocated from the first department. These "steps" continue until all service costs are allocated.

   b. Once a department's costs have been allocated, no further allocations are made to it from other departments. (**Reciprocal** services among departments are **not** considered.)

Example 7 ▶ Service Cost Allocation

	Production Departments		Service Departments	
	A	B	General plant	Maintenance
Overhead—Production depts.	$40,000	$50,000		
Total costs—Service depts.			$20,000	$10,000
Square footage occupied	50,000	30,000	5,000	4,000
Direct labor hours	60,000	40,000	15,000	20,000

Allocation bases: General plant services are allocated on the basis of direct labor hours. Maintenance services are allocated on the basis of square footage occupied.

Required:

A. Allocate each service department's cost to the production departments using the (1) direct and (2) step methods.

B. Compute the overhead rate based on direct labor hours for the production departments using the (1) direct and (2) step methods.

Solution A: Schedules of Cost Allocation

(1) Direct Method	Dept. A	Dept. B	General plant	Maintenance
Total cost			$ 20,000	$ 10,000
Initial production overhead	$40,000	$50,000		
Reallocation:				
General plant:			(20,000)	
(60,000 / 100,000*) × $20,000	12,000			
(40,000 / 100,000) × $20,000		8,000		
Maintenance:				(10,000)
(50,000 / 80,000*) × $10,000	6,250			
(30,000 / 80,000) × $10,000		3,750		
Final production overhead	$58,250	$61,750	$ 0	$ 0

(2) Step Method	Dept. A	Dept. B	General plant	Maintenance
Total cost			$ 20,000	$ 10,000
Initial production overhead	$40,000	$50,000		
Reallocation:				
General plant:			(20,000)	
(60,000 / 120,000*) × $20,000	10,000			
(40,000 / 120,000) × $20,000		6,667		
(20,000 / 120,000) × $20,000				3,333
Maintenance:				(13,333)
(50,000 / 80,000*) × $13,333	8,333			
(30,000 / 80,000) × $13,333		5,000		
Final production overhead	$58,333	$61,667	$ 0	$ 0

Solution B: Overhead Rates

	Dept. A		Dept. B	
(1) Direct Method	($58,250 / 60,000) =	$0.9708	($61,750 / 40,000) =	$1.5438
(2) Step Method	($58,333 / 60,000) =	$0.9722	($61,667 / 40,000) =	$1.5417

* The denominator must equal the sum of the allocation bases used in order for the service departments' total costs to be allocated.

V. Activity-Based Costing

A. Overview

Activity-based costing (ABC) in many cases is an improvement over traditional methods of allocating overhead to product costs on a volume-related basis. In the past, when production was more labor intensive, nonvolume-related costs were a much smaller portion of total product costs compared to the high technology environments in which companies operate today, thus volume plays a smaller role in driving overhead costs. ABC follows the idea that products consume activities. ABC's purpose is to assign costs to activities performed in an organization and then assign them to products according to each product's use of the activities.

1.   **Activities** Procedures or processes that cause work. Materiality and the cost/benefit of relevant information determines the need for dividing the organization into smaller and smaller pieces. In a large company, an example of an activity as it relates to accounts payable might be matching invoices, purchase orders, and receiving reports. Another activity could be batching vouchers for data entry. For a small company, an activity could incorporate the whole accounts payable function.

   •   Activities may be identified as batch-level activities and product-level activities. A batch-level activity would be the manufacture of breaker panels for which customers have specified the number and size of holes to be cut in ordered boards. The setup activity for this order benefits the entire batch, as opposed to performing the activity for each product unit.

2. **Cost Drivers** May be thought of as the root cause of a cost or the factor used to measure how a cost is incurred and how best to charge the cost to activities or products. Cost drivers are used to reflect the consumption of costs by activities and products. An example for an accounts payable department may be the number of invoices processed.

3. **Occupancy Group** The occupancy group is the most appropriate cost driver for distributing fixed costs based on the physical location of activities or assets. An example would be the distribution of property taxes, building depreciation, and security guard service charges based upon square footage occupied by each activity.

4. **Cost Centers** The lowest level of detail for which costs are accumulated and distributed, and can consist of a single activity or group of activities.

5. **Product Diversity** Occurs when products consume activities and inputs in different proportions. Thus, there is a difference in the size, complexity, material components, and other characteristics and demands made on a firm's resources by product lines.

6. **Volume Diversity** Occurs when there is a difference in the number of units manufactured by product lines.

7. **Material Diversity** Occurs when products having materials that take longer to process consume a disproportionate share of the unit-level inputs.

B. **Application**
Activity-based costing is appropriate for selling, administrative, and general business functions as well as manufacturing and revenue-producing service processes. ABC assigns costs of activities to products using both volume- and nonvolume-based cost drivers. Thus, if some product-related activity is unrelated to the number of units manufactured, using only volume-based allocations would distort the product's cost. As an example, for determining overhead allocation, cost accountants should instead apply the factors that cause activities to occur. This establishes the requirements placed on an activity by a product. Once costs are assigned to activities performed in an organization, the costs can be allocated to products (or services) based on each product's use of the activities. General steps in establishing an ABC system are:

1. Identify relevant activities.

2. Organize activities by cost centers.

3. Identify major elements of indirect costs.

4. Identify cost drivers, assign costs to activities, assign activities to products.

5. Establish a cost flow chart.

6. Establish appropriate cost conversion tools.

7. Gather data information for the ABC system.

8. Establish the cost flow model to develop costing rates.

Exhibit 4 ▶ Activity-Based Costing

This exhibit illustrates how an inappropriate cost system can lead an organization to make pricing decisions that reward the company with contracts for which the company has actually underpriced itself, and at the same time, making itself noncompetitive by overpricing bids that could have created a profit at a lower price.

A homeowner obtained quotes from two remodeling companies for renovations on her home. The two remodeling companies are identical except for their method of costing and pricing their services. The Overhaul Remodeling Company uses the standard industry practice of charging 50 percent of the material's sales price for its installation, whereas the ABC Remodeling Company uses the activity-based costing method for determining costs incurred and the prices to charge for various installation activities. Both companies submitted bids of $2,430 for the following materials and services:

- Provide and install two 3' × 9' French doors
- Provide and install one 48" × 72" bay window
- Provide and install three rolls Grade A wallpaper
- Paint and trim out new window and door

Material Portion of Bid:		Overhaul	ABC
2-3' × 9' French doors	@$400/ea.	$ 800	$ 800
1-48" × 72" bay window	@$300	300	300
3-Rolls of wallpaper	@$40/ea.	120	120
Paint and trim	@$20/ft.	400	400
Total Material Bid		$1,620	$1,620

Installation/Application Portion of Bid:	Overhaul (@50%)	ABC	ABC charge per unit
Installation of French doors	$400	$500	(@$100/hr.)
Installation of bay window	150	200	(@$100/hr.)
Application of wallpaper	60	30	(@$10/roll)
Application of paint & trim	200	80	(@$4/ft.)
Total Installation Bid	$810	$810	

The actual costs of providing the materials and services, using activity-based costing, are as follows:

	Materials		Installation/Application		Total
2-3' × 9' French doors	@$380/ea.	$ 760	@$90/hr.	$450	$1,210
1-48" × 72" bay window	@$275	275	@$90/hr.	180	455
3-Rolls wallpaper	@$20/ea.	60	@$5/roll	15	75
Paint and trim	@$10/ft.	200	@$3/ft.	60	200
Total Actual Cost		$1,295		$705	$2,000

The Overhaul Company actually is losing money by pricing the installation of the French doors and bay windows using the old method. This is because the installation of these items is labor intensive (since more employees are required for these procedures) and also because special tools are needed, adding the cost of maintenance, depreciation, and so forth, that are all part of the cost of using this equipment. Overhaul is making up for the loss in performing the finishing work. If the homeowner contracts with Overhaul to install the French doors and bay windows and with the ABC Company for the finishing work, the Overhaul Company would lose money due to an inappropriate bid.

VI. Standard Cost Accounting

A. Purpose

Comparison of standard (or estimated) to actual costs aids management in identifying problems and is a basis for judging performance. Standard costing is used to value inventory, plan and control costs, measure performance, prepare budgets, and motivate employees. Standard costing can be used in a wide variety of organizations; it is not limited to manufacturing activities. Standard costing can be used with process or job-order costing.

1. **Variances** Variances are the differences between standard and actual costs. A variance is favorable if actual costs are less than standard costs, and unfavorable if actual costs exceed

standard costs. Analysis of variances reveals the causes of deviations between actual and standard costs. This feedback aids in setting goals, estimating future costs, and evaluating performance.

2. **Management by Exception** Reports of activities and performance show actual and budgeted amounts, and variances. Attention is focused on deviations from the budget, rather than on those parts of the operation that adhere to the budget.

B. Development of Standard Costs

Standard costs are predetermined, or target, unit costs that should be attained under efficient conditions. A standard cost system records activities at both standard and actual costs. Physical standards are determined by analyses of the kinds and amounts of material, labor, and factory overhead needed to produce one unit. The entire production cycle is divided into various operations, and inputs are estimated for each operation. Physical standards are multiplied by appropriate price factors to determine standard costs. Standards can be set at different levels, depending on management's objectives.

1. **Basic Cost Standards** Standards that are unchanged year after year. Useful in tracing trends in price effects and efficiency, except when products change frequently.

2. **Perfection (Ideal) Cost Standards** Absolute minimum costs attainable under perfect operating conditions (i.e., "factory heaven"). No allowance is made for factors beyond management's control. They may depress employee morale since they frequently result in unfavorable variances.

3. **Currently Attainable Cost Standards** Standards that can be attained under efficient operating conditions. Widely used because they serve a variety of purposes. Useful for employee motivation, product costing, and budgeting.

C. Overhead Costs

Variances in overhead costs represent differences between budgeted (predetermined) and actual overhead.

1. **Variable Overhead** Application of **variable** overhead requires that the **incremental** overhead costs of production be determined. A standard variable overhead rate is obtained and applied to production on the basis of some common denominator, such as direct labor cost, direct labor hours, or machine hours. Note that, by definition, the total amount of **variable** overhead incurred and applied varies **directly** with the level of production.

2. **Fixed Overhead** Since the total amount of **fixed** overhead remains **constant** over the relevant range of activity, the amount of fixed overhead per unit varies **inversely** with the level of production. Therefore, in order to obtain a standard fixed overhead rate it is necessary to select a predetermined (budgeted) level of activity. This activity should be measured on the basis of standard inputs allowed, such as direct labor cost, direct labor hours, or machine hours. If the fixed overhead rate was determined on the basis of actual outputs (i.e., finished units), it would be influenced by how **efficiently** those units were produced.

Exhibit 5 ▶ Fixed OH Standard Rate Formula

$$\text{Fixed overhead standard rate} = \frac{\text{Budgeted fixed manufacturing overhead}}{\text{Predetermined level of activity (measured in standard inputs)}}$$

D. Isolating Variances

Accounting depends upon when variances are isolated in the flow of elements through the accounts. A common method is to isolate material price variances at the time of purchase and to isolate all other variances in the work-in-process account. (This method makes the formulas for variances, discussed later, relatively easy to remember.)

1. Accumulate direct materials at actual quantity times standard prices. The difference between actual and standard price is charged or credited to the direct material price variance account.

2. Accumulate actual cost of direct labor and manufacturing overhead.

3. Transfer direct material, direct labor, and overhead to the work-in-process account at standard quantity times standard price. The differences between actual and standard direct material and labor prices are isolated in material quantity, labor rate, and labor efficiency variances. Thus, work-in-process includes no inefficiencies.

4. The cost of completed units is transferred to finished goods at standard quantities times standard prices. No variances are recognized at this time.

E. Disposition of Variances

At the end of the period, the variances must be **disposed** of to arrive at the proper net income. The commonly used alternatives for disposing of these variances are

Example 8 ▶ Variance Disposition

Midge Company has under-applied overhead of $55,000 for the calendar year. Before disposition of the under-applied overhead, selected year-end balances from Midge's accounting records are as follows:

Sales	$1,200,000
Cost of goods sold	900,000
Inventories:	
Direct materials	150,000
Work-in-process	200,000
Finished goods	100,000

Under Midge's cost accounting system, over or under-applied overhead is allocated to appropriate inventories and cost of goods sold based on year-end balances.

Required: Determine the amounts that Midge should report for costs of goods sold and the year-end inventories.

Solution: The under (or over) applied overhead is prorated to the balances of work-in-process, finished goods, and cost of goods sold. The under (or over) applied overhead should not be applied to the raw materials inventory.

	Dec. 31 unadjusted balance	%	% × under-applied overhead	Dec. 31 adjusted balance
Cost of goods sold	$ 900,000	75	$41,250	$ 941,250
Finished goods	100,000	8 1/3	4,583	104,583
Work-in-process	200,000	16 2/3	9,167	209,167
	$1,200,000	100	$55,000	$1,255,000

1. **Expense or Income Item** Close out the variance to the income summary account and present the net variance as an income or expense item in the income statement.

2. **Cost of Goods Sold** Close out the variance to cost of goods sold and present the net variance as an adjustment to cost of goods sold in the income statement.

3. **All Inventories** Close out the variances by allocating them between inventories and cost of goods sold. This is the most conceptually sound and most commonly used approach.

    a. Inventories may be carried at standard costs for external reporting purposes only if the standards are frequently adjusted so as to approximate the costs that would be inventories under one of the cost flow assumptions recognized by GAAP.

b. Each specific variance is allocated in proportion to the related standard cost included in each account. For example, the material price variance would be allocated based on the ratio of total material price variance to the total material cost included in the raw materials, work-in-process, and finished goods inventories and cost of goods sold. All other variances should be allocated to work-in-process and finished goods inventories, and cost of goods sold.

F. Variances in Prime Costs
Efficiency variances are generally more controllable by management than price variances, and are thus of more interest to most enterprises.

1. Price Variances Price variances are differences between **actual unit prices** and **standard unit prices,** multiplied by **actual inputs.** A positive result (i.e., a positive V_p) indicates an **increase** in costs (i.e., an unfavorable variance), while a negative V_p indicates a cost **reduction** (i.e., a favorable variance). Price variances reflect changes between the expected price and actual price of direct materials and labor.

Exhibit 6 ▶ Prime Cost Price Variance Formula

$$V_p = (AP - SP) \times AQ$$

Example 9 ▶ Material Price Variance

Bell Company recognizes any material price variance when materials are purchased. The following information pertains to the production of one unit of Bell's product during the month of June:

Standard quantity of materials	5 lbs.
Standard cost per lb.	$0.40
Materials purchased	100,000 lbs.
Actual cost of materials purchased per lb.	$0.34
Materials consumed for manufacture of 10,000 units	60,000 lbs.

Required: Determine Bell's materials price variance for June.

Solution: $6,000 favorable variance.

Discussion: The materials price variance is computed by multiplying the difference between the actual price (AP) and the standard price (SP) by the actual quantity (AQ) of material purchased, i.e., (AP − SP) × AQ. Thus, the materials price variance is equal to ($0.34 − $0.40) × 100,000, or $6,000. Because the actual cost is less than the standard cost, it is a <u>favorable</u> variance.

a. Unfavorable direct **material** price variances may be related to unwise purchasing decisions. However, price variances are often caused by price fluctuations that cannot be controlled by management. Therefore, in many enterprises, the price variance is isolated solely to separate it from efficiency variances.

b. Material price variances may be isolated at the time of purchase to remove the influence of price changes from efficiency reports, or to control purchasing activities.

c. Unfavorable **labor** price variances may be the result of unavoidable increases in labor rates or the use of overqualified persons for a job, resulting in payment of higher rates than standard.

2. Efficiency Variances Efficiency variances are differences between the quantity of inputs (materials or labor) that should have been used and inputs that were actually used, based on the **standard unit price.**

Exhibit 7 ▶ Prime Cost Efficiency Variance Formula

$$V_e = (AQ - SQ) \times SP$$

    a.   Unfavorable material efficiency variances indicate excessive usage of materials.

    b.   Unfavorable labor efficiency variances indicate that inefficient labor methods resulted in more hours worked than would be budgeted for the level of production achieved.

   3.   **Distinguishing the Variance Formulas of Prime Costs** Remembering these two formulas is easy, if one assumes isolation of the material price variances at the time of purchase (a common practice). At the time of purchase, the standard quantity is not known, so it cannot be used in the price variance formula. Then keep in mind that the efficiency variance formula must account for all of the remaining variance from standard cost.

G.   **Variances in Variable Overhead Costs**

   1.   **Efficiency Variance** The variable overhead efficiency variance reflects the differences in actual and budgeted variable overhead costs that are incurred because of the inefficient use of resources such as direct labor or machine hours.

Exhibit 8 ▶ Variable OH Cost Efficiency Variance Formula

$$VOHV_e = (AQ - SQ) \times SP$$

   2.   **Spending Variance** The variable overhead spending variance reflects the differences in actual and budgeted variable costs that result from price changes in indirect materials and labor, poor budget estimates, and insufficient control of costs of specific overhead items.

Exhibit 9 ▶ Variable OH Cost Spending Variance Formula

$$VOHV_s = (AP - SP) \times AQ$$

H.   **Variances in Fixed Overhead Costs**

   1.   **Total Fixed Overhead Variance (FOHV)** Total FOHV (i.e., **under-** or **overapplied** overhead) is the difference between **actual** fixed overhead incurred and FOH applied to production (generally on the basis of standard direct labor hours, machine hours, etc., allowed for good production output). Total FOHV combines the FOH **volume** variance and the FOH **budget** (spending) variance.

Exhibit 10 ▶ Fixed OH Cost Total Variance Formula

Total *FOHV*	=	*FOH* **incurred** − *FOH* **applied**	
	=	*FOH incurred* −	$\left[\begin{array}{l} FOH\ standard \\ rate \end{array} \times \begin{array}{l} Standard\ inputs\ allowed \\ (DLH,\ mach.\ hours,\ etc.) \end{array}\right]$

   2.   **Volume Variance** Fixed overhead volume (denominator) variance results when the actual activity level (direct labor, machine hours, etc.) differs from the budgeted quantity used in determining the fixed overhead application rate. In developing a predetermined fixed overhead rate, the denominator represents the expected activity level. The denominator variance arises when the activity level for a period does not coincide with the predetermined activity level. A volume variance is a measure of the cost of failure to operate at the budgeted activity level, and may be caused by failure to meet sales goals or idleness due to poor scheduling, machine breakdowns, etc.

Exhibit 11 ▶ Fixed OH Cost Volume Variance Formula

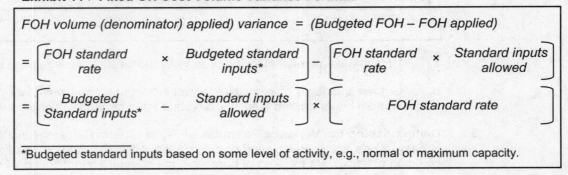

FOH volume (denominator) applied) variance = (Budgeted FOH − FOH applied)

$$= \left[\begin{array}{c} \text{FOH standard} \\ \text{rate} \end{array} \times \begin{array}{c} \text{Budgeted standard} \\ \text{inputs*} \end{array} \right] - \left[\begin{array}{c} \text{FOH standard} \\ \text{rate} \end{array} \times \begin{array}{c} \text{Standard inputs} \\ \text{allowed} \end{array} \right]$$

$$= \left[\begin{array}{c} \text{Budgeted} \\ \text{Standard inputs*} \end{array} - \begin{array}{c} \text{Standard inputs} \\ \text{allowed} \end{array} \right] \times \left[\quad \text{FOH standard rate} \quad \right]$$

*Budgeted standard inputs based on some level of activity, e.g., normal or maximum capacity.

3. **Budget (Spending) Variance** Fixed overhead budget (spending) variance is the difference between actual fixed overhead incurred and fixed overhead budgeted. *This difference is not affected by the level of production.* Fixed overhead, by definition, does not change in total with the level of activity within the relevant range. The budget variance is caused solely by events such as unexpected changes in prices, unforeseen repairs, etc.

Exhibit 12 ▶ Fixed OH Cost Budget Variance Formula

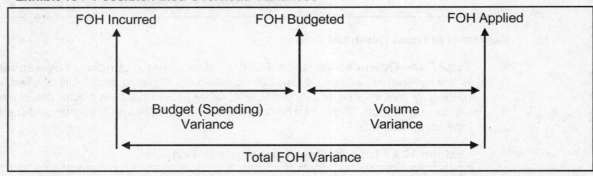

FOH budget variance = Actual FOH − Budgeted FOH

$$= \text{Actual FOH} - \left[\begin{array}{c} \text{FOH} \\ \text{Standard rate} \end{array} \times \begin{array}{c} \text{Budgeted production} \\ \text{(DL, machine hours, etc.} \end{array} \right]$$

4. **Efficiency Variance** There are no FOH efficiency variances because fixed overhead does not change regardless of whether productive resources are used **efficiently** or not (e.g., real estate taxes are not affected by whether production is being carried on efficiently or not).

Exhibit 13 ▶ Possible Fixed Overhead Variances

```
     FOH Incurred              FOH Budgeted                FOH Applied
          ↑                         ↑                          ↑
          |                         |                          |
          |←——— Budget (Spending) ——→|←———— Volume ————————————→|
          |        Variance          |        Variance          |
          |                                                     |
          |←——————————————— Total FOH Variance ————————————————→|
```

I. Variance Analysis

Variances between standard and actual costs may be analyzed to discover price or efficiency differences in prime costs (labor and direct material), spending or efficiency differences in variable overhead costs, and budget or volume differences in fixed overhead costs. Variance analysis is subject to the same cost-benefit tests as other phases of an information system.

1. **Purpose** Variances that are material in amount may indicate that further investigation is warranted to pinpoint their exact cause. For example, a material efficiency variance may be caused by faulty workmanship or an improper mix of materials. Consistently high variances (favorable **or** unfavorable) may be indicative of faulty standards. Standards should be examined and revised if appropriate.

2. **Methods** Variance analysis generally consists of a two-way prime cost variance analysis and a two-, three-, or four-way overhead variance analysis, depending on the significance of the variance amounts compared to the cost of analysis. Note that the three-way analysis is a refinement on the two-way analysis and the four-way analysis is a refinement on the three-way analysis.

a. **Two-way** direct material and direct labor variance analysis involves the computation of **price** and **efficiency** variances for each of those cost elements.

b. **Two-way** overhead variance analysis

    (1)   Volume variance   =   Fixed overhead (OH) volume variance

    (2)   Budget variance   =   Variable OH efficiency variance +
    Variable OH spending variance +
    Fixed OH budget variance

c. **Three-way** overhead variance analysis

    (1)   Volume variance   =   Fixed OH volume variance

    (2)   Efficiency variance   =   Variable OH efficiency variance

    (3)   Spending variance   =   Variable OH spending variance +
    Fixed OH budget variance

d. **Four-way** overhead variance analysis

    (1)   Fixed OH volume variance

    (2)   Variable OH efficiency variance

    (3)   Variable OH spending variance

    (4)   Fixed OH budget variance

Example 10 ▶ Variance Analysis

| | Standard | | Standard cost for one |
	Quantity	Price	completed unit
Material	3 lbs.	$2.00	$ 6.00
Labor	2 hrs.	4.00	8.00
Overhead:			
Variable	2 hrs.	1.00	2.00
Fixed	2 hrs.	2.00	4.00
			$20.00

Budgeted Activity: 50 Standard direct labor hours

Actual Data:	Units produced	20
	Material = 100 pounds at a total cost of	$225
	Labor—30 hours at $4.10	$123
	Overhead	
	Variable	$ 45
	Fixed	$115

Required: Compute the following variances:

a.   Material price
b.   Material quantity
c.   Labor rate
d.   Labor quantity
e.   Total net overhead

Solution:

a.   *Material price variance (AP – SP)AQ*

     Price difference ($2.25 – $2.00) times Actual quantity or:
     $0.25 × 100 = $25 Unfavorable

b.   *Material quantity variance (AQ – SQ)SP*

     Quantity difference (100 – 60) times Standard price or:
     40 × $2 = $80 Unfavorable
     Note: AP = $225 / 100 = $2.25, SQ = 20 units × 3 lbs. = 60

c.   *Labor rate variance (AP – SP)AQ*

     Rate difference ($4.10 – $4.00) times Actual quantity or:
     $0.10 × 30 = $3.00 Unfavorable

d.   *Labor efficiency variance (AQ – SQ)SP*

     Quantity difference (30 – 40) times Standard rate or:
     (10) × $4 = $(40) Favorable
     Note: SQ = 20 units × 2 hrs./unit = 40 hrs.

e.   *Total net overhead variance*

Actual overhead ($45 + $115)	$ 160	
Less: Overhead appl. (SQ × SP = 40 × $3)	(120)	
Underapplied overhead	$ 40	Unfavorable

Exhibit 14 ▶ Relationships of 1-, 2-, and 3-Way Analyses

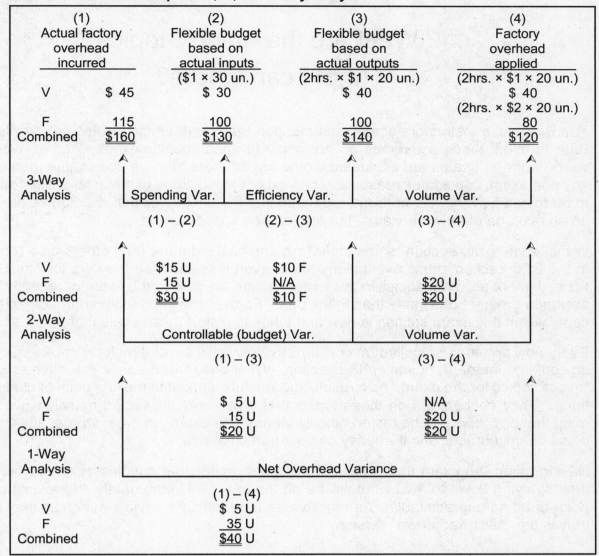

What are the "minor" topics
that I can ignore?

The Bisk video instructors sometimes mention that some topics are tested heavily or lightly. Bear in mind, these comments do not apply to each specific exam. Rather, when several years' worth of exams are evaluated, some topics average more point value than others. On any one exam, candidates reasonably can expect at least one of these so-called "minor" topics to be tested heavily. Do not read too much into these evaluations: candidates are not tested on an average of several exams, but only on one specific exam.

Within each exam section, some topics are emphasized more than others on a regular basis. In the BEC section, these evaluations are of even less use than they are for other exam sections. First of all, many topics in this exam section are new to the exam or recently have been assigned greater point value than in the past. Further, the integrative approach to testing concepts within this exam section is new and tends to distort these evaluations.

Every now and then so-called "minor" topics show up in several multiple choice questions and so could count for 10 points on the section. What does this mean? You have to know these "minor" topics for the exam. As a result, successful candidates make a point of studying everything. They concentrate on those topics that repeatedly are tested heavily while bearing in mind that any topic can be tested heavily on any one exam. In other words, any "minor" topic could be uncharacteristically heavy on your particular exam.

Having taken the exam themselves, the editors realize that candidates would like to narrow their studying down to "just what will be on the exam." Unfortunately, the examiners make a point of being unpredictable. As massive as the Bisk CPA review materials may seem, this truly is the "narrowed down" version.

Remember, with the techniques and information in your material,

A passing score is well within reach!

CHAPTER 53—COST ACCOUNTING

Problem 53-1 MULTIPLE CHOICE QUESTIONS (60 to 75 minutes)

1. Under Pick Co.'s job order costing system, manufacturing overhead is applied to work in process using a predetermined annual overhead rate. During January, Pick's transactions included the following:

Direct materials issued to production	$ 90,000
Indirect materials issued to production	8,000
Manufacturing overhead incurred	125,000
Manufacturing overhead applied	113,000
Direct labor costs	107,000

Pick had neither beginning nor ending work-in-process inventory. What was the cost of jobs completed in January?
a. $302,000
b. $310,000
c. $322,000
d. $330,000 (5/94, AR, #42, amended, 4647)

2. In a traditional job order cost system, the issue of indirect materials to a production department increases
a. Stores control
b. Work-in-process control
c. Factory overhead control
d. Factory overhead applied
(5/93, Theory, #41, 4228)

3. The following information pertains to Lap Co.'s Palo Division for the month of April:

	Number of units	Cost of materials
Beginning work-in-process	15,000	$ 5,500
Started in April	40,000	18,000
Units completed	42,500	
Ending work-in-process	12,500	

All materials are added at the beginning of the process. Using the weighted-average method, the cost per equivalent unit for materials is
a. $0.59
b. $0.55
c. $0.45
d. $0.43 (5/94, AR, #40, 4645)

4. In computing the current period's manufacturing cost per equivalent unit, the FIFO method of process costing considers current period costs
a. Only
b. Plus cost of beginning work-in-process inventory
c. Less cost of beginning work-in-process inventory
d. Plus cost of ending work-in-process inventory
(11/92, Theory #47, 3480)

5. In process 2, material G is added when a batch is 60% complete. Ending work-in-process units, which are 50% complete, would be included in the computation of equivalent units for

	Conversion costs	Material G
a.	Yes	No
b.	No	Yes
c.	No	No
d.	Yes	Yes

(5/90, Theory, #42, 2185)

6. A process costing system was used for a department that began operations in January. Approximately the same number of physical units, at the same degree of completion, were in work in process at the end of both January and February. Monthly conversion costs are allocated between ending work-in-process and units completed. Compared to the FIFO method, would the weighted-average method use the same or a greater number of equivalent units to calculate the monthly allocations?

	Equivalent units for weighted-average compared to FIFO	
	January	February
a.	Same	Same
b.	Greater number	Greater number
c.	Greater number	Same
d.	Same	Greater number

(5/91, Theory, #42, amended, 2175)

7. During March, Hamilton Company incurred the following costs on Job 10 for the manufacture of 200 motors:

Direct materials	$ 330
Direct labor	400
Factory overhead (150% of direct labor)	600
Original cost accumulation:	$1,330
Direct materials	$ 50
Direct labor	80
Direct costs of reworked 10 units:	$ 130

The rework costs were attributable to exacting specifications of Job 10 and the full rework costs were charged to this specific job. The cost per finished unit of Job 10 was
a. $7.90
b. $7.30
c. $7.00
d. $6.65 (Editors, 1501)

8. In its April production, Hern Corp., which does not use a standard cost system, incurred total production costs of $900,000, of which Hern attributed $60,000 to normal spoilage and $30,000 to abnormal spoilage. Hern should account for this spoilage as
a. Period cost of $90,000
b. Inventoriable cost of $90,000
c. Period cost of $60,000 and inventoriable cost of $30,000
d. Inventoriable cost of $60,000 and period cost of $30,000   (5/95, AR, #41, amended, 5459)

9. The Forming Department is the first of a two-stage production process. Spoilage is identified when the units have completed the Forming process. Costs of spoiled units are assigned to units completed and transferred to the second department in the period spoilage is identified. The following information concerns Forming's conversion costs in May:

	Units	Conversion costs
Beginning work-in-process (50% complete)	2,000	$10,000
Units started during May	8,000	75,500
Spoilage—normal	500	
Units completed & transferred	7,000	
Ending work-in-process (80% complete)	2,500	

Using the weighted average method, what was Forming's conversion cost transferred to the second production department?
a. $59,850
b. $64,125
c. $67,500
d. $71,250   (11/95, AR, #46, amended, 5789)

10. A processing department produces joint products Ajac and Bjac, each of which incurs separable production costs after split-off. Information concerning a batch produced at a $60,000 joint cost before split-off follows:

Product	Separable costs	Sales value
Ajac	$ 8,000	$ 80,000
Bjac	22,000	40,000
Total	$30,000	$120,000

What is the joint cost assigned to Ajac if costs are assigned using the relative net realizable value?
a. $16,000
b. $40,000
c. $48,000
d. $52,000   (R/00, AR, #17, 6922)

11. For purposes of allocating joint costs to joint products, the sales price at point of sale, reduced by cost to complete after split-off, is assumed to be equal to the
a. Joint costs
b. Total costs
c. Net sales value at split-off
d. Sales price less a normal profit margin at point of sale   (11/95, AR, #48, 5791)

12. Kode Co. manufactures a major product that gives rise to a by-product called May. May's only separable cost is a $1 selling cost when a unit is sold for $4. Kode accounts for May's sales by deducting the $3 net amount from the cost of goods sold of the major product. There are no inventories. If Kode were to change its method of accounting for May from a by-product to a joint product, what would be the effect on Kode's overall gross margin?
a. No effect
b. Gross margin increases by $1 for each unit of May sold.
c. Gross margin increases by $3 for each unit of May sold.
d. Gross margin increases by $4 for each unit of May sold.   (5/95, AR, #43, 5461)

13. Parat College allocates support department costs to its individual schools using the step method. Information for May is as follows:

	Support departments	
	Maintenance	Power
Costs incurred	$99,000	$54,000
Services percentages provided to:		
Maintenance	—	10%
Power	20%	—
School of Education	30%	20%
School of Technology	50%	70%
	100%	100%

What is the amount of May support department costs allocated to the School of Education?
a. $40,500
b. $42,120
c. $46,100
d. $49,125   (11/95, AR, #49, amended, 5792)

14. Which of the following is true about activity-based costing?
a. It should **not** be used with process or job costing.
b. It can be used only with process costing.
c. It can be used only with job costing.
d. It can be used with either process or job costing.   (R/03, BEC, #30, 7693)

15. What is the normal effect on the numbers of cost pools and allocation bases when an activity-based cost (ABC) system replaces a traditional cost system?

	Cost pools	Allocation bases
a.	No effect	No effect
b.	Increase	No effect
c.	No effect	Increase
d.	Increase	Increase

(5/94, AR, #41, 4646)

16. A basic assumption of activity-based costing (ABC) is that
a. All manufacturing costs vary directly with units of production.
b. Products or services require the performance of activities, and activities consume resources.
c. Only costs that respond to unit-level drivers are product costs.
d. Only variable costs are included in activity cost pools. (R/00, AR, #13, 6918)

17. Book Co. uses the activity-based costing approach for cost allocation and product costing purposes. Printing, cutting, and binding functions make up the manufacturing process. Machinery and equipment are arranged in operating cells that produce a complete product starting with raw materials. Which of the following are characteristic of Book's activity-based costing approach?

I. Cost drivers are used as a basis for cost allocation.
II. Costs are accumulated by department or function for purposes of product costing.
III. Activities that do not add value to the product are identified and reduced to the extent possible.

a. I only
b. I and II
c. I and III
d. II and III (5/92, Theory, #55, 2748)

18. In an activity-based costing system, cost reduction is accomplished by identifying and eliminating

	All cost drivers	Nonvalue-adding activities
a.	No	No
b.	Yes	Yes
c.	No	Yes
d.	Yes	No

(11/93, Theory, #45, 4550)

19. In an activity-based costing system, what should be used to assign a department's manufacturing overhead costs to products produced in varying lot sizes?
a. A single cause and effect relationship
b. Multiple cause and effect relationships
c. Relative net sales values of the products
d. A product's ability to bear cost allocations

(5/95, AR, #44, 5462)

Items 20 and 21 are based on the following information pertaining to 1,200,000 papers that were processed by DEP Company:

Total cost	$1,050,000
Labor cost	$ 950,000
Labor hours	190,000

The following processing standards have been set for DEP Co.'s clerical workers:

Number of hours per 1,000 papers processed	150
Normal number of papers processed per year	1,600,000
Wage rate per 1,000 papers	$ 750
Standard variable cost of processing 1,600,000 papers	$1,280,000
Fixed costs per year	$ 200,000

20. DEP Company's expected total cost to process 1,200,000 papers, assuming standard performance, is
a. $1,480,000
b. $1,280,000
c. $1,160,000
d. $1,100,000 (Editors, 1509)

21. DEP's labor rate variance is
a. $50,000 unfavorable
b. $40,000 favorable
c. $10,000 unfavorable
d. $0 (Editors, 1510)

22. Companies in what type of industry may use a standard cost system for cost control?

	Mass production industry	Service industry
a.	Yes	Yes
b.	Yes	No
c.	No	No
d.	No	Yes

(5/95, AR, #42, 5460)

23. In connection with a standard cost system being developed by Flint Co., the following information is being considered with regard to standard hours allowed for output of one unit of product:

Average historical performance for the past
   three years   1.85
Production level to satisfy average consumer
   demand over a seasonal time span   1.60
Engineering estimates based on attainable
   performance   1.50
Engineering estimates based on ideal
   performance   1.25

To measure controllable production inefficiencies, what is the best basis for Flint to use in establishing standard hours allowed?
a. 1.25
b. 1.50
c. 1.60
d. 1.85   (11/92, PII, #31, amended, 3365)

24. Nile Co. uses a predetermined factory overhead application rate based on direct labor cost. Nile's budgeted factory overhead was $300,000, based on a budgeted volume of 25,000 direct labor hours, at a standard direct labor rate of $6.00 per hour. Actual factory overhead amounted to $310,000, with actual direct labor cost of $162,500. Overapplied factory overhead was
a. $10,000
b. $12,500
c. $15,000
d. $25,000   (Editors, 1512)

Items 25 and 26 are based on the following:

Hart Company uses job order costing. Factory overhead is applied to production at a determined rate of 150% of direct-labor cost. Any over- or under-applied factory overhead is closed to the cost of goods sold account at the end of each month.

- Job 1001 was the only job in process at the end of April, with accumulated costs as follows:

Direct materials	$4,000
Direct labor	2,000
Applied factory overhead	3,000
	$9,000

- Jobs 1002, 1003, and 1004 were started during May.
- Direct materials requisitions for May totaled $26,000.

- Direct-labor cost of $20,000 was incurred for May.
- Actual factory overhead was $32,000 for May.
- The only job still in process at the end of May was Job 1004, with costs of $2,800 for direct materials and $1,800 for direct labor.

25. The cost of goods manufactured for May was
a. $77,700
b. $78,000
c. $79,700
d. $85,000   (Editors, 7395)

26. Over- or underapplied factory overhead should be closed to the cost of goods sold account at the end of May, in the amount of
a. $ 700 overapplied
b. $1,000 overapplied
c. $1,700 underapplied
d. $2,000 underapplied   (Editors, 7396)

Items 27 and 28 are based on the following inventory balances and manufacturing cost data for the month of January for Summit Company. Under Summit's cost system, any over- or under-applied overhead is closed to the cost of goods sold account at the end of the calendar year.

Inventories:	Beginning	Ending
Direct materials	$15,000	$20,000
Work-in-process	7,500	10,000
Finished goods	32,500	25,000

	Month of January
Cost of goods manufactured	$257,500
Factory overhead applied	75,000
Direct materials used	95,000
Actual factory overhead	72,000

27. What was the total amount of direct-material purchases during January?
a. $ 90,000
b. $ 95,000
c. $ 97,500
d. $100,000   (Editors, 7397)

28. How much direct-labor cost was incurred during January?
a. $85,000
b. $87,500
c. $90,000
d. $93,000   (Editors, 7398)

29. The following information pertains to Roe Co.'s June manufacturing operations:

Standard direct labor hours per unit	2
Actual direct labor hours	10,500
Number of units produced	5,000
Standard variable overhead per standard direct labor hour	$ 3
Actual variable overhead	$28,000

Roe's June unfavorable variable overhead efficiency variance was
a. $0
b. $1,500
c. $2,000
d. $3,500   (11/92, PII, #25, amended, 3359)

30. Mason Company uses a job-order cost system and applies manufacturing overhead to jobs using a predetermined overhead rate based on direct-labor dollars. The rate for the current year is 200 percent of direct-labor dollars. This rate was calculated last December and will be used throughout the current year. Mason had one job, No. 150, in process on August 1 with raw materials costs of $2,000 and direct-labor costs of $3,000. During August, raw materials and direct labor added to jobs were as follows:

	No. 150	No. 151	No. 152
Raw materials	—	$4,000	$1,000
Direct labor	$1,500	5,000	2,500

Actual manufacturing overhead for the month of August was $20,000. During the month, Mason completed Job Nos. 150 and 151. For August, manufacturing overhead was
a. Overapplied by $4,000
b. Underapplied by $7,000
c. Underapplied by $2,000
d. Underapplied by $1,000   (R/00, AR, #12, 6917)

Problem 53-2 ADDITIONAL MULTIPLE CHOICE QUESTIONS (106 to 133 minutes)

31. Birk Co. uses a job order cost system. The following debits (credit) appeared in Birk's work-in-process account for the month of April:

April	Description	Amount
1	Balance	$ 4,000
30	Direct materials	24,000
30	Direct labor	16,000
30	Factory overhead	12,800
30	To finished goods	(48,000)

Birk applies overhead to production at a predetermined rate of 80% of direct labor cost. Job No. 5, the only job still in process at the end of April, has been charged with direct labor of $2,000. What was the amount of direct materials charged to Job No. 5?
a. $ 3,000
b. $ 5,200
c. $ 8,800
d. $24,000   (5/92, PII, #44, amended, 2676)

32. In a job order cost system, the use of direct materials previously purchased usually is recorded as an increase in
a. Work-in-process control
b. Factory overhead applied
c. Factory overhead control
d. Stores control   (Editors, 2205)

33. A job order cost system uses a predetermined factory overhead rate based on expected volume and expected fixed cost. At the end of the year, underapplied overhead might be explained by which of the following situations?

	Actual volume	Actual fixed costs
a.	Greater than expected	Greater than expected
b.	Greater than expected	Less than expected
c.	Less than expected	Greater than expected
d.	Less than expected	Less than expected

(11/90, Theory, #42, 2181)

34. In a process cost system, the application of factory overhead usually would be recorded as an increase in
a. Finished goods inventory control
b. Factory overhead control
c. Cost of goods sold
d. Work-in-process inventory control
          (5/92, Theory, #51, 2744)

35. In developing a predetermined factory overhead application rate for use in a process costing system, which of the following could be used in the numerator and denominator?

	Numerator	Denominator
a.	Actual factory overhead	Actual machine hours
b.	Actual factory overhead	Estimated machine hours
c.	Estimated factory overhead	Actual machine hours
d.	Estimated factory overhead	Estimated machine hours

(5/91, Theory, #46, 2179)

36. In the computation of manufacturing cost per equivalent unit, the weighted-average method of process costing considers
a. Current cost less cost of beginning work-in-process inventory
b. Current costs plus cost of ending work-in-process inventory
c. Current costs plus cost of beginning work-in-process inventory
d. Current costs only   (Editors, 2224)

37. Mart Co. adds materials at the beginning of the process in Department M. The following information pertains to units in Department M's work-in-process during April:

Work-in-process, April 1
(60% complete as to conversion cost)   1,500
Started in April   12,500
Completed   10,000
Work-in-process, April 30
(75% complete as to conversion cost)   4,000

Under the weighted-average method, the equivalent units for conversion cost are
a. 13,000
b. 12,500
c. 12,000
d. 10,900   (Editors, 1487)

Items 38 through 40 are based on the following information.

Kerner Manufacturing uses a process cost system to manufacture laptop computers. The following information summarizes operations relating to laptop computer model #KJK20 during the quarter ending March 31:

	Units
Work-in-process inventory, January 1	100
Started during the quarter	500
Completed during the quarter	400
Work-in-process inventory, March 31	200

Beginning work-in-process inventory was 50% complete for direct materials and direct labor costs. Ending work-in-process inventory was 75% complete for direct materials and direct labor costs.

38. Direct labor work-in-process inventory on January 1 was $25,000. Direct labor costs added during the quarter were $360,000. What is the total value of direct labor costs in ending work-in-process inventory using the weighted-average unit cost inventory valuation method?
a. $ 91,500
b. $ 97,000
c. $105,000
d. $108,000   (R/02, AR, #11, amended, 7076)

39. Direct material work-in-process inventory on January 1 was $50,000. Direct material costs added during the quarter were $720,000. What is the total value of material costs in ending work-in-process inventory using the weighted-average unit cost inventory valuation method?
a. $183,000
b. $194,000
c. $210,000
d. $216,000   (R/02, AR, #12, 7077)

40. Direct material work-in-process inventory on January 1 was $50,000. Direct material costs added during the quarter were $720,000. What is the total value of material costs in ending work-in-process inventory using the FIFO unit cost, inventory valuation method?
a. $183,000
b. $194,000
c. $210,000
d. $216,000   (R/01, AR, #15, 7000)

41. Yarn Co.'s inventories in process were at the following stages of completion at the end of April:

No. of units	Percent complete
200	90
100	80
400	10

Equivalent units of production amounted to
a. 300
b. 360
c. 660
d. 700   (Editors, 2677)

42. Kerner Manufacturing uses a process cost system to manufacture laptop computers. The following information summarizes operations relating to laptop computer model #KJK20 during the quarter ending March 31:

	Units	Direct Materials
Work-in-process inventory, January 1	100	$ 70,000
Started during the quarter	500	
Completed during the quarter	400	
Work-in-process inventory, March 31	200	
Costs added during the quarter		$750,000

Beginning work-in-process inventory was 50% complete for direct materials. Ending work-in-process inventory was 75% complete for direct materials. Kerner uses a FIFO cost-flow assumption. What were the equivalent units of production with regard to materials for the quarter?
a. 450
b. 500
c. 550
d. 600   (R/01, AR, #12, amended, 6997)

43. Bing Company had no beginning work-in-process inventory, and the ending work-in-process inventory is 50% complete as to conversion costs. The number of equivalent units as to conversion costs would be
a. The same as the units completed
b. The same as the units placed in process
c. Less than the units placed in process
d. Less than the units completed   (Editors, 2229)

44. Which of the following is a disadvantage of using a process costing system versus job-order costing?
a. It is difficult to determine cost of goods sold when partial shipments are made before completion.
b. It is difficult to ensure that material and labor are accurately charged to each specific job.
c. It involves the calculation of stage of completion of goods-in-process and the use of equivalent units.
d. It is expensive to use as a good deal of clerical work is required.   (R/03, BEC, #3, 7665)

45. Simpson Company manufactures electric drills to the exacting specifications of various customers. During April, Job 43 for the production of 1,100 drills was completed at the following costs per unit:

Direct materials	$ 5
Direct labor	4
Applied factory overhead	6
	$15

Final inspection of Job 43 disclosed 50 defective units and 100 spoiled units. The defective drills were reworked at a total cost of $250, and the spoiled drills were sold to a jobber for $750. What would be the unit cost of the good units produced on Job 43?
a. $16.50
b. $16.00
c. $15.00
d. $14.50   (Editors, 7394)

46. The sale of scrap from a manufacturing process usually would be recorded as a(an)
a. Decrease in factory overhead control
b. Decrease in finished goods control
c. Increase in factory overhead control
d. Increase in finished goods control
(Editors, 2204)

47. A department adds material at the beginning of a process and identifies defective units when the process is 40% complete. At the beginning of the period, there was no work in process. At the end of the period, the number of work-in-process units equaled the number of units transferred to finished goods. If all units in ending work-in-process were 66-2/3% complete, then ending work-in-process should be allocated
a. 50% of all normal defective unit costs
b. 40% of all normal defective unit costs
c. 50% of the material costs and 40% of the conversion costs of all normal defective unit costs
d. None of the normal defective unit costs
(5/91, Theory, #41, 2174)

48. During June, Delta Co. experienced scrap, normal spoilage, and abnormal spoilage in its manufacturing process. The cost of units produced includes
a. Scrap, but **not** spoilage
b. Normal spoilage, but **neither** scrap **nor** abnormal spoilage
c. Scrap and normal spoilage, but **not** abnormal spoilage
d. Scrap, normal spoilage, and abnormal spoilage
(11/91, Theory, #44, 2552)

49. The diagram below represents the production and sales relationships of joint products P and Q. Joint costs are incurred until split-off, then separable costs are incurred in refining each product. Market values of P and Q at split-off are used to allocate joint costs.

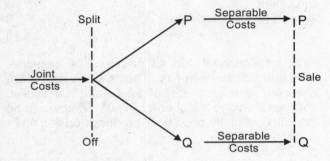

If the market value of P at split-off increases and all other costs and selling prices remain unchanged, then the gross margin of

	P	Q
a.	Increases	Decreases
b.	Increases	Increases
c.	Decreases	Decreases
d.	Decreases	Increases

(5/90, Theory, #44, 7402)

50. Actual sales values at the split-off point for joint products Y and Z are not known. For purposes of allocating joint costs to products Y and Z, the relative sales value at split-off method is used. An increase in the costs beyond split-off occurs for product Z, while those of product Y remain constant. If the selling prices of finished products Y and Z remain constant, the percentage of the total joint costs allocated to product Y and product Z would
a. Decrease for product Y and increase for product Z
b. Decrease for product Y and product Z
c. Increase for product Y and product Z
d. Increase for product Y and decrease for product Z (Editors, 2189)

51. Rome Co. produces two joint products, BEC and CAL. Joint production costs for June were $30,000. During June, further processing costs beyond the split-off point, needed to convert the products into saleable form, were $25,000 and $35,000 for 800 units of BEC and 400 units of CAL, respectively. BEC sells for $100 per unit, and CAL sells for $200 per unit. Rome uses the net realizable value method for allocating joint product costs. For June, the joint costs allocated to product BEC were
a. $20,000
b. $16,500
c. $13,500
d. $10,000 (Editors, 1489)

52. In accounting for by-products, the value of the by-product may be recognized at the time of

	Production	Sale
a.	Yes	Yes
b.	No	Yes
c.	No	No
d.	Yes	No	(Editors, 2206)

53. Alley Co. produces main products Kul and Ju. The process also yields by-product Bef. Net realizable value of by-product Bef is subtracted from joint production cost of Kul and Ju. The following information pertains to production in July at a joint cost of $54,000:

Product	Units produced	Market value	Additional cost after split-off
Kul	1,000	$40,000	$0
Ju	2,500	60,000	0
Bef	500	9,000	5,000

If Alley uses the net realizable value method for allocating joint cost, how much of the joint cost should be allocated to product Kul?
a. $13,500
b. $14,286
c. $20,000
d. $33,333 (Editors, 7403)

54. The following information pertains to a by-product called Moy:

Sales in July	5,000 units
Selling price per unit	$6
Selling costs per unit	2
Processing costs	0

Inventory of Moy was recorded at net realizable value when produced in June. No units of Moy were produced in July. What amount should be recognized as profit on Moy's July sales?
a. $0
b. $10,000
c. $20,000
d. $30,000 (5/92, PII, #47, amended, 2679)

55. Mig Co. produces gasoline and a gasoline by-product. The following information is available pertaining to sales and production of the first year of operations:

Total production costs to split-off point	$120,000
Gasoline sales	270,000
By-product sales	30,000
Gasoline inventory, ending	15,000
Additional by-product costs:	
Marketing	10,000
Production	15,000

Mig accounts for the by-product at the time of production. What are Mig's cost of sales for gasoline and the by-product for the first year of operations?

	Gasoline	By-product
a.	$105,000	$25,000
b.	$115,000	$0
c.	$108,000	$37,000
d.	$100,000	$0

(11/92, PII, #32, amended, 3366)

56. A standard cost system may be used in
a. Neither process costing nor job order costing
b. Process costing but **not** job order costing
c. Either job order costing or process costing
d. Job order costing but **not** process costing

(11/91, Theory, #42, 2550)

57. Which of the following standard costing variances would be **least** controllable by a production supervisor?
a. Overhead volume
b. Overhead efficiency
c. Labor efficiency
d. Material usage

(5/93, Theory, #43, 4230)

58. Rigley Company has underapplied overhead of $55,000 for the calendar year. Before disposition of the underapplied overhead, selected year-end balances from Rigley's accounting records are:

Sales	$1,200,000
Cost of goods sold	900,000
Direct materials inventory	150,000
Work-in-process inventory	200,000
Finished goods inventory	100,000

Under Rigley's cost accounting system, over or underapplied overhead is allocated to appropriate inventories and cost of goods sold based on year-end balances. In its annual income statement, Rigley should report costs of goods sold as
a. $858,750
b. $863,333
c. $936,667
d. $941,250

(Editors, 1519)

59. The following were among Gage Co.'s April costs:

Normal spoilage	$ 5,000
Freight out	10,000
Excess of actual manufacturing costs over standard costs	20,000
Standard manufacturing costs	100,000
Actual prime manufacturing costs	80,000

Gage's April actual manufacturing overhead was
a. $ 40,000
b. $ 45,000
c. $ 55,000
d. $120,000

(5/92, PII, #43, amended, 2675)

60. Which of the following variances would be useful in calling attention to a possible short-term problem in the control of overhead costs?

	Spending variance	Volume variance
a.	Yes	Yes
b.	No	Yes
c.	Yes	No
d.	No	No

(Editors, 2188)

61. Baby Frames, Inc., evaluates manufacturing overhead in its factory by using variance analysis. The following information applies to the month of May:

	Actual	Budgeted
Number of frames manufactured	19,000	20,000
Variable overhead costs	$4,100	$2 per direct labor hour
Fixed overhead costs	$22,000	$20,000
Direct labor hours	2,100 hours	0.1 hour per frame

What is the fixed overhead spending variance?
a. $1,000 favorable
b. $1,000 unfavorable
c. $2,000 favorable
d. $2,000 unfavorable

(R/01, AR, #13, 6998)

62. Fount Company uses a standard cost system. For April, total overhead is budgeted at $80,000 based on the normal capacity of 10,000 direct-labor hours. At standard, each unit of finished product requires two direct-labor hours. The following data are available for April production activity:

Equivalent units of product	4,750
Direct-labor hours worked	9,250
Actual total overhead incurred	$79,500

What amount should Fount credit to the applied factory overhead account for April?
a. $76,000
b. $78,000
c. $79,500
d. $80,000 (Editors, 1520)

63. When a manager is concerned with monitoring total cost, total revenue, and net profit conditioned upon the level of productivity, an accountant would normally recommend

	Flexible budgeting	Standard costing
a.	Yes	Yes
b.	Yes	No
c.	No	Yes
d.	No	No

(11/90, Theory, #45, 2182)

64. The standard direct material cost to produce a unit of Lem is 4 meters of material at $2.50 per meter. During May, 4,200 meters of material costing $10,080 were purchased and used to produce 1,000 units of Lem. What was the material price variance for May?
a. $400 favorable
b. $420 favorable
c. $ 80 unfavorable
d. $480 unfavorable

(11/95, AR, #47, amended, 5790)

65. Yola Co. manufactures one product with a standard direct labor cost of four hours at $12.00 per hour. During June, 1,000 units were produced using 4,100 hours at $12.20 per hour. The unfavorable direct labor efficiency variance was
a. $1,220
b. $1,200
c. $ 820
d. $ 400 (11/92, PII, #21, 3355)

66. For April, Stork Co.'s records disclosed the following data relating to direct labor:

Actual cost	$10,000
Rate variance	1,000 favorable
Efficiency variance	1,500 unfavorable
Standard cost	$ 9,500

For April, actual direct labor hours totaled 1,000. Stork's standard direct labor rate per hour was
a. $11.00
b. $10.00
c. $ 9.50
d. $ 9.00 (Editors, 1515)

67. Tyro Co. uses a standard cost system. The following information pertains to direct labor for product B for the month of May:

Actual rate paid	$8.40 per hour
Standard rate	$8.00 per hour
Standard hours allowed for actual production	2,000 hours
Labor efficiency variance	$ 800 unfavorable

What were the actual hours worked?
a. 1,900
b. 1,905
c. 2,095
d. 2,100 (Editors, 1511)

68. The following direct labor information pertains to the manufacture of product Glu:

Time required to make one unit	2 direct labor hours
Number of direct workers	50
Number of productive hours per week, per worker	40
Weekly wages per worker	$500
Workers' benefits treated as direct labor costs	20% of wages

What is the standard direct labor cost per unit of product Glu?
a. $30
b. $24
c. $15
d. $12 (5/92, PII, #46, 2678)

69. Kemper Company follows a practice of isolating variances at the earliest point in time. When is the appropriate time to isolate and recognize a direct material price variance?
a. When a purchase order is originated
b. When material is purchased
c. When material is used in production
d. When material is issued (Editors, 2234)

70. Under the two-variance method for analyzing overhead, which of the following variances consists of both variable and fixed overhead elements?

	Controllable (budget) variance	Volume variance
a.	No	No
b.	Yes	No
c.	Yes	Yes
d.	No	Yes

(Editors, 7404)

71. Information on Wright Company's overhead costs for the June production activity is as follows:

Budgeted fixed overhead	$ 37,500
Standard fixed overhead rate per direct-labor hour	$ 3
Standard variable overhead rate per direct-labor hour	$ 6
Standard direct-labor hours allowed for actual production	12,000
Actual total overhead incurred	$110,000

Wright has a standard absorption and flexible budgeting system, and uses the two-variance method (two-way analysis) for overhead variances. The volume (denominator) variance for June is
a. $1,500 unfavorable
b. $1,500 favorable
c. $2,000 unfavorable
d. $2,000 favorable   (Editors, 7405)

72. Under the two-variance method for analyzing factory overhead, which of the following is used in the computation of the controllable (budget) variance?

	Budget allowance based on actual hours	Budget allowance based on standard hours
a.	No	No
b.	Yes	No
c.	Yes	Yes
d.	No	Yes

(Editors, 2202)

73. When using the two-variance method for analyzing factory overhead, the difference between the budget allowance based on standard hours allowed and the factory overhead applied to production is the
a. Controllable variance
b. Net overhead variance
c. Volume variance
d. Efficiency variance   (Editors, 2225)

74. Columbia Company uses a standard cost system and prepared the following budget at normal capacity for the month of June:

Direct-labor hours	12,000
Variable factory overhead	$24,000
Fixed factory overhead	$54,000
Total factory overhead per direct-labor hour	$ 6.50
Actual June direct labor hours worked	11,000
Actual June total factory overhead	$73,500
Standard direct labor hours allowed for capacity attained in June	10,500

Using the two-way analysis of overhead variances, what is the budget (controllable) variance for June?
a. $1,500 favorable
b. $2,500 favorable
c. $4,500 favorable
d. $5,250 unfavorable   (Editors, 1523)

Items 75 and 76 are based on the following information pertaining to Baby Frames, Inc., applicable to the month of May. Baby Frames evaluates manufacturing overhead by using variance analysis.

	Actual	Budgeted
Number of frames manufactured	19,000	20,000
Variable overhead costs	$ 4,100	$2 per DL hour
Fixed overhead costs	$22,000	$20,000; $1 per unit
Direct labor hours	2,100 hours	0.1 hour per frame

75. What is the variable overhead efficiency variance?
a. $200 favorable
b. $200 unfavorable
c. $400 favorable
d. $400 unfavorable   (R/02, AR, #13, 7078)

76. What is the production volume variance?
a. $1,000 favorable
b. $1,000 unfavorable
c. $2,000 favorable
d. $2,000 unfavorable   (R/02, AR, #14, 7079)

Items 77 through 79 are based on the following information pertaining to Rand Company:

Units actually produced	76,000
Actual direct labor hours worked	160,000
Actual variable overhead incurred	$500,000
Actual fixed overhead incurred	384,000

Based on monthly normal volume of 100,000 units (200,000 direct labor hours), Rand's standard cost system contains the following overhead costs:

Variable	$6 per unit
Fixed	4 per unit

77. The fixed overhead budget variance was
a. $ 8,000 unfavorable
b. $ 8,000 favorable
c. $16,000 unfavorable
d. $16,000 favorable   (Editors, 7399)

78. The unfavorable variable overhead spending variance was
a. $12,000
b. $20,000
c. $24,000
d. $44,000   (Editors, 1513)

79. The fixed overhead volume variance was
a. $96,000 unfavorable
b. $96,000 favorable
c. $80,000 unfavorable
d. $80,000 favorable   (Editors, 1514)

80. Under the three-variance method for analyzing factory overhead, which of the following is used in the computation of the spending variance?

	Actual factory overhead	Budget allowance based on actual hours
a.	Yes	No
b.	No	No
c.	No	Yes
d.	Yes	Yes

(Editors, 2212)

Items 81 and 82 are based on the following information available from Rust Company:

Actual factory overhead	$30,000
Fixed overhead, actual	$14,400
Fixed overhead, budgeted	$14,000
Actual hours	7,000
Standard hours	7,600
Variable overhead rate per direct-labor hour	$ 2.50

Rust uses a three-way analysis of overhead variances.

81. What is the spending variance?
a. $1,500 favorable
b. $1,500 unfavorable
c. $1,900 favorable
d. $3,000 unfavorable   (Editors, 7400)

82. What is the efficiency variance?
a. $1,500 favorable
b. $1,500 unfavorable
c. $1,900 favorable
d. $3,000 unfavorable   (Editors, 7401)

83. A department's three-variance overhead standard costing system reported unfavorable spending and volume variances. The activity level selected for allocating overhead to the product was based on 80% of practical capacity. If 100% of practical capacity had been selected instead, how would the reported unfavorable spending and volume variances be affected?

	Spending variance	Volume variance
a.	Increased	Unchanged
b.	Increased	Increased
c.	Unchanged	Increased
d.	Unchanged	Unchanged

(5/91, Theory, #43, amended, 2176)

SIMULATIONS

The editors encourage candidates to answer simulations as part of their review because such studying provides for content reinforcement, regardless of question format. FYI: Simulations currently are not part of the BEC exam; simulations are not expected on the BEC exam section until 2007, at earliest. Bisk Education updating supplements will notify readers when this situation changes; updating supplements are posted at www.cpaexam.com/content/support.asp.

Problem 53-3 (7 to 15 minutes)

On the accompanying diagram, the line OW represents the standard labor cost at any output volume expressed in direct labor hours. Point S indicates the actual output at standard cost, and Point A indicates the actual hours and actual costs required to produce S.

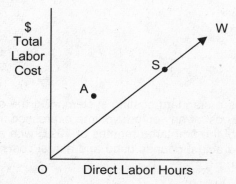

Indicate if each variance is favorable (F) or unfavorable (U).

1. Rate variance
2. Efficiency variance

(11/90, Theory, #41, amended, 7479)

The accompanying diagram depicts a factory overhead flexible budget line DB and standard overhead application line OA. Activity is expressed in machine hours with Point V indicating the standard hours required for the actual output in September. Point S indicates the actual machine hours (inputs) and actual costs in September.

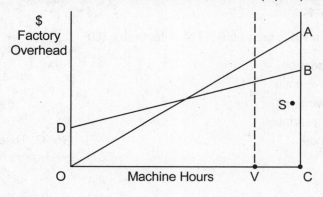

1. Indicate if the volume (capacity) variance is favorable (F) or unfavorable (U).
2. Indicate if the efficiency variance is favorable (F) or unfavorable (U).
3. The budgeted total variable overhead cost for C machine hours is
   A. AB
   B. BC
   C. AC minus DO
   D. BC minus DO

(11/90, Theory, #42-44, amended, 7479)

Problem 53-4 (15 to 20 minutes)

Bilco, Inc. produces bricks and uses a standard costing system. On the accompanying diagram, the line OP represents Bilco's standard material cost at any output volume expressed in direct material pounds to be used. Bilco had identical outputs in each of the first three months of 1997, with a standard cost of V in each month. Points Ja, Fe, and Ma represent the actual pounds used and actual costs incurred in January, February, and March, respectively.

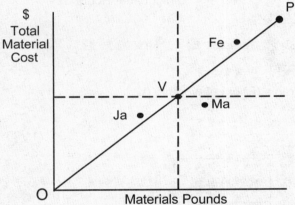

Determine whether each variance is favorable (F) or unfavorable (U).

1. January material price variance
2. January material usage variance
3. February material price variance
4. February material usage variance
5. March material net variance

(5/92, Theory, #61-65, amended, 9911)

Problem 53-5 (7 to 12 minutes)

The accompanying diagram depicts a manufacturing total cost flexible budget line KI and standard cost line OI. Line OJ is parallel to line KI, and revenues are represented by line OH.

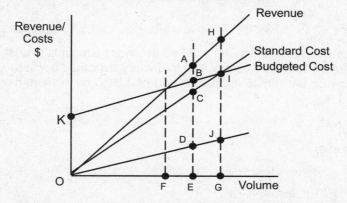

Identify the line on the graph that represents each item.

1. The budgeted fixed cost at volume OE
2. The budgeted variable cost at volume OE
3. The standard gross profit at volume OE
4. The budgeted gross profit at volume OE, assuming no change between beginning and ending inventories
5. The normal capacity, assuming standard costs are based on normal capacity

(11/92, Theory, #69-73, 7477)

Problem 53-6 (10 to 15 minutes)

The Tyler Company has the following amounts related to its first-year operations.

Materials and supplies (all purchased on account)	$220,000
Direct materials issued for production	170,000
Unused direct materials returned to storeroom	5,000
Supplies issued (to production departments)	18,000
Direct labor (on production)	150,000
Indirect labor (on production)	40,000
Depreciation—factory, plant, and equipment	11,000
Miscellaneous factory overhead incurred (normally detailed)	25,000
Factory overhead applied (60% of direct labor cost)	90,000
Cost of completed production	305,000
Sales (all on account)	320,000
Cost of goods sold	260,000

Present general journal entries to record this activity.

Present the general journal entry to close the manufacturing overhead accounts to cost of goods sold. Show the T-accounts for factory department overhead control and for factory overhead applied. (Editor's Note: While the preparation of T-accounts may be unlikely to appear as part of a BEC simulation, most candidates will benefit from doing this at least once.)

Problem 53-7 (10 to 15 minutes)

ABC Company keeps inventory records using a FIFO cost flow assumption. Product enters Department B from Department A. Product conversion costs are incurred evenly in Department B, and material is added to the product at the end of the process. In May, there was no ending WIP inventory for Department B. In June, 3,000 units were transferred from Department A to Department B, at a total cost of $7,500. At the end of June, 1,000 units were finished and 2,000 units were 40% complete. During June, $9,000 was incurred for conversion costs and $500 for material costs in Department B.

Department C is unrelated to Departments A and B. In Department C, ABC produces two products, Y and Z, from the same raw material. Joint product costs are $900. The process yields 200 units of Y and 400 units of Z. Sales values at split-off are estimated to be $5 and $3.50 per unit, respectively.

1. What is the unit cost of WIP inventory in Department B at the end of June?
2. What is the total cost of WIP inventory in Department B at the end of June?
3. What is the unit cost of the product finished in June in Department B?
4. What is the total cost of the product finished in June in Department B?   (5/90, Theory, #4, 9911)

Determine the amount of joint costs to allocate to each product in Department C on the basis of relative sales value at split-off.

1. Product Y
2. Product Z

Problem 53-8 (10 to 15 minutes)

		Standard Cost		Standard cost for one completed unit
		Quantity	Price	
Material		3 lbs.	$2.00	$ 6.00
Labor		2 hrs.	4.00	8.00
Overhead:	Variable	2 hrs.	1.00	2.00
	Fixed	2 hrs.	2.00	4.00
Total				$20.00

<u>Budgeted Activity</u>: 50 Standard direct labor hours

<u>Actual Data</u>:

Units produced		20
Material—Actual usage = 100 pounds at a total cost of		$225
Labor—Actual hours 30 at $4.10		
Overhead:	Variable	$45
	Fixed	$115

Compute the following variances.

1. Material price
2. Material quantity
3. Labor rate
4. Labor quantity
5. Total net overhead variance
6. Variable overhead spending variance
7. Variable overhead efficiency variance
8. Fixed overhead budget variance
9. Fixed overhead volume variance
10. Fixed overhead denominator variance (Two-way analysis of overhead)
11. Fixed overhead controllable (budget) variance (Two-way analysis of overhead)
12. Volume variance (Three-way analysis of overhead)
13. Efficiency variance (Three-way analysis of overhead)
14. Spending variance (Three-way analysis of overhead)   (5/90, Theory, #4, 9911)

Prepare journal entries based on the transactions in Response #1.

Solution 53-1 MULTIPLE CHOICE ANSWERS

Job Order Costing

1. (b) Indirect materials are a part of manufacturing overhead. Therefore, they are included in the manufacturing overhead cost and should not be added again. Doing so would result in double counting the cost of indirect materials. The jobs complete during January should be charged with the manufacturing overhead applied, not the manufacturing overhead incurred. Some overhead costs are not incurred uniformly during the year. Applying overhead to production using a predetermined annual overhead rate helps to prevent some jobs from being overcosted and others from being undercosted.

Direct materials issued to production	$ 90,000
Direct labor costs	107,000
Manufacturing overhead applied	113,000
Total manufacturing costs	310,000
Add: Beginning WIP	0
Total costs in WIP	310,000
Less: Ending WIP	0
Cost of jobs completed during January	$310,000

2. (c) In a job order cost system, the issue of indirect materials to a production department is recorded as an increase to the *Factory Overhead Control* account, as follows.

Factory Overhead Control	XX	
Stores Control		XX

Process Costing

3. (d) The weighted-average method of process costing assumes that all units in the beginning inventory were completed during the current period. The equivalent units (EU) of production are the completed units plus the units in the ending work-in-process (WIP) inventory times the percentage of completion. In this case, all materials are added at the beginning of the process. Thus, the units in the ending inventory are 100% complete as to materials. To determine unit costs under the weighted-average method, the cost of beginning WIP is added to costs incurred during the period. The total cost is then divided by the EU of production. The result is the cost per EU: $23,500 / 55,000 = $0.43/unit.

Units completed	42,500
Units in ending WIP (12,500 × 100%)	12,500
Equivalent units of production	55,000
Cost of materials in beginning WIP	$ 5,500
Cost of materials added during period	18,000
Total cost of materials	$23,500

4. (a) The first-in, first-out (FIFO) method of process costing separates the costs of the beginning work-in-process inventory from the costs of current production. Current-period costs are divided by current-period equivalent units (EU) to determine the current period's manufacturing cost per EU.

5. (a) In the process, material G is added when a batch is 60% complete. Since the ending work-in-process (WIP) units are only 50% complete, they have not reached the stage of production where material G is added. Therefore, we do not assume that there are any equivalent units (EU) of material G in the ending WIP units. On the other hand, conversion costs (i.e., direct labor and manufacturing overhead) are assumed to be incurred evenly throughout the process. Therefore, the ending WIP units are assumed to be 50% complete as to conversion costs. Note that the answer to this question is not dependent on whether the weighted-average method or the FIFO method of process costing is used. Both of these methods use the EU in the ending WIP units to compute the EU of production of the period.

6. (d) Under the FIFO method of process costing, the costs of the beginning work-in-process (WIP) are separated from the cost of current production. Therefore, in the computation of equivalent units (EU) for the period under FIFO, the EU in beginning WIP are subtracted. In the weighted-average method, all costs (including that of beginning WIP) are lumped together and a single cost of EU of production is computed. Thus, for any period for which there is a beginning WIP, EU for the weighted-average method will exceed the EU for the FIFO method by the number of EU in beginning WIP. Since there was no WIP at January 1, both methods yield the same results in January. However, since there was WIP at February 1, the number of EU is greater for the weighted-average method in February.

Spoilage

7. (a) Job 10 unit cost = $1,580/200 = $7.90.

	Original cost accumulation	Rework costs	Total costs
Direct materials	$ 330	$ 50	$ 380
Direct labor	400	80	480
Factory overhead			
(150% of DL)	600	120	720
Total	$1,330	$250	$1,580

8. (d) Normal spoilage is considered as a necessary cost of production. Therefore, the $60,000

normal spoilage cost is treated as a product or inventoriable cost. The $30,000 in abnormal spoilage cost is treated as a period cost because this cost is not usually incurred in making the product.

9.　(c)　The weighted average method treats partially completed units in the beginning work-in-process inventory as if they were started and completed in the current period. Normal spoilage is treated as a normal cost of production, and the cost of spoilage is transferred to the second production department. The equivalent units (EUs) of production for purposes of determining the costs to be transferred also include the spoiled units. The conversion cost per EU is $9.00 ($85,500 / 9,500). $9.00 × 7,500 = $67,500.

Units completed and transferred	7,000
Spoiled units	500
Ending work-in-process (2,500 × 80%)	2,000
Equivalent units of production	9,500

Beginning WIP conversion costs	$10,000
Conversion costs added during May	75,500
Total conversion costs	$85,500

Joint Product Costing

10.　(c)　As Ajac has 80% of net realizable value [($80,000 − $8,000) / ($120,000 − $30,000) = 80%], it is assigned 80% of joint cost. [$60,000 × 80% = $48,000]

11.　(c)　Sales price after further processing less the costs of further processing is assumed to be equal to the net sales value at the split-off point. Subtracting the cost to process further after the split-off point from the sales price would not equal joint costs or total costs because subtracting further processing costs from sales price would not equal costs. Such a difference would not equal the sales price less a normal profit margin.

By-Products

12.　(b)　There would be no effect on Kode Co.'s overall profit, but there will be an effect on the company's gross margin. The gross margin will be $1 higher for each unit of May sold if May is accounted for as a joint product rather than as a by-product. The reason is that selling expenses are not subtracted in arriving at overall gross margin. This problem is best illustrated with an example. Assume that the major product sells for $100 and costs $60 to make. If May is accounted for as a by-product, the overall gross margin is $43.

Sales		$100
Cost of major product	$60	
Less: Sale of May ($4 − $1)	(3)	
Cost of goods sold		57
Overall gross margin (by-product)		$ 43

If May is accounted for as a joint product, the overall gross margin is $44, although the overall profit is $43. Therefore, the overall gross margin will be $1 higher for each unit of May sold if May is accounted for as a joint product rather than as a by-product.

Sales ($100 + $4)	$104
Less: Cost of goods sold	(60)
Overall gross margin (joint product)	44
Less: Selling expense	(1)
Overall profit	$ 43

Service Costs

13.　(c)　Under the step method, costs are allocated from the service departments to other service departments and to the operating departments. In this case, the maintenance department costs must be allocated first because if the power department costs are allocated first, the answer doesn't appear in the options. Once costs are allocated from a service department, costs are not allocated back to that department. Neither can costs be allocated from a service department to the same service department based on a measure of service that such service department receives. Any percentage of use by the same service department or by a service department that already has had its costs allocated are ignored and new ratios must be computed using the relative usage of the remaining departments. The power department costs are allocated 2/(2 + 7) = 2 / 9 to the School of Education and 7/9 to the School of Technology.

	Maintenance	Power	School of Education	School of Technology
Costs	$ 99,000	$ 54,000		
Allocation of Maintenance Costs:				
2/10 × $99,000	(19,800)	19,800		
3/10 × $99,000	(29,700)		$29,700	
5/10 × $99,000	(49,500)			$ 49,500
Total Power Costs		73,800		
Allocation of Power Costs:				
2/9 × $73,800		(16,400)	16,400	
7/9 × $73,800		(57,400)		57,400
Totals	$　　0	$　　0	$46,100	$106,900

Activity-Based Costing

14.　(d)　Compared to traditional costing methods, ABC increases the number of cost drivers used in assigning overhead costs to products. It is appropriate whether costs are identified with specific units (job-order costing) or aggregated by departments or production phases (process costing).

15. (d) In such a system, costs are assigned to cost centers or cost pools and then to products using a volume basis. The most commonly used bases for allocating overhead are direct labor hours, direct labor cost, and machine hours. In an ABC system, costs are first charged to activities and then to products using cost drivers. Activities may be combined into homogeneous cost pools if the products consume the activities in the same proportion. Cost drivers should have a causal relationship to the incurrence of cost. Thus, in an ABC system there are usually more cost pools and more allocation bases (cost drivers). An ABC system is more complex, but generally it is more accurate than a traditional cost system.

16. (b) ABC assumes that creating production requires activities that consume resources. ABC allows for more complex relationships to be included in costing than traditional methods. An ABC system may use unit-, batch-, and plant-level drivers and both variable and fixed costs.

17. (c) Activity-based accounting systems have activities as the fundamental cost objects (they do not accumulate costs by department or function for purposes of product costing). Activity-based accounting systems use cost drivers as a basis for cost allocation (a cost driver is any factor whose effects cause an increase in the total cost of a related cost object). Under an activity-based accounting system, activities that do not add to the value of the product are identified and reduced to the extent possible.

18. (c) ABC systems have activities as the fundamental cost objects; they do not accumulate costs by department, or function for purposes of product costing. ABC systems identify cost drivers as a basis for cost allocation. No attempt is made to eliminate the cost drivers. A cost driver is any factor whose effects cause an increase in the total cost of a related cost object. Under an ABC system, activities that do not add to the value of the product are identified and eliminated to the extent possible.

19. (b) In an ABC system, costs are first assigned to activities based upon the costs those activities consume. Next, the costs are assigned to cost objects such as products based upon the activities those cost objects consume. For example, some costs are batch level costs, such as the cost to set up a machine. Other costs are related to volume. There may be various kinds of batch level costs related to different activities. ABC uses a multiple cause and

effect relationship in an attempt to arrive at the most accurate cost possible.

Standard Cost Concepts

20. (c) The expected total cost to process the papers is comprised of the expected variable and fixed costs of processing, given standard performance.

Standard variable cost of processing 1.6M papers	$ 1,280,000
Divide by: 1,600,000 papers	/ 1,600,000
Standard variable cost of processing one paper	0.80
Papers processed during period	× 1,200,000
Expected variable cost of processing 1.2M papers	960,000
Expected fixed cost of processing (given)	200,000
Expected total cost to process papers produced	$ 1,160,000

21. (d) Since there is no difference between the standard and actual labor rate, there is no labor rate variance. To determine the labor rate variance it is necessary to determine the standard rate and actual rate per labor hour.

Standard labor cost to process 1,000 papers	$	750
Standard labor hours to process 1,000 papers	/	150
Standard rate per labor hour	$	5.00
Labor cost incurred to process 1,200,000 papers		$950,000
Labor hours incurred to process 1,200,000 papers		/ 190,000
Actual rate per labor hour	$	5.00

22. (a) Standard costing is appropriate for mass production industries, as well as for service industries. Standard costing may be used in various types of companies in which repetitive tasks are performed in making and selling a product or in delivering a service.

23. (b) Engineering standards based on attainable performance is the best basis to use in establishing standard hours allowed because they reflect the costs that should be incurred under efficient operating conditions. Standards based on attainable performance are less stringent than those based on ideal performance because of allowance for normal spoilage, ordinary machine breakdowns, and lost time. However, standards based on attainable performance usually are set strict enough so that the achievement of standard performance is a satisfying accomplishment for the workers. The average historical performance for the past three years may contain many inefficiencies, which should not be permitted to influence future performance measurement. In addition, the past may not be reflective of current economic conditions, technology, and supply and demand characteristics. Engineering estimates based on ideal performance do not allow for imperfections or inefficiencies of any type. Standards based on ideal performance rarely, if ever, are attained. The production level to satisfy average consumer demand over a seasonal time span also should not be used.

24. (c) The predetermined factory overhead application rate is based on direct labor cost. Budgeted factory overhead was $300,000 and budgeted direct labor cost was $150,000 (25,000 DLH × $6.00) resulting in a predetermined factory overhead application rate of 200% ($300,000 / $150,000) of direct labor cost.

Factory overhead applied ($162,500 × 200%)	$325,000
Factory overhead incurred	310,000
Overapplied factory overhead	$ 15,000

25. (a) Cost of goods manufactured for May is determined by first adding the costs in beginning WIP, direct costs incurred during May, and OH applied; this is then reduced by ending WIP. Note that any over- or underapplied OH is closed to cost of goods sold; it is not reflected in cost of goods manufactured or ending WIP.

Beginning WIP	$ 9,000	
Direct materials	26,000	
Direct labor	20,000	
Applied OH ($20,000 × 150%)	30,000	
Total manufacturing costs applied		$85,000
Direct materials	2,800	
Direct labor	1,800	
Applied OH ($1,800 × 150%)	2,700	
Less ending WIP		(7,300)
Cost of goods manufactured		$77,700

26. (d) Hart does not allocate over- or underapplied OH to inventories and cost of goods sold. Thus, the entire $2,000 is charged to CGS.

Factory overhead incurred	$ 32,000
Factory overhead applied ($20,000 × 150%)	(30,000)
Underapplied overhead	$ 2,000

Prime Cost Variances

27. (d) To compute the amount of direct materials purchased in January, it is necessary to analyze the changes in the direct materials inventory.

Beg. inventory + Purchases = Materials used + End. inventory

$$\$15,000 + X = \$95,000 + \$20,000$$
$$X = \$100,000$$

28. (c) In computing the amount of direct-labor cost, it is necessary to isolate the costs that were applied during January. The cost-of-goods manufactured of $257,500 includes the $7,500 of cost in beginning WIP. Beginning WIP must be subtracted because it involves costs applied in a prior period. In the same respect, the $10,000 of costs of the ending WIP must be added in because such costs were applied in January. Now that the total costs applied in January are isolated, the amounts applied for direct materials used and factory overhead are subtracted, yielding $90,000 direct-labor costs ($260,000 − $75,000 − $95,000). It should be noted that the amount of actual factory overhead is *not* subtracted because any over- or underapplied overhead is closed to cost of goods sold at the *end* of the year.

Variances in OH Costs

29. (b) In the four-way analysis of factory overhead, the variable overhead efficiency variance is computed by multiplying the difference between the actual direct labor hours incurred and the standard direct labor hours (DLH) allowed for the units produced by the variable overhead rate (DLH).

Actual direct labor hours	10,500
Standard DLH allowed for quantity produced (5,000 units × 2 hours/unit)	10,000
Excess of actual DLH over standard DLH	500
Times: Variable overhead rate per standard DLH	× $3
Variable overhead efficiency variance (unfavorable)	$ 1,500

30. (c) In August, $9,000 ($1,500 + $5,000 + $2,500) of direct labor was added to jobs, so $18,000 ($9,000 × 2) of manufacturing overhead was applied, or $2,000 less than actual manufacturing overhead of $20,000.

Solution 53-2 ADDITIONAL MULTIPLE CHOICE ANSWERS

Job Order Costing

31. (b)

Beginning work-in-process		$ 4,000
Direct materials	$24,000	
Direct labor	16,000	
Factory overhead applied	12,800	
Manufacturing costs added during month		52,800
Manufacturing costs to account for		56,800
Less: Transfer to finished goods		48,000
Ending work-in-process—Job No. 5		8,800
Less: Direct labor (given)		(2,000)
Factory overhead applied		
($2,000 × 80%)		(1,600)
Direct materials charged to Job No. 5		$ 5,200

32. (a) In a job order cost system, use of direct materials previously purchased usually is recorded as an increase in the *WIP Control* account.

Work-in-Process Control—Job "x"	XX	
Stores Control		XX

33. (c) The predetermined factory overhead rate is determined by dividing the estimated factory overhead cost by the estimated level of activity. Underapplied overhead could result if the actual level of activity was less than the estimated level of activity used to determine the overhead rate. Underapplied overhead could also result if actual fixed costs were greater than the estimated fixed costs used to determine the overhead rate.

Process Costing

34. (d) In either a process or job order cost system, the application of factory overhead is usually recorded as an increase in the *Work-in-Process Control* account.

Work-in-Process Control—Job "x"	XX	
Factory Overhead Applied		XX

Finished Goods Inventory Control is increased when goods are completed. *Factory Overhead Control* is increased when factory overhead costs are incurred. Cost of goods sold is increased when finished goods are sold.

35. (d) The predetermined factory overhead application rate is computed by dividing the estimated factory overhead costs by the estimated level of activity, usually measured in direct labor hours, direct labor cost, or machine hours.

36. (c) The weighted-average method of process costing intermingles the costs in beginning work-in-process (WIP) inventory with the costs incurred in the current period. These costs are then allocated to all the equivalent units of production, including the equivalent units in beginning inventory. By contrast, the first-in, first-out (FIFO) method of process costing treats the beginning WIP as a separate batch.

37. (a) Under the weighted-average method, the equivalent units (EU) for conversion cost are determined by adding the EU of conversion cost embodied in the units completed and in ending WIP.

	Physical units	Percentage complete as to conversion cost	Equivalent units of conversion cost
Completed	10,000 ×	100%	10,000
Ending WIP	4,000 ×	75%	3,000
			13,000

38. (c) The weighted average method adds beginning inventory (BI) costs to current costs and allocates them across BI units plus currently started units. During the quarter, 550 [100 × (50% + 500)] equivalent finished units (EFU) are in process. Total quarter costs are BI costs plus costs added: $25,000 + $360,000 = $385,000. Cost per EFU is $385,000 / 550 EFU = $700/EFU. Ending inventory (EI) is 550 − 400 = 150 EFU. 150 EFU × $700 / EFU = $105,000.

39. (c) The weighted average method adds beginning inventory (BI) costs to current costs and allocates them across BI units plus currently started units. During the quarter, 550 [100 × (50% + 500)] equivalent finished units (EFU) are in process. Total quarter costs are BI costs plus costs added: $50,000 + $720,000 = $770,000. Cost per EFU is $770,000 / 550 EFU = $1,400/EFU. Ending inventory (EI) is 550 − 400 = 150 EFU. Alternatively, EI is calculated as 100 + 500 − 400 = 200; 200 units at 75% completion = 150 EFU. 150 EFU × $1,400 / EFU = $210,000.

40. (d) FIFO assumes the WIP beginning inventory, 100 units 50% complete, are among the 400 units completed during the quarter. That would use 50 equivalent finished units (EFU) of direct materials (DM). Of the 500 units started during the quarter, 300 EFU were completed, using 300 units of DM. Finally, 200 of the 500 units started were only 75% completed, using (75% × 200 units) 150 EFU of DM. Production units used during the quarter are 50 EFU to complete the original 100, plus 300 started & completed, plus the 150 EFU used to process 200 units to 75% of completion, for a total of 500 EFU. Divide the DM costs added during the quarter, $720,000, by the 500 EFU of DM used during the quarter, to get DM cost per unit, $1,440. 150 EFU's × $1,440 / EFU equals $216,000.

41. (a) Equivalent units (EU) of production are used in process costing to express a given number of partially completed units in terms of a smaller number of fully completed units. The EU of production for the inventories in question is 300 [i.e., (200 × 90%) + (100 × 80%) + (400 × 10%)].

42. (b) Assume the WIP beginning inventory, 100 units 50% complete, are among the 400 units completed during the quarter. That would use 50 equivalent units (EU) of direct materials. Of the 500 units started during the quarter, 300 were completed, using 300 units of direct materials (DM). Finally, 200 of the 500 units started were only 75% completed, using (75% × 200 units) 150 EU of DM. Production units used during the quarter would be 50 to complete the original 100, plus 300 started & completed during the quarter, plus the 150 used to process 200 units to 75% completion, for a total of 500 units. Notice that the dollar figures given in the question are irrelevant to the solution.

43. (c) Assuming no beginning work-in-process (WIP), the number of equivalent units (EU) as to conversion costs will be the sum of the number of units finished during the period, plus the product of multiplying the number of units in ending WIP by the percentage of completion of those units. Thus, the number of EU of conversion costs will be greater than the number of units finished, but less than the number of units initially placed in production.

44. (c) Calculation of stage of completion of work-in-process and equivalent units is somewhat complex; this can be confusing for some. Process costing is a cost accumulation method that aggregates product costs by departments or production phases, ensuring that material and labor are charged accurately to each job. Job-order costing is the accumulation of costs by specific jobs. Process costing facilitates determination of cost of goods sold on a unit basis; partial batches represent minimal incremental work to determine the cost of goods sold. Process costing typically involves less clerical work than job-order costing.

Spoilage

45. (b) The original production of 1,100 drills cost $16,500 (1,100 drills × $15/drill). The reworking of the 50 defective drills increased the cost total to $16,750. The $750 received from the sale of the 100 spoiled units should be subtracted from the total cost incurred in producing the 1,100 drills. Therefore, the total cost for producing 1,000 good drills equals $16,000 ($16,500 + $250 – $750).

46. (a) Scrap is the residue from manufacturing operations that has measurable but relatively minor recovery value. The sales value of scrap is usually recorded as a decrease to the *Factory Overhead Control* account. An alternative method in a job-cost situation would be to trace sales of scrap to the jobs that yielded the scrap and decrease the *Work-in-Process Control* account.

47. (a) Because defective units are identified when production is 40% complete, and all of the completed units and all of the work-in-process (WIP) units are past that point, all units should receive the same amount of spoilage cost. Because, at the end of the period, the number of WIP units equaled the number of completed units, the ending WIP should be allocated 50% of the defective unit costs.

48. (c) The cost of units produced usually includes scrap and normal spoilage, but not abnormal spoilage. *Scrap* is the residue from manufacturing operations that has measurable but relatively minor recovery value. The sales value of scrap is *usually* recorded as a decrease to the *Factory Overhead Control* account (although it is important to note that an alternative in a job order cost situation would be to trace sales of scrap to the job that yielded the scrap and decrease the *Work-in-Process Control* account). The cost of the units produced should include *normal spoilage* because it is an inherent result of the particular process; it was expected to occur under efficient operating conditions. On the other hand, *abnormal spoilage* is not inventoried because it is not an inherent result of the selected production process; it was not expected to be incurred under efficient operating conditions.

Joint Product Costing

49. (d) The market values of joint products P and Q at split-off are used to allocate their joint costs. If the market value of P at split-off increases, while the market value of Q at split-off remains unchanged, the relative market value at split-off increases for P and decreases for Q. Thus, more of the joint product costs would be allocated to P and less would be allocated to Q. Since the separable costs and the final selling prices of P and Q remain constant, the gross margin of P would decrease due to its increased allocation of joint costs, and the gross margin of Q would increase due to its decreased allocation of joint costs.

50. (d) When the actual sales values at the split-off point for joint products are not known, joint costs are allocated on the basis of each product's net realizable value. Net realizable value is the excess of the product's sales value less costs beyond the split-off point. Since the selling prices of products Y

and Z remain constant, and the costs beyond the split-off point increase for product Z, its net realizable value decreases. Less joint costs will be allocated to product Z and more will be allocated to product Y.

51. (b) The joint costs (in 1,000's) are allocated as follows.

	Total sales value	Costs beyond split-off	NRV at split-off	%	Joint costs to allocate	Joint costs allocated
BEC	$ 80	$25	$ 55	55%	$30	$16.5
CAL	80	35	45	45	30	13.5
	$160	$60	$100	100%		$30.0

By-Products

52. (a) There are two general approaches to accounting for the value of by-products. First of all, the value of by-products may be recognized at the time of production. Under this approach, the net realizable value of the by-products produced is deducted from the cost of the major products produced. Alternatively, the value of the by-products may be recognized at the time of sale. Under this approach, the net revenue from the by-products sold is deducted from the cost of the major products sold.

53. (c) Subtracting the net realizable value (NRV) of Bef (i.e., $9,000 – $5,000) from the joint cost of $54,000 leaves $50,000 to be allocated to products Kul and Ju. Kul's portion of this cost is computed as follows.

$$\text{Sales value} - \text{Additional cost} = \text{NRV}$$
$$\$40,000 - \$0 = \$40,000$$

$$\text{NRV ratio} \times \text{Joint cost} = \text{Allocated portion}$$
$$40/(40+60) \times \$50,000 = \underline{\$20,000}$$

54. (a) Net realizable value (NRV) is the estimated selling price of an inventory item less the estimated costs that will be incurred in preparing the item for sale and selling it. Since the inventory in question was recorded at net realizable value when produced, no profit will be recognized on its sale.

Selling price per unit		$6.00
Less: Selling costs per unit	$2.00	
Carrying amount per unit ($6.00 – $2.00)	4.00	6.00
Profit recognized on each unit at time of sale		$ 0

55. (d) Mig accounts for the by-product at the time of production, whereby the net realizable value (i.e., sales value less additional costs) of the by-product is deducted from the total cost of production of the main product. This method directly matches the cost-reduction power of the by-product to the production costs of the main product. No cost of sales is reported for the gasoline by-product because its NRV is deducted from the total cost of production of the gasoline.

Total production costs to split-off point (i.e., the joint product costs)	$120,000
Less: Net realizable value of by-product [$30,000 – ($15,000 + $10,000)]	5,000
Net production costs of gasoline	115,000
Less: Gasoline inventory, ending	15,000
Cost of sales for gasoline	$100,000

Standard Cost Concepts

56. (c) A standard cost system is one whereby costs are charged to work-in-process on the basis of predetermined standard rates. Standard costs may be applied to a single unit as in job order costing or to many units as in process costing.

57. (a) The overhead volume variance is a measure of the utilization of available plant facilities; it does not measure the efficient use of inputs used in production. The volume variance is considered to be beyond the immediate control of a production supervisor because it is an activity-related variance that is explainable only by activity and is controllable only by activity—which is often geared to anticipated sales. Efficiency variances (e.g., overhead efficiency, labor efficiency, and material usage) measure the difference between the quantity of inputs that should have been used at the actual output level achieved and the quantity of inputs that were actually used. Efficiency variances are considered to be controllable by a production supervisor.

58. (d) The under (over) applied overhead should be prorated to the balances of work-in-process, finished goods, and cost of goods sold.

	Dec. 31 unadjusted balance	%	% × under-applied overhead	Dec. 31 adjusted balance
Cost of goods sold	$ 900,000	75	$41,250	$ 941,250
Finished goods	100,000	8 1/3	4,583	104,583
Work-in-process	200,000	16 2/3	9,167	209,167
	$1,200,000	100	$55,000	$1,255,000

59. (a)

Standard manufacturing costs	$100,000
Add: Excess of actual manufacturing costs over standard costs	20,000
Actual manufacturing (conversion) costs	120,000
Actual prime manufacturing costs	80,000
Actual manufacturing overhead costs, April	$ 40,000

60. (c) The relationships in the three-variance method for analyzing factory overhead are identified below.

Actual Factory overhead incurred	Budget allowance based on actual hours	Budget allowance based on standard hours	Factory overhead applied
ʌ	ʌ	ʌ	ʌ
	Spending variance	Efficiency variance	Volume variance

The spending variance is affected by (1) price increases over what was shown in the flexible budget and (2) waste or excessive usage of overhead materials. Since the spending variance represents the difference between the actual factory overhead incurred and the budget allowance based on actual hours, waste will automatically show up as part of this variance, along with any excessive prices paid for overhead items. Generally the price element in this variance will be small, so the variance permits a focusing of attention on that thing over which the supervisor probably has the greatest control—the usage of overhead in production. On the other hand, the volume variance is a measure of utilization of available plant facilities; it does not measure over- or underspending. Most companies consider the volume variance to be beyond immediate control because it is an activity-related variance that is explainable only by activity and is controllable only by activity—which often is geared to anticipated sales.

61. (d) An unfavorable variance exists when actual cost exceeds standard cost. Since Baby Frames actually overspent the fixed overhead budget by $2,000, the spending variance is $2,000 unfavorable.

62. (a) Fount should apply factory overhead based on the equivalent units of production, the standard direct-labor hours (DLH) per unit, and the overhead rate. The overhead rate is the total overhead that is budgeted divided by the normal capacity.

Equivalent units (EU) of product	4,750
Standard direct-labor hours per EU	× 2
Standard direct-labor hours	9,500
Overhead rate ($80,000/10,000 DLH)	× $8
Applied factory overhead	$76,000

63. (a) Whenever levels of production change, cost variances should be calculated based on a flexible budget. Standard costing allows control over variances from actual costs to standard flexible budget cost at the appropriate level of production.

Prime Cost Variances

64. (b) The material price variance (MPV) is equal to the difference between the actual price and the standard price times the actual quantity purchased: MPV = (AP – SP) AQ. The actual price is $2.40 ($10,080 / 4,200). MPV = ($2.40 – $2.50) × 4,200 = ($420). The cost variance is considered favorable because the actual cost is less than the standard cost.

65. (b)

Actual direct labor hours	4,100
Standard direct labor hours (1,000 × 4 DLH)	4,000
Excess of actual over standard direct labor hours	100
Times: Standard direct labor rate	× $12
Direct labor efficiency variance—Unfavorable	$1,200

66. (a)

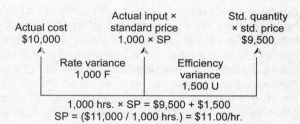

$$1,000 \text{ hrs.} \times SP = \$9,500 + \$1,500$$
$$SP = (\$11,000 / 1,000 \text{ hrs.}) = \$11.00/\text{hr.}$$

67. (d) The labor efficiency variance is $800 unfavorable and the standard rate per direct labor hour (DLH) is $8.00; thus, 100 ($800 / $8) DLH were incurred above the 2,000 standard DLH allowed for actual production. Actual hours worked were 2,100 hours (2,000 + 100).

68. (a)

Weekly wages per worker	$ 500
Number of productive hours per week per worker	/ 40
Hourly wage	12.50
Add: Workers' benefits treated as direct labor cost ($12.50 × 20%)	2.50
Direct labor cost per productive hour	15.00
Times: DLH required to produce one unit	× 2
Standard direct labor cost per unit	$30.00

69. (b) If the company follows a practice of isolating variances at the earliest point in time, a direct material price variance will be isolated at purchase time. This is the earliest time at which the company knows that the actual price differs from its standard price.

2-Variance OH Method

70. (b) This diagram identifies the relationships in the two-variance method for analyzing factory overhead.

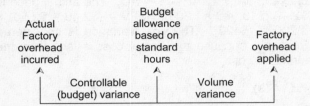

The controllable (budget) variance consists of both variable and fixed overhead elements. The amount of the variable overhead element included in the actual factory overhead incurred (i.e., the actual variable overhead incurred) and that included in the flexible budget based on standard hours allowed (i.e., the variable overhead rate multiplied by the standard hours allowed) differ. The amount of the fixed overhead element included in the actual factory overhead incurred (i.e., the actual fixed overhead incurred) and that included in the flexible budget based on standard hours allowed (i.e., the original estimate of budgeted fixed overhead for the period) also differ. On the other hand, the volume variance consists only of a fixed overhead element. The amount of the variable overhead element included in the flexible budget based on standard hours allowed is the same as that included in the amount of factory overhead applied (i.e., the variable overhead rate multiplied by the standard hours allowed). On the other hand, the amount of the fixed overhead element included in the flexible budget based on standard hours allowed (i.e., the original estimate of budgeted fixed overhead for the period) differs from the amount of the fixed factory overhead included in the amount of factory overhead applied (i.e., the fixed overhead rate multiplied by the standard hours allowed).

71. (a) The volume (denominator) variance in either the two-, three-, or four-way analysis of overhead can be computed as the difference between the budgeted fixed overhead and the fixed overhead applied to production.

Budgeted fixed overhead	$37,500
Standard DLHs allowed for actual production	12,000
Standard fixed overhead rate per DLH	$ 3.00
Fixed overhead applied to production	36,000
Volume (denominator) variance (unfavorable)	$ 1,500

The volume variance is unfavorable because the company operated at an activity level (12,000 DLH) below that planned for the period [12,500 DLH (i.e., $37,500 / $3.00)].

72. (d) The budget allowance based on standard hours is used in the computation of the controllable (budget) variance. The budget allowance based on actual hours is not used in the two-variance method of analyzing factory overhead. The following diagram identifies relationships in the two-variance method of analyzing factory overhead.

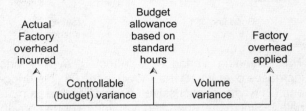

73. (c) The difference between the budget allowance based on standard hours allowed and the factory overhead applied to production is the volume variance. (Also see the diagram in the explanation to question #72.)

74. (a) The budget (controllable) variance is the difference between the actual OH incurred and the budgeted OH based on the standard costs for the attained capacity. The actual OH incurred was $73,500. Total OH is 12 hours × $6.50/hr. = $78,000. Variable OH is $78,000 − $54,000 = $24,000 and the variable OH rate is $24,000 / 12,000 hr. = $2/hr. Thus, the total OH for the attained capacity is 10,500/hr. × $2/hr. + $54,000 = $75,000. Thus, the actual OH incurred was $1,500 less than the budgeted OH for the capacity attained.

75. (d) The variable overhead efficiency variance is the difference between the actual quantity (AQ) of inputs in units and the standard quantity (SQ) of inputs in units for the outputs achieved (19,000 × 0.1 = 1,900) times the standard price per unit. [(2,100 − 1,900) × $2 = $400] As AQ is greater than SQ, the variance is unfavorable.

76. (b) The production volume variance is the budgeted fixed overhead (FOH) less the FOH units for output achieved times the budgeted FOH rate. $20,000 − (19,000 × $1) = $1,000. As AQ of inputs is greater than SQ of inputs, the variance is unfavorable.

3-Variance OH Method

77. (d) The fixed overhead budget variance in the four-way analysis of overhead is computed as the difference between the budgeted fixed overhead and the actual fixed overhead incurred. The fixed overhead budget variance is favorable because less fixed overhead was incurred than was budgeted.

Budgeted fixed overhead (100,000 units × $4/unit)	$ 400,000
Actual fixed overhead incurred (given)	(384,000)
Fixed overhead budget variance (favorable)	$ 16,000

78. (b)

$$\text{Variable FOH spending variance} = \text{Actual VFOH} - \begin{array}{c}\text{Flexible budget based on actual inputs} \\ \times \text{ application rate}\end{array}$$

$$\text{Standard direct labor hours per unit} = \frac{200,000 \text{ hrs.}}{100,000 \text{ units}} = 2 \text{ hrs./unit}$$

$$\text{Application rate per DLH} = \frac{\$6}{2} = \$3 \text{ per DLH}$$

$$\begin{array}{c}\text{Flexible budget based on actual input}\end{array} \times \begin{array}{c}\text{Application rate}\end{array} = 160,000 \text{ hours} \times \frac{\$3}{\text{per hour}} = \$480,000$$

$$\text{Variable FOH spending variance} = \$500,000 - \$480,000 = \mathbf{\$20,000}$$

79. (a)

$$\begin{aligned}\text{FOH Volume Variance} &= \text{Budgeted FOH} - \text{Applied FOH} \\ &= (100,000 \times \$4) - (76,000 \times \$4) \\ &= \$400,000 - \$304,000 \\ &= \underline{\$96,000} \text{ Unfavorable}\end{aligned}$$

80. (d) Actual factory overhead and the budget allowance based on actual hours are used to determine the spending variance under the three-variance method for analyzing factory overhead. The relationships in the three-variance method for analyzing factory overhead are identified below:

Actual Factory overhead incurred	Budget allowance based on actual hours	Budget allowance based on standard hours	Factory overhead applied
↑	↑	↑	↑
Spending variance	Efficiency variance	Volume variance	

81. (a) Under the three-way analysis of overhead, the spending variance is computed as the difference between the amount of actual factory overhead (FOH) incurred and the amount of FOH budgeted for the actual hours incurred. The spending variance is favorable because less FOH was incurred than that budgeted for the actual direct labor hours (DLH) incurred.

Actual factory overhead (given)		$30,000
Actual DLH incurred	7,000	
Times: Variable FOH per DLH	× $2.50	
Budgeted variable FOH for actual DLH	17,500	
Budgeted fixed FOH (given)	14,000	
Budgeted FOH for actual DLH		31,500
Spending variance (favorable)		$ 1,500

82. (a) Under the three-way analysis of overhead, the efficiency variance is computed as the difference between the amount of budgeted factory overhead (FOH) for the actual hours incurred and the amount of budgeted FOH for the standard hours allowed. The efficiency variance is favorable because less FOH is budgeted at the actual hours incurred than that for the standard hours allowed.

Actual DLH incurred	7,000	
Times: Variable FOH rate per DLH	× $2.50	
Budgeted variable FOH for actual DLH	17,500	
Budgeted fixed FOH (given)	14,000	
Budgeted FOH for actual DLH		$31,500
Standard DLH	7,600	
Times: Variable FOH rate per DLH	× $2.50	
Budgeted variable FOH for DLH	19,000	
Budgeted fixed FOH (given)	14,000	
Budgeted FOH for allowed DLH		33,000
Efficiency variance (favorable)		$ 1,500

83. (c) The spending variance is **not** affected by the activity level selected for applying overhead because the computation of the spending variance involves the comparison of standard variable overhead costs and actual variable overhead costs, holding quantity constant at the actual quantity used. The volume variance results when the actual activity level differs from the budgeted quantity used in determining the fixed overhead application rate. If the application rate had been based on 100% capacity rather than 80%, a lower application rate would have resulted. Because the volume variance was unfavorable at an 80% level of application, standard production must have been lower than 80% of capacity. The lower application rate based on 100% would have made the underapplication of fixed costs even greater.

PERFORMANCE BY SUBTOPICS

Each category below parallels a subtopic covered in Chapter 53. Record the number and percentage of questions you correctly answered in each subtopic area.

Job Order Costing

Question #	Correct	√
1		
2		
# Questions	2	
# Correct		
% Correct		

Process Costing

Question #	Correct	√
3		
4		
5		
6		
# Questions	4	
# Correct		
% Correct		

Spoilage

Question #	Correct	√
7		
8		
9		
# Questions	3	
# Correct		
% Correct		

Joint Product Costing

Question #	Correct	√
10		
11		
# Questions	2	
# Correct		
% Correct		

By-Products

Question #	Correct	√
12		
# Questions	1	
# Correct		
% Correct		

Service Costs

Question #	Correct	√
13		
# Questions	1	
# Correct		
% Correct		

Activity-Based Costing

Question #	Correct	√
14		
15		
16		
17		
18		
19		
# Questions	6	
# Correct		
% Correct		

Standard Cost Concepts

Question #	Correct	√
20		
21		
22		
23		
24		
25		
26		
# Questions	7	
# Correct		
% Correct		

Prime Cost Variances

Question #	Correct	√
27		
28		
# Questions	2	
# Correct		
% Correct		

Variances in OH Costs

Question #	Correct	√
29		
30		
# Questions	2	
# Correct		
% Correct		

SIMULATION SOLUTIONS

Solution 53-3

Response #1: Variances & Graphs (2 points)

1. U

The direct labor rate variance is unfavorable because the direct labor cost incurred for the actual direct labor hours incurred was more than the amount that would have been incurred if the actual direct labor hours had been incurred at the standard direct labor hour rate. This can be determined by noting where lines drawn from the following points intersect the direct labor cost axis: (1) Point A and (2) the point where a line drawn from Point A intersects line OW (a point we will now refer to as Point Z). Actual direct labor cost incurred is determined where the line drawn from Point A intersects the direct labor cost axis. The standard direct labor cost allowed for the actual hours incurred is determined where the line drawn from Point Z intersects the direct labor hours axis (i.e., the point at which the line drawn from Point A intersects line OW represents the actual direct labor hours incurred at the standard direct labor hour rate; since line OW represents the standard labor cost at any output volume, all points on line OW are a function of the standard direct labor hour rate). Since the line drawn from Point A intersects the direct labor cost axis further away from the origin than the line drawn from Point Z, the direct labor cost incurred for the actual direct labor hours incurred was more than the amount that would have been incurred if the actual direct labor hours had been incurred at the standard direct labor hour rate.

2. F

The direct labor efficiency variance is favorable because the actual direct labor hours incurred were less than the direct labor hours allowed for the output achieved. This can be easily determined by noting where lines drawn from Points A and S intersect the direct labor hour axis. Actual direct labor hours incurred is determined where the line drawn from Point A intersects the direct labor hours axis. Standard direct labor hours allowed for the output achieved is determined where the line drawn from Point S intersects the direct labor hours axis. Since the line drawn from Point A intersects the direct labor hours axis closer to the origin than the line drawn from Point S, the actual direct labor hours incurred were less than the direct labor hours allowed for the output achieved.

Response #2: Variances & Graphs (3 points)

1. F

At volume V, overhead cost applied (shown on Line OA) exceeds budgeted overhead costs (shown on Line DB). Therefore, more overhead was applied than was budgeted and the volume variance is favorable.

2. U

Actual machine hours (Point S) exceed standard hours allowed for good production (Point V); therefore, the efficiency variance is unfavorable.

3. D

Line DB depicts the factory overhead flexible budget line. At zero volume, Point O, no variable costs are budgeted. Thus, Line DO represents budgeted fixed costs. Fixed costs are budgeted to remain constant in total within the relevant range, regardless of changes in volume. Therefore, budgeted variable costs at Point C are equal to total budgeted costs at Point C (Line BC) less budgeted fixed costs at Point C (Line DO).

———————————————

Solution 53-4

Response: Direct Material Variances (5 points)

1. U

The January material price variance is unfavorable because the actual cost incurred for the actual materials pounds used is greater than the amount that would have been incurred if the actual materials pounds used had been purchased at their standard price. This can be determined by noting where horizontal lines drawn from the following points intersect the total material cost axis: (1) Point Ja and (2) the point where a vertical line drawn from Point Ja intersects line OP (a point we will now refer to as Z). Actual total material cost is determined where the horizontal line drawn from Point Ja intersects the total material cost axis. Standard total material cost for the actual materials pounds used is determined where the horizontal line drawn from Point Z intersects the total material cost axis (i.e., the point at which the vertical line drawn from Point Ja intersects line OP represents actual materials pounds used at standard price; since line OP represents standard material cost at any output volume, all points on line OP are a function of the standard price of the material). Since the horizontal line drawn from Point Ja intersects the total material cost axis further away from the origin than the horizontal line drawn from Point Z, actual material cost is more than the amount that would have been incurred if the actual materials pounds used had been acquired at their standard price. Hence, the January material price variance is unfavorable.

2. F

The January material usage variance is favorable because actual materials pounds used is less than standard materials pounds allowed for the output volume achieved. This can be easily seen by noting where vertical lines drawn from Points Ja and V intersect the materials pounds axis. Actual materials pounds is determined where the vertical line from Point Ja intersects the materials pounds axis. Standard materials pounds allowed for the output volume achieved is determined where the vertical line drawn from Point V intersects the materials pounds axis. Since the vertical line drawn from Point Ja intersects the materials pounds axis closer to the origin than the vertical line drawn from Point V, actual materials pounds used is less than standard materials pounds allowed for the output volume achieved. Hence, the January material usage variance is favorable.

3. U

The February material price variance is unfavorable because the actual cost incurred for the actual materials pounds used is greater than the amount that would have been incurred if the actual materials pounds used had been purchased at their standard price. This can be determined by noting where horizontal lines drawn from the following points intersect the total material cost axis: (1) Point Fe and (2) the point where a vertical line drawn from Point Fe intersects line OP (a point we will now refer to as S). Actual total material cost is determined where the horizontal line drawn from Point Fe intersects the total material cost axis. Standard total material cost for the actual materials pounds used is determined where the horizontal line drawn from Point S intersects the total material cost axis (i.e., the point at which the vertical line drawn from Point Fe intersects line OP represents actual materials pounds used at standard price; since line OP represents standard material cost at any output volume, all points on line OP are a function of the standard price of the material). Since the horizontal line drawn from Point Fe intersects the total material cost axis further away from the origin than the horizontal line drawn from Point S, actual material cost is more than the amount that would have been incurred if the actual material pounds used had been acquired at their standard

price. Hence, the February material price variance is unfavorable.

4. U

The February material usage variance is unfavorable because actual materials pounds used is greater than standard materials pounds allowed for the output volume achieved. This can be easily seen by noting where vertical lines drawn from Points Fe and V intersect the materials pounds axis.

Actual material pounds is determined where the vertical line from Point Fe intersects the materials pounds axis. Standard materials pounds allowed for the output volume achieved is determined where the vertical line drawn from Point V intersects the materials pounds axis. Since the vertical line drawn from Point Fe intersects the materials pounds axis further away from the origin than the vertical line drawn from Point V, actual materials pounds used is greater than standard materials pounds allowed for the output volume achieved. Hence, the February material usage variance is unfavorable.

5. F

The March material net variance is favorable because Point Ma (actual material cost incurred in March) is below the horizontal line drawn through Point V which represents the standard cost for the output volume achieved in March.

Solution 53-5

Response: Budgets & Standard Costs (5 points)

1. BD

Budgeted variable cost is the line which begins at the origin that is below and parallel to the budgeted cost line. Budgeted cost is comprised of budgeted variable cost and budgeted fixed cost. At volume OE, budgeted cost is represented by the line BE and budgeted variable cost is represented by line DE. Thus, budgeted fixed cost at volume OE is represented by line BD.

2. DE

Budgeted variable cost is the line which begins at the origin that is below and parallel to the budgeted cost line. At volume OE, budgeted variable cost is represented by line DE.

3. AC

Standard gross profit is the difference between revenue and standard cost. At volume OE, revenue is represented by line AE and standard cost is represented by line CE. Thus, standard gross profit at volume OE is represented by line AC.

4. AB

Budgeted gross profit is the difference between revenue and budgeted cost. At volume OE, revenue is represented by line AE and budgeted cost is represented by line BE. Thus, budgeted gross profit at volume OE is represented by line AB.

5. OG

Normal capacity is the point at which standard costs equal budgeted costs since standard costs are determined by dividing budgeted costs by normal volume. As these costs are equal at point I, normal capacity is represented by line OG.

Solution 53-6

Response #1: Job Order Journal Entries (8 points)

| 1 | Stores Control | 220,000 | |
| | Accounts Payable | | 220,000 |

| 2 | Work-in-Process Control | 170,000 | |
| | Stores Control | | 170,000 |

| 3 | Stores Control | 5,000 | |
| | Work-in-Process Control | | 5,000 |

| 4 | Factory Overhead Control | 18,000 | |
| | Stores Control | | 18,000 |

5/6	Work-in-Process Control	150,000	
	Factory Overhead Control	40,000	
	Accrued Factory Payroll		190,000

Note: Nos. 5 & 6 may be shown as separate or combined entries.

| 7 | Factory Overhead Control | 11,000 | |
| | Accumulated Depreciation | | 11,000 |

| 8 | Factory Overhead Control | 25,000 | |
| | Misc. Payables, Cash, Etc. | | 25,000 |

| 9 | Work-in-Process Control | 90,000 | |
| | Factory Overhead Applied | | 90,000 |

| 10 | Finished Goods Control | 305,000 | |
| | Work-in-Process Control | | 305,000 |

| 11 | Accounts Receivable | 320,000 | |
| | Sales | | 320,000 |

| 12 | Cost of Goods Sold | 260,000 | |
| | Finished Goods Control | | 260,000 |

Response #2: T-Accounts (2 points)

Factory Overhead Control		Factory Overhead Applied	
(4) 18,000			90,000 (9)
(6) 40,000			
(7) 11,000			
(8) 25,000			
94,000			90,000

Note: The numbers in the T-accounts in parentheses refer to the journal entries in Response #1.

Factory Overhead Applied	90,000	
Cost of Goods Sold	4,000	
Factory Overhead Control		94,000

To close the manufacturing overhead accounts to cost of goods sold.

Solution 53-7

Response #1: FIFO, Multiple Departments (4 points)

1. $4.50

The total cost of ending WIP is $9,000. The unit cost of ending WIP is calculated as follows: $9,000 / 2,000 units = $4.50.

2. $9,000

3. $8.00 / unit

The total cost of finished goods is $8,000. The unit cost of finished goods is $8,000 / 1,000 units = $8.00. Also see Step Four in the explanation to item #4.

4. $8,000

The following explanation pertains to all of Response #1.

Step One: Calculate the physical flow in units.

	Units		Units
Beginning WIP	0	Units completed	1,000
Units started	3,000	Ending WIP (40% complete)	2,000
Units to account for	3,000	Units accounted for	3,000

Step Two: Compute the equivalent units of production.

	Equivalent Units					
	Prior Dept.		Conversion		Material	
Units completed	(1K × 100%)	1,000	(1K × 100%)	1,000	(1K × 100%)	1,000
Ending WIP	(2K × 100%)	2,000	(2K × 40%)	800	(2K × 0%)	0
WA EU		3,000		1,800		1,000
Begining WIP		0		0		0
FIFO EU		3,000		1,800		1,000

Step Three: Determine total costs.

	Beginning WIP costs	Current costs	Total costs
Prior department costs	$-0-	$ 7,500	$ 7,500
Conversion costs	-0-	9,000	9,000
Material costs	-0-	500	500
Total costs	$-0-	$17,000	$17,000

Step Four: Calculate equivalent unit cost.

	Current costs	FIFO EU divisor	Equivalent unit cost
Prior department costs	$ 7,500	3,000	$2.50
Conversion costs	9,000	1,800	5.00
Material costs	500	1,000	0.50
Total costs	$17,000		$8.00

Step Five: Allocate total costs between work-in-process and finished goods.

	Total costs
Ending WIP prior department costs (2,000 units × 100% × $2.50/unit)	$ 5,000
Ending WIP conversion costs (2,000 units × 40% × $5.00/unit)	4,000
Ending WIP material costs (2,000 units × 0% × $0.50 unit)	0
Ending WIP costs	$ 9,000

	Total costs
Total costs	$17,000
Less: Ending WIP costs	9,000
Cost of finished goods	$ 8,000

---

1. $375

2. $525

Product	Sales value at split-off	% of Total	Allocated joint costs
Y	$1,000	10/24	$375
Z	1,400	14/24	525
	$2,400		$900

Solution 53-8

Response #1: Variance Calculation (7 points)

1. $25 U

Price difference ($2.25 – $2.00)	$ 0.25	
Actual quantity	× 100	
Material price variance (AP – SP) AQ	$ 25	Unf.

2. $80 U

Quantity difference (100 – 60)	40	
Standard price	×$ 2	
Material quantity variance (AQ – SQ)SP	$ 80	Unf.

Note: AP = $225 / 100 = $2.25/unit; SQ = 20 units × 3 lbs. = 60 lbs.

3. $3.00 U

Rate difference ($4.10 – $4.00)	$ 0.10	
Actual quantity	× 30	
Labor rate variance (AP – SP)AQ	$ 3.00	Unf.

4. $240 F

Quantity difference (30 – 40)	(10)	
Standard rate	×$ 4	
Labor efficiency variance (AQ – SQ)SP	$ (40)	Fav.

Note: SQ = 20 units × 2 hrs/unit = 40 hrs

5. $40 U

Actual overhead ($45 + $115)	$ 160	
Overhead appl.(SQ × SP = 40 × $3)	(120)	
Total net overhead variance (under-applied)	$ 40	Unf.

6. $15 U

Cost difference [($45 ÷ 30) – $1	$ 0.50	
Actual variable overhead hrs.	× 30	
Variable OH spending variance (AP – SP)AQ	$ 15	Unf.

7. $10 F

Quantity difference (30 – 40)	$ (10)	
Standard cost	×$ 1	
Variable OH efficiency variance (AQ – SQ)SP	$ (10)	Fav.

8. $15 U

Actual fixed overhead	$ 15	
Budgeted fixed overhead (50 × $2)	(100)	
Fixed OH budget variance (actual – budgeted)	$ 15	Unf.

9. $20 U

Budgeted fixed overhead		$ 100
Applied fixed overhead (20 × 2 × $2)		(80)
Fixed OH volume variance (budgeted – applied)		$ 20 Unf.

10. $20 U

Budget based on standard		$ 100
Applied (20 × 2 × $2)		(80)
Volume variance (fixed OH denominator variance)		$ 20 Unf.

11. $20 U

Actual		$ 160
Fixed	$100	
Variable (20 × 2 × $1)	40	
Budget based on standard		(140)
Controllable (budget) variance		$ 20 Unf.

12. $20 U

Budget based on standard		$ 140
Applied (40 × $3)		(120)
Volume variance		$ 20 Unf.

13. $10 F

Budget based on actual		$ 130
Budget based on standard		(140)
Efficiency variance		$ (10) Fav.

14. $30 U

Actual		$ 160
Fixed	$100	
Variable (30 × $1)	30	
Budget based on actual		(130)
Spending Variance		$ 30 Unf.

_____

Response #2: Standard Cost Journal Entries (3 points)

Stores Control (AQ × DP), 100 × $2	200	
Direct Material Price Variance (U)	25	
Cash, A/P (AQ × AP) (100 × $2.25)		225

To record acquisition of direct materials and record related price variances.

Work-in-Process (SQ × SP), 60 × $2	120	
Direct Material Quantity Variance (U)	80	
Stores Control (AQ × SP), 100 × $2		200

To charge WIP for DM (at std.) and to record DM quantity variance.

Work-in-Process		
(40 std. hrs. × $4 std. DL rate)	160	
Direct Labor Rate Variance (U)	3	
Factory Wages Payable		
(30 actual hrs. × $4.10 actual rate)		123
Direct Labor Efficiency Variance (F)		40

To charge WIP for DL (at std.) and record DL rate and efficiency variances.

Work-in-Process		
(40 std. DLH × $3 std. OH rate)	120	
Overhead Variance (U)	40	
Overhead Control (Actual)		
($45 + $115)		160

To charge WIP for OH (standard).

Finished Goods (20 units × $20 / unit)	400	
Work-in-Process		400

To transfer WIP to finished goods inventory.

_____

Updating Supplements

Bisk Education's updating supplements are small publications available from either customer representatives or our CPA review website (http://www.cpaexam.com/content/support.asp). The editors recommend checking the website for new supplements a month and again a week before your exam. Version 35 (and higher) updating supplements are appropriate for candidates with the 35th edition. Information from earlier supplements (for instance, Version 34.2) are incorporated into this edition. Supplements are issued no more frequently than every three months. Supplements are not necessarily issued every three months; supplements are issued only as information appropriate for supplements becomes available.

The BEC exam section currently does not have simulations. The AICPA plans to have BEC simulations at a future undisclosed date. This date likely will be no earlier than 2007. Bisk Education's updating supplements will notify candidates when simulations will be on the BEC exam section.

CHAPTER 54

PLANNING & CONTROL

EXAM COVERAGE: The *Planning and Management* portion of the BEC section of the CPA exam is designated by the examiners to be 22 to 28 percent of the section's point value. Candidates should plan their use of study time accordingly. More information about the point value of various topics is included in the **Practical Advice** section of this volume.

CHAPTER 54

PLANNING & CONTROL

I. Budgets

A. Overview

A budget is a quantitative expression of the objectives and goals of an enterprise. Budgeting compels management planning, provides definite expectations that are a objective framework for judging subsequent performance, and promotes communication and coordination among the various segments of the enterprise. Budgets may be used for planning, evaluating performance, implementing plans, communicating plans, motivating personnel, and authorizing actions. **Zero-based budgeting** involves scrutiny of every proposed expenditure.

B. Master Budget

A master budget represents a comprehensive plan for the overall activities of the enterprise. A master budget generally summarizes the forecasts contained in the operating budget, the capital expenditures budget, and the financial budget. Formulating a master budget involves preparing the operating income budget and using that information to develop a financial budget and a capital expenditure budget.

1. **Operating Budget** An operating budget forecasts income, predicts sales volume, as well as estimates cost of goods sold and operating expenses.

    a. Prepare a sales forecast, generally based on estimates by the sales staff, statistical analyses, and group executive judgment.

    b. Prepare a schedule of desired ending inventory levels.

    c. Prepare a production budget based on the sales forecast. Production is affected by both finished goods inventory levels and the sales budget. The production budget has an added benefit for enterprises whose sales fluctuate on a seasonal basis. The budget can be used to coordinate the manufacturing and sales functions, so that production can proceed at an orderly and efficient pace and still fulfill the need for finished goods at peak periods. Units to produce = Desired ending finished goods inventory + Budgeted sales (units) − Beginning finished goods inventory

    d. Prepare a schedule of inventory costs based on production level.

        Example 1 ▶ Material Purchase Schedule

        Mien Co. is budgeting sales of 53,000 units of product Lye for April. The manufacture of one unit of Lye requires 4 kilos of chemical Loire. During April, Mien plans to reduce the inventory of Loire by 50,000 kilos and increase the finished goods inventory of Lye by 6,000 units. There is no Lye work-in-process inventory.

        Required: How many kilos of Loire is Mien budgeting to purchase in April?

        Solution:

Budgeted sales of Lye (in units)	53,000
Add: Increase in finished goods inventory of Lye	6,000
Units of Lye to produce	59,000
Times: Kilos of Loire per unit of Lye	× 4
Kilos of Loire needed	236,000
Less: Decrease in inventory of Loire	(50,000)
Kilos of Loire to purchase	186,000

(1) Prepare a schedule of direct material usage and purchases. Usage will depend on the level of production as budgeted. Purchases will depend on the desired ending material inventory plus usage less beginning material inventory.

(2) Prepare a schedule of direct labor costs based on estimated production, labor rates, and labor methods.

(3) Prepare a schedule of manufacturing overhead costs. This schedule consists of two parts: variable overhead and fixed overhead. Variable overhead is determined by the production budget and the per-unit budgeted costs. Fixed overhead remains stable over a wide production range.

e. Prepare a cost of goods sold budget, using the information already gathered.

f. Prepare a budget of selling, administrative, and other expenses, often determined by group executive judgment and statistical analyses.

g. Prepare a budgeted income statement, based on the information gathered thus far.

2. **Financial Budget** A financial budget forecasts the flow of cash and other funds in the business and charts the expected balance sheet for the end of the planning period.

Example 2 ▶ Payments Forecast

For the 2011 purchases of Toyi, a merchandise item, budget data are

Annual cost of goods sold	$300,000
Accounts payable, beginning balance	20,000
Inventory, beginning balance	30,000
ending balance	42,000

Purchases will be made in equal monthly amounts and paid for in the following month.

Required: What is the 2011 budgeted cash payment for purchases of Toyi?

Solution: The cost of goods available for sale is equal to the sum of the ending inventory and the cost of goods sold. Therefore, the cost of goods available for sale is $342,000 ($42,000 + $300,000). By subtracting the beginning inventory from the cost of goods available for sale, the annual purchases can be obtained. Thus, the 2011 purchases are $312,000 ($342,000 − $30,000). Because the purchases are made in equal monthly amounts, the monthly purchases are $26,000 ($312,000 / 12). The purchases are paid for one month after purchase.

Cash payment for accounts payable at 1/1/11	$ 20,000
Cash payments for purchases made during year ($26,000/month × 11 months)	286,000
Budgeted cash payment for purchases	$306,000

a. Prepare a cash budget, predicting the effects on cash position of the level of operation forecast in step g., above. Note that noncash expenses such as depreciation and amortization are not included. Future dividend payments may or may not be included in the cash budget. Financing requirements include repayments of obligations, interest expense, and other investments that may be planned. Prepare a budgeted statement of cash flows using the information gathered for other budgets.

(1) Beginning cash + Cash collections = Total cash available before financing activity

(2) Cash disbursements = Purchases of materials + Salaries and wages + Other cash outlays + Purchases of fixed assets + Investments

    (3) Ending cash balance = Beginning cash balance + Cash collections – Cash disbursements

b. Prepare a budgeted balance sheet, using the information gathered for other budgets. For example, accounts receivable equals budgeted sales, plus beginning accounts receivable balance, less estimated cash receipts.

3. Capital Expenditures Budget A capital expenditures budget summarizes expenditures for individual capital projects. The time period of this budget depends on the entity's planning horizon. Capital expenditures that are budgeted include replacement, acquisition, or construction of plants and major equipment. Prepare a capital expenditures budget taking into account the facilities, equipment, etc., required to achieve the budgeted level of production, long-range expansion plans, and the cash available for capital expenditures (from the cash budget).

C. Flexible Budget

A flexible budget does not confine itself to one activity level, but rather aims toward an activity range. A flexible budget may be prepared for production, selling, or administrative activities.

Exhibit 1 ▸ Flexible Budget for Production Costs

	Cost formula (per unit)	Various Production Levels 10,000	12,000	14,000
		Production Department X **Flexible Budget**		
Direct materials	$1.00	$10,000	$ 12,000	$ 14,000
Direct labor	2.00	20,000	24,000	28,000
Variable factory overhead	3.00	30,000	36,000	42,000
Total variable manufacturing costs	$6.00	60,000	72,000	84,000
Depreciation		20,000	20,000	20,000
Supervisory salaries		10,000	10,000	10,000
Insurance		5,000	5,000	5,000
Total fixed manufacturing costs		35,000	35,000	35,000
Total manufacturing costs		$95,000	$107,000	$119,000

1. Variable Budget Use A static budget is not adjusted or altered, regardless of changes in volume during the period. In the planning phase, the flexible budget can be geared toward all levels of activity within the relevant range. In the controlling phase, the flexible budget can be tailored for the level of activity achieved. That is, a manager can look at what activity level was attained during a period and then turn to the flexible budget to determine what costs should have been at that level.

2. Effects on Costs When using a flexible budget, it is important to know the effect that changes in production levels within the relevant range have on variable, fixed, and total costs.

a. Variable Costs Variable costs are costs that remain constant per unit but that vary in total in direct proportion to changes in the level of production. Thus, with an increase in production levels within the relevant range, total variable costs increase; with a decrease in production levels within the relevant range, total variable costs decrease.

b. Fixed Costs Fixed costs are costs that tend to remain constant in total, regardless of changes in production levels within the relevant range. However, fixed costs per unit have an inverse relationship with changes in production levels. Fixed costs per unit decrease with an increase in production levels because total fixed costs are spread over more units. Fixed costs per unit increase with a decrease in production levels because total fixed costs are spread over fewer units.

c. **Total Costs** Total costs vary with changes in the level of production due to the change in total variable costs. Thus, with an increase in production levels within the relevant range, total costs increase; with a decrease in production levels within the relevant range, total costs decrease.

D. Responsibility Accounting

Responsibility accounting systems recognize various decision centers (or responsibility centers) throughout an organization and trace costs (and revenues, assets, and liabilities, where pertinent) to the individual managers who are primarily responsible for the costs in question. Generally, the manager in question is not held responsible for her/his own salary or other factors beyond control. Controllable costs for responsibility accounting purposes are those costs that are directly influenced by a given manager within a given period of time.

1. **Cost Center** The manager is responsible only for **controllable costs.** The manager has no control over sales or over the generating of revenue. Cost centers are evaluated by means of performance reports, in terms of meeting cost standards that have been set.

2. **Revenue Center** The manager is responsible only for **controllable revenues.** For instance, a sales manager has no control over manufacturing costs.

3. **Profit Center** The manager is responsible for both controllable **revenues and costs.** Profit centers are evaluated by means of contribution income statements, in terms of meeting revenue and cost objectives.

4. **Investment Center** The manager is responsible for controllable revenues, costs, and **investment funds.** Investment centers also are evaluated by means of contribution income statements, but normally in terms of the rate of return they are able to generate on invested funds.

II. Forecasting Tools

A. Probability Theory

Probability theory helps formulate quantitative models to deal with situations involving uncertainty. Such situations are formally described by means of random variables. A **random variable** can take several values, each with a specified probability. The set of values that a random variable can take, together with the associated probabilities, constitutes a **probability distribution.** The probabilities are non-negative numbers, each being less than or equal to one. Since the variable must take one of the values, the probabilities add up to one. Probability analysis is an extension of sensitivity analysis.

Example 3 ▶ Probability

The Wing Manufacturing Corporation has manufactured a chemical compound, product X, for the past 20 months. Demand for product X has been irregular and at present there is no consistent sales trend. During this period, there have been five months with 8,000 units sold, twelve months with 9,000 units sold, and three months with 10,000 units sold.

Required: Compute the probability of sales of 8,000, 9,000, or 10,000 units in any month.

Solution:

Units sales per month	Number of months	Probability
8,000	5	5/20 = 25%
9,000	12	12/20 = 60%
10,000	3	3/20 = 15%
	20	100%

1. **Expected Value** The information provided by a probability distribution can be summarized by means of the expected value of the random variable. This is a weighted average of all the values the variable can take, with the respective probabilities as weights. To compute the expected value, the various values are multiplied by their probabilities and then added together. The expected value concept furnishes business managers with a decision-making tool when dealing with situations characterized by uncertainty. Suppose the decision maker has to choose from among several courses of action. There are several possible outcomes, with known probabilities. The decision maker would compute the monetary value (gain or loss) that would result from each action/outcome combination. For each action, the **expected monetary value** would be calculated next. The action whose expected monetary value is the highest (the highest gain or the least loss) would be selected as the optimum course of action.

   Example 4 ▶ Expected Monetary Value

   Lex Co. is considering introducing a new product, Vee. The following probability distribution indicates the relative likelihood of monthly sales volume levels and related income (loss) for Vee.

Monthly sales volume	Probability	Income (loss)
6,000	0.10	$ (70,000)
12,000	0.20	10,000
18,000	0.40	60,000
24,000	0.20	100,000
30,000	0.10	140,000

   Required: Determine the expected value of the added monthly income if Lex markets Vee.

   Solution:

Probability	×	Income (loss)	=	Expected value
0.10		$ (70,000)		$ (7,000)
0.20		10,000		2,000
0.40		60,000		24,000
0.20		100,000		20,000
0.10		140,000		14,000

   Expected value of added monthly income $53,000

2. **Standard Deviation** The conventional measure of the dispersion of a probability distribution for a single variable is the standard deviation. The standard deviation is the square root of the mean of the squared differences between the observed values and the expected value.

3. **Joint Probability** Two events (A and B) may be either independent or dependent.

   a. **Independent** If they are **independent,** the probability that either one of them will occur does not depend on the probability of the other event occurring. The **joint probability,** P(AB), which is the probability that both A and B occur, is equal to P(A) × P(B).

   b. **Dependent** If two events are dependent, the probability that A occurs, given that B has occurred, is different from P(A). This is called the conditional probability of A given B, denoted by P(A/B). P(AB) = P(A/B) × P(B) = P(B/A) × P(A).

B. **Regression Analysis**
   Regression analysis tries to estimate the relationship between a *dependent* variable and one or more *independent* variables from a set of actual observations on these variables. Regression analysis produces a measure of *probable* error, but does not establish a cause and effect relationship. *Simple* regression analysis measures the change in one dependent variable associated with the change in one independent variable. *Multiple* regression analysis measures the change in *one* dependent variable associated with the change in *more than one* independent variable.

Exhibit 2 ▸ Regression Equation

y	=	A + Bx
y	=	dependent variable (e.g., total overhead cost)
A	=	the y intercept (e.g., fixed overhead cost)
B	=	the slope of the line (e.g., the variable overhead cost per direct labor hour)
x	=	independent variable (e.g., direct labor hours)
Bx	=	total variable overhead cost

1.   **Time Series** Time series models provide an analysis of serially correlated data in both time and frequency domains.

2.   **Econometrics** Econometrics is the use of mathematical and statistical techniques to study economics problems. An econometric model is an economic model formulated so that its parameters can be estimated if one determines that the model is appropriate for a given situation.

C.   Coefficient of Correlation

The coefficient of correlation (R) measures the degree of linearity in the relationship between two variables—one dependent and one independent variable. It can vary only between +1 and −1. These two values (perfect correlation) imply a perfect linear relationship between the two variables. The data points in a scatter diagram would lie on a straight line in such a case. The two variables move in the same direction when the correlation coefficient is positive and in opposite directions if it is negative. If the data points in a scatter diagram appear as random points, the coefficient of correlation between the two variables is zero.

Exhibit 3 ▸ Scatter Diagrams Depicting Different Degrees of Correlation

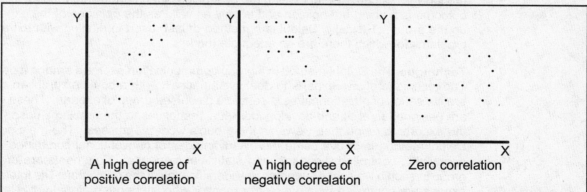

| A high degree of positive correlation | A high degree of negative correlation | Zero correlation |

D.   Coefficient of Determination

The coefficient of determination, which is the square of the coefficient of correlation (R^2), lies between 0 and 1. As the coefficient of determination approaches +1, we are given a higher level of assurance that the independent variable accounts for most of the variability in the dependent variable.

Example 5 ▶ Coefficient of Determination

Box Co. has developed the following regression equation to analyze the behavior of its maintenance costs (Y) as a function of machine hours (X):

Y = $12,000 + $10.50X

Box used 30 monthly observations to develop the foregoing equation. The related coefficient of determination (R^2) was 0.90.

Required: Determine the related point estimate of total maintenance cost if 1,000 machine hours are worked in one month.

Solution: Total maintenance costs = $12,000 + $10.50 (1,000) = <u>$22,500</u>

The 0.90 coefficient of determination does **not** affect the above computation. However, since it approaches +1, we are given a high level of assurance that the independent variable, machine hours, accounts for most of the variability in the dependent variable, total maintenance cost.

E. Delphi Method

Lacking full knowledge, decision-makers have to rely on their own intuition or on expert opinion. The objective of the Delphi method is the reliable and creative exploration of ideas or the production of suitable information for decision making. The Delphi method a structured process for collecting and distilling knowledge from a group of experts by means of a series of questionnaires interspersed with controlled opinion feedback, designed to minimize "groupthink."

1. **Outcome** Expert judgment is a legitimate and useful input in generating forecasts; however, single experts sometimes suffer biases and groups may suffer from "follow the leader" tendencies or "groupthink." The Delphi method attempts to overcome these shortcomings; it primarily is concerned with making the best of less than perfect information. A Delphi method outcome is nothing but opinion and is only as valid as the opinions of the experts who make up the group. Typically, Delphi is a method of last resort in dealing with extremely complex problems for which there are no adequate models.

2. **Technique** The Delphi method is a group communication exercise among a panel of experts. The technique allows experts to deal systematically with a complex problem or task. A reiterative series of questionnaires is sent to a disbursed group of experts. These questionnaires are designed to elicit and develop individual responses to the problems posed and to enable the experts to refine their views as the group's work progresses. The main point behind the Delphi method is to overcome the disadvantages of conventional committee action through anonymity, controlled feedback, and statistical response. Comments are presented to the group in such a way as to suppress any identification of the originator. The interactions among experts are controlled by a director or monitor who filters out material not related to the purpose of the group, circumventing usual group dynamic problems.

III. Performance Measures

A. Entity-Wide Measures

Organizational performance is multi-faceted. Because GAAP financial statements focus on presenting financial position and activity in accordance with established criteria, they are not always the best measure of performance. Scorecards with selected financial and nonfinancial elements can provide different insights than financial statements prepared in accordance with GAAP.

1. **Nature** Scorecards don't attempt to meet such criteria as income determination or expense allocation; neither do they attempt to reveal the same level of detail as in financial statements. Their objective is to summarize the status or operations of an entity into a few bullet points. As such, they should concentrate only on the measures essential to achieving entity objectives at the level of the intended audience.

2. **Content** As scorecards typically are tailored for a particular audience, they can be both more concise and more informative than financial statements. Scorecards may require more judgment to prepare: (a) elements appropriate for one industry or company could be irrelevant or misleading for another; and (b) scorecard preparation is not as well defined or standardized as financial statement preparation. Among other things, strategic management attempts to delineate what makes a **balanced scorecard.** An entity might include the following information.

    a. **Customer** The customer information elements tend to answer the question, "How do we appear to customers?"

    b. **Innovation** The innovation information elements tend to answer the question, "Can we continue to improve?" This also may be called the learning and growth perspective.

    c. **Strategic** The internal business information elements tend to answer the questions, "At what functions must we excel?" and "Are we excelling?" This also may be called the internal process perspective.

    d. **Financial** The financial information elements tend to answer the question, "How do we appear to owners and creditors?"

B. **Quality Control Programs**

1. **Cost Categories** Quality control programs commonly recognize four, or occasionally five, costs categories. Quality control programs are also applicable when the "product" is a service.

    a. **Prevention Costs** The costs of avoiding producing products not conforming to specifications.

    b. **Appraisal Costs** The costs of discovering which individual units don't conform to the specifications.

    c. **Interior Failure Costs** The costs incurred when a non-conforming product is discovered before shipment to the customer; for example, rework of a partially complete product.

    d. **Exterior Failure Costs** The costs incurred when a non-conforming product is discovered after shipment to the customer; for example, rework of returned product and reshipping charges.

    e. **Opportunity Costs** These include the estimated "costs" of lost sales or dissatisfied customers. An example of an opportunity cost is lost margin on products that could have been produced when a full capacity plant was instead reworking defective parts. These indistinct costs are included in quality program reports less frequently than the other costs listed here, as they rarely are readily available or verifiable.

2. **Cost Management Systems**

    a. **Traditional** Traditional methods usually base production on forecast sales. Standard cost systems often are used to measure variances that result in operations improvement. However, using variances without discretion may lead to dysfunctional behavior. (For example, an extreme emphasis on the materials price variance may encourage the purchaser to obtain the lowest price without regard for quality or warehousing costs.)

    b. **Process Value Analysis** Process value analysis (or value chain analysis) attempts to reduce all nonvalue added costs, keeping costs low and flexibility to customer requirements at a maximum. This system is also referred to as a just-in-time (JIT) system.

(1) **Suppliers** Companies applying PVA techniques often negotiate long-term contracts with a limited number of vendors that specify acceptable prices and quality, eliminating the need to compute a material price variance. By only working with suppliers who deliver quality raw materials on a timely basis, less raw material inventory is required as a safety stock.

(2) **Value-Added Focus** By eliminating nonvalue-adding work (for example, materials handling) and costs (for example, warehousing costs), throughput time is minimized, enabling customer demand to stimulate production (inventory is produced after a sale is made), so excess and obsolete finished goods inventory is reduced. This is referred to as a "pull" system (each department's work is initiated by demand from the department ahead of it), as opposed to a "push" system (work is pushed from beginning to end, based on forecasts of customer demand).

(3) **Quality Focus** By concentrating on quality, rework and reshipping costs are minimized and customer satisfaction is maximized.

3. **Inventory Tracking Systems**

a. **Sequential Costing** Sequential (or synchronous) tracking methods attempt to time entries with physical production events. This can be expensive, especially when material and time tickets are linked to individual products or operations.

b. **Backflush Costing** Backflush costing systems eliminate the need to record work-in-process inventory by delaying recording production changes until finished goods (or sometimes even sales) occur. At this point, standard costs are used to allocate manufacturing costs to finished goods. Other names for this system include delayed costing or endpoint costing. Although backflush costing can be used with any production system, it frequently appears with a just-in-time (JIT) inventory system. Entities using backflush costing usually (a) want a simple accounting system, (b) have a standard cost for each product, and (c) achieve about the same end results with backflush costing as with sequential tracking.

4. **Quality Measures** Several different types of measures, or combinations of measures, of quality may be used by different companies in the same markets.

a. **Aesthetics** The product's appearance, feel, sound, taste, or smell. Does the refrigerator color match, contrast, or clash with other kitchen furnishings?

b. **Conformance** Degree to which a product meets standards: Does the refrigerator delivered from the factory match the one displayed on the showroom floor?

c. **Durability** Time that the consumer reasonably may expect a product to perform before significant deterioration: How many years does the refrigerator run? Note that a product can be durable and still require considerable maintenance.

d. **Features** Additional functions that supplement the basic operating characteristic: Does the refrigerator have a self-defrosting mechanism or ice-cube maker?

e. **Perceived Quality** Overall reputation becomes particularly important when the product or service has no readily objective measure of quality. For example, while certification and professional associations are important, overall reputation often is highly significant for customers selecting an accountant's services.

f. **Performance** Basic characteristic: Does the refrigerator keep food cold?

g. **Reliability** The extent to which the product will function without substantial maintenance: Does the refrigerator require an annual or 10-year maintenance call? Note that a product can be durable and still require considerable maintenance.

      h.   **Serviceability** Ease of repair. Does the refrigerator require repair in a location with specialized equipment and a technician certified by the manufacturer or can any average appliance repair service handle repairs in the owner's home?

C. **Best Practices**

An analysis of entity's processes reveals practices common to those entities with highly effective and efficient operations. Often the difference in costs from the most and the least efficient entities varies not by ten or twenty percent, but by three or four hundred percent. With a frequent event, such as issuing payments, savings are magnified into significant advantages for efficient organizations. Examples of best practices include the following.

  1.   **Organization** Work is organized around results, not tasks. Instead of dividing the work into small tasks and units completed in sequence by multiple task experts, best-practice organizations often structure work so that it can be completed by one individual or one team. This eliminates the time wasted and potential for error that occurs in hand-off of tasks from one individual to another, and it puts one employee in control of the customer relationship.

  2.   **Data Capture** Data is captured once, accurately. Two of the major forms of waste in transaction processing are multiple entry of data due to lack of integration of the information system, and re-keying or correcting faulty data. To avoid this, data capture is structured so that there is both a transaction and an information focus and usability. Supporting diverse users requires accurate information on demand.

  3.   **Controls** To garner the benefits of technology, controls are incorporated into information processing systems used to gather and analyze data. Active at the point of data entry, these controls seek zero-defect information through the use of limits and ranges. Random sampling of transactions identifies errors.

  4.   **Data Integration** Users create, maintain, and use data for decision making. The individuals who do the work are given the responsibility, authority, and accountability for the activities they perform and the data they create. For example, the accounting function is to integrate and analyze transactions, not originate transactions, such as material move tickets. The accountant is a data steward, rather than a data producer.

  5.   **Concurrent Operations** Work in parallel instead of sequence, and then integrate results. Parallel work flows allow information and insights to be shared, processes and programs to be piloted with minimal disruption of operations, and feedback to be incorporated into the systems. For example, the accounting department performs analysis of inventory accounts on an ongoing basis, so that at closing, little remains to be analyzed or corrected.

  6.   **Geographical Integration** Treat geographically dispersed resources as one. Shared databases, telecommunications networks, and standardized processing systems make it possible to gain the benefits of scale and centralization while maintaining the flexibility and service that comes from being dispersed and close to the customer.

  7.   **Online Processing** Companies speed up expense reimbursement and related transactions through online (rather than printed) approvals. Queries for customers are conducted online with the support of flexible databases or data warehouses and automated tracking and recording technologies. Queries by customers themselves enable customized answers to routine customer questions without customer service representative labor.

D. **Benchmarking Techniques**

Benchmarking is the process of examining an exemplary process similar in nature to a process being considered for improvement. The exemplary process under observation typically exists at a different company that is not a competitor. Alternatively, the exemplary process may exist at a single unit of a large organization. The exemplary process is identified and examined to determine criteria for excellence. Benchmarking implies assigning quantifiable measures of best practices. Contrast benchmarking with current-use assessment: current-use assessment traces every aspect of process to customer (internal or external) needs. Benchmarking might be considered as partly leveraging other entities' current-use assessment work.

1. **Internal vs. External Benchmarks** In periods of rapid significant change, improvements based only on current internal processes may result in overlooking substantial improvement opportunities. For example, reducing the cost to issue checks from $1.50/check to $1.25/check seems impressive until it is benchmarked against a $0.50/payment cost to issue an electronic funds transfer.

2. **Measures** Aside from the obvious measure of monetary units, other measures provide insight into processes. Cycle time is a common measure.

3. **Value Classifications** Value added, or real value added, refers to activities that are essential in meeting customer expectations. Business value added refers to activities that are essential to conducting business (such as regulation compliance) but do not add value from the customer's viewpoint. No value added refers to activities that are essential neither to meet customer expectations nor to conducting business.

4. **Process Map** A process map is a tool to illustrate the manner in which information, documents, and materials are moved through a business process. A process map can be used for training or for pinpointing potential problem areas, such as bottlenecks or process disconnects. Examples of problem areas typically highlighted by process mapping include rework (redundant data entry, modification of paperwork, or changes in data structures), redundant databases, complex hand-offs or transaction processing due to legacy systems, and manual report preparation due to data fragmentation. Process reengineering involves examining current processes and either improving them or designing replacement processes.

IV. Strategic Management

A. Overview
Strategic management concentrates on decisions that map an entity's long-run operations. Business policy concentrates on integrating an entity's diverse functions. Strategic management tends to be more externally focused than business policy. The basic strategic management model includes four components: (1) environmental analysis, (2) strategy development, (3) strategy implementation, and (4) evaluation and control.

1. **Decision Level** Strategic decisions are rare, consequential, and directive. They typically are rare in both timing and nature; in other words, unusual and unprecedented. Strategic decisions commit substantial resources to plans. Strategic decisions set the stage for future decisions and actions.

2. **Benefits** Strategic management benefits include an improved (a) vision for the entity; (b) perception of what is important; and (c) perception of the changing environment. The largest benefits from strategic planning may be from the increased awareness of the external environment and the focus on the future gained from the process of the plan development rather than the written plan itself.

3. **Evolution** As businesses evolve to become large entities operating in volatile environments, strategic management becomes more relevant. The magnitude of a large entity's operations increases the risk and cost of error: Where previously a poor decision might have lost capital for dozens of investors and thrown dozens of employees out of work, now a similar mistake might impact thousands of stakeholders. The accelerated speed of change also increases the importance of strategic management. Previously, entities may have had as much as a decade to absorb the shock of fundamental industry or societal changes. In a dynamic environment, failure to recognize and adapt to such changes could cause financial strain within a year or less.

a. **Basic Financial Planning** Basic financial planning concentrates on a one-year budget. Projects are evaluated mainly based on internal information. External environmental information typically is from the sales force only; it may be largely anecdotal information. Normal entity operations may be suspended to accommodate planning.

b. **Forecast-Based Planning** Three- or five-year plans involving consideration of long-term projects are typical of forecast-based planning. Management collects some environmental information and extrapolates current trends into the future. Normal entity operations may be suspended to accommodate planning. Adversarial situations may develop as lower-level managers compete for resources, critiquing proposals and justifying assumptions.

c. **Strategic Planning (Externally Oriented Planning)** Strategic planning seeks to increase an entity's responsiveness to dynamic markets and competition. Strategic planning generally is characterized by removing primary planning from low-level managers' hands and assigning it to a dedicated planning group. Top-down planning is typical, with top management developing five-year plans with input from consultants and the planning group, but with minimal direct input from lower-level management. Top management formulates a formal strategy and lower-level management addresses implementation.

d. **Strategic Management** Strategic management combines the external focus of strategic planning with the input and commitment of lower-level management and other employees. These groups develop plans to achieve the company's primary objectives that include implementation, evaluation, and control issues. These plans outline probable scenarios and contingency strategies rather than attempting accurate forecasts. Rather than suspending normal operations for a month, planning is a year-round activity. Rather than a isolated planning group, the planning staff mediates strategy sessions of planning groups formed from employees at many levels and functions. Top management tends to initiate strategic planning, but planning typically is interactive across levels and functions, rather than top down.

4. **Learning Organization** Dynamic environments favor flexible entities that downplay bureaucracy, commit to nurturing critical resources, and become learning organizations. A learning organization is skilled at acquiring and disseminating knowledge and modifying organization operations to incorporate insights gained from new knowledge. Learning organizations have several common characteristics: (a) systematic problem-solving ability; (b) experimentation with new approaches; (c) ability to learn from their own experience as well as that of others; and (d) timely and efficient dissemination of knowledge.

5. **Trigger** Strategy development typically is an irregular process. Organizations often continue with a course of action that has worked in the past until the organization is forced to question its actions. Often this questioning is triggered when something goes wrong. For instance, credit may become difficult to obtain. A new CEO may destroy a company's complacency with questions that have embarrassing answers. A significant gap in expected and actual performance may act as a trigger. The possibility of a change in ownership may be a company's wake-up call.

6. **Hypercompetition** Before the phenomenon known as hypercompetition, competitive advantages provided by strategic initiatives could last years. Hypercompetition shortens this cycle to months or, at most, a few years. A company in a hypercompetitive market must defend and improve its competitive advantage continually. Computer hardware and software industries are examples of hypercompetitive markets.

a. **Focus** Concentrating on the concept of hypercompetition can cause a company's management overlook long-term strategy in favor of short-term tactics. In other words, this excessive focus on short-term concerns can undermine development of long-term advantages.

b. **Cycle** Companies initially compete on cost and quality until there is an abundance of high-quality, low-cost goods; then they move into untapped markets. After they move into the markets that their competitors tapped (and their competitors have moved into the markets that they tapped), entry barriers are raised (such as economies of scale, strategic alliances, and distribution agreements) and consolidation of companies starts. To maintain competitive advantage at this point, a company must be willing to replace its own currently successful products with the next generation of products before competitors do so.

B. **Environmental Scanning**

Environmental scanning is the monitoring, evaluating, and distribution of information regarding external and internal environments to identify strategic factors. **Strategic factors** are factors that impact the future performance of an entity and typically are not within the short-term control of management. A tool commonly used for this component is SWOT (or TOWS) analysis. SWOT is an acronym for strengths, weaknesses, opportunities, and threats.

Exhibit 4 ▶ Blank SWOT Analysis Matrix With Descriptions

Internal Factors / External Factors	**S**trengths <Listing of 5 to 8 internal strengths>	**W**eaknesses <Listing of 5 to 8 internal weaknesses>
Opportunities <Listing of 5 to 8 external opportunities>	<Strategies that use strengths to take advantage of opportunities>	<Strategies that overcome weaknesses to take advantage of opportunities>
Threats <Listing of 5 to 8 external threats>	<Strategies that use strengths to circumvent threats>	<Strategies that minimize weaknesses to circumvent threats>

1. **External Analysis** Opportunities and threats are variables of the external environment. The external environmental often is divided further into societal environment (general variables) and task environment (industry variables). For instance, the aging of baby boomers often is cited as a general trend; recent concerns over food additives is an example of an industry force for the food processing industry.

   a. **Societal Environment** The societal environment includes socio-cultural, political-legal, economic, and technological forces. Forces in the United States currently include the following.

   (1) **Environmental Awareness** Recycling and conservation are entering mainstream lifestyles.

   (2) **Mass Customization** The mass market declines as consumers seek products tailored for their individual needs. In many markets, mass production is replaced by the production of products from a set of standard components, adapted to each consumer's specifications. Dell Computers is an example of a company that uses mass customization.

   (3) **Market & Workforce Diversity** As a percentage of the total U.S. population, minority groups are increasing in size and being identified as desirable markets.

Exhibit 5 ▶ Partial SWOT Analysis: Blinking Cosmetic Company

Internal Factors / External Factors	**Strengths**	**Weaknesses**
	• Loyal independent sales representatives make in-person sales as well as recruit and mentor others • Strong training program • Efficient distribution system delivers 95% of products within 24 hours of order receipt • No animal testing	• Rely on sales parties to keep overhead low; Internet sales could damage relationships with representatives • Containers promote high perceived quality, but are not recyclable in most areas
Opportunities • Animal right activists protest animal testing • Increased health awareness • Increased environmental awareness • Mass customization • Market diversity • Generation Y	• Highlight no-animal testing policy in promotional materials • Include protection against UV rays in products • Create new product line with custom mixed foundations; include mixing in training program • Target Generation Y with consultation-and-product packages as prizes for high school and college events; tie in with recruitment	• Establish container return program
Threats • Fewer women at home during workday or with time for parties • Competitors sell on Internet	• Encourage sales representatives to schedule weekend, lunch, and evening times • Highlight distribution system in promotional materials	• Replace parties with individual consultations • Establish appointment scheduling service on Internet; customers can schedule appointments, Blinking can monitor demand for representatives automatically • Establish re-order service on Internet; sales representative gets a reduced commission, but also has less work

(4) **Household Change** Single person households and households with married couples with no children are increasing. Families with children often have fewer children than in the past.

(5) **Communication** Mobile phones, email, and overnight delivery services offer increased efficiency and choices for employees and consumers, but they also increase pressure to respond quickly.

(6) **Boomlet** The children of the baby boomers, called the boomlet or Generation Y, have a impact similar to their parents.

(7) **Seniors' Market Growth** As seniors' numbers increase, they become a more significant market. With improved medical techniques, current seniors are often more healthy and active for more years in retirement than previous generations.

b. **Task Environment** The task environment includes shareholders, creditors, governments, communities, customers, employees, labor unions, competitors, trade associations, suppliers, and special interest groups.

2. **Entity (Internal) Analysis** Strengths and weaknesses relate to the internal environment. This evaluation includes analysis of the entity's: (a) culture (beliefs, expectations, and values); (b) structure (chain of command); and (c) resources (assets, skills, competencies, and knowledge).

C. **Strategy Development**
Strategy development is the formulation of long-term plans to effectively take advantage of opportunities and manage threats depending on the entity's strengths and weaknesses. Strategy development encompasses development of a mission, objectives, strategies, and policies. Objectives are quantifiable results with deadlines. Strategies are plans to achieve the mission and objectives. Policies are broad guidelines for implementation and decision making. Before considering alternate strategies, a review of the entity's mission and objectives provides a check that the mission and objectives are still appropriate in nature and scope.

1. **Mission** A mission is the purpose for the entity's existence. An ideal mission statement defines the essential reason of an entity's existence, separates it from similar entities, and delineates the scope of operations in terms of products and customers. A mission statement may include a description of what the entity seeks to become, or that may be separate. If separate, a statement exclusive to the future typically is called a **vision** statement. Mission statements may be broad or narrow. Broad statements may fail to clearly identify what an entity makes or the markets it plans to emphasize and thus provide little guidance to users. Narrow statements may unduly restrict the scope of activities in terms of products, means, or customers.

2. **Objectives** Ideally, objectives quantify what is to be done within a given deadline. Some strategic management practitioners differentiate between goals and objectives; they classify **unquantified** open-ended statements of desired accomplishments without deadlines as **goals.** Correspondingly, a quantified goal with a deadline is also an objective. Objectives frequently are based on several common goals: profitability, efficiency, growth, shareholder wealth increases, efficient resource utilization, building entity reputation, employee rewards, contributions to society, market leadership, technological leadership, survival (avoiding bankruptcy), and meeting the needs of top management. **Market leadership** generally is having the largest market share; **technological leadership** is focused on innovation or creativity.

3. **Hierarchy of Strategies** A strategy is a comprehensive master plan outlining how an entity will meet its mission and objectives. Ideally, it maximizes competitive advantages and minimizes competitive disadvantages. A hierarchy of strategies is the nesting of strategies by organizational level. An entity may have unstated, incremental, or intuitive strategies rather than formally articulated or analyzed strategies.

a. **Corporate Strategy** The corporate strategy addresses issues facing the whole company. Directional strategy charts a corporation's overall direction. Portfolio strategy decides a corporation's markets and industries. Parenting strategy coordinates resources among product lines and business units.

(1) **Growth Strategy** Growth strategies include concentration (focusing on product lines in one industry) and diversification (developing product lines in other industries). **Concentration** may be through **vertical** growth (assuming a function previously filled by a supplier or distributor) or horizontal growth (increasing market share). **Diversification** may be **concentric** (a company using its strengths in an original industry to expand into a related industry) or conglomerate (operating in an unrelated industry). **Synergy** is the concept that businesses in two related industries will generate greater profits than either of them separately. The link between two businesses in concentric diversification may be a common distribution network, customer base, technology, or managerial skills. The link between two businesses in **conglomerate** diversification generally is financial. Companies pursuing conglomerate diversification generally are either cash-rich companies that have no expansion room in current markets or are seeking to counter cyclical fluctuations (for instance, a snowplowing business combined with a camping equipment rental business). Diversification involving both very similarly related businesses and very unrelated businesses typically improve returns only marginally. Diversification involving synergy with a somewhat related business typically have significantly greater profitability than what the two businesses operating independently of each other would have.

(2) **Stability Strategy** Stability strategies generally are classified into three categories. The **pause/proceed with caution** strategy essentially is a time-out strategy: a deliberate attempt is made to make only incremental changes until a particular situation is resolved. For instance, after a period of tremendous growth, a pause may be needed to fortify the organization's infrastructure: managers, facilities, etc. The **no change** strategy often is employed in a stable market with no obvious threats or opportunities; it rarely is adopted explicitly. The **profit** strategy is to support profits during a period of declining sales by limiting short-term discretionary expenditures; in other words, treating the company's problems as temporary so as not to alarm stakeholders.

(3) **Retrenchment Strategy** Retrenchment strategies generally are classified into four categories. If a company's problems are pervasive but manageable, it may employ a **turnaround** strategy, which involves streamlining the company in two stages. The first stage of a turnaround is **contraction,** or across the board cuts in size and costs designed to improve cash flow. In the second stage, **consolidation,** the company implements stabilization programs. The **captive company** strategy typically involves a long-term contract with a strong customer involving a majority of product; some supporting functions, such as marketing, are reduced because of the long-term contract, but the company is dependent on that customer. A **divestment** strategy involves selling a product line; taken to its extreme, a **sell-out** strategy involves selling a business and exiting an industry entirely. A **bankruptcy** strategy involves giving control of the company to the courts in exchange for debt relief. Termination of the company is involved in a **liquidation** strategy.

(4) **Portfolio Strategy** Companies with multiple product lines or businesses may analyze these assets like a portfolio or series of investments. Products are managed differently at various stages in the **product life cycle.** New, untried products in markets with potential need cash for development. Proven products at the peak of their product life cycle generate enough cash to maintain their market share. As these proven product mature, they bring in more money than they need to maintain market share. Product lines in markets with low potential need either to be sold or carefully managed to reap the small returns that they can generate. Cost containment is a high concern with these products.

(5) **Parenting Strategy** Parenting strategy concentrates on building synergies among different businesses within the corporation, allocating resources among units, and coordinating shared unit functions to take advantage of economies of scale.

b. **Business Strategy** In a fragmented industry, where many small and medium local companies compete for relatively small shares of the total market, focus strategies often predominate. An industry consolidates as minimum quality and features become standardized and competition increasingly distills to cost and service. Maneuvering to circumvent market boundaries (either geographical or niche) frequently increase the market share of a few companies. In a consolidated industry, a few large companies tend to predominate, under the impact of knowledgeable buyers, slow growth, and over-capacity. All of these strategies are subject to failure due to imitation by competitors.

(1) **Competitive Strategy** The breadth of the company's target market (broad or niche markets) and the basis of competition (low cost or differentiation—superior value in terms of quality, special features, or service). A differentiation strategy typically is more likely to generate higher profits than a low-cost strategy, as differentiation is a more difficult entry barrier to overcome than low costs. A low-cost strategy is more likely to increase market share than a differentiation strategy. There are four generally recognized generic types of competitive strategies.

(a) **Cost Leadership Strategy** Competing on the basis of low cost in a broad market commonly is called cost leadership. Cost leadership involves aggressive cost minimization, avoidance of marginal customers, and economies of scale. Low costs allow a cost leader to earn profits even during heavily competitive times. High market share generally means bargaining power relative to suppliers. Low prices serve as a barrier to entry, as new entrants have difficulty establishing the same economies of scale. Cost leaders can be challenged by competitors' cost reduction actions or changing technologies. Further, companies using cost focus may achieve even lower costs than the company that attempts a cost leadership strategy.

(b) **Differentiation** Competing on the basis of superior value in terms of quality, special features, or service in a broad market commonly is called differentiation. Buyer loyalty serves as an entry barrier and allows cost increases to be passed on to customers. Companies using differentiation can be challenged by the basis for differentiation becoming less significant to customers. Further, companies using differentiation focus may achieve even higher quality than the company that attempts a differentiation strategy.

(c) **Cost Focus** Competing on the basis of low cost in a narrow market commonly is called cost focus. By focusing on a narrow market, companies are able to streamline operations and thus minimize costs. Companies using either focus strategy are challenged if the target market becomes attractive to broadly targeted competitors or is further segmented by more narrowly focused competitors (business is "too good") or demand disappears (business is poor).

(d) **Differentiation Focus** Competing on the basis of superior value in terms of quality in a narrow market commonly is called differentiation focus. By focusing on a narrow market, companies are able to best meet the special needs of their target customers.

(2) **Cooperative Strategy** The two generic types of cooperative strategies are collusion and strategic alliances. Collusion is illegal in many countries, including the United States. A strategic alliance is a partnership of companies to achieve strategic and mutually beneficial objectives. The partnership may be temporary or may be the precursor to a merger. Reasons for an alliance include: gaining technology or manufacturing capacity; gaining access to additional markets; minimizing financial or political risk; and gaining or maintaining competitive advantage. Alliances range from weak and distant to strong and close (integral to the partners' operations). Joint ventures and licensing arrangements tend to fall in the mid point of that range.

(a) **Mutual Service Consortium** Mutual service consortia generally are at the weak-and-distant end of the scale of alliances. They involve partnerships of similar companies in similar industries to gain economies of scale, typically research. A consortium generally is characterized by little interaction among partners.

(b) **Joint Venture** Joint ventures are popular because they often avoid financial, legal, and political restraints. Their creation frequently is the result of an unwillingness or inability to merge permanently. Disadvantages include the likely transfer of technological expertise to a partner, loss of control, lower profits, and probability of partner conflicts. When partners have equal ownership and mutual dependence, joint ventures tend to be more successful than joint ventures where ownership is unequal or of less consequence to one partner.

(c) **Licensing Arrangement** Licensing is particularly useful when a multinational company has a widely known trademark or brand, but insufficient capital to finance direct international expansion. Licensing typically provides technical expertise and grants rights to a separate entity to produce or sell a product in another market. Disadvantages include the potential for the licensee to develop its competence to the degree that it becomes a competitor.

(d) **Value-Chain Partnership** A value-chain partnership generally is at the strong-and-close end of the scale of alliances. Typical situations include a contract to run a financing or service arm of a retail business and the long-term relationships with suppliers or distributors. A manufacturer may work with few suppliers and involve them in product design, as opposed to merely placing orders. For instance, a glass supplier may suggest to its car manufacturing customer that it include UV filtering capabilities in windows.

(e) **Collusion** Collusion is agreeing to limit output and thus raise prices. Explicit collusion might involve a meeting and agreement between market leaders. Implicit collusion might involve widespread advertising that promises to not lower prices without refunding the difference to previous purchasers (ensuring that a significant reduction will not occur) and corresponding price-matching actions by competitors. Both explicit and implicit collusion are illegal in the United States.

c. **Functional Strategy** The functional strategy focuses on developing a distinguishing (or distinctive) competency to establish or maintain a competitive advantage. A **core competency** or capability is a function at which a company performs well. A **distinctive competency** is a function: (1) at which a company outperforms its competition; (2) which makes a disproportionate contribution to the customer's perception of value; and (3) that can be transferred to development of new products or markets. While a distinctive competency is a key **strength,** by this definition, not all key strengths are distinctive competencies. If a competency is copied successfully by a competitor, it ceases being a distinctive competency. If copied by enough competitors, it could become merely a minimum requirement for competition within the industry.

(1) **Financial** Financial strategy decisions include equity vs. debt financing, short-term vs. long-term debt, and current vs. long-term assets.

(2) **Human Resources** Human resources strategy addresses the type of employ-ees to hire (permanent vs. temporary, highly trained vs. low skilled, etc.) as well as whether to hire any at all (hiring vs. leasing through a third party).

(3) **Information Technology** IT strategies involve using systems to develop com-petitive advantages. For example, a delivery service may provide a web-site where customers can track their packages.

(4) **Logistic** Logistic strategy decisions address distribution of raw materials as well as finished product.

(5) **Marketing** Marketing strategy details how a product is priced, sold, and distrib-uted. With a **market development** strategy, an entity either gains a increased share of an existing market through market saturation and penetration for current products or develops new markets for current products. With a **product devel-opment** strategy, an entity either develops new products for existing markets or develops new products for new markets. A **push** strategy concentrates on get-ting shelf space for a product, so it is everywhere purchasers would go to buy that type of product. A **pull** strategy concentrates on making consumers aware of a product, so that they will request it wherever they ordinarily shop. When pricing a new product, companies use either **skim** or **penetration** pricing. Skim-ming typically is used when introducing a unique product: the price is set high and gradually lowered as all consumers who will purchase at that price have bought the product and competitors introduce similar products. Skimming allows the initial seller to reap large profits from the first sales. Penetration pricing involves setting the price low (or issuing coupons or another form of discounts) in order to gain a large market share and dominance.

(6) **Operations** Operation strategy decisions involve the production locations and processes (job shop vs. assembly line, mass customization vs. mass production, etc.), the degree of vertical integration, suppliers relationships, and the optimum technology level.

(7) **Purchasing** Purchasing strategy addresses the sources of raw materials and supplies. **Multiple** sourcing involves many suppliers. **Sole** sourcing involves one supplier chosen for commitment to the purchaser's goals and quality levels.

(8) **R&D** R&D strategy decisions involve product and process change and improve-ment, including the type of R&D (basic, product, or process) and the source of new technology (internal development, acquisition, or strategic alliances).

4. **Policy** Policies promote support of the company's strategies in the decisions that employees make.

D. **Implementation**
Implementation is influenced by strategies and polices. Typically it involves establishing programs, budgets, and procedures. Programs are the actions necessary to implement a strategy. Budgets are developed based on the programs. Procedures are sequences of steps to perform a particular task within a program.

1. **Entity Structure** Often when a new strategy is implemented, new administrative problems appear and economic performance declines until the structure is changed to accommodate the strategy.

a. **Simple** A simple or entrepreneurial, structure is feasible only with a small entity. One person makes all important decisions and is involved actively with all aspects of the entity, generally including supervision of all employees.

b. **Functional** The functional structure replaces most of an entrepreneurial leader's roles with a team of managers with functional specializations. The advantage of this centralized structure is that specialization is highly efficient for one industry. Its concentration is also its greatest weakness; if the industry dramatically changes and the entity is unprepared, the entity may not survive.

c. **Divisional** Multiple product lines generally are best accommodated by a divisional, or conglomerate, structure which decentralizes decisions. The advantage of a divisional structure is usually its wide and vast resources; its biggest disadvantage tends to be inflexibility.

d. **Advanced** In an effort to overcome the inflexibility of functional and divisional structures, corporations are developing advanced structures.

   (1) **Matrix** In a matrix structure, each employee reports to two superiors: a product manager and a functional manager. The functional manager typically is permanent. Conflicts may arise with this structure due to vague goals. The matrix structure typically is used when the projects are multi-functional, resources are scarce, and information processing and decision making need to be improved.

   (2) **Network** A network attempts to eliminate most of the structure, so the entity becomes a middleman between various suppliers and its customers, rather than a producer. A network typically is used when the environment is dynamic and expected to remain so. In-house business functions are eliminated. Instead of employees, the company contracts for labor for specific projects or lengths of time. Long-term contracts generally replace manufacturing and distribution functions. Network advantages include flexibility and ability to concentrate on distinctive competencies; disadvantages include lack of opportunities to develop synergies, lack of potential partners, and the danger of selecting competencies that become obsolete.

2. **Organizational Life Cycle** An organizational life cycle may include birth, growth, maturity, decline, and termination. These first three stages of a life cycle closely correspond to structure evolution. An entity in maturity or decline may re-enter another growth cycle. These stages are not necessarily sequential; an entity leap from birth to maturity without significant time in a growth stage; an entity in the birth or growth stage may enter decline. The structures listed in Exhibit 6 are only likely or typical structures; for instance, a mature entity entering a growth period may decide to retain a decentralized or advanced structure.

Exhibit 6 ▶ Organizational Life Cycle

	Common Strategies	Likely Structure
Birth	Niche concentration	Simple structure
Growth	Horizontal and vertical growth	Divisional structure
Maturity	Concentration and conglomerate diversification	Decentralized structure
Decline	Profit followed by retrenchment	Remnants of former structure
Termination	Bankruptcy or liquidation	None

E.   Evaluation & Control
Evaluation and control are processes to monitor performance and take corrective action, which can be as minor as a change in procedures or as major as an overhaul of the mission statement. Feedback from evaluation and control impacts future environmental scanning, strategy development, and strategy implementation.

1.   **Feedback Model** Feedback involves several steps. Organizations often complete the first two listed here, but fail to establish procedures to ensure that the last three are performed for all of the factors, particularly nonfinancial measures.

   a.   Specify what to measure

   b.   Establish targets and tolerance ranges

   c.   Measure actual performance

   d.   Compare actual performance and target

   e.   If actual performance is below target, initiate corrective action

2.   **Measurement Problems** Objectives may be difficult to quantify. Information systems in place may not collect information reliably or timely.

   a.   **Goal Displacement** Goal displacement is the replacement of objectives with the procedures intended to achieve those objectives.

      (1)   **Behavior Substitution** Activities that are difficult to measure rarely are rewarded. Often activities that are easy to measure are substituted as the basis for rewards. Rational employees will work for the rewards that the system offers, substituting ignored activities that support the objectives with activities that earn rewards, regardless of whether they support objectives. In other words, quantifiable goals crowd out nonquantifiable goals.

      (2)   **Suboptimization** Suboptimization occurs when a subdivision's actions optimize its performance at the expense of the entity as a whole.

   b.   **Short-Term Focus** Many accounting measures encourage a short-term focus. Further, some executives avoid evaluation of long-term factors because: (1) they believe short-term considerations are more important than long-term considerations; (2) they are not evaluated on a long-term basis; or (3) a lack of time.

3.   **Selecting Controls** A control system should support strategy; unless a control supports the strategy, it should not exist. To avoid confusion, controls should involve the minimum information need to evaluate events. Controls should monitor only relevant activities, otherwise goal displacement is encouraged. Controls must be timely and reliable. Both short- and long-term controls should be used, to maintain a balanced focus. Controls should target exceptions, to concentrate efforts on activity outside of acceptable ranges. Controls should emphasize rewards rather than punishments; punishments increase the likelihood of negative reception of new policies as well as goal displacement.

———————————————

CHAPTER 54—PLANNING & CONTROL

Problem 54-1 MULTIPLE CHOICE QUESTIONS (70 to 88 minutes)

1. Mien Co. is budgeting sales of 53,000 units of product Nous for April. The manufacture of one unit of Nous requires 4 kilos of chemical Loire. During April, Mien plans to reduce the inventory of Loire by 50,000 kilos and increase the finished goods inventory of Nous by 6,000 units. There is no Nous work-in-process inventory. How many kilos of Loire is Mien budgeting to purchase in April?
a. 138,000
b. 162,000
c. 186,000
d. 238,000   (11/95, AR, #40, amended, 5783)

2. The basic difference between a master budget and a flexible budget is that a master budget is
a. Only used before and during the budget period and a flexible budget is only used after the budget period
b. For an entire production facility and a flexible budget is applicable to single departments only
c. Based on one specific level of production and a flexible budget can be prepared for any production level within a relevant range
d. Based on a fixed standard and a flexible budget allows management latitude in meeting goals
    (11/95, AR, #41, 5784)

3. Lean Company is preparing its cash budget for November. The following information pertains to Lean's past collection experience from its credit sales:

Current month's sales	12%
Prior month's sales	75%
Sales two months prior to current month	6%
Sales three months prior to current month	4%
Cash discounts (2/30, net 90)	2%
Doubtful accounts	1%

Credit sales:

November—estimated	$100,000
October	90,000
September	80,000
August	95,000

How much is the estimated credit to accounts receivable as a result of collections expected during November?
a. $85,100
b. $87,100
c. $88,100
d. $90,000   (Editors, 1471)

4. A flexible budget is appropriate for a

	Marketing budget	Direct material usage budget
a.	No	No
b.	No	Yes
c.	Yes	Yes
d.	Yes	No

(5/94, AR, #37, 4642)

5. When a flexible budget is used, an increase in production levels within the relevant range would
a. Not change variable costs per unit
b. Not change fixed costs per unit
c. Not change total variable costs
d. Change total fixed costs   (Editors, 7586)

6. Cook Co.'s total costs of operating five sales offices last year were $500,000, of which $70,000 represented fixed costs. Cook has determined that total costs are significantly influenced by the number of sales offices operated. Last year's costs and number of sales offices can be used as the bases for predicting annual costs. What would be the budgeted costs for the coming year if Cook were to operate seven sales offices?
a. $700,000
b. $672,000
c. $614,000
d. $586,000   (11/92, PII, #34, 3368)

7. Wages earned by machine operators in producing the firm's product should be categorized as

	Direct labor	Controllable by the machine operators' foreman
a.	Yes	Yes
b.	Yes	No
c.	No	Yes
d.	No	No

(11/90, Theory, #41, 2180)

8. Controllable revenue would be included in a performance report for a

	Profit center	Cost center
a.	No	No
b.	No	Yes
c.	Yes	No
d.	Yes	Yes

(11/93, Theory, #49, 4554)

9. The following is a summarized income statement of Carr Co.'s profit center No. 43 for December:

Contribution margin		$70,000
Period expenses:		
Manager's salary	$20,000	
Facility depreciation	8,000	
Corporate expense allocation	5,000	33,000
Profit center income		$37,000

Which of the following amounts would most likely be subject to the control of the profit center's manager?
a. $70,000
b. $50,000
c. $37,000
d. $33,000   (5/92, PII, #51, amended, 2683)

10. Which of the following forecasting methods relies mostly on judgment?
a. Time series models
b. Econometric models
c. Delphi
d. Regression   (R/03, BEC, #15, 7677)

11. Probability (risk) analysis is
a. Used only for situations involving five or fewer possible outcomes
b. Used only for situations in which the summation of probability weights is greater than one
c. An extension of sensitivity analysis
d. Incompatible with sensitivity analysis
                    (5/94, AR, #47, 4652)

12. Which tool would most likely be used to determine the best course of action under conditions of uncertainty?
a. Cost-volume-profit analysis
b. Expected value (EV)
c. Program evaluation and review technique (PERT)
d. Scattergraph method   (R/99, AR, #25, 6814)

13. Under frost-free conditions, Cal Cultivators expects its strawberry crop to have a $60,000 market value. An unprotected crop subject to frost has an expected market value of $40,000. If Cal protects the strawberries against frost, then the market value of the crop is still expected to be $60,000 under frost-free conditions and $90,000 if there is a frost. What must be the probability of a frost for Cal to be indifferent to spending $10,000 for frost protection?
a. .167
b. .200
c. .250
d. .333   (11/95, AR, #53, 5796)

14. In probability analysis, the square root of the mean of the squared differences between the observed values and the expected value is the
a. Economic order quantity (EOQ)
b. Objective function
c. Optimum corner point
d. Standard deviation   (Editors, 2266)

15. Using regression analysis, Fairfield Co. graphed the following relationship of its cheapest product line's sales with its customers' income levels:

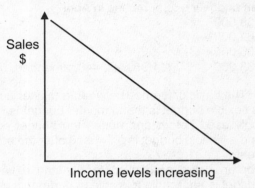

Sales $

Income levels increasing

If there is a strong statistical relationship between the sales and customers' income levels, which of the following numbers best represents the correlation coefficient for this relationship?
a. −9.00
b. −0.93
c. +0.93
d. +9.00   (5/93, Theory, #50, 4237)

16. To determine the best cost driver of warranty costs relating to glass breakage during shipments, Wymer Co. used simple linear regression analysis to study the relationship between warranty costs and each of the following variables: type of packaging, quantity shipped, type of carrier, and distance shipped. The analysis yielded the following statistics:

Independent Variable	Coefficient of Determination	Standard Error of Regression
Type of packaging	0.60	1,524
Quantity shipped	0.48	1,875
Type of carrier	0.45	2,149
Distance shipped	0.20	4,876

Based on these analyses, the best driver of warranty costs for glass breakage is
a. Type of packaging
b. Quantity shipped
c. Type of carrier
d. Distance shipped   (11/97, AR, #19, 6547)

17. Sago Co. uses regression analysis to develop a model for predicting overhead costs. Two different cost drivers (machine hours and direct materials weight) are under consideration as the independent variable. Relevant data were run on a computer using one of the standard regression programs, with the following results:

	Machine hours	Direct materials weight
Y intercept coefficient	2,500	4,600
B coefficient	5.0	2.6
R^2	0.70	0.50

Which regression equation should be used?
a. Y = 2,500 + 5.0X
b. Y = 2,500 + 3.5X
c. Y = 4,600 + 2.6X
d. Y = 4,600 + 1.3X (11/92, PII, #22, 3356)

18. Multiple regression differs from simple regression in that it
a. Provides an estimated constant term
b. Has more dependent variables
c. Allows the computation of the coefficient of determination
d. Has more independent variables
(R/00, AR, #11, 6916)

19. Under the balanced scorecard concept developed by Kaplan and Norton, employee satisfaction and retention are measures used under which of the following perspectives?
a. Customer
b. Internal business
c. Learning and growth
d. Financial (R/03, BEC, #6, 7668)

20. Key Co. changed from a traditional manufacturing operation with a job order costing system to a just-in-time operation with a back-flush costing system. What is(are) the expected effect(s) of these changes on Key's inspection costs and recording detail of costs tracked to jobs in process?

	Inspection costs	Detail of costs tracked to jobs
a.	Decrease	Decrease
b.	Decrease	Increase
c.	Increase	Decrease
d.	Increase	Increase

(11/95, AR, #51, 5794)

21. Rework costs should be regarded as a cost of quality in a manufacturing company's quality control program when they are

I. Caused by the customer.
II. Caused by internal failure.

a. I only
b. II only
c. Both I and II
d. Neither I nor II (R/01, AR, #18, 7003)

22. Which measures would be useful in evaluating the performance of a manufacturing system?

I. Throughput time
II. Total setup time for machines/Total production time
III. Number of rework units/Total number of units completed

a. I and II only
b. II and III only
c. I and III only
d. I, II, and III (5/95, AR, #46, 5464)

23. Which changes in costs are most conducive to switching from a traditional inventory ordering system to a just-in-time ordering system?

	Cost per purchase order	Inventory unit carrying costs
a.	Increasing	Increasing
b.	Decreasing	Increasing
c.	Decreasing	Decreasing
d.	Increasing	Decreasing

(5/95, AR, #47, 5465)

24. Which of the following is **not** a typical characteristic of a just-in-time (JIT) production environment?
a. Lot sizes equal to one
b. Insignificant setup times and costs
c. Push-through system
d. Balanced and level workloads
(R/99, AR, #24, 6813)

25. What characteristic would most likely **not** be a best practice for an accounting department?
a. Have the accounting department originate transactions
b. Have online approvals and queries
c. Treat geographically dispersed resources as one
d. Data entry controls seek zero-defect information through the use of limits and ranges
e. Capture data once and accurately
(Editors, 7416)

26. Which of the following definitions best characterizes benchmarking?
a. A technique that examines product and process attributes to identify areas for improvements
b. The comparison of existing activities with the best levels of performance in other, similar organizations
c. The development of the most effective methods of completing tasks in a particular industry
d. The complete redesign of a process within an organization (R/03, BEC, #29, 7692)

27. What is least characteristic of a learning organization?
a. Ability to learn from its own experience as well as that of others
b. Efficient dissemination of knowledge
c. Experimentation with new approaches
d. Stringent adherence to company policy
e. Systematic problem-solving ability
(Editors, 7407)

28. Which of the following generally is considered the **least** beneficial result of strategic management?
a. Focus on the future
b. Perception of a changing environment
c. Vision for the entity
d. Written strategic plan (Editors, 7408)

29. What is the typical link between two businesses being combined in a conglomerate diversification strategy?
a. Customer base
b. Distribution network
c. Financial
d. Managerial skills
e. Technology (Editors, 7409)

30. Strategic management has which of the following **two** characteristics?
a. Emphasis on accurate forecasts
b. Ideally includes a review of the entity's mission and objectives
c. Incorporates external information
d. Input primarily from top management, consultants, and employees dedicated to the planning function
e. Top-down planning (Editors, 7410)

31. What strategy involves increasing market share in the same industry?
a. Concentric growth
b. Conglomerate growth
c. Horizontal growth
d. Synergy growth
e. Vertical growth (Editors, 7411)

32. Which of the following steps in the strategic planning process should be completed first?
a. Translate objectives into goals
b. Determine actions to achieve goals
c. Develop performance measures
d. Create a mission statement
(R/03, BEC, #13, 7675)

33. Aim Company manufactures residential windows. It has a long-term contract with only two glass suppliers who are involved in Aim's design process. What is the best description of this relationship?
a. Collusion
b. Competitive strategy
c. Cost focus
d. Sole sourcing
e. Value-chain partnership (Editors, 7415)

34. When introducing a unique product, Aviator Company sets a high price and gradually lowers it as all consumers who will purchase at each price have bought the product and competitors introduce similar products. Which of the following best describes this practice?
a. Market leadership
b. Penetration pricing
c. Sole sourcing
d. Skim pricing (Editors, 7700)

35. Which of the following best describes an entity with a divisional entity structure?
a. Andy's Puppies has one person supervising most employees and making most decisions.
b. Eve's Exotics has a web of independent contractors instead of employees.
c. Fido & Friends has each employee report to both a functional and a product manager.
d. Harold's Hunt has a team of managers with functional specializations that supervises employees and make most decisions within each of their specializations.
e. Pete's Pets has multiple product lines and decentralized decision making. (Editors, 7701)

Problem 54-2 ADDITIONAL MULTIPLE CHOICE QUESTIONS (58 to 73 minutes)

36. The flexible budget for a production department may include

	Direct labor	Factory overhead
a.	Yes	No
b.	No	No
c.	No	Yes
d.	Yes	Yes

(Editors, 2219)

37. When production levels are expected to decline within a relevant range, and a flexible budget is used, what effect would be anticipated with respect to each of the following?

	Variable costs per unit	Fixed costs per unit
a.	No change	No change
b.	Increase	No change
c.	No change	Increase
d.	Increase	Increase

(11/91, Theory, #46, 2554)

38. Rolling Wheels purchases bicycle components in the month prior to assembling them into bicycles. Assembly is scheduled one month prior to budgeted sales. Rolling pays 75% of component costs in the month of purchase and 25% of the costs in the following month. Component costs included in budgeted cost of sales are:

April	May	June	July	August
$5,000	$6,000	$7,000	$8,000	$8,000

What is Rolling's budgeted cash payments for components in May?
a. $5,750
b. $6,750
c. $7,750
d. $8,000

(R/01, AR, #20, 7005)

39. Lanta Restaurant compares monthly operating results with a static budget. When actual sales are less than budget, would Lanta usually report favorable variances on variable food costs and fixed supervisory salaries?

	Variable food costs	Fixed supervisory salaries
a.	Yes	Yes
b.	Yes	No
c.	No	Yes
d.	No	No

(5/91, Theory, #44, 2177)

40. Which of the following is the best description of a budget?
a. A delineation of the scope of operations in terms of products and customers
b. An expression of the essential reason of an entity's existence
c. The rules and regulations that govern the internal management of a corporation
d. A quantitative expression of the objectives and goals of an enterprise (Editors, 7739)

41. Controllable revenues would be included in the performance reports of which of the following types of responsibility centers?

	Cost centers	Investment centers
a.	Yes	No
b.	Yes	Yes
c.	No	No
d.	No	Yes

(5/91, Theory, #47, 7417)

42. Which of the following may be used to estimate how inventory warehouse costs are affected by both the number of shipments and the weight of materials handled?
a. Economic order quantity analysis
b. Probability analysis
c. Correlation analysis
d. Multiple regression analysis

(11/90, Theory, #50, 2246)

43. Kane Corp. estimates that it would incur a $100,000 cost to prepare a bid proposal. Kane estimates also that there would be an 80% chance of being awarded the contract if the bid is low enough to result in a net profit of $250,000. What is the expected value of the payoff?
a. $0
b. $150,000
c. $180,000
d. $220,000 (5/92, PII, #55, 2687)

44. During 20X1, Deet Corp. experienced the following power outages:

Number of outages per month	Number of months
0	3
1	2
2	4
3	3
	12

Each power outage results in out-of-pocket costs of $400. For $500 per month, Deet can lease an auxiliary generator to provide power during outages. If Deet leases an auxiliary generator in 20X2, the estimated savings (or additional expenditures) for 20X2 would be
a. ($3,600)
b. ($1,200)
c. $1,600
d. $1,900   (11/95, AR, #54, amended, 5797)

45. To assist in an investment decision, Gift Co. selected the most likely sales volume from several possible outcomes. Which of the following attributes would selected sales volume reflect?
a. The midpoint of the range
b. The median
c. The greatest probability
d. The expected value   (11/92, Theory, #50, 3483)

46. A vendor offered Wyatt Co. $25,000 compensation for losses resulting from faulty raw materials. Alternately, a lawyer offered to represent Wyatt in a lawsuit against the vendor for a $12,000 retainer and 50% of any award over $35,000. Possible court awards with their associated probabilities are:

Award	Probability
$75,000	0.6
0	0.4

Compared to accepting the vendor's offer, the expected value for Wyatt to litigate the matter to verdict provides a
a. $ 4,000 loss
b. $18,200 gain
c. $21,000 gain
d. $38,000 gain   (R/00, AR, #20, 6925)

47. In statistical analysis, a weighted average using probabilities as weights is the
a. Objective function
b. Coefficient of variation
c. Expected value
d. Standard deviation   (5/90, Theory, #50, 2250)

48. Much Co. has developed a regression equation to analyze the behavior of its maintenance costs (Q) as a function of machine hours (Z). The following equation was developed by using 30 monthly observations with a related coefficient of determination of .90: Q = $5,000 + $6.50Z. If 1,000 machine hours are worked in one month, the related point estimate of total maintenance costs would be
a. $11,500
b. $11,000
c. $ 6,500
d $ 5,850   (Editors, 1531)

49. Multiple regression analysis
a. Produces measures of probable error
b. Establishes a cause and effect relationship
c. Involves the use of independent variables only
d. Is **not** a sampling technique   (Editors, 2268)

50. Box Co. uses regression analysis to estimate the functional relationship between an independent variable (cost driver) and overhead cost. Assume that the following equation is being used:

$$y = A + Bx$$

What is the symbol for the independent variable?
a. y
b. x
c. Bx
d. A   (5/92, PII, #54, 2686)

51. What measures might appear on a balanced scorecard?

	Quick ratio	Number of customer returns
a.	Yes	No
b.	Yes	Yes
c.	No	Yes
d.	No	No

(Editors, 7419)

52. The benefits of a just-in-time system for raw materials usually include
a. Elimination of nonvalue adding operations
b. Increase in the number of suppliers, thereby ensuring competitive bidding
c. Maximization of the standard delivery quantity, thereby lessening the paperwork for each delivery
d. Decrease in the number of deliveries required to maintain production   (5/93, Theory, #44, 4231)

53. Nonfinancial performance measures are important to engineering and operations managers in assessing the quality levels of their products. Which of the following indicators can be used to measure product quality?

I.   Returns and no allowances
II. Number and types of customer complaints
III. Production cycle time

a. I and II only
b. I and III only
c. II and III only
d. I, II, and III   (5/93, Theory, #49, 4236)

54. Bell Co. changed from a traditional manufacturing philosophy to a just-in-time philosophy. What are the expected effects of this change on Bell's inventory turnover and inventory as a percentage of total assets reported on Bell's balance sheet?

	Inventory turnover	Inventory percentage
a.	Decrease	Decrease
b.	Decrease	Increase
c.	Increase	Decrease
d.	Increase	Increase

(5/94, AR, #50, 4655)

55. Which of the following is generally not included in cost/cycle time analysis task categories?
a. Business value
b. No value
c. Priority value
d. Real value   (Editors, 7406)

56. Which of the following objectives are focused on innovation or creativity?
a. Market leadership
b. Parenting strategy
c. Portfolio strategy
d. Technology leadership   (Editors, 7702)

57. What strategy involves supporting profits during a period of declining sales by limiting discretionary expenditures?
a. Divestment strategy
b. Liquidation strategy
c. No change strategy
d. Profit strategy   (Editors, 7412)

58. What strategy involves streamlining the company by contraction and consolidation?
a. Captive company strategy
b. Divestment strategy
c. Sell-out strategy
d. Turnaround strategy   (Editors, 7413)

59. Which of the following bases of competition are **not** related to a differentiation focus strategy?
a. Low cost
b. Superior service
c. Superior quality
d. Special features   (Editors, 7414)

Items 60 through 62 are based on the following.

Blue Ridge Crafters is a co-operative that distributes traditional household furnishings, such as home-spun textiles, hand-thrown pottery, and hand-carved wood items. These items invariably are more expensive than mass-produced goods with similar functions, but customers prefer the artistry in Blue Ridge's goods. Because of subtle variations in color and grain, customers typically insist on handling these goods before committing to a sale. Each artisan decides which products to make. Blue Ridge relies on sales parties for about 20% and craft fairs for about 60% of its sales, with the remainder sold through a combination outlet-exhibit along a popular vacation route and independent boutiques and art galleries.

60. Blue Ridge is conducting environmental scanning as part of its strategic management initiative. Which **two** of the following factors are least likely considered opportunities for Blue Ridge?
a. An Internet retail site, as opposed to a physical site, has relatively low overhead costs.
b. Attendance at craft fairs has increased 20% from five years ago.
c. Blue Ridge artisans are a highly trained group.
d. The general population shows a decreased interest in modern-style furnishings.
e. Increased national income   (Editors, 7703)

61. Blue Ridge is considering admitting metalworkers to the cooperative, who will add hand-forged fireplace tools, latches, light fixtures, and iron gates to its product line. Of the following, what best describes this strategy?
a. Concentric diversification strategy
b. Conglomerate diversification strategy
c. Horizontal growth strategy
d. Profit strategy
e. Vertical growth strategy   (Editors, 7704)

62. Fiber Rugs, Inc., manufactures rugs with unusual designs and borders from coir, jute, sea-grass, and sisal. It sells its products using craft fairs, its own factory outlet, and retail chains. Fiber Rugs makes rugs using mostly mechanized processes, as opposed to Blue Ridge's craft processes. Fiber Rugs' management is dominated by its sole owner, as opposed to Blue Ridge's decentralized structure. Because their products appeal to a similar group of customers, Fiber Rugs and Blue Ridge are forming an alliance. Instead of a merger, the two entities are going to form a third, related entity to sell their products at craft fairs. Both Blue Ridge and Fiber Rugs will continue using their other distribution avenues. Of the following, what best describes this strategy?

a. Collusion
b. Licensing arrangement
c. Mutual service consortium
d. Sole sourcing
e. Value-chain partnership   (Editors, 7705)

63. Seawall Industries has a decentralized structure and is experiencing concentric growth. Which stage in the organizational life cycle is Seawall most likely experiencing?

a. Birth
b. Decline
c. Growth
d. Maturity
e. Termination   (Editors, 7706)

64. Which of the following is not an element of the strategic management feedback model?

a. Compare actual and target performance
b. Establish target and tolerance ranges
c. Initiate corrective action, if actual performance is below target
d. Review mission statement
e. Specify what to measure   (Editors, 7707)

SIMULATION

FYI: The editors encourage candidates to answer simulations as part of their review because such studying provides for content reinforcement, regardless of question format. Simulations currently are not part of the BEC exam; Bisk Education updating supplements will notify readers when this situation changes.

Problem 54-3 (25 to 35 minutes)

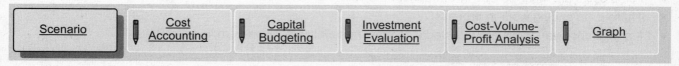

Editor's note: Candidates may want to review all the managerial chapters before answering this simulation.

Isle, Inc., commenced operations on January 2, Year 1. Isle's three products (Aran, Bute, Cilly) are produced in different plants located in the same community. Apart from initial build-ups in raw materials and finished goods inventories, production schedules are based on sales forecasts. The following selected information is taken from Isle's internal Year 1 contribution income statement, based on standard costs:

Isle, Inc.
Year 1 Contribution Income Statement

	Products			
	Aran	Bute	Cilly	Total
Sales (Aran 80,000 units)	$1,200,000	$800,000	$500,000	$2,500,000
Standard Costs:				
Direct Materials	180,000			
Direct Labor (Aran 20,000 hours)	240,000			
Variable Manufacturing Overhead	80,000			
Total Variable Manufacturing Costs	500,000	*(Detail omitted)*		
Less: Finished Goods Inventory				
December 31	100,000			
Variable Cost of Goods Sold	400,000			
Variable Selling and Administrative Costs	120,000			
Total Variable Costs	520,000			
Standard Contribution Margin	680,000	176,000	144,000	1,000,000
Fixed Manufacturing Overhead Costs	440,000	*(Detail omitted)*		
Fixed Selling and Administrative Costs	140,000			
Total Fixed Costs	580,000			
Standard Operating Income	100,000	35,000	25,000	160,000
Variances—Favorable (F)/Unfavorable (U):				
Direct Materials—Price	2,000(F)			
Usage	16,000(U)			
Direct Labor—Rate	12,000(U)	*(Detail omitted)*		
Efficiency	24,000(U)			
Manufacturing Overhead—Total	43,000(U)			
Selling and Administrative—Total	7,000(U)			
Operating Income, Net of Variances	$ 0	$ 41,000	$ 36,000	$ 77,000

Additional Information:

Manufacturing Capacity Utilization	75%	80%	70%
Average Investment	$1,000,000	$800,000	$400,000

- Demand for Aran is somewhat seasonal and moderately difficult to project more than 3 years
- Demand for Bute is constant and easy to project more than 3 years
- Demand for Cilly is very seasonal and very difficult to project more than 3 years
- Isle also prepared standard absorption costing statements using full capacity (based on machine hours) to allocate overhead costs.
- Fixed costs are incurred evenly throughout the year.
- There is no ending work-in-process.
- Material price variances are reported when raw materials are taken from inventory.

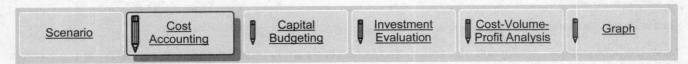

1. Does Isle practice a just-in-time philosophy?

2. Should Isle include standard indirect material costs in standard fixed overhead costs?

3. Should Isle categorize the operation of production equipment as a value-adding activity?

4. If Isle's three products were produced in a single plant, would activity-based costing provide more useful total production cost information for Aran, Bute, and Cilly than traditional standard costing?

5. Is the regression analysis technique helpful in determining the variable cost component of Isle's manufacturing overhead costs?

6. In Isle's internal performance reports, should normal spoilage costs be reported in fixed manufacturing overhead costs?

7. The computation of Bute's normal spoilage assumes 10 units in 1,000 contain defective materials, and, independently, 15 units in 1,000 contain defective workmanship. Is the probability that is used in computing Bute's normal spoilage less than 0.025?

8. Isle has contracted to sell units of Aran to a customer in a segregated market during the off-season. Ignore variances and the costs of developing and administering the contract, and assume that standard cost patterns are unchanged except that variable selling and administrative costs are one-half the standard rate. Isle will sell Aran at a price which recoups the variable cost of goods sold at the standard rate, plus variable selling and administrative costs at one-half of the standard rate. Will Isle break even on the contract?

9. Were the actual Year 1 direct labor hours used in manufacturing Aran less than the standard hours?

10. Would Aran's Year 1 operating income reported using absorption cost be lower than the amount reported using variable costing?

11. Was the total amount paid for direct materials put into process for the manufacture of Aran more than the standard cost allowed for the work done?   (11/94, AR, #100-110, amended, 6164-6174)

Items on this tab are based on the following as well as the information provided on the scenario tab.

Isle is considering investing $60,000 in a 10-year property lease that will reduce Aran's annual selling and administration costs by $12,000. Isle's cost of capital is 12%. The present value factor for a 10-year annuity at 12% is 5.65.

1. Is there a positive net present value for the lease investment?
2. Is the internal rate of return for the lease investment lower than the cost of capital?

(11/94, AR, #111-112, amended, 6175-6176)

Select the best answer from the following responses.

A. Aran
B. Bute
C. Cilly

1. For which product is evaluation of investments by the payback method likely to be more appropriate?

2. For which product is the economic order quantity formula likely to be most useful when purchasing raw materials to be used in manufacturing?

3. Ignore Year 1 reported variances and assume that Isle used expected demand to allocate manufacturing overhead costs. Which product would be most likely to have a substantial percentage of underapplied or overapplied fixed manufacturing overhead costs on quarterly statements?

4. Which product had the greatest actual return on investment?

(11/94, AR, #113-116, amended, 9911, 6177-6179)

1. If Isle sells $10,000 more of Bute and $10,000 less of Cilly, what is the effect on Isle's standard dollar break-even point: (A) increase, (B) decrease, or (C) no effect?

2. What is Aran's budgeted standard per unit cost for variable selling and administrative costs on sales of 75,000 units?

3. What is Aran's budgeted standard fixed selling and administrative costs on sales of 75,000 units?

4. What is Isle's standard breakeven point in sales dollars for the actual sales mix achieved?

5. What amount of Aran's direct material and direct labor variances might be regarded, wholly or partially, as direct labor employees' responsibility? (11/94, AR, #117-122, amended, 6180-6184)

Scenario	Cost Accounting	Capital Budgeting	Investment Evaluation	Cost-Volume-Profit Analysis	Graph

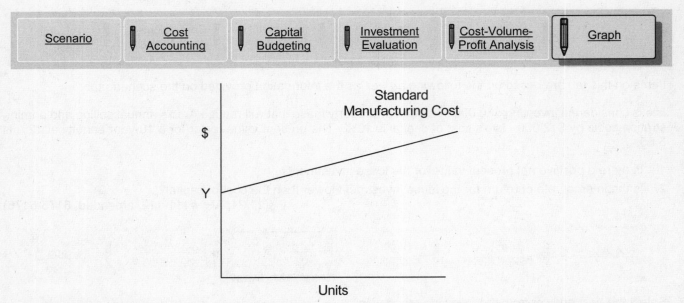

Isle uses the accompanying graph shown to estimate Aran's total standard manufacturing costs. What amount does Y represent?   (11/94, AR, #122, amended, 9911)

Solution 54-1 MULTIPLE CHOICE ANSWERS

Budgets

1. (c)

Budgeted Sales of Nous, in units	53,000
Add: Increase in Finished Goods Inventory of Nous	6,000
Units of Nous to produce	59,000
Times: Kilos of Loire per unit of Nous	× 4
Kilos of Loire needed	236,000
Less: Decrease in inventory of Loire	(50,000)
Kilos of Loire to purchase	186,000

2. (c) A master budget is based on the anticipated activity level for the period the budget covers. A flexible budget shows costs by behavior. A flexible budget shows total fixed costs and variable costs on a per unit basis. Thus, a flexible budget can be prepared for any activity level within the relevant range.

3. (c) The question asks for the computation of the estimated *credit* to *Accounts Receivable*—not the estimated amount of cash received—as a result of November collections. Therefore, cash discounts are disregarded. The doubtful accounts adjustment of 1% also can be discarded because it would be a credit to *Allowance for Doubtful Accounts,* not to *Accounts Receivable.*

Collections from Nov. sales	12% ×	$100,000	$12,000
Collections from Oct. sales	75% ×	90,000	67,500
Collections from Sept. sales	6% ×	80,000	4,800
Collections from Aug. sales	4% ×	95,000	3,800
			$88,100

4. (c) A flexible budget is one that shows budgeted costs for different activity levels. A flexible budget is appropriate for a direct materials usage budget because the quantity of direct materials used will vary with the level of production. Therefore, the cost of direct materials used also will vary with the level of production.

A flexible budget is also appropriate for a marketing budget because some marketing costs are variable. The variable marketing costs would tend to vary with sales rather than production. Other marketing costs may be semi-variable or fixed. The semi-variable costs would be broken down into their variable and fixed elements. The purely variable costs are added to the variable cost element of the semi-variable costs and the resulting total variable costs are estimated for various levels of activity. The purely fixed costs and the fixed element of the semi-variable costs also are shown. Finally, the total budgeted marketing costs for various levels of activity are shown.

5. (a) Variable costs do not change on a per unit basis with changes in the level of activity. Total variable costs increase in direct proportion to an increase in the level of activity. Fixed costs decrease on a per unit basis with an increase in the level of activity. Total fixed costs remain constant regardless of changes in the level of activity within the relevant range.

6. (b)

Total costs of operating 5 offices	$500,000
Less: Portion representing fixed costs	(70,000)
Portion representing variable costs	430,000
Divide by: Number of offices in operation	/ 5
Variable cost per office	86,000
Times: New number of offices in operation	× 7
Budgeted variable costs of 7 offices	602,000
Add: Budgeted fixed costs	70,000
Budgeted costs of operating 7 offices	$672,000

Responsibility Accounting

7. (a) Direct labor includes all labor that is physically traceable to the finished goods in an economically feasible manner. The labor of a factory machine operator and an assembler are common examples of direct labor. Controllable costs are defined as those that are influenced directly by a given manager within a given time span. Therefore, the expense of wages earned by machine operators considered to be a controllable cost of the machine operators' foreman because the foreman controls these costs by scheduling who operates the machines, how they work, and by controlling when they work (i.e., overtime).

8. (c) The manager of a profit center is responsible for controllable revenues and controllable costs. The manager of a cost center is responsible only for controllable costs. Thus, controllable revenues would be included in a performance report for a profit center but would not be included in such a report for a cost center.

9. (a) The manager of a profit center is responsible for both controllable revenues and controllable costs. Controllable costs are defined as those that are influenced directly by a given manager within a given time span and, thus, would include the center's variable costs. Therefore, the manager of a profit center most likely would be responsible for the center's contribution margin (i.e., the center's revenues less the center's variable costs). On the other hand, the manager of a profit center should not be held responsible for costs that cannot be influenced directly by the manager within a given time frame

(i.e., uncontrollable costs). The manager of a profit center normally would not be held responsible for her/his salary, facility depreciation, or the corporate expense allocation.

Forecasting Tools

10. (c) Lacking full knowledge, decision-makers have to rely on their own intuition or on expert opinion. Expert judgment is a legitimate and useful input in generating forecasts; however, single experts sometimes suffer biases, while groups may suffer from "follow the leader" tendencies or "groupthink." The Delphi method is a group communication exercise among a panel of experts that attempts to overcome these shortcomings; it primarily is concerned with making the best of imperfect information. A series of questionnaires is sent to a group of experts. These questionnaires are designed to elicit and develop individual responses to the issues posed and to enable the experts to refine their views as the group's work progresses. The Delphi method attempts to overcome the disadvantages of conventional committee action through anonymity, controlled feedback, and statistical response. A Delphi method outcome is nothing but opinion (i.e., judgments) and is only as valid as the opinions of the experts who make up the group. Time series models provide an analysis of serially correlated data in both time and frequency domains. Econometrics is the use of mathematical and statistical techniques to study economics problems. An econometric model is an economic model formulated so that its parameters can be estimated if one determines that the model is appropriate for a given situation. Regression is a form of statistical modeling that attempts to evaluate the relationship between one dependent variable and one or more independent variables.

Probability & Expected Value

11. (c) Probability (risk) analysis is an extension of sensitivity analysis. Sensitivity analysis involves determining how sensitive the result is to a change in one or more variables. Probability analysis involves weighting scenarios by the probability of their occurrence. Both are used to assess the risk that the predicted outcome may not occur. They are used for such activities as operational budgeting, capital budgeting, and linear programming.

12. (b) The expected value of a random variable summarizes probability distribution information. Cost-volume-profit analysis examines the operating income effect of sale and cost decisions. PERT is a project control technique. A scattergraph is used to consider correlation.

13. (b) The difference in the value of the crop between protecting and not protecting it if frost occurs is $50,000 ($90,000 – $40,000). Dividing the $10,000 cost to protect the crop by this $50,000 difference equals 0.20. Thus, 0.20 is the probability of frost occurring at which Cal would be indifferent between the two courses of action. $50,000 × 0.20 = $10,000

14. (d) By definition, the standard deviation in probability analysis is the square root of the mean of the squared differences between the observed values and the expected value. It is the conventional measure of the dispersion of a probability distribution.

Regression & Correlation

15. (b) The coefficient of correlation measures the degree of linearity in the relationship between two variables. It can range only between +1 and –1. The two variables move in the same direction when the correlation coefficient is positive and in opposite directions if it is negative. Since the dollar amount of Fairfield's sales (i.e., the dependent variable) decreases as customer income levels (i.e., the independent variable) increase, the correlation coefficient is negative. Therefore, only answer (b), –0.93 satisfies these requirements. Answers (a) and (d) cannot be correct because the correlation coefficient must range between +1 and –1. Answer (c) is incorrect because the correlation coefficient for the relationship in question is negative (i.e., the dollar amount of Fairfield's sales decreases as customer income levels increase).

16. (a) As the coefficient of determination approaches positive 1, users are given a higher level of assurance that the independent variable accounts for most of the variability in the dependent variable.

17. (a) The coefficient of determination (R^2), which is the square of the coefficient of correlation, lies between 0 and 1. As the coefficient of determination approaches 1, we are given a higher level of assurance that the independent variable accounts for most of the variability in the dependent variable.

Since the regression equation using machine hours has a higher coefficient of determination than the regression equation using direct materials weight (i.e., 0.70 > 0.50), the regression equation using machine hours should be used.

$$y = A + Bx$$
$$y = 2{,}500 + 5.0x$$

In this equation:
y = dependent variable (i.e., total overhead costs)
A = the y intercept (i.e., fixed overhead costs)
B = the slope of the line (i.e., the variable overhead cost per machine hour)
x = the independent variable (i.e., machine hours)
Bx = total variable overhead cost

18.　(d)　Multiple regression uses several independent variable to predict one dependent variable. Both simple and multiple regression have an estimated constant term, have one dependent variable, and allow the computation of the coefficient of determination.

Performance Measures

19.　(c)　The Kaplan and Norton Balanced Scorecard is a strategic tool that enables organizations to implement a company's vision and strategy, working from four perspectives: (1) financial, (2) customer, (3) internal process, and (4) learning and growth. The **learning and growth** perspective (also referred to as innovation) includes employee training and corporate cultural attitudes related to both individual and corporate self-improvement. In a knowledge-worker entity, people are the main resource. In a climate of rapid technological change, it is necessary for knowledge workers to be learning continuously, as entities often are unable to hire new trained workers. Learning also includes things like mentors and tutors within the organization, as well as that ease of communication among workers that allows them to get help readily as needed. **Financial** perspective: Kaplan and Norton do not disregard the traditional need for timely and accurate financial data; however, they recognize that the typical emphasis on financials leads to an unbalanced situation with regard to other perspectives. Poor performance from the **customer** perspective is a leading indicator of future decline, even though the current financial picture looks good; if customers are not satisfied, they eventually will find other suppliers that meet their needs. The **internal process** (or strategic) perspective evaluates how well a business is running, and whether its products and services conform to customer requirements (the mission).

20.　(a)　When a company changes from a job order cost system to a just-in-time (JIT) system with backflush costing, inspection costs should decrease. A JIT system places a high emphasis on quality. The company would buy from fewer vendors and these vendors would have been approved as to the quality of their materials. Also, the line workers take on more responsibility for quality. Quality should improve because of a greater emphasis on prevention. Inspection costs would go down as quality improves. The amount of detail tracked to jobs should also decrease under a backflush costing system. There are different levels of backflush costing systems. At the extreme, all production costs are charged to cost of goods sold. Any inventories at the end of a period are backflushed to the inventory accounts by reducing cost of goods sold. Under these systems, little detail is tracked to individual jobs.

21.　(b)　Rework costs caused by internal failure are within the control of the manufacturer and therefore should be considered costs of quality. Rework costs caused by the customer, not by product failure, are beyond the manufacturer's control, and are not costs of quality.

22.　(d)　All three measures should be useful in evaluating the performance of a manufacturing system. Total throughput time is a measure of how long the system takes to manufacture a product from start to finish. (Some companies may begin counting throughput time when a customer places an order and may end the counting of throughput time when the product is received by the customer.) Setup time is time devoted to a low-value-added activity. By measuring setup time as a percentage of total production time, the company obtains a ratio of time devoted to this low-value-added activity to the total time the product spends in production. Quality is important in the manufacturing environment. The cost of rework is an internal failure cost of quality. By dividing the number of reworked units by the total number of units completed, the company can better assess its quality control procedures in an attempt to minimize total quality costs.

23.　(b)　In a just-in-time (JIT) system there are frequent orders and the company maintains little, if any, inventory. If the cost of placing a purchase order is decreasing, this is conducive to a JIT system because the company will be placing more orders in a JIT system than in a traditional inventory ordering system. If the unit carrying cost is increasing, this will be conducive to switching to a JIT system.

24.　(c)　By eliminating non-value-adding work and costs, JIT techniques seek to minimize throughput time, enabling customer demand to stimulate production, so excess and obsolete finished goods inventory is minimal. This is referred to as a "pull" system, rather than a "push" system.

25.　(a)　Typical best practices include having the accounting department integrate and analyze transactions—to be a steward—not to originate transactions; having online approvals and queries; treating geographically dispersed resources as one;

having limit and range controls for zero-defect information; and capturing data once—accurately.

26. (b) Benchmarking is the process of examining an exemplary process similar in nature to a process being considered for improvement. The observed process typically exists at a different company. Benchmarking concentrates on process, rather than product, attributes. Companies are unlikely to share benchmarking information with entities in the same industry, as they are competitors. Drastic process changes may result, but complete redesign is not the focus of benchmarking.

Strategic Management

27. (d) Dynamic environments favor flexible entities that downplay bureaucracy, commit to nurturing critical resources, and become learning organizations. Learning organizations have several common characteristics: (a) systematic problem-solving ability; (b) experimentation with new approaches; (c) ability to learn from its own experience as well as that of others; and (d) timely and efficient dissemination of knowledge.

28. (d) The largest benefits from strategic planning may be from the increased awareness of the external environment and the focus on the future gained from the process of the plan development rather than the written plan itself. Strategic management benefits include an improved (a) vision for the entity; (b) perception of what is important; and (c) perception of the changing environment.

29. (c) The link between two businesses in conglomerate diversification generally is financial. Companies pursuing conglomerate diversification generally are either cash-rich companies that have no room for expansion in current markets or are seeking to counter cyclical fluctuations. The link between two businesses in concentric diversification may be a common distribution network, customer base, technology, or managerial skills.

30. (b, c) Two responses are required for full point value. Before considering alternative strategies, a review of the entity's mission and objectives provides a check that the mission and objectives are still appropriate in nature and scope. Strategic management combines the external focus of strategic planning with the input and commitment of low-level management and other employees. Input primarily from top management, consultants, and employees dedicated to the planning function is more typical of strategic planning. Strategic management tends to outline probable scenarios and contingency strategies rather than attempting accurate forecasts.

31. (c) Horizontal growth involves increasing market share in the same industry. Concentric diversification involves a company using its strengths in an original industry to expand into a related industry. Conglomerate diversification involves expanding into an unrelated industry. Vertical growth involves assuming a function previously filled by a supplier or distributor.

32. (d) An ideal mission statement defines the essential reason of an entity's existence, separates it from similar entities, and delineates the scope of operations in terms of products and customers. Generally, a mission statement is reviewed, created, or amended before any other strategic management steps, as the mission statement has a broad impact on goals and objectives. Performance measures typically are set after goals and objectives are determined.

33. (e) Typical value-chain partnership situations include a contract to run a financing or service arm of a retail business and the long-term relationships with suppliers or distributors. Collusion is agreeing to limit output and thus raise prices. A value-chain partnership is one means of implementing a cooperative strategy, not a competitive strategy. Competing on the basis of low cost in a narrow market commonly is called cost focus.

34. (d) Skim pricing is setting a high price and gradually lowering it as all consumers who will purchase at each price level have bought the product and competitors introduce similar products. Market leadership generally is having the largest market share. Penetration pricing involves setting the price low in order to gain a large market share. Sole sourcing involves purchasing from one supplier chosen for commitment to the purchaser's goals and quality levels.

35. (e) Multiple product lines and decentralized decision making is characteristic of a divisional structure. A simple or entrepreneurial structure has one person supervising most employees and making most decisions. A network attempts to eliminate most structure, so the entity becomes a middleman between various suppliers and its customers, rather than a producer; typically a network entity contracts for labor rather than hiring employees. A matrix structure involves each employee reporting to both a functional manager and a product manager. A functional structure has a team of managers with functional specializations each of whom supervises employees and makes most decisions within their own specializations.

Solution 54-2 ADDITIONAL MULTIPLE CHOICE ANSWERS

Budgets

36.　(d)　The flexible budget for a production department is based upon different levels of activity and takes into account the department's cost of direct materials, *direct labor,* and *factory overhead* at such different levels of activity. It allows a comparison for measuring the actual costs incurred against the costs that were budgeted for the particular activity level achieved.

37.　(c)　Variable costs do not change on a per unit basis with changes in the level of activity within the relevant range. Since total fixed costs remain constant in total within the relevant range of activity, a decline in the level of production increases the fixed cost per unit because the same total fixed cost is allocated over fewer units.

38.　(c)　In May, Rolling Wheels purchases components for bicycles it would assemble in June for sales in July. It pays in May for 75% of these components' costs. July's budgeted component costs are $8,000, so Rolling Wheels will pay ($8,000 × 75%) $6,000 in May for these components. In May, it also will pay for the remaining 25% for components purchased in April for June sales ($7,000 × 25%), or $1,750. Total payments in May for components ($6,000 + $1,750) equal $7,750.

39.　(b)　A static budget is of limited usefulness because it is based upon only one level of volume. When actual sales are less than that level, total variable costs should be lower simply because of lower volume (the variable cost per unit does not change). Total fixed costs, however, should not change with a change in volume. Thus, total fixed costs should be the same at the level of volume assumed in the static budget and that actually achieved.

40.　(d)　A budget is a quantitative expression of the objectives and goals of an enterprise. A mission statement is an expression of the essential reason of an entity's existence that delineates the scope of operations in terms of products and customers. A corporation's bylaws are the rules and regulations that govern the internal management of a corporation.

Responsibility Accounting

41.　(d)　The manager of a cost center is responsible only for controllable costs. Thus, controllable revenues would not be included in the performance report of a cost center. The manager of an investment center is responsible for controllable revenues, controllable costs, and investment funds. Thus, controllable revenues would be included in the performance report of an investment center.

Forecasting Tools

42.　(d)　Multiple regression analysis could be used to estimate the relationship between the dependent variable (e.g., inventory warehouse costs) and the two independent variables (e.g., number of shipments, weight of materials handled), based on a set of actual observations in these variables. Correlation analysis could not be used in this fact situation because there are three variables. Correlation analysis relates only two variables (i.e., one independent variable and the dependent variable). Economic order quantity analysis and probability analysis are not used to relate behavior of variables.

Probability & Expected Value

43.　(c)　The expected value of the payoff is computed adding the products of each level of income (loss) multiplied by its probability.

Probability	×	Income(loss)	=	Expected value
0.20		$(100,000)		$ (20,000)
0.80		250,000		200,000
1.00				$180,000

44.　(c)

Months with zero outages (0 × 3)	0
Months with one outage (1 × 2)	2
Months with two outages (2 × 4)	8
Months with three outages (3 × 3)	9
Total number of expected outages, annually	19
Times: Out-of-pocket costs per outage	$ 400
Expected out-of-pocket costs	7,600
Less: Cost of auxiliary generator ($500 × 12)	(6,000)
Estimated net savings by leasing generator	$ 1,600

45.　(c)　The "most likely sales volume" is the sales volume with the greatest probability. The midpoint of the range and the median are statistics derived by combining the estimates of likely sales volume. The expected value of a random variable is a weighted average of all the values the variable can take, with the respective probabilities as weights.

46.　(a)　The expected value is a weighted average of all the values the variable can take, with the respective probabilities as weights. The value of winning the case is $43,000 = $75,000 − [$12,000 + 1/2 × ($75,000 − $35,000)]. The expected value of accepting the offer is $4,000 greater than the expected value of litigation ($25,800 − $4,800 = $21,000).

Outcome	Probability	Value of Outcome	Weighted Average
Win	0.6	$43,000	$25,800
Lose	0.4	$0 – $12,000	(4,800)

47.   (c)   The information provided by a probability distribution can be summarized by means of the expected value of the random variable. This is a weighted average of all the values the variable can take, with the respective probabilities as weights. To compute the expected value, the various values are multiplied by their probabilities and then added together.

Regression & Correlation

48.   (a)   The estimated total maintenance cost incurred at 1,000 machine hours is determined by multiplying the variable cost per machine hour times 1,000 machine hours and adding the fixed cost. Total cost = $5,000 + $6.50 × 1,000 = $11,500. The 0.90 coefficient of determination does not affect the above computation. However, since it approaches +1, we are given a high level of assurance that the independent variable, machine hours, accounts for most of the variability in the dependent variable, total maintenance cost.

49.   (a)   Regression analysis (multiple or simple) produces measures of the probable error associated with both the uncertainty associated with the location of the regression line (standard error of the estimate) and the uncertainty associated with the variance of the predicted dependent variable. Regression analysis only identifies the association between variables without establishing a cause and effect relationship. Multiple regression almost always involves a sample of observations. Multiple regression analysis involves the use of more than one independent variable in estimating the value of the dependent variable.

50.   (b)   The equation being used is that for a straight line: $y = A + Bx$. In this equation:

y = dependent variable (i.e., total overhead cost)
A = the y intercept (i.e., fixed overhead cost)
B = the slope of the line (i.e., the variable overhead cost per cost driver)
x = independent variable (i.e., the cost driver)
Bx = total variable overhead cost

Performance Measures

51.   (b)   The quick ratio may appear on a balanced scorecard as an indication of creditworthiness. Information on customer returns may appear on a balanced scorecard as an indication of product quality and customer satisfaction.

52.   (a)   The benefits of a just-in-time (JIT) system usually include elimination of non-value-added operations—that is, operations that do not affect how customers perceive a product. Eliminating non-value-added operations saves the manufacturer money and does no harm to customer relations. Holding inventory is a non-value-added activity. Hence, under a JIT system, inventory is regarded as an evil, and rigid limits are therefore imposed on all inventories, from raw materials through all stages of production. Maximizing the standard delivery quantity of raw materials or decreasing the number of deliveries of raw materials required to maintain production conflicts with the JIT objective to minimize inventory levels. Use of a JIT system does not necessarily increase the number of suppliers and ensure competitive bidding.

53.   (a)   Both (I) returns and allowances and (II) number and types of customer complaints are indicators which can be used to measure product quality. The production cycle time cannot be used to measure product quality directly.

54.   (c)   The just-in-time philosophy emphasizes the reduction of waste and maintaining low inventories. Shipments should arrive frequently and just in time to go into production. Inventory turnover is determined by dividing cost of goods sold by the average inventory. Assuming that cost of goods sold remains constant, the inventory turnover will increase because average inventory will decrease. Inventory as a percentage of total assets will decrease because the average inventory will decrease. Although the total assets also will decrease by the reduction in the average inventory, the percentage will still decrease.

55.   (c)   Tasks are categorized according to the type of value they contribute: real value, business value, and no value. Value added, or real value added, refers to activities that are essential in meeting customer expectations. "Business-value-added" tasks refers to activities that are essential to conducting business (such as regulation compliance) but do not add value from the customer's viewpoint. No-value-added" tasks refers to activities that are essential neither to meet customer expectations nor to conduct business.

Strategic Management

56.   (d)   Technological leadership focuses on innovation or creativity. Market leadership generally is having the largest market share. Portfolio and parenting strategies generally are not objectives. Portfolio strategy refers to analyzing multiple product lines or businesses like a portfolio or series of investments. Parenting strategy concentrates on building synergies among different businesses within a larger entity, allocating resources among units, and coordinating shared unit functions to take advantage of economies of scale.

57. (d) The profit strategy is to support profits during a period of declining sales by limiting short-term discretionary expenditures; in other words, treating the company's problems as temporary so as not to alarm stakeholders. The no-change strategy often is employed in a stable market with no obvious threats or opportunities. A divestment strategy involves selling a product line. Termination of the company is involved in a liquidation strategy.

58. (d) A turnaround strategy involves streamlining the company in two stages: contraction (cuts in size and costs designed to improve cash flow) and consolidation (implementation of stabilization programs). The captive company strategy typically involves a long-term contract with a strong customer involving a majority of product; some supporting functions, such as marketing, are reduced because of the long-term contract, but the company is dependent on that customer. A divestment strategy involves selling a product line. A sell-out strategy involves selling a business and exiting an industry entirely.

59. (a) Competing on the basis of low cost in a narrow market commonly is called cost focus. Competing on the basis of superior value in terms of quality, special features, or service in a narrow market commonly is called differentiation focus.

60. (a, c) Relatively low Internet retail costs favor competitors who ship uniform goods, rather than an enterprise with unique products that customers must handle physically before purchasing. Generally, internal positive factors are classified as strengths and external positive factors are classified as opportunities. A highly trained work force is a positive factor generally classified as a strength. Increased attendance at craft fairs tends to increase sales at those fairs. Increased national income tends to increase sales of luxury items. (Also refer to the *Economic Theory* chapter.)

61. (a) Diversification may be concentric (involving an entity using its strengths in an original industry to expand into a related industry) or conglomerate (expansion into an unrelated industry). The link between two businesses in concentric diversification may be a common distribution network, customer base, technology, or managerial skills. The link in conglomerate diversification generally is financial. Vertical growth involves assuming a function previously filled by a supplier or distributor. Horizontal growth involves increasing market share. A profit strategy is to support profits during a period of declining sales by limiting short-term discretionary expenditures.

62. (c) A mutual service consortium involves a partnership of companies in a similar industry to gain economies of scale. (The arrangement described in this question also might be considered a joint venture, but that was not an answer option.) A licensing arrangement typically involves the provision of technical expertise and rights to produce and sell products under a brand name in another, specific market. Collusion is agreeing to raise prices by limiting output; it is illegal. Sole sourcing involves one supplier chosen for commitment to the purchaser's goals and quality levels. Typical value-chain partnership situations include a contract to run a financing or service arm of a single retail business and the long-term relationships with suppliers or distributors.

63. (d) Maturity typically is characterized by concentration or conglomerate diversification and a decentralized organizational structure. Birth is characterized by a niche concentration and a simple structure. Decline is characterized by profit followed by retrenchment and the remnants of the former structure. Growth is characterized by horizontal or vertical growth and a divisional structure. Termination is characterized by bankruptcy or liquidation.

64. (d) The elements of a feedback model commonly are described as follows: (1) specify what to measure; (2) establish targets and tolerance ranges; (3) measure actual performance; (4) compare actual performance and target; and (5) if actual performance is below target, initiate corrective action. Reviewing the mission statement is often part of strategic management, but typically not included as part of the feedback model.

PERFORMANCE BY SUBTOPICS

Each category below parallels a subtopic covered in Chapter 54. Record the number and percentage of questions you correctly answered in each subtopic area.

Budgets

Question #	Correct	√
1		
2		
3		
4		
5		
6		
# Questions	6	
# Correct		
% Correct		

Responsibility Accounting

Question #	Correct	√
7		
8		
9		
# Questions	3	
# Correct		
% Correct		

Forecasting Tools

Question #	Correct	√
10		
# Questions	1	
# Correct		
% Correct		

Probability & Expected Value

Question #	Correct	√
11		
12		
13		
14		
# Questions	4	
# Correct		
% Correct		

Regression & Correlation

Question #	Correct	√
15		
16		
17		
18		
# Questions	4	
# Correct		
% Correct		

Performance Measures

Question #	Correct	√
19		
20		
21		
22		
23		
24		
25		
26		
# Questions	8	
# Correct		
% Correct		

Strategic Management

Question #	Correct	√
27		
28		
29		
30		
31		
32		
33		
34		
35		
# Questions	9	
# Correct		
% Correct		

SIMULATION SOLUTION

Solution 54-3

Response #1: Cost Accounting (8 points)

1. N

Isle does not practice a just-in-time (JIT) philosophy. Having no work-in-process inventories is characteristic of a JIT system. However, other facts lead to the conclusion that Isle does not practice a JIT philosophy. For one thing, production schedules are based upon sales forecasts. In a JIT system, customer demand is what stimulates production. There is a substantial finished goods inventory for the Aran product. In addition, Isle uses a standard cost system to measure variances that lead to attempts to improve operations. Using variances under a standard cost system can lead to dysfunctional behavior. For example, a materials price variance encourages the purchaser to obtain the lowest price with less attention paid to quality. High quality is a key aspect of a JIT system. Also, in a JIT system, the company often negotiates long-term contracts with vendors that specify acceptable prices and quality, eliminating the need for a materials price variance to be computed.

2. N

Indirect materials costs are costs that are variable, not fixed. These costs vary with production. Thus, they should not be included in standard fixed overhead costs.

3. Y

A value-adding activity is one that a customer is willing to pay for. Customers are willing to pay for the reasonable cost of operating the equipment necessary to produce a product. Examples of non-value-adding activities include material moves, inspections, and rework.

4. Y

If Isle's three products were produced in a single plant, activity-based costing (ABC) would provide more accurate, and thus more useful, production cost information than would traditional standard costing. Traditional standard costing uses a volume-based measure to allocate overhead costs to production. If some of the overhead costs are not related to volume, high volume products are over costed and low volume products are undercosted. ABC overcomes this systematic bias by tracing the cost of the activities necessary to produce each product to each product.

5. Y

When overhead costs are mixed or semivariable, there are a number of ways to separate the costs into their fixed and variable components. One such way is the high-low method. However, this method is deficient in that it takes only the high cost point and the low cost point and their corresponding activity levels into account. Another method is the scatter-graph method in which the analyst uses judgment to draw a line of best fit through the points representing total costs. Regression analysis is superior to both of these methods, taking all points into account and plotting a line of best fit through the points. This regression line minimizes the sum of the squared deviations between the points and the regression line. The point where the line intercepts the Y axis represents the fixed cost element. The slope of the line represents the variable costs per unit of activity.

6. N

Normal spoilage would be expected to increase or decrease as production increases or decreases. Thus, normal spoilage represents a variable cost, not a fixed cost.

7. Y

Because the estimate of the number of units containing defective materials and the number of units containing defective workmanship were made independently, the probability used to determine normal spoilage is less than 0.025. The reason is that some of the units that contain defective workmanship are likely to contain defective materials also. Although the probability estimates were made independently, the two types of defects are not independent events. Indeed, a unit with defective materials would be more likely to have defective workmanship also. The probability estimate would be 0.025 less the probability that a unit has defective materials and defective workmanship.

8. Y

Isle will break even on the contract using variable costing. The fixed costs do not change in total. The sales price exactly offsets the variable costs that would be incurred. Under absorption costing, Isle would show a loss on the contract because fixed manufacturing overhead costs would be allocated to the products sold under the contract.

9. N

The direct labor hours used in producing Aran were greater than the standard hours allowed because the direct labor efficiency variance is unfavorable. The direct labor efficiency variance is the standard labor rate times the difference between the actual hours and the standard hours: SR (AH – SH). If this variance is positive, it is unfavorable because the actual hours were greater than the standard hours. If this variance is negative, the negative sign is dropped and the variance is called favorable because the actual hours were less than the standard hours. Since the direct labor variance was unfavorable for the production of Aran, the direct labor hours used were greater than the standard hours.

10. N

Because Isle began operations in 20X1, there was no beginning inventory of Aran. The ending variable cost of finished goods inventory of Aran is reported to be $100,000. Thus, inventory increased. Absorption costing would result in a greater net income because under absorption costing, some of the fixed manufacturing overhead costs would be deferred as a part of the ending finished goods inventory. Thus, costs charged against income would be less and the net income would be higher. Under variable costing, all fixed manufacturing overhead costs are charged as an expense of the period. If inventory were to decrease during a period, then variable costing would yield a greater net income than would absorption costing.

11. Y

The total amount paid for the direct materials put into process was more than the standard cost allowed for the work done because the total materials variance was unfavorable. The total materials variance was $14,000 unfavorable. It consists of the combination of the $16,000 unfavorable usage variance and the $2,000 favorable price variance. Although the price paid for the materials was favorable, Isle used far more than the standard quantity of materials allowed for the work done. Thus, the total amount paid is more than the standard cost allowed for the work done.

Response #2: Capital Budgeting (2 points)

1. Y

The present value of the cash inflows is $67,800 (5.65 × $12,000). Subtracting the $60,000

investment from this amount gives a positive net present value of $7,800 ($67,800 – $60,000).

2. N

The internal rate of return (IRR) on the lease is greater than the cost of capital. The IRR is the rate of return that, when used in the discount rate in the net present value computations, yields a net present value of exactly zero. Because the net present value of this investment is positive, the IRR is greater than the cost of capital. The internal rate of return on this investment is approximately 15.1%.

Response #3: Investment Evaluation (4 points)

1. B or C

(The editors prefer answer C.) Of the three products, the payback method is likely to be more appropriate for evaluating investments in Cilly. The payback method is not a discounted cash flow method. The payback method is often used as a crude measure of risk. The payback period is computed by dividing the cost of the investment by the cash flows per year, assuming the cash flows are constant. If the cash flows are not constant, the cash flows for each year are subtracted from the investment. The payback period is the point in time from the time the investment was made to the point where the cost of the investment is recovered in full. Investments in Cilly are more risky because demand is difficult to project for more than 3 years. Thus, the payback method would be important because the company would want to recover any investment in Cilly as soon as possible.

2. B

Of the three products that Isle produces, the economic order quantity would be most useful when purchasing raw materials for Bute. The reason is that the demand for Bute is constant and easy to project. Estimating demand is important because the economic order quantity is determined by taking the square root of the following formula:

$$\sqrt{\frac{2 \times \text{the order cost for each order x the annual demand in units}}{\text{cost to carry one unit of inventory for one year}}}$$

3. C

Cilly would be more likely to have a substantial percentage of under- or overapplied fixed manufacturing overhead costs on quarterly statements because demand for Cilly is very seasonal, yet fixed costs are incurred evenly throughout the year.

4. C

The actual return on investment is determined by dividing the operating income, net of variances, by the average investment. The return on investment for each of the three products is computed as follows:

Aran: $0 / $1,000,000   = 0.000%
Bute: $41,000 / $800,000 = 5.125%
Cilly: $36,000 / $400,000 = 9.000%

Response #4: Cost-Volume Profit Analysis (5 points)

1. A

Bute's standard contribution margin ratio is 22% ($176,000/$800,000). Cilly's standard contribution margin ratio is 28.8% ($144,000/ $500,000). Thus, by selling $10,000 more of Bute and $10,000 less of Cilly, Isle would lower its standard weighted average contribution margin ratio. The breakeven point in sales dollars is fixed costs divided by the weighted average contribution margin ratio. Therefore, by lowering its standard weighted average contribution margin ratio, Isle would increase its standard dollar break-even point.

2. $1.50

Aran's standard variable selling and administrative costs per unit can be computed by dividing the standard variable selling and administrative costs by the 80,000 units sold. Thus, the variable selling and administrative costs per unit are $1.50 ($120,000 / 80,000 units). Because variable costs are fixed per unit, Aran's budgeted standard per unit cost for variable selling and administrative costs at a sales level of 75,000 units is the same $1.50.

3. $140,000

Fixed costs are fixed in total and vary on a per unit basis. If Aran's standard fixed selling and administrative costs are $140,000 at a sales level of 80,000 units, such fixed costs should remain at $140,000 at a sales level of 75,000 units.

4. $2,100,000

Isle's standard break-even point in sales dollars can be determined by dividing the standard total fixed costs by the standard weighted average contribution margin ratio. Isle's standard total fixed costs can be determined by subtracting the standard operating income from the standard contribution margin. Thus, Isle's standard total fixed costs are $840,000 ($1,000,000 – $160,000). Isle's standard weighted average contribution margin ratio can be determined by dividing the standard contribution margin by the standard sales revenue. Thus, Isle's standard weighted average contribution margin ratio is 40% or 0.4 ($1,000,000 / $2,500,000). Therefore, the standard break-even point in sales dollars is $2,100,000 ($840,000 / 0.4).

5. $40,000

The direct materials usage variance and the direct labor efficiency variance might be partially or wholly the responsibility of the direct labor employees. Thus, the total amount of the variances that might be regarded partially or wholly as the responsibility of the direct labor employees is $40,000 ($16,000 + $24,000). The direct materials price variance would be the responsibility of the purchasing manager. The direct labor rate variance is the responsibility of management.

Response #5: Graph (1 point)

1. $440,000

The Y represents the total standard manufacturing cost that would be incurred at a production level of zero units. If no units were produced, the only manufacturing costs that would be incurred would be the fixed manufacturing costs.

FYI: Question Reference Numbers

This page is included due to questions editors have received from some candidates using previous editions; however, it is not essential for your review.

In the lower right-hand corner of a multiple choice question, you may note a question reference. This reference is included primarily so that editors may trace a question to its source and readily track it from one edition to another and from one media to another.

The reference indicates the source of the question and, possibly, a similar question in the software. For instance, a question with reference 11/93, Aud., #4, 4241, was question number 4 from the November 1993 AICPA Auditing & Attestation examination. When the reference has an "R" instead of 5 or 11, the AICPA released the question from a "nondisclosed" exam without specifying the exam month. Questions marked "Editors" are questions that are modeled after AICPA questions, but are not actually from the examiners. The examiners occasionally move topics from one exam section to another. You may see a question from a former AUD exam, for instance, in the REG or BEC volume. The following abbreviations indicate former exam section titles.

BLPR Business Law & Professional Responsibilities   BL   Business Law
AR   Accounting & Reporting   PI   Accounting Practice, Part I
T   Accounting Theory   PII   Accounting Practice, Part II

At first glance, candidates may assume that very early questions are irrelevant for preparation for upcoming exams. Provided that they are updated appropriately, many early questions are excellent review questions. When the exam was fully disclosed, editors noted that it was **more** likely that questions from early exams would reappear than questions from relatively recent exams. For instance, on a 1994 exam, it was more likely than an updated question from a 1988 exam would appear than an updated question from a 1993 exam. Second-guessing what questions the examiners will ask typically is more difficult and less reliable than merely learning the content eligible to be tested on the exam.

The four-digit number in these references often corresponds to a four-digit ID number in our software and online courses. Sometimes questions are removed from the software but not the book (and vice versa), so a question in the book is not necessarily in the software. Also, questions may vary slightly between the book and software. The four digit number has no significance for a candidate who is not using our software. If you need help finding a question from the book in the software using this four-digit ID number, please contact our technical support staff at support@cpaexam.com or 1-800-742-1309 and ask them to explain using the "jump" feature for questions.

More helpful exam information is included in the **Practical Advice** appendix in this volume.

CHAPTER 55

INFORMATION TECHNOLOGY

EXAM COVERAGE: The *Information Technology* portion of the Business Environment & Concepts section of the CPA exam is designated by the examiners to be 22 to 28 percent of the BEC section's point value. Candidates reviewing for both sections of the exam may notice considerable overlap between this chapter and the AUD IT chapter. While IT itself is tested in the BEC exam section, an understanding of IT is necessary to answer AUD questions that deal with IT considerations. Because we expect a significant number of candidates to review for one exam section at a time and we cannot count on them reviewing in any particular order, we must duplicate some of this information. More information about the point value of various topics is included in the **Practical Advice** section of this volume.

CHAPTER 55

INFORMATION TECHNOLOGY

I. Overview

A. Hardware, Software & Networks

Exhibit 1 ▶ Computer Hardware Configuration

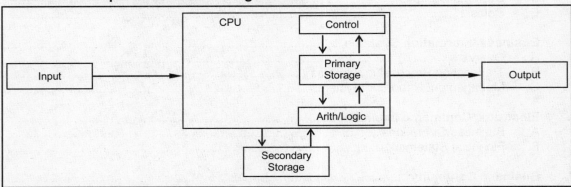

1. **Application Program** Designed to perform the processing of a specific application. For example, an accounts receivable update program is an application program that processes accounts receivable data to update the accounts receivable master file.

2. **Central Processing Unit (CPU, Mainframe)** Primary hardware component. The actual processing of data occurs in the CPU. It contains primary storage, a control unit, and an arithmetic/logic unit.

   a. **Primary Storage (Main Memory)** Portion of the CPU that holds the program, data, and results (intermediate and final) **during** processing; therefore, this includes only temporary storage. The primary storage contains the data and program steps that are being processed by the CPU and is divided into RAM (random-access memory) and ROM (read-only memory).

   b. **Control Unit** Portion of the CPU that **controls** and **directs** the operations of the computer. It interprets the instructions from the program and directs the computer system to perform them.

   c. **Arithmetic/Logic Unit** Portion of the CPU that has special circuitry for performing arithmetic calculations and logical operations. This may be combined with the control unit.

3. **Collaborative Computing Applications (Groupware, Shareware)** A program that allows several people to have access to the same information and attempts to track the authors of changes.

4. **Database Management System (DBMS)** A set of programs (software) that manages a database (i.e., creates, accesses, and maintains a database).

5. **Email, eMail** Electronic messages, typically delivered through the Internet. The messages may have attached files, including documents and programs.

6. **Enterprise Resource Planning Software** Complex, highly integrated, multi-module applications that manage a business' different aspects, from traditional accounting to inventory management and advanced planning and forecasting. These systems that share data and are used to support all aspects of the entity's financial reporting, operations, and compliance objectives.

7. **Firewall** Software designed to prevent unauthorized access to data by separating one segment from another.

8. **Gateway** Software or hardware that links two or more computer networks.

9. **Groupware** A program designed to allow several people to work on a single project. While this allows for greater flexibility, there is a loss of accountability. (Also see collaborative computing applications.)

10. **Hardware Maintenance** Involves equipment service. Routine service is scheduled. Unscheduled maintenance arises when there are unanticipated problems. Downtime is time when the computer is not functioning. This may be scheduled or unscheduled.

11. **Heuristic** In computing, the adjective *heuristic* signifies *able to change;* it is used to describe a computer program that can modify itself in response to the user, for example, a spell check program that allows the user to add words or voice recognition software that adapts to an individual user's speech.

12. **Input/Output Devices** Devices for transferring data in and out of the CPU. Examples include the following.

    a. **Bar Code Reader** An input device to scan bar codes, such as universal product codes on merchandise.

    b. **Keyboard** Typewriter-like device to allow the user to type information into the computer.

    c. **Magnetic Ink Character Recognition (MICR)** Sensing information recorded in special magnetized ink. MICR commonly is used by the banking industry for check processing.

    d. **Magnetic Tape Reader** A device to sense information recorded as magnetized spots on magnetic tape (e.g., the magnetic strips used on credit cards and ATM cards).

    e. **Modem** A device to allow users to transfer files over telephone lines to distant computers.

    f. **Monitor, Screen** A television-like screen to display information, providing feedback to the user.

    g. **Mouse, Trackball** A pointing device to manipulate representations displayed on a screen.

    h. **Optical Character Recognition (OCR) Scanner** A device to sense printed information through the use of light-sensitive devices.

    i. **Printer** A device to produce output on paper, including invoices and checks.

13. **Inventory Control System** A system that tracks the quantity of inventory bought and sold.

14. **Network** A network is an arrangement of computers to allow users access to common data, hardware, and/or software. An internet is network of networks. The Internet is a public network of many networks, also called the Web. An intranet is a network generally restricted to employee access. LANs are typically intranets. An extranet is a password-protected internet,

usually for established vendors and customers. A local area network (LAN) is a network of computers within a small area (i.e., a building) to transmit information electronically and share files and peripheral equipment among members (compare to wide area network). A value-added network (VAN) is a network service that provides additional services beyond mere connections to the Internet, particularly services enabling EDI. A wide area network (WAN) is a computer network encompassing a large area (i.e., city-wide or globally) to transmit information electronically and share files among members (typically company-wide only).

    a.   **Concentrator** A device that combines multiple communication channels into one. A concentrator differs from a multiplexer in that the total bandwidth of a concentrators' inputs don't necessarily equal the total bandwidth of its outputs. A concentrator temporarily stores data to compensate for this imbalance.

    b.   **Multiplexer (Multiplexor)** A device that converts several low-speed transmissions into one high-speed transmission and back again for communication purposes.

15. **Library Program (Library Routine)** Programs that frequently are used by several other programs. They are kept within the system and "called up" whenever necessary. One example is generating random numbers.

16. **Management Information System (MIS)** An information system within an organization that provides management with the information needed for planning and control. This involves an integration of the functions of gathering and analyzing data, and reporting (i.e., communicating) the results to management in a meaningful form.

17. **Operating System (O/S)** Manages the coordinating and scheduling of various application programs and computer functions. Examples include the following.

    a.   **Job control language (JCL)** A command language that launches applications, specifying priorities, program sizes, running sequences, databases used, and files used.

    b.   **Multiprocessing** Allows the execution of two or more programs at the same time and requires the utilization of more than one CPU.

    c.   **Multiprogramming** A program is processed until some type of input or output is needed. The O/S then delegates the process to a piece of peripheral equipment, and the CPU begins executing other programs. Processing speed is enhanced considerably, making it appear as if more than one program is being processed concurrently, while utilizing only one CPU.

    d.   **Virtual Storage** The O/S divides a program into segments (called pages) and brings only sections of the program into memory as needed to execute the instructions. This saves memory and processing cost because the majority of the program remains in less expensive secondary storage.

18. **Pass (Run)** A complete cycle of input, processing, and output in the execution of a computer program.

19. **Patch** Addition of a new part to a program. It may be added to correct or update a program. For example, if a new government regulation affecting withholding tax becomes effective, a patch may be added to the payroll program to provide for this. A patch also may be added for a fraudulent purpose. For example, an employee might insert a patch into a payroll program to print an extra check.

20. **Peripheral Equipment** Equipment that is **not** part of the CPU but that may be placed under the control of the CPU, i.e., which may be accessed directly by the CPU. Input/output devices and secondary storage devices are peripheral equipment.

21. **Program** Set of instructions that the computer follows to accomplish a specified task (e.g., accounts receivable update program, inventory management program, and payroll program). Program maintenance refers to making changes in the program in order to keep it current and functioning properly. For example, maintenance of the payroll program may involve modifying it because of changes in the social security law or to provide for a greater number of employees.

22. **Router** Switches that transfer incoming messages to outgoing links via the most efficient route possible, for example, over the Internet.

23. **Secondary Storage** Devices external to the CPU that store data.

    a. **Disk, Diskette** Randomly accessible data is represented in concentric circles called "tracks." A magnetic disk is a platter coated on both sides with a material on which data can be represented as magnetized dots according to a predetermined code. Diskettes are more common than disks, as they hold more data. Still more data can be stored on CDs (also called laser disks). A disk drive is used to read data from the disk into the CPU and to write data from the CPU onto the disk. A hard drive is fixed more permanently than a disk or diskette, with faster retrieval. Disks usually are moved from one computer to another more easily than a hard drive.

    b. **Magnetic Tape** Plastic tape that is coated with a material on which data can be represented as magnetized dots according to a predetermined code. It resembles audio tape.

    c. **Off-Line Storage** Not in direct communication with the CPU. Human intervention is needed for the data to be processed. For example, a disk must be inserted in a disk drive before it can be accessed.

    d. **Online Storage** In direct communication with the CPU without human intervention. For example, a hard drive ordinarily is accessed by the CPU without human intervention.

    e. **Randomly Accessible (Direct Access)** Data records can be accessed directly. Disks are an example. For example, if the customer records are stored in a file on a disk, the disk drive could go directly to Joe Zablonski's record without having to read any of the other customer records.

    f. **Sequentially Accessible** Requires the reading of all data between the starting point and the information sought. Magnetic tape is sequentially accessible. For example, if alphabetized records are on magnetic tape and none are read, most of the tape must be read to get to the Joe Zablonski data.

24. **Software** Programs, routines, documentation, manuals, etc., that make it possible for the computer system to operate and process data. (Compare to hardware.)

25. **Systems Programs (Supervisory Programs)** Perform the functions of coordinating and controlling the overall operation of the computer system.

26. **Video Conference** Real-time meeting over the Internet.

27. **Voice Mail** A system that records, directs, stores, and re-plays telephone messages.

28. **Universal Inbox** A system to collect email and voice mail in one "place", accessible by either a regular phone or computer.

29. **Utility Program (Utility Routine)** Standard program for performing routine functions, e.g., sorting and merging.

30. **Web Crawler** A program used to search the World Wide Web for files meeting user criteria.

B.   Data

Generally, the term data relates to information that is transmitted, processed, maintained, and/or accessed by electronic means (e.g., using a computer, scanner, sensor, and/or magnetic media). Many of the issues related to data also are applicable to records in the form of computer-printed documents and reports, particularly if there is no way to independently review or validate the printed information.

1.   **Alteration** Easily-altered records lack credibility. Manual records are difficult to alter without detection. Users have a reasonable likelihood of detecting significant alterations that have been made to paper documents. This quality provides users with some assurance that the evidence represents original information. Alterations due to the operation of a IT system may not be detected without specifically-designed tests.

2.   **Prima Facie Credibility** Paper documents (e.g., incoming purchase orders) usually have a high degree of credibility. However, a purchase order transmitted electronically from a customer derives its credibility primarily from the controls within the electronic environment. A fraudulent or altered electronic purchase order exhibits no apparent difference, compared to a valid purchase order, when extracted from an IT environment.

3.   **Documents Completeness** Paper evidence typically includes all of the essential terms of a transaction. Paper evidence also includes information regarding other parties to the transaction (e.g., customer name and address, or preferred shipping methods), on the face of the document. Paper documents often include acknowledgments of data entry and postings. An electronic environment may mask this evidence with codes or by cross-references to other data files that may not be visible to the users of the data.

4.   **Approvals** Paper documents typically show approvals on their face. For example, incoming purchase orders may have marketing department price approvals and credit department approvals written on the face of each original document. The same treatment may apply to electronic approvals by integrating approvals into the electronic record. Electronic elements may require additional interpretation.

5.   **Use** Users may access traditional paper records without additional tools or expert analysis. Electronic evidence often requires extraction of the desired data by an person knowledgeable in electronic data extraction techniques or through use of a specialist.

6.   **Structure** A bit is a binary digit (0 or 1, on or off, etc.), representing the smallest unit of data possible. A byte is a group of bits that represents a single character, whether alphabetic or numeric. Characters are letters, numbers, and special symbols (e.g., periods, commas, and hyphens). A record is a group of related fields; for example, a customer record would include ID number, name, address, etc. A field is a group of related characters; for example, a customer name. A file is a group of related records; for example, a customer file. (Also see master file and transaction file.) Editing refers to the addition, deletion, and/or rearrangement of data. **Input editing** refers to editing before processing and **output editing** refers to editing after processing.

   a.   A master file contains relatively permanent data. For example, an accounts receivable master file would contain a record for each customer and each record would include fields for customer number, name, address, credit limit, amount owed, etc. (Compare to transaction file.)

   b.   A transaction (detail) file contains current, temporary data. A transaction file is used to update a master file. For example, the day's charge sales would be accumulated on a transaction file that would be used to update the accounts receivable master file during an update run.

7.   **Database** A structured set of interrelated files combined to eliminate redundancy of data items within the files and to establish logical connections between data items. For example,

within personnel and payroll files, some of the data in the two sets of records will be the same; in a database system, these files would be combined to eliminate the redundant data.

8.   **Document Management** Electronic document storage and retrieval.

9.   **Encode / Decode** Encoding (or encrypting) is scrambling data to prevent unauthorized use. Decoding is convert data from an encoded state to its original form.

C.   Development & Implementation
The development and implementation process generally involves the following phases.

1.   **Systems Analysis (Feasibility Study)** The system's overall objectives and requirements are clearly determined. The existing system then is studied to see if it is meeting them adequately. Broad alternative approaches also are considered.

2.   **Systems Design**

    a.   **General** The alternative approaches are evaluated in more detail and a specific proposal is developed for implementing the alternative that is felt to be best.

    b.   **Detailed** The recommended system is designed in greater detail. This includes designing files, determining resource requirements, and developing plans for the following phases.

3.   **Program Specifications & Implementation Planning** Detailed specifications are developed for the computer programs that will be required, and plans are made for testing the program and implementing the system. This process usually includes hardware installation, coding programs, training users, systems testing, conversion, and volume testing.

    a.   **Coding Programs** Programmers write and test the required programs.

    b.   **Systems Testing** The system is tested thoroughly. The results of the tests are compared with the specifications and requirements of the system to determine whether it does what it is supposed to do.

    c.   **Conversion Testing** Conversion is done comparing the old system to the new system. This involves such things as converting and verifying files and data. Frequently, conversion involves parallel processing (i.e., parallel operations) in which the old system and the new system are run at the same time with the actual data for the period and the results compared. This checks the new system and avoids disaster if the new system fails the first time it is used.

    d.   **Volume Testing** Updating a large database for a few items may appear instantaneous to the user. When that same database is updated for normal levels of processing, unacceptable delays may be apparent. Volume testing ensures that operation with typical processing levels meet acceptable performance levels. For instance, a catalog business with 25% of its sales occurring on the day after Thanksgiving probably would need to ensure inventory updates in fractions of seconds, so that its phone representatives could confirm orders quickly.

4.   **Implementation** The system is released to the user.

5.   **Monitoring** Once the system is operating routinely, it is reviewed to be sure it is attaining the original objectives set for it, and to correct any problems.

D.   Systems Operation

1.   **Processing Methodology** Transactions may be processed either in batches or online.

a. **Batch Processing** Transactions to be processed are accumulated in groups (batches) before processing and are then processed as a batch. Batch processing frequently involves sequential access to the data files. For example, a company may accumulate a day's charge sales before processing them against the master file during the night. Before they are processed, the transactions would be sorted into the order of the records on the master file. One disadvantage of batch processing is that, because of the time delays, errors may not be detected immediately.

b. **Online Processing** Transactions are processed and the file is updated as the transactions occur. Online processing usually involves files that can be accessed directly. For example, a cash register terminal automatically may update the inventory file when a sale is made.

c. **Real-Time Processing** An online system is operating in real-time if the data is processed fast enough to get the response back in time to influence the process. For example, an airline reservation system is an online, real-time (OLRT) system since the customer receives reservations after waiting only a few moments.

d. **Integrated System** All files affected by a transaction are updated in one transaction-processing run, rather than having a separate run for each file. For example, in an integrated system, a sales transaction may update the sales summary file, the accounts receivable master file, and the inventory file during one processing run.

2. **File Updating** With sequential access, the updating process is most efficient when the transaction file has been sorted into the same order as the master file. There are four basic steps in the process of updating a batch of records in a master file that is kept on a magnetic disk. First, a transaction enters the CPU. Second, the record to be updated is read from its location on the disk into the CPU. Third, the record is updated in the CPU. Fourth, the updated record is written onto the disk in the same location as the original record. The result is that the original record is replaced by the updated record. This results in the original record being erased. This can be contrasted with the updating of a tape file (Exhibit 2) in which the original record still exists on the original tape after the updating process.

Exhibit 2 ▶ Updating a Master File Kept on Tape

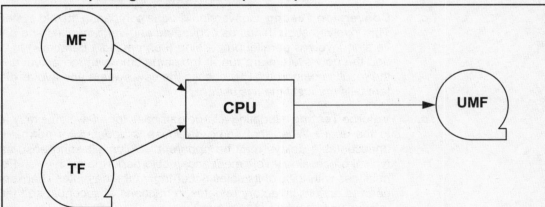

Three reels of tape are required: the **master file** (MF), the **transaction file** (TF), and the reel that becomes the **updated master file** (UMF). There are three basic steps in the updating process. **First,** records are read into the CPU from the master file (MF) and the transaction file (TF). **Second,** the records from the master file are updated in the CPU. **Third,** the updated records are written onto the output reel to form the updated master file (UMF). It is important to note that **after** updating is complete, **all** three tapes will still be intact.

3. **Outside Processing** While many companies have their own equipment to do their processing within the company (i.e., in-house), others utilize outside processors. Several common arrangements are as follows.

    a. **Block Time** Client rents a certain block of computer time from an outside party. For example, a company may rent time from a bank that does not utilize its computer system 24 hours per day.

    b. **Time-Sharing** A number of users share a computer system. Each may have a terminal that it can use to access a CPU located outside of the client. Each user can access the system whenever it wishes.

    c. **Service Bureau** An outside organization that provides a wide range of data processing services for a fee.

E. **Roles**

Segregation of functions between the IT department and users is a general internal control. Provision for general authorization over the execution of transactions should occur outside of the IT department (prohibiting the IT department from initiating or authorizing transactions). Segregation of functions within the IT department is also part of proper internal control. Among the various functions that should be segregated are the control group, operators, programmer, system analyst, and librarian.

Exhibit 3 ▶ Segregation Mnemonic

C	CONTROL GROUP	Responsible for internal control within IT department.
O	OPERATORS	Convert data into machine readable form.
P	PROGRAMMER	Develops and writes the computer programs. Responsible for debugging of programs. Writes the run manual.
A	ANALYST	Designs the overall system and prepares the system flowchart.
L	LIBRARIAN	Keeps track of program and file use. Maintains storage of all data and backups. Controls access to programs.

1. **Operator** Computer operators physically run the equipment. This includes loading (i.e., entering) the program and data into the computer at the correct time, mounting tapes and disks on the appropriate tape and disk drives, and dealing with problems that occur during processing. The input preparation process converts the input data into machine-readable form. Input methods include key-to-tape (i.e., keying the information directly onto the magnetic tape), key-to-disk, and OCR.

2. **Programmer** Applications programmers write, test, and debug the application programs from the specifications provided by the systems analyst. Systems programmers implement, modify, and debug the software necessary to make the hardware operate.

3. **Systems Analyst** Systems analysts investigate a business system and decide how the computer can be applied. This includes designing the system, deciding what the programs will do, and determining how the outputs should appear.

4. **Librarians** Provide control over the various programs, data tapes, disks, and documentation (manuals, etc.) when they are not in use; also, librarians are responsible for restricting access to IT materials to authorized personnel only. Library-control software may be used in some systems to keep control over programs, data, etc., that is kept online.

5. **Control Group** Data must be safeguarded for maximum control. To this end, users are given passwords or IDs to ensure that only authorized persons can access selected data.

These passwords and IDs are changed frequently to further ensure the integrity of the system and its data. Passwords can be used to limit access to the entire system and to limit what the individual can access and/or change once in the system.

6. **Administrators** The database administrator is responsible for maintaining one or more databases and restricting access to authorized personnel. Network administrators usually are responsible for maintaining the efficiency and effectiveness of an internal network. Web administrators usually are responsible for maintaining external network interfaces (web sites). These administrators may be primarily responsible for security, or primary responsibility for security may be assigned to a separate person so that security considerations are not obscured by day-to-day operations.

7. **Web Site Team** Several skills are involved in developing the best e-commerce sites; usually several people are involved.

   a. **Accountant/Auditor** Specialists who understand how business processes work and the kinds of controls that need to be in place to avoid, for instance, fraudulent orders being shipped.

   b. **Graphics Designer** An artist who uses colors and images to design a site to complement the site's mission.

   c. **Marketing Specialist** A specialist who understands how the designing of a web site can impact the success of marketing efforts, including the features that get a site frequent hits by search engines.

   d. **Usability Specialist** A specialist who understands human behavior and can evaluate the user-friendliness of a site. For instance, a usability specialist can offer insights on whether high shopping cart abandonment statistics are due to the site organization or appearance, a long waiting period to get an order confirmation, or some other factor.

   e. **Webmaster** A programmer responsible for the functionality of a site, generally including web site security.

   f. **Writer** One who composes prose for the web site. The short and punchy prose typical on the Web is unlike prose appropriate for a magazine, book, or newspaper article.

II. Business Information Systems

A. Overview
The use of IT often changes the fundamental manner in which transactions are initiated, recorded, processed, and reported from paper-based systems that rely primarily on manual controls to electronic systems using a combination of manual and automated controls. As **enterprise resource planning** (ERP) systems become more comprehensive and more widely in use, this issue becomes more prevalent—even for small and mid-sized entities. An IT system includes (1) hardware, (2) software, (3) documentation, (4) personnel, (5) data, and (6) controls. There can be significant differences between IT activities and non-IT activities.

1. **Manual** In a manual system, an entity uses manual procedures and records in paper format (e.g., to enter sales orders, authorize credit, prepare shipping reports and invoices, and maintain accounts receivable records). Controls in a "traditional" system also are manual, and may include procedures such as approvals and reviews of activities, and reconciliations and follow-up of reconciling items.

2. **Automatic** An entity may have complex IT systems that use automated procedures to initiate, record, process, and report transactions, in which case, records in electronic format replace paper documents such as purchase orders, invoices, and shipping documents. Controls in systems that use IT consist of a combination of automated controls (e.g., controls embedded in computer programs) and manual controls. Manual controls may be independent of the

IT system and may use information produced by the IT system, or may be limited to monitoring the effective functioning of the system and the automated controls and handling exceptions. An entity's mix of manual and automated controls varies with the nature and complexity of the entity's use of IT.

3. **Benefits** An IT environment provides benefits related to effectiveness and efficiency because it enables the entity to perform the following.

   a. Consistently apply predefined business rules and perform complex calculations in processing large volumes of transactions or data.

   b. Enhance the timeliness, availability, and accuracy of information.

   c. Facilitate the additional analysis of information.

   d. Enhance the ability to monitor the performance of the entity's activities and compliance with its policies and procedures.

   e. Reduce the risk that controls will be circumvented, especially if controls over changes to the IT system are effective.

4. **Risks** Risks within an IT environment include the following.

   a. Overreliance on information provided by the IT system that could be processing data incorrectly or consistently processing inaccurate data.

   b. Unauthorized access to data that may result in destruction of data or improper changes to data including the recording of unauthorized or nonexistent transactions or inaccurate recording of transactions.

   c. Unauthorized changes to computer programs.

   d. Failure to make necessary changes to computer programs.

   e. Inappropriate manual intervention.

   f. Potential loss of data.

5. **Considerations**

   a. **Documentation** Many procedures in IT systems do not leave evidence of performance automatically.

   b. **Electronic Information** Files and records are usually in machine-readable form and cannot be read without using a computer.

   c. **Knowledge** An user may need specialized knowledge to use the system.

   d. **Difficulty of Change** Once implemented, it is harder to change an IT system than it is to change a manual system. Therefore, accountants will want to become familiar with a new IT system at an early stage of the development process so that the accountant can anticipate possible future accounting and audit problems.

6. **Reliability** IT systems are more reliable than manual systems because all data is subject to the same controls; manual systems are subject to human error on a random basis. Computer processing virtually eliminates computational errors associated with manual processing; however, computer processing may obscure errors that a human would notice while handling a transaction.

B.   Transaction Processing Systems
Common systems are as follows.

1.   **Inventory Control** An inventory control application generally tracks the nature, quantity, location, and cost of inventory.

2.   **Sales** A sales application generally manages customer orders from order receipt to fulfillment billing. It interacts with the inventory control system to ensure adequate goods available for sale and with the general ledger to report sales. Accounts receivable and credit management functions may be included within the sales application or in separate applications.

3.   **Purchasing** A purchasing application may simply store and report details of purchasing activity or may be highly automated, initiating automatic orders electronically as inventory levels and sales indicate.

4.   **Payroll** The payroll application prepares and reports payroll, deductions, and withholding. It typically interacts closely with a separate human resources application.

5.   **Production** A production application schedules and tracks manufacturing activity. Material requirements planning (MRP) is a system for effectively managing material requirements in a manufacturing process, typically in a computerized environment. Using bills of material, inventory data, and master production schedules, MRP applications make recommendations to reorder materials and, as appropriate, reschedule open orders when due dates and required dates are out of synchronization.

6.   **General Ledger** The general ledger application facilitates chart of accounts maintenance and financial reporting. All applications that manage financial data report transactions to the general ledger application.

C.   Management Reporting Systems

1.   **Financial Statements** Financial statements are generated readily from IT records. Standard financial statements (income statement, balance sheet, statement of cash flows, etc.) are designed once and then generated on a fairly automatic basis. *Ad hoc* reports (for example, a comparative report of overtime and sick days before and after a scheduling policy change) are developed in response to a particular situation, often by the user or non-IT personnel.

2.   **Data Mining** Data mining (also known as relationship mapping, data interrogation, or knowledge discovery) is the distillation of previously unknown information from raw data. The largest strength of data mining is identification of unexpected relationships. Manual review may be inefficient for entities with a high number of transactions. Data mining is used for many purposes (streamlining operations, marketing analysis). Data mining tools can assist users to perceive patterns in voluminous databases in a timely manner.

Exhibit 4 ▶ Data Mining: Fraud Profile Examples for Accounts Payable

Vendor records that list more than one payment address. (Vendors may have multiple branches, or payments to a legitimate vendor may have been fraudulently redirected.)

Vendor records showing only post office box addresses. (While payments are frequently sent to lock boxes, usually there is one address—for instance, shipping or purchasing—that is a street address.)

In a large organization, records for one vendor showing the same authorized signer on every check and/or the same receiving clerk accepting every delivery connected with that vendor. (In an organization with several possible signers and receiving clerks for any given transaction, this circumstance is an unlikely coincidence.)

Matching employee and vendor addresses. (It is rare that an employee's home-based business is a legitimate vendor.)

> Mailing addresses that are shared by vendors. (Several false vendors may share the same address or payments may be fraudulently redirected to the same address for a perpetrator's convenience.)
>
> Payments close to payment-review thresholds. (Management review is not necessary up to the threshold. Employees may aim to commit fraud for the largest amount possible per transaction.)
>
> Invoice numbers from the same vendor that are close in sequence. (Legitimate vendors typically have many customers.)

a. **Sieve** A data mining tool is like a sieve, allowing a user to sift through large amounts of data quickly, providing an overview of an entity. These preliminary procedures can be performed on entire populations, instead of relatively small samples. Users can readily identify relationships, allowing them to concentrate on analyzing relationships. Analysis tools also can highlight individual transactions that fit a profile.

b. **Customer Profiling** For example, a store may notice several apparently unrelated items commonly are purchased at the same time; a change in merchandise arrangement may result in increased sales. A credit card company may flag and delay transactions that don't fit its customers' profiles.

c. **Auditing** For example, a bank may have the same employees who authorized a loan to a debtor named Jones being named on checks drawn on the account that Jones opened with the loan proceeds. This coincidence might escape manual detection and yet warrant extra auditor scrutiny. A fraud profile is a summary of expected data characteristics that an auditor expects to find in a particular type of fraudulent transaction, based on an understanding of a given entity's internal control weaknesses. Not all transactions fitting a fraud profile are fraudulent, but an auditor may increase audit efficiency by selecting transactions to examine based on a fraud profile.

3. **Key Performance Indicators** Using data mining, an entity may be able to locate key performance indicators relevant to that particular entity. Managers may be able to review these indicators and be alerted to take corrective action before feedback from traditional financial statements is ready.

III. Electronic Commerce Implications

A. Business Operations

Electronic commerce (eCommerce) is business via the Internet, including EDI. Electronic commerce involves the electronic initiation, processing, and conclusion of the sales cycle (from order entry to payment) by electronic means. Because few businesses are engaged exclusively in electronic commerce, inventory information at physical sites must be integrated with the electronic commerce operation to avoid, for instance, selling the final item both on the Web and at a store (because inventory records were not updated) and having insufficient inventory to cover both orders.

1. **Web Site** Electronic commerce often is implemented through a web site where customers browse through a database of merchandise or offered services, place orders, and make payment. A simple web site might have little more than a business' name, address, and the product lines the entity sells. Some sites have an online catalog and order entry, but the back-end transaction processing is manual. True electronic commerce involves automatic interaction between the web site and the order processing, inventory, shipment, and other applications.

    a. **Back-End Transaction Processing** Sales reporting, order inquiry, inventory updating, shipping order generation, etc.

b. **Connectionless Environment** The Internet (or Web) is a connectionless environment, meaning a web site can interact with many users simultaneously. In contrast, a typical telephone call is a connected exchange—while a caller speaks with one person, others cannot call.

c. **Shopping Cart** Shopping cart technology allows the software to identify an individual customer, an essential in a connectionless environment, keeping track of that customer's journey through the site and items in that customer's order.

d. **Product Space** Also called catalog or shelf space. A database of products or services. Marketing or sales people, rather than programmers, can update a user-friendly database. This keeps programmer involvement to a minimum.

e. **Transaction Network** A transaction network allows the exchange of money. An instance is the use of credit cards or exchanges between checking accounts.

f. **Security Assurance** Without processes to ensure confidentiality and safety of financial information, few customers would release financial information necessary to complete the revenue cycle. For instance, CPA WebTrust is a symbol that appears on web sites to indicates that the site meets joint Canadian Institute of Chartered Accountants and AICPA business practice disclosures, transaction integrity, and information protection criteria. A digital signature is an encryption feature used to authenticate the originator of a document and insure that the message is intact.

2. **EDI** Electronic data interchange (EDI) is electronic communication among entities such as financial institutions and customer-vendor partners (typically involving order placement, invoicing, and payment and may involve inventory monitoring and automatic restocking). ANSI X12 is a domestic EDI format. EDIFACT is an international EDI format. Typically, a standing agreement (usually business-to-business) for electronic data interchange (EDI) transactions also is considered electronic commerce. EDI typically involves automatic monitoring of inventory levels and sales orders (by the business customer's system), purchase order placement and fulfillment, and payment. While there is not necessarily a web site, the back-end transaction processing is similar.

3. **Electronic Document Submission** Electronic document submission is submission of documents such as federal tax returns and securities reports in electronic form, usually over the Internet.

4. **Point-of-Sale (POS) System** A point-of-sale (POS) system is a system that records goods sold and figures the amount due at the cash register, frequently also verifying credit cards or checks.

5. **Self-Service Application** A self-service application is software that allows customers to provide much of their own customer service.

6. **Telecommuting** Telecommuting is working outside of a traditional office, remaining connected by the Internet, phone, et cetera. Telecommuting usually implies an office in the employee's home, although sales agents or insurance adjusters also might work from a vehicle and customer sites.

B. **Financial Statements**
IT allows for quick generation of financial statements, increasing the feedback value. Rather than taking weeks to close a fiscal period, even global organizations can close books in days or hours. Also greater detail (more frequent reports and information at a lower organizational level) to the user is a practical option, especially if delivered in electronic form. Customized reports can be generated from the same information, allowing for greater relevance to each user's needs.

1. *Ad Hoc* **Report** Non-standardized report composed when the need arises. Frequently developed by users, rather than programmers with extensive training, for limited use.

2. **Management Information** Rather than having managers read daily traditional financial statements (which could be voluminous reports), entities may use data mining to discover a handful of items that indicate the day-to-day entity performance and deliver only selected items of information on a routine basis. Sophisticated systems have drill-down capabilities so managers quickly can link to the detail behind this targeted snapshot of the entity.

IV. Business Continuity

A. Security

As organizations integrate IT functions within their operations, operation of the organization becomes dependent on operation of the IT system. Mere loss of IT functionality, intentional or unintentional, could prove damaging to the continuing survival of an organization. Further, fraudulent activity within a compromised IT environment could cause significant loss of other assets. Protection involves awareness at management and staff levels, appropriate funding, having business processes in place to identify vulnerabilities, intrusion detection tools, and security audits on an ongoing basis.

1. **Hackers** A **classic** hacker is a computer enthusiast—someone who's interested in learning the nitty-gritty of how computers and computer networks work, simply for the joy of it or for peer recognition. Hackers coined the term **crackers** (criminal + hackers) to describe hackers intentionally involved in unethical activity. Crackers break into systems to violate laws, to steal information, or otherwise to use computers inappropriately. Perhaps more dangerous than crackers are **script kiddies**. Script kiddies use tools—oftentimes, in an automated fashion—and cause damage without understanding what they're doing.

2. **Hacker Tools** **Demon dialers** are software tools that will dial through a series of phone numbers. Once a demon dialer finds modems, it issues standard or default passwords, username combinations, or a brute force-type attack (where it will go through a dictionary or try every combination up to, for instance, eight alphabet letter combination passwords) until it breaks into a system. **Port scanners** are tools that will scan a network and network devices, and produce, automatically, reports that say these particular services are available and open; thus, it's important to turn off services that are not being used and to restrict services that are being used. Automated **scripts** will interrogate or investigate machines, finding out what accounts exist on the machine and whether a limit on password attempts is enabled on the machine. Once loaded on any machine in an office, a **sniffer** will report all the user names and passwords that it sees on a network, allowing the operator access to an unaware user's e-mail or other accounts. A **Trojan horse** is a seemingly legitimate program that operates in an unauthorized manner, usually causing damage. A **virus** is a program that replicates and attaches itself to other programs. The effects of a virus can be merely an annoying message or malicious activity, such as reformatting a hard drive or flooding an email system. A **virus hoax** is an e-mail message with a false warning; its originator tries to get it circulated as widely as possible.

3. **Digital Signature** A digital signature is a guarantee that information has not been modified, like a tamper-proof seal on a bottle of aspirin. Digital signatures are used for establishing secure web site connections and verifying the validity, but not the privacy, of transmitted files. A digital signature does not verify the receiving person or address.

4. **Encryption** Encryption is a mathematical process of coding data so that it cannot be read by unauthorized people. Decryption is transforming an encrypted file into the file that existed before the encryption process. A key is used to lock and unlock the data. To encrypt a file, one performs some mathematical functions on the data and the result of these functions produces a file that is meaningless without decryption (reversing the process). For instance, a file containing a credit card number may be sent across the Internet safely once it is encrypted. Information users cannot read encrypted files. The recipient has to decrypt the file once it is received to read it. The two broad encryption categories are distinguished by the key.

a. **Key** Encryption and decryption software accepts a file, performs some predefined mathematical operations on the data, and produces an encrypted file. A key is the set of mathematical operations and any random initial values that are used to encrypt and decrypt the data. Encryption and decryption algorithms describe the mathematical operations as opposed to the key, which describes the exact process, including the algorithms and any other random initial values used by the algorithms.

b. **Symmetric Encryption** With symmetric (or private key) encryption, the same algorithm is used for encryption and decryption. Anyone who knows the method used to encrypt the message can decrypt the message. Using this method for secure transmissions requires that the key be kept secret between the person sending the data and the person receiving the data. Accordingly, the two users must communicate and agree on the algorithm and key beforehand so that the recipient can decrypt the messages.

(1) **Feature** Both parties use the same key to encrypt and decrypt messages.

(2) **Disadvantage** The key must be known by both the sender and receiver beforehand. This means that this is a poor system for entities that send or receive a few messages with many correspondents. For instance, it is awkward for an online retailer to establish a key for each customer because (a) to be effective, keys must be secret, meaning that they should not be sent in messages that are not encrypted; (b) the keys must be assigned before encrypted messages can be sent; and (c) there is no means for the recipient to decrypt an encrypted message that contains an unknown key.

c. **Asymmetric Encryption** Public key (asymmetric) encryption is a system that uses a public key that may be made widely known and a private key that is intended to be kept secret and known only by the recipient of the encrypted messages. The private key is not released or disclosed. The sender encrypts messages to each particular recipient with that particular recipient's public key. The recipient decrypts messages with that particular recipient's private key.

(1) **Feature** Only the related public key can be used to encrypt messages by the corresponding private key. Only the corresponding private key can be used to decrypt them. It is extremely difficult to deduce the private key, even knowing the public key. Therefore, secure communication may take place between the recipient and the sender without advance communication through another means.

(2) **Disadvantage** A sender must know the recipient's public key to send a recipient something encrypted. Either the potential recipient must let each potential sender know the public key explicitly or a public registry of public keys needs to be established.

5. **Passwords** A typical password policy might require passwords to be at least eight characters long and include a special character (?, &, or *) as well as numeric characters. This is because a password cracker (a hacker tool) typically tries the words in a dictionary as passwords. A prudent operator may set the number of password attempts to something like three; however, for each one of the accounts that a password cracker discovers, it may try two passwords: password equal to blank and then password equal to "username." These two passwords are defaults that frequently are not changed. With wireless networks, access to the network is particularly easy, making password policies even more important than with wired networks.

B. **Disaster Recovery**
Disaster recovery is restoration of data and business function after loss. Conceivably, additional copies of off-the-shelf software and hardware could be purchased as needed, if it is widely available; however, with a situation affecting an entire geographic area, such as a flood, temporary shortages and transportation problems probably would render this plan inadequate for most entities.

Example 1 ▶ Contingency Plan: Lack of Testing

Mellow Construction has a disaster recovery plan that outlines contact protocols for employees, customers, and essential vendors; off-site data backup; laptops for use from employee's homes, and a small contingency site for central computer operations in a construction site trailer. Fire occurs in the building where Mellow leases office space. Its offices suffer heat, smoke, water, and possible structural damage, making it impossible to enter the offices until officials inspect the entire building, in about a week. Further, even after such approval, it will be weeks before the offices will be ready for occupancy again. In accordance with the disaster recovery plan, the managing partner starts to contact each of the managers, who in turn contact their staff members. The IT manager initiates restoration at the backup computer center. Hours into the recovery, weaknesses in the contingency plan become apparent.

One of the managers is on vacation; a copy of the contact information for her staff is locked away at her vacant home. Thus, the managing partner has no access to these employee's home phone numbers until the central computer is operating unless those employees contact Mellow.

Customers, employees, and vendors are calling the backup computer center with questions regarding projects' status and delivery details, because that is the only phone number they have for Mellow that anybody is answering. The staff at various construction trailers also is getting similar calls; while they take messages regarding these calls, they have little idea of who to give most of them to.

Further, employees are swamping the IT staff with questions about help remote connections, tying up the phone lines further and delaying work on the restoration of the very files and programs that the callers are trying to access.

Two months ago, Mellow updated a human resources program that tracks employee information, yet there is no copy of the new software at the contingency site. Some of the current backup data files are incompatible with the former software. Payday for 250 full and part-time employees is in three days; while information regarding time, rates, and type of pay is linked to employee numbers, the information on names, addresses, and phone numbers linked to those employee numbers is unavailable.

Discussion: Had Mellow done some scenario testing before the disaster, it likely would have noted weaknesses and refined the disaster recover plan. Such testing likely would have initiated development of procedures that allowed for unavailability of essential employees and redundant backups of essential information such as employee phone numbers; a backup receptionist and message distribution plan; and established priorities for IT tasks (restoration versus technical support, etc.). Such testing also would have kept the importance of software backups fresh in the minds of the IT staff.

1. **Files** Back-up data and software are essential to recovery. Back-up data stored off-site is perhaps the minimum requirement for a disaster recovery plan. Back-ups of customized software must be kept so that full functionality is available.

2. **Hardware** To restore function, hardware must be available to use the data software files. The more essential an IT function, the greater the investment in back-up hardware should be. At one end of the spectrum, an entity may plan to order replacement personal computers in the event of a disaster. At the other end of the spectrum, large organizations with minimal downtime contracts may have alternate sites and detailed plans to transport regular personnel or hire temporary personnel for essential functions. Low-downtime plans might include power generation as well as living and child care accommodations for, and commitments from, essential personnel. Backup arrangements frequently are made with service bureaus or with subsidiaries. Backup facilities are referred to as "hot" or "cold" sites, depending on their state of readiness.

   a. **Hot Site** Location where a functioning system is planned for use with minimal preparation in the event of a disaster at the primary work location.

      b.   **Cold Site** Location where equipment and power is available in the event of disaster at the primary location, but requiring considerable effort to get an operational system functioning.

  3. **Plan** Continuity planning should include notification procedures, recovery management, temporary operating procedures, and back-up and recovery procedures.

      a.   **Notification Procedures** Notification procedures outline how staff and external stakeholders will contact each other. This includes locating people as well as communications. A plan might include general notification through a web-site to streamline notification to stakeholders who are not involved directly in the restoration, especially initially. After a flood, for instance, a website may tell employees of their recovery-period assignments and reassure vendors and customers that payments and shipping will resume in a week.

      b.   **Recovery Management** The relative importance of various aspects of the contingency plan should be determined before a disaster and must be understood for appropriate decisions to be made during recovery from disasters that differ from tested scenarios. Physical facilities, communications, data processing, and staffing requirements are all part of recovery.

      c.   **Temporary Operating Procedures** Along with having IT employees work at an off-site facility, a plan also may call for a receptionist to handle calls and a non-IT manager who can authorize unforeseen purchases, to ensure that the IT employees can concentrate on restoring systems. As it may take weeks or months for regular facilities to become available, a plan may call for office employees to work from their homes. If this is not normal for the entity, IT resources will be needed to establish and support this off-site computer use as well as reestablish regular IT functions.

  4. **Testing** Given the domino effect that disasters may create and the difficulty of adapting during a disaster, continuity plans should be tested.

      a.   **Scenario Testing** The expense and lost productivity to simulate a company-wide disaster could be significant and unnecessary. A dry run (or table-top testing) would discover many weaknesses and allow contingency plans to be refined. Several limited-scope disaster simulations could pinpoint additional weaknesses with minimal disruption to regular operations.

      b.   **Secondary Effects** When a widespread disaster occurs, infrastructure that normally is in place may be unavailable or burdened more than usual.

      c.   **Recovery Plan Team** Having a multi-functional team responsible for creating, updating, and executing a recovery plan keeps the plan relevant, updated, and realistic.

C. **Documentation**

Documentation is an important aspect of control and communication. It generally provides (1) an understanding of the system's objectives, concepts, and output, (2) a source of information for systems analysts and programmers when involved in program maintenance and revision, (3) information that is needed for a supervisory review, (4) a basis for training new personnel, (5) a means of communicating common information, (6) a source of information about accounting controls, and (7) a source of information that will aid in providing continuity in the event experienced personnel leave. There are several types of documentation.

Exhibit 6 ♦ Common Flowchart Symbols

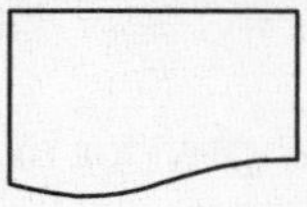

DOCUMENT: Paper documents and reports of all kinds, e.g., sales invoices, purchase orders, employee paychecks, and computer-prepared error listings.

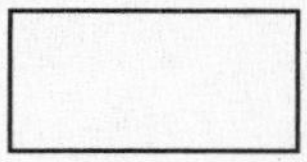

COMPUTER OPERATION/PROCESS: Execute defined operations resulting in some change in the information or the determination of flow direction, e.g., checking customer's credit limit.

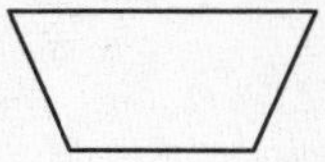

MANUAL OPERATION: Off-line process that is performed manually, e.g., preparing a three-part sales invoice or manually posting to customer accounts.

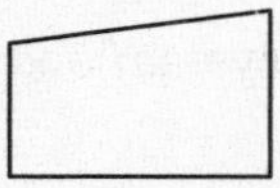

MANUAL INPUT: Represents input entered manually at the time of processing, e.g., using a keyboard.

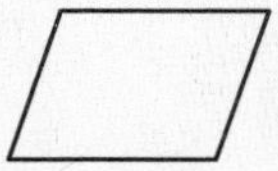

INPUT/OUTPUT: General input/output symbol, e.g., general ledger, can be used regardless of the type of medium or data.

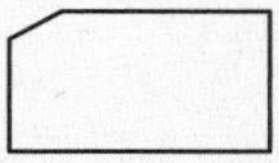

PUNCHED CARD: Input/output function in which the medium is a punched card, e.g., payroll earnings card.

PUNCHED TAPE: Input/output function in which the medium is punched tape.

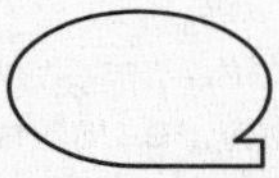

MAGNETIC TAPE: Input/output function in which the medium is magnetic tape, e.g., master payroll data file.

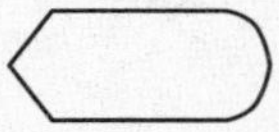

DISPLAY: Input/output device in which the information is displayed at the time of processing for human use, e.g., display customer number.

ONLINE STORAGE: Storage that is connected to and under the control of the computer, e.g., disk, drum, magnetic tape, etc.

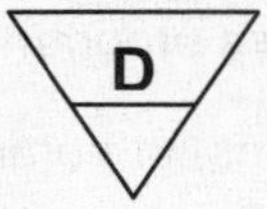

OFF-LINE STORAGE: Any off-line storage of information regardless of the medium on which the information is recorded. This includes filing documents such as sales invoices and purchase orders. An "A" signifies an alphabetic file, an "N" is for a numeric file, and a "D" indicates a file organized by date.

OFF-PAGE CONNECTOR: Designates entry to or exit from a page. For example, it can be used to indicate sending a copy of an invoice to a customer.

ANNOTATION: Provides additional information.

DECISION: Determines next action. Used in program flowcharts, e.g., is A = B?

1. **Problem Definition Documentation** Permits the auditor to gain a general understanding of the system without having to become involved in the details of the programs. Contents include the following.

   a. Description of the reasons for implementing the system.

    b.   Description of the operations performed by the system.

    c.   Project proposals.

    d.   Evidence of approval of the system and subsequent changes (for example, a particular individual may have to sign a form to indicate these).

    e.   A listing of the assignment of project responsibilities.

2.   **Systems Documentation** Provides sufficient information to trace accounting data from its original entry to system output. Contents include the following.

    a.   A description of the system.

    b.   A systems flowchart shows the flow of data through the system and the interrelationships between the processing steps and computer runs.

    c.   Input descriptions.

    d.   Output descriptions.

    e.   File descriptions.

    f.   Descriptions of controls.

    g.   Copies of authorizations and their effective dates for systems changes that have been implemented.

3.   **Program Documentation** Primarily used by systems analysts and programmers to provide a control over program corrections and revisions. However, it may be useful to the auditor to determine the current status of a program. Contents include the following.

    a.   Brief narrative description of the program.

    b.   A program flowchart shows the steps followed by the program in processing the data. A decision table describes a portion of the logic used in the program. Although it is not always used, it can replace or supplement the program flowchart. A detailed logic narrative is a narrative description of the logic followed by a program.

    c.   Source statements (i.e., a listing of the program instructions) or parameter listings.

    d.   List of control features.

    e.   Detailed description of file formats and record layouts.

    f.   Table of code values used to indicate processing requirements.

    g.   Record of program changes, authorizations, and effective dates.

    h.   Input and output formats.

    i.   Operating instructions.

    j.   Descriptions of any special features.

4.   **Operations Documentation** Information provided to the computer operator. It can be used by the auditor to obtain an understanding of the functions performed by the operator and to determine how data is processed. Contents include the following.

    a.   A brief description of the program.

    b.   Description of the inputs and outputs that are required (e.g., the forms used).

    c.   Sequence of cards, tapes, disks, and other files.

    d.   Set-up instructions and operating system requirements.

    e.   Operating notes listing program messages, halts, and action necessary to signal the end of jobs.

    f.   Control procedures to be performed by operations.

    g.   Recovery and restart procedures (to be used for hardware or software malfunctions).

    h.   Estimated normal and maximum run time.

    i.   Instructions to the operator in the event of an emergency.

5.   **User Documentation** Description of the input required for processing and an output listing. The auditor may use it to gain an understanding of the functions performed by the user and the general flow of information. Contents include a description of the system, description of the input and output, list of control procedures and an indication of the position of the person performing the procedures, error correction procedures, cutoff procedures for submitting the data to the IT department, and a description of how the user department should check reports for accuracy.

6.   **Operator Documentation** Documentation should be prepared that will indicate the jobs run and any operator interaction.

    a.   **Daily Computer Log** May be prepared manually by the computer operator or automatically by the system software. It indicates the jobs run, the time required, who ran them, etc.

    b.   **Console Log** A listing of all interactions between the console and the CPU. Prepared by the computer as messages are entered from the console, it can be a valuable control for detecting unauthorized intervention of the computer operator during the running of a program. It also shows how the operator responded to processing problems.

7.   **Decision Tables** Decision tables are a type of documentation. They emphasize the relationships among conditions and actions, and present decision choices. Decision tables often supplement systems flowcharts.

Exhibit 5 ▶ IT Documentation Mnemonic

O	Operations Documentation
P	Problem Definition Documentation
S	Systems Documentation
O	Operator Documentation
U	User Documentation
P	Program Documentation

V. General Controls (GC)

A. Organization & Operation Controls

1.   **GC 1:**   Segregation of functions between the IT department and users.

2.   **GC 2:**   Provision for general authorization over the execution of transactions (prohibiting the IT department from initiating or authorizing transactions).

3.   **GC 3:**   Part of proper internal control is the segregation of functions within the IT department.

B.   Systems Development & Documentation Controls

1.   **GC 4:**   The procedures for system design, including the acquisition of software packages, should require active participation by representatives of the users and, as appropriate, the accounting department and internal auditors.

2.   **GC 5:**   Each system should have written specifications that are reviewed and approved by an appropriate level of management and users in applicable departments.

3.   **GC 6:**   Systems testing should be a joint effort of users and IT personnel and should include both the manual and computerized phases of the system.

4.   **GC 7:**   Final approval should be obtained prior to placing a new system into operation.

5.   **GC 8:**   All master file and transaction file conversions should be controlled to prevent unauthorized changes and to provide accurate and complete results.

6.   **GC 9:**   After a new system has been placed in operation, all program changes should be approved before implementation to determine whether they have been authorized, tested, and documented.

7.   **GC 10:**   Management should require various levels of documentation and establish formal procedures to define the system at appropriate levels of detail.

C.   Hardware & Systems Software Controls
Hardware controls are controls that are built into the computer.

1.   **Parity Bit (Redundant Character Check)** In odd parity, an odd number of magnetized dots (on tape, disk, etc.) should always represent each character. When recording data, the computer automatically checks this. Then, when reading the data, the computer checks to see if there is still an odd number. In even parity, an even number of magnetized dots is used to represent each character. For example, the use of a parity bit probably would discover a distortion caused either by dust on a tape or by sending data over telephone lines.

2.   **Echo Check** CPU sends a signal to activate an input or output device in a certain manner. The device then sends a signal back to verify activation. The CPU then compares the signals.

3.   **Hardware Check** Computer checks to make sure the equipment is functioning properly. For example, periodically the computer may search for circuits that are failing.

4.   **Boundary Protection** Keeps several files or programs separate when they share a common storage. For example, in time-sharing, several users may share primary storage. Boundary protection would prevent their data and/or programs from becoming mixed and from accessing each other's data.

5.   **GC 11:**   The control features inherent in the computer hardware, operating system, and other supporting software should be utilized to the maximum possible extent to provide control over operations and to detect and report hardware malfunctions.

6.   **GC 12:**   Systems software should be subjected to the same control procedures as those applied to the installation of, and changes to, application programs.

D.   Access Controls
Only authorized personnel should have access to the facilities housing IT equipment, files, and documentation. Access control software is available to limit system access electronically. Access to program documentation and computer hardware should be limited to those persons who require it in the performance of their duties. Access to data files and programs should be limited to those individuals authorized to process or maintain particular systems.

E.   Data & Procedural Controls

1.   File Labels External labels are human-readable labels attached to the outside of a secondary storage device, indicating the name of the file, expiration date, etc. Internal labels are labels in machine-readable form.

   a.   Header Label Appears at the *beginning* of the file and contains such information as the file name, identification number, and the tape reel number.

   b.   Trailer Label Appears at the *end* of the file and contains such information as a count of the number of the records in the file and an end-of-file code.

2.   File Protection Ring A plastic ring that must be attached to a reel of magnetic tape before the tape drive will write on the tape. Since writing on magnetic tape automatically erases the data already there, the file protection ring guards against the inadvertent erasure of the information on the tape.

3.   File Protection Plans

   a.   Duplicate Files The most important data files are duplicated and the duplicates are safely stored away from the computer center.

   b.   Grandparent-Parent-Child (or Vice Versa) Retention Concept This also is known as Grandfather-Father-Son Retention. The master file is updated at the end of each day by the day's transaction file, illustrated in Exhibit 7. After updating on Thursday, the Thursday updated master file (TUMF) is the child, the Wednesday updated master file (WUMF) is the parent, and the Tuesday updated master file (TSUMF) is the grandparent. These three files plus Wednesday's and Thursday's transaction files (WTF and TTF, respectively) are retained. If there is a problem during Friday's update run, the TUMF can be regenerated by running the copy of the WUMF with Thursday's transaction file. If necessary the WUMF could be reconstructed by processing TSUMF with Wednesday's transaction file. Once updating is completed on Friday, Friday's updated master file (FUMF) becomes the child, TUMF becomes the parent and WUMF becomes the grandparent. Therefore, at that time, TSUMF and Wednesday's transaction file can be erased.

Exhibit 7 ▶ Grandparent-Parent-Child Retention Concept

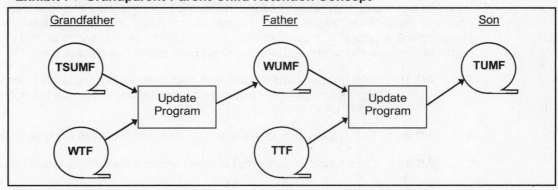

    c.   **Disk Reconstruction Plan** In updating a record in a disk file, the record is read from the disk into the CPU, altered, and then written back to its previous location on the disk, thereby erasing the preupdated record. Therefore, a "disk dump" is used in which a copy of the contents of the disk is made on magnetic tape periodically, say each morning. Then, as the day's transactions are processed against the disk file, copies of the transactions are recorded on another tape. If it becomes necessary to reconstruct the disk file at any time during the day, the old file can be read from the tape to the disk and reupdated with the transactions from the transaction tape.

4.   **Physical Safeguards**

    a.   **Proper Physical Environment** Consider extreme temperature, humidity, dust, etc.

    b.   **Environment Free From Possibility of Disasters** Includes proper fire-proofing and locating the computer in a safe place (for example, not in the basement if there is a danger of flooding).

    c.   **Control Access to Computer Room** Only authorized personnel should have access. For example, computer operators would be authorized to be in the computer room, but programmers should not be. A weakness in internal control exists when a client uses personal computers, because these computers rarely are isolated in a limited-access location and operators may remove hardware and software components and modify them at home more readily.

5.   **GC 16:**   A control function should be responsible for receiving all data to be processed, for ensuring that all data are recorded, for following up on errors detected during processing to see that the transactions are corrected and resubmitted by the proper party, and for verifying the proper distribution of output.

6.   **GC 17:**   A written manual of systems and procedures should be prepared for all computer operations and should provide for management's general or specific authorizations to process transactions.

7.   **GC 18:**   Internal auditors or an other independent group within an organization should review and evaluate proposed systems at critical stages of development.

8.   **GC 19:**   On a continuing basis, internal auditors, or an other independent group within an organization should review and test computer processing activities.

VI. Application Controls (AC)

A. Input Controls

Input controls are designed to provide reasonable assurance that data received by the IT department have been properly authorized, converted into machine sensible form, and identified, and that data have not been lost, suppressed, added, duplicated, or otherwise changed improperly. Basic categories of input to be controlled are (1) transaction entry, (2) file maintenance transactions (e.g., changing sales prices on a product master file), (3) inquiry transactions (e.g., how many units of a particular inventory item are on hand), and (4) error correction transactions.

    1.   **AC 1:**   Only properly authorized and approved input, prepared in accordance with management's general or specific authorization, should be accepted for processing by the IT department.

    2.   **AC 2:**   The system should verify all significant codes used to record data.

    3.   **AC 3:**   Conversion of data into machine-sensible form should be controlled.

    4.   **Common Errors in Conversion** Keying errors and the losing or dropping of records.

5.   **Input Control Techniques**

a.   **Control Totals** A total is computed and then recomputed at a later time. The totals are compared and should be the same. Control totals can be used as *input*, processing, and output controls.

    (1)   **Financial Total** Has financial meaning in addition to being a control. For example, the dollar amount of accounts receivable to be updated can be compared with a computer-generated total of the dollar amount of updates read from the tape.

    (2)   **Hash Total** Has meaning only as a control. For example, a total of the account numbers of those accounts that should have been updated can be compared with a computer-generated total of those account numbers actually entered.

    (3)   **Record Count (Document Count)** A count of the number of transactions processed. For example, the computer can be programmed to print the total number of A/R records actually inputted.

b.   **Computer Editing** Computers can be programmed to perform a wide range of edit tests (i.e., edit checks) on records as they are being entered into the system. If a particular record does not meet the test, it is not processed. Edit tests include the following:

    (1)   **Limit (Reasonableness) Test** A particular field of an input transaction record is checked to be sure it is not greater (or smaller) than a prespecified amount, or that it is within a prespecified range of acceptable values. For example, "hours worked" on a payroll record may be checked to be sure it does not exceed 50 hours.

    (2)   **Valid Field and/or Character Test** The particular field is examined to be sure it is of the proper size and composition. For example, if a customer account number should be seven numeric digits appearing in the first 7 spaces of the record, the first 7 spaces can be examined to be sure there are 7 numerals there.

    (3)   **Valid Number or Code Test** Verifies that a particular number or code is one of those that is recognized by the system. For example, if a company has 5 retail outlets and records sales by using a location code of 1-5, the computer can check to be sure the code digit on the transaction record is a 1, 2, 3, 4, or 5.

    (4)   **Sequence Check** If the input records should be in some particular sequence, the computer can be programmed to verify the sequence. For example, after sorting, the day's transaction file that is being entered should be in ascending order by customer account number.

    (5)   **Missing Data Test** Verifies that all of the data fields actually contain data. For example, a point-of-sale terminal may be programmed not to accept a transaction unless the clerk has entered 10 pieces of required data.

    (6)   **Valid Transaction Test** Since there are only a certain number of transaction types that would be expected for most files, the computer can be programmed to verify that a particular transaction is an appropriate type for a particular file. For example, in the case of inventory, the only valid transaction may be to debit the inventory account when inventory is added and credit the account when inventory is taken away.

    (7)   **Valid Combination of Fields** Checks to be sure a certain combination of fields is reasonable. For example, a large retail outlet may program its computer to check the reasonableness of the product code field and the quantity-sold field.

This would disclose a clerical error that resulted in a sale being entered for 11 television sets when only 1 was sold; i.e., it is not reasonable that one retail customer would purchase 11 television sets.

    (8)   **Check Digit (Self-Checking Digit)** Digit (determined according to a prespecified mathematical routine) that is added to the end of a piece of numeric data to permit the numeric data to be checked for accuracy during input, processing, or output. For example, a customer account number may be 1234. A check digit could be formed by adding the first and third digits and using the sum. Since the sum of the two digits is 4 (i.e., 1 + 3), the check digit is 4. It is added to the end of the number that is assigned to the customer. The new customer account number becomes 12344. The computer can be programmed to verify the check digit at appropriate times. For instance, if the number is accidentally entered as 13244, the check digit would not match and the transaction would not be accepted. In practice, the mathematical routine generally is more complex than the one illustrated here.

    (9)   **Valid Sign Test** A particular field can be checked to be sure it has the proper sign. For example, the quantity received in an inventory record should not be negative.

6.   **AC 4:**   Movement of data between one processing step and another, or between departments, should be controlled.

7.   **AC 5:**   The correction of all errors detected by the application system and the resubmission of corrected transactions should be reviewed and controlled.

- **Error Log (Error Listing)** A computer-prepared list of those transactions that were not processed because of some error condition (e.g., an invalid customer account number). When an error is encountered, the usual procedure is for the computer to not process the erroneous transaction but to skip it and continue processing the valid transactions rather than to halt processing altogether. A control function should be responsible for following up on errors detected during processing to see that the transactions are corrected and resubmitted by the proper party. This control function should ideally be delegated to a special IT control group that is independent from system analysis, programming, and operation.

B.   **Processing Controls**
(**NOTE:** Many of the input controls are also valid processing controls.)

1.   **AC 6:**   Control totals should be produced and reconciled with input control totals.

2.   **AC 7:**   Controls should prevent processing the wrong file, detect errors in file manipulation, and highlight operator-caused errors.

3.   **AC 8:**   Limit and reasonableness checks should be incorporated within programs.

4.   **AC 9:**   Run-to-run controls should be verified at appropriate points in the processing cycle.

C.   **Output Controls**
Primarily balancing, visual scanning or verification, and distribution.

1.   **AC 10:**   Output control totals should be reconciled with input and processing controls.

2.   **AC 11:**   Output should be scanned and tested by comparison to original source documents.

3.   **AC 12:**   Systems output should be distributed only to authorized users.

VII. Special Systems

A. Online, Real Time (OLRT) Systems

These also are called quick response systems. Transactions are *processed* and files *updated* as transactions occur. The data is processed fast enough to get the response back in time to influence the process. Common examples include airline reservations systems in which the customer receives the reservations after waiting only a few moments and point-of-sale (POS) terminals in retail stores where a customer's credit limit is checked while the customer waits.

1. Common Characteristics

    a. Online terminals usually are used.

    b. Data files are usually disk files.

    c. A supervisory program (software) is used to manage the OLRT system.

2. General Controls Hardware controls that control the transmittal of the transactions from the terminal to the CPU and back are important (for example, a parity bit). Documentation of the transaction is often produced as a by-product of processing. For example, in point-of-sale terminals, a multicopy sales receipt is usually prepared when the transaction is processed. Further, many terminals automatically prepare an input log (input listing) that includes the code number of the employees who entered the data as well as information about the transactions.

3. Application Controls Due to the nature of OLRT systems, application controls are particularly important. They include the following.

    a. Passwords In some systems, only certain passwords can input certain kinds of transactions or access certain data files. For example, a sales representative could input sales orders under a password, but not change payroll records.

    b. Input Edit Tests Limit and reasonableness tests, valid customer number tests, missing data tests, etc. Transactions that are found to contain an error will not be accepted for processing and the clerk will be notified immediately. Normal error correction is through correction and resubmission.

    c. Control Totals Control totals can be prepared by the terminal and later checked against totals prepared by the CPU, e.g., the number of transactions processed or the dollar value of sales processed for a day. Either of these totals also could be checked against the copies of the sales slips.

B. Personal Computer Systems

The basic considerations in a small computer environment are the same as those in a large and complex IT system.

1. Planning Since the number of records that can be stored in a personal computer system is limited, detailed records often are retained for a limited period of time.

2. General Controls

    a. System Design & Documentation Since the choice of software in small systems is influenced by the hardware, users should be involved in the selection of both hardware and software. Although access to program documentation should be limited, it is difficult to enforce in many small computer environments where the data processing group is small.

    b. File Conversion & System Testing Frequently, an organization's initial IT applications include the use of a small business computer system. File conversion and system testing are particularly important in these initial applications. Before relying on the contents of converted files, the user should evaluate the controls used to ensure against lost or distorted data during conversion.

c. **Hardware Control** Limiting access to computer hardware is difficult in a small computer environment. Often, these systems lack controls that would prevent access to the actual hardware. Such a situation may cause the auditor to reduce reliance on stored data records. However, good application controls usually can compensate for problems caused by the absence or ineffectiveness of hardware controls.

d. **Software Control** All program changes should be authorized, tested, and documented. It is also important to control disks with stored data when not in use. Files should be copied or backed up to ensure against loss of data. The use of hard disk drives calls for access protection with the use of passwords, IDs, and the like.

3. **Application Controls** Most application controls have the same relevance in the personal computer environment as they do in large IT systems. The following are problems characteristic of small computer environments.

a. Many of the protection controls available in large systems to prohibit file manipulation or processing errors are not available in personal computer systems.

b. Limit (reasonableness) checks generally are not adapted to specific situations since most small system software is purchased off the shelf.

c. Most data is **not** converted into machine-readable form before input into a personal computer system. This should cause more concern with data input controls and less concerned with data conversion controls.

4. **Distributed Systems** Distributed systems are a network of remote computer sites where small computers are connected to a main computer system. A reduced work load on the main computer results, since edit and processing functions can be performed at the small computer station, as well as increased efficiency from faster turnaround of information.

C. **Service Center (Service Bureau)**
A service center provides IT services to its clients for a fee. Processing of client data occurs at the service center and the client's computerized master files are usually maintained at the center. Certain controls are particularly important because of the *nature* of the client-service center relationship.

Exhibit 8 ▶ IT Service Center Controls

T	Transmission
E	Error Correction
A	Audit trail
M	Master file changes
O	Output
S	Security

1. **Transmission** Document counts, hash totals, financial totals, etc., may be used to control the transmission of data to and from the client's office.

2. **Error Correction** Client should receive an error listing that identifies all of the errors that occurred in the system. Correction, review, and approval procedures should be established and used.

3. **Audit Trail** An audit trail must be maintained. This may be done through proper filing and sequencing of original transaction documents, and also through periodic reports of journal and ledger balances.

4. **Master File Changes** Printout of all master file changes should be sent to the client. Control counts of master file records and control totals of items within master file records may be used.

5. **Output** Output must be *restricted* to the client. An output distribution list (indicating who should receive the output) and control tests on samples of output may be used.

6. **Security** Service center must have adequate controls to protect the client's data (while being stored and during processing). Further, there must be adequate *reconstruction* procedures so that the client's data files can be reconstructed (i.e., recreated) if all or part of them are destroyed.

D. **Time-Sharing Systems**
A time-sharing center *rents* time on its central computer to a number of users, with each user having one or more remote input and output devices. The user usually accesses the central computer over telephone lines. To each user, it seems as if they are the only one using the system. User files and programs are maintained at the time-sharing center.

1. Controls are needed (a) to prevent *alteration* and *destruction* of the client's programs and data files, (b) to prevent the *unauthorized* use of the client's programs and data files, (c) to *reconstruct* the data files and other data in the event of a catastrophe or computer breakdown, and (d) to guard against *inaccurate transmission* of data between the client's terminal and the time-sharing center, and vice versa.

2. Common controls include programmed application controls (as discussed earlier); control totals for data transmission; control totals for processing; boundary protection features (to prevent programs from entering storage, both primary and secondary, that they are not authorized to enter); and the use of passwords or codes that must be furnished by the user to access programs and files.

CPA Exam Week Checklist

What to pack for exam week:

1. CPA exam registration material (Notice to Schedule and **two** proper forms of ID).

2. Hotel confirmation.

3. Cash and/or a major credit card.

4. Alarm clock—Don't rely on a hotel wake-up call.

5. Comfortable clothing that can be layered to suit varying temperatures.

6. An inexpensive watch (to leave in a testing site locker).

7. Appropriate review materials (don't take to exam site).

8. Healthy snack foods.

Evenings before exam sections:

1. Read through your Bisk Education chapter outlines for the next day's section(s).

2. Eat lightly and monitor your intake of alcohol and caffeine. Get a good night's rest.

3. Do not try to cram. A brief review of your notes will help to focus your attention on important points and remind you that you are well prepared, but too much cramming can shatter your self-confidence. If you have reviewed conscientiously, you already are well-prepared for the CPA exam.

The morning of each exam section:

1. Eat a satisfying breakfast. It will be several hours before your next meal. Eat enough to ward off hunger, but not so much that you feel uncomfortable.

2. Dress appropriately. Wear layers you can loosen to suit varying temperatures in the room.

3. Arrive at the exam center at least 30 minutes early. Check in as soon as you are allowed to do so.

More helpful exam information is included in the **Practical Advice** appendix in this volume.

———————————

CHAPTER 55—INFORMATION TECHNOLOGY

Problem 55-1 MULTIPLE CHOICE QUESTIONS (120 to 150 minutes)

1. Which of the following is considered a component of a local area network?
a. Program flowchart
b. Loop verification
c. Transmission media
d. Input routine   (5/98, Aud., #7, 6624)

2. What is the primary advantage of using an application firewall rather than a network firewall?
a. It is less expensive.
b. It offers easier access to applications.
c. It provides additional user authentication.
d. It is easier to install.   (R/03, BEC, #7, 7669)

3. What term is used to describe the display of more than one program on a portion of a monitor at the same time, but permits only one of those programs to be active?
a. Distributed processing
b. Multiprocessing
c. Multiprogramming
d. Windowing   (Editors, 7423)

4. What best describes an allocation of computer tasks located throughout a nationwide entity's various facilities?
a. Distributed processing
b. Local area network
c. Online processing
d. Multiprocessing
e. Timesharing   (Editors, 7424)

5. A bus network is characterized by communication channels
a. Directly linked to a single host computer
b. Linked to a loop, with each message passed neighbor to neighbor until the message reaches its destination
c. Linked to one common line with direct access to the message destination
d. Organized along hierarchical channels that eventually are linked to a single host computer
(Editors, 7450)

6. What reliable and economic automatic device do banks commonly use for data entry for check processing?
a. Bar coding
b. Electronic data interchange
c. Magnetic ink character recognition
d. Magnetic tape   (Editors, 7449)

7. Which of the following statements is inapplicable to database management systems (DBMS)?
a. The database administrator is that part of the software that directs the program operation when data is added to, located within, or deleted from the database.
b. DBMS maintain data and programs separately except during processing.
c. DBMS include a set of data definitions that help describe the logical structure of the database.
d. A primary goal of DBMS is to minimize data redundancy.   (Editors, 7447)

8. Batch processing
a. Allows users to inquire about information within the system
b. Groups transactions for incorporation into a master file
c. Processes individual transactions on input
d. Reduces the audit trail   (Editors, 7448)

9. Each record in a database is assigned a unique identification key. Which of the following is **not** an attribute of keys?
a. A given record may have multiple secondary keys.
b. A primary key is the main means to locate records within the file.
c. A secondary key may replace the primary key.
d. A secondary key may be used to locate a record when the primary key is unknown.
(Editors, 7452)

10. Which of the following is an example of how specific internal controls in a database environment may differ from controls in a nondatabase environment?
a. Controls should exist to ensure that users have access to and can update only the data elements that they have been authorized to access.
b. Controls over data sharing by diverse users within an entity should be the same for every user.
c. The employee who manages the computer hardware should also develop and debug the computer programs.
d. Controls can provide assurance that all processed transactions are authorized, but cannot verify that all authorized transactions are processed.   (R/00, Aud., #8, 7552)

11. Timeliness of data availability is most significant when designing which **two** of the following?
a. General ledger system
b. Internet catalog and order system
c. Payroll system
d. Purchasing system
e. Sales call center system (Editors, 7451)

12. Which of the following is the primary reason that many auditors hesitate to use embedded audit modules?
a. Embedded audit modules **cannot** be protected from computer viruses.
b. Auditors are required to monitor embedded audit modules continuously to obtain valid results.
c. Embedded audit modules can easily be modified through management tampering.
d. Auditors are required to be involved in the system design of the application to be monitored.
(R/02, Aud., #20, 7553)

13. System objectives most likely will **not** be met in the development of a new system when
a. Programmers take longer to write programs than scheduled.
b. Users are trained during system implementation.
c. User specifications are misunderstood.
d. Written user specifications are required by the system analysts. (Editors, 7453)

14. The process of determining business rules to incorporate into a system is called system
a. Analysis
b. Design
c. Feasibility study
d. Implementation
e. Maintenance (Editors, 7454)

15. Rover Installations is evaluating systems to keep its crews at remote construction sites in contact with a central office. When evaluating proposed system changes, which of the following feasibility studies is **least** likely to be performed?
a. Economic
b. Environmental
c. Operational
d. Technical (Editors, 7455)

16. System errors are most expensive to correct during
a. Analysis
b. Design
c. Implementation
d. Programming (Editors, 7456)

17. The least risky strategy for conversion from a manual to computerized payroll system would be a
a. Direct conversion
b. Mainframe conversion
c. Parallel conversion
d. Pilot conversion (Editors, 7457)

18. Kiln Corporation is learning how its current system functions, determining user needs, and developing its objectives for a future system. In what stage in the system development life cycle is Kiln's software project?
a. Analysis
b. Design
c. Implementation
d. Maintenance
e. Programming (Editors, 7468)

19. The greatest financial threat to an organization that implemented the financial accounting module of an enterprise resource planning (ERP) system from a major vendor exists from errors detected during which of the following times?
a. Project initiation
b. Requirements determination
c. Table configuration
d. Implementation (R/03, BEC., #27, 7690)

20. Which of the following statements about multiprocessing and multiprogramming are false?
a. Multiprocessing allows multiple programs to execute simultaneously.
b. Multiprocessing allows a central memory to be shared by multiple programs.
c. Multiprogramming allows multiple programs to execute simultaneously.
d. Multiprogramming involves alternating between programs during processing. (Editors, 7420)

21. In computer processing, access time is the time that it takes
a. For data from a keyboard to reach memory
b. For data to be retrieved from memory
c. To perform a computer instruction
d. To transmit data from a remote computer to a central computer (Editors, 7421)

22. Which of the following statements most likely represents a disadvantage for an entity that keeps microcomputer-prepared data files rather than manually prepared files?
a. Attention is focused on the accuracy of the programming process rather than errors in individual transactions.
b. It is usually easier for unauthorized persons to access and alter the files.
c. Random error associated with processing similar transactions in different ways is usually greater.
d. It is usually more difficult to compare recorded accountability with physical count of assets.
(5/94, Aud., #16, 7554)

23. Which of the following control procedures most likely could prevent IT personnel from modifying programs to bypass programmed controls?
a. Periodic management review of computer utilization reports and systems documentation
b. Segregation of duties within IT for computer programming and computer operations
c. Participation of user department personnel in designing and approving new systems
d. Physical security of IT facilities in limiting access to IT equipment
(11/95, Aud., #14, amended, 7555)

24. A database administrator ordinarily is **not** responsible for
a. Assigning passwords for database access
b. Database design
c. Database operation
d. Data input preparation (Editors, 7585)

25. Which activity is a systems analyst least likely to perform?
a. Application design
b. Coding programs
c. Evaluating user requirements
d. Specification development (Editors, 7425)

26. An executive information system is **not** characterized by
a. Supplying advice to top management from an expert (knowledge-based) system
b. Supplying financial and nonfinancial information
c. Supplying immediate information about an entity's critical success factors
d. Use on both mainframes and personal computer networks (Editors, 7426)

27. What distinguishes accounting information systems (AIS) from management information systems (MIS)?
a. AIS manage financial information and MIS manage only nonfinancial information.
b. AIS are subsystems of MIS.
c. Information from AIS is restricted to financial employees and information from MIS is available throughout an entity.
d. AIS focus on information for financial reporting and MIS focus on information for management decisions. (Editors, 7427)

28. What system derives an answer using a logical problem-solving approach developed by an expert and input from the user?
a. Decision support system
b. Knowledge-based system
c. Natural language processing
d. Neural network (Editors, 7428)

29. What attribute is **not** characteristic of a decision support system?
a. Expert system
b. Interactive computer-based modeling processes
c. Judgment on the part of the decision maker
d. Models
e. Specialized databases (Editors, 7429)

30. Database queries are **not** characterized by which of the following?
a. Both batch and real-time processing of queries is feasible.
b. Responses may be sorted in a specified format.
c. Users with inquiry authorization may change the records that are retrieved.
d. Users with inquiry authorization may change which records are retrieved. (Editors, 7430)

31. Which of the following represents an additional cost of transmitting business transactions by means of electronic data interchange (EDI) rather than in a traditional paper environment?
a. Redundant data checks are needed to verify that individual EDI transactions are **not** recorded twice.
b. Internal audit work is needed because the potential for random data entry errors is increased.
c. Translation software is needed to convert transactions from the entity's internal format to a standard EDI format.
d. More supervisory personnel are needed because the amount of data entry is greater in an EDI system. (5/98, Aud., #9, 6626)

32.   Which of the following is usually a benefit of using electronic funds transfer for international cash transactions?
a.   Improvement of the audit trail for cash receipts and disbursements
b.   Creation of self-monitoring access controls
c.   Reduction of the frequency of data entry errors
d.   Off-site storage of source documents for cash transactions   (R/99, Aud., #8, 7556)

33.   Many entities use the Internet as a network to transmit electronic data interchange (EDI) trans-actions.   An advantage of using the Internet for electronic commerce rather than a traditional value-added network (VAN) is that the Internet
a.   Permits EDI transactions to be sent to trading partners as transactions occur
b.   Automatically batches EDI transactions to multi-ple trading partners
c.   Possesses superior characteristics regarding dis-aster recovery
d.   Converts EDI transactions to a standard format without translation software
                (5/98, Aud., #10, 6627)

34.   Which of the following statements is correct concerning the security of messages in an electronic data interchange (EDI) system?
a.   When the confidentiality of data is the primary risk, message authentication is the preferred con-trol rather than encryption.
b.   Encryption performed by physically secure hard-ware devices is more secure than encryption performed by software.
c.   Message authentication in EDI systems performs the same function as segregation of duties in other information systems.
d.   Security at the transaction phase in EDI systems is **not** necessary because problems at that level will usually be identified by the service provider.
                (R/99, Aud., #12, 7557)

35.   Which of the following characteristics distin-guishes electronic data interchange (EDI) from other forms of electronic commerce?
a.   EDI transactions are formatted using standards that are uniform worldwide.
b.   EDI transactions need **not** comply with generally accepted accounting principles.
c.   EDI transactions ordinarily are processed without the Internet.
d.   EDI transactions are usually recorded without security and privacy concerns.
                (R/01, Aud., #7, 7022)

36.   Which of the following would an auditor ordi-narily consider the greatest risk regarding an entity's use of electronic data interchange (EDI)?
a.   Authorization of EDI transactions
b.   Duplication of EDI transmissions
c.   Improper distribution of EDI transactions
d.   Elimination of paper documents
                (6/99, Aud., #3, 7558)

37.   Which of the following is an essential element of the audit trail in an electronic data interchange (EDI) system?
a.   Disaster recovery plans that ensure proper back-up of files
b.   Encrypted hash totals that authenticate mes-sages
c.   Activity logs that indicate failed transactions
d.   Hardware security modules that store sensitive data   (R/99, Aud., #13, 7559)

38.   Jones, an auditor for Farmington Co., noted that the Acme employees were using computers con-nected to Acme's network by wireless technology. On Jones' next visit to Acme, Jones brought one of Farmington's laptop computers with a wireless net-work card.   When Jones started the laptop to begin work, Jones noticed that the laptop could view sev-eral computers on Acme's network and Jones had access to Acme's network files.   Which of the follow-ing statements is the most likely explanation?
a.   Acme's router was improperly configured.
b.   Farmington's computer had the same adminis-trator password as the server.
c.   Jones had been given root account access on Acme's computer.
d.   Acme was not using security on the network.
                (R/03, BEC, #9, 7671)

39.   To obtain evidence that on-line access controls are properly functioning, an auditor most likely would
a.   Create checkpoints at periodic intervals after live data processing to test for unauthorized use of the system
b.   Examine the transaction log to discover whether any transactions were lost or entered twice due to a system malfunction
c.   Enter invalid identification numbers or passwords to ascertain whether the system rejects them
d.   Vouch a random sample of processed transac-tions to assure proper authorization
                (5/93, Aud., #41, 7560)

40. Which of the following is an encryption feature that can be used to authenticate the originator of a document and ensure that the message is intact and has **not** been tampered with?
a. Heuristic terminal
b. Perimeter switch
c. Default settings
d. Digital signatures   (R/01, Aud., #9, 7024)

41. Which of the following procedures would an entity **most** likely include in its disaster recovery plan?
a. Convert all data from EDI format to an internal company format
b. Maintain a Trojan horse program to prevent illicit activity
c. Develop an auxiliary power supply to provide uninterrupted electricity
d. Store duplicate copies of files in a location away from the computer center
                    (R/03, BEC., #28, 7691)

42. A client is concerned that a power outage or disaster could impair the computer hardware's ability to function as designed. The client desires off-site backup hardware facilities that are fully configured and ready to operate within several hours. The client most likely should consider a
a. Cold site
b. Cool site
c. Warm site
d. Hot site   (5/98, Aud., #6, 7708)

43. Decision tables differ from program flowcharts in that decision tables emphasize
a. Ease of manageability for complex programs
b. Logical relationships among conditions and actions
c. Cost benefit factors justifying the program
d. The sequence in which operations are performed
                    (5/92, Aud., #55, 2808)

44. Which of the following is a pictorial illustration of a system's data flow and information processing, including hardware?
a. Data-flow diagram
b. Decision table
c. PERT chart
d. Program flowchart
e. System flowchart   (Editors, 7444)

45. Which of the following are **not** essential data-flow diagram elements?
a. Data destination
b. Data source
c. Data storage
d. System flowchart
e. Transformation processes   (Editors, 7445)

46. Which of the following illustrates the path of data as it is processed by a system?
a. Decision table
b. Program flowchart
c. Pseudo code
d. System flowchart   (Editors, 7446)

47. Processing data through the use of simulated files provides an auditor with information about the operating effectiveness of control policies and procedures. One of the techniques involved in this approach makes use of
a. Controlled reprocessing
b. An integrated test facility
c. Input validation
d. Program code checking (11/92, Aud., #36, 7563)

48. An auditor most likely would test for the presence of unauthorized software changes by running a
a. Program with test data
b. Check digit verification program
c. Source code comparison program
d. Program that computes control totals
                    (11/92, Aud., #37, amended, 7562)

49. An auditor would most likely be concerned with which of the following controls in a distributed data processing system?
a. Hardware controls
b. Systems documentation controls
c. Access controls
d. Disaster recovery controls
                    (5/91, Aud., #16, 7561)

50. Which of the following computer-assisted auditing techniques allows fictitious and real transactions to be processed together without client operating personnel being aware of the testing process?
a. Integrated test facility
b. Input controls matrix
c. Parallel simulation
d. Data entry monitor   (11/94, Aud., #70, 7564)

51. Which of the following controls is a processing control designed to ensure the reliability and accuracy of data processing?

	Limit test	Validity check test
a.	Yes	Yes
b.	No	No
c.	No	Yes
d.	Yes	No

                    (11/94, Aud., #38, 7565)

52. The completeness of IT-generated sales figures can be tested by comparing the number of items listed on the daily sales report with the number of items billed on the actual invoices. This process uses
a. Check digits
b. Control totals
c. Process tracing data
d. Validity tests   (Editors, 7566)

Items 53 and 54 are based on the following:

Invoice #	Product	Quantity	Unit price
201	F10	150	$ 5.00
202	G15	200	$10.00
203	H20	250	$25.00
204	K35	300	$30.00

53. Which of the following numbers represents the record count?
a.   1
b.   4
c.   810
d.   900   (5/98, Aud., #3, 7548)

54. Which of the following most likely represents a hash total?
a. FGHK80
b. 4
c. 204
d. 810   (5/98, Aud., #4, 7549)

55. An IT input control is designed to ensure that
a. Only authorized personnel have access to the computer area.
b. Machine processing is accurate.
c. Data received for processing are properly authorized and converted to machine readable form.
d. Electronic data processing has been performed as intended for the particular application.
                    (Editors, 7567)

56. A customer intended to order 100 units of product Z96014, bur incorrectly ordered nonexistent product Z96015. Which of the following controls most likely would detect this error?
a. Check digit verification
b. Record count
c. Hash total
d. Redundant data check   (R/03, BEC., #26, 7689)

57. Which of the following input controls is a numeric value computed to provide assurance that the original value has **not** been altered in construction or transmission?
a. Hash total
b. Parity check
c. Encryption
d. Check digit   (5/98, Aud., #8, 7569)

58. Which of the following is an attribute of an interactive system?
a. Data is processed as it is input.
b. Groups of data processed at regular intervals.
c. Sorting transaction files prior to processing.
d. Transaction files with sequential arrangement of records.   (Editors, 7458)

59. What risk typically is **not** associated with outsourcing data processing?
a. Inflexibility
b. Lack of control
c. Lack of confidentiality
d. Reduction in expertise availability (Editors, 7459)

60. A commonly used measure of the relative effectiveness of an online site functioning as retail store is the
a. Abandonment ratio
b. Portability ratio
c. Volatility ratio
d. Volume   (Editors, 7460)

Problem 55-2 ADDITIONAL MULTIPLE CHOICE QUESTIONS (94 to 118 minutes)

61. Which of the following refers to implementing controls that protect the completeness, accuracy, and security of files?
a. File integrity
b. Machine language
c. Random access memory (RAM)
d. Software control   (Editors, 7461)

62. Which of the following is a network node that is used to improve network traffic and to set up as a boundary that prevents traffic from one segment to cross over to another?
a. Router
b. Gateway
c. Firewall
d. Heuristic   (R/00, Aud., #7, 6932)

63. The part of the central processing unit that stores data and programs temporarily during processing is the
a. Floppy disk memory
b. Operating system
c. Random-access memory (RAM)
d. Read-only memory (ROM) (Editors, 7463)

64. Which of the following is **not** an example of software?
a. Database management system
b. Firewall
c. Operating system
d. Router
e. Spreadsheet application (Editors, 7464)

65. Which is **not** part of the main components of a central processing unit (CPU)?
a. Arithmetic-logic unit
b. Control unit
c. Disk drive
d. Primary memory (Editors, 7465)

66. A local area network (LAN) is
a. A system that connects computers and other devices in a limited physical area.
b. A system that rents time on a central computer to several entities, with each entity having remote input and output devices.
c. Facilitates meetings among several people at different physical locations.
d. Facilitates working outside of a traditional office, remaining connected by the Internet, phone, etc. (Editors, 7466)

67. What is the most common advantage of a compact disk (CD) over a hard disk in a personal computer system?
a. Greater access speed
b. Greater portability
c. Greater protection against surface contamination
d. Greater storage capacity (Editors, 7467)

68. Misstatements in a batch computer system caused by incorrect programs or data may **not** be detected immediately because
a. Errors in some transactions may cause rejection of other transactions in the batch.
b. The identification of errors in input data typically is **not** part of the program.
c. There are time delays in processing transactions in a batch system.
d. The processing of transactions in a batch system is **not** uniform. (11/94, Aud., #37, 7570)

69. Matthews Corp. has changed from a system of recording time worked on clock cards to a computerized payroll system in which employees record time in and out with magnetic cards. The IT system automatically updates all payroll records. Because of this change
a. A generalized computer audit program must be used.
b. Part of the audit trail is altered.
c. Transactions must be processed in batches.
d. The potential for payroll-related fraud is diminished. (Editors, 7571)

70. Which of the following statements is false regarding a personal computer network?
a. An integrated package is a type of operating system software appropriate for a personal computer network.
b. Language translation software is appropriate for a personal computer network.
c. Operating system software is essential for a personal computer network.
d. A spreadsheet application is a type of software appropriate for a personal computer network. (Editors, 7470)

71. The process of monitoring, evaluating, and modifying a current system as appropriate is called system
a. Analysis
b. Design
c. Feasibility study
d. Implementation
e. Maintenance (Editors, 7471)

72. What stage of a system's life cycle involves hiring and training new employees and testing new procedures?
a. Analysis
b. Design
c. Implementation
d. Maintenance
e. Programming (Editors, 7472)

73. Systems implementation is unlikely to include
a. Conversion
b. Documentation
c. System design
d. Testing
e. User training (Editors, 7469)

74. A software tool used to access database records infrequently most likely is
a. An emulator
b. A program generator
c. A query utility program
d. A report generator (Editors, 7473)

75. Which of the following policies is most appropriate?
a. Always sorting transactions before updating the master file
b. Always sorting transactions after updating the master file
c. Sorting transactions before updating the master file only if random access storage is used
d. Sorting transactions before updating the master file only if sequential access storage is used
(Editors, 7474)

76. System design usually includes design of
a. Data, input, and user interface
b. Data, process, and user interface
c. Input, data, and output
d. Input, process, and output   (Editors, 7475)

77. What is the most likely reason that a systems designer would specify disk storage as opposed to magnetic tape storage?
a. Disk storage capacity can be measured in bits.
b. Disk storage has substantially less cost than magnetic tape storage.
c. Disk storage offers random access to data.
d. Disk storage offers sequential access to data.
(Editors, 7436)

78. What activity is **least** likely to occur during the analysis stage of system development?
a. Determine user information needs
b. Develop program specifications
c. Evaluate the current system
d. Identify problems in the current system
e. Identify system objectives   (Editors, 7437)

79. What tool would a systems analyst use in selecting the best system among alternatives?
a. Cost-benefit analysis
b. Data-flow diagram
c. PERT chart
d. Pilot test
e. System flowchart   (Editors, 7438)

80. Which of the following is not part of the definition of a system?
a. Boundary
b. Environment
c. Feedback
d. Subsystems   (Editors, 7439)

81. In an accounting information system, which of the following types of computer files most likely would be a master file?
a. Inventory subsidiary
b. Cash disbursements
c. Cash receipts
d. Payroll transactions   (R/03, BEC, #14, 7676)

82. Which of the following characteristics distinguishes computer processing from manual processing?
a. Computer processing virtually eliminates the occurrence of computational error normally associated with manual processing
b. The potential for systematic error is ordinarily greater in manual processing than in computerized processing
c. Errors or fraud in computer processing will be detected soon after their occurrences
d. Most computer systems are designed so that transaction trails useful for audit purposes do not exist   (Editors, 7572)

83. What attribute is characteristic of a decision support system?
a. Database management system
b. Expert system
c. Interactive system
d. Transaction processing system   (Editors, 7431)

84. What best describes an electronic meeting among several people at different physical locations?
a. Interactive system
b. Interfacing
c. Telecommuting
d. Teleconferencing   (Editors, 7432)

85. What attribute is **least** descriptive of an accounting information system?
a. Best suited to solving problems involving uncertainty and ambiguous reporting requirements
b. Provides information to management for use in planning and controlling an entity's activities
c. Subsystem of a management information system
d. Transaction processing system   (Editors, 7433)

86. What attribute is **least** descriptive of an accounting information system?
a. Data records typically are historical
b. Data records are chiefly financial
c. Most data records are quantifiable in nature
d. Output includes answers to problems through use of a knowledge base   (Editors, 7434)

87. What attribute is **least** descriptive of an executive information system?
a. Combines, integrates, and summarizes data from many sources
b. Designed to monitor business conditions and assist in strategic planning
c. Provides immediate and interactive access to information
d. Provides only highly aggregated information
(Editors, 7435)

88. In building an electronic data interchange (EDI) system, what process is used to determine which elements in the entity's computer system correspond to the standard data elements?
a. Mapping
b. Translation
c. Encryption
d. Decoding   (R/01, Aud., #18, 7033)

89. Which of the following is usually a benefit of transmitting transactions in an electronic data interchange (EDI) environment?
a. A compressed business cycle with lower year-end receivables balances
b. A reduced need to test computer controls related to sales and collections transactions
c. An increased opportunity to apply statistical sampling techniques to account balances
d. No need to rely on third-party service providers to ensure security   (R/99, Aud., #9, 6825)

90. A system that provides vendor and customer access to each other's internal computer data to facilitate service, deliveries, and payment is called
a. Distributed processing
b. Electronic data interchange
c. Electronic mail
d. Timesharing   (Editors, 7440)

91. Which of the following best describes a non-standard computer-generated report that is generated as need arises?
a. *Ad hoc*
b. ANSI X12
c. Automated script
d. EDIFACT   (Editors, 7740)

92. Which of the following is a computer program that appears to be legitimate but performs some illicit activity when it is run?
a. Hoax virus
b. Web crawler
c. Trojan horse
d. Killer application   (R/01, Aud., #5, 7020)

93. Which of the following is a term for an attest engagement in which a CPA assesses a client's commercial Internet site for predefined criteria that are designed to measure transaction integrity, information protection, and disclosure of business practices?
a. ElectroNet
b. EDIFACT
c. TechSafe
d. WebTrust   (R/99, Aud., #2, 7573)

94. Which of the following risks can be minimized by requiring all employees accessing the information system to use passwords?
a. Collusion
b. Data entry errors
c. Failure of server duplicating function
d. Firewall vulnerability   (R/03, BEC, #19, 7681)

95. Which of the following is a password security problem?
a. Users are assigned passwords when accounts are created, but do **not** change them.
b. Users have accounts on several systems with different passwords.
c. Users copy their passwords on note paper, which is kept in their wallets.
d. Users select passwords that are **not** listed in any online dictionary.   (R/01, Aud., #19, 7034)

96. Which of the following passwords would be most difficult to crack?
a. OrCa!FlSi
b. language
c. 12 HOUSE 24
d. pass56word   (R/01, Aud., #20, 7035)

97. Which of the following procedures would an entity most likely include in its disaster recovery plan?
a. Convert all data from EDI format to an internal company format
b. Maintain a Trojan horse program to prevent illicit activity
c. Develop an auxiliary power supply to provide uninterrupted electricity
d. Store duplicate copies of files in a location away from the computer center (R/01, Aud., #6, 7021)

98. Which of the following strategies would a CPA most likely consider in auditing an entity that processes most of its financial data only in electronic form, such as a paperless system?
a. Continuous monitoring and analysis of transaction processing with an embedded audit module
b. Increased reliance on internal control activities that emphasize the segregation of duties
c. Verification of encrypted digital certificates used to monitor the authorization of transactions
d. Extensive testing of firewall boundaries that restrict the recording of outside network traffic   (R/99, Aud., #23, 7574)

99.   What is an echo check?
a.   A CPU compares signals sent and received by the CPU to and from an input or output device.
b.   A CPU continually confirms that an odd number of magnetized dots represent each character when receiving input.
c.   A CPU periodically searches for circuits that are failing.
d.   A plastic ring must be attached to a reel before the tape drive will write to the tape.
(Editors, 7741)

100.   Computer files have various types of labels. What is a header label?
a.   An external label attached to the outside of a secondary storage media, such as a disk
b.   A machine-readable label appearing at the beginning of a file containing information such as a file identification number
c.   A machine-readable label appearing at the end of a file containing information such as an end-of-file code
d.   A manual log prepared by the computer operator indicating jobs run, the duration of jobs, who ran jobs, etc.   (Editors, 7742)

101.   Preventive controls typically
a.   Are found only in accounting applications
b.   Are less costly than detective controls
c.   Are more costly than detective controls
d.   Do not require updating once in place
(Editors, 7441)

102.   A clerk entered information regarding a new employee's home address, but unintentionally omitted a city from the mailing address. The best control to detect this omission is a
a.   Batch total
b.   Completeness test
c.   Hash total
d.   Limit or reasonableness test   (Editors, 7442)

103.   A clerk entered information regarding a new employee's home address, but entered year 2070, instead of 1970, as a birth year. The best control to detect this omission is a
a.   Batch total
b.   Completeness test
c.   Hash total
d.   Limit or reasonableness test   (Editors, 7443)

104.   Which of the following is an example of a validity check?
a.   The computer ensures that a numerical amount in a record does **not** exceed some predetermined amount.
b.   As the computer corrects errors and data are successfully resubmitted to the system, the causes of the errors are printed out.
c.   The computer flags any transmission for which the control field value did **not** match that of an existing file record.
d.   After data for a transaction are entered, the computer sends certain data back to the terminal for comparison with data originally sent.
(11/95, Aud., #10, 5957)

105.   A customer intended to order 100 units of product Z96014, but incorrectly ordered nonexistent product Z96015. Which of the following controls most likely would detect this error?
a.   Check digit verification
b.   Record count
c.   Hash total
d.   Redundant data check   (5/98, Aud., #5, 7568)

106.   Which of the following is likely to be more of a consideration for a personal computer system used to keep records for a business, as opposed to a large computer?
a.   Limit or reasonableness checks generally are not adapted to specific situations.
b.   The most important program and data files should be duplicated and stored safely off-site.
c.   A physical environment free from extreme temperatures and humidity must be maintained.
d.   A physical location protected from likely emergencies, such as fire or flooding   (Editors, 7743)

107.   Which of the following best describes a time-sharing center?
a.   A center that process client data for a fee
b.   A computer remotely accessed by a number of different users, who are unaware of each other
c.   A center than distils previously unknown relationships from information in an existing database
d.   A location where equipment and power is available to geographically dispersed subscribers in the event of a disaster at one of their business sites   (Editors, 7744)

SIMULATIONS

The editors encourage candidates to answer simulations as part of their review because such studying provides for content reinforcement, regardless of question format. FYI: Simulations currently are not part of the BEC exam; Bisk Education updating supplements will notify readers when this situation changes.

Problem 55-3 (30 to 50 minutes)

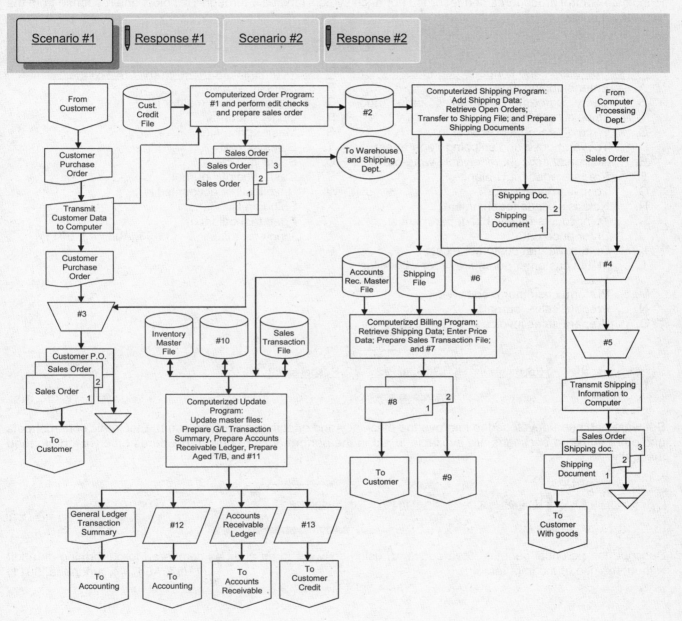

The accompanying flowchart depicts part of a client's revenue cycle. Some of the flowchart symbols are labeled to indicate control procedures and records. For each symbol labeled 1 through 13, select one response from the answer list below.

Answer List

	Operations and control procedures		*Documents, journals, ledgers, and files*
A.	Enter shipping data	P.	Shipping document
B.	Verify agreement of sales order and shipping document	Q.	General ledger master file
		R.	General journal
C.	Write off accounts receivable	S.	Master price file
D.	To warehouse and shipping department	T.	Sales journal
E.	Authorize account receivable write-off	U.	Sales invoice
F.	Prepare aged trial balance	V.	Cash receipts journal
G.	To sales department	W.	Uncollectible accounts file
H.	Release goods for shipment	X.	Shipping file
I.	To accounts receivable department	Y.	Aged trial balance
J.	Enter price data	Z.	Open order file (11/93, Aud., #2, 9911)
K.	Determine that customer exists		
L.	Match customer purchase order with sales order		
M.	Perform customer credit check		
N.	Prepare sales journal		
O.	Prepare sales invoice		

Software has been developed to improve the efficiency and effectiveness of the audit. Electronic spreadsheets and other software packages are available to aid in the performance of audit procedures otherwise performed manually.

Describe the potential benefits to an auditor of using software in an audit as compared to performing an audit without the use of a computer. (11/87, Aud., #4, amended, 9911)

Problem 55-4 (20 to 30 minutes)

Brown, CPA, is auditing the financial statements of Big Z Wholesaling, Inc., a continuing audit client, for the year ended January 31, 20X1. Brown issued an unqualified opinion on the prior year's financial statements. On January 5, 20X1, Brown observed the tagging and counting of Big Z's physical inventory and made appropriate test counts. All inventory is purchased for resale and located in a single warehouse. These test counts have been recorded on a computer file. As in prior years, Big Z gave Brown two computer files. One file represents the perpetual inventory (FIFO) records for the year ended January 31, 20X1. The other file represents the January 5 physical inventory count. Brown has appropriate computerized audit software.

The perpetual inventory file contains the following information in item number sequence:

(1) Beginning balances at February 1, 20X0; item number, item description, total quantity, and prices.
(2) For each item purchased during the year: date received, receiving report number, vendor, item number, item description, quantity, and total dollar amount.
(3) For each item sold during the year: date shipped, invoice number, item number, item description, quantity shipped, and dollar amount of the cost removed from inventory.
(4) For each item adjusted for physical inventory count differences: date, item number, item descriptions, quantity, and dollar amount.

The physical inventory file contains the following information in item number sequence: tag number, item number, item description, and count quantity.

Describe the substantive auditing procedures Brown may consider performing with computerized audit software using Big Z's two computer files and Brown's computer file of test counts. The substantive auditing procedures described may indicate the reports to be printed out for Brown's follow-up by subsequent application of manual procedures. Do not describe subsequent manual auditing procedures. Group the procedures by those using (1) the perpetual inventory file and (2) the physical inventory and test count files.

(5/92, Aud., #4, amended, 6297)

Based on the accompanying flowchart of a client's revenue cycle, what do the symbols marked A and B most likely represent?

<u>Answer List</u>

A.   Accounts receivable master file.
B.   Cash disbursements transaction file.
C.   Customer checks.
D.   Customer orders.

E.   Receiving reports.
F.   Receiving report file.
G.   Remittance advice file.
H.   Sales invoices.

(11/95, Aud., #7 and #8, amended, 9434)

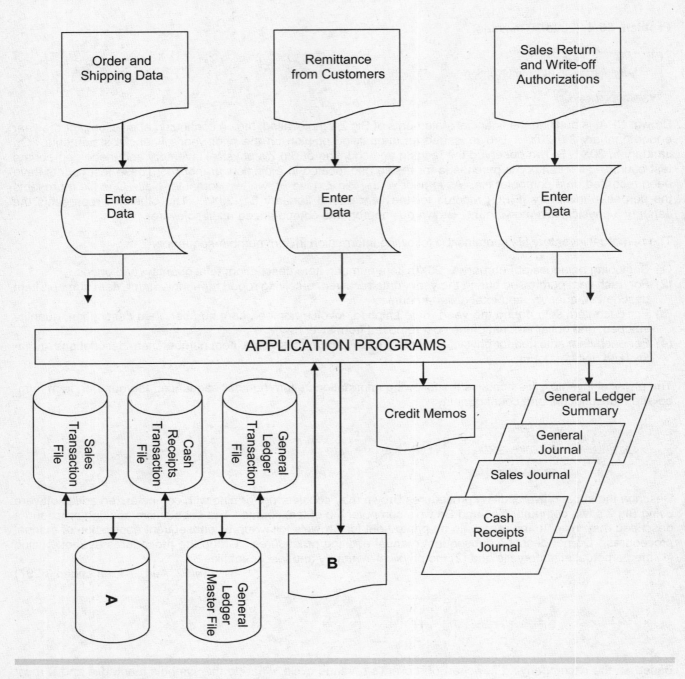

Solution 55-1 MULTIPLE CHOICE ANSWERS

Hardware, Software & Networks

1. (c) A local area network is a network of computers within a small area to transmit information among network members. By its nature, it requires a means of transmission. Program flowcharts relate to software. An input routine generally is a program that relates to the acceptance of information (data entry). Loop verification is not a commonly used term.

2. (c) A network firewall protects the network as a whole, but avoids issues specific to a particular application hosted on that network. An application firewall, providing additional defenses, typically is used as a supplement to the network firewall, resulting in incremental costs and installation issues. An application firewall results in more difficult access to applications for unauthorized users; if anything changed, authorized users probably would encounter more difficult access, rather than less. If application firewalls were used without a network firewall,

application firewalls would be required for each application, which would tend to make them more expensive and difficult to install.

3. (d) Windowing involves the display of more than one program on a portion of a monitor at the same time, but has only one of those programs active. It typically is used in connection with a graphical user interface (GUI), which uses pictorial icons to represent software, files, and processes. Distributed processing is an allocation of various processing tasks to various business divisions, with some tasks centralized and some decentralized. Multiprogramming involves the operating system (OS) processing a program to the point where input or output is involved, at which point, the OS delegates further work on that program to peripheral hardware, and processing an alternative program until the first program's input is received or output is finished. Ideally, no interruption occurs that is discernable to the user, so multiple programs appear to run simultaneously. Multiprocessing involves the OS using multiple CPUs to run multiple programs simultaneously.

4. (a) Distributed processing is an allocation of various processing tasks to various business divisions, with some tasks centralized and some decentralized. A local area network (LAN) typically is restricted to a small physical location, such as a building. Online processing refers to processing as data is input, as opposed to batch processing. Multiprocessing involves the operating system using multiple CPUs to run multiple programs simultaneously. Timesharing involves using another entity's computer.

5. (c) A bus network links communication channels to one common line with direct access to the message destination. A star network links channels to a single host computer. A ring network links channels to a loop, with each message passed neighbor to neighbor until the message reaches its destination. A tree configuration is organized along hierarchical channels that eventually are linked to a single host computer.

Data

6. (c) Banks commonly use magnetic ink character recognition for data entry for check processing. Bar coding is used commonly in inventory management systems, but rarely by banks for check processing. Electronic data interchange is not involved closely with data entry or check processing. Magnetic tape is a storage medium, not a data entry device.

7. (a) A database administrator (DBA) is a person who usually has overall responsibility for designing and maintaining a database. DBMS separately maintain data and programs except during processing. DBMS include a data definition language that helps describe the schema, which is a logical structure or organization of a database. A primary goal of DBMS is to minimize data redundancy.

8. (b) Batch processing involves accumulating transactions for processing in groups, or batches. Typically, batches are ordered to facilitate posting to a similarly ordered master file. Batch processing is a method of data input and has nothing to do with inquiries, other than that the delay in posting transactions may cause master files to be outdated. As opposed to processing individual transactions at the time of input, there is some delay as batches are created. Batch and online processing can provide the same audit trail.

9. (c) A primary key uniquely identifies a record; in order to maintain file integrity, a record without a primary key is not accepted. While a secondary key may be used when a primary key is unknown, the primary key must still be in existence. Assume a database of customer records has the account number as the primary key and the phone number and address both as secondary keys. If a customer leaves a voice-mail message or sends a letter without her/his account number, a service representative could search for the record based on either phone number or address. However, the system would not have accepted the record in the first place without assigning an account number.

10. (a) Controls in a database environment can be very specific as to which elements of a record can be accessed or changed, resulting in a more detailed set of authorizations. [Note: The examiners' say to select the best answer.] Controls over data sharing should be appropriate for each user, usually resulting in diverse controls. Preferably, hardware management and software development are segregated. The relationship between authorization and processing usually is the same within a database and a non-database environment.

Development & Implementation

11. (b, e) This question requires two answers for full credit. An Internet system generally returns a response to the user almost immediately after data entry. A sales call center requires quick response so representatives can meet customers' expectations. With these two systems, lack of a speedy response can cost sales as well as diminish goodwill and employee morale. While the general ledger, payroll,

and purchasing systems need responses within a reasonable time, their response times generally are measured in seconds, rather than milliseconds. A system supporting retail operations has more significant timeliness needs than, for instance, a payroll system.

12. (d) Embedded audit modules can be difficult to install once the application program is operational, but efficiently included during system design. Embedded audit modules can be protected from viruses as well as other applications. Sporadic or occasional monitoring of embedded audit modules can produce valid results. Management tampering can modify other applications as easily as embedded audit modules.

13. (c) The overall system design is based on user specifications; a serious misunderstanding of those specifications could impact the functionality of the system so that it doesn't meet the objectives. While programming delays are unwelcome, they are less likely to prevent reaching system objectives than confusion regarding specifications. Users typically are trained during system implementation. Written user specifications may be referenced readily by system developers, making them preferable to oral specifications.

14. (b) Systems design involves determining specifications for inputs, processing (business rules), security, output, and storage. Systems analysis involves defining user needs and evaluating any current systems. A feasibility study determines whether a proposed system is practicable from technical, operational, and economical standpoints. Implementation is the process of installing and testing software, training users, and converting to a new system. System maintenance occurs continuously throughout most of a system's life, starting after implementation.

15. (b) A feasibility study determines whether a proposed system is practicable from technical, operational, and economical standpoints. An environment's impact on the system typically is considered part of an operational study.

16. (c) Any kind of change, including correction of an error, is less expensive to make the earlier in the system life cycle that it is made. The life cycle order is analysis, design, programming, implementation, and maintenance.

17. (c) A parallel conversion involves operating two systems concurrently. If some component of the new computerized system doesn't work, the manual system provides an up-to-date backup. Further, the results from the two systems are compared

as an accuracy check. These two features reduce the risk involved. A direct conversion is when use of the former and new systems is mutually exclusive; only the former system is used through a certain time and all transactions after that time are entered only on the new system. A mainframe conversion is not a commonly used term; the type of hardware involved would not have a significant difference on the riskiness of conversion. A pilot conversion involves converting a trial group or division before converting the whole entity, to identify any potential problems on a small scale; while less risky than a direct conversion, it doesn't offer the same protection as a parallel conversion.

18. (a) The system life cycle order is analysis, design, programming, implementation, and maintenance. The analysis stage is characterized by evaluation of the current system and future needs, and identifying objectives for the new system.

19. (d) Errors that exist during implementation may allow access to unauthorized users or provide incorrect information; even if discovered during implementation, some time has elapsed when the system was operating with an error. Project initiation, requirements determination, and table configuration occur during system development. Errors that exist during system development cause fewer problems because users don't take action based on information provided by a system under development and a system under development isn't integrated with the live system to the point where it authorizes access.

System Operations

20. (c) Multiprogramming involves the operating system (OS) processing a program to the point where input or output is involved, at which point, the OS delegates further work on that program to peripheral hardware, and processing an alternative program until the first program's input is received or output is finished. Ideally, no interruption occurs that is discernable to the user, so multiple programs **appear** to run simultaneously. Multiprocessing involves the OS using multiple CPUs to run multiple programs simultaneously.

21. (b) Access time is the time that it takes for data to be retrieved from memory from the time that the control unit calls it. Random access memory generally is faster than sequential access memory. Entering data, transmitting data, and performing a computer instruction are different from accessing data.

Roles

22. **(b)** Many internal control procedures once performed by separate individuals in manual systems may be concentrated in systems that use computer processing. Therefore, an individual who has access to the computer may be in a position to perform incompatible functions. Answers (a) and (c) are false statements. Detailed ledger accounts may be maintained as easily with microcomputer data files as with manually prepared files.

23. **(b)** A control procedure for preventing employees from modifying programs to bypass programmed controls is to segregate the functions of programming and computer operations. Answers (a), (c), and (d) are all appropriate practices but in themselves would not prevent employees from modifying programs.

24. **(d)** Typically, users are responsible for input preparation. A database administrator (DBA) usually has overall responsibility for designing and maintaining a database, including security measures (assigning passwords) and operations.

25. **(b)** System analysts concentrate on developing system specifications to meet user needs. They assess any current systems, evaluate user needs, and design future systems, supplying programmers with specifications for coding. Under an ideal internal control system, system analysts don't write programs or have access to operational equipment, programs, or data files—although system analysts might use copies, facsimiles, or samples of operational resources when assessing current systems.

Business Information Systems

26. **(a)** An expert system is based on the rules developed by an expert to address specified situations. For example, a business valuation expert's complex set of rules developed from years of experience may be incorporated into a software program for use by inexperienced business valuation specialists. An executive information system (EIS) focuses on long-range objectives. Unlike an expert system, the EIS addresses situations that often don't have an expert with a proven history of managing such situations. An EIS typically provides summary financial and nonfinancial information from other systems about critical success factors so that top management can develop solutions that may contain considerable innovation. An EIS is appropriate for both mainframes and personal computer networks.

27. **(b)** MIS provide information for management decisions. AIS are subsystems of MIS that process financial and some nonfinancial information that is necessary for financial reporting and useful for management decisions. Restrictions on information rarely are set by the source system; rather, utility and sensitivity criteria guide disbursement policies.

28. **(b)** Expert, or knowledge-based, systems provide answers based on information provided by the user and rules developed by an expert to address specified situations. For example, a tax planning expert's set of rules may be incorporated into a software program for use by inexperienced tax planning specialists. As new circumstances or decision-making techniques are developed, expert systems must be updated. Decision support systems (DSS) are used primarily for semi-structured problems requiring the exercise of judgment. Rather than providing answers, a DSS provides information to assist a user to develop answers. Natural language processing is an input-output tool. Neural networks are similar to expert systems, but they also learn from their mistakes.

29. **(a)** Decision support systems (DSS) are used primarily for semi-structured problems requiring the exercise of judgment. Rather than providing answers, a DSS provides information to assist a user to develop answers. Expert, or knowledge-based, systems provide answers based on information provided by the user and the rules developed by an expert to address specified situations. By comparison, DSS facilitate problem-solving by providing computational capacity and data for use in interactive models.

30. **(c)** Users with inquiry authorization may alter the specifications that determine which records are retrieved, but may not change the records. Changing records requires edit authorization. Database queries may be processed either in batch or real-time. The response order often is sorted based on user-specified criteria or system defaults.

E-Commerce Implications

31. **(c)** EDI involves electronic communication among two or more entities. These entities need a common standard transmission format. Individual EDI transactions are no more likely to be recorded twice than transactions performed in a paper environment. One primary advantage of EDI is the reduction of data entry and a corresponding reduction of associated errors. Random data entry errors are generally reduced in an EDI system, because information is entered once (allowing one opportunity for errors), instead of entered, printed, and reentered (allowing multiple opportunities for errors).

32. (c) With EDI, information is entered into a system once and transmitted to other parties. These other parties do not have to re-enter the information into their systems, eliminating an opportunity for errors to occur. Using EDI, audit trails typically are less clear, if anything. Creation of self-monitoring access controls and off-site storage of source documents for cash transactions could occur with or without EDI.

33. (a) The Internet is a no-frills option, but it does offer immediacy. VANs can offer services to customers such as batching EDI transactions, providing disaster recovery services, and converting EDI transactions to and from a standard format.

34. (b) Physically secure hardware devices are less likely to be compromised than software. Message authentication provides assurance about messages' sources. Encryption provides assurance about privacy. Message authentication performs similarly to control duties in non-IT systems, but not the segregation of duties aspect. Service providers usually do **not** provide security at the transaction level.

35. (a) Electronic data interchange is a method of conducting routine business transactions. It relies on standardized guidelines that everyone can use. EDI transactions need to follow GAAP just as paper transactions do, they may be processed over the Internet, and that makes them more vulnerable to security violations.

36. (c) Improper transactions, regardless of the media, are usually the greatest risk. Appropriate authorization of EDI transactions doesn't present a risk. Duplication of EDI transactions would likely be found by one of the involved parties upon reconciliation. Elimination of paper documents is a goal of EDI.

37. (c) Logs with failed transactions are examined to determine whether the corrected transactions were eventually executed and to detect attempts of unauthorized system use. Proper file backup is a recovery issue. Message authentication and hardware security modules are security issues.

Security

38. (d) That Jones notices that Acme's network files are available without entering a password provided by Acme indicates that Acme is not using security on the network. The scenario implies that Jones did not make an effort directed to testing the security of, or accessing files on, the client's system, but became aware of this access during tasks that did not require such access. A router is a switch that transfers messages; this function seems to be working only too well on Acme's system. For the laptop and Acme's server to have the same password is an unusual (i.e., unlikely) coincidence or both are set to the default password. Changing default passwords is an elementary security step. Appropriate security implies that those with access are aware of such access, so they may restrict it from unauthorized users.

39. (c) Password controls, used in restricting access to computers, are designed to preclude access capabilities of those employees whose regular functions are incompatible with computer use. To obtain evidence that user identification and password controls are functioning as designed, an auditor would most likely examine a sample of invalid passwords or numbers to determine whether the computer is recognizing the invalid passwords and rejecting access. Answer (a) checks the level of authorization an employee has once within the system rather than access to the online system. Answer (b) is a procedure for determining the completeness of transaction processing. Answer (d) does not address whether the online access is being limited or circumvented.

40. (d) Digital signatures are forgery-resistant encrypted files used to prove identity. Heuristic terminals, perimeter switches and default settings are irrelevant to the answer.

Disaster Recovery

41. (d) While an auxiliary power supply is important, duplicate copies are an essential element of a disaster recovery plan; recovery may be delayed without auxiliary power, but may be impossible without essential files. Converting data from EDI format to an internal company format is typically a communication, rather than disaster-recovery, issue. A Trojan program typically initiates illicit activity; preventing illicit activity is a security, rather than a disaster-recovery, issue.

42. (d) A cold site is space where furnishings and power is available in the event of a disaster at a primary location, but a computer system is not installed. A hot site is one that is ready for use with minimal preparation—for example, with hardware and software installed, links established, and backups of information available. The terms *warm site* and *cool site* are not generally used.

Documentation

43. (b) A systems flowchart shows the flow of data through the system and the interrelationships between the processing steps and computer runs. A decision table describes a portion of the logic used in the program.

44. (e) A system flowchart is a graphic portrayal of a system's data flow and information processing, including hardware. A data-flow diagram doesn't include information on hardware. A decision table illustrates all the various possibilities in a given situation. A PERT chart is a scheduling tool for use on many types of projects, not merely IT projects. A program flowchart illustrates details of a program, not a system.

45. (d) A system flowchart is an illustration of a system's data flow and information processing, including hardware. A data-flow diagram typically includes information on data flows, data destination, data source, data storage, and transformation processes, but not hardware.

46. (d) A system flowchart is an illustration of a system's data flow and information processing, including hardware. A decision table illustrates all the various possibilities in a given situation. A program flowchart illustrates details of a program, not a system. Pseudo code is a structured language (sometimes called structured English) designed to assist in coding; programmers may write programs in pseudo code and then translate those notes to a formal computer language.

General Controls

47. (b) Processing data through the use of simulated files makes use of an integrated test facility. Using this method, the auditor creates a fictitious entity within the client's actual data files. S/he then processes fictitious data for the entity as part of the client's regular data processing. Controlled reprocessing involves the processing of the client's actual data through the auditor's controlled copy of the client's program. Input validation is concerned only that the inputted data is accurate. Program code checking involves analysis of the client's actual program.

48. (c) A source code comparison program could be used to compare the original code written for a specific program to the current code in use for that program. Thus, it would make note of any differences in the program from the time it was originally written. Test data would generally be used to test the output of the program but would provide no evidence as to whether the program code had been changed. A check digit program involves the use of a digit that is added to the end of a piece of numeric data to permit the data to be checked for accuracy during input, processing, or output. Control totals are totals computed at different times in the computer process and are used as input, processing, and output controls. They would not provide evidence as to whether any changes were made to the original program code.

49. (c) A distributed data processing system is one in which many different users have access to the main computer through various computer locations. Thus, access controls, which restrict access to the main computer, are necessary to maintain a strong internal control structure, since those with access to the computer are in a position to perform incompatible functions. Hardware controls, systems documentation controls, and disaster recovery controls would not be as important in assessing control risk and would not likely present unusual problems in a distributed system.

50. (a) An integrated test facility (ITF) processes fictitious data with real data in order to test computer controls; client personnel are unaware of the testing. An input control matrix documents controls and their presence. Parallel simulation processes client input data on an auditor-controlled program to test controls; test data is not utilized. The term "data entry monitor" is not commonly used.

Application Controls

51. (a) Computers can be programmed to perform a wide range of edit tasks on records as they are being inputted into the system. If a particular record does not meet the test, it would not be processed. Edit tests include limit tests, validity check tests, check digit tests, etc.

52. (b) The use of control totals is an example of a processing control which is designed to provide reasonable assurances that processing occurred as intended for the particular application, i.e., that all transactions are processed as authorized, that no authorized transactions were omitted, and that no unauthorized transactions were added. A *check digit* is a number that is added at the end of a numerical entry to check its accuracy. A *validity test,* is designed to ensure that only data meeting specific criteria are allowed. Answer (c) apparently refers to "tagging" of data, a technique used by auditors to follow a transaction through the processing cycle.

53. (b) A record count is a count of the number of records in a batch or file or similar group.

54. (d) A hash total is a numeric total with meaning only as a control. Because of the alpha characters in the product codes, a hash total cannot be derived from product codes without a conversion of letters into numeric amounts. Totals of quantities have meaning beyond a control.

55. (c) Input controls are designed to provide reasonable assurance that data received by IT have been properly authorized, converted into machine sensible form and identified and that data have not been lost, added, duplicated, or otherwise improperly changed. Answer (a) describes an access control. Answer (b) describes an output control. Answer (d) describes a processing control.

56. (a) A check digit is a digit that is appended to a piece of numeric data following a pre-specified routine. A record count is a count of the number of records in a batch or file or similar group; the number of order records would not be different if the customer ordered a nonexistent product. A hash total is a numeric total with meaning only as a control; with one part number, there is nothing to total. A redundant data check (also known as a parity bit check) is a general control designed to check that storage or transmission media are not distorted on a character level.

57. (d) A check digit is a digit that is appended to a piece of numeric data following a pre-specified routine. A hash total is a numeric total with meaning only as a control. A parity check is an extra bit attached to the end of a string of bits to detect errors resulting from electronic interference when transmitting the string. Encryption is the conversion of a message into a coded message.

Special Systems

58. (a) In an interactive system, data is processed as it is input and feedback is provided to the user; transaction files are not batched or sorted before processing, as this introduces a delay. Random memory is most likely to be used in an interactive system. Sequential record access almost requires sorting transaction files prior to processing, or master files take a long time to update.

59. (d) Typical advantages of outsourcing data processing are cost savings and predictability, superior service quality, low capital investment, and greater expertise supplied by specialists. Typical disadvantages include inflexibility, lack of control, and concerns about confidentiality.

60. (a) Abandonment ratios are based on the number of visitors who start, but don't complete, transactions. Information on the point at which visitors abandon their selections provides feedback to the web site sponsor. Using these ratios, the site can be changed, for example, to make it easier for customers to find complementary products or to provide assurance that payment information is secure. Portability is used in this question as a nonsense term. Volatility is concerned with how often files are updated. Volume addresses the amount of traffic on the site or the quantity of data transmission.

Solution 55-2 ADDITIONAL MULTIPLE CHOICE ANSWERS

Hardware, Software & Networks

61. (a) Implementing controls that protect the completeness accuracy, and security of files achieves file integrity. Machine language is recognized and executed by a computer directly. RAM is a means of storage that allows direct access to data, as compared to sequential access. Software control refers to the librarian's control of programs.

62. (c) A firewall is designed to prevent unauthorized access to data by separating one segment from another. Routers (switches that transfer incoming messages to outgoing links via the most efficient route possible, for example, over the Internet) and gateways (software or hardware that link two computer networks) allow traffic. In computing, heuristic signifies *able to change;* it is used to describe a computer program that can modify itself in response to the user, for example, a spell check program.

63. (c) The central processing unit (CPU) is the component that manipulates data. Data is stored in RAM (within the CPU) during processing. Files may be saved on a floppy disk after CPU processing is finished; a floppy disk is not required for CPU processing. An operating system is software, not hardware. ROM would not function as temporary storage because it is read-only; temporary storage must be rewritten frequently. ROM is used for permanent storage of essential programs.

64. (d) A router is a hardware switch that manages messages to links via the most efficient route possible. A database management system, firewall, operating system, and spreadsheet application are all software.

65. (c) A disk drive typically is considered a peripheral device. The CPU generally is considered

to be composed of an arithmetic-logic unit, a control unit, and primary memory.

66. (a) A LAN is a system that connects computers and other devices in a limited physical area, typically within the same building. A time-sharing center rents time on a central computer to several entities, with each entity having remote input and output devices. To each entity, it seems as if it is the only one using the system. A meeting among several people at different physical locations facilitated by electronics is a teleconference. Working outside of a traditional office, but remaining connected by the Internet, phone, etc., is called telecommuting.

67. (b) A CD's greatest advantage over a hard disk is its portability. A hard disk typically has greater access speed, protection against surface or head contamination, and storage capacity.

Data

68. (c) There are time delays when data is processed in batches, so errors may not be detected immediately. The time delays in processing cause a delay in error detection. The identification of errors in input data would be identified through various means such as the use of batch totals and would generally be made part of the program. The processing of transactions in a batch system is uniform; for example, all sales invoices would be part of a group of transactions entered together in a batch system.

69. (b) When time clock cards are used, they constitute a form of physical evidence that can be examined in determining the proper amount of wage expense. By changing to an IT system, part of the audit trail is altered—although not necessarily destroyed. The IT system can be audited in numerous ways that don't require the use of a generalized audit program. The potential for payroll fraud may or may not change depending on the internal controls incorporated into the new payroll system. The system automatically updates the payroll records whenever anyone punches in or out. Batch processing is eliminated in this system.

Development & Implementation

70. (a) An integrated package is a bundle of application software, not operating system software, usually with similar user interfaces. A common package includes a word processor, a spreadsheet, and presentation software. Without operating system software, a personal computer or network will not function. Language translation software translates computer code written in human-readable language into machine language (binary code).

71. (e) System maintenance occurs continuously throughout most of a system's life, starting after implementation. Maintenance involves modifications to the system to meet new needs or correct design flaws. Systems analysis involves defining user needs and evaluating any current systems. Systems design involves determining specifications. A feasibility study determines whether a proposed system is practicable from technical, operational, and economical standpoints. Implementation is the process of installing and testing software, training users, and converting to a new system.

72. (c) The implementation stage of a system's life cycle involves training users to use the system's features properly and overcome resistance to change; testing inputs, outputs, and procedures to confirm that the system meets users' needs; converting data files as necessary, and documenting the system. Testing new procedures should occur before the maintenance stage of the life cycle. It is difficult to train new or old employees on a new system before details of that new system are established. In the analysis and design phases, major changes could occur; the programming phase also is called the detailed design phase.

73. (c) The system life cycle order is analysis, design, programming, implementation, and maintenance. The implementation stage of a system's life cycle involves converting data files as necessary; documenting the system; training users to use the system's features properly and overcome resistance to change; and testing inputs, outputs, and procedures to confirm that the system meets users' needs.

74. (c) A query utility program generally is used for one-time database inquires. An emulator is a device that allows one system to imitate another; the first system uses the same data and programs to obtain the same results as a second system. A program generator creates applications based on specifications that users supply in a specific format. A report generator is used to develop reports for frequent or repetitive database inquires.

75. (d) When sequential access storage is used, having transactions in the same order as the master file significantly expedites the updating process, particularly when the activity ratio is high. Sorting the transaction file is not beneficial if random access storage is used or after the master file is updated.

76. (b) System design typically is classified into three categories: data design, process design, and user interface design. Input and output design may be considered sub-elements of user interface design.

77. (c) Disk storage offers random, rather than sequential, access to data, facilitating real-time updates. Historically, magnetic tape storage is less expensive than disk storage. Storage capacity can be measured for both disk and magnetic tape. To update a master file with an unsorted transaction file involves finding the particular record to be updated. With sequential access, the software starts at the file beginning to search for the master record for each unsorted transaction, taking substantial time. If the transactions are sorted, the software can start the search at the record pertaining to the last transaction, significantly reducing search time. Sequential access rarely is deemed to be a favorable attribute, particularly for real-time systems.

78. (b) A system life cycle order is analysis, design, programming, implementation, and maintenance. Developing program specifications generally is considered part of design. The analysis stage is characterized by evaluation of the current system and future needs; thus, this phase generally includes determining user needs, evaluating the current system, identifying problems in the current system, and identifying objectives for the new system.

79. (a) A feasibility study determines whether a proposed system is practicable from technical, operational, and economical standpoints. Thus, feasibility studies should include cost-benefit analysis once a set of acceptable alternatives is established. A data-flow diagram portrays a system's data flow. A PERT chart is a scheduling tool. Pilot testing involves testing a trial group or division before testing the whole entity, to identify any potential problem areas on a small scale. A system flowchart portrays a system's data flow and information processing, including hardware.

80. (b) System theory describes systems as having common attributes: a boundary that separates a system from its environment; a super-system, or environment; subsystems or components; and feedback. While a system exists in an environment, the environment itself is not part of a system. Lasting systems have countermeasures to offset to adjust for undesirable performance; without such countermeasures, the resulting disorder undermines the system.

Systems Operations

81. (a) Cash disbursements, cash receipts, and payroll transactions are all examples of transactions; records pertaining to these events are maintained in transaction files which update master files. Editor's Note: "Inventory subsidiary" is not a common name for a master file. The editors don't expect similar questions to appear on future exams.

Business Information Systems

82. (a) An advantage of computer processing is that it virtually eliminates computational errors. Errors or fraud are not detected more quickly when computer processing is used. The potential for systematic errors is greater in computer processing than in manual processing. Transaction trails useful for audit purposes are created but the data may be available for only a short period of time.

83. (c) Decision support systems (DSS) are used primarily for semi-structured problems requiring the exercise of judgment. Rather than providing answers, a DSS provides information to assist a user to develop answers. Database management systems (DBMS) create and manage databases. Expert, or knowledge-based, systems provide answers based on information provided by the user and rules developed by an expert to address specified situations. By comparison, DSS facilitate problem-solving by providing computational capacity and data for use in interactive models. DSS support decisions, rather than process transactions.

84. (d) A teleconference is a meeting among several people at different physical locations facilitated by electronics. An interactive system is a system that quickly responds to user input, as opposed to a system with punch-card entry, for example. Interfacing refers to the direct connection of multiple computer systems. Telecommuting involves working outside of a traditional office, remaining connected by the Internet, phone, et cetera.

85. (a) Decision support systems (DSS) are used primarily for semi-structured problems involving uncertainty and ambiguous reporting requirements and requiring the exercise of judgment. An accounting information system (AIS) is a management information subsystem that provides information to management for use in measuring, planning, and controlling an entity's activities. An AIS typically includes such functions as accounts receivable, accounts payable, and payroll, and hence, processes a large number of transactions.

86. (d) Knowledge-based, or expert, systems provide answers based on information provided by the user and rules developed by an expert to address specified situations. By comparison, an accounting information system (AIS) is a transaction processing system that provides information to management for use in measuring, planning, and controlling an entity's activities.

87. (d) While an executive information system (EIS) provides highly aggregated information, details supporting that information ideally are readily available. An EIS combines, integrates, and summarizes data from many sources (external as well as internal) to monitor business conditions and assist in strategic planning. An EIS typically provides immediate and interactive access to information.

E-Commerce Implications

88. (a) Mapping converts data between EDI applications and a standard EDI form. Translation changes representations between a standard EDI form and an encoded standard EDI form. Encryption scrambles files and communications to prevent unauthorized use. Decoding means converting data back to its original form.

89. (a) EDI generally results in a compressed cycle of orders, purchases, deliveries, and payments. EDI generally increases the need to test computer controls and the need for security. EDI has no impact on the application of sampling techniques for account balances.

90. (b) Electronic data interchange is a method of conducting routine business transactions, such as inventory purchases. It relies on standardized guidelines that everyone can use. Distributed processing is an allocation of various processing tasks to various business divisions, with some tasks centralized and some decentralized. Electronic mail (email) refers to the electronic transmission of messages, including attached files from programs unrelated to the email software. A time-sharing center rents time on a central computer to several entities, with each entity having remote input and output devices. To each entity, it seems as if it is the only one using the system.

91. (a) An *ad hoc* report is a non-standardized report composed when the need arises, typically for limited use. ANSI X12 is a domestic EDI format. An automated script is a hacker program that investigates computers, discovering what accounts exist and whether a limit on the number of password attempts is enabled on a machine. EDIFACT is an international EDI format.

Security

92. (c) A Trojan horse is a seemingly legitimate program that causes damage when executed. A hoax virus is a false e-mail warning that tries to get circulated as widely as possible. A web crawler is used to search the World Wide Web for documents containing specific words or phrases. A killer application is extremely useful or interesting.

93. (d) The CPA WebTrust symbol on a web site indicates that the organization meets AICPA business practice disclosures, transaction integrity, and information protection criteria. A specially trained and licensed CPA reviews compliance with these criteria every 90 days. EDIFACT is an international EDI format. (ANSI X12 is a domestic EDI format.) ElectroNet and TechSafe are not widely used terms.

94. (d) Requiring the use of well-developed passwords to access systems increases the effectiveness of a firewall. Passwords will not reduce collusion, data entry errors, or the failure of server duplication significantly. An appropriate environment is a better aid against collusion. Data entry errors can be minimized by various input controls, such as edit checks. As an issue of business continuity, server duplication failure is better avoided by redundant systems than by the use of passwords.

95. (a) Assigned passwords are known by the assigner, thereby defeating their access-restricting ability. Users must make their passwords unknown to the greatest number of people. Different passwords for different systems help promote this; if one password is discovered, the others remain unknown. Employees will protect notes in wallets with the passwords as they protect their cash. If the password isn't in the dictionary, a hacker will not be successful when trying words in an electronic dictionary as passwords in an attempt to gain access.

96. (a) The more complicated a password is, the less susceptible it would be to discovery by hackers. This password uses both upper and lower case, and the non-alphanumeric exclamation point symbol. Words in dictionaries should not be used as passwords.

Disaster Recovery

97. (d) Having duplicate off-site copies of critical files is a relatively inexpensive and highly effective disaster recovery measure. An auxiliary power supply is a secondary concern in disaster recovery. Converting data to internal company format and maintaining Trojan horse programs are more closely related to security than disaster recovery.

General Controls

98. (a) When a client processes financial data in electronic form without paper documentation, the auditor may audit on a more continuous basis than a traditional system, as a convenience, and may be required to audit on a more continuous basis to obtain sufficient, competent evidence as documentation for some transactions may only be available for a limited time. An embedded audit module can facilitate

this "continuous" auditing. If anything, an auditor may rely less on internal control activities that emphasize the segregation of duties. Digital certificate verification and testing of firewall boundaries are more concerned with security than internal control.

99. (a) When performing an echo check, a CPU compares the signals sent to a device and to the signals received from that device. When performing an parity check, a CPU that has odd parity confirms that an odd number of magnetized dots represent each character. A hardware check is a search for circuits that are failing. A file protection ring is a plastic ring that must be attached to a reel before the tape drive will write to the tape; it generally is considered a data control.

100. (b) A header label appears at the beginning of a file, in machine-readable form. External labels are human-readable labels attached to the outside of a secondary storage media, such as a disk. A trailer label appears at the end of a file containing information. A daily computer log is a log prepared by the computer operator indicating jobs run, the duration of jobs, who ran jobs, etc.

Application Controls

101. (b) Preventive controls are designed to anticipate and forestall errors. Detective controls merely uncover errors after they occur. Because they prevent errors from ever occurring, both the loss from the error and the cost of correcting the error are avoided, making preventive controls more cost-effective than detective controls. All types of controls should be reviewed and updated to meet changing circumstances. Controls should be included in most applications; for instance, inappropriate distribution of non-financial, but confidential, information from clients or employees could have severe adverse consequences.

102. (b) A completeness test confirms that all required data fields are present before accepting the transaction for processing. Frequently, the system is programmed to notify the user as to which element is missing. A batch total is the total of one element in several different records. A hash total is also the total of one element in several different records, except that a hash total has no meaning except as a control total; for instance, the total of social security numbers might be checked from one payroll period to another. A limit or reasonableness test confirms information against established limits.

103. (d) A limit or reasonableness test confirms information against established limits. A payroll program might limit acceptable birth dates to any date indicating an employee is older than a minimum hiring age, or perhaps the current date. A completeness test confirms that all required data fields are present before accepting the transaction for processing. A batch total is the total of one element in several different records. A hash total is also the total of one element in several different records, except that a hash total has no meaning except as a control total; for instance, the total of social security numbers might be checked from one payroll period to another.

104. (c) A validity check ensures that only authorized data codes will be entered into and accepted by the system. Answer (a) is an example of a limit (reasonableness) check. Answer (b) is an example of an error report being generated. There is no comparison performed as in answer (d).

105. (a) A check digit is a digit that is appended to a piece of numeric data following a pre-specified routine. A record count is a count of the number of records in a batch or file or similar group. A hash total is a numeric total with meaning only as a control. A redundant data check would check one piece of data against another, not the elements of a product code label against each other.

Special Systems

106. (a) Limit (or reasonableness) checks generally are not adapted to specific situations in personal computer systems since most small system software is purchased off the shelf. Off-site storage of duplicate files, an appropriate environment, and a location unlikely to be damaged by fire or flooding are all important for both large and small computer systems.

107. (b) A time-sharing center has a computer remotely accessed by a number of different users, who are unaware of each other. A service bureau processes client data for a fee. Data mining involves distilling previously unknown relationships from information in an existing database; it can be done in-house or out-sourced. A cold site is a location where equipment and power is available in the event of a disaster at regular business sites; geographically dispersed subscribers are unlikely to need the site at the same time; a time-sharing center typically is used routinely.

PERFORMANCE BY SUBTOPICS

Each category below parallels a subtopic covered in Chapter 55. Record the number and percentage of questions you correctly answered in each subtopic area.

Hardware, Software & Networks

Question #	Correct	√
1		
2		
3		
4		
5		
# Questions	5	
# Correct		
% Correct		

Data

Question #	Correct	√
6		
7		
8		
9		
10		
# Questions	5	
# Correct		
% Correct		

Development & Implementations

Question #	Correct	√
11		
12		
13		
14		
15		
16		
17		
18		
19		
# Questions	9	
# Correct		
% Correct		

System Operations

Question #	Correct	√
20		
21		
# Questions	2	
# Correct		
% Correct		

Roles

Question #	Correct	√
22		
23		
24		
25		
# Questions	4	
# Correct		
% Correct		

Business Information Systems

Question #	Correct	√
26		
27		
28		
29		
30		
# Questions	5	
# Correct		
% Correct		

E-Commerce Implications

Question #	Correct	√
31		
32		
33		
34		
35		
36		
37		
# Questions	7	
# Correct		
% Correct		

Security

Question #	Correct	√
38		
39		
40		
# Questions	3	
# Correct		
% Correct		

Disaster Recovery

Question #	Correct	√
41		
42		
# Questions	2	
# Correct		
% Correct		

Documentation

Question #	Correct	√
43		
44		
45		
46		
# Questions	4	
# Correct		
% Correct		

General Controls

Question #	Correct	√
47		
48		
49		
50		
# Questions	4	
# Correct		
% Correct		

Application Controls

Question #	Correct	√
51		
52		
53		
54		
55		
56		
57		
# Questions	7	
# Correct		
% Correct		

Special Systems

Question #	Correct	√
58		
59		
60		
# Questions	3	
# Correct		
% Correct		

SIMULATION SOLUTIONS

Solution 55-3

Response #1: Flowchart (8 points)

1. M

Before preparing a sales order, the computer processing department should perform a credit check to determine that the sale will be made to a creditworthy customer. This information may be obtained from the customer credit file or from outside sources.

2. Z

Once the sales order has been prepared, it will be recorded and placed in the open order file.

3. L

This manual operation represents the process of matching customer purchase orders with sales orders for agreement.

4. B

This manual operation represents matching the shipping document with the sales order for agreement.

5. H

Once the shipping document and sales order have been matched, the goods will be released for shipment.

6. S

In order to prepare the customer bill, the computerized billing program will retrieve the shipping data from the shipping file and enter the price data from the master price file.

7. O

Once the shipping data and price data have been retrieved and the sale to the customer generated, the sales invoice will be prepared.

8. U

This document represents the duplicate copy sales invoice generated by the computerized billing program.

9. I

One copy of the sales invoice will be sent to the customer, and one will be sent to the accounts receivable department as support for the entry to the accounts receivable ledger—to be held until remittance is made by the customer.

10. Q

The computer processing department will (daily, weekly, or monthly) update the master files, such as the accounts receivable ledger, the inventory master file, the sales transaction file, and the general ledger master file.

11. N

The computer processing department will prepare, based upon the update program, an accounts receivable ledger, an aged trial balance, a general ledger transaction summary, and a sales journal.

12. T

This output function represents the sales journal which was generated by the computerized update program for the day, week, or month, depending upon the frequency of report generation established by management.

13. Y

This output report represents the aged trial balance generated by the computerized update program, which combined information from the general ledger master file, the sales transaction file, and the inventory master file.

Response #2: CAAT Advantages (6 points)

The potential benefits to an auditor of using software in an audit as compared to performing an audit without the use of a computer include the following:

1. **Time** may be **saved** by eliminating manual footing, cross-footing, and other routine calculations.

2. **Calculations,** comparisons, and other data manipulations are **more accurately performed.**

3. **Analytical procedures** calculations may be **more efficiently performed.**

4. The **scope** of analytical procedures may be **broadened.**

5. Audit **sampling** may be **facilitated.**

6. Potential **weaknesses** in a client's internal control structure may be more readily **identified.**

7. Preparation and **revision of flowcharts** depicting the flow of financial transactions in a client's structure may be **facilitated.**

8. **Working papers** may be easily **stored** and accessed.

9. **Graphics capabilities** may allow the auditor to generate, display, and evaluate various financial and nonfinancial relationships graphically.

10. Engagement-management information such as **time budgets** and the monitoring of **actual time vs. budgeted amounts** may be more easily generated and analyzed.

11. **Customized working papers** may be developed with greater ease.

12. **Standardized audit correspondence,** such as engagement letters, client representation letters, and attorney letters **may be stored and easily modified.**

13. **Supervisory-review time** may be **reduced.**

14. Staff morale and productivity may be improved by reducing the time spent on clerical tasks.

15. **Client's personnel may not need to manually prepare** as many **schedules** and otherwise spend as much time assisting the auditor.

16. Computer-generated working papers are generally more **legible** and consistent.

Solution 55-4

Response #1: Auditing Procedures (7 points)

The **substantive auditing procedures** Brown may consider performing include the following:

Using the **perpetual** inventory file,

- **Recalculate the beginning and ending balances** (prices × quantities), foot, and print out a report to be used to reconcile the totals with the general ledger (or agree beginning balance with the prior year's working papers).

- **Calculate the quantity balances** as of the physical inventory date **for comparison to** the **physical inventory file.** (Alternatively, update the physical inventory file for purchases and sales from January 6 to January 31, 20X1, for comparison to the perpetual inventory at January 31, 20X1.)

- Select and print out a **sample of items received and shipped** for the periods (a) before and after January 5 and 31, 20X1, **for cut-off testing,** (b) between January 5 and January 31, 20X1, **for vouching or analytical procedures,** and (c) prior to January 5, 20X1, **for tests of details** or analytical procedures.

- Compare quantities sold during the year to quantities on hand at year end. Print out a **report of items for which turnover is less than expected.** (Alternatively, calculate the number of days' sales in inventory for selected items.)

- **Select items** noted as possibly **unsalable** or **obsolete** during the physical inventory observation and print out information about purchases and sales for further consideration.

- **Recalculate** the prices used to value the year-end FIFO inventory by matching prices and quantities to the most recent purchases.

- Select a **sample** of **items for comparison** to **current sales prices.**

- **Identify** and print out **unusual transactions.** (These are transactions other than purchases or sales for the year, or physical inventory adjustments as of January 5, 20X1.)

- **Recalculate the ending inventory** (or selected items) by taking the beginning balances plus purchases, less sales, (quantities and/or amounts) and print out the differences.

- **Recalculate the cost of sales** for selected items sold during the year.

Using the **physical inventory** and test count files,

- **Account for all inventory tag numbers** used and print out a report of missing or duplicate numbers for follow-up.

- **Search for tag numbers** noted during the physical inventory observation as being **voided or not used.**

- **Compare the physical inventory file to the file of test counts** and print out a report of differences for auditor follow-up.

- **Combine the quantities** for each item appearing on more than one inventory tag number for comparison to the perpetual file.

- **Compare** the **quantities** on the file to the calculated quantity balances on the perpetual inventory file as of January 5, 20X1. (Alternatively, compare the physical inventory file updated to year end to the perpetual inventory file.)

- **Calculate the quantities and dollar amounts of the book-to-physical adjustments** for each item and the total adjustment. Print out a report to reconcile the total adjustment to the adjustment recorded in the general ledger before the year end.

- Using the calculated book-to-physical adjustments for each item, **compare the quantities and dollar amounts of each adjustment to the perpetual inventory file** as of January 5, 20X1, and print out a report of differences for follow-up.

Response #2: Flowchart (2 points)

1. A

This symbol represents a file. In the revenue cycle application process, the most likely output among the choices given is an accounts receivable master file, especially since there is a cash receipts transaction file. A remittance file (G) is not typically a separately constructed file. Answers F and B are not part of the revenue cycle.

2. H

This symbol represents some sort of printed output. Sales invoices are the most likely output from the system at this point. The customer orders would most likely be at the beginning of the revenue cycle. Receiving reports are not part of the revenue cycle. Customer checks are not created by the system but are received from the customer.

Education Requirements

Most states (and other jurisdictions) now require candidates to obtain 150 semester hours of education prior to taking the examination. Jurisdictions with 150-hour requirements may have alternate options available for candidates. Naturally, this information is subject to change without notice. Contact the jurisdiction in question for all applicable requirements to sit for the exam.

New York has a 150-hour requirement that will not be effective until August 1, 2009.

Some jurisdictions with 150-hour requirements may substitute experience for some education. Others may allow candidates to sit for the exam without the experience required for the license. Two of these are California and Pennsylvania.

Colorado, Delaware, New Hampshire, Vermont, and the Virgin Islands currently don't have a 150-hour requirement.

Out-of-State Candidates

Each state has separate requirements for candidates who wish to proctor within the state. Contact individual states or NASBA (www.nasba.org) for more information on individual states' requirements. Contact both the state where you plan to apply for a certificate and the state where you plan to sit for the examination.

Most states require candidates with degrees from schools outside of the United States to have their credentials evaluated by a member of the National Association of Credential Evaluation Services (NACES). View the NASBA web-site for a list of NACES members.

APPENDIX A
PRACTICE EXAMINATION

Editor's Note: Note that (1) 20% of multiple choice questions on the actual CPA exam are not scored; and (2) there are no simulations in the BEC exam section until further notice (probably, no earlier than 2007). There is only one practice (or final) examination in this book. Do not take this exam until you are ready for it. If you did not mark the answers on the diagnostic exam, it can be used as a second "final" exam.

Testlet 1 MULTIPLE CHOICE QUESTIONS (60 to 75 minutes)

1. Which of the following statements best describes the effect of the assignment of an interest in a general partnership?
a. The assignee becomes a partner.
b. The assignee is responsible for a proportionate share of past and future partnership debts.
c. The assignment automatically dissolves the partnership.
d. The assignment transfers the assignor's interest in partnership profits and surplus. (5888)

2. The partnership agreement for Owen Associates, a general partnership, provided that profits be paid to the partners in the ratio of their financial contribution to the partnership. Moore contributed $10,000, Noon contributed $30,000, and Kale contributed $50,000. For the year ended December 31, Owen had losses of $180,000. What amount of the losses should be allocated to Kale?
a. $ 40,000
b. $ 60,000
c. $ 90,000
d. $100,000 (5199)

3. Which of the following statements is correct regarding the apparent authority of a partner to bind the partnership in dealings with third parties? The apparent authority
a. Must be derived from the express powers and purposes contained in the partnership agreement
b. Will be effectively limited by a formal resolution of the partners of which third parties are unaware
c. May allow a partner to bind the partnership to representations made in connection with the sale of goods
d. Would permit a partner to submit a claim against the partnership to arbitration (6443)

4. Wind, who has been a partner in the PLW general partnership for four years, decides to withdraw from the partnership despite a written partnership agreement that states, "no partner may withdraw for a period of five years". What is the result of Wind's withdrawal?
a. Wind's withdrawal causes a dissolution of the partnership by operation of law.
b. Wind's withdrawal has **no** bearing on the continued operation of the partnership by the remaining partners.
c. Wind's withdrawal is **not** effective until Wind obtains a court ordered decree of dissolution.
d. Wind's withdrawal causes a dissolution of the partnership despite being in violation of the partnership agreement. (7042)

5. The partners of College Assoc., a general partnership, decided to dissolve the partnership and agreed that none of the partners would continue to use the partnership name. Which of the following events will occur on dissolution of the partnership?

	Each partner's existing liability would be discharged	Each partner's apparent authority would continue
a.	Yes	Yes
b.	Yes	No
c.	No	Yes
d.	No	No (5201)

6. Which of the following statements regarding a limited partner is(are) generally correct?

	The limited partner is subject to personal liability for partnership debts	The limited partner has the right to take part in the control of the partnership
a.	Yes	Yes
b.	Yes	No
c.	No	Yes
d.	No	No (0670)

7. What is the effect on the market price when both the supply and demand for a good increase?
a. Decrease only with inelastic demand
b. Decrease only with inelastic supply
c. Increase only with inelastic demand
d. Indeterminate from the given information (7213)

8. Which of the following is characteristic of an oligopoly market?
a. Mutual influence among industry firms on each others' prices
b. No entry or exit barriers
c. No promotional or informational advertising
d. One seller of a product with no close substitutes
e. Technological conditions permit only one efficient supplier (7232)

9. The federal government measures inflation with which of the following indicators?
a. Dow Jones index
b. Consumer price index
c. Consumer confidence index
d. Corporate profits (7664)

10. On March 15, Year 1, Ashe Corp. adopted a plan to accumulate $1,000,000 by September 1, Year 5. Ashe plans to make four equal annual deposits to a fund that will earn interest at 10% compounded annually. Ashe made the first deposit on September 1, 20X1. Future value and future amount factors are as follows:

Future value of 1 at 10% for 4 periods   1.46
Future amount of ordinary annuity of 1
   at 10% for 4 periods   4.64
Future amount of annuity in advance of 1
   at 10% for 4 periods   5.11

Ashe should make four annual deposits (rounded) of
a. $250,000
b. $215,500
c. $195,700
d. $146,000 (2397)

11. Velocity Company estimates the following for the next year, when common stock is expected to trade at a price-earnings ratio of seven.

Earnings before interest and taxes	$45 million
Interest expense	$5 million
Effective income tax rate	30%
Preferred stock dividends	$10 million
Common shares outstanding	2 million
Common stock payout ratio	25%

What is Velocity's approximate expected common stock market price per share next year?
a. $ 63
b. $ 75
c. $ 98
d. $105 (7278)

12. What ratios are characteristic of an entity with high financial risk?

	Debt-to-equity	Interest coverage
a.	High	High
b.	Low	High
c.	High	Low
d.	Low	Low (7282)

13. Zig Corp. provides the following information:

Pretax operating profit	$ 300,000,000
Tax rate	40%
Capital used to generate profits	
(50% debt, 50% equity)	$1,200,000,000
Cost of equity	15%
Cost of debt	5%

What of the following represents Zig's year-end economic value-added amount?
a. $0
b. $ 60,000,000
c. $120,000,000
d. $180,000,000 (7670)

14. To maximize shareholder wealth, which of the following measures is most appropriate for management focus?
a. Earnings per share
b. Profits
c. Stock value
d. Total return per share (7729)

15. Which of the following are characteristic of the growth or exploitation phase of a product life cycle?
a. High promotional expenses as a percentage of sales
b. Little direct competition
c. Profits shrink as direct competition increases.
d. Sales increase dramatically. (7730)

16. Which of the following is the **least** likely reason for an entity to hold cash and marketable securities?
a. Maintain sufficient cash to meet transaction requirements
b. Maintain a reserve for unexpected events
c. Fulfill compensating balance requirements
d. Earn maximum returns on assets (7360)

17. Rolling Wheels purchases bicycle components in the month prior to assembling them into bicycles. Assembly is scheduled one month prior to budgeted sales. Rolling pays 75% of component costs in the month of purchase and 25% of the costs in the following month. Component costs included in budgeted cost of sales are:

April	May	June	July	August
$5,000	$6,000	$7,000	$8,000	$8,000

What is Rolling's budgeted cash payments for components in May?
a. $5,750
b. $6,750
c. $7,750
d. $8,000 (7005)

18. Controllable revenues would be included in the performance reports of which of the following types of responsibility centers?

	Cost centers	Investment centers
a.	Yes	No
b.	Yes	Yes
c.	No	No
d.	No	Yes	(7417)

19. Multiple regression differs from simple regression in that it
a. Provides an estimated constant term
b. Has more dependent variables
c. Allows the computation of the coefficient of determination
d. Has more independent variables (6916)

20. What characteristic would most likely **not** be a best practice for an accounting department?
a. Have the accounting department originate transactions
b. Have online approvals and queries
c. Treat geographically dispersed resources as one
d. Data entry controls seek zero-defect information through the use of limits and ranges
e. Capture data once and accurately (7416)

21. What is the typical link between two businesses being combined in a conglomerate diversification strategy?
a. Customer base
b. Distribution network
c. Financial
d. Managerial skills
e. Technology (7409)

22. Which of the following bases of competition are **not** related to a differentiation focus strategy?
a. Low cost
b. Superior service
c. Superior quality
d. Special features (7414)

23. Blue Ridge Crafters is a co-operative that distributes traditional household furnishings, such as home-spun textiles, hand-thrown pottery, and hand-carved wood items. These items invariably are more expensive than mass-produced goods with similar functions, but customers prefer the artistry in Blue Ridge's goods. Because of subtle variations in color and grain, customers typically insist on handling these goods before committing to a sale. Each artisan decides which products to make. Blue Ridge relies on sales parties for about 20% and craft fairs for about 60% of its sales, with the remainder sold through a combination outlet-exhibit along a popular vacation route and independent boutiques and art galleries. Blue Ridge is conducting environmental scanning as part of its strategic management initiative. Which **two** of the following factors are least likely considered opportunities for Blue Ridge?
a. An Internet retail site, as opposed to a physical site, has relatively low overhead costs.
b. Attendance at craft fairs has increased 20% from five years ago.
c. Blue Ridge artisans are a highly trained group.
d. The general population shows a decreased interest in modern-style furnishings.
e. Increased national income (7703)

24. A bus network is characterized by communication channels
a. Directly linked to a single host computer
b. Linked to a loop, with each message passed neighbor to neighbor until the message reaches its destination
c. Linked to one common line with direct access to the message destination
d. Organized along hierarchical channels that eventually are linked to a single host computer (7450)

25. What reliable and economic automatic device do banks commonly use for data entry for check processing?
a. Bar coding
b. Electronic data interchange
c. Magnetic ink character recognition
d. Magnetic tape (7449)

26. The greatest financial threat to an organization that implemented the financial accounting module of an enterprise resource planning (ERP) system from a major vendor exists from errors detected during which of the following times?
a. Project initiation
b. Requirements determination
c. Table configuration
d. Implementation (7690)

27. Which activity is a systems analyst least likely to perform?
a. Application design
b. Coding programs
c. Evaluating user requirements
d. Specification development (7425)

28. Jones, an auditor for Farmington Co., noted that the Acme employees were using computers connected to Acme's network by wireless technology. On Jones' next visit to Acme, Jones brought one of Farmington's laptop computers with a wireless network card. When Jones started the laptop to begin work, Jones noticed that the laptop could view several computers on Acme's network and Jones had access to Acme's network files. Which of the following statements is the most likely explanation?
a. Acme's router was improperly configured.
b. Farmington's computer had the same administrator password as the server.
c. Jones had been given root account access on Acme's computer.
d. Acme was not using security on the network. (7671)

29. A client is concerned that a power outage or disaster could impair the computer hardware's ability to function as designed. The client desires off-site backup hardware facilities that are fully configured and ready to operate within several hours. The client most likely should consider a
a. Cold site
b. Cool site
c. Warm site
d. Hot site (7708)

30. Decision tables differ from program flowcharts in that decision tables emphasize
a. Ease of manageability for complex programs
b. Logical relationships among conditions and actions
c. Cost benefit factors justifying the program
d. The sequence in which operations are performed (2808)

Testlet 2 MULTIPLE CHOICE QUESTIONS (60 to 75 minutes)

1. Jones, Smith, and Bay wanted to form a company called JSB Co. but were unsure about which type of entity would be most beneficial based on their concerns. They all desired the opportunity to make tax-free contributions and distributions where appropriate. They wanted earnings to accumulate tax-free. They did not want to be subject to personal holding tax and did not want double taxation of income. Bay was going to be the only individual giving management advice to the company and wanted to be a member of JSB through his current company, Channel, Inc. Which of the following would be the most appropriate business structure to meet all of their concerns?
a. Proprietorship
b. S corporation
c. C corporation
d. Limited liability partnership   (7680)

Items 2 and 3 are based on the following:

Lange, Maine, and Nemo formed a general partnership, LMN. Their written partnership agreement provided that the profits would be divided so that Lange would receive 50%; Maine, 30%; and Nemo, 20%. There was no provision for allocating losses. At the end of its first year, the partnership had losses of $210,000. Before allocating losses, the partners' capital account balances were: Lange, $130,000; Maine, $165,000; and Nemo, $10,000. Nemo refuses to make any further contributions to the partnership. After losses were allocated to the partners' capital accounts and all liabilities were paid, the partnership's sole asset was $95,000 in cash. Ignore the effects of partnership tax law.

2. What would be Nemo's share of the partnership losses?
a. $12,000
b. $21,000
c. $42,000
d. $70,000   (9911)

3. How much would Maine receive on dissolution of the partnership?
a. $37,000
b. $40,000
c. $47,500
d. $50,000   (9911)

4. The corporate veil is most likely to be pierced and the shareholders held personally liable if
a. The corporation has elected S corporation status under the Internal Revenue Code.
b. The shareholders have commingled their personal funds with those of the corporation.
c. An ultra vires act has been committed.
d. A partnership incorporates its business solely to limit the liability of its partners.   (4317)

5. Which of the following statements is correct concerning the similarities between a limited partnership and a corporation?
a. Each is created under a statute and must file a copy of its certificate with the proper state authorities.
b. All corporate stockholders and all partners in a limited partnership have limited liability.
c. Both are recognized for federal income tax purposes as taxable entities.
d. Both are allowed statutorily to have perpetual existence.   (3083)

6. Under the Revised Model Business Corporation Act, a corporate director is authorized to
a. Rely on information provided by the appropriate corporate officer
b. Serve on the board of directors of a competing business
c. Sell control of the corporation
d. Profit from insider information   (6423)

7. What is characteristic of a business cycle trough?
a. Decreasing purchasing power
b. Increasing capital investments
c. Rising costs
d. Shortages of essential raw materials
e. Unused productive capacity   (7239)

8. Which of the following circumstances is **not** characteristic of structural unemployment?
a. All labor is employed, although some people are working at jobs for which they are overqualified.
b. The economic cycle is in recessionary phase.
c. The labor shortage in Calgary is equal to the labor surplus in Atlanta.
d. A placement agency has unfilled programming positions and resumes from airline pilots, but no unfilled pilot positions.   (7242)

9. What is the effect on prices of U.S. imports and exports when the dollar depreciates?
a. Import prices and export prices will decrease.
b. Import prices will decrease and export prices will increase.
c. Import prices will increase and export prices will decrease.
d. Import prices and export prices will increase.
(7682)

10. Which of the following ratios provides the most appropriate liquidity measure?
a. Current assets to current liabilities
b. Current liabilities to long-term liabilities
c. Net income to current liabilities
d. Total assets to total liabilities
(7286)

11. Which of the following is **least** appropriate for use as a cash substitute?
a. Banker's acceptances
b. Commercial paper
c. Convertible bonds
d. U.S. Treasury bills
(7364)

12. Net working capital is the difference between
a. Capital assets and long-term liabilities
b. Current assets and current liabilities
c. Current assets, except for inventories, and current liabilities
d. Fixed assets and long-term liabilities
e. Total equity and stock par value
(7358)

13. What is the largest source of short-term credit for small businesses?
a. Commercial paper
b. Debentures
c. Mortgages
d. Notes payables
e. Trade credit
(7373)

14. The estimates necessary to compute the economic order quantity are
a. Annual usage in units, cost per order, and annual cost of carrying one unit in stock
b. Annual usage in units, cost per unit of inventory, and annual cost of carrying one unit in stock
c. Annual cost of placing orders, and annual cost of carrying one unit in stock
d. Cost per unit of inventory, annual cost of placing orders, and annual carrying cost
(9911)

15. Pan Company's bonds are yielding 6% currently. Why is Pan's cost of debt lower than 6%?
a. Additional debt is issued less expensively than initial debt.
b. Interest is deductible in calculating taxable income.
c. Interest rates decreased since Pan issued these bonds.
d. Interest rates increased since Pan issued these bonds.
(7381)

16. A direct labor overtime premium should be charged to a specific job when the overtime is caused by the
a. Increased overall level of activity
b. Customer's requirement for early completion of job
c. Management's failure to include the job in the production schedule
d. Management's requirement that the job be completed before the annual factory vacation closure
(2551)

17. Break-even analysis assumes that over the relevant range
a. Unit revenues are nonlinear.
b. Unit variable costs are unchanged.
c. Total costs are unchanged.
d. Total fixed costs are nonlinear.
(5787)

18. In the profit-volume chart below, EF and GH represent the profit-volume graphs of a single-product company for 20X1 and 20X2, respectively.

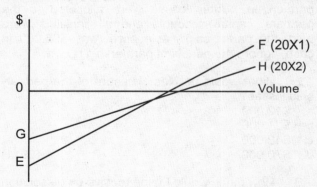

If 20X1 and 20X2 unit sales prices are identical, how did total fixed costs and unit variable costs of 20X2 change compared to 20X1?

	20X2 Total fixed costs	20X2 Unit variable costs
a.	Decreased	Increased
b.	Decreased	Decreased
c.	Increased	Increased
d.	Increased	Decreased (7384)

19. Day Glow Co. applied the high-low method of cost estimation to inventory purchase order data for the first four months of the year.

Month	Orders	Cost
January	120	$ 412
February	130	425
March	180	502
April	170	489
	600	$1,828

What is Day Glow's estimated monthly fixed cost of filling purchase orders?
a. $230
b. $232
c. $234
d. $412 (9911)

20. Plainfield Company manufactures Part G for use in its production cycle. The costs per unit for 10,000 units of Part G are as follows:

Direct materials	$ 3
Direct labor	15
Variable overhead	6
Fixed overhead	8
	$32

Verona Company has offered to sell Plainfield 10,000 units of Part G for $30 per unit. If Plainfield accepts Verona's offer, the released facilities could be used to save $45,000 in relevant costs in the manufacture of Part H. In addition, $5 per unit of the fixed overhead applied to Part G would be totally eliminated. What alternative is more desirable and by what amount is it more desirable?

	Alternative	Amount
a.	Manufacture	$10,000
b.	Manufacture	$15,000
c.	Buy	$35,000
d.	Buy	$65,000 (9911)

21. Cuff Caterers quotes a price of $60 per person for a dinner party. This price includes the 6% sales tax and the 15% service charge. Sales tax is computed on the food plus the service charge. The service charge is computed on the food only. At what amount does Cuff price the food?
a. $56.40
b. $51.00
c. $49.22
d. $47.40 (5468)

22. During May, Roy Co. produced 10,000 units of Product X. Costs incurred by Roy during May were as follows.

Direct Materials	$10,000
Direct labor	20,000
Variable manufacturing overhead	5,000
Variable selling and general	3,000
Fixed manufacturing overhead	9,000
Fixed selling and general	4,000
Total	$51,000

Under absorption costing, Product X's unit cost was
a. $5.10
b. $4.40
c. $3.80
d. $3.50 (9911)

23. During the Year 1 ski season, Sunglow Ski Resort had its three access roads blocked by snow.

Number of blocked roads per day	Number of days
0	120
1	16
2	10
3	1

Sunglow estimates that each blocked road results in lost revenue of $4,500 per day, unless all three roads are blocked. When all three roads are blocked, estimated lost revenue is $35,000 for that day. Sunglow can retain a snowplow service for $50,000 to clear blocked roads. The variable cost of operating the snowplow is $500 per day per blocked road. If Sunglow uses a snowplow service in Year 2, the estimated benefit for Year 2 would be
a. $267,000
b. $127,500
c. $125,500
d. $106,000 (9911)

24. The part of the central processing unit that stores data and programs temporarily during processing is the
a. Floppy disk memory
b. Operating system
c. Random-access memory (RAM)
d. Read-only memory (ROM) (7463)

25. Misstatements in a batch computer system caused by incorrect programs or data may **not** be detected immediately because
a. Errors in some transactions may cause rejection of other transactions in the batch.
b. The identification of errors in input data typically is **not** part of the program.
c. There are time delays in processing transactions in a batch system.
d. The processing of transactions in a batch system is **not** uniform. (7570)

26. Which of the following computer-assisted auditing techniques allows fictitious and real transactions to be processed together without client operating personnel being aware of the testing process?
a. Integrated test facility
b. Input controls matrix
c. Parallel simulation
d. Data entry monitor (7564)

Items 27 and 28 are based on the following:

Invoice #	Product	Quantity	Unit price
201	F10	150	$ 5.00
202	G15	200	$10.00
203	H20	250	$25.00
204	K35	300	$30.00

27. Which of the following numbers represents the record count?
a. 1
b. 4
c. 810
d. 900 (7548)

28. Which of the following most likely represents a hash total?
a. FGHK80
b. 4
c. 204
d. 810 (7549)

29. Which of the following is an attribute of an interactive system?
a. Data is processed as it is input.
b. Groups of data processed at regular intervals
c. Sorting transaction files prior to processing
d. Transaction files with sequential arrangement of records (7458)

30. A local area network (LAN) is
a. A system that connects computers and other devices in a limited physical area.
b. A system that rents time on a central computer to several entities, with each entity having remote input and output devices.
c. Facilitates meetings among several people at different physical locations.
d. Facilitates working outside of a traditional office, remaining connected by the Internet, phone, etc. (7466)

Testlet 3 MULTIPLE CHOICE QUESTIONS (60 to 75 minutes)

1. Which of the following statements is (are) correct regarding the methods a target corporation may use to ward off a takeover attempt?

I. The target corporation may make an offer ("self-tender") to acquire stock from its own shareholders.
II. The target corporation may seek an injunction against the acquiring corporation on the grounds that the attempted takeover violates federal antitrust law.

a. I only
b. II only
c. Both I and II
d. Neither I nor II (7045)

2. Which of the following facts is(are) generally included in a corporation's articles of incorporation?

	Name of registered agent	Number of authorized shares
a.	Yes	Yes
b.	Yes	No
c.	No	Yes
d.	No	No	(5890)

3. After proper incorporation of Alpha, it was decided to purchase a plant site. Gold, a newly elected director, has owned a desirable site for many years. He purchased the property for $60,000, and its present fair value is $100,000. What would be the result if Gold offered the property to Alpha for $100,000 in an arm's-length transaction with full disclosure at a meeting of the seven directors of the corporation?
a. The sale would be proper only upon requisite approval by the appropriate number of directors and at no more than Gold's cost, thus precluding his profiting from the sale to the corporation.
b. The sale would be void under the self-dealing rule.
c. The sale would be proper and Gold would not have to account to the corporation for his profit if the sale was approved by a disinterested majority of the directors.
d. The sale would not be proper, if sold for the present fair value of the property, without the approval of all of the directors in these circumstances. (9911)

4. Under the Revised Model Business Corporation Act, when a corporation's bylaws grant stockholders preemptive rights, which of the following rights is(are) included in that grant?

	The right to purchase a proportionate share of newly-issued stock	The right to a proportionate share of corporate assets remaining on corporate dissolution
a.	Yes	Yes
b.	Yes	No
c.	No	Yes
d.	No	No (6752)

5. A corporate stockholder is entitled to which of the following rights?
a. Elect officers
b. Receive annual dividends
c. Approve dissolution
d. Prevent corporate borrowing (2831)

6. A parent corporation owned more than 90% of each class of the outstanding stock issued by a subsidiary corporation and decided to merge that subsidiary into itself. Under the Revised Model Business Corporation Act, which of the following actions must be taken?
a. The subsidiary corporation's board of directors must pass a merger resolution.
b. The subsidiary corporation's dissenting stockholders must be given an appraisal remedy.
c. The parent corporation's stockholders must approve the merger.
d. The parent corporation's dissenting stockholders must be given an appraisal remedy. (5202)

7. To what does the term "managed float" refer in foreign exchange markets?
a. Commercial activity between businesses of different nations that sets exchange rates
b. Discretionary currency trading by central banks
c. The International Monetary Fund's role in covering short-term deficits in balance of payments
d. The tendency of currencies of nation's experiencing inflation to depreciate (7257)

8. What is the primary reason for nations to devalue their currencies?
a. Discourage exports without using quotas
b. Encourage citizens to make foreign investments
c. Improve the balance of trade
d. Slow inflation by increasing imports (7258)

9. When deciding on transfer pricing used in compiling internal financial statements used to evaluate a division's performance for managerial purposes, what factor should receive the least consideration?
a. Controllability of costs
b. Effect of random shocks
c. Minimize world-wide corporate taxes
d. Possible dysfunctional behavior induced by the evaluation system (7728)

10. Para Co. is reviewing the following data relating to an energy saving investment proposal:

Cost	$50,000
Residual value at the end of 5 years	10,000
Present value of an annuity of 1 at 12% for 5 years	3.60
Present value of 1 due in 5 years at 12%	0.57

What would be the annual savings needed to make the investment realize a 12% yield?
a. $ 8,189
b. $11,111
c. $12,306
d. $13,889 (4643)

11. Kim Co.'s profit center Zee had Year 1 operating income of $200,000 before a $50,000 imputed interest charge for using Kim's assets. Kim's aggregate net income from all of its profit centers was $2,000,000. During Year 1, Kim declared and paid dividends of $30,000 and $70,000 on its preferred and common stock, respectively. Zee's Year 1 residual income was
a. $140,000
b. $143,000
c. $147,000
d. $150,000 (3362)

12. Which of the following is characteristic of primary capital markets?
a. Exchanges of existing debt and equity securities
b. Exchanges of future commodity contracts
c. Exchanges of future commodity contracts and new issues of debt and equity securities
d. New issues of debt and equity securities (7368)

13. Aardvark Company's beta coefficient is 1.2. The current rates for U.S. treasury bonds and expected corporate returns are 7% and 12%, respectively. What is Aardvark's approximate expected rate of return using the capital asset pricing model (CAPM)?
a. 8.4%
b. 10.6%
c. 13.0%
d. 14.4% (7382)

14. Which of the following is an assumption of the residual theory of dividends?
a. The rate of return that investors require is not affected by dividend policy.
b. Dividend payments should be a percentage of earnings.
c. Dividend payments should be stable.
d. The number of dividend distributions should be minimized. (7316)

15. Which of the following is (are) acceptable regarding the allocation of joint product cost to a by-product?

	Some portion allocated	None allocated
a.	Acceptable	Not acceptable
b.	Acceptable	Acceptable
c.	Not acceptable	Acceptable
d.	Not acceptable	Not acceptable

(9911)

16. Carr Co. had an unfavorable materials usage variance of $900. What amounts of this variance should be charged to each department?

	Purchasing	Warehousing	Manufacturing
a.	$0	$0	$900
b.	$0	$900	$0
c.	$300	$300	$300
d.	$900	$0	$0

(3358)

17. Yarn Co.'s inventories in process were at the following stages of completion at the end of April:

No. of units	Percent complete
200	90
100	80
400	10

Equivalent units of production amounted to
a. 300
b. 360
c. 660
d. 700 (2677)

18. Simpson Company manufactures electric drills to the exacting specifications of various customers. During April, Job 43 for the production of 1,100 drills was completed at the following costs per unit:

Direct materials	$ 5
Direct labor	4
Applied factory overhead	6
	$15

Final inspection of Job 43 disclosed 50 defective units and 100 spoiled units. The defective drills were reworked at a total cost of $250, and the spoiled drills were sold to a jobber for $750. What would be the unit cost of the good units produced on Job 43?
a. $16.50
b. $16.00
c. $15.00
d. $14.50 (7394)

19. Clean Power, Inc., allocates support department costs to its individual divisions using the step method, starting with the finance department costs. Information for July is as follows.

	Support departments	
	Finance	Legal
Costs incurred	$80,000	$56,000
Services percentages provided to:		
Finance department	—	20%
Legal department	10%	—
Photovoltaic division	60%	20%
Windmill division	30%	60%
	100%	100%

What is the amount of support department costs allocated to the photovoltaic division for July?
a. $72,000
b. $64,000
c. $60,800
d. $59,200   (9911)

20. In an activity-based costing system, cost reduction is accomplished by identifying and eliminating

	All cost drivers	Nonvalue-adding activities
a.	No	No
b.	Yes	Yes
c.	No	Yes
d.	Yes	No (4550)

21. Tyro Co. uses a standard cost system. The following information pertains to direct labor for product B for the month of May:

Actual rate paid	$8.40 per hour
Standard rate	$8.00 per hour
Standard hours allowed for actual production	2,000 hours
Labor efficiency variance	$ 800 unfavorable

What were the actual hours worked?
a. 1,900
b. 1,905
c. 2,095
d. 2,100   (1511)

22. When using the two-variance method for analyzing factory overhead, the difference between the budget allowance based on standard hours allowed and the factory overhead applied to production is the
a. Controllable variance
b. Net overhead variance
c. Volume variance
d. Efficiency variance   (2225)

23. System design usually includes design of
a. Data, input, and user interface
b. Data, process, and user interface
c. Input, data, and output
d. Input, process, and output   (7475)

24. In an accounting information system, which of the following types of computer files most likely would be a master file?
a. Inventory subsidiary
b. Cash disbursements
c. Cash receipts
d. Payroll transactions   (7676)

25. What attribute is characteristic of a decision support system?
a. Database management system
b. Expert system
c. Interactive system
d. Transaction processing system   (7431)

26. What attribute is **least** descriptive of an accounting information system?
a. Best suited to solving problems involving uncertainty and ambiguous reporting requirements
b. Provides information to management for use in planning and controlling an entity's activities
c. Subsystem of a management information system
d. Transaction processing system   (7433)

27. Which of the following is usually a benefit of transmitting transactions in an electronic data interchange (EDI) environment?
a. A compressed business cycle with lower year-end receivables balances
b. A reduced need to test computer controls related to sales and collections transactions
c. An increased opportunity to apply statistical sampling techniques to account balances
d. No need to rely on third-party service providers to ensure security   (6825)

28. Which of the following is a computer program that appears to be legitimate but performs some illicit activity when it is run?
a. Hoax virus
b. Web crawler
c. Trojan horse
d. Killer application   (7020)

29. What is an echo check?
a. A CPU compares signals sent and received by the CPU to and from an input or output device.
b. A CPU continually confirms that an odd number of magnetized dots represent each character when receiving input.
c. A CPU periodically searches for circuits that are failing.
d. A plastic ring must be attached to a reel before the tape drive will write to the tape. (7741)

30. Which of the following is an example of a validity check?
a. The computer ensures that a numerical amount in a record does **not** exceed some predetermined amount.
b. As the computer corrects errors and data are successfully resubmitted to the system, the causes of the errors are printed out.
c. The computer flags any transmission for which the control field value did **not** match that of an existing file record.
d. After data for a transaction are entered, the computer sends certain data back to the terminal for comparison with data originally sent. (5957)

SIMULATIONS

Editor's Note: Simulations are not included on the BEC exam section currently, although the AICPA plans to add them at an unspecified date. These simulations still provide a good review of topics covered by the exam.

Testlet 4 (15 to 25 minutes)

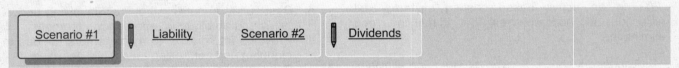

Mill, Web, and Trent own all the outstanding and issued voting common stock of Sack Corp. Mill owns 40%, Web owns 30%, and Trent owns 30%. They also executed a written stockholders' agreement in which Mill, Web, and Trent agreed to vote for each other as directors of Sack.

At the initial meeting of the incorporators, Mill, Web and Trent were elected to the board of directors together with three non-stockholders. At the initial board of directors meeting, Mill, Web, and Trent were appointed as officers of the corporation and given three-year employment contracts.

During its first year of operations, Sack began experiencing financial difficulties, which caused disagreements among Mill, Web, and Trent as to how the business should be operated.

At the next annual stockholders' meeting, Mill was not elected to the board of directors. The new board fired Mill in a management reorganization despite there being two years left on the employment contract. The board, reasonably relying on assurances from Web and Trent regarding financial statements Web and Trent knew to be materially misstated, declared and paid a dividend that caused Sack to become insolvent.

Answer the following questions based on Scenario #1.

1. According to the stockholders' agreement, what party(ies) must be elected as director(s) of Sack?
2. According to the stockholders' agreement, what party(ies) must be appointed as officer(s) of the corporation?
3. What party(ies) is (are) liable to Mill for Mill's firing?
4. What party(ies) must return the dividend to the corporation?
5. What party(ies) would be liable for declaring the illegal dividend?

Responses

A. Mill only	F. Web and Trent only
B. Web only	G. Mill, Web, and Trent
C. Trent only	H. Neither Mill, Web, nor Trent
D. Mill and Web only	I. All directors
E. Mill and Trent only	J. Sack Corp

(6519-6523)

Mace, Inc. wishes to acquire Creme Corp., a highly profitable company with substantial retained earnings. Creme is incorporated in a state that recognizes the concepts of stated capital (legal capital) and capital surplus.

In conjunction with the proposed acquisition, Mace engaged Gold & Co., CPAs, to audit Creme's financial statements. Gold began analyzing Creme's stated capital account and was provided the following data:

- Creme was initially capitalized in 2000 by issuing 40,000 shares of common stock, 50¢ par value, at $15 per share. The total number of authorized shares was fixed at 100,000 shares.
- Costs to organize Creme were $15,000.
- During 2002, Creme's board of directors declared and distributed a 5% common stock dividend. The fair market value of the stock at that time was $20 per share.
- On June 1, 2003, the president of Creme exercised a stock option to purchase 1,000 shares of common stock at $21 per share when the market price was $25 per share.
- During 2004, Creme's board of directors declared and distributed a 2-for-1 stock split on its common stock when the market price was $28 per share.
- During 2005, Creme acquired as treasury stock 5,000 shares of its common stock at a market price of $30 per share. Creme uses the cost method of accounting and reporting for treasury stock.
- During 2006, Creme reissued 3,000 shares of the treasury stock at the market price of $32 per share.

Discuss the requirements necessary to properly declare and pay cash dividends based on Scenario #2. Set forth reasons for any conclusions stated.

(9661)

Testlet 5 (15 to 25 minutes)

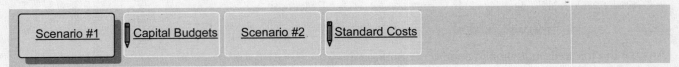

Scenario #1   Capital Budgets   Scenario #2   Standard Costs

A company has two mutually exclusive projects, A and B, which have the same initial investment requirements and lives. Project B has a decrease in estimated cash inflows each year, and project A has an increase in estimated net cash inflows each year. Project A has a greater total net cash inflow. Diagram I below depicts the net cash inflows of each project by year. Diagram II depicts the net present value (NPV) of each project assuming various discount rates.

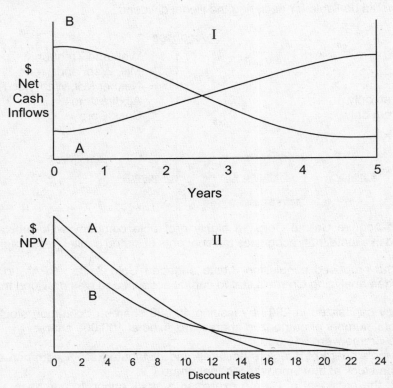

Select your answer from the following list, based on Scenario #1.

A. Project A
B. Project B
C. Both projects equal
D. Indeterminate from information given

1. Which project would be likely to have the shorter payback period?

2. Which project would have the greater average accounting rate of return?

3. Which project would have the greater internal rate of return?

4. Assume, due to innovation, the projects were to terminate at the end of year 4 with cash flows remaining as projected for the first 4 years and no cash flows in year 5. Which project would have the greater internal rate of return?   (7478)

The accompanying diagram depicts a manufacturing total cost flexible budget line KI and standard cost line OI. Line OJ is parallel to line KI, and revenues are represented by line OH.

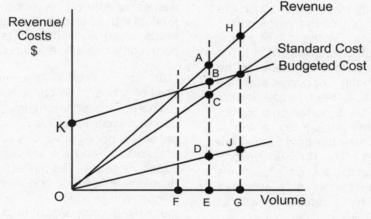

Identify the line on the graph in Scenario #2 that represents each item.

1. The budgeted fixed cost at volume OE

2. The budgeted variable cost at volume OE

3. The standard gross profit at volume OE

4. The budgeted gross profit at volume OE, assuming no change between beginning and ending inventories

5. The normal capacity, assuming standard costs are based on normal capacity   (7477)

Solution 1 MULTIPLE CHOICE ANSWERS

Chapter 48: Partnerships

1. (d) A general partner's interest in the partnership refers to that partner's right to participate in profit distributions and a return of capital upon dissolution. Thus, a general partner may transfer this interest without dissolving the partnership. The assignee receives nothing more that the assignor's interest in partnership profits and surplus. The assignee does not become a partner and, thus, incurs no liability for partnership debts.

2. (d) The partners of Owen Associates have entered into an enforceable agreement providing that a partner's distributive share of profits would represent each partner's percentage of capital contribution. The Revised Uniform Partnership Act provides that a partner's liability for losses is the same percentage as their right to profits unless the partners agree otherwise. Kale contributed 5/9 of all capital, thus is entitled to 5/9 of all profits and for 5/9 of all losses. $180,000 × 5/9 = $100,000.

3. (c) Apparent authority arises in situations where a third party could reasonably believe the principal (partnership) has authorized the actions of the agent (partner). The actions of a partner which are apparently for the carrying on of the partnership's business in the usual way, such as the sale of goods, even though not actually authorized, will still bind the partnership if the third party does not know of the partner's lack of actual authority. Apparent authority is not necessarily derived from the express powers and purposes contained in the partnership agreement, and is not effectively limited by a formal resolution of the partners when the third parties are unaware of such resolution. The Revised Uniform Partnership Act imposes limitations on a partner's authority, including that no partner may submit a partnership claim or liability to arbitration without authorization to do so.

4. (d) Under RUPA, every partner has the power to dissolve the partnership whether or not the partner has that right under the partnership agreement. When the dissolving partner acts in violation of the agreement, the partner may be held liable for any losses caused by the dissolution.

5. (c) The Revised Uniform Partnership Act (RUPA) provides that all partners have personal liability for partnership liabilities incurred while they were partners. Their liability would continue even after dissociation. RUPA also provides that unless a partnership dissolves by operation of law, the partnership, to terminate the partners' apparent authority, must give actual notice to all third parties who have had dealings with the partners and constructive notice to all others. Since College Assoc. has not provided any notice, the partners continue to have apparent authority.

6. (d) A limited partner is not subject to personal liability for partnership debts, because a limited partner's liability is limited to the amount of her/his capital contribution. In addition, generally, a limited partner has no right to control (manage) the partnership (there are a few limited exceptions).

Chapter 50: Economic Theory

7. (d) With the same demand, an increase in supply will lower the price. With the same supply, an increase in demand will raise the price. When both change concurrently, the effect on the market price depends on the size of the changes and the slopes of the supply and demand curves.

8. (a) An oligopoly is characterized by price leadership (mutual influence among industry firms on each others' prices) and interdependence on output decisions. Oligopolies typically have entry barriers as well as advertising. A monopoly has one seller of a product with no close substitutes. A natural monopoly exists when economic or technological conditions permit only one efficient supplier.

9. (b) Inflation is an increase in the general level of prices. The consumer price index is a comparison of the price of items in a "typical" shopping cart to a base value. A Dow Jones index is a comparison of prices of various lists of stocks; the stocks are selected and the indices are complied by Dow Jones Indexes, an independent company that develops, maintains, and licenses market indices for investment products. The consumer confidence index is a comparison of a consumer assurance survey to a base consumer assurance survey. Corporations, not the federal government, report corporate profits.

Chapter 51: Financial Management

10. (c) To determine the amount of the periodic payments required to accumulate to a given sum, with the first payment to be made immediately, the factor for the future amount of an annuity in advance is used. The factor for the future amount of an annuity in advance of 1 at 10% for 4 periods is given as 5.11.

Annual deposit amount	×	*Applicable factor for future amount of annuity in advance*	=	*Future annuity in advance*

Annual deposit × 5.11 = $1,000,000
Annual deposit = $1,000,000 / 5.11 = $195,700

11. (a) Estimated earnings are $28 million [($45 million − $5 million) × (1 − 0.30)]. After paying preferred stock dividends, there is $18 million available to common shareholders, or EPS of $9 ($18 million / 2 million shares). To figure price when the price/earnings ratio is known, multiply the ratio by earnings. 7 × $9 / share = $63 / share.

12. (c) A high debt-to-equity ratio puts an entity at a high risk of insolvency; debt payments legally must be made in recessive periods as well as boom periods, while dividends never are required to be declared. A low interest coverage ratio signifies that earnings before interest and taxes with which to pay interest are small in proportion to required interest payments. A small earnings drop for an entity with high interest coverage would have minimal impact on financial condition. A drop of the same dollar amount could throw an entity with low interest coverage into insolvency.

13. (b) Economic value added is the net operating profit after tax less the opportunity cost of capital. The post-tax operating profit is $180,000,000 [$300,000,000 × (1 − 0.40)] The equity capital is $600M (50% of $1,200M) so the cost of equity capital is $90M ($600M × 15%). The cost of debt capital is $30M ($600M × 5%). $180M − ($90M + $30M) = $60M.

14. (d) To maximize shareholder wealth, management should concentrate on total return per share, rather than other measures. Total return per share includes earnings per share (EPS) and stock value changes. Maximization of earnings per share ignores the potential decrease in share value. Maximization of profits ignores the potential dilution of widespread ownership. Maximization of stock value ignores the potential decrease in earnings.

15. (d) In the growth or exploitation stage, sales increase dramatically. When a product is introduced initially in the infancy phase, it has little direct competition, but also may have limited consumer acceptance, prompting relatively high promotional expenses to gain widespread acceptance. In the maturity stage, profits shrink as direct competition increases.

16. (d) Cash and marketable securities rarely earn high returns; businesses try to minimize the amount they hold in order to maximize return on assets. Entities must hold enough cash to pay bills as they become due, or face bankruptcy. Entities also hold cash and marketable securities to be able to take advantage of unexpected events or fund occasional projects, such as fixed asset purchases. A compensating balance is held in an account at a financial institution to cover the cost of services to the account holder, typically including check processing.

Chapter 54: Planning & Control

17. (c) In May, Rolling Wheels purchases components for bicycles it would assemble in June for sales in July. It pays in May for 75% of these components' costs. July's budgeted component costs are $8,000, so Rolling Wheels will pay ($8,000 × 75%) $6,000 in May for these components. It will also pay in May for the remaining 25% for components purchased in April for June sales ($7,000 × 25%), or $1,750. Total payments in May for components ($6,000 + $1,750) equal $7,750.

18. (d) The manager of a cost center is responsible only for controllable costs. Thus, controllable revenues would not be included in the performance report of a cost center. The manager of an investment center is responsible for controllable revenues, controllable costs, and investment funds. Thus, controllable revenues would be included in the performance report of an investment center.

19. (d) Multiple regression uses several independent variable to predict one dependent variable. Both simple and multiple regression have an estimated constant term, have one dependent variable, and allow the computation of the coefficient of determination.

20. (a) Typical best practices include having the accounting department integrate and analyze transactions—to be a steward—not to originate transactions; having online approvals and queries; treating geographically dispersed resources as one; having limit and range controls for zero-defect information; and capturing data once—accurately.

21. (c) The link between two businesses in conglomerate diversification generally is financial. Companies pursuing conglomerate diversification generally are either cash-rich companies that have no room for expansion in current markets or are seeking to counter cyclical fluctuations. The link between two businesses in concentric diversification may be a common distribution network, customer base, technology, or managerial skills.

22. (a) Competing on the basis of low cost in a narrow market commonly is called cost focus. Competing on the basis of superior value in terms of quality, special features, or service in a narrow market commonly is called differentiation focus.

23. (a, c) Relatively low Internet retail costs favor competitors who ship uniform goods, rather than an enterprise with unique products that customers must handle physically before purchasing. Generally, internal positive factors are classified as strengths and external positive factors are classified as opportunities. A highly trained work force is a positive factor generally classified as a strength. Increased attendance at craft fairs tends to increase sales at those fairs. Increased national income tends to increase sales of luxury items.

Chapter 55: Information Technology

24. (c) A bus network links communication channels to one common line with direct access to the message destination. A star network links channels to a single host computer. A ring network links channels to a loop, with each message passed neighbor to neighbor until the message reaches its destination. A tree configuration is organized along hierarchical channels that eventually are linked to a single host computer.

25. (c) Banks commonly use magnetic ink character recognition for data entry for check processing. Bar coding is used commonly in inventory management systems, but rarely by banks for check processing. Electronic data interchange is not involved closely with data entry or check processing. Magnetic tape is a storage medium, not a data entry device.

26. (d) Errors that exist during implementation may allow access to unauthorized users or provide incorrect information; even if discovered during implementation, some time has elapsed when the system was operating with an error. Project initiation, requirements determination, and table configuration occur during system development. Errors that exist during system development cause fewer problems because users don't take action based on information provided by a system under development and a system under development isn't integrated with the live system to the point where it authorizes access.

27. (b) System analysts concentrate on developing system specifications to meet user needs. They assess any current systems, evaluate user needs, and design future systems, supplying programmers with specifications for coding. Under an ideal internal control system, system analysts don't write programs or have access to operational equipment, programs, or data files—although system analysts might use copies, facsimiles, or samples of operational resources when assessing current systems.

28. (d) That Jones notices that Acme's network files are available without entering a password provided by Acme indicates that Acme is not using security on the network. The scenario implies that Jones did not make an effort directed to testing the security of, or accessing files on, the client's system, but became aware of this access during tasks that did not require such access. A router is a switch that transfers messages; this function seems to be working only too well on Acme's system. For the laptop and Acme's server to have the same password is an unusual (i.e., unlikely) coincidence or both are set to the default password. Changing default passwords is an elementary security step. Appropriate security implies that those with access are aware of such access, so they may restrict it from unauthorized users.

29. (d) A cold site is space where furnishings and power is available in the event of a disaster at a primary location, but a computer system is not installed. A hot site is one that is ready for use with minimal preparation—for example, with hardware and software installed, links established, and backups of information available. The terms *warm site* and *cool site* are not generally used.

30. (b) A systems flowchart shows the flow of data through the system and the interrelationships between the processing steps and computer runs. A decision table describes a portion of the logic used in the program.

Solution 2 MULTIPLE CHOICE ANSWERS

Chapter 48: Partnerships

1. (d) A limited liability partnership (LLP) can accept contributions, make distributions, and accumulate earnings without incurring taxes or penalties. A LLP is not subject to personal holding tax or double taxation of income. A corporation has no implied power to enter into a partnership; however, it may enter into a partnership if authorized to do so by its corporate charter or state corporation statute. By definition, a proprietorship has only one owner. Corporations may not be shareholders of S corporations. Before 2003, corporations typically incurred double taxation and could not accumulate earnings without penalty. Note: Recent tax changes make similar questions less likely to be asked on future exams.

2. (c) When a partnership agreement is silent regarding the allocation of partnership losses, losses are allocated in the same manner as partnership profits. Since Nemo has a 20 percent profit share percentage, she also is attributed with 20 percent of the losses ($210,000 × 0.20 = $42,000). Capital balances play no part in calculating the loss attributable to the partners.

3. (a) When a partnership agreement is silent regarding the allocation of partnership losses, losses are allocated in the same manner as partnership profits. Accordingly, Maine is allocated 30% of the $210,000 loss, or $63,000. Maine also is responsible for 3/8 of Nemo's deficit capital balance [30 / (50 + 30)]. Nemo has a negative capital balance of $32,000 as a result of allocating Nemo's 20% portion of the $210,000 loss to a $10,000 capital balance. It is Nemo's responsibility to eliminate this deficit; however, Nemo refuses to make any further contribution. Therefore, the other partners must make up the difference. Maine's 3/8 share of Nemo's deficit ($12,000) leaves Maine's capital account at $90,000.

	L(50%)	M(30%)	N(20%)	T
Beg. capital	130	165	10	305
Allocate loss	<105>	<63>	<42>	<210>
Subtotal	25	102	<32>	95
Allocate deficit	<20>	<12>	32	-0-
Total	5	90	0	95

Chapter 49: Corporations

4. (b) Four factors that frequently cause the courts to pierce the corporate veil are listed below:

1. Fraudulently inducing someone into dealing with the corporation rather than the individual

2. "Thinly capitalized" corporations

3. Failure to act as a corporation

4. Commingling personal and corporate assets to the extent that the corporation has no identity of its own

Answer (b) falls within the description of Factor #4; thus, it would be most likely to cause the courts to pierce the corporate veil.

5. (a) Both a limited partnership and a corporation may be created only under a state statute, and each must file a copy of its certificate with the proper state authorities. Further, both a corporation's stock and a limited partnership interest are subject to the federal securities laws registration requirements if they are "securities" under the federal securities laws. General partners in a limited partnership do not have limited liability. Partnerships are not recognized for federal income tax purposes as taxable entities. Instead, the income flows through to the partners and is taxed on their individual returns. Partnerships do not have perpetual existence. Their existence can be affected by the death of a partner.

6. (a) The Revised Model Business Corporation Act authorizes corporate directors to rely on information provided by the appropriate corporate officer. Directors have the duty of loyalty to the corporation, which would prevent them from serving on the board of directors of a competing business and from selling control of the corporation. Profiting from insider information would also be a breach of the fiduciary duty of loyalty, and is prohibited by the federal securities laws.

Chapter 50: Economic Theory

7. (e) The business cycle trough is characterized by low levels of economic activity, underuse of resources (productive capacity), and investors unwilling to risk new investments in productive capacity. In the absence of inflation or deflation, purchasing power remains stable during a trough. Costs generally don't rise and shortages rarely occur during a trough because of the excess capacity.

8. (b) Cyclical unemployment occurs during low points in the economic cycle, when aggregate demand is less than aggregate labor supply. Structural unemployment is when aggregate labor demanded is equal to aggregate labor supplied, but the nature of the supply doesn't match the nature of the demand. Mismatches can occur in terms of skills, occupations, industries, or geographic locations.

9. (c) A decline in the value of a currency relative to the currencies of that nation's trading partners is called depreciation. When depreciation occurs, generally export prices decrease, as the nation's goods are cheaper to foreign purchasers than before the decline. When depreciation occurs, generally import prices increase, as foreign sellers want more of the devalued currency in exchange for their goods.

Chapter 51: Financial Management

10. (a) Liquidity is the ability to use assets to meet maturing debts (i.e., short-term liabilities). The current ratio (current assets to current liabilities) and the quick ratio (current assets less inventory to current liabilities) provide measures of the amount of assets to settle short-term liabilities. Comparing short-term and long-term debt ignores the impact of current assets. Net income typically includes non-cash items (such as depreciation) that cannot be used to settle debts. Comparing total assets to total liabilities introduces irrelevant considerations: assets that are not converted into cash readily and debts that need not be retired shortly.

11. (c) Convertible bonds are long-term securities issued by entities with varying degrees of creditworthiness. Bankers' acceptances are drafts for which the bank guarantees payment; they are designed to facilitate transfers; thus, they must be low risk and liquid. Commercial paper is short-term unsecured notes issued by large, financially strong commercial enterprises, typically to institutional investors. A U.S. Treasury bill is a highly liquid short-term government obligation that is considered practically risk-free.

12. (b) Net working capital (also called merely working capital) is the difference between current assets and current liabilities; only current items are components of working capital.

13. (e) Trade credit (accounts payable) is called a spontaneous financing source because it originates automatically from purchasing transactions. Commercial paper typically is issued by large, financially strong commercial enterprises to institutional investors; it is unlikely that a small business would be able to issue commercial paper at reasonable rates. A debenture is an unsecured bond. Debentures, mortgages, and notes payable tend to be long-term.

14. (a) The three numbers necessary to compute the economic order quantity are the annual demand or usage, the cost of placing each order, and the annual cost of carrying one unit in inventory.

The cost per unit of inventory is **not** used to compute the economic order quantity.

15. (b) Because interest is deductible to calculate taxable income, the true cost of debt is the interest payment less the related tax deduction. Additional debt may be issued at a higher or lower rates; such issues have no impact on the current cost of debt. Any change in interest rates after Pan issued the debt will change the yield that bondholders receive if they sell in the secondary markets, but it will not affect Pan's payments to bondholders.

Chapter 52: Decision Making

16. (b) A direct labor overtime premium is generally considered to be attributable to the heavy overall volume of work, and its cost is thus regarded as part of manufacturing overhead, which is borne by all units produced. Sometimes the direct labor overtime premium is not random. For example, a special or rush job may clearly be the sole source of the overtime. In such instances, the premium is regarded as a direct cost of the products made for that job.

17. (b) Break-even analysis assumes that costs behave in a linear relationship within the relevant range. Break-even analysis assumes that fixed costs remain constant in total and that variable costs are fixed or unchanged on a per-unit basis.

18. (a) Lines EF and GH depict profit lines for 20X1 and 20X2, respectively. Points E and G, the points at which the profit lines intersect the vertical axis, represent the total fixed costs for 20X1 and 20X2, respectively, because there are no variable costs at zero volume. Since Line OG (20X2) is less than Line OE (20X1), total fixed costs decreased in 20X2. The profit lines slope upward from the fixed cost points at the rate of the unit contribution margin. Since the 20X2 profit line (GH) has a less steep slope than the 20X1 profit line (EF), the unit contribution margin decreased in 20X2, meaning that variable costs increased in 20X2.

19. (b) The high month is March with 180 orders at a cost of $492. The low month is January with 120 orders at a cost of $312. The estimated variable order cost can be obtained by dividing the change in cost by the change in orders, because only variable costs change in total with a change in the order volume. The monthly fixed cost of filling orders is determined by subtracting the variable cost from the total cost for either the high or low months. January: $412 − ($1.50 / order × 120 orders) = $232; March: $502 − ($1.50 / order × 180 orders) = $232.

$$\frac{\$502 - \$412}{180 - 120} = \frac{\$90}{60} = \$1.50/\text{order}$$

20. (c) Buying the parts will result in $35,000 savings (i.e., $290,000 – $255,000).

	Make	Buy
Variable cost		
[($3 + $15 + $6) × 10,000]	$240,000	
Fixed OH [($8 – $3) × 10,000]	50,000	
Purchase ($30 × 10,000)		$300,000
Savings, Part H		(45,000)
Total Relevant Costs	$290,000	$255,000

21. (c) Let F = sales price of the food only. Then, the service charge is 0.15F and the sales tax is 0.06 (F + 0.15F) = 0.06 (1.15F) = 0.069F

$60 = F + service charge + sales tax
$60 = F + 0.15F + 0.069F = 1.219F
F = $60 / 1.219 = $49.22

22. (b) Absorption costing considers fixed manufacturing overhead to be a product cost. A portion of fixed manufacturing overhead is included in the cost of a unit of product, along with direct materials, direct labor, and variable manufacturing overhead. The selling and general administrative costs ($3,000 and $4,000, respectively) are period costs and are expensed when incurred.

Direct materials	$ 10,000
Direct labor	20,000
Variable manufacturing overhead	5,000
Fixed manufacturing overhead	9,000
Total product costs incurred	44,000
Units produced during period	/ 10,000
Unit cost, absorption costing, Product X	$ 4.40

Chapter 54: Planning & Control

23. (a)

Days with zero blocked roads (0 × 120)	0
Days with one blocked road (1 × 16)	16
Days with two blocked roads (2 × 10)	20
Days with three blocked roads (3 × 1)	3
Total number of blocked roads	39
Expected lost revenue per blocked road	$ 4,500
Lost revenue, with less than 3 roads blocked	175,500
Additional lost revenue, 3 roads blocked	
[3 × ($35,000 - $4,500)]	91,500
Less: Snowplow cost ($50,000 + $500 × 39)	(69,500)
Estimated net revenue saved with snowplow	$267,000

Chapter 55: Information Technology

24. (c) The central processing unit (CPU) is the component that manipulates data. Data is stored in RAM (within the CPU) during processing. Files may be saved on a floppy disk after CPU processing is finished; a floppy disk is not required for CPU

processing. An operating system is software, not hardware. ROM would not function as temporary storage because it is read-only; temporary storage must be rewritten frequently. ROM is used for permanent storage of essential programs.

25. (c) There are time delays when data is processed in batches, so errors may not be detected immediately. The time delays in processing cause a delay in error detection. The identification of errors in input data would be identified through various means such as the use of batch totals and would generally be made part of the program. The processing of transactions in a batch system is uniform; for example, all sales invoices would be part of a group of transactions entered together in a batch system.

26. (a) An integrated test facility (ITF) processes fictitious data with real data in order to test computer controls; client personnel are unaware of the testing. An input control matrix documents controls and their presence. Parallel simulation processes client input data on an auditor-controlled program to test controls; test data is not utilized. The term "data entry monitor" is not commonly used.

27. (b) A record count is a count of the number of records in a batch or file or similar group.

28. (d) A hash total is a numeric total with meaning only as a control. Because of the alpha characters in the product codes, a hash total cannot be derived from product codes without a conversion of letters into numeric amounts. Totals of quantities have meaning beyond a control.

29. (a) In an interactive system, data is processed as it is input and feedback is provided to the user; transaction files are not batched or sorted before processing, as this introduces a delay. Random memory is most likely to be used in an interactive system. Sequential record access almost requires sorting transaction files prior to processing, or master files take a long time to update.

30. (a) A LAN is a system that connects computers and other devices in a limited physical area, typically within the same building. A time-sharing center rents time on a central computer to several entities, with each entity having remote input and output devices. To each entity, it seems as if it is the only one using the system. A meeting among several people at different physical locations facilitated by electronics is a teleconference. Working outside of a traditional office, but remaining connected by the Internet, phone, etc., is called telecommuting.

Solution 3 MULTIPLE CHOICE ANSWERS

Chapter 49: Corporations

1. (c) Most courts hold that a corporation may purchase its own shares, provided such action promotes the corporate business. A corporation has express power to perform any act authorized by state law, its articles of incorporation, or its bylaws. The existence of a takeover attempt doesn't restrict these actions.

2. (a) Most state enabling acts (incorporation statutes) require both the name of the registered agent and the number of authorized shares.

3. (c) The sale would be proper and Gold would not have to account to the corporation for his profit if the sale was approved by a disinterested majority of the directors. The directors are then answerable to the stockholders for any wrongdoing.

4. (b) Preemptive rights, under the Revised Model Business Corporation Act, grant the stockholders the right to purchase a proportionate share of newly-issued stock. Although stockholders generally have the right to a proportionate share of corporate assets remaining on dissolution after the creditors are paid, this right is not part of the definition of preemptive rights.

5. (c) Certain types of changes, such as amendments to the articles, merger, consolidation, dissolution, or sale of a substantial part of the corporate assets, require approval by an absolute majority of the shareholders, unless a greater proportion is required by the articles of incorporation. The board of directors is responsible for electing officers. Stockholders do not have a right to receive *annual* dividends nor to prevent corporate borrowing.

6. (b) The Revised Model Business Corporation Act (RMBCA) 11.04 provides a simplified procedure for the merger of a substantially owned subsidiary corporation into its parent corporation, referred to as a "short-form merger" or a "parent-subsidiary merger." This form of merger can be used only when the parent corporation owns at least 90% of the outstanding shares of each class of stock of the subsidiary corporation. The plan only need be approved by the board of directors of the parent corporation, not the board of directors of the subsidiary corporation, before it is filed with the state. A copy of the merger plan must be sent to each shareholder of record of the subsidiary corporation and the subsidiary corporation's dissenting stockholders must be given an appraisal remedy. The dissenting stockholders, upon fulfilling the proper procedures, have the right to obtain payment for the fair market value of their shares. This form of merger can be accomplished without the approval of the shareholders of either corporation.

Note that this simplified procedure differs from mergers and consolidations where the parent owns less than 90% of the subsidiary corporation. When the parent owns less than substantially all of the subsidiary, the board of directors and the shareholders of each corporation involved must approve a merger or consolidation plan before the plan can be filed with the state, and dissenting shareholders of each corporation may have appraisal rights.

Chapter 50: Economic Theory

7. (b) Under current international agreements, foreign exchange rates are allowed to float; supply and demand for currencies set the exchange rates. "Managed float" refers to central banks temporary management of exchange rates to maintain market stability; such efforts rapidly become prohibitively expensive. Exporters and importers influence exchange rates only insofar as they affect supply and demand. While the IMF's role is to cover short-term deficits in balance of payments and currencies of nation's experiencing inflation tend to depreciate, neither of these are managed float.

8. (c) Currency devaluation makes a nation's exports cheaper in foreign markets, increasing exports and improving the balance of trade. Currency devaluation also may increase domestic inflation (money is worth less than it was before devaluation) and reduce foreign investment, as prices for foreign goods and investments higher priced (in terms of local currency).

9. (c) Currently, most companies set transfer prices primarily to minimize overall corporate taxes. This approach ignores other important areas: management incentives among various divisions, allocation of production capacities, and guidance for future capital investment. It's legal to maintain two sets of transfer prices. Most people think of transfer pricing as a tax optimization issue, yet transfer prices also are management tools. They have important decision-making functions, valuing intermediate product so that regional managers may maximize the profit of the company as a whole. A company may seek to generate information that provides a clear basis for internal decision making. For managerial purposes, when deciding what metric should be selected to evaluate a unit's performance, the following should be considered: controllability of costs, the

effect by random shocks, and possible dysfunctional behavior induced by the evaluation system.

Chapter 51: Financial Management

10. (c) The annual savings needed to realize a 12% yield can be obtained by dividing the $44,300 by the present value of an annuity at 12% for 5 years. Thus, the annual savings needed are $12,306 ($44,300 / 3.60), rounded to the nearest dollar.

Cost	$50,000
Less: PV of Residual Value ($10,000 × 0.57)	(5,700)
Present Value of Annual Savings Needed	$44,300

11. (d) Zee's residual income is $150,000 (i.e., $200,000 – $50,000). The residual income of a profit center is computed by subtracting an imputed interest charge for invested capital from the operating income of the center.

12. (d) In the primary capital markets, investment bankers buy new debt and equity securities and sell them to investors. The issuers receive the proceeds. Exchanges of existing debt and equity securities occur in the secondary capital markets. Future commodity contracts are sold in the futures market.

13. (c) The market risk premium is the difference between the average market rate and the risk-free rate (12% – 7% = 5%). The capital asset pricing model (CAPM) estimates an individual issuer's expected rate of return is the risk-free rate plus the market risk premium, adjusted by the individual issuer's beta coefficient, which is a measure of how closely an individual issuer's return correlates to the market average. 7% + (5% × 1.2) = 13%.

14. (a) Residual dividend theory holds that earnings should be reinvested to the extent that profitable projects exist, consistent with the target capital structure, and only earnings remaining after profitable projects are funded should be distributed. This policy assumes (1) the corporation can reinvest earnings at a higher rate of return than investors can find though another investment with comparable risk, (2) investors prefer to have the corporation re-invest the earnings, and (3) the rate of return that investors require is not affected by dividend policy. The constant payout ratio assumes that dividend payments should be a percentage of earnings. A stable dividend policy involves a dividend amount that increases only when future earnings seem sufficient to support the higher dividend indefinitely. Residual dividend theory doesn't address the number of dividend distributions.

Chapter 53: Cost Accounting

15. (b) By-products result from the joint production process and have a relatively minor sales value compared to the main product. Conceptually, a portion of the joint process costs should be allocated to by-products proportionally to their relative sales value. Due to the immaterial amounts involved, however, it is acceptable to account for the sales value of by-products as a reduction of the cost of the main product.

16. (a) The material usage variance measures the difference between the quantity of materials used in production and the quantity that should have been used according to an established standard. Generally, it is the responsibility of the production department to ensure this standard is met. Therefore the material usage variance usually is not allocated to either the purchasing or warehousing departments. (Conceivably, the material usage variance would be allocated to one of these departments if the variance was the result of either the purchase of inferior quality or improper storage or handling, resulting in excessive waste. There is no indication that this is the case in this situation.)

17. (a) Equivalent units (EU) of production are used in process costing to express a given number of partially completed units in terms of a smaller number of fully completed units. The EU of production for the inventories in question is 300 [i.e., (200 × 90%) + (100 × 80%) + (400 × 10%)].

18. (b) The original production of 1,100 drills cost $16,500 (1,100 drills × $15/drill). The reworking of 50 defective drills increased the cost total to $16,750. The $750 received from the sale of the 100 spoiled units should be subtracted from the total cost incurred in producing the 1,100 drills. Therefore, the total cost for producing *1,000* good drills equals $16,000 ($16,500 + $250 – $750).

19. (b) Under the step method, costs are allocated from the service departments to other service departments and to operating divisions. Once costs are allocated from a department, costs are not allocated back to that department. Any percentage of use by the same service department or by a service department that already has had its costs allocated are ignored and new ratios must be computed using the remaining departments or divisions (20% + 60% = 80%; 20% / 80% = 2/8). The legal department costs are allocated 2/8 to the photovoltaic (PV) division and 6/8 to the windmill (WM) division.

	Finance	Legal	PV	WM
Costs before allocation (in 1,000s)	$ 80	$56		
Allocation of finance costs:				
1/10 × $80	(8)	8		
6/10 × $80	(48)		$48	
3/10 × $80	(24)			$24
Total legal costs		64		
Allocation of legal costs:				
2/8 × $64		(16)	16	
6/8 × $64		(48)		48
Totals	$ 0	$ 0	$64	$72

20. (c) ABC systems have activities as the fundamental cost objects; they do not accumulate costs by department, or function for purposes of product costing. ABC systems identify cost drivers as a basis for cost allocation. No attempt is made to eliminate the cost drivers. A cost driver is any factor whose effects cause an increase in the total cost of a related cost object. Under an ABC system, activities that do not add to the value of the product are identified and eliminated to the extent possible.

21. (d) The labor efficiency variance is $800 unfavorable and the standard rate per direct labor hour is $8.00; thus, 100 ($800 / $8) direct labor hours were incurred above the 2,000 standard hours allowed for actual production. Actual hours worked were 2,100 hours (2,000 + 100).

22. (c) The difference between the budget allowance based on standard hours allowed and the factory overhead applied to production is the volume variance.

```
Actual              Budget
Factory             allowance                    Factory
overhead            based on                     overhead
incurred            standard                     applied
                    hours

        Controllable            Volume
        (budget) variance       variance
```

Chapter 55: Information Technology

23. (b) System design typically is classified into three categories: data design, process design, and user interface design. Input and output design may be considered sub-elements of user interface design.

24. (a) Cash disbursements, cash receipts, and payroll transactions are all examples of transactions; records pertaining to these events are maintained in transaction files which update master files. Editor's Note: "Inventory subsidiary" is not a common name for a master file. The editors don't expect similar questions to appear on future exams.

25. (c) Decision support systems (DSS) are used primarily for semi-structured problems requiring the exercise of judgment. Rather than providing answers, a DSS provides information to assist a user to develop answers. Database management systems (DBMS) create and manage databases. Expert, or knowledge-based, systems provide answers based on information provided by the user and rules developed by an expert to address specified situations. By comparison, DSS facilitate problem-solving by providing computational capacity and data for use in interactive models. DSS support decisions, rather than process transactions.

26. (a) Decision support systems (DSS) are used primarily for semi-structured problems involving uncertainty and ambiguous reporting requirements and requiring the exercise of judgment. An accounting information system (AIS) is a management information subsystem that provides information to management for use in measuring, planning, and controlling an entity's activities. An AIS typically includes such functions as accounts receivable, accounts payable, and payroll, and hence, processes a large number of transactions.

27. (a) EDI generally results in a compressed cycle of orders, purchases, deliveries, and payments. EDI generally increases the need to test computer controls and the need for security. EDI has no impact on the application of sampling techniques for account balances.

28. (c) A Trojan horse is a seemingly legitimate program that causes damage when executed. A hoax virus is a false e-mail warning that tries to get circulated as widely as possible. A web crawler is used to search the World Wide Web for documents containing specific words or phrases. A killer application is extremely useful or interesting.

29. (a) When performing an echo check, a CPU compares the signals sent to a device and to the signals received from that device. When performing an parity check, a CPU that has odd parity confirms that an odd number of magnetized dots represent each character. A hardware check is a search for circuits that are failing. A file protection ring is a plastic ring that must be attached to a reel before the tape drive will write to the tape; it generally is considered a data control.

30. (c) A validity check ensures that only authorized data codes will be entered into and accepted by the system. Answer (a) is an example of a limit (reasonableness) check. Answer (b) is an example of an error report being generated. There is no comparison performed as in answer (d).

PERFORMANCE BY TOPICS

The practice examination questions corresponding to each chapter of the Business Environment & Concepts text are listed below. The number preceding the colon is the testlet number; the number after the colon is the question number. To assess your preparedness for the CPA exam, record the number and percentage of questions you correctly answered in each topic area. The point distribution of the multiple choice questions approximates that of the exam.

Chapter 48:
Partnerships

Question #	Correct	√
1:1		
1:2		
1:3		
1:4		
1:5		
1:6		
2:1		
2:2		
2:3		
# Questions	9	
# Correct		
% Correct		

Chapter 49:
Corporations

Question #	Correct	√
2:4		
2:5		
2:6		
3:1		
3:2		
3:3		
3:4		
3:5		
3:6		
# Questions	9	
# Correct		
% Correct		

Chapter 50:
Economic Theory

Question #	Correct	√
1:7		
1:8		
1:9		
2:7		
2:8		
2:9		
3:7		
3:8		
3:9		
# Questions	9	
# Correct		
% Correct		

Chapter 51:
Financial Management

Question #	Correct	√
1:10		
1.11		
1:12		
1:13		
1:14		
1:15		
1:16		
2:10		
2:11		
2:12		
2:13		
2:14		
2:15		
3:10		
3:11		
3:12		
3:13		
3:14		
# Questions	18	
# Correct		
% Correct		

Chapter 52:
Decision Making

Question #	Correct	√
2:16		
2:17		
2:18		
2:19		
2:20		
2:21		
2:22		
# Questions	7	
# Correct		
% Correct		

Chapter 53:
Cost Accounting

Question #	Correct	√
3:15		
3:16		
3:17		
3:18		
3:19		
3:20		
3:21		
3:22		
# Questions	8	
# Correct		
% Correct		

Chapter 54:
Planning & Control

Question #	Correct	√
1:17		
1:18		
1:19		
1:20		
1:21		
1:22		
1:23		
2:23		
# Questions	8	
# Correct		
% Correct		

Chapter 55:
Information Technology

Question #	Correct	√
1:24		
1:25		
1:26		
1:27		
1:28		
1:29		
1:30		
2:24		
2:25		
2:26		
2:27		
2:28		
2:29		
2:30		
3:23		
3:24		
3:25		
3:26		
3:27		
3:28		
3:29		
3:30		
# Questions	22	
# Correct		
% Correct		

PERFORMANCE BY AICPA CONTENT SPECIFICATION

The practice examination questions are listed below by content specification category. The point distribution of the multiple choice questions approximates that of the exam.

CSO I		CSO II		CSO III		CSO IV		CSO V	
Question #	Correct√	Question #	Correct√	Question #	Correct√	Question #	Correct√	Question #	Correct√
1:1		1:7		1:10		1:24		1:17	
1:2		1:8		1:11		1:25		1:18	
1:3		1:9		1:12		1:26		1:19	
1:4		2:7		1:13		1:27		1:20	
1:5		2:8		1:14		1:28		1:21	
1:6		2:9		1:15		1:29		1:22	
2:1		3:7		1:16		1:30		1:23	
2:2		3:8		2:10		2:24		2:16	
2:3		3:9		2:11		2:25		2:17	
2:4		# Questions 9		2:12		2:26		2:18	
2:5				2:13		2:27		2:19	
2:6		# Correct ____		2:14		2:28		2:20	
3:1		% Correct ____		2:15		2:29		2:21	
3:2				3:10		2:30		2:22	
3:3				3:11		3:23		2:23	
3:4				3:12		3:24		3:15	
3:5				3:13		3:25		3:16	
3:6				3:14		3:26		3:17	
# Questions 18				# Questions 18		3:27		3:18	
						3:28		3:19	
# Correct ____				# Correct ____		3:29		3:20	
% Correct ____				% Correct ____		3:30		3:21	
						# Questions 22		3:22	
								# Questions 23	
						# Correct ____			
						% Correct ____		# Correct ____	
								% Correct ____	

SIMULATION SOLUTIONS

Solution 4 (15 to 25 minutes)

Response #1: Liability (5 points)

1. G

According to the stockholders' agreement, Mill, Web, and Trent agreed to vote for each other as directors of Sack.

2. H

According to the stockholders' agreement, Mill, Web, and Trent agreed to vote for each other as *directors* of Sack, but no mention is made about the appointment of officers. Corporate officers generally are elected by the board of directors and serve at the board's pleasure.

3. J

Sack Corp. is liable to Mill for Mill's firing. The corporation is the employer of Mills and the one who entered into the employment contract with Mills, and therefore, the corporation would be the one in breach of contract.

4. G

Dividends paid that cause a corporation to become insolvent are considered illegal dividends and are required to be returned by any shareholders receiving the dividends.

5. F

Directors are personally liable for dividends that are wrongfully or unlawfully paid. In this case, Web and Trent are liable because they knowingly made assurances to the board regarding materially misstated financial statements resulting in an illegal declaration and payment of dividends. The other directors are protected under the Business Judgment Rule because they reasonably relied on assurances from other board members in declaring the illegal dividend. Directors acting in good faith are not liable for errors of judgment unless they are clearly and grossly negligent.

Response #2: Dividends (5 points)

Cash dividends may be declared and paid if the corporation is **solvent** and payment of the dividends would not render the corporation insolvent. Furthermore, each state imposes **additional restrictions** on what funds are **legally available** to pay dividends. One of the more restrictive tests adopted by many states permits the payment of dividends only out of **unrestricted** and **unreserved earned surplus** (retained earnings). The Model Business Corporation Act **prohibits dividend distributions** if, after giving effect to the distribution, the **corporation's total assets would be less than its total liabilities.**

Solution 5 (15 to 25 minutes)

Response #1: Capital Budgets (4 points)

1. B

The payback period is the period of time it takes for the cumulative sum of annual net cash inflows from a project to equal the initial cash outlay. When cash inflows are not uniform, the payback period computation takes a cumulative form. That is, each year's net cash inflows are accumulated until the initial cash outlay is recovered. The question states that Projects A and B have the same initial cash outlay and lives. Per a review of Diagram I, most of the net cash inflows of Project B occur in the first three years of the project's life, and most of the net cash inflows of Project A occur in the last three years of that project's life. Therefore, Project B would be more likely to have the shorter payback period.

2. A

The average annual accounting income generated by a project is the numerator of the average accounting rate of return (ARR) method of capital budgeting. This amount is computed by subtracting average annual depreciation expense from the average annual net cash inflows generated by the project. Projects A and B have the same initial investment requirements and lives. Therefore, annual average depreciation expense is the same for both projects. Project A has a greater total net cash inflow. Therefore, Project A has greater average annual net cash inflows and thus a greater average ARR.

3. B

The internal rate of return (IRR) is the discount rate which would make the present value of the project equal to zero. Per a review of Diagram II, projects A and B have a zero present value at discount rates of 16% and 22%, respectively. Hence, projects A and B have internal rates of return of 16% and 22%, respectively. The 22% IRR of project B exceeds the 16% IRR of project A.

4. B

The internal rate of return (IRR) is the discount rate which would make the present value of a project equal to zero. Per a review of Diagram II, based on 5-year lives, projects A and B have a zero present value at discount rates of 16% and 22%, respectively. Hence, based on 5-year lives, projects A and B have internal rates of return of 16% and 22%, respectively. The 22% internal rate of return of project B based on a 5-year life exceeds the 16% internal rate of return of project A based on a 5-year life. If both projects were to terminate at the end of year 4 with cash flows remaining as projected for the first 4 years and no cash flows in year 5, per a review of Diagram I, the present value of net cash inflows lost by project B is less than that lost by project A. Therefore, although the IRR of both projects would decrease if the projects were to terminate at the end of year 4, the IRR of project B would still exceed that of project A.

Response #2: Budgets & Standard Costs (5 points)

1. BD

Budgeted variable cost is the line which begins at the origin that is below and parallel to the budgeted cost line. Budgeted cost is comprised of budgeted variable cost and budgeted fixed cost. At volume OE, budgeted cost is represented by the line BE and budgeted variable cost is represented by line DE. Thus, budgeted fixed cost at volume OE is represented by line BD.

2. DE

Budgeted variable cost is the line which begins at the origin that is below and parallel to the budgeted cost line. At volume OE, budgeted variable cost is represented by line DE.

3. AC

Standard gross profit is the difference between revenue and standard cost. At volume OE, revenue is represented by line AE and standard cost is represented by line CE. Thus, standard gross profit at volume OE is represented by line AC.

4.   AB

Budgeted gross profit is the difference between revenue and budgeted cost. At volume OE, revenue is represented by line AE and budgeted cost is represented by line BE. Thus, budgeted gross profit at volume OE is represented by line AB.

5.   OG

Normal capacity is the point at which standard costs equal budgeted costs since standard costs are determined by dividing budgeted costs by normal volume. These costs are equal at point I. Therefore, normal capacity is represented by line OG.

APPENDIX B
PRACTICAL ADVICE

Your first step toward an effective CPA Review program is to **study** the material in this appendix. It has been carefully developed to provide you with essential information that will help you succeed on the CPA exam. This material will assist you in organizing an efficient study plan and will demonstrate effective techniques and strategies for taking the CPA exam.

SECTION ONE: GENERAL COMMENTS ON THE CPA EXAM

The difficulty and comprehensiveness of the CPA exam is a well-known fact to all candidates. However, success on the CPA exam is a **reasonable, attainable** goal. You should keep this point in mind as you study this appendix and develop your study plan. A positive attitude toward the examination, combined with determination and discipline, will enhance your opportunity to pass.

Purpose of the CPA Exam

The CPA exam is designed as a licensing requirement to measure the technical competence of CPA candidates. Although licensing occurs at the state level, the exam is uniform at all sites and has national acceptance. In other words, passing the CPA exam in one jurisdiction generally allows a candidate to obtain a reciprocal certificate or license, if they meet all the requirements imposed by the jurisdiction from which reciprocity is sought.

Boards of accountancy also rely upon other means to ensure that candidates possess the necessary technical and character attributes, including interviews, letters of reference, affidavits of employment, ethics examinations, and educational requirements. Boards' addresses are listed in this section of the **Practical Advice** appendix or (along with applicable links) on the web site of the National Association of the State Boards of Accountancy (http://www.nasba.org).

The CPA exam essentially is an academic examination that tests the breadth of material covered by good accounting curricula. It emphasizes the body of knowledge required for the practice of public accounting. It is to your advantage to take the exam as soon as possible after completing the formal education requirements.

We recommend that most candidates study for two examination sections at once, since there is a **synergistic** learning effect to be derived through preparing for more than one part. That is, all sections of the exam share some common subjects (particularly Financial Accounting & Reporting and Auditing & Attestation); so as you study for one section, you are also studying for the others. This advice will be different for different candidates. Candidates studying full-time may find that studying for all four sections at once is most beneficial. Some candidates with full-time jobs and family responsibilities may find that studying for a single exam section at once is best for them.

Score

A passing score for each exam section is 75 points. The objective responses are scored electronically. The written communication response (essay) portions of simulations (essay elements) are graded manually. Scores are released to candidates during the next exam window by boards of accountancy. Scores are not available from the testing sites.

Format

The CPA exam is split into four sections of differing length.

1. **Financial Accounting & Reporting**—This section covers generally accepted accounting principles for business enterprises and governmental and nonprofit organizations. This section's name frequently is abbreviated as FAR or FARE. (4 hours)

2. **Auditing & Attestation**—This section covers the generally accepted auditing standards, procedures, and related topics. The CPA's professional responsibility is no longer tested in this area. This section's name often is abbreviated as AUD. (4½ hours)

3. **Regulation**—This section covers the CPA's professional responsibility to the public and the profession, the legal implications of business transactions generally confronted by CPAs, and federal taxation. This section's name commonly is abbreviated as REG. (3 hours)

4. **Business Environment & Concepts**—This section covers business organizations, economic concepts, financial management, planning, measurement, and information technology. This section's name typically is abbreviated as BEC. The AICPA has announced that initially, it will not test

candidates using simulations in this section. The AICPA has not specified when simulations will first appear in this exam section. (2½ hours)

Schedule

There are four exam windows annually; the first one starts in January. A candidate may sit for any particular exam section only once during a window. Between windows there is a dark period of about a month when the exam is not administered. Once a candidate has a passing score for one section, that candidate has a certain length of time (typically 18 months) to pass the other three exam sections, or lose the credit for passing that first exam section. Candidates should check with the governing Board of Accountancy concerning details on the length of time to pass all four sections. Exam sites typically are open Mondays through Fridays; some are open on Saturdays as well.

January	February	March
April	May	June
July	August	September
October	November	December

Writing Skills Content

Written communication responses (commonly called essays) are used to assess candidates' writing skills. Additional information is included in the **Writing Skills** section. Only those writing samples that generally are responsive to the topic will be graded. If the response is off topic or offers advice that is clearly incorrect, no credit will be given for the response.

Written communication responses are scored holistically. Scores are based on three general writing criteria:

1. Organization

2. Development

3. Expression

Reference Materials

All the material you need to review to pass the CPA exam is in your Bisk Education *CPA Comprehensive Review* texts! However, should you desire more detailed coverage in any area, you may consult the actual promulgations. Individual copies of recent pronouncements are available from the FASB, AICPA, SEC, etc. To order printed materials from the **FASB** or **AICPA** contact:

FASB Order Department
P.O. Box 5116
Norwalk, CT 06856-5116
Telephone (203) 847-0700

AICPA Order Department
P.O. Box 1003
New York, NY 10108-1003
Telephone (800) 334-6961   www.aicpa.org

The AICPA has made available, to candidates with their Notice to Schedule (NTS), a **free** six-month's subscription to some of the databases used in the exam. Bisk Education is unable to fill orders for these subscriptions; they are available only through the AICPA exam web site (www.cpa-exam.org).

If you do not yet have your NTS, the FASB offers a student discount that varies depending on the publication. The AICPA offers a 30% educational discount, which students may claim by submitting proof of their eligibility (e.g., copy of ID card or teacher's letter). AICPA members get a 20% discount and delivery time is speedier because members may order by phone. Unamended, full-text FASB statements are available without charge in PDF format on the FASB Web site (www.fasb.org/st). Bear in mind that these statements are not provided in a searchable format, nor are they the only authoritative literature used in the research element of simulations.

STATE BOARDS OF ACCOUNTANCY

Certified Public Accountants are licensed to practice by individual State Boards of Accountancy. Application forms and requirements to sit for the CPA exam should be requested from your individual State Board. IT IS EXTREMELY IMPORTANT THAT YOU COMPLETE THE APPLICATION FORM CORRECTLY AND RETURN IT TO YOUR STATE BOARD BEFORE THE DEADLINE. Errors and/or delays may result in the rejection of your application. Be extremely careful in filling out the application and be sure to enclose all required materials. Requirements as to education, experience, internship, and other matters vary. If you have not already done so, take a moment to call the appropriate board for specific and current requirements. Complete the application in a timely manner. Some states arrange for an examination administrator, such CPA Examination Services [a division of the National Association of State Boards of Accountancy (NASBA), (800) CPA-EXAM (272-3926)], to handle candidate registration, examination administration, etc.

It may be possible to sit for the exam in another state as an out-of-state candidate. Candidates wishing to do so should also contact the Board of Accountancy in the state where they plan to be certified. NASBA has links (**http://www.nasba.org**) to many state board sites.

At least 45 days before you plan to sit for the exam, check to see that your application to sit for the exam has been processed. DON'T ASSUME THAT YOU ARE PROPERLY REGISTERED UNLESS YOU HAVE RECEIVED YOUR NOTICE TO SCHEDULE (NTS). You must present your NTS and proper identification to be admitted to the testing room at an exam site. Contact the applicable board of accountancy if you have any doubts about what constitutes proper ID.

The AICPA publishes a booklet entitled *Information for CPA Candidates,* usually distributed by Boards of Accountancy to candidates upon receipt or acceptance of their applications. To request a complimentary copy, contact your **state board** or the **AICPA,** Examination Division, 1211 Avenue of the Americas, New York, NY 10036. This publication is also available on the AICPA's exam web site: www.cpa-exam.org.

Candidates requiring medication during the exam should make sure to notify the state board and other examining entities as appropriate during registration.

Contacting Your State Board

CPA Examination Services, a division of the National Association of State Boards of Accountancy (NASBA) administers the examination for 25 states. Contact CPA Examination Services at (800) CPA-EXAM (272-3926), (615) 880-4250, or www.nasba.org.

CO CT DE FL GA HI IA IN KS LA MA ME MI MN MO MT
NE NH NJ NM NY OH PA PR RI SC TN UT VA VT WI

Castle Worldwide at (800) 655-4845 administers the examination for WA.

Following are the telephone numbers for the boards in the other states.

AK	(907) 465-2580	IL	(217) 333-1565	OK	(405) 521-2397
AL	(334) 242-5700	KY	(502) 595-3037	OR	(503) 378-4181
AR	(501) 682-1520	MD	(410) 333-6322	SD	(605) 367-5770
AZ	(602) 255-3648	MS	(601) 354-7320	TX	(512) 305-7850
CA	(916) 263-3680	NC	(919) 733-4222	VI	(340) 773-2226
DC	(202) 442-4461	ND	(800) 532-5904	WV	(304) 558-3557
GU	(671) 477-1050	NE	(402) 471-3595	WY	(307) 777-7551
ID	(208) 334-2490	NV	(775) 786-0231		

The web sites for the state boards that administer the exam themselves are listed here. Each address has www. as a prefix, except WY. The Bisk Education web site (**www.cpaexam.com**) has links to the AICPA and NASBA. These numbers and addresses are subject to change without notice. Bisk Education doesn't assume responsibility for their accuracy.

AK	dced.state.ak.us/occ/pcpa.htm	MT	discoveringmontana.com/dli/bsd
AL	asbpa.state.al.us	NE	nol.org/home/BPA
AZ	accountancy.state.az.us	NV	accountancy/state.nv.us
AR	state.ar.us/asbpa	NH	state.nh.us/accountancy
CA	dca.ca.gov/cba	NC	state.nc.us/cpabd
DC	dcra.org/acct/newboa.shtm	ND	state.nd.us/ndsba
FL	myflorida.com	OK	state.ok.us/~oab
GU	guam.net/gov/gba	OR	boa.state.or.us/boa.html
ID	state.id.us/boa	SD	state.sd.us/dcr/accountancy
IL	illinois-cpa-exam.com/cpa.htm	TX	tsbpa.state.tx.us
KY	state.ky.us/agencies/boa	UT	commerce.state.ut.us
MD	dllr.state.md.us/license/occprof/account.html	VI	usvi.org/dlca/licensing/cpa.html
MN	boa.state.mn.us	WV	state.wv.us/wvboa
MS	msbpa.state.ms.us	WY	cpaboard.state.wy.us

COMPUTER-BASED TESTING (CBT)

The information presented here is intended to give candidates an overall idea of what their exam will be like. This information is as accurate as possible; however, circumstances are subject to change after this publication goes to press. Candidates should check the AICPA's web site (www.cpa-exam.org) 45 days before their exam for the most recent bulletin.

Registration Process

To sit for the exam, candidates apply to the appropriate state board of accountancy. Some state boards contract with NASBA's service to handle candidate applications. Once a state board or its agent determines that a candidate is eligible to sit for the exam, the board informs NASBA of candidate eligibility and NASBA adds the candidate to its database. With a national database, NASBA is able to ensure that no candidate can sit for the same exam section more than once during a single exam window. Within 24 hours, NASBA sends Prometric a notice to schedule (NTS). At that point, a candidate can schedule a date and time to sit for the exam with Prometric. With a NTS, a candidate also can subscribe to electronic databases of professional literature for free through the AICPA's exam website, www.cpa-exam.org. Please note that at Prometric's call center, Monday tends to have the longest wait times.

Scheduling

Candidates to whom taking the exam on a particular day is important should plan to schedule their exam dates **45 days** in advance. Upon receipt of the NTS, candidates have a limited amount of time to sit for the specified exam sections; this time is set by states. The exam is called on-demand because candidates may sit at anytime for any available date in the open window.

Candidate Medical Condition

If any medical conditions exist that need to be considered during the exam, candidates should supply information about that situation when scheduling. Ordinarily, candidates may not bring anything into the exam room—including prescription medications.

Granting of Credit

Once candidates have been granted credit for one exam section, they typically have 18 months to pass the three other exam sections. As this issue is decided by 54 boards of accountancy which are independent of each other, the length of time varies among jurisdictions. With CBT implementation, the AICPA uses the term *granting of credit* as opposed to the former term, *conditioning*. Candidates who conditioned in paper-and-pencil exams should contact the appropriate accountancy board regarding its transition conditioning policies.

Prometric

Prometric, a commercial testing center, has facilities at different security levels; the CPA exam is administered only at locations that have the highest restrictions. In other words, not all Prometric facilities may administer the CPA exam. These locations have adjustable chairs, 17-inch monitors, and uninterruptible power supplies (UPS). Prometric generally is closed on Sundays. A few locations are open on Saturdays. Candidates can register either at individual Prometric locations or through Prometric's national call center (800-864-8080). Candidates also may schedule, reschedule, cancel, or confirm an exam as well as find the closest testing location online at www.prometric.com.

Prometric doesn't score the exam. Candidates do not know their scores when they leave the exam site. Prometric sends a result file to NASBA that includes candidate responses, attendance information, and any incident reports.

Incident Reports

Prometric prepares an incident report for any unusual circumstances that occur during the exam. While Prometric has UPS available at qualified testing centers, if some problem similar to a power outage should occur, an incident report is included with the information that Prometric sends to NASBA after the candidate is finished with the exam. An incident report would be filed for such events as missing scratch sheets or a mid-testlet absence from the testing room.

Exam Day

On the day of their exam, candidates sign in and confirm their appointments. An administrator checks notices to schedule and two forms of identification. Digital photos are created. Candidates stow their belongings in designated locations. Candidates may not bring purses, watches, bottles of water, tissues, etc. into the exam room. Each candidate may receive six pages of scratch paper. Candidates may exchange used sheets for six more sheets. Candidates must account for the six pages at the conclusion of the exam. After the exam, candidates complete a survey to provide feedback.

Fees

States inform candidates of the total applicable fee. The total fee includes fees for NASBA, AICPA, Prometric, the state board, and the digital photo. Cancellations in advance generally result in a partially refunded fee. Cancellations (as opposed to a missed appointment) with no notice result in no refund. If a candidate misses an appointment, there generally is a $35 to $50 rescheduling fee unless due to circumstances beyond the candidate's control. Those situations are decided on a case-by-case basis. Some states structure their fees to provide incentive for taking more than one exam section in the same exam window.

Testing Room

Ordinarily, candidates are not permitted to bring any supplies into the testing room, including pencils, water, or aspirin. Candidates requiring medication during the exam should make sure to notify the state board as appropriate during the registration process. Exam proctors supply "scratch" or note paper. These pages must be returned to proctors before leaving the examination site.

Testlets

Multiple choice questions and simulations are grouped into testlets. A testlet typically has either from 24 to 30 multiple choice questions or a single simulation. The typical exam has three multiple choice testlets and two simulation testlets. Candidates may not pick the order in which they answer testlets. In other words, candidates cannot choose to answer the simulation testlets first and then the multiple choice question testlets. Within any one testlet, questions cover the entire content specification outline and are presented in random order.

Adaptive Testing

Each testlet is designed to cover all of the topics for an exam section. After the first testlet is finished, the software selects a second testlet based on the candidate's performance on the first testlet. If a candidate did well on the first testlet, the second testlet will be a little more difficult than average. Conversely, if a candidate did poorly on the first testlet, the second testlet will be a little less difficult than average. The examiners plan on adaptive testing eventually allowing for less questions, resulting in more time for testing skills.

Initially, testlets with different levels of difficulty will have the same number of questions; however, the point value of a question from an "easy" testlet will be less than a question from a "difficult" testlet. Thus, some candidates may think that they are not doing well because they are finding the questions difficult; when in reality, they are getting difficult questions because of exceptional performance on previous testlets. Other candidates may think that they are doing well because they are finding the questions easy; when in reality, they are getting easy questions because of poor performance on previous testlets.

The BEC exam section is not adaptive in the initial CBT exams. The AICPA has not announced when this will change.

Breaks

Once a testlet is started, a candidate ordinarily may not leave the workstation until that testlet is finished. Once a testlet is finished, a candidate may not return to it to change responses. After each testlet, a candidate has the option to take a break, but the clock is still running; a candidate's time responding to questions is reduced by the amount of time spent on breaks.

For a well-prepared candidate, time should not be an issue. Candidates will receive a five or ten minute warning. The software stops accepting exam responses at the end of the exam time automatically. All information entered before that time is scored.

Multiple Choice Questions

If there are six answer options and a candidate is told to choose one, the software will allow the selection of a second option and automatically unselect the previously selected option. If there are six answer options and a candidate is told to choose two, the software will not allow the selection of a third option without the candidate unselecting one of the other selected options.

In Bisk Education's printed book, letter answers appear next to each answer option to simplify indicating the correct answer. In the exam, a radio button appears instead of this letter. During the exam, candidates will indicate their response by clicking the appropriate radio button with a mouse device.

Simulations

A simulation is a collection of related items. A single simulation likely will have several response types. In other words, objective and essay responses may be included in the same simulation. Simulations typically are 20% or less of the exam score. The BEC exam section will not have simulations in the initial CBT exams. The AICPA has not announced yet when simulations will first appear in the BEC section.

Simulation Appearance Simulations generally appear as a collection of tabbed pages. Each tab requiring a candidate response will be designated by a pencil icon that changes appearance when any response is entered on that tab. Candidates should be alert to the fact that the altered icon does not indicate that all responses on that tab are entered, but rather that one response is entered.

Scenario Elements Simulations generally have one or two scenarios providing the basis for answers to all of the questions in the simulations.

Objective Response Elements Simulations may require candidates to select answers from drop-down lists or to enter numbers into worksheets or tax forms. Tax forms or schedules may appear on the REG exam section, but not all simulations on tax topics will include tax forms. Candidates don't need to know how to create a spreadsheet from scratch to earn full points on the exam; they do need to know how to categorize, determine value, and add to a previously constructed worksheet.

Written Communication Elements Initially, written communication will continue to be hand-graded. The "essay" score focuses primarily on writing skills. The essay content must be on topic to earn the full point value, but the examiners plan to focus on testing content in the objective response questions. Candidates should use their own words in essays; cut-and-paste excerpts from the standards may result in a zero-point score for that element.

Word Processor Tool There is a word processor tool with limited features in some simulations. The word processor tool has cut, paste, copy, do, and undo features. Spell check likely will be available. The word processor intentionally does **not** have bold, underline, or bullet features; the examiners don't want candidates spending much time on formatting.

Spreadsheet Tool The exam has a blank spreadsheet for use like a piece of electronic scratch paper. Anything in such a spreadsheet generally is not graded. In other words, if a candidate calculates an amount in a spreadsheet, it must be transferred to the appropriate answer location in order to earn points.

Research Elements Each simulation in the FAR, AUD, and REG exam sections has a research element, probably for one point. With an estimated two simulations per exam section, this means that the point value on any one of these three exam sections for the research element of a simulation will total two percent of that section's point value. The initial BEC exam section simulations will not have research elements. The AICPA has not announced yet when simulations, let alone research elements, first will appear in the BEC exam section.

A research element involves a search of an electronic database of authoritative literature for guidance. The examiners devise research questions with references unlikely to be known, requiring candidates to search the material. No written analysis of the reference is required; candidates merely provide the most appropriate reference(s) to a research question. Each research question will specify the number of references to provide.

The research skill evaluation distills down to the ability to structure a search of an electronic database and select the appropriate guidance from the "hits" generated by that search. Candidates may search using **either** Boolean protocols or the table of contents of the relevant guidance. Qualified candidates may get a **free** six month subscription to the databases used in the FAR and AUD exam sections from the AICPA and NASBA. Any difficulties candidates encounter in accepting the joint AICPA-NASBA offer should be brought to the attention of AICPA or NASBA. Qualified candidates may subscribe at www.cpa-exam.org. Only candidates who have applied to take the exam, been deemed eligible by one of the 54 boards of accountancy, and have a valid Notice to Schedule (NTS) may have access to this complimentary package of professional literature. Further information may be found at www.cpa-exam.org. For further inquiries after subscribing at this site, candidates may contact either: Joel Allegretti, AICPA, 212.596.6111; or Thomas Kenny, NASBA, 615.880.4237.

Tutorial

The AICPA provides a web-based tutorial for the CBT. This tutorial has samples of all the different types of simulation elements. The examiners believe that an hour spent with this tutorial will eliminate any point value loss due merely to unfamiliarity with the CBT system. It is important that you become familiar with the latest version of the AICPA testing software. The simulations use both a word processor and a spreadsheet program; however, these applications are not Microsoft Excel™ or Word™. It may be unsettling to encounter an unfamiliar interface on your exam day.

Advice to Candidates

Arrive at the testing center **at least** ½ hour before your appointment. Midweek appointments probably will be easiest to schedule. If taking the exam on a certain day is important, **schedule 45 days in advance.** Prometric doesn't overbook like airlines do—that is why there is a rescheduling fee for missed appointments.

Don't go to exam without spending at least an hour with the practice materials (also called a tutorial) available on the AICPA exam web-site. This tutorial is intended to familiarize candidates with the features of the exam software, so that when they take the exam, they are not worried about functionality and, hence, can concentrate on the content. The AICPA does **not** intend its tutorial to demonstrate content. The Bisk Education editors recommend viewing this tutorial at least a month before taking the exam and again a second time a week before your exam date.

THE NONDISCLOSED EXAM

Exam Disclosure

The Uniform CPA Examination is nondisclosed. This means that candidates are not allowed to receive a copy of their examination questions after the test. Also, candidates are required to sign a statement of confidentiality in which they promise not to reveal questions or answers. Only the AICPA have access to the test questions and answers. (In the past, the AICPA has released a small number of questions with unofficial answers from each nondisclosed exam; it makes no guarantees that it will continue this practice.) Bisk Education's editors update the diagnostic, study, and practice questions, based upon content changes, items from previously disclosed tests, and the teaching expertise of our editors. Due to the nondisclosure requirements, Bisk Education's editors are no longer able to address questions about specific examination questions, although we continue to supply help with similar study problems and questions in our texts.

The AICPA no longer discloses the exam in order to increase consistency, facilitate computer administration of the test, and improve examination quality by pretesting questions. Because the examination is no longer completely changed every year, statistical equating methods are more relevant, and the usefulness of specific questions as indicators of candidates' knowledge can be tested.

Time Management

Approximately 20% of the multiple choice questions in every section of every exam are questions that are being pretested. These questions are not included in candidates' final grades; they are presented only so that the Board of Examiners may evaluate them for effectiveness and possible ambiguity. The Scholastic Achievement Test and the Graduate Record Exam both employ similar but not identical strategies: those tests include an extra section that is being pretested, and test-takers do not know which section is the one which will not be graded. On the Uniform CPA Examination, however, the extra questions are mixed in among the graded questions. This makes time management even more crucial. Candidates who are deciding how much time to spend on a difficult multiple choice question must keep in mind that there is a 20% chance that the answer to the question will not affect them either way. Also, candidates should not allow a question that seems particularly difficult or confusing to shake their confidence or affect their attitude towards the rest of the test; it may not even count. This experimental 20% works against candidates who are not sure whether they have answered enough questions to earn 75%. Candidates should try for a safety margin, so that they will have accumulated enough correct answers to pass, even though some of their correctly answered questions will not be scored.

Post-Exam Diagnostics

The AICPA Board of Examiners' Advisory Grading Service provides boards of accountancy with individual diagnostic reports for all candidates along with the candidates' grades. The accountancy boards may mail the diagnostic reports to candidates along with their grades. Candidates should contact the state board in their jurisdiction to find out its policy on this issue. Grades are mailed in the first month of the next exam window; the examiners plan to reduce this waiting time gradually as they speed up the grading process.

Question Re-Evaluation

Candidates who believe that an examination question contains errors that will affect the grading should contact the AICPA Examinations Division, in accordance with the AICPA's *Uniform CPA Examination Candidate Bulletin: Information for Applicants* within **four days** of taking the examination. The Advisory Grading Service asks candidates to be as precise as possible about the question and their reason for believing that it should be re-evaluated, and, if possible, to supply references to support their position. Since candidates are not able to keep a copy of examination questions, it is important to remember as much detail as possible about a disputed question.

TEN ATTRIBUTES OF EXAMINATION SUCCESS

1.	Positive Mental Attitude	6.	Examination Strategies
2.	Development of a Plan	7.	Examination Grading
3.	Adherence to the Plan	8.	Solutions Approach™
4.	Time Management	9.	Focus on Ultimate Objective—Passing!
5.	Knowledge	10.	Examination Confidence

We believe that successful CPA candidates possess these ten characteristics that contribute to their ability to pass the exam. Because of their importance, we will consider each attribute individually.

1. Positive Mental Attitude

Preparation for the CPA exam is a long, intense process. A positive mental attitude, above all else, can be the difference between passing and failing.

2. Development of a Plan

The significant commitment involved in preparing for the exam requires a plan. We have prepared a study plan in the preceding **Getting Started** section. Take time to read this plan. **Amend it to your situation.** Whether you use our study plan or create your own, the importance of this attribute can't be overlooked.

3. Adherence to the Plan

You cannot expect to accomplish a successful and comprehensive review without adherence to your study plan.

4. Time Management

We all lead busy lives and the ability to budget study time is a key to success. We have outlined steps to budgeting time in the **Personalized Training Plan** found in the **Getting Started** section.

5. Knowledge

There is a distinct difference between understanding the material and knowing the material. A superficial understanding of accounting, auditing, and the business environment is not enough. You must know the material likely to be tested on the exam. Your Bisk Education text is designed to help you acquire the working knowledge that is essential to exam success.

6. Examination Strategies

You should be familiar with the format of the CPA exam and know exactly what you will do when you enter the examination room. In Section Two, we discuss the steps you should take from the time you enter the testing room, until you hand in your note (or scratch) sheets. Planning in advance how you will spend your examination time will save you time and confusion on exam day.

7. Examination Grading

An understanding of the CPA exam written communication (essay) grading procedure will help you to maximize grading points on the exam. Remember that your objective is to score 75 points on each section. Points are assigned to essay questions by the human grader who reads your exam. In essence, your job is to satisfy the grader by writing answers that closely conform to the grading guide. In Section Three, we explain AICPA grading procedures and show you how to tailor your answer to the grading guide and thus earn more points on the exam.

8. Solutions Approach™

The Solutions Approach™ is an efficient, systematic method of organizing and solving questions found on the CPA exam. This Approach will permit you to organize your thinking and your written answers in a logical manner that will maximize your exam score. Candidates who do not use a systematic answering method often neglect to show all their work on free form response questions—work that could earn partial credit if it were presented to the grader in an orderly fashion. The Solutions Approach™ will help you avoid drawing "blanks" on the exam; with it, you always know where to begin.

Many candidates have never developed an effective problem-solving methodology in their undergraduate studies. The "cookbook" approach, in which students work problems by following examples, is widespread among accounting schools. Unfortunately, it is not an effective problem-solving method for the CPA exam or for problems you will encounter in your professional career. Our Solutions Approach™ teaches you to derive solutions independently, without an example to guide you.

Our **Solutions Approach™** and grader orientation skills, when developed properly, can be worth at least 10 to 15 points for most candidates. These 10 to 15 points can often make the difference between passing and failing.

The **Solutions Approach™** for objective questions and essays is outlined in Section Four. Examples are worked and explained.

9. Focus on Ultimate Objective—Passing!

Your primary goal in preparing for the CPA exam is to attain a grade of 75 or better on all sections and, thus, **pass the examination**. Your review should be focused on this goal. Other objectives, such as learning new material or reviewing old material, are important only insofar as they assist you in passing the exam.

10. Examination Confidence

Examination confidence is actually a function of the other nine attributes. If you have acquired a good working knowledge of the material, an understanding of the grading system, a tactic for answering simulations, and a plan for taking the exam, you can go into the examination room **confident** that you are in control.

SECTION TWO: EXAMINATION STRATEGIES

The CPA exam is more than a test of your knowledge and technical competence. It is also a test of your ability to function under psychological pressure. You easily could be thrown off balance by an unexpected turn of events during the days of the exam. Your objective is to avoid surprises and eliminate hassles and distractions that might shake your confidence. You want to be in complete control so that you can concentrate on the exam material, rather than the exam situation. By taking charge of the exam, you will be able to handle pressure in a constructive manner. The keys to control are adequate preparation and an effective examination strategy.

Overall Preparation

Advance preparation will arm you with the confidence you need to overcome the psychological pressure of the exam. As you complete your comprehensive review, you will cover most of the material that will be tested on the exam; it is unlikely that an essay, problem, or series of objective questions will deal with a topic you have not studied. But if an unfamiliar topic **is** tested, you will not be dismayed because you have learned to use the **Solutions Approach™** to derive the best possible answer from the knowledge you possess. Similarly, you will not feel pressured to write "perfect" essay answers, because you understand the grading process. You recognize that there is a limit to the points you can earn for each answer, no matter how much you write.

The components of your advance preparation program have previously been discussed in this appendix. Briefly summarizing, they include the following.

1. Comprehensive review materials such as your Bisk Education CPA Review Program.

2. A method for pre-review and ongoing self-evaluation of your level of proficiency.

3. A study plan that enables you to review each subject area methodically and thoroughly.

4. A **Solutions Approach™** for each type of examination question.

5. An understanding of the grading process and grader orientation skills.

CPA Exam Strategies

The second key to controlling the exam is to develop effective strategies for the days you take the exam. Your objective is to avoid surprises and frustrations so that you can focus your full concentration on the questions and your answers.

You should be familiar with the format of the CPA exam and know exactly what you will do when you enter the testing room. Remember to read all instructions carefully, whether general or specific to a particular question. Disregarding the instructions may mean loss of points.

On the following pages, we discuss the steps you should take on exam day. Planning in advance how you will spend your examination time will save you time and confusion.

Examination Inventory

You should spend the first few minutes the exam and planning your work. **Do not** plunge head-first into answering the questions without a plan of action. You do not want to risk running out of time, becoming frustrated by a difficult question, or losing the opportunity to answer a question that you could have answered well. Your inventory should take no longer than five minutes. The time you spend will help you "settle in" to the examination and develop a feel for your ability to answer the questions.

1.   Carefully read the "Instructions to Candidates".

2.   Note the number and type of testlets, as well as any other information provided by the examiners.

3.   Devise a time schedule on your "scratch" paper, taking into account the number and type of testlets.

Order of Answering Questions

Objective questions comprise a majority of the point value of each section. Because of their objective nature, the correct solution often is listed as one of the answer choices. (The exception is when a numeric response is required.) By solving these questions, not only do you gain confidence, but they often involve the same or a related topic to that covered in any essays that may appear in the simulations.

A very effective and efficient manner of answering the objective questions is to make **two passes** through the questions. On the first pass, you should answer those questions that you find the easiest. If you come across a question that you find difficult to solve, note it on your scratch paper and proceed to the next one. This will allow you to avoid wasting precious time and will enable your mind to clear and start anew on your **second pass.** On the second pass, you should return and solve those questions you left unanswered on the first pass. Some of these questions you may have skipped over without an attempt, while in others you may have been able to eliminate one or two of the answer choices. Either way, you should come up with an answer on the second pass, even if you have to guess! Once you leave a testlet, you may not return to it. Before leaving a testlet, make sure you have answered all of the individual questions. Be careful not to overlook any items; use particular care in simulations.

Written communication responses (commonly called essays) should be worked only through the key word outlines on the first pass. Then take a fresh look at the question and return to write your essay solution.

Examination Time Budgeting

You must **plan** how you will use your examination time and adhere faithfully to your schedule. If you budget your time carefully, you should be able to answer all parts of all questions. You should subtract a minute or two for your initial inventory on each section. Assuming you will use the **Solutions Approach™** and there will be two simulations in all sections except BEC, your time budgets may be similar to these. Your actual exam may differ from this scenario. You may benefit by taking more breaks than are included in this schedule. Be sure to adjust your time budget to accommodate the number and type of questions asked as well as your individual needs and strengths.

	Minutes			
	FAR	AUD	REG	BEC
Inventory examination	1	1	1	1
Answer multiple choice question testlet	51	58	33	49
Answer multiple choice question testlet	51	58	33	50
Answer multiple choice question testlet	51	58	33	50
Break	6	5	0	0
Answer simulation testlet	40	45	40	n/a
Answer simulation testlet	40	45	40	n/a
	240	270	180	150

Your objective in time budgeting is to avoid running out of time to answer a question. Work quickly but efficiently (i.e., use the **Solutions Approach™**). Remember that when you are answering an essay question, a partial answer is better than no answer at all. If you don't write anything, how can a grader justify giving you any points?

Page Numbering

Identify and label your scratch pages to avoid confusing yourself during the stress of the exam.

Psychology of Examination Success

As stated previously, the CPA exam is in itself a physical and mental strain. You can minimize this strain by avoiding all unnecessary distractions and inconveniences during your exam week. For example, consider the following.

- **Use the AICPA's free tutorial and sample examination** at www.cpa-exam.org at least a week before your examination. Because the exam interface is subject to change, re-visit the site to be sure that you are familiar with the current interface if you took an exam in a previous window. The site also has the most current *Uniform CPA Examination Candidate Bulletin,* a publication with useful information for candidates. These are **not** available at the test center.

- **Carefully register for the examination.** You must bring two forms of identification and your notice to schedule to the test center on the day of your exam. The name you use to make the appointment must match **exactly** your name on the identification and your notice to schedule (which also must match each other exactly).

- **Make any reservations for lodging well in advance.** If you are traveling, it's best to reserve a room for the preceding night so that you can check in, get a good night's sleep, and locate the exam site well before the exam.

- **Stick to your normal eating, sleeping, and exercise habits.** Eat lightly before the exam. Watch your caffeine and alcohol intake. If you are accustomed to regular exercise, continue a regular routine leading up to your exam day.

- **Locate the examination facilities** before the examination and familiarize yourself with the surroundings and alternate routes.

- **Arrive early for the exam.** Allow plenty of time for unexpected delays. Nothing is more demoralizing than getting caught in a traffic jam ten minutes before your exam is scheduled to begin. Your appointment time is the time that the actual examination process is scheduled to start, not the start of the test center pre-exam procedures: identification verification, digital photography, storage locker assignment, etc. The examiners recommend that you arrive **at least** 30 minutes before your scheduled appointment. If your examination doesn't begin within 30 minutes of your scheduled start time, you may have to reschedule. This means that if you show up 30 minutes after your scheduled start time, you may have to reschedule—pre-exam procedures are neither instantaneous nor factored into your scheduled appointment.

- **Avoid possible distractions,** such as friends and pre-exam conversation, immediately before the exam.

- In general, **you should not attempt serious study on the nights before exam sessions.** It's better to relax—watch a movie, exercise, or read a novel. If you feel you must study, spend half an hour or so going over the chapter outlines in the text. Some candidates develop a single page of notes for each chapter (or each exam section) throughout their review process to review for a few minutes during the evening before the exam. This single page includes only those things that are particularly troublesome for that candidate, such as the criteria for a capital lease or the economic order quantity formula.

- **Don't discuss exam answers with other candidates.** Not only have you signed a statement of confidentiality, but someone is sure to disagree with your answer, and if you are easily influenced by his or her reasoning, you can become doubtful of your own ability. If you are writing more than one exam section within a two-month exam window, you will not have the reliable feedback that only your score can provide from your first section before you sit for the second section. Wait and analyze your performance by yourself when you are in a relaxed and objective frame of mind.

- **Avoid self-evaluation** of your exam performance until after you receive your official score. The Bisk editors have heard from several candidates who were sure that they failed by a large margin, only to receive subsequent messages rejoicing in scores in the 80s and 90s. Self-evaluation without an official score is unreliable. Not all of the examiners' questions are the same point value. Further, approximately 20% of multiple choice questions are not scored; candidates have no reliable way to know which questions are not scored. Instead of speculating, focus on preparing for your next exam section.

General Rules Governing Examinations

1. Read carefully any paperwork assigned to you; make note of numbers for future reference; when it is requested, return it to the examiner. Only the examination number on your card shall be used on your exam for the purpose of identification. If a question calls for an answer involving a signature, **do not** use your own name or initials.

2. Use the exact same name as on your notice to schedule (NTS) when scheduling your appointment. Two pieces of identification are required; one must have a photo. The name on your identification must match your name on your notice to schedule **exactly.**

3. Seating during the exam is assigned by Prometric.

4. Supplies furnished by the Board remain its property and must be returned whether used or not.

5. Any reference during the examination to books or other matters or the exchange of information with other persons shall be considered misconduct sufficient to bar you from further participation in the examination.

6. The only aids most candidates are permitted to have in the examination room are supplied by the proctors. Wallets, briefcases, files, books, phones, watches, and other material brought to the examination site by candidates must be placed in a designated area before the start of the examination. Candidates get a key to a **small** storage locker. The test center is not responsible for lost items.

7. Do not leave your workstation during a testlet. Breaks are allowed only before starting and after finishing testlets.

8. Smoking is allowed only in designated areas away from the general examination area.

9. No telephone calls are permitted during the examination session.

10. Answers must be completed in the total time allotted for each exam section. The fixed time for each session must be observed by all candidates. One time warning is given five or ten minutes before the end of the exam. The testing software will end the test at the end of the specified time.

CPA Exam Week Checklist

What to pack for exam week:

1. CPA exam notice to schedule and matching identification.

2. If traveling, your hotel confirmation and an alarm clock. (Don't rely on a hotel wake-up call.)

3. Cash and/or a major credit card.

4. An inexpensive watch (will not be allowed in the testing room) to facilitate your timely arrival at the exam site.

5. Comfortable clothing that can be loosened to suit varying temperatures. What is worn into the testing room must be worn throughout the testing period; however, once at the testing center, you can remove a sweater or coat, for instance, before entering the testing room.

6. Appropriate review materials and tools for final reviews during the last days before the exam.

7. Healthy snack foods (will not be allowed in testing room).

Evenings before exam sections:

1. Read through your Bisk Education chapter outlines for the next day's section(s).

2. Eat lightly and monitor your intake of alcohol and caffeine. Get a good night's rest.

3. Do **not** try to cram. A brief review of your notes will help to focus your attention on important points and remind you that you are well prepared, but too much cramming can shatter your self-confidence. If you have reviewed conscientiously, you are already well-prepared for the CPA exam.

The morning of each exam section:

1. Eat a satisfying meal before your exam. It will be several hours before your next meal. Eat enough to ward off hunger, but not so much that you feel uncomfortable.

2. Dress appropriately. Wear layers you can loosen to suit varying temperatures in the room.

3. Arrive at the exam center at least 30 minutes early.

What to bring to the exam:

1. Appropriate identification (two forms, one with a picture) and notice to schedule (NTS). Your name on the identification must match your name on your NTS **exactly.** Use the exact same name when scheduling your appointment.

2. An inexpensive watch (to be left outside of the exam room) to ensure that you arrive 30 minutes early.

3. Take only those articles that you need to get to and from the exam site. Avoid taking any articles that are not allowed in the exam room, especially valuable ones. There are **small** storage lockers outside of the testing room to hold purses, etc. The test center is not responsible for lost items. Watches, phones, pencils, purses, tissues, candy, and gum are not allowed in the exam room. Even medication is not allowed except by previous arrangement.

During the exam:

1. Always read all instructions and follow the directions of the exam administrator. If you don't understand any written or verbal instructions, or if something doesn't seem right, ASK QUESTIONS as allowed. Remember that an error in following directions could invalidate your **entire** exam.

2. Budget your time. Always keep track of the time and avoid getting too involved with one question.

3. **Satisfy the grader.** Remember that the grader cannot read your mind. You must explain every point in written communications. Focus on key words and concepts. Tell the grader what you know, don't **worry** about any points you don't know.

4. Answer every question, even if you must guess.

5. Use **all** the allotted time. If you finish a testlet early, go back and reconsider the more difficult questions.

6. Get up and stretch between testlets, if you feel sluggish. Walk around as allowed. Breathe deeply; focus your eyes on distant objects to avoid eye strain. Do some exercises to relax muscles in the face, neck, fingers, and back.

7. Do not leave your workstation. except between testlets. Leaving your workstation during a testlet may invalidate your score.

8. Take enough time to organize written answers. Well-organized answers will impress the grader.

9. Remember that you are well-prepared for the CPA exam, and that you can **expect to pass!** A confident attitude will help you overcome examination anxiety.

SECTION THREE: EXAMINATION GRADING ORIENTATION

The CPA exam is prepared and graded by the AICPA Examinations Division. It is administered by a commercial testing center, Prometric. Candidates register for the exam through various State Boards of Accountancy.

An understanding of the grading procedure will help you maximize grading points on the CPA exam. Remember that your objective is to pass the exam. You cannot afford to spend time on activities that will not affect your grade, or to ignore opportunities to increase your points. The following material abstracted from the *Information for CPA Candidates* booklet summarizes the important substantive aspects of the Uniform CPA Examination itself and the grading procedures used by the AICPA.

Security

The examination is prepared and administered under tight security measures. The candidates' anonymity is preserved throughout the examination and grading process. Unusual similarities in answers among candidates are reported to the appropriate accountancy boards.

Objective Questions

Objective questions consist of multiple-choice questions and objective answer format questions in simulations, which include: yes-no, true-false, matching, and questions requiring a numerical response. Objective questions are machine graded. It is important to understand that there is **no grade reduction** for incorrect responses to objective questions—your total objective question grade is determined solely by the number of correct answers. Thus, you **should answer every question.** If you do not know the answer, make an intelligent guess.

The point to remember is to avoid getting "bogged down" on one answer. Move along and answer all the questions. This helps you avoid leaving questions unanswered or panic-answering questions due to poor budgeting of test time.

Written Communication Responses

Essay responses also appear on the computer-based exam, as components of simulations. On the actual exam, essays are not computer graded. Note that the initial BEC exams will not have simulations and therefore will not have essays. Information on essays is provided as the examiners have not announced when they will start including simulations in the BEC exam section. The examiners might not include simulations in the BEC exam section until 2007 or later, or they may include simulations in the BEC exam section as early as 2006. Essay responses are graded for writing skills, but the essay content must answer the question that the examiners asked. Essay responses are graded by CPAs and AICPA staff members, using the following procedures.

First Grading

The first grading is done by graders assigned to individual questions. In other words, each essay is graded by a specific grader. A grader assigned to a single question becomes an expert in the subject matter of the question and in the evaluation of the candidates' answers. Thus, grading is objective and uniform.

The purpose of the first grading is to separate the candidates' answers into three groups: obvious passes, marginal, and obvious failures.

Second Grading

Upon completion of the first grading, a second grading is done by reviewers. Obvious passes and failures are subjected to cursory reviews as part of the grading controls. Marginal answers receive an extensive review.

The graders who make the extensive reviews have had years of experience grading the CPA examination. They have also participated in the development of the grading bases and have access to item analysis for objective questions, identifying concepts as discriminating (those included by most candidates passing the exam) or as rudimentary (those included by candidates both passing and failing the exam). An important indicator of the competence of the candidate is whether grade points were earned chiefly from discriminating concepts or from rudimentary concepts.

Third Grading

After the papers have been through the second grading for all parts of the examination, the resultant grades are listed by candidate number and compared for consistency among subjects. For example, if a candidate passes two subjects and receives a marginal grade in a third, the marginal paper will receive a third grading in the hope that the candidate, now identified as possessing considerable competence, can have the paper raised to a passing grade by finding additional points for which to grant positive credit. This third grading is done by the section head or a reviewer who did not do the second grading of the paper.

Fourth Grading

The Director of Examinations applies a fourth grading to papers that have received the third grading but have grades that are inconsistent. The Director knows that the papers have already been subjected to three gradings, and that it would be difficult to find additional points for which the candidates should be given credit. Obviously, very few candidates are passed in this manner, but this fourth grading assures that marginal candidates receive every possible consideration.

Written Communication Question Example—Grading Guide

Points are assigned to essay questions on the basis of **key concepts.** A key concept is an idea, thought, or option that can be clearly defined and identified. Through a grading of sample papers, a list of key concepts related to each question is accumulated. These key concepts become the **grading bases** for the question. That is, your answer will be scored according to the number of key concepts it contains. Note that you need not include **all** possible key concepts to receive full credit on a question. The total number of grading bases exceeds the point value of the question. For example, a 10-point question may have 15 or more grading bases. Thus, a candidate would not have to provide all the key concepts to get the maximum available points. Conversely, a candidate cannot receive more points even if he or she provides more than 10 key concepts.

To illustrate the grading procedure and the importance of using key concepts in your answers, we will develop a hypothetical grading guide for a question adapted from a past exam. We will assume that the entire question is worth 10 points.

Written Communication Question Example (15 to 25 minutes)

Best Aviation Associates is a general partnership engaged in the business of buying, selling and servicing used airplanes. Best's original partners were Martin and Kent. They formed the partnership on January 1, 2002, under an oral partnership agreement which provided that the partners would share profits equally. There was no agreement as to how the partners would share losses. At the time the partnership was formed, Martin contributed $320,000 and Kent contributed $80,000.

On December 1, 2003, Best hired Baker to be a salesperson and to assist in purchasing used aircraft for Best's inventory. On December 15, 2003, Martin instructed Baker to negotiate the purchase of a used airplane without disclosing that Baker was acting on Best's behalf. Martin thought that a better price could be negotiated by Baker if Jackson was not aware that the aircraft was being acquired for Best. The agreement provided that Jackson would deliver the airplane to Baker on January 2, 2004, at which time the purchase price was to be paid. On January 2, 2004, Jackson attempted to deliver the used airplane purchased for Best by Baker. Baker, acting on Martin's instructions, refused to accept delivery or pay the purchase price.

On December 20, 2003, Kent assigned Kent's partnership interest in Best to Green. On December 31, 2003, Kent advised Martin of the assignment to Green. On January 11, 2004, Green contacted Martin and demanded to inspect the partnership books and to participate in the management of partnership affairs, including voting on partnership decisions.

On January 13, 2004, it was determined that Best had incurred an operating loss of $160,000 in 2003. Martin demanded that Kent contribute $80,000 to the partnership to account for Kent's share of the loss. Kent refused to contribute.

On January 28, 2004, Laco Supplies, Inc., a creditor of Best, sued Best and Martin for unpaid bills totaling $92,000. Best had not paid the bills because of a cash shortfall caused by the 2003 operating loss.

Jackson has taken the following position:

- Baker is responsible for any damages incurred by Jackson as a result of Best's refusal to accept delivery or pay the purchase price.

Martin has taken the following positions:

- Green is not entitled to inspect the partnership books or participate in the management of the partnership.
- Only the partnership is liable for the amounts owed to Laco, or, in the alternative, Martin's personal liability is limited to 50% of the total of the unpaid bills.

Kent has taken the following positions:

- Only Martin is liable for the 2003 operating loss because of the assignment to Green of Kent's partnership interest.
- Any personal liability of the partners for the 2003 operating loss should be allocated between them on the basis of their original capital contributions.

Required:

a. Determine whether Jackson's position is correct and state the reasons for your conclusions.

b. Determine whether Martin's positions are correct and state the reasons for your conclusions.

c. Determine whether Kent's positions are correct and state the reasons for your conclusions.

Now let's look at the unofficial answer. Notice that we have boldfaced the key concepts in the answer. Later, as we develop a grading guide for the answer, you will see the importance of using key concepts to tailor your answer to parallel the grading guide.

Unofficial Solution: Partnership Agent and Assignment

a. Jackson is correct. Baker, as an **agent** acting on behalf of an **undisclosed principal** (Best), is **personally liable** for any contracts entered into in that capacity.

b. Martin's first position that Green is not entitled to inspect the partnership books or participate in partnership management is correct. Green, as an **assignee** of Kent's **partnership interest,** is entitled to receive Kent's **share of partnership profits only.** Green is **not entitled,** as an assignee of Kent's partnership interest, to **inspect** the partnership **records** or to **participate in the management** of the partnership.

Martin's second position that only the partnership is responsible for the debt owed Laco is incorrect. Although the partnership is **primarily liable** for the unpaid bills, both Martin and Kent, as Best's partners, are personally liable for the **unpaid** amount of the debt. Laco will be entitled to seek recovery against Martin or Kent for the full amount owed.

c. Kent's first position that only Martin is liable for the 2003 operating loss because of the assignment of Kent's partnership interest to Green is incorrect. A partner's **assignment** of a partnership interest does **not terminate** that partner's **liability** for the partnership's losses and debts.

Kent's second position that any personal liability of the partners for the 2003 operating loss should be allocated on the basis of their original capital contributions is incorrect. The 2003 loss will be **allocated in the same way** that **profits were to be allocated** between the parties, that is, equally, because Martin and Kent had not agreed on the method for allocating losses between themselves.

Example Grading Guide for Written Communication Response

STATE _____

CANDIDATE NO. _____

POINTS	KEY WORD CONCEPTS
2	**Agent** acting on behalf of an **undisclosed principal** (Best), is **personally liable**
1	**Assignee** of **partnership interest** is entitled to receive a **share of partnership profits only**
1	Assignee is **not entitled** to **inspect** the partnership **records** or to **participate in management**
2	Partnership is **primarily liable** for the unpaid bills; partners are personally liable for the **unpaid** amount of the debt
2	A partner's **assignment** of a partnership interest does **not terminate** that partner's **liability** for the partnership's losses and debts
_2_	Losses are **allocated in the same way** that **profits were to be allocated** between the parties
10	

GRADE	1	2	3	4	5
POINTS	1	2 3	4 5	6 7	8 9 10

Importance of Key Concepts

A grading guide similar to the one above is used to evaluate every candidate's work, with the key concepts or grading bases for each question. On the first grading, answers may be scanned first for key words, then read carefully to ascertain that no key concepts were overlooked. Each key concept in the answer increases the candidate's grade. The candidate's total grade for the question is determined easily by converting raw points, using a conversion chart. For example, a candidate who earns 8 of the 10 points for key concepts for this question would earn a grade of 5 for the answer. The process is repeated by the second grader and subsequent graders if necessary (i.e., borderline papers).

The point you should notice is that **key concepts earn points.** The unofficial answer closely conforms to the grading guide, making the grader's task simple. In turn, the unofficial answer also conforms to the format of the question. That is, each answer is numbered and lettered to correspond to the requirements. This should be your standard format.

There are two more points you should observe as you study the unofficial answer for our example. First, the answer is written in standard English, with clear, concise sentences and short paragraphs. A simple listing of key words is **unacceptable;** the concepts and their interrelationships must be presented logically. Secondly, remember that the unofficial answer represents the most acceptable solution to a question. This is not to say, however, that alternative answers are not considered or that other answers are not equally acceptable. During the accumulation of grading bases, many concepts are added to the original "correct answer." Additionally, an answer that is near the passing mark receives a third (and perhaps fourth) grading, at which time individual consideration is given to the merits of each answer.

Parenthetically, we should mention that all the Bisk Education *CPA Review* essays within simulations are solved using the unofficial AICPA answers. Thus, you have ample opportunity to accustom yourself to the favored answer format.

Importance of Writing Skills

Essay responses are graded mainly for writing skills; however, the essay response must address the essay question to earn the full point value. For more coverage of this area, refer to the **Writing Skills** section.

Grading Implications for CPA Candidates

To summarize this review of the AICPA's grading procedure, we can offer the following conclusions that will help you to **satisfy the grader** and maximize your score:

1.   Attempt an answer on every question.

2.   Respond directly to the requirements of the questions.

3.   Use schedules and formats favored by the AICPA examiners.

4.   Answer all requirements.

5.   Develop a **Solutions Approach™** to each question type.

6.   Written communication questions:

   Label your solutions parallel to the requirements.

   Offer reasons for your conclusions.

   Emphasize key words by underlining them.

   Separate grading concepts into individual sentences or paragraphs.

   Use of a well-chosen example is an easy way of expressing an understanding of the subject or supporting a conclusion.

   Do **not** present your answer in outline format.

   Note that the editors strongly recommend **against** cutting-and-pasting excerpts from the professional literature provided for research questions.

7.   Allocate your examination time based on AICPA point value or recommended time, if provided.

———————————

SECTION FOUR: THE SOLUTIONS APPROACH™

The **Bisk Education Solutions Approach™** is an efficient, systematic method of organizing and solving questions found on the CPA exam. Remember that all the knowledge in the world is worthless unless you can get it down on paper. Conversely, a little knowledge can go a long way if you use a proper approach. The **Solutions Approach™** was developed by our Editorial Board in 1971; all subsequently developed stereotypes trace their roots from the original "Approach" that we formulated. Our **Solutions Approach™** and grader orientation skills, when properly developed, can be worth at least 10 to 15 points for most candidates. These 10 to 15 points often make the difference between passing and failing.

We will suggest a number of steps for deriving a solution that will help maximize your grade on the exam. Although you should remember the important steps in our suggested approach, don't be afraid to adapt these steps to your own taste and requirements. When you work the questions at the conclusion of each chapter, make sure you use your variation of the **Solutions Approach™**. It is also important for you to attempt to pattern the organization and format of your written solution to the unofficial answer. However, DO NOT CONSULT THE UNOFFICIAL ANSWER UNTIL YOU FINISH THE QUESTION. The worst thing you can do is look at old questions and then turn to the answer without working the problem. This will build false confidence and provide **no** skills in developing a **Solutions Approach™**. Therefore, in order to derive the maximum number of points from an essay solution, you should **first** apply the **Solutions Approach™** to reading and answering the question, and **secondly,** write an essay answer using an organization and format identical to that which would be used by the AICPA in writing the unofficial answer to that essay question.

Solutions Approach™ for Written Communication Questions

Our **six steps** are as follows.

1. Scan the text of the question for an overview of the subject area and content of the question.
2. Study the question requirements slowly and thoroughly. Note portions of the requirements on your scratch paper as needed.
3. Visualize the unofficial answer format based on the requirements of the question.
4. Carefully study the text of the question. Note important data on your scratch paper.
5. Outline the solution in key words and phrases. Be sure to respond to the requirements, telling the grader only what s/he needs to know. Explain the reasons for your conclusions.
6. Write the solution in the proper format based upon your key word outline. Write concise, complete sentences. Do not forget to proofread and edit your solution.

Written Communication Question Example

To illustrate the **Solutions Approach™** for essay questions, we consider a question from a past examination.

Sample Written Communication

Edwards, a director and a 10% stockholder in National Corp., is dissatisfied with the way National's officers, particularly Olsen, the president, have been operating the corporation.

Edwards has made many suggestions that have been rejected by the board of directors, and has made several unsuccessful attempts to have Olsen removed as president.

National and Grand Corp. had been negotiating a merger that Edwards has adamantly opposed. Edwards has blamed Olsen for initiating the negotiation and has urged the board to fire Olsen. National's board refused to fire Olsen. In an attempt to defeat the merger, Edwards approached Jenkins, the president of Queen Corp., and contracted for Queen to purchase several of National's assets. Jenkins knew Edwards was a National director, but had never done business with National. When National learned of the contract, it notified Queen that the contract was invalid.

Edwards filed an objection to the merger before the stockholders' meeting called to consider the merger proposal was held. At the meeting, Edwards voted against the merger proposal.

Despite Edward's efforts, the merger was approved by both corporations. Edwards then orally demanded that National purchase Edwards' stock, citing the dissenters rights provision of the corporation's by-laws, which reflects the Model Business Corporation Act.

National's board has claimed National does not have to purchase Edward's stock.

As a result of the above:

- Edwards initiated a minority stockholder's action to have Olsen removed as president and to force National to purchase Edward's stock.

- Queen sued National to enforce the contract and/or collect damages.

- Queen sued Edwards to collect damages.

Required: Answer the following questions and give the reasons for your answers.

a. Will Edwards be successful in a lawsuit to have Olsen removed as president?

b. Will Edwards be successful in a lawsuit to have National purchase the stock?

c. 1. Will Queen be successful in a lawsuit against National?

   2. Will Queen be successful in a lawsuit against Edwards?

Applying the Solutions Approach™

Let's look at the steps you go through to arrive at your solution:

In **Step 1,** you scan the question. Do not read thoroughly, simply get an overview of the subject area and content of the question. You notice the question addresses a UCC sale of goods consisting of several transactions.

In **Step 2,** you study the question requirements thoroughly. **Part a** addresses Edwards' right to remove an officer of the corporation, while **Parts b** and **c** addresses Edwards' authority to act for the corporation. Underline key phrases and words.

In **Step 3,** you visualize the format of your solution. The solution will be in paragraph form. **Part a** will discuss Edwards' claim, whether it is correct, and why. **Part b** addresses Edwards' authority to act for the corporation. **Part c** will discuss Queen's claims, whether they are correct, and why. It will be important to identify each of these claims in the text of the question to aid in organizing your thoughts.

In **Step 4,** you carefully study the text of the question, given the requirements you want to satisfy, *i.e.*, read the question carefully, noting Edwards' rights and authority and each of Queen's claims. You should note important information on your scratch paper.

In **Step 5,** you outline your answer in keyword form. This will include an answer of "correct" or "incorrect" for the claim in **Parts a** and **b** as well as each of the claims in **Part c** plus additional key concepts you want to include in your final answer. In your exam preparation, as you work business law essays in particular, notice that sometimes you are not asked to render a decision in the case, but rather you are asked to discuss **both sides** of the case.

Outline Answer

a.   Edwards' claim—incorrect
        Board of directors holds right to hire and fire officers
        Individual stockholders have no vote in the selection of officers
                Regardless of the size of their holding
                Vote for directors at the annual stockholders' meeting

b.   Edwards' lawsuit—will lose
        Dissenting stockholder has appraisal remedy
                Dissents from merger plan
                Purchase stockholder's shares
                If the statutory requirements are met
                Entitled to the fair value of the stock

c.   Queen's lawsuit against National—will lose
        Edwards had no authority to contract with Queen
        A director has a fiduciary duty to the stockholders of a corporation
                A director has no authority to contract on behalf of the corporation unless expressly authorized
        Jenkins may have assumed that Edwards was acting as National's agent
                No implied agency authority merely by being a director

        Queen's lawsuit against Edwards—will win
                Edwards had no authority to act for National
                Edwards will be personally liable

In **Step 6**, you write your solution in a format similar to the unofficial answer. Notice how clear and concise the AICPA unofficial answers are. There is no doubt as to their decision or the reasoning supporting the decision. Notice also how they answer each requirement separately and in the same order as in the question. Be sure to proofread and edit your solution.

In general, each requirement in a business law topic is designed to elicit from you at least one rule of law which is different from any other rule of law covered by any other part of the question. Finally, if you discuss two sides of an issue, be sure to indicate that this is what you are doing so that it does not appear that you have inconsistencies in you answer.

Sample Essay Unofficial Answer

a.   Edwards will not win the suit to have Olsen removed as president. The **right to hire and fire** officers is held by the **board of directors. Individual stockholders,** regardless of the size of their holding, **have no vote in the selection of officers.** Individual stockholders may exert influence in this area by voting for directors at the annual stockholders' meeting.

b.   Edwards will lose the suit to have National purchase the stock. A stockholder who **dissents from a merger** may require the corporation to purchase her/his shares if the statutory requirements are met and would be entitled to the fair value of the stock **(appraisal remedy).** To **compel the purchase,** Edwards would have had to **file an objection** to the merger before the stockholders meeting at which the merger proposal was considered, **vote against** the merger proposal, and make a **written demand** that the corporation purchase the stock at an appraised price. Edwards will lose because the first two requirements were met but Edwards failed to make a written demand that the corporation purchase the stock.

c.   1.   Queen will lose its suit against National to enforce the contract, even though Edwards was a National director. Jenkins may have assumed that Edwards was **acting as National's agent,** but Edwards had **no authority** to contract with Queen. A director has a **fiduciary duty** to the stockholders of a corporation but, unless **expressly authorized** by the board of directors or the officers of the corporation, has **no authority to contract on behalf of the corporation.** There is **no implied agency authority** merely **by being a director.**
        2.   Queen will win its suit against Edwards because Edwards had **no authority to act** for National. Edwards will be **personally liable** for Queen's damages.

Solutions Approach™ for Objective Questions

The **Solutions Approach™** is also adaptable to objective questions. We recommend the following framework:

1. Read the "Instructions to Candidates" section on your particular exam to determine if the AICPA's standard is the same. Generally, your objective portion will be determined by the number of correct answers with no penalty for incorrect answers.

2. Read the question carefully, noting exactly what the question is asking. Negative requirements are easily missed. Note key words and when the requirement is an exception (e.g., "except for...," or "which of the following does **not**..."). Perform any intermediate calculations necessary to the determination of the correct answer.

3. Anticipate the answer by covering the possible answers and seeing if you **know** the correct answer.

4. Read the answers given.

5. Select the best alternative. Very often, one or two possible answers will be clearly incorrect. Of the other alternatives, be sure to select the alternative that **best answers the question asked.**

6. After completing all of the individual questions in a testlet, **go back** and double check that you have answered each question.

7. Answer the questions in order. This is a proven, systematic approach to objective test taking. You generally are limited to an average of 2 to 2½ minutes per multiple choice question. Under no circumstances should you allow yourself to fall behind schedule. If a question is difficult or long, be sure you remain cognizant of the time you are using. If after a minute or so you feel that it is too costly to continue on with a particular question, select the letter answer you tentatively feel is the best answer and go to the next question. Return to these questions at a later time and attempt to finally answer them when you have time for more consideration. If you cannot find a better answer when you return to the question, use your preliminary answer because your first impressions are often correct. However, as you read other question(s), if something about these subsequent questions or answers jogs your memory, return to the previous tentatively answered question(s) or make a note of the idea for later consideration (time permitting).

A simulation is a particularly challenging format for many candidates. A simulation is a group of objective and free-response questions, generally based on one hypothetical situation. In this case, you should skim all the related questions (but not the answer possibilities) before you begin answering, since an overall view of the problem will guide you in the work you do.

Note also that many incorrect answer choices are based on the erroneous application of one or more items in the text of the question. Thus, it is extremely important to **anticipate** the answer before you read the alternatives. Otherwise, you may be easily persuaded by an answer choice that is formulated through the incorrect use of the given data.

Let's consider a multiple choice question adapted from a past examination.

Sample Objective Question

Lean Company is preparing its cash budget for November. The following information pertains to Lean's past collection experience from its credit sales:

Current month's sales	12%
Prior month's sales	75%
Sales two months prior to current month	6%
Sales three months prior to current month	4%
Cash discounts (2/30, net 90)	2%
Doubtful accounts	1%

Credit sales:

November—estimated	$100,000
October	90,000
September	80,000
August	95,000

How much is the estimated credit to accounts receivable as a result of collections expected during November?
a. $85,100
b. $87,100
c. $88,100
d. $90,000

APPLYING THE SOLUTIONS APPROACH™

Let's look at the steps you should go through to arrive at your objective question solution.

In **Step 1,** you must carefully read the **"Instructions"** that precede your particular objective CPA exam portion.

In **Step 2,** you must read the question and its requirements carefully. Look out for questions that require you to provide those options **not** applicable, **not** true, etc...

In **Step 3,** you must anticipate the correct answer **after** reading the question **but before** reading the possible answers.

In **Step 4,** you must read the answer carefully and select the alternative that best answers the question asked. Ideally, the best alternative will immediately present itself because it roughly or exactly corresponds with the answer you anticipated before looking at the other possible choices.

In **Step 5,** you select the best alternative. If there are two close possibilities, make sure you select the **best** one in light of the **facts** and **requirements** of the question.

In **Step 6,** you must make sure you answer each question in the testlet, with due regard to time constraints.

Sample Objective Question Solution

Solution: The answer is (c). The question asks for the computation of the estimated *credit* to *Accounts Receivable*—not the estimated amount of cash received—as a result of November collections. Therefore, cash discounts are disregarded. The doubtful accounts adjustment of 1% can also be discarded because it would be a credit to *Allowance for Doubtful Accounts,* not to *Accounts Receivable.*

Collections from Nov. sales	12% ×	$100,000	$12,000
Collections from Oct. sales	75% ×	90,000	67,500
Collections from Sept. sales	6% ×	80,000	4,800
Collections from Aug. sales	4% ×	95,000	3,800
			$88,100

Benefits of the Solutions Approach™

The **Solutions Approach™** may seem cumbersome the first time you attempt it; candidates frequently have a tendency to write as they think. Such a haphazard approach often results in a disorganized answer. The Solutions Approach™ will help you write a solution that parallels the question requirements. It will also help you recall information under the pressure of the exam. The technique assists you in directing your thoughts toward the information required for the answer. Without a Solutions Approach™, you are apt to become distracted or confused by details that are irrelevant to the answer. Finally, the Solutions Approach™ is a **faster** way to answer exam questions. You will not waste time on false starts or rewrites. The approach may seem time-consuming at first, but as you become comfortable using it, you will see that it actually saves time and results in a better answer.

We urge you to give the **Solutions Approach™** a good try by using it throughout your CPA review. As you practice, you may adapt or modify it to your own preferences and requirements. The important thing is to develop a system so that you do not approach exam questions with a storehouse of knowledge that you can not express to the graders.

———————————

SECTION FIVE: CONTENT SPECIFICATION OUTLINE

The AICPA Board of Examiners has developed a **Content Specification Outline** for each section of the exam to be tested. These outlines list the areas, groups, and topics to be tested and indicate the approximate percentage of the total test score devoted to each area. The content of the examination is based primarily on the results of national studies of public accounting practice and the evaluation of CPA practitioners and educators.

BUSINESS ENVIRONMENT & CONCEPTS

I. Business Structure (17% - 23%)

A. Advantages, Implications, and Constraints of Legal Structures for Business

  1. Sole Proprietorships and General and Limited Partnerships
  2. Limited Liability Companies (LLC), Limited Liability Partnerships (LLP), and Joint Ventures
  3. Subchapter C and Subchapter S Corporations

B. Formation, Operation, and Termination of Businesses

C. Financial Structure, Capitalization, Profit and Loss Allocation, and Distributions

D. Rights, Duties, Legal Obligations and Authority of Owners and Management (Directors, Officers, Stockholders, Partners, and Other Owners)

II. Economic Concepts Essential to Obtaining an Understanding of an Entity's Business and Industry (8% - 12%)

A. Business Cycles and Reasons for Business Fluctuations

B. Economic Measures and Reasons for Changes in the Economy, Such as Inflation, Deflation and Interest Rate Changes

C. Market Influences on Business Strategies, Including Selling, Supply Chain, and Customer Management Strategies

D. Implications to Business of Dealings in Foreign Currencies, Hedging and Exchange Rate Fluctuations

III. Financial Management (17% - 23%)

A. Financial Modeling, Including Factors Such as Financial Indexes, Taxes and Opportunity Costs, and Models Such as Economic Value Added, Cash Flow, Net Present Value, Discounted Payback, and Internal Rate of Return

  1. Objectives
  2. Techniques
  3. Limitations

B. Strategies for Short-Term and Long-Term Financing Options, Including Cost of Capital and Derivatives

C. Financial Statement and Business Implications of Liquid Asset Management

  1. Management of Cash and Cash Equivalents, Accounts Receivable, Accounts Payable, and Inventories
  2. Characteristics and Financial Statement and Business Implications of Loan Rates (Fixed vs. Variable) and Loan Covenants

IV. Information Technology (IT) Implications in the Business Environment (22% - 28%)

A. Role of Business Information Systems

  1. Reporting Concepts and Systems
  2. Transaction Processing Systems
  3. Management Reporting Systems
  4. Risks

B. Roles and Responsibilities Within the IT Function

    1. Roles and Responsibilities of Database/Network/Web Administrators, Computer Operators, Librarians, Systems Programmers and Applications Programmers

    2. Appropriate Segregation of Duties

C. IT Fundamentals

    1. Hardware and Software, Networks, and Data Structure, Analysis, and Application, Including Operating Systems, Security, File Organization, Types of Data Files, and Database Managements Systems

    2. Systems Operation, Including Transaction Processing Modes, Such as Batch, On-Line, Real-Time, and Distributed Processing, and Application Processing Phases, Such as Data Capture; Edit Routines; Master File Maintenance; Reporting, Accounting, Control, and Management; Query, Audit Trail, and Ad Hoc Reports; and Transaction Flow

D. Disaster Recovery and Business Continuity, Including Data Backup and Data Recovery Procedures, Alternate Processing Facilities (Hot Sites), and Threats and Risk Management

E. Financial Statement and Business Implications of Electronic Commerce, Including Electronic Fund Transfers, Point of Sale Transactions, Internet-Based Transactions and Electronic Data Interchange

V. **Planning and Measurement (22% - 28%)**

A. Planning and Budgeting

    1. Planning Techniques, Including Strategic and Operational Planning

    2. Forecasting and Projection Techniques

    3. Budgeting and Budget Variance Analysis

B. Performance Measures

    1. Organizational Performance Measures, Including Financial and Nonfinancial Scorecards

    2. Benchmarking, Including Quality Control Principles, Best Practices, and Benchmarking Techniques

C. Cost Measurement

    1. Cost Measurement Concepts (Standard, Joint Product, and By-Product Costing)

    2. Accumulating and Assigning Costs (Job Order, Process, and Activity-Based Costing)

    3. Factors Affecting Production Costs

APPENDIX C
WRITING SKILLS

CONTENTS

INTRODUCTION

Before skipping this appendix, review at least the following writing samples and the "Writing an Answer to an Exam Question" starting on page C-5. Be sure to take the Diagnostic Quiz on C-8.

In place of essays, an assessment of written communication skills has been incorporated into the simulation portion of the examination. These skills are tested by written communications which require the candidate to write memoranda, letters to clients, or other communications an entry-level CPA would write on the job. Simulations are presented in the Financial Accounting & Reporting, Auditing & Attestation, and Regulation sections. The Business Environment & Concepts exam section eventually will have simulations, and therefore, written communication questions.

For this simulation element, candidates must read a situation description and then write an appropriate document relating to the situation. The instructions will state in what form the document should be presented and its focus. The candidate's response should provide the correct information in writing that is clear, complete, and professional. Only those writing samples that are in your own words and responsive to the topic will be graded. If the response is off-topic, or offers advice that is clearly illegal, no credit will be given for the response.

Constructed responses will be scored holistically. Scores will be based on three general writing criteria: organization, development, and expression.

1. **Organization:** The document's structure, ordering of ideas, and linking of one idea to another:

    Overview/thesis statement
    Unified paragraphs (topic and supporting sentences)
    Transitions and connectives

2. **Development:** The document's supporting evidence/information to clarify thoughts:

    Details
    Definitions
    Examples
    Rephrasing

3. **Expression:** The document's use of conventional standards of business English:

    Grammar (sentence construction, subject/verb agreement, pronouns, modifiers)
    Punctuation (final, comma)
    Word usage (incorrect, imprecise language)
    Capitalization
    Spelling

WRITING SKILLS SAMPLES

The following problems taken from past exams are answered in various ways to illustrate good, fair, and poor writing skills.

Essex Company has a compensation plan for future vacations for its employees. What conditions must be met for Essex to accrue compensation for future vacations? FAR Problem—From Chapter 7—Liabilities

Good: Essex must accrue compensation for future vacations if all of the following criteria are met. Essex's obligation relating to employees' rights to receive compensation for future vacations is attributable to employees' services already rendered. The obligation relates to rights that vest or accumulate. Payment of the vacation benefits is probable. The amount can be reasonably estimated.

Explanation: This essay is coherent, concise, and well organized. The first sentence uses the wording of the question to introduce the elements of the answer. Each point is then made clearly and concisely. There are no unnecessary words or elements. The language and vocabulary are appropriate, and there are no mistakes in grammar or spelling.

Fair: In order for Essex to accrue compensation for future vacations, they must attribute their obligation to employees services already rendered, recognize that the obligation relates to vested and accumulated rights, and that payment is probable and the amount can be reasonably estimated.

Explanation: This passage is also coherent and concise; however, it lacks the clarity and detail of the previous answer. The language is appropriate, but the grammatical construction is somewhat weak.

Poor: It is based on accrual. The employees must have vested or accumulated rights. They must be able to estimate amounts of compensation and their payment. Vested rights means that the employer must pay the employees even if he is fired or quits.

Explanation: This answer is so poorly worded and disorganized as to be virtually incoherent. There are also some grammar mistakes. The final sentence is additional information but not necessary to answer the question.

PARAGRAPHS

The kind of writing you do for the CPA exam is called **expository writing** (writing in which something is explained in straightforward terms). Expository writing uses the basic techniques we will be discussing here. Other kinds of writing (i.e., narration, description, argument, and persuasion) will sometimes require different techniques.

Consider a paragraph as a division of an essay that consists of one or more sentences, deals with one point, and begins on a new, indented line. Paragraphs provide a way to write about a subject one point or one thought at a time.

Usually, a paragraph begins with a **topic sentence.** The topic sentence communicates the main idea of the paragraph, and the remainder of the paragraph explains or illuminates that central idea. The paragraph sometimes finishes with a restatement of the topic sentence. This strategy is easily read by the exam graders.

Often the topic sentence of the first paragraph is the central idea of the entire composition. Each succeeding paragraph then breaks down this idea into subtopics with each of the new topic sentences being the central thought of that subtopic.

Let's take a look at a simple paragraph to see how it's put together.

    The deductibility of home mortgage interest has been under recent review by Congress as a way to raise revenue. There have been two major reasons for this scrutiny. First, now that consumer interest is nondeductible and investment interest is limited to net investment income, taxpayers have been motivated to rearrange their finances to maximize their tax deductions. Second, most voters do not own homes costing more than $500,000 and, therefore, putting a cap on mortgage loans does not affect the mass of voters. Given the pressure to raise revenue, two major changes have occurred in this area.

The first sentence of the example is the **topic sentence.** The second sentence introduces the supporting examples which appear in the next two sentences beginning with *first* and *second.* The final sentence of the paragraph acts as a preview to the contents of the next paragraph.

Now, let's examine the makeup of a single paragraph answer to an essay question from a previous CPA Exam.

Question: Dunhill fraudulently obtained a negotiable promissory note from Beeler by misrepresentation of a material fact. Dunhill subsequently negotiated the note to Gordon, a holder in due course. Pine, a business associate of Dunhill, was aware of the fraud perpetrated by Dunhill. Pine purchased the note for value from Gordon. Upon presentment, Beeler has defaulted on the note.

Required: Answer the following, setting forth reasons for any conclusions stated.

1. What are the rights of Pine against Beeler?
2. What are the rights of Pine against Dunhill?

Examples of possible answers:

1.   The rights of Pine against Beeler arise from Pine's having acquired the note from Gordon, who was a holder in due course. Pine himself is not a holder in due course because he had knowledge of a defense against the note. The rule wherein a transferee, not a holder in due course, acquires the rights of one by taking from a holder in due course is known as the "shelter rule." Through these rights, Pine is entitled to recover the proceeds of the note from Beeler. The defense of fraud in the inducement is a personal defense and not valid against a holder in due course.

The first sentence of the paragraph is the topic sentence in which the basic answer to the question is given. The third and fourth sentence explains the rule governing Pine's rights. (The *shelter rule* would be considered a *key phrase* in this answer.) The final sentence of the paragraph is not really necessary to answer the question but was added as an explanation of what some might mistakenly believe to be the key to the answer.

2.   As one with the rights of a holder in due course, Pine is entitled to proceed against any person whose signature appears on the note, provided he gives notice of dishonor. When Dunhill negotiated the note to Gordon, Dunhill's signature on the note made him secondarily liable. As a result, if Pine brings suit against Dunhill, Pine will prevail because of Dunhill's secondary liability.

The first sentence of this paragraph restates the fact that Pine has the rights of a holder in due course and what these rights mean. The second sentence explains what happened when Dunhill negotiated the note, and the third sentence states the probable outcome of these results.

Note that in both answers 1. and 2., the sentences hang together in a logical fashion and lead the reader easily from one thought to the next. This is called coherence, a primary factor in considerations of conciseness and clarity.

Transitions

To demonstrate how to use **transitions** in a paragraph to carry the reader easily from one thought or example to another, let's consider a slightly longer and more detailed paragraph. The transitions are indicated in italics.

A concerted effort to reduce book income in response to AMT could have a significant impact on corporations. *For example,* the auditor-client relationship may change. *Currently,* it isn't unusual for corporate management to argue for higher rather than lower book earnings, *while* the auditor would argue for conservative reported numbers. Such a corporate reporting posture may change as a consequence of the BURP adjustment. *Furthermore,* stock market analysts often rely on a price/earnings ratio. Lower earnings for essentially the same level of activity may have a significant effect on security prices.

The first sentence of the paragraph is the topic sentence. The next sentence, beginning with the transition *for example,* introduces the example with a broad statement. The following sentence, beginning with *currently,* gives a specific example to support the basic premise. The sentence beginning *furthermore* leads us into a final example. Without these transitions, the paragraph would be choppy and lack coherence.

What follows is a list of some transitions divided by usage. We suggest you commit some of these to memory so that you will never be at a loss as to how to tie your ideas together.

Transitional Words & Phrases

One idea plus one idea:

again	equally important	in addition	likewise	similarly
also	finally	in the same fashion	moreover	third
and	first	in the same respect	next	thirdly
and then	further	last	second	too
besides	furthermore	lastly	secondly	

To show time or place:

after a time	at that time	immediately	presently	thereafter
after a while	at the same time	in due time	second	thereupon
afterwards	before	in the meantime	shortly	to the left
as long as	earlier	lately	since	until
as soon as	eventually	later	soon	when
at last	finally	meanwhile	temporarily	while
at length	first	next	then	
	further	of late		

To contrast or qualify:

after all	at the same time	however	nevertheless	on the other hand
although true	but	in any case	nonetheless	otherwise
and yet	despite this fact	in contrast	notwithstanding	still
anyway	for all that	in spite of	on the contrary	yet

To introduce an illustration

for example	in particular	incidentally	specifically	to illustrate
for instance	in other words	indeed	that is	
in fact	in summary	namely	thus	

To indicate concession

after all	I admit
although this may be	naturally
at the same time	of course
even though	

To indicate comparison:

in a likewise manner
likewise
similarly

WRITING AN ANSWER TO AN EXAM QUESTION

Now that we have examined the makeup of an answer to an exam question, let's take another essay question from a past CPA Exam and see how to go about writing a clear, comprehensive answer, step by step, sentence by sentence. A question similar to the one that follows would very likely be one the examiners would choose to grade writing skills.

Question:

Bar Manufacturing and Cole Enterprises were arch rivals in the high technology industry, and both were feverishly working on a new product that would give the first to develop it a significant competitive advantage. Bar engaged Abel Consultants on April 1, 20X3, for one year, commencing immediately, at $7,500 a month to aid the company in the development of the new product. The contract was oral and was consummated by a handshake. Cole approached Abel and offered them a $10,000 bonus for signing, $10,000 a month for nine months, and a $40,000 bonus if Cole was the first to successfully market the new product. In this connection, Cole stated that the oral contract Abel made with Bar was unenforceable and that Abel could walk away from it without liability. In addition, Cole made certain misrepresentations regarding the dollar amount of its commitment to the project, the state of its development, and the expertise of its research staff. Abel accepted the offer.

Four months later, Bar successfully introduced the new product. Cole immediately dismissed Abel and has paid nothing beyond the first four $10,000 payments plus the initial bonus. Three lawsuits ensued: Bar sued Cole, Bar sued Abel, and Abel sued Cole.

Required: Answer the following, setting forth reasons for any conclusions stated.

Discuss the various theories on which each of the three lawsuits is based, the defenses that will be asserted, the measure of possible recovery, and the probable outcome of the litigation.

Composing an Answer:

Analyze requirements.

Plan on one paragraph for each lawsuit. Each paragraph will contain four elements: theory, defenses, recovery, and outcome.

Paragraph one:

Step 1: Begin with the first lawsuit mentioned, Bar vs. Cole. Write a topic sentence that will sum up the theory of the suit.

> **Topic sentence:** Bar's lawsuit against Cole will be based upon the intentional tort of wrongful interference with a contractual relationship.

Step 2: Back up this statement with law and facts from the question scenario.

> The primary requirement for this cause of action is a valid contractual relationship with which the defendant knowingly interferes. This requirement is met in the case of Cole.

Step 3: State defenses.

> The contract is not required to be in writing since it is for exactly one year from the time of its making. It is, therefore, valid even though oral.

Step 4: Introduce subject of recovery (damages).

> Cole's knowledge of the contract is obvious.

Step 5: Explain possible problems to recovery.

The principal problem, however, is damages. Since Bar was the first to market the product successfully, it would seem that damages are not present. It is possible there were actual damages incurred by Bar (for example, it hired another consulting firm at an increased price).

Step 6: Discuss possible outcome.

It also might be possible that some courts would permit the recovery of punitive damages since this is an intentional tort.

Paragraph one completed:

Bar's lawsuit against Cole will be based upon the intentional tort of wrongful interference with a contractual relationship. The primary requirement for this cause of action is a valid contractual relationship with which the defendant knowingly interferes. The requirement is met in the case of Cole. The contract is not required to be in writing since it is for exactly one year from the time of its making. It is, therefore, valid even though oral. Cole's knowledge of the contract is obvious. The principal problem, however, is damages. Since Bar was the first to market the product successfully, it would seem that damages are not present. It is possible there were actual damages incurred by Bar (for example, it hired another consulting firm at an increased price). It also might be possible that some courts would permit the recovery of punitive damages since this is an intentional tort.

Paragraph two:

Step 1: Discuss second lawsuit mentioned, Bar vs. Abel. Write a topic sentence that will sum up the theory of the suit.

Topic sentence: Bar's cause of action against Abel would be for breach of contract.

Step 2: State defenses. [Same as for first paragraph; this could be left out.]

The contract is not required to be in writing since it is for exactly one year from the time of its making. It is, therefore, valid even though oral.

Step 3: Introduce subject of recovery (damages).

Once again, [*indicating similarity and tying second paragraph to first*] damages would seem to be a serious problem.

Step 4: Explain possible problems to recovery.

Furthermore, punitive damages would rarely be available in a contract action. Finally, Bar cannot recover the same damages twice.

Step 5: Discuss possible outcome.

Hence, if it proceeds against Cole and recovers damages caused by Abel's breach of contract, it will not be able to recover a second time.

Paragraph two completed:

Bar's cause of action against Abel would be for breach of contract. [The contract is not required to be in writing since it is for exactly one year from the time of its making. It is, therefore, valid even though oral.] Once again, damages would seem to be a serious problem. Furthermore, punitive damages would rarely be available in a contract action. Finally, Bar cannot recover the same damages twice. Hence, if it proceeds against Cole and recovers damages caused by Abel's breach of contract, it will not be able to recover a second time.

Paragraph three:

Step 1: Discuss third lawsuit mentioned, Abel vs. Cole. Write a topic sentence that will sum up the theory of the suit.

Topic sentence: Abel's lawsuit against Cole will be based upon fraud and breach of contract.

Step 2: State defenses.

There were fraudulent statements made by Cole with the requisite intent and that were possibly to Abel's detriment. The breach of contract by Cole is obvious.

Step 3: Back up these statements with law and facts from the question scenario.

However, the contract that Cole induced Abel to enter into and which it subsequently breached was an illegal contract, that is, one calling for the commission of a tort.

Step 4: Explain possible problems to recovery and possible outcome.

Therefore, both parties are likely to be treated as wrongdoers, and Abel will be denied recovery.

Paragraph three completed:

Abel's lawsuit against Cole will be based upon fraud and breach of contract. There were fraudulent statements made by Cole with the requisite intent and that were possibly to Abel's detriment. The breach of contract by Cole is obvious. However, the contract that Cole induced Abel to enter into and which it subsequently breached was an illegal contract, that is, one calling for the commission of a tort. Therefore, both parties are likely to be treated as wrongdoers, and Abel will be denied recovery.

Paragraph Editing:

After you have written your essay, go back over your work to check for the six characteristics that the AICPA will be looking for; coherent organization, conciseness, clarity, use of standard English, responsiveness to the requirements of the question, and appropriateness to the reader.

DIAGNOSTIC QUIZ

The following quiz is designed to test your knowledge of standard English. The correct answers follow the quiz, along with references to the sections that cover that particular area. By identifying the sections that are troublesome for you, you will be able to assess your weaknesses and concentrate on reviewing these areas. If you simply made a lucky guess, you'd better do a review anyway.

Circle the correct choice in the brackets for items 1 through 17.

1. The company can assert any defenses against third party beneficiaries that [they have/it has] against the promisee.

2. Among those securities [which/that] are exempt from registration under the 1933 Act [are/is] a class of stock given in exchange for another class by the issuer to its existing stockholders without the [issuer's/ issuer] paying a commission.

3. This type of promise will not bind the promisor [as/because/since] there is no mutuality of obligation.

4. Under the cost method, treasury stock is presented on the balance sheet as an unallocated reduction of total [stockholders'/stockholders/stockholder's] equity.

5. Jones wished that he [was/were] not bound by the offer he made Smith, while Smith celebrated [his/him] having accepted the offer.

6. [Non-cash/Noncash] investing and financing transactions are not reported in the statement of cash flows because the statement reports only the [affects/effects] of operating, investing, and financing activities that directly [affect/effect] cash flows.

7. Since [its/it's] impossible to predict the future and because prospective financial statements can be [effected/ affected] by numerous factors, the accountant must use [judgment/judgement] to estimate when and how conditions are [likely/liable] to change.

8. A common format of bank reconciliation statements [is/are] to reconcile both book and bank balances to a common amount known as the "true balance."

9. Corporations, clubs, churches, and other entities may be beneficiaries so long as they are sufficiently identifiable to permit a determination of [who/whom] is empowered to enforce the terms of the trust.

10. None of the beneficiaries [was/were] specifically referred to in the will.

11. Either Dr. Kline or Dr. Monroe [have/has] been elected to the board of directors.

12. The letter should be signed by Bill and [me/myself].

13. Any trust [which/that] is created for an illegal purpose is invalid.

14. When the nature of relevant information is such that it cannot appear in the accounts, this [principal/ principle] dictates that such relevant information be included in the accompanying notes to the financial statements. Financial reporting is the [principal/principle] means of communicating financial information to those outside an entity.

15. The inheritance was divided [between/among] several beneficiaries.

16. Termination of an offer ends the offeree's power to [accept/except] it.

17. The consideration given by the participating creditors is [their/there] mutual promises to [accept/except] less than the full amount of [their/there] claims. Because [their/there] must be such mutual promises [between/ among] all the participating creditors, a composition or extension agreement requires the participation of at least two or more creditors.

Follow instructions for items 18 through 20.

18. The duties assigned to the interns were to accompany the seniors on field work assignments and the organization and filing of the work papers.

    Fix this sentence so that it will read more smoothly. _____

    _____

    _____

19. Circle the correct spelling of the following pairs of words.

    liaison laison   privilege priviledge   paralleled paraleled

    achieve acheive   occasion occassion   accommodate accomodate

20. Each set of brackets in the following example represents a possible location for punctuation. If you believe a location needs no punctuation, leave it blank; if you think a location needs punctuation, enter a comma, a colon, or a semicolon.

    If the promises supply the consideration [ ] there must be a mutuality of obligation [ ] in other words [ ] both parties must be bound.

ANSWERS TO DIAGNOSTIC QUIZ

Each answer includes a reference to the section that covers what you need to review.

1.	it has	Pronouns—Antecedents, p. C-27.
2.	that; is; issuer's	Subordinating Conjunctions, p. C-30; Verbs—Agreement, p. C-23; Nouns—Gerunds, p. C-26.
3.	because	Subordinating Conjunctions, p. C-30.
4.	stockholders'	Possessive Nouns, p. C-25.
5.	were; his	Verbs, Mood, p. C-22; Nouns—Gerunds, p. C-26.
6.	Noncash; effects; affect	Hyphen, p. C-20; Syntax: Troublesome Words, p. C-13.
7.	it's; affected; judgment, likely	Syntax: Troublesome Words, p. C-13; Spelling: Troublesome Words, p. C-22; Diction: List of Words, p. C-11.
8.	is	Verbs—Agreement, p. C-23.
9.	who	Pronouns, Who/Whom, p. C-26.
10.	were	Verbs—Agreement with Each/None, p. C-24.
11.	has	Verbs—Agreement, p. C-23.
12.	me	Pronouns, that follow prepositions, p. C-27.
13.	that	Subordinating Conjunctions, p. C-30.
14.	principle; principal	Syntax: Troublesome Words, p. C-12.
15.	among	Diction: List of Words, p. C-10.
16.	accept	Syntax: Troublesome Words, C-12

17. their; accept; their; there; among;   Syntax: Troublesome Words, p. C-12; Diction: List of Words, p. C-10.

18. Two possible answers: Parallelism: p. C-15.

The duties assigned to the interns were *accompanying* the seniors on field work assignments and *organizing* and filing the work papers.
or
The duties assigned to the interns were to accompany the seniors on field work assignments and *to organize* and *file* the work papers.

19. In every case, the **first choice** is the correct spelling.
Refer to Spelling: Troublesome Words, p. C-21.

20. If the promises supply the consideration [,] there must be a mutuality of obligation [;] in other words [,] both parties must be bound.   Refer to Punctuation, p. C-16.

Scoring

Count one point for each item (some numbers contain more than one item) and one point for question number 18 if your sentence came close to the parallelism demonstrated by the answer choices. There are a total of 40 points.

If you scored 37-40, you did very well. A brief review of the items you missed should be sufficient to make you feel fairly confident about your grammar skills.

If you scored 33-36, you did fairly well—better than average—but you should do a thorough review of the items you missed.

If you scored 29-32, your score was average. Since "average" will probably not make it on the CPA exam, you might want to consider a thorough grammar review, in addition to the items you missed.

If you scored below average (28 or less), you **definitely** should make grammar review a high priority when budgeting your exam study time. You should consider using resources beyond those provided here.

SENTENCE STRUCTURE

A sentence is a statement or question, consisting of a subject and a predicate. A subject, at a minimum is a noun, usually accompanied by one or more modifiers (for example, "The Trial Balance"). A predicate consists, at a minimum, of a verb. Cultivate the habit of a quick verification for a subject, predicate, capitalized first word, and ending punctuation in each sentence of an essay. A study of sentence structure is essentially a study of grammar but also moves just beyond grammar to diction, syntax, and parallelism. As we discuss how sentences are structured, there will naturally be some overlapping with grammar.

DICTION

Diction is appropriate word choice. There is no substitute for a diversified vocabulary. If you have a diversified vocabulary or "a way with words," you are already a step ahead. A good general vocabulary, as well as a good accounting vocabulary, is a prerequisite of the CPA exam. Develop your vocabulary as you review for the Exam.

An important aspect of choosing the right words is knowing the audience for whom you are choosing those "perfect words." A perfect word for accountants is not necessarily the perfect word for mechanics or lawyers or English professors. If a CPA exam question asks you to write a specific document for a reader other than another accountant or CPA, you need to be very specific but less technical than you would be otherwise.

Accounting, auditing, and related areas have a certain diction and syntax peculiar unto themselves. Promulgations, for instance, are written very carefully so as to avoid possible misinterpretations or misunderstandings. Of course, you are not expected to write like this—for the CPA exam or in other situations. Find the best word possible to explain clearly and concisely what it is you are trying to say. Often the "right word" is simply just not the "wrong word," so be certain you know the exact meaning of a word before you use it. As an accountant writing for accountants, what is most important is knowing the technical terms and the "key words" and placing them in your sentences properly and effectively. Defining or explaining key words demonstrates to graders that you understand the words you are using and not merely parroting the jargon.

The following is a list of words that frequently either are mistaken for one another or incorrectly assumed to be more or less synonymous.

Among—preposition, refers to more than two
Between—preposition, refers to two; is used for three or more if the items are considered severally and individually

> If only part of the seller's capacity to perform is affected, the seller must allocate deliveries *among* the customers, and he or she must give each one reasonable notice of the quota available to him or her.
> *Between* merchants, the additional terms become part of the contract unless one of the following applies. (This sentence is correct whether there are two merchants or many merchants.)

Amount—noun, an aggregate; total number or quantity
Number—noun, a sum of units; a countable number
Quantity—noun, an indefinite amount or number

> The checks must be charged to the account in the order of lowest *amount* to highest *amount* to minimize the *number* of dishonored checks.
> The contract is not enforceable under this paragraph beyond the *quantity* of goods shown in such writing.

Allude—verb, to state indirectly
Refer—verb, to state clearly and directly

> She *alluded* to the fact that the company's management was unscrupulous.
> She *referred* to his poor management in her report.

Bimonthly—adjective or adverb; every two months
Semimonthly—adjective or adverb; twice a month

> Our company has *bimonthly* meetings.
> We get paid *semimonthly.*

Continual—adjective, that which is repeatedly renewed after each interruption or intermission
Continuous—adjective, that which is uninterrupted in time, space, or sequence

> The *continuous* ramblings of the managing partner caused the other partners to *continually* check the time.

Cost—noun, the amount paid for an item
Price—noun, the amount set for an item
Value—noun, the relative worth, utility, or importance of an item
Worth—noun, value of an item measured by its qualities or by the esteem in which it is held

> The *cost* of that stock is too much.
> The *price* of that stock is $100 a share.
> I place no *value* on that stock.
> That stock's *worth* is overestimated.

Decide—verb, to arrive at a solution
Conclude—verb, to reach a final determination; to exercise judgment

Barbara *decided* to listen to what the accountant was saying; she then *concluded* that what he was saying was true.

Fewer—adjective, not as many; consisting or amounting to a smaller number (used of numbers; comparative of few)
Less—adjective, lower rank, degree, or importance; a more limited amount (used of quantity—for the most part)

My clients require *fewer* consultations than yours do.
My clients are *less* demanding than yours are.

Good—adjective, of a favorable character or tendency; noun, something that is good
Well—adverb, good or proper manner; satisfactorily with respect to conduct or action; adjective, being in satisfactory condition or circumstances

It was *good* [adjective] of you to help me study for the CPA exam.
The decision was for the *good* [noun] of the firm.
He performed that task *well* [adverb].
His work was *well* [adjective] respected by the other accountants.

Imply—verb, to suggest
Infer—verb, to assume; deduce

Her report seems to *imply* that my work was not up to par.
From reading her report, the manager *inferred* that my work was not up to par.

Oral—adjective, by the mouth, spoken; not written
Verbal—adjective, relating to or consisting of words
Vocal—adjective, uttered by the voice, spoken; persistence and volume of speech

Hawkins, Inc. made an *oral* agreement to the contract.
One partner gave his *verbal* consent while the other partner was very *vocal* with his objections.

State—verb, to set forth in detail; completely
Assert—verb, to claim positively, sometimes aggressively or controversially
Affirm—verb, to validate, confirm, state positively

The attorney *stated* the facts of the case.
The plaintiff asserted that his rights had been violated.
The judge *affirmed* the jury's decision.

SYNTAX

Syntax is the order of words in a sentence. Errors in syntax occur in a number of ways; the number one way is through hasty composition. The only way to catch errors in word order is to read each of your sentences carefully to make sure that the words you meant to write or type are the words that actually appear on the page and that those words are in the best possible order. The following list should help you avoid errors in both diction and syntax and gives examples where necessary.

Troublesome Words

Accept—verb, to receive or to agree to willingly
Except—verb, to take out or leave out from a number or a whole; conjunction, on any other condition but that condition

Except for the items we have mentioned, we will *accept* the conditions of the contract.

Advice—noun, information or recommendation
Advise—verb, to recommend, give advice

The *accountant advised* us to take his *advice*.

Affect—verb, to influence or change (**Note:** affect is occasionally used as a noun in technical writing only.)
Effect—noun, result or cause; verb, to cause

The effect [noun] of Ward, Inc.'s decision to cease operations affected many people.
He quickly *effected* [verb] policy changes for office procedures.

All Ready—adjectival phrase, completely prepared
Already—adverb, before now; previously

Although the tax return was *all ready* to be filed, the deadline had *already* passed.

All Right; Alright—adjective or adverb, beyond doubt; very well; satisfactory; agreeable, pleasing. (Although many grammarians insist that **alright** is not a proper form, it is widely accepted.)

Appraise—verb, set a value on
Apprise—verb, inform

Dane Corp. *apprised* him of the equipment's age, so that he could *appraise* it more accurately.

Assure—verb, to give confidence to positively
Ensure—verb, to make sure, certain, or safe
Insure—verb, to obtain or provide insurance on or for; to make certain by taking necessary measures and precautions

The accountant assured his client that he would file his return in a timely manner.
He added the figures more than once to *ensure* their accuracy.
She was advised to *insure* her diamond property.

Decedent—noun, a deceased person
Descendant—noun, proceeding from an ancestor or source

The decedent left her vast fortune to her *descendants*.

Eminent—adjective, to stand out; important
Imminent—adjective, impending

Although he was an *eminent* businessman, foreclosure on his house was *imminent.*

Its—possessive
It's—contraction, **it is**

The company held *its* board of directors meeting on Saturday. *It's* the second meeting this month.

Lay—verb, to place or set
Lie—verb, to recline

He *lies* down to rest.
He *lays* down the book.

Percent—used with numbers only
Percentage—used with words or phrases

Each employee received 2 *percent* of the profits.
They all agreed this was a small *percentage*.

Precedence—noun, the fact of preceding in time, priority of importance
Precedent—noun, established authority; adjective, prior in time, order, or significance

>The board of directors meeting took *precedence* over his going away.
>The president set a *precedent* when making that decision.

Principal—noun, a capital sum placed at interest; a leading figure; the corpus of an estate; adjective, first, most important
Principle—noun, a basic truth or rule

>Paying interest on the loan's *principal* [noun] was explained to the company's *principals* [noun].
>The principal [adjective] part of…
>She refused to compromise her *principles*.

Than—conjunction, function word to indicate difference in kind, manner, or identity; preposition, in comparison with (indicates comparison)
Then—adverb, at that time; soon after that (indicates time)

>BFE Corp. has more shareholders *than* Hills Corp.
>First, we must write the report, and *then* we will meet with the clients.

Their—adjective, of or relating to them or themselves
There—adverb, in or at that place

>*There* were fifty shareholders at the meeting to cast *their* votes.

Modifier Placement

Pay close attention to where modifiers are placed, especially adverbs such as **only** and **even**. In speech, inflection aids meaning but, in writing, placing modifiers improperly can be confusing and often changes the meaning. The modifier should usually be placed before the word(s) it modifies.

>She *almost* finished the whole report.
>She finished *almost* the whole report.

>*Only* she finished the report.
>She *only* finished the report.
>She finished *only* the report.

Phrases also must be placed properly, usually, but not always, following the word or phrase they modify. Often, **reading the sentence aloud** will help you decide where the modifier belongs.

>Fleming introduced a client to John with a counter-offer. (*With a counter-offer* modifies *client,* not *John,* and should be placed after *client.*)
>The accountant recommended a bankruptcy petition to the client under Chapter 7. (*Under Chapter 7* modifies *bankruptcy petition,* not *the client,* and should be placed after *bankruptcy petition.*)

Split Infinitives

Infinitives are the root verb form (e.g., to be, to consider, to walk). Generally speaking, infinitives should not be split except when to do so makes the meaning clearer.

Awkward: Management's responsibility is to clearly represent its financial position.
Better: Management's responsibility is to represent its financial position clearly.

Exception: Management's responsibility in the future is to better represent its financial position.

Sentence Fragments

To avoid sentence fragments, read over your work carefully. Each sentence needs at least (1) a subject and (2) a predicate.

> Unlike the case of a forged endorsement, a drawee bank charged with the recognition of its drawer-customer's signature. (The verb *is*, before the word *charged,* has been left out.)

PARALLELISM

Parallelism refers to a similarity in structure and meaning of all parts of a sentence or a paragraph. In parallelism, parts of a sentence (or a paragraph) that are parallel in meaning are also parallel in structure. Sentences that violate rules of parallelism will be difficult to read and may obscure meaning. The following are some examples of different **violations** of parallelism.

(1) A security interest can be effected through a financing statement or the creditor's taking possession of it. (The two prepositional phrases separated by **or** should be parallel.)

Corrected: A security interest can be effected through a financing statement or through possession by the creditor.

(2) The independent auditor should consider whether the scope is appropriate, adequate audit programs and working papers, appropriate conclusions, and reports prepared are consistent with results of the work performed. (The clause beginning with **whether** (which acts as the direct object of the verb **should consider**) is faulty. The items mentioned must be similarly constructed to each other.)

Corrected: The independent auditor should consider whether the scope is appropriate, audit programs and working papers are adequate, conclusions are appropriate, and reports prepared are consistent with results of the work performed.

(3) The CPA was responsible for performing the inquiry and analytical procedures and that the review report was completed in a timely manner. (The prepositional phrase beginning with **for** is faulty.)

Corrected: The CPA was responsible for performing the inquiry and analytical procedures and ensuring that the review report was completed in a timely manner.

(4) Procedures that should be applied in examining the stock accounts are as follows:

   (1) Review the corporate charter…
   (2) Obtain or preparing an analysis of…
   (3) Determination of authorization for… (All items in a list must be in parallel structure.)

   Corrected:

   1. Review the corporate charter…
   2. Obtain or prepare an analysis of…
   3. Determine the authorization for…

There are many other types of faulty constructions that can creep into sentences—too many to detail here. Furthermore, if any of the above is not clear, syntax may be a problem for you and you might want to consider a more thorough review of this subject.

NUMBERS

1. The basic rule for writing numbers is to write out the numbers ten and under and use numerals for all the others. More formal writing may dictate writing out all round numbers and numbers under 101. Let style, context of the sentence and of the work, and common sense be your guide.

The partnership was formed 18 years ago.
Jim Bryant joined the firm four years ago.
Baker purchased 200 shares of stock.

2.   When there are two numbers next to each other, alternate the styles.

three 4-year certificates of deposit   5 two-party instruments

3.   Never begin a sentence with numerals, such as:

1989 was the last year that Zinc Co. filed a tax return.

This example can be corrected as follows:

Nineteen hundred and eighty-nine was the last year that Zinc Co. filed a tax return. (For use only in very formal writing)
or
Zinc Co. has not filed a tax return since 1989.

CAPITALIZATION

This section mentions only areas that seem to cause particular difficulties.

1.   The first word **after a colon** is capped only when it is the beginning of a complete sentence.

We discussed several possibilities at the meeting: Among them were liquidation, reorganization, and rehabilitation.
We discussed several possibilities at the meeting: liquidation, reorganization, and rehabilitation.

2.   The capitalization of titles and headings is especially tricky. In general, the first word and all other important words, no matter what length they are, should be capped. Beyond this general rule, there are several variations relating to the capitalization of pronouns. The important thing here is to pick a style and use it consistently within a single document, article, etc.

For example, the following pair of headings would both be acceptable depending on the style and consistency of style:

Securities to which SFAS 115 Applies   **or**   Securities to Which SFAS 115 Applies
Issues for Property other than Cash   **or**   Issues For Property Other Than Cash

PUNCTUATION

PERIOD

Probably the two most common errors involving periods occur when incorporating quotation marks and/or parentheses with periods.

1.   When a period is used with closing quotation marks, the period is always placed **inside,** regardless of whether the entire sentence is a quote or only the end of the sentence.

2.   When a period is used with parentheses, the period goes **inside** the closing parenthesis if the entire sentence is enclosed in parentheses. When only the last word or words is enclosed in parentheses, the period goes **outside** the closing parenthesis.

(See Chapter 34, Contracts.)
The answer to that question is in the section on contracts (Chapter 34).

EXCLAMATION POINT

An exclamation point is used for emphasis and when issuing a command. In many cases, this is determined by the author when he or she wants to convey urgency, irony, or stronger emotion than ordinarily would be inferred.

COLON

A colon is used to introduce something in the sentence—a list of related words, phrases, or items directly related to the first part of the sentence; a quotation; a **direct** question; or an example of what was stated in the first part of the sentence. The colon takes the place of **that is** or **such as** and should never be used **with** such phrases.

> The accountant discussed two possibilities with the clients: first, a joint voluntary bankruptcy petition under Chapter 7, and second,…

> The following will be discussed: life insurance proceeds; inheritance; and property.

> My CPA accounting review book states the following: "All leases that do not meet any of the four criteria for capital leases are operating leases."

Colons are used in formal correspondence after the salutation.

> Dear Mr. Bennett:
> To Whom it May Concern:

Note: When **that is** or **such as** is followed by a numeric list, it may be followed by a colon.

> When writing a sentence, if you're not sure whether or not a colon is appropriate, it probably isn't. When in doubt, change the sentence so that you're sure it doesn't need a colon.

SEMICOLON

A semicolon is used in a number of ways:

1. Use a **semicolon in place of a conjunction** when there are two or more closely related thoughts and each is expressed in a coordinate clause (a clause that could stand as a complete sentence).

    > A marketable title is one that is free from plausible or reasonable objections; it need not be perfect.

2. Use a **semicolon** as in the above example **with a conjunction** when the sentence is very long and complex. This promotes **clarity** by making the sentence easier to read.

    > Should the lease be prematurely terminated, the deposit may be retained only to cover the landlord's actual expenses or damages; *and* any excess must be returned to the tenant.

    > An assignment establishes privity of estate between the lessor and assignee; *[and]* therefore, the assignee becomes personally liable for the rent.

3. When there are commas in a series of items, use a **semicolon** to separate the main items.

    > Addison, Inc. has distribution centers in Camden, Maine; Portsmouth, New Hampshire; and Rock Island, Rhode Island.

COMMA

Informal English allows much freedom in the placement or the omission of commas, and the overall trend is away from commas. However, standard, formal English provides rules for its usage. Accounting "language" can be so complex that using commas and using them correctly and appropriately is a necessity to avoid obscurity and promote clarity. Accordingly, we encourage you to learn the basics about comma placement.

What follows is not a complete set of rules for commas but should be everything you need to know about commas to make your sentences clear and concise. Because the primary purpose of the comma is to clarify meaning, it is the opinion of the authors that in the case of a complex subject such as accounting, it is better to overpunctuate than to underpunctuate. If you are concerned about overpunctuation, try to reduce an unwieldy sentence to two or more sentences.

1.   Use a comma to **separate a compound sentence** (one with two or more independent coordinate clauses joined by a conjunction).

> Gil Corp. has current assets of $90,000, but the corporation has current liabilities of $180,000. Jim borrowed $60,000, and he used the proceeds to purchase outstanding common shares of stock.

> **Note:** In these examples, a comma would **not** be necessary if the **and** or the **but** were not followed by a noun or pronoun (the subject of the second clause). In other words, if by removing the conjunction, the sentence could be separated into two complete sentences, it needs a comma.

2.   Use a comma after an introductory word or phrase.

> During 1992, Rand Co. purchased $960,000 of inventory.
> On April 1, 1993, Wall's inventory had a fair value of $150,000.

> **Note:** Writers often choose to omit this comma when the introductory phrase is very short. Again, we recommend using the comma. It will never be incorrect in this position.

3.   Use a comma after an introductory adverbial clause.

> Although insurance contracts are not required by the Statute of Frauds to be in writing, most states have enacted statutes that now require such.

4.   Use commas to separate items, phrases, or clauses in a series.

> To be negotiable, an instrument must be in writing, signed by the maker or drawer, contain an unconditional promise or order to pay a sum certain in money on demand or at a specific time, and be payable to order or to bearer.

> **Note:** Modern practice often omits the last comma in the series (in the above example, the one before **and**). Again, for the sake of clarity, we recommend using this comma.

5.   In most cases, use a comma or commas to separate **a series of adjectives.**

> Silt Co. kept their inventory in an old, decrepit, brick building.
> He purchased several outstanding shares of common stock. (*No* commas are needed.)

When in doubt as to whether or not to use a comma after a particular adjective, try inserting the word **and** between the adjectives. If it makes sense, use a comma. (In the second example, above, **several and outstanding,** or **outstanding and several** don't make sense.)

---

6.   Use a comma or commas to set off any **word or words, phrase, or clause that interrupts the sentence** but does not change its essential meaning.

> SLD Industries, as drawer of the instrument, is only secondarily liable.

7.   Use commas to set off **geographical names** and **dates.**

> Feeney Co. moved its headquarters to Miami, Florida, on August 16, 1992.

QUOTATION MARKS

Quotation marks are used with **direct quotations; direct discourse and direct questions;** and **definitions or explanations of words.** Other uses of quotation marks are used rarely in the accounting profession and, therefore, are not discussed in this review.

HYPHEN

1.   Use a hyphen to separate words into syllables. It is best to check a dictionary, because some words do not split where you might imagine.

2.   Modern practice does not normally hyphenate prefixes and their root words, even when both the prefix and the root word begin with vowels. A common exception is when the root word begins with a capital letter or a date or number.

| prenuptial | nonexempt | semiannual |
| pre-1987 | nonnegotiable | non-American |

3.   Although modern practice is moving away from using hyphens for **compound adjectives** (a noun and an adjective in combination to make a single adjective), clarity dictates that hyphens still be used in many cases.

| long-term investments | two-party instrument |
| a noninterest-bearing note | short-term capital losses |

4.   Use a hyphen **only** when the compound adjective or compound adjective-adverb **precedes the noun.**

> The well-known company is going bankrupt.
> The company is well known for its quality products.

Note: There are certain word combinations that are always hyphenated, always one word, or always two words. Use the dictionary.

5.   **Suspended hyphens** are used to avoid repetition in compound adjectives. For example, instead of having to write **himself or herself,** especially when these forms are being used repeatedly as they often must be in our newly nongender-biased world, use **him- or herself.**

> 10-, 15-, and 18-year depreciation   first-, second-, and third-class

SPELLING

Just as many of us believe that arithmetic can be done always by our calculators, we also believe that spelling will be done by our word processors and, therefore, we needn't worry too much about it. There is no doubt that these devices are tremendous boons. However, sometimes a spell-checker cannot tell the difference between words that you have misspelled which are nonetheless real words, such as **there** and **their.** (See the list in this section of words often confused.)

Let's hit some highlights here of troublesome spellings with some brief tips that should help you become a better speller.

1.   **IE** or **EI**? If you are still confused by words containing the **ie** or **ei** combinations, you'd better relearn those old rhymes we ridiculed in grade school.

"**i** before **e** except after **c.**" (This works only for words where the ie-ei combination sounds like **ee.**)

ach**ie**ve   bel**ie**ve   ch**ie**f
ceiling   re**cei**ve   re**cei**pt

Of course there are always **exceptions** such as:

either   neither   seize   financier

When **ie** or **ei** have a different sound than **ee**, the above rule does not apply. For example:

fr**ie**nd   s**ie**ve   effic**ie**nt
for**ei**gn   sover**ei**gn   surf**ei**t

2. **Doubling final consonants.** When an ending (**suffix**) beginning with a vowel is added to a root word that ends in a single consonant, that final consonant is **usually doubled**.

lag—lagging   bid—bidding   top—topped

The exceptions generally fall under three rules.

First, double only after a short vowel and **not** after a double vowel.

big—bigger   tug—tugging   get—getting
need—needing   keep—keeping   pool—pooled

Second, a **long** vowel (one that "says its own name"), which is almost always followed by a silent **e** that must be dropped to add the suffix, is **not** doubled.

hope—hoping   tape—taped   rule—ruled

Note: Sometimes, as in the first two examples above, doubling the consonants would create entirely new words.

Third, with root words of two or more syllables ending in a single consonant, double the consonant **only** when the last syllable is the **stressed syllable.**

Double: be**gin**—beginning, beginner   pre**fer**—preferred, preferring
re**gret**—**regretted**, regrettable   ad**mit**—admitted, admittance
Don't   pro**hib**it—prohibited, prohibitive   **ben**efit—benefited, benefiting
Double: de**vel**op—developing   **pref**erence—preferable

3. **Drop** the silent **e** before adding a suffix **beginning with a vowel.**

store—storing   take—taking   value—valuing

Keep the **e** before adding a suffix **beginning with a consonant,** such as:

move—movement   achieve—achievement

Again, there are **exceptions**.

e: mile—mileage   dye—dyeing

No e: argue—argument   due—duly   true—truly

4. Change **y** to **ie** before adding **s** when it is the single final vowel.

country—countries   study—studies   quantity—quantities

Change **y** to **i** before adding other endings **except s.**

busy—business   dry—drier   copy—copier

Exceptions: Keep **y** for the following:

copying   studying   trying

Y is also usually preserved when it follows another vowel.

delays   joys   played

Exceptions:

day—daily   lay—laid   pay—paid   say—said

5.   **Forming Plurals.** The formation of some plurals does not follow the general rule of adding **s** or **es** to the singular. What follows are some of the more troublesome forms.

Some singular nouns that end in **o** form their plurals by adding **s**; some by adding **es**.

ratio**s**   zero**s**   hero**es**   potato**es**

Many nouns taken directly from **foreign languages** retain their original plural. Below are a few of the more common ones.

alumnus—alumni   basis—bases   crisis—crises
criterion—criteria   datum—data   matrix—matrices

Other nouns taken directly from foreign languages have **two acceptable plural forms:** the foreign language plural and the anglicized plural. Here are some of the more common:

medium—media, mediums   appendix—appendices, appendixes
formula—formulae, formulas   memorandum—memoranda, memorandums

Finally, in this foreign language category are some commonly used Latin nouns that form their plurals by adding **es.**

census—censuses   consensus—consensuses
hiatus—hiatuses   prospectus—prospectuses

Troublesome Words: Spelling

Spelling errors occur for different reasons; probably the most common reason is confusion with the spelling of similar words. The following is a list of commonly misspelled words. You will find those you may have misspelled in taking the Diagnostic Quiz, and you may recognize others you have problems with. Memorize them. (Note: some of these words may have acceptable alternative spellings; however, the spellings listed below are the preferred form.)

accommodate	bankruptcy	irrelevant	paralleled	skillful
achieve	deferred	judgment	privilege	supersede
acknowledgment	existence	liaison	receivable	surety
balance	fulfill	occasion	resistance	trial

GRAMMAR

This section on grammar is intended to be a brief overview only. Consequently, the authors have chosen to focus on items that seem to cause the most problems. If you did not do well on the Diagnostic Quiz, you would be well advised to go over all the material in this section and consider a more thorough grammar study than provided here.

VERBS

The verb is the driving force of the sentence: it is the word or words to which all other parts of the sentence relate. When trying to analyze a sentence to identify its grammatical parts or its meaning, or when attempting to amend a sentence, you should always identify the verb or verbs first. A verb expresses action or being.

Action: The accountant *visits* his clients regularly.
Being: Kyle *is* an accountant.

Voice

1.   The **active voice** indicates that the subject of the sentence (the person or thing) does something. The **passive voice** indicates that the subject is acted upon.

Active: *The accountant worked* on the client's financial statements.
Passive: The client's financial statements *were worked on by the accountant.*

2.   The most important thing to understand about voice is that it should be consistent; that is, you should avoid shifts from one voice to another, especially within the same sentence as below.

Taylor Corporation *hired* an independent computer programmer to develop a simplified payroll application for its new computer, and an on-line, data-based microcomputer system *was developed.*

Use the active voice for the entire sentence:

Taylor Corporation *hired* an independent computer programmer to develop a simplified payroll application for its new computer, and he *developed* an on-line, data-based microcomputer system.

Mood

1.   Common errors in syntax are made when **more than one mood** is used in a single sentence. The first example that follows begins with the **imperative** and shifts to the **indicative.** The second example corrects the sentence by using the imperative in both clauses, and the third example corrects the sentence by using the indicative in both clauses. The fourth example avoids the problem by forming two sentences.

Pick up (imperative) that work program for me at the printer, and then we will go (indicative) to the client.
Pick up that work program for me at the printer, and then go to the client with me.
After you pick up that work program for me at the printer, we will go to the client.
Pick up that work program for me at the printer. Then we will go to the client.

2.   There are three moods: the indicative, the imperative, and the subjunctive. We do not examine the subjunctive. Most sentences are **indicative:**

The percentage of completion method is justified. Declarative indicative.
Is the percentage of completion method justified? Interrogative indicative.

3.   Sentences that give a command are called **imperative** sentences:

Pick up your books!
Be sure to use the correct method of accounting for income taxes.

Tense

1. Tense is all about *time.* If the proper sequence of tenses is not used, confusion can arise as to what happened when. Consider:

    > *Not getting* the raise he was expecting, John was unhappy about the additional work load. [???]
    > *Having not gotten* the raise he was expecting, John was unhappy about the additional work load. [Much clearer]

2. The **present tense** is used to express action or a state of being that is taking place in the present. The present tense is also used to express an action or a state of being that is habitual and when a definite time in the future is stated.

    > Dan *is taking* his CPA exam.
    > Robin *goes* to the printer once a week.
    > The new computer *arrives* on Monday.

3. The **present perfect tense** is used to indicate action that began in the past and has continued to the present.

    > From the time of its founder, the CPA firm *has celebrated* April 16 with a fabulous dinner party.

4. The **future tense** is used to indicate action that takes place in the indefinite future.

    > A plan of reorganization *will determine* the amount and the manner in which the creditors *will be paid*, in what form the business *will continue,* and any other necessary details.

5. The **future perfect tense** is used to indicate action that has not taken place yet but will take place before a specific future time.

    > Before Susan arrives at the client's office, the client *will have prepared* the documents she needs.

6. The **past tense** is used to indicate an action that took place in the past. The **past tense** is also used to indicate a condition or state occurring at a specific time in the past.

    > The predecessor auditor *resigned* last week.
    > The company *contacted* its auditor the first of every new year.

7. The **past perfect tense** is used to indicate an action that is completed before another action that also took place in the past.

    > The work load *had been* so heavy that she was required to work overtime. (Not *was*)

Agreement

1. The first element of agreement to examine is **verb** and **subject.** These two components must agree **in number.** Number is just one of several things to consider when examining the agreement of the components of a sentence.

2. The subject of the sentence is the noun or pronoun (person, place, or thing) doing the action stated by the verb (in the case of the active voice) or being acted upon by the verb (in the case of the passive voice). Although the subject normally precedes the verb, this is not always the case. Thus, you must be able to identify sentence elements no matter where they happen to fall. This is not a difficult matter, at least most of the time. Consider:

    (1) Lewis, Bradford, Johnson & Co. [is or are] the client with the best pay record.

    (2) For me, one of the most difficult questions on the exam [was or were] concerned with correcting weaknesses in internal controls.

In both examples, the first choice, the singular verb form, is correct. In sentence (1), Lewis, Bradford, Johnson & Co. is considered singular in number because we are talking about the company, not Lewis, Bradford, and Johnson per se. In sentence (2), the verb is also singular because **one** is the subject of the sentence, not **questions. Questions** is the object of the preposition **of.** If this seems confusing, rearrange the sentence so that the prepositional phrase appears first, and the agreement of subject and verb will be clearer. Thus:

Of the most difficult questions, one *was concerned* with correcting weaknesses in internal controls.

We will address special problems associated with prepositional phrases in other sections.

3. Beware of the word **number.** When it is preceded by the word **the,** it is always singular, and when it is preceded by the word **a,** it is always plural.

    The number of listings generated by the new EDP system *was* astounding.
    A number of listings *were generated* by the new EDP system.

4. A **compound subject,** even when made up of nouns singular in number, always takes a plural verb.

    The balance sheet, the independent auditor's report, and the quarterly report *are lying* on the desk. (Not *is lying*)

5. Continuing now with **compound subjects,** let's address the problem of when there are two or more subjects—one (or more) singular and one (or more) plural. When the sentence contains subjects connected by **or** or **nor,** or **not only…but also,** the verb should agree with the subject nearer to the verb.

    Either the auditors or the partner *is going* to the client.
    Not only the partner but also the auditors *are going* to the client.

    In the case of the first example above, which sounds awkward, simply switch the order of the subjects **(the partner; the auditors)** and use the verb **are going** to make it read better.

6. When one subject is **positive** and one is **negative,** the verb always agrees with the positive.

    The partner, and not the auditors, *is going* to the client.
    Not the partner but the auditors frequently go to the client.

7. You should use singular verbs with the following: each, every, everyone, everybody, anyone, anybody, either, neither, someone, somebody, no one, nobody, and one.

    Anybody who wants to go *is* welcome.
    Neither the accountant nor the bookkeeper ever *arrives* on time.
    One never *knows* what to expect.

Watch out for the words **each** and **none.** They can trip up even careful writers.

---

8. Improper placement of **each** in the sentence will confuse the verb agreement.

    The balance sheet, the income statement, and the statement of cash flows each [has/have] several errors.

In this example, we know that the verb must be **has** (to agree with **each**), but then again, maybe it should be **have** to agree with the subjects. The problem is that we have a sentence with a compound subject that must take a plural verb, but here it is connected with a singular pronoun (each). This is a very common error. This particular example may be fixed in one of two ways. First, if the word **each** is not really necessary in the sentence, simply drop it. Second, simply place the word **each** in a better position in the sentence. In the example below, placing the word **each** at the end of the sentence properly connects it to **errors;** also it no longer confuses verb agreement.

The balance sheet, the income statement, and the statement of cash flows *have* several errors *each.*

9.   The word **none** has special problems all its own. Not too many years ago, it was the accepted rule that every time **none** was the subject of the sentence, it should take a **singular verb.** Most modern grammarians now agree that the plural may be used when followed by a prepositional phrase with a plural object (noun) or with an object whose meaning in the sentence is plural.

None of the statements *were* correct.

When **none** stands alone, some purists believe it should take the singular and others believe that the plural is the proper form when the meaning conveys plurality. Consequently, in the following example, either the singular or plural is generally acceptable.

All the financial statements had been compiled, but none *was* **or** *were* correct.

> When in doubt, use **not one** in place of **none** (with a singular verb, of course).

NOUNS

Nouns are people, places, and things and can occur anywhere in the sentence. Make sure that, when necessary, the nouns are the same in number.

Do the exercises at the end of each chapter by answering the *questions* true or false. (Not singular *question*)
At the end of the engagement, everyone must turn in their *time sheets.* (Not singular *time sheet*)

Possessive Nouns

1.   The basic rule for making a **singular noun** possessive is to add an **apostrophe and an s.** If a singular noun ends in s, **add apostrophe and an s.** To make a **plural noun** possessive, add an **apostrophe alone** when the plural ends in **s** or an **apostrophe and an s** when the plural does not end in an **s.**

Singular:	client*'s*	system*'s*	beneficiary*'s*	*Chris'*
Plural:	client*s'*	system*s'*	beneficiar*ies'*	

2.   A common area of difficulty has to do with **ownership,** that is, when two or more individuals or groups are mentioned as owning something. If the ownership is **not common** to all, apostrophes appear after each individual or group. If the ownership **is common** to all, only the last individual or group in the series takes an apostrophe.

Not common to all: The accountant's and the attorney's offices…
Common to all: Robert, his brother, and their sons' company…

> Most of the confusion associated with possessives seems to be with the plural possessive. Remember to make the noun **plural** first and **possessive** second.

3.   Modern usage tends to make possessive forms into adjectives where appropriate. Thus:

Company's (possessive) management becomes *company* (adjective) management.
A *two weeks'* (possessive) vacation becomes a *two weeks* or *two-week* (both adjectives) vacation.

> In most instances, either the possessive form or the adjectival form is acceptable. Go with the form that seems most appropriate for that particular sentence.

Gerunds

1.   A gerund is a verb changed to a noun by adding **ing.** A noun preceding a gerund must be possessive so that it may be construed as **modifying the noun.**

> *Caroline's telecommuting* was approved by the partner.

In this example, the subject of the sentence is **telecommuting,** not Caroline or Caroline's. Since we know that nouns cannot modify nouns, Caroline must become **Caroline's** to create a possessive form that can modify the noun **telecommuting.**

2.   The same holds true for **gerunds** used as **objects of prepositions:**

> The partner objected to *Caroline's telecommuting.*

In this example, **telecommuting** is the object of the preposition **to.** Caroline's is an appositive (or possessive) form modifying **telecommuting.**

PRONOUNS

Like Latin where most words have "cases" according to their function in the sentence, English **pronouns** also have cases. Sometimes you may be aware that you are using a case when determining the proper form of the pronoun and sometimes you may not.

> *He* met *his* partner at *their* office.

1.   Let's begin by tackling everybody's favorite: **who** and **whom.** We're going to take some time reviewing this one since it seems to be a major area of confusion. There is little or no confusion when **who** is clearly the **subject** of the sentence:

> *Who* is going with us?

And little or no confusion when **whom** is clearly (1) the **object** of the sentence or (2) the **object** of the preposition.

> (1)   Jenny audited *whom*? *Whom* did Jenny audit?

> (2)   Jenny is working for *whom*? For *whom* is Jenny working?

If you are having difficulty with **questions,** try changing them into declarative sentences (statements) and substituting another pronoun. Thus: Jenny audits **them** (objective), obviously not **they** (subjective), or Jenny is working for **her,** obviously not **she.**

---

2.   **Who** or **whoever** is the subjective case, and **whom** or **whomever** is the objective case. Common errors occur frequently in two instances: (1) when **who or whoever** is interrupted by a parenthetical phrase and (2) when an entire clause is the subject of a preposition.

> (1)   *Whoever* she decides is working with her should meet her at six o'clock.

In this example, **she decides** is a parenthetical phrase (one that could be left out of the sentence and the sentence would still be a complete thought). When you disregard **she decides,** you can see that **whoever** is the subject of the sentence, not **she.** The error occurs when **she** is believed to be the subject and **whomever,** the object of **decides.**

> (2)   Jenny will work with *whoever* shows up first.

This example represents what seems the most problematic of all the areas relating to who or whom. We have been taught to use the objective case after the preposition (in this case **with**). So why isn't **whomever** the correct form in this example? The answer is that it would be the correct form if the sentence ended with the word **whomever.** (**Whomever** would be the object of the preposition **with.**) In this case, it is not the last word but, rather, it is the **subject** of the clause **whoever shows up first.**

> Again, make the substitution of another pronoun as a test of whether to use the subjective or objective case.

Let's look at a few more examples. See if you are better able to recognize the correct form.

    (1)   I'm sure I will be comfortable with [*whoever/whomever*] the manager decides to assign.

    (2)   To [*who/whom*] should she speak regarding that matter?

    (3)   He always chooses [*whoever/whomever*] in his opinion is the best auditor.

    (4)   She usually enjoys working with [*whoever/whomever*] the partner assigns.

    (5)   [*Who/Whom*] should I ask to accompany me?

Let's see how well you did.

    (1)   **Whomever** is correct. The whole clause after the preposition **with** is the object of the preposition, and **whomever** is the object of the verb **to assign.** Turn the clause around and substitute another pronoun. Thus, **the manager decides to assign** *him.*

    (2)   **Whom** is correct. **Whom** is the object of the preposition **to.** Make the question into a declarative sentence and substitute another pronoun. Thus, **She should speak to** *him* **regarding that matter.**

    (3)   **Whoever** is correct. The entire clause **whoever is the best auditor** is the object of the main verb **chooses. Whoever** is the subject of that clause. **In his opinion** is a parenthetical phrase and doesn't affect the rest of the sentence.

    (4)   **Whomever** is correct. The entire clause **whomever the partner assigns** is the object of the preposition **with,** and **whomever** is the object of the verb **assigns.** Again, turn the clause around and substitute another pronoun. Thus, **the partner assigns** *him.*

    (5)   **Whom** is correct. **Whom** is the object of the main verb **ask.** Turn the question into a regular declarative sentence and substitute another pronoun. Thus, **I should ask** *her* **to accompany me.**

3.   Pronouns that follow prepositions are always in the **objective case,** except when serving as the subject of a clause, as discussed above. The most popular misuse occurs when using a pronoun after the preposition **between.** (**I, he, she, they,** are never used after **between,** no matter where the prepositional phrase falls in the sentence.)

> Between you and me, I don't believe our client will be able to continue as a going concern.
> That matter is strictly between her and them.

Antecedents

1.   An antecedent is the word or words for which a pronoun stands. Any time a pronoun is used, its antecedent must be clear and agree with the word or words for which it stands.

> *The accountant* placed *his* work in the file.

In this example, **his** is the pronoun with **the accountant** as its antecedent. **His** agrees with **the accountant** in person and number. **His** is used so as not to repeat **the accountant.**

2.   Confusion most often occurs when using indefinite pronouns such as **it, that, this,** and **which.**

> The company for *which* he works always mails *its* paychecks on Friday.

In this example, the pronouns **which** and **its** both clearly refer to **the company.** Consider the next example. Since it is not clear what the antecedent for **it** is, we can't tell for sure whether the company or the paycheck is small.

The company always mails my paycheck on Friday and *it* is a small one.

3. So far in our discussion of antecedents, we have talked about agreement in person. We have not addressed agreement in **number.** The following examples demonstrate pronouns that **do not agree** in number with their antecedents.

The company issued quarterly financial reports to *their* shareholders. (*Its* is the correct antecedent to agree in number with *company*.)

Each of the methods is introduced on a separate page, so that the student is made aware of *their* importance. (*Its* is the correct antecedent to agree in number with *each*.) **Note: Importance** refers to **each,** the subject of the sentence, not to **methods,** which is the object of the preposition **of.**

4. When a pronoun refers to singular antecedents that are connected by **or** or **nor**, the pronoun should be **singular.**

Joe or Buddy has misplaced *his* workpapers.

Neither Joe nor Buddy has misplaced *his* workpapers.

5. When a pronoun refers to a singular and a plural antecedent connected by **or** or **nor**, the pronoun should be **plural.**

Neither Joe nor his associates can locate *their* workpapers.

6. Pronouns must also agree with their antecedents in **gender.** Because English language has no way of expressing gender-neutral in pronoun agreement, it has been the custom to use **his** as a convenience when referring to both sexes. To avoid this "gender bias" in writing, there is a growing use of a more cumbersome construction in order to be more politically correct.

Old: When a new partner's identifiable asset contribution is less than the ownership interest *he* is to receive, the excess capital allowed *him* is considered as goodwill attributable to *him.*

New: When a new partner's identifiable asset contribution is less than the ownership interest *he or she* is to receive, the excess capital allowed *the new partner* is considered as goodwill attributable to *him or her.*

You will note in the above example that **he or she (he/she)** and **him or her (him/her)** have been used only once each and the antecedent **new partner** has been repeated once.

> The idea is to not overload a single sentence with too many repetitions of each construction. When it seems that **he/she** constructions are overwhelming the sentence, repeat the noun antecedent where possible, even if it sounds a bit labored.

7. **Reflexive pronouns** are pronouns that are used for **emphasizing their antecedents** and should **not be used as substitutes** for regular pronouns. The reflexive pronouns are **myself, yourself, himself, herself, itself, ourselves, yourselves, and themselves.**

The financing is being handled by the principals *themselves.* (Demonstrates emphasis)
The partner *himself* will take care of that matter. (Demonstrates emphasis)
My associate and *I* accept the engagement. (Not my associate and *myself*...)
I am fine; how about *you*? (Not how about *yourself*?)

ADJECTIVES & ADVERBS

1. Most of us understand that adjectives and adverbs are **modifiers,** but many of us can't tell them apart. In fact, there are many words that can be used as either depending on their use. Consequently, differentiating adjectives from adverbs is really not very important as long as you know how to use them. Understanding, however, that **adjectives modify nouns or pronouns,** and **adverbs modify verbs** and adjectives will help you choose the correct form.

    > Falcone Co. purchased *two* computers from Wizard Corp., a very *small* manufacturer. (*two* is an adjective describing the noun *computers, very* is an adverb modifying the adjective *small,* and *small* is an adjective describing the noun *manufacturer.*)

    > Acme advised Mason that it would deliver the appliances on July 2 as *originally* agreed. (*originally* is an adverb describing the verb *agreed.*)

2. In writing for the CPA exam, avoid colloquial uses of the adjectives **real** and **sure.** In the following examples, adverbs are called for.

    > I am *very* (not *real*) sorry that you didn't pass the exam.
    > He will *surely* (not *sure*) be glad if he passes the exam.

3. **Comparisons** using adjectives frequently present problems. Remember that when comparing two things, the **comparative** (often **er**) form is used, and when comparing more than two, the **superlative** (often **est**) form is used.

    > This report is *larger* than the other one.
    > This report is the *largest* of them all.
    > This report is *more* detailed than the others.
    > This report is the *most* detailed of them all.

4. **Articles** are adjectives. **An** precedes most vowels, but when the vowel begins with a **consonant sound,** we should use **a.**

    > *a* usual adjustment…
    > *a* one in a million deal…

    Similarly, when **a** or **an** precedes abbreviations or initials, it is the next **sound** that we should consider, not the next letter. In other words, if the next sound is a vowel sound, **an** should be used. Usually, your reader will be reading the abbreviations or initials and not the whole term, title, etc.

    > *An S.A.* will be used to head up the field work on this engagement.
    > *An F.O.B.* contract is a *contract* indicating that the seller will bear that degree of risk and expense that is appropriate to the F.O.B. terms.

CONJUNCTIONS

There are three types of conjunctions: coordinating, subordinating, and correlative.

Coordinating Conjunctions

Coordinating conjunctions are conjunctions that connect equal elements in a sentence. These conjunctions include **and, but, for, yet, so, or,** and **nor.** Examples of common problems involving coordinating conjunctions:

1. Leaving out the **and,** leading to difficulties with comprehension and clarity.

    > The accountant studied some of management's representations, marked what she wanted to discuss in the meeting. (The word *and* should be in the place of the comma.)

Mike's summer job entails opening the mail, stamps it with a dater, routing it to the proper person. (Should be: …opening the mail from other offices, *stamping* it with a dater, *and* routing it to the proper person. **This example also demonstrates a lack of parallelism,** which is addressed in an earlier section.)

2.   Omission of **and** is correct when the sentence is a compound sentence (meaning that it contains two independent clauses), in which case a semicolon takes the place of **and.** When the semicolon is used, the ideas of each independent clause should be closely related.

The security is genuine; it has not been materially altered.

3.   Although the rules for **or** and **nor** have become less strict over time, you should understand proper usage for the sake of comprehension and clarity. Most of us are familiar with **either**…**or** and **neither**…**nor:**

Either the creditor must take possession *or* the debtor must sign a security agreement that describes the collateral.

The company would neither accept delivery of the water coolers, nor pay for them, because Peterson did not have the authority to enter into the contract.

Subordinating Conjunctions

Subordinating conjunctions are conjunctions that introduce subordinate elements of the sentence. The most common and the ones we want to concentrate on here are **as, since, because, that, which, when, where,** and **while.**

1.   **As; Since; Because**

Because is the only word of the three that **always** indicates cause. **Since** usually indicates **time** and, when introducing adverbial clauses, may mean either **when** or **because.** **As** should be avoided altogether in these constructions and used only for comparisons. We strongly recommend using the exact word to avoid any confusion, especially when clarity is essential.

Attachment of the security interest did not occur because Pix failed to file a financing statement. (Specifically indicates *cause.*)
Green has not paid any creditor since January 1, 1992. (Specifically indicates *time.*)

The following example is a typical misuse of the conjunction **as** and demonstrates why **as** should not be used as a substitute for **because:**

As the partners are contributing more capital to the company, the stock prices are going up.

The meaning of this sentence is ambiguous. Are the stock prices going up **while** the partners are contributing capital or are the stock prices going up **because** the partners are contributing more capital?

2.   **That; Which**

Many people complain about not understanding when to use **that** and when to use **which** more *than just* about anything else. The rule to follow requires that you know the difference between a restrictive and a nonrestrictive clause. A **restrictive clause** is one that must remain in the sentence for the sentence to make sense. A **nonrestrictive** clause is one that may be removed from a sentence and the sentence will still make sense.

That is used with restrictive clauses; *which* is used with nonrestrictive clauses.

(1)   An accountant who breaches his or her contract with a client may be subject to liability for damages and losses *which* the client suffers as a direct result of the breach.

(2)   As a result, the accountant is responsible for errors resulting from changes *that* occurred between the time he or she prepared the statement and its effective date.

(3)   A reply *that* purports to accept an offer but which adds material qualifications or conditions is not an acceptance; rather, it is a rejection and a counter-offer.

In example (1) above, the clause beginning with **which** is nonrestrictive (sentence would make sense without it). In examples (2) and (3), the clauses that follow **that** are restrictive (necessary for the meaning of the sentence).

If you can put commas around the clause in question, it is usually nonrestrictive and thus takes **which**. Occasionally, there will be a fine line between what one might consider restrictive or nonrestrictive. In these cases, make your choice based on which sounds better and, if there is another **which** or **that** nearby, let that help your decision. (Unless truly necessary, don't have two or three uses of **which** or two or three uses of **that** in the same sentence.)

---

3.   **When; Where**

The most common incorrect usage associated with these words occurs when they are used to define something.

(1)   Exoneration is *where* the surety takes action against the debtor, which seeks to force the debtor to pay his or her debts.

(2)   A fiduciary relationship is where the agent acts for the benefit of the principal.

(3)   Joint liability is *when* all partners in a partnership are jointly liable for any contract actions against the partnership.

The above three examples are **faulty constructions**. The verb **to be** (**is,** in this case) must be followed by a predicate adjective (an adjective modifying the subject) or a predicate nominative (a noun meaning the same as the subject), **not** an adverbial phrase or clause. These sentences should be rewritten as follows:

(1)   Exoneration is *an action* by the surety against the debtor, which seeks to force the debtor to pay his or her debts.

(2)   A fiduciary relationship is *the association* of the agent and the principal whereby the agent acts for the benefit of the principal.

(3)   Joint liability is *the liability* of all partners in a partnership for any contract actions against the partnership.

4.   **While**

Formerly, **while** was acceptable only to denote time. Modern practice accepts **while** and **although** as nearly synonymous. In example (1), either while or although is acceptable. In example (2), **while** is **not** a proper substitution for **although.**

(1)   *While/Although* Acme contends that its agreement with Mason was not binding, it is willing to deliver the goods to Mason.

(2)   Under a sale or return contract, the sale is considered as completed *although* it is voidable at the buyer's election.

Correlative Conjunction

The third type of conjunction is the **correlative conjunction.** We have briefly mentioned and presented examples of **either…or** and **neither…nor** earlier in connection with nouns, verbs, and agreement. Now we want to discuss these correlatives in connection with **parallelism.**

1.   **Not only** should be followed by **but (also).**

In determining whether a mere invitation or an offer exists, the courts generally will look *not only* to the specific language *but also* to the surrounding circumstances, the custom within the industry, and the prior practice between the parties.

2.   Watch out for **placement of correlatives.** Faulty placement leads to faulty construction and obstructs clarity.

The lawyer *either* is asked to furnish specific information *or* comment as to where the lawyer's views differ from those of management.

Below is the same sentence in much clearer form. Note that the phrases introduced by *either* and *or* are now in parallel construction: *either to furnish…or to comment.*

The lawyer is asked *either* to furnish specific information *or to* comment as to where the lawyer's views differ from those of management.

———————————

APPENDIX D
COMPOUND INTEREST TABLES & FINANCIAL RATIOS

Table 1—Future Value of $1

$$FV = PV(1 + r)^n$$

r = interest rate; n = number of periods until valuation; PV = \$1

	1%	2%	3%	4%	5%	6%	7%	8%	10%	12%	15%	20%	25%
$n=1$	1.010000	1.020000	1.030000	1.040000	1.050000	1.060000	1.070000	1.080000	1.100000	1.120000	1.150000	1.200000	1.250000
2	1.020100	1.040400	1.060900	1.081600	1.102500	1.123600	1.144900	1.166400	1.210000	1.254400	1.322500	1.440000	1.562500
3	1.030301	1.061208	1.092727	1.124864	1.157625	1.191016	1.225043	1.259712	1.331000	1.404928	1.520875	1.728000	1.953125
4	1.040604	1.082432	1.125509	1.169859	1.215506	1.262477	1.310796	1.360489	1.464100	1.573519	1.749006	2.073600	2.441406
5	1.051010	1.104081	1.159274	1.216653	1.276282	1.338226	1.402552	1.469328	1.610510	1.762342	2.011357	2.488320	3.051758
6	1.061520	1.126162	1.194052	1.265319	1.340096	1.418519	1.500730	1.586874	1.771561	1.973823	2.313061	2.985984	3.814697
7	1.072135	1.148686	1.229874	1.315932	1.407100	1.503630	1.605781	1.713824	1.948717	2.210681	2.660020	3.583181	4.768372
8	1.082857	1.171659	1.266770	1.368569	1.477455	1.593848	1.718186	1.850930	2.143589	2.475963	3.059023	4.299817	5.960464
9	1.093685	1.195093	1.304773	1.423312	1.551328	1.689479	1.838459	1.999005	2.357948	2.773079	3.517876	5.159781	7.450581
10	1.104622	1.218994	1.343916	1.480244	1.628895	1.790848	1.967151	2.158925	2.593743	3.105848	4.045558	6.191737	9.313226
11	1.115668	1.243374	1.384234	1.539454	1.710339	1.898299	2.104852	2.331639	2.853117	3.478550	4.652391	7.430084	11.64153
12	1.126825	1.268242	1.425761	1.601032	1.795856	2.012197	2.252192	2.518170	3.138428	3.895976	5.350250	8.916101	14.55192
13	1.138093	1.293607	1.468534	1.665074	1.885649	2.132928	2.409845	2.719624	3.452271	4.363493	6.152788	10.69932	18.18989
14	1.149474	1.319479	1.512590	1.731676	1.979932	2.260904	2.578534	2.937194	3.797498	4.887112	7.075706	12.83918	22.73737
15	1.160969	1.345868	1.557967	1.800943	2.078928	2.396558	2.759032	3.172169	4.177248	5.473566	8.137062	15.40702	28.42171
16	1.172579	1.372786	1.604706	1.872981	2.182875	2.540352	2.952164	3.425943	4.594973	6.130394	9.357621	18.48843	35.52714
17	1.184304	1.400241	1.652848	1.947900	2.292018	2.692773	3.158815	3.700018	5.054471	6.866041	10.76126	22.18611	44.40892
18	1.196147	1.428246	1.702433	2.025816	2.406619	2.854339	3.379932	3.996019	5.559917	7.689965	12.37545	26.62333	55.51115
19	1.208109	1.456811	1.753506	2.106849	2.526950	3.025599	3.616528	4.315701	6.115909	8.612761	14.23177	31.94800	69.38894
20	1.220190	1.485947	1.806111	2.191123	2.653298	3.207135	3.869684	4.660957	6.727500	9.646293	16.36654	38.33760	86.73618
22	1.244716	1.545980	1.916103	2.369919	2.925261	3.603537	4.430402	5.436540	8.140275	12.10031	21.64475	55.20615	135.5253
24	1.269735	1.608437	2.032794	2.563304	3.225100	4.048934	5.072367	6.341180	9.849733	15.17863	28.62518	79.49685	211.7582
26	1.295256	1.673418	2.156591	2.772470	3.555673	4.549383	5.807353	7.396353	11.91818	19.04007	37.85680	114.4755	330.8723
28	1.321291	1.741024	2.287928	2.998703	3.920129	5.111687	6.648839	8.627106	14.42099	23.88387	50.06562	164.8447	516.9879
30	1.347849	1.811362	2.427262	3.243397	4.321942	5.743491	7.612255	10.06266	17.44940	29.95992	66.21178	237.3763	807.7936
32	1.374941	1.884541	2.575083	3.508059	4.764942	6.453386	8.715271	11.73708	21.11378	37.58172	87.56509	341.8219	1262.177
34	1.402577	1.960676	2.731905	3.794316	5.253348	7.251025	9.978113	13.69013	25.54767	47.14251	115.8048	492.2236	1972.152
36	1.430769	2.039887	2.898278	4.103932	5.791816	8.147252	11.42394	15.96817	30.91268	59.13557	153.1519	708.8019	3081.488
38	1.459527	2.122299	3.074783	4.438813	6.385478	9.154252	13.07927	18.62527	37.40435	74.17966	202.5434	1020.675	4814.825
40	1.488864	2.208040	3.262038	4.801021	7.039989	10.28572	14.97446	21.72452	45.25926	93.05096	267.8636	1469.772	7523.164
45	1.564811	2.437854	3.781596	5.841176	8.985008	13.76461	21.00245	31.92045	72.89049	163.9876	538.7694	3657.262	22958.88
50	1.644632	2.691588	4.383906	7.106683	11.46740	18.42015	29.45703	46.90161	117.3909	289.0022	1083.658	9100.439	70064.92
100	2.704814	7.244646	19.21863	50.50494	131.5013	339.3020	867.7164	2199.761	13780.61	83522.24	117×10^4	828×10^6	491×10^7

Example 1 ▶ Future Value of a Single Sum

Required: Find the future value of a \$100 certificate of deposit at 8% for three years, (A) compounded annually and (B) compounded quarterly.

Solution A: Let Principal = P = \$100, Interest Rate = r = 8%, Period = n = 3 years
Future Value Interest Factor at r Rate for n Periods = FVIF(r, n)
Future Value = FV = P × FVIF(r, n)

FVIF(8%, 3 years) = 1.2597 (from Table 1)

FV = \$100 × 1.2597 = \$125.97

Solution B: Let Principal = P = \$100
Interest Rate = r = 8% / 4 quarters = 2%, Period = n = 12 quarters
Future Value Interest Factor at r Rate for n Periods = FVIF(r, n)
Future Value = FV = P × FVIF(r, n)

FVIF(2%, 12 quarters) = 1.2682 (from Table 1)

FV = \$100 × 1.2682 = \$126.82

Table 2—Present Value of $1

$$PV = \frac{FV}{(1 + r)^n}$$

r = discount rate; n = number of periods until payment; FV = $1

	1%	2%	3%	4%	5%	6%	7%	8%	10%	12%	15%	20%	25%
$n=1$	0.990099	0.980392	0.970874	0.961538	0.952381	0.943396	0.934579	0.925926	0.909091	0.892857	0.869565	0.833333	0.800000
2	0.980296	0.961169	0.942596	0.924556	0.907029	0.889996	0.873439	0.857339	0.826446	0.797194	0.756144	0.694444	0.640000
3	0.970590	0.942322	0.915142	0.888996	0.863838	0.839619	0.816298	0.793832	0.751315	0.711780	0.657516	0.578704	0.512000
4	0.960980	0.923845	0.888487	0.854804	0.822702	0.792094	0.762895	0.735030	0.683013	0.635518	0.571753	0.482253	0.409600
5	0.951466	0.905731	0.862609	0.821927	0.783526	0.747258	0.712986	0.680583	0.620921	0.567427	0.497177	0.401878	0.327680
6	0.942045	0.887971	0.837484	0.790315	0.746215	0.704961	0.666342	0.630170	0.564474	0.506631	0.432328	0.334898	0.262144
7	0.932718	0.870560	0.813092	0.759918	0.710681	0.665057	0.622750	0.583490	0.513158	0.452349	0.375937	0.279082	0.209715
8	0.923483	0.853490	0.789409	0.730690	0.676839	0.627412	0.582009	0.540269	0.466507	0.403883	0.326902	0.232568	0.167772
9	0.914340	0.836755	0.766417	0.702587	0.644609	0.591898	0.543934	0.500249	0.424098	0.360610	0.284262	0.193807	0.134218
10	0.905287	0.820348	0.744094	0.675564	0.613913	0.558395	0.508349	0.463194	0.385543	0.321973	0.247185	0.161506	0.107374
11	0.896324	0.804263	0.722421	0.649581	0.584679	0.526788	0.475093	0.428883	0.350494	0.287476	0.214943	0.134588	0.085899
12	0.887449	0.788493	0.701380	0.624597	0.556837	0.496969	0.444012	0.397114	0.318631	0.256675	0.186907	0.112157	0.068719
13	0.878663	0.773033	0.680951	0.600574	0.530321	0.468839	0.414964	0.367698	0.289664	0.229174	0.162528	0.093464	0.054976
14	0.869963	0.757875	0.661118	0.577475	0.505068	0.442301	0.387817	0.340461	0.263331	0.204620	0.141329	0.077887	0.043980
15	0.861349	0.743015	0.641862	0.555265	0.481017	0.417265	0.362446	0.315242	0.239392	0.182696	0.122894	0.064905	0.035184
16	0.852821	0.728446	0.623167	0.533908	0.458112	0.393646	0.338735	0.291890	0.217629	0.163122	0.106865	0.054088	0.028147
17	0.844378	0.714163	0.605016	0.513373	0.436297	0.371364	0.316574	0.270269	0.197845	0.145644	0.092926	0.045073	0.022518
18	0.836017	0.700159	0.587395	0.493628	0.415521	0.350344	0.295864	0.250249	0.179859	0.130040	0.080805	0.037561	0.018014
19	0.827740	0.686431	0.570286	0.474642	0.395734	0.330513	0.276508	0.231712	0.163508	0.116107	0.070265	0.031301	0.014412
20	0.819544	0.672971	0.553676	0.456387	0.376889	0.311805	0.258419	0.214548	0.148644	0.103667	0.061100	0.026084	0.011529
22	0.803396	0.646839	0.521892	0.421955	0.341850	0.277505	0.225713	0.183941	0.122846	0.082643	0.046201	0.018114	0.007379
24	0.787566	0.621722	0.491934	0.390121	0.310068	0.246979	0.197147	0.157699	0.101526	0.065882	0.034934	0.012579	0.004722
26	0.772048	0.597579	0.463695	0.360689	0.281241	0.219810	0.172195	0.135202	0.083905	0.052521	0.026415	0.008735	0.003022
28	0.756836	0.574375	0.437077	0.333477	0.255094	0.195630	0.150402	0.115914	0.069343	0.041869	0.019974	0.006066	0.001934
30	0.741923	0.552071	0.411987	0.308319	0.231377	0.174110	0.131367	0.099377	0.057309	0.033378	0.015103	0.004213	0.001238
32	0.727304	0.530633	0.388337	0.285058	0.209866	0.154957	0.114741	0.085200	0.047362	0.026609	0.011420	0.002926	0.000792
34	0.712973	0.510028	0.366045	0.263552	0.190355	0.137912	0.100219	0.073045	0.039143	0.021212	0.008635	0.002032	0.000507
36	0.698925	0.490223	0.345032	0.243669	0.172657	0.122741	0.087535	0.062625	0.032349	0.016910	0.006529	0.001411	0.000325
38	0.685153	0.471187	0.325226	0.225285	0.156605	0.109239	0.076457	0.053690	0.026735	0.013481	0.004937	0.000980	0.000208
40	0.671653	0.452890	0.306557	0.208289	0.142046	0.097222	0.066780	0.046031	0.022095	0.010747	0.003733	0.000680	0.000133
45	0.639055	0.410197	0.264439	0.171198	0.111297	0.072650	0.047613	0.031328	0.013719	0.006098	0.001856	0.000273	0.000044
50	0.608039	0.371528	0.228107	0.140713	0.087204	0.054288	0.033948	0.021321	0.008519	0.003460	0.000923	0.000110	0.000014
100	0.369711	0.138033	0.052033	0.019800	0.007604	0.002947	0.001152	0.000455	0.000073	0.000012	0.000001	0.000000	0.000000

Note: The future value factor is equal to 1 divided by the present value factor.

Example 2 ▶ Present Value of a Single Sum

Required: Find the present value of $100 paid three years from now if the market rate of interest is 8% (A) compounded annually and (B) compounded quarterly.

Solution A: Let   Principal = P = $100,   Interest Rate = r = 8%,   Period = n = 3 years
Present Value Interest Factor at r Rate for n Periods = PVIF(r, n)
Present Value = PV = P × PVIF(r, n)

PVIF(8%, 3 years) = 0.7938 (from Table 2)

PV = $100 × 0.7938 = $79.38

Solution B: Let   Principal = P = $100,   Interest Rate = r = 2%,   Period = n = 12 quarters
Present Value Interest Factor at r Rate for n Periods = PVIF(r, n)
Present Value = PV = P × PVIF(r, n)

PVIF(2%, 12 quarters) = 0.7885 (from Table 2)

PV = $100 × 0.7885 = $78.85

Table 3—Future Value of Annuity of $1 in Arrears

$$FV = \frac{(1 + r)^n - 1}{r} \qquad r = \text{interest rate; } n = \text{number of payments}$$

	1%	2%	3%	4%	5%	6%	7%	8%	10%	12%	15%	20%	25%
n = 1	1.000000	1.000000	1.000000	1.000000	1.000000	1.000000	1.000000	1.000000	1.000000	1.000000	1.000000	1.000000	1.000000
2	2.010000	2.020000	2.030000	2.040000	2.050000	2.060000	2.070000	2.080000	2.100000	2.120000	2.150000	2.200000	2.250000
3	3.030100	3.060400	3.090900	3.121600	3.152500	3.183600	3.214900	3.246400	3.310000	3.374400	3.472500	3.640000	3.812500
4	4.060401	4.121608	4.183627	4.246464	4.310125	4.374616	4.439943	4.506112	4.641000	4.779328	4.993375	5.368000	5.765625
5	5.101005	5.204040	5.309136	5.416323	5.525631	5.637093	5.750739	5.866601	6.105100	6.352847	6.742381	7.441600	8.207031
6	6.152015	6.308121	6.468410	6.632976	6.801913	6.975318	7.153291	7.335929	7.715610	8.115189	8.753738	9.929920	11.25879
7	7.213535	7.434283	7.662462	7.898294	8.142009	8.393838	8.654021	8.922803	9.487171	10.08901	11.06680	12.91590	15.07349
8	8.285670	8.582969	8.892336	9.214226	9.549109	9.897468	10.25980	10.63663	11.43589	12.29969	13.72682	16.49908	19.84186
9	9.368527	9.754628	10.15911	10.58280	11.02656	11.49132	11.97799	12.48756	13.57948	14.77566	16.78584	20.79890	25.80232
10	10.46221	10.94972	11.46388	12.00611	12.57789	13.18079	13.81645	14.48656	15.93742	17.54873	20.30372	25.95868	33.25290
11	11.56683	12.16872	12.80780	13.48635	14.20679	14.97164	15.78360	16.64549	18.53117	20.65458	24.34928	32.15042	42.56613
12	12.68250	13.41209	14.19203	15.02581	15.91713	16.86994	17.88845	18.97713	21.38428	24.13313	29.00167	39.58050	54.20766
13	13.80933	14.68033	15.61779	16.62684	17.71298	18.88214	20.14064	21.49530	24.52271	28.02911	34.35192	48.49660	68.75957
14	14.94742	15.97394	17.08632	18.29191	19.59863	21.01507	22.55049	24.21492	27.97498	32.39260	40.50471	59.19592	86.94947
15	16.09690	17.29342	18.59891	20.02359	21.57856	23.27597	25.12902	27.15211	31.77248	37.27971	47.58041	72.03511	109.6868
16	17.25786	18.63929	20.15688	21.82453	23.65749	25.67253	27.88805	30.32428	35.94973	42.75328	55.71748	87.44213	138.1086
17	18.43044	20.01207	21.76159	23.69751	25.84037	28.21288	30.84022	33.75023	40.54470	48.88367	65.07510	105.9306	173.6357
18	19.61475	21.41231	23.41443	25.64541	28.13239	30.90565	33.99903	37.45024	45.59917	55.74971	75.83636	128.1167	218.0446
19	20.81090	22.84056	25.11687	27.67123	30.53900	33.75999	37.37896	41.44626	51.15909	63.43968	88.21181	154.7400	273.5558
20	22.01900	24.29737	26.87037	29.77808	33.06596	36.78559	40.99549	45.76196	57.27500	72.05244	102.4436	186.6880	342.9447
22	24.47159	27.29898	30.53678	34.24797	38.50521	43.39229	49.00574	55.45675	71.40275	92.50258	137.6317	271.0307	538.1011
24	26.97346	30.42186	34.42647	39.08260	44.50200	50.81557	58.17667	66.76476	88.49733	118.1552	184.1679	392.4843	843.0330
26	29.52563	33.67091	38.55304	44.31174	51.11345	59.15638	68.67647	79.95441	109.1818	150.3339	245.7120	567.3773	1319.489
28	32.12910	37.05121	42.93092	49.96758	58.40258	68.52811	80.69769	95.33883	134.2099	190.6989	327.1041	819.2233	2063.951
30	34.78489	40.56808	47.57542	56.08494	66.43885	79.05818	94.46078	113.2832	164.4940	241.3327	434.7452	1181.882	3227.174
32	37.49407	44.22703	52.50276	62.70147	75.29883	90.88978	110.2182	134.2135	201.1378	304.8477	577.1005	1704.110	5044.710
34	40.25770	48.03380	57.73018	69.85791	85.06696	104.1838	128.2588	158.6267	245.4767	384.5210	765.3655	2456.118	7884.609
36	43.07688	51.99437	63.27594	77.59831	95.83633	119.1209	148.9135	187.1021	299.1268	484.4631	1014.346	3539.010	12321.95
38	45.95272	56.11494	69.15945	85.97034	107.7095	135.9042	172.5610	220.3159	364.0435	609.8305	1343.622	5098.374	19255.30
40	48.88637	60.40198	75.40126	95.02551	120.7998	154.7620	199.6351	259.0565	442.5926	767.0914	1779.091	7343.858	30088.66
45	56.48108	71.89271	92.71986	121.0294	159.7002	212.7435	285.7493	386.5056	718.9048	1358.230	3585.129	18281.31	91831.50
50	64.46318	84.57940	112.7969	152.6671	209.3480	290.3359	406.5289	573.7701	1163.909	2400.018	7217.718	45497.20	280255.7
100	170.4814	312.2323	607.2877	1237.624	2610.025	5638.368	12381.66	27484.51	137796.1	696010.5	783×10⁴	414×10⁶	196×10⁹

Note: To convert from this table to values of an annuity in advance, determine the annuity in arrears factor above for one more period and subtract 1.

Example 3 ▶ Future Value of an Annuity in Arrears

Required: Jones plans to save $300 a year for three years. If Jones deposits money at the end of each period in a savings plan that yields 24%, how much will Jones have at the end of the three years if Jones deposits (A) $75 at the end of each quarter? (B) $25 at the end of every month?

Solution A: Let   Payment = P = $75,   Interest Rate = r = 6%,   Period = n = 12 quarters
             Future Value of an Annuity Factor at r Rate for n Periods = FVAF(r, n)
             Future Value of the Annuity = FVA = P × FVAF(r, n)

             FVAF(6%, 12 quarters) = 16.8699 (from Table 3)

       FVA = $75 × 16.8699 = $1,265.24

Solution B: Let   Payment = P = $25,   Interest Rate = r = 2%,   Period = n = 36 months
             Future Value of an Annuity Factor at r Rate for n Periods = FVAF(r, n)
             Future Value of the Annuity = FVA = P × FVAF(r, n)

             FVAF(2%, 36 months) = 51.9944 (from Table 3)

       FVA = $25 × 51.9944 = $1,299.86

Table 4—Present Value of Annuity of $1 in Arrears

$$PV = \frac{1 - (1 + r)^{-n}}{r} \qquad r = \text{discount rate; } n = \text{number of payments}$$

	1%	2%	3%	4%	5%	6%	7%	8%	10%	12%	15%	20%	25%
n = 1	0.990099	0.980392	0.970874	0.961538	0.952381	0.943396	0.934579	0.925926	0.909091	0.892857	0.869565	0.833333	0.800000
2	1.970395	1.941561	1.913470	1.886095	1.859410	1.833393	1.808018	1.783265	1.735537	1.690051	1.625709	1.527778	1.440000
3	2.940985	2.883883	2.828611	2.775091	2.723248	2.673012	2.624316	2.577097	2.486852	2.401831	2.283225	2.106482	1.952000
4	3.901966	3.807729	3.717098	3.629895	3.545950	3.465106	3.387211	3.312127	3.169865	3.037349	2.854978	2.588735	2.361600
5	4.853431	4.713459	4.579707	4.451822	4.329477	4.212364	4.100197	3.992710	3.790787	3.604776	3.352155	2.990612	2.689280
6	5.795476	5.601431	5.417192	5.242137	5.075692	4.917325	4.766540	4.622880	4.355261	4.111407	3.784483	3.325510	2.951424
7	6.728195	6.471991	6.230283	6.002055	5.786374	5.582381	5.389289	5.206370	4.868419	4.563756	4.160419	3.604592	3.161139
8	7.651678	7.325481	7.019692	6.732745	6.463213	6.209794	5.971299	5.746639	5.334926	4.967640	4.487321	3.837160	3.328911
9	8.566017	8.162237	7.786109	7.435332	7.107821	6.801692	6.515232	6.246888	5.759024	5.328250	4.771584	4.030966	3.463129
10	9.471305	8.982585	8.530203	8.110896	7.721735	7.360087	7.023582	6.710082	6.144567	5.650223	5.018768	4.192472	3.570503
11	10.36763	9.786848	9.252625	8.760477	8.306415	7.886875	7.498674	7.138964	6.495061	5.937699	5.233712	4.327060	3.656403
12	11.25508	10.57534	9.954004	9.385074	8.863252	8.383844	7.942686	7.536078	6.813692	6.194374	5.420619	4.439217	3.725122
13	12.13374	11.34837	10.63496	9.985648	9.393573	8.852683	8.357651	7.903776	7.103356	6.423549	5.583147	4.532681	3.780098
14	13.00370	12.10625	11.29607	10.56312	9.898641	9.294984	8.745468	8.244237	7.366687	6.628168	5.724475	4.610567	3.824078
15	13.86505	12.84926	11.93793	11.11839	10.37966	9.712249	9.107914	8.559479	7.606080	6.810864	5.847370	4.675473	3.859262
16	14.71787	13.57771	12.56110	11.65230	10.83777	10.10590	9.446649	8.851369	7.823709	6.973986	5.954235	4.729560	3.887410
17	15.56225	14.29187	13.16612	12.16567	11.27407	10.47726	9.763223	9.121638	8.021553	7.119631	6.047161	4.774634	3.909928
18	16.39827	14.99203	13.75351	12.65930	11.68959	10.82760	10.05909	9.371887	8.201412	7.249670	6.127965	4.812195	3.927943
19	17.22601	15.67846	14.32380	13.13394	12.08532	11.15812	10.33560	9.603600	8.364920	7.365777	6.198231	4.843496	3.942354
20	18.04555	16.35143	14.87747	13.59033	12.46221	11.46992	10.59401	9.818148	8.513564	7.469444	6.259331	4.869580	3.953883
22	19.66038	17.65805	15.93692	14.45112	13.16300	12.04158	11.06124	10.20074	8.771541	7.644646	6.358663	4.909431	3.970485
24	21.24339	18.91393	16.93554	15.24696	13.79864	12.55036	11.46933	10.52876	8.984744	7.784316	6.433771	4.937104	3.981111
26	22.79520	20.12104	17.87684	15.98277	14.37519	13.00317	11.82578	10.80998	9.160945	7.895660	6.490564	4.956323	3.987911
28	24.31644	21.28127	18.76411	16.66306	14.89813	13.40616	12.13711	11.05108	9.306566	7.984423	6.533508	4.969668	3.992263
30	25.80771	22.39646	19.60044	17.29203	15.37245	13.76483	12.40904	11.25778	9.426914	8.055184	6.565979	4.978936	3.995048
32	27.26959	23.46833	20.38877	17.87355	15.80268	14.08404	12.64655	11.43500	9.526376	8.111594	6.590533	4.985373	3.996831
34	28.70267	24.49859	21.13184	18.41120	16.19290	14.36814	12.85401	11.58693	9.608575	8.156565	6.609098	4.989842	3.997972
36	30.10751	25.48884	21.83225	18.90828	16.54685	14.62099	13.03521	11.71719	9.676508	8.192414	6.623137	4.992946	3.998702
38	31.48466	26.44064	22.49246	19.36786	16.86789	14.84602	13.19347	11.82887	9.732652	8.220994	6.633752	4.995101	3.999169
40	32.83469	27.35548	23.11477	19.79277	17.15909	15.04630	13.33171	11.92461	9.779051	8.243777	6.641778	4.996598	3.999468
45	36.09451	29.49016	24.51871	20.72004	17.77407	15.45583	13.60552	12.10840	9.862807	8.282516	6.654293	4.998633	3.999826
50	39.19612	31.42361	25.72976	21.48219	18.25593	15.76186	13.80075	12.23349	9.914814	8.304499	6.660514	4.999451	3.999943
100	63.02888	43.09835	31.59891	24.50500	19.84791	16.61755	14.26925	12.49432	9.999274	8.333234	6.666661	5.000000	4.000000

Note: To convert from this table to values of an annuity in advance, determine the annuity in arrears factor above for one less period and add 1.

Example 4 ▶ Present Value of an Annuity in Arrears and Present Value of an Annuity Due

Required: Smith can make annual mortgage payments (not including taxes, etc.) of $4,800. How much can Smith borrow at 8% interest and repay in 20 years: (A) making 20 equal payments at the end of the year? (B) making 20 equal payments at the beginning of the year?

Solution A: Let   Payment = P = $4,800,   Interest Rate = r = 8%,   Period = n = 20 years
Present Value of an Annuity Factor at r Rate for n Periods = PVAF(r, n)
Present Value of the Annuity = PVA = P × PVAF(r, n)

PVAF(8%, 20 years) = 9.8181 (from Table 4)

Loan = PVA = $4,800 × 9.8181 = $47,126.88

Solution B: Let   Payment = P = $4,800,   Interest Rate = r = 8%,   Period = n = 20 years
Present Value of an Annuity Factor at r Rate for n Periods = PVAF(r, n)
Present Value of the Annuity in Advance = PVAA = P × [PVAF(r, n − 1) + 1]

PVAF(8%, 19 years) = 9.6036 (from Table 4)

Loan = PVAA = $4,800 × (9.6036 + 1) = $50,897.28

Example 5 ▶ Capital Lease Obligation

Alpha Company has a 10 year capital lease with an implicit interest rate of 8%. The $40,000 payments are made at the beginning of each year.

Required: What is the capital lease obligation (the present value of the lease payments)?

Solution: Let   Payment = P = $40,000,   Interest Rate = r = 8%,   Period = n = 10 years
Present Value of an Annuity Factor at r Rate for n Periods = PVAF(r, n)
Present Value of the Annuity in Advance = PVAA = P × [PVAF(r, n – 1) + 1]

PVAF(8%, 9 years) = 6.246888 (from Table 4)

Capital Lease Obligation = PVAA = $40,000 × (6.246888 + 1) = $289,875.52

This is the same as: Capital Lease Obligation = Initial Payment + PVA (where r = 8%, n = 9)
= Initial Payment + P × PVAF(8%, 9)
= $40,000   + $40,000 × 6.246888
= $289,875.52

Example 6 ▶ Internal Rate of Return

Beta Company is considering the purchase of a machine for $12,500. Beta expects a net year-end cash inflow of $5,000 annually over the machine's 3-year life. [The IRR is that rate at which NPV = 0. For more information on internal rate of return (IRR) and net present value (NPV), see Chapter 26 in the ARE volume.]

Required: What is this project's approximate internal rate of return?

Solution: This example involves a present single sum and an annuity. The present value of the single sum paid today is $12,500. In this situation, NPV is the present value of the purchase price (P) less the present value of the future annual cash inflow (PVA).

Let   Single Payment = P = $12,500   Interest Rate = r = ?
Annual Cash Inflow = A = $5,000   Period = n = 3 years
Present Value of an Annuity Factor at r Rate for n Periods = PVAF(r, n)

NPV = P – PVA   and NPV = 0   Thus,   P – PVA = 0

PVA = A × PVAF(r, n) so P – [A × PVAF(r, n)] = 0   or
P = A × PVAF(r, n)   or
P / A = PVAF(r, n)   and substituting known values:
$12,500 / $5,000 = PVAF(r, 3 years) or
PVAF(r, 3 years) = 2.5

Looking in the 3 period row of Table 4, we find the interest rate that produces the interest factor closest to 2.5 is in the 10% column. (Examiners generally narrow the field somewhat by supplying half a dozen values instead of a whole table, but they frequently also provide values from tables that are misleading. For instance, they may supply future values of annuities or present values of single sums.)

PVAF(8%, 3 years) = 2.577097 rounds to 2.6
PVAF(10%, 3 years) = 2.486852 rounds to 2.5 Thus, r (or IRR) is about <u>10%</u>.
PVAF(12%, 3 years) = 2.401831 rounds to 2.4

Financial Ratios

Analytics (or analytical procedures) concern the test of plausible relationships. In the absence of changes in conditions, it is reasonable to expect relationships among the elements of financial statements to remain similar from one period to the next. Several common financial statement ratios are reproduced here for your information. For more coverage of ratio analysis, consult your FAR volume.

When computing a ratio, remember to consider the following:

1. Net or gross amounts (e.g., receivables).

2. Average for the period or year-end (e.g., receivables, inventories, common shares outstanding).

3. Adjustments to income (e.g., interest, income taxes, preferred dividends).

We suggest that you concern yourself with knowing how to arrive at the less common ratios, rather than rote memorization of ratios. For instance, when *margin* is in the ratio name, it usually is a reference to sales. Thus *gross margin percentage* is the gross margin divided by sales, expressed as a percentage, and *net operating margin percentage* is operating income divided by sales, expressed as a percentage. *Turnover* refers to the number of cycles in a fiscal period. Thus *total asset turnover* is sales divided by total assets.

1. Working Capital — Current Assets - Current Liabilities

2. Current Ratio — $\dfrac{\text{Current Assets}}{\text{Current Liabilities}}$

3. Acid-Test or Quick Ratio — $\dfrac{\text{Cash + Marketable Securities + Net Receivables}}{\text{Current Liabilities}}$

4. Defensive-Interval Ratio — $\dfrac{\text{Cash + Marketable Securities + Net Receivables}}{\text{Average Daily Cash Expenditures}}$

5. Debt to Equity — $\dfrac{\text{Total Liabilities}}{\text{Owners' Equity}}$

6. Times Interest Earned — $\dfrac{\text{Income Before Income Taxes and Interest Charges}}{\text{Interest Charges}}$

7. Times Preferred Dividends Earned — $\dfrac{\text{Net Income}}{\text{Annual Preferred Dividend Requirement}}$

8. Accounts Receivable Turnover — $\dfrac{\text{Net Credit Sales}}{\text{Average Net Receivables}}$

9. Number of Days' Sales in Average Receivables — $\dfrac{360}{\text{Receivables Turnover}}$

10. Inventory Turnover — $\dfrac{\text{Cost of Goods Sold}}{\text{Average Inventory}}$

11. Return on Total Assets — $\dfrac{\text{Net Income + Interest Expense (Net of Tax)}}{\text{Average Total Assets}}$

12. Number of Days' Supply in Average Inventory — $\dfrac{360}{\text{Inventory Turnover}}$

- The number of days' supply in average (ending) inventory can also be computed in the following manner:

$$\frac{\text{Average (Ending) Inventory}}{\text{Average Daily Cost of Goods Sold}}$$

- Average daily cost of goods sold is determined by dividing cost of goods sold by the number of business days in the year (e.g., 365, 360, 300, or 250).

13. Length of Operating Cycle

$$\frac{\text{Number of days' sales}}{\text{in average receivables}} + \frac{\text{Number of days' supply}}{\text{in average inventory}}$$

14. Book Value Per Common Share

$$\frac{\text{Common Stockholders' Equity}}{\text{Number of Common Shares Outstanding}}$$

- To determine common stockholders' equity, preferred stock is subtracted from total stockholders' equity at the greater of its liquidation, par or stated value. Cumulative preferred stock dividends in arrears are also similarly subtracted. Treasury stock affects the denominator as the number of common shares outstanding is reduced.

15. Book Value Per Preferred Share

$$\frac{\text{Preferred Stockholders' Equity}}{\text{Number of Preferred Shares Outstanding}}$$

- Preferred stockholders' equity is comprised of (a) preferred stock at the greater of its liquidation, par or stated value and (b) cumulative preferred stock dividends in arrears.

16. Return on Common Stockholders' Equity

$$\frac{\text{Net Income} - \text{Preferred Dividends}}{\text{Average Common Stockholders' Equity}}$$

17. Return on Stockholders' Equity

$$\frac{\text{Net Income}}{\text{Average Stockholders' Equity}}$$

18. Earnings Per Share

$$\frac{\text{Net Income} - \text{Preferred Dividends}}{\text{Average Number of Common Shares Outstanding}}$$

19. Price-Earnings Ratio

$$\frac{\text{Market Price Per Common Share}}{\text{Earnings Per Common Share}}$$

20. Dividend Payout Ratio

$$\frac{\text{Cash Dividend Per Common Share}}{\text{Earnings Per Common Share}}$$

21. Yield on Common Stock

$$\frac{\text{Dividend Per Common Share}}{\text{Market Price Per Common Share}}$$

APPENDIX E
RECENTLY RELEASED AICPA QUESTIONS

In May 2005, the AICPA released several questions labeled as "Year 2005 CPA Exams." The BEC questions and the related unofficial solutions are reproduced here, along with the exclusive Bisk Education explanations. The AICPA did not state whether these questions were used on an exam. These questions are intended only as a study aid and should not be used to predict the content of future exams. It is extremely unlikely that released questions will appear on future examinations. The alphanumeric identifications associated with these questions were assigned by the AICPA.

Problem 1 MULTIPLE CHOICE QUESTIONS (100 to 125 minutes)

1. Johnson Co. is preparing its master budget for the first quarter of next year. Budgeted sales and production for one of the company's products are as follows:

Month	Sales	Production
January	10,000	12,000
February	12,000	11,000
March	15,000	16,000

Each unit of this product requires four pounds of raw materials. Johnson's policy is to have sufficient raw materials on hand at the end of each month for 40 percent of the following month's production requirements. The January 1 raw materials inventory is expected to conform with this policy. How many pounds of raw materials should Johnson budget to purchase for January?
a. 11,600
b. 46,400
c. 48,000
d. 65,600　　　　(R/05, BEC, 0116M, #1, 7888)

2. In the past, four direct labor hours were required to produce each unit of product Y. Material costs were $200 per unit, the direct labor rate was $20 per hour, and factory overhead was three times direct labor cost. In budgeting for next year, management is planning to outsource some manufacturing activities and to further automate others. Management estimates these plans will reduce labor hours by 25%, increase the factory overhead rate to 3.6 times direct labor costs, and increase material costs by $30 per unit. Management plans to manufacture 10,000 units. What amount should management budget for cost of goods manufactured?
a. $4,820,000
b. $5,060,000
c. $5,200,000
d. $6,500,000　　　　(R/05, BEC, 0184M, #2, 7889)

3. Mighty, Inc. processes chickens for distribution to major grocery chains. The two major products resulting from the production process are white breast meat and legs. Joint costs of $600,000 are incurred during standard production runs each month, which produce a total of 100,000 pounds of white breast meat and 50,000 pounds of legs. Each pound of white breast meat sells for $2 and each pound of legs sells for $1. If there are **no** further processing costs incurred after the split-off point, what amount of the joint costs would be allocated to the white breast meat on a relative sales value basis?
a. $120,000
b. $200,000
c. $400,000
d. $480,000　　　　(R/05, BEC, 0299M, #3, 7890)

4. Black, Inc. employs a weighted average method in its process costing system. Black's work in process inventory on June 30 consists of 40,000 units. These units are 100% complete with respect to materials and 60% complete with respect to conversion costs. The equivalent unit costs are $5.00 for materials and $7.00 for conversion costs. What is the total cost of the June 30 work in process inventory?
a. $200,000
b. $288,000
c. $368,000
d. $480,000　　　　(R/05, BEC, 0336M, #4, 7891)

5. Virgil Corp. uses a standard cost system. In May, Virgil purchased and used 17,500 pounds of materials at a cost of $70,000. The materials usage variance was $2,500 unfavorable and the standard materials allowed for May production was 17,000 pounds. What was the materials price variance for May?
a. $17,500 favorable
b. $17,500 unfavorable
c. $15,000 favorable
d. $15,000 unfavorable
　　　　(R/05, BEC, 0341M, #5, 7892)

6. Waldo company, which produces only one product, provides its most current month's data as follows:

Selling price per unit	$80

Variable costs per unit:

Direct materials	21
Direct labor	10
Variable manufacturing overhead	3
Variable selling and administrative	6

Fixed costs:

Manufacturing overhead	$76,000
Selling and administrative	58,000

Units:

Beginning inventory	0
Month's production	5,000
Number sold	4,500
Ending inventory	500

Based upon the above information, what is the total contribution margin for the month under the variable costing approach?
a. $ 46,000
b. $180,000
c. $207,000
d. $226,000   (R/05, BEC, 0342M, #6, 7893)

7. A management accountant performs a linear regression of maintenance cost vs. production using a computer spreadsheet. The regression output shows an "intercept" value of $322,897. How should the accountant interpret this information?
a. Y has a value of $322,897 when X equals zero.
b. X has a value of $322,897 when Y equals zero.
c. The residual error of the regression is $322,897.
d. Maintenance cost has an average value of $322,897.   (R/05, BEC, 0381M, #7, 7894)

8. Which of the following statements is correct concerning the security of messages in an electronic data interchange (EDI) system?
a. Removable drives that can be locked up at night provide adequate security when the confidentiality of data is the primary risk.
b. Message authentication in EDI systems performs the same function as segregation of duties in other information systems.
c. Encryption performed by a physically secure hardware device is more secure than encryption performed by software.
d. Security at the transaction phase in EDI systems is **not** necessary because problems at that level will be identified by the service provider.
          (R/05, BEC, 1432A, #8, 7895)

9. Which of the following documents would most likely contain specific rules for the management of a business corporation?
a. Articles of incorporation
b. Bylaws
c. Certificate of authority
d. Shareholders' agreement
          (R/05, BEC, 5103L, #9, 7896)

10. Following the formation of a corporation, which of the following terms best describes the process by which the promoter is released from, and the corporation is made liable for, pre-incorporation contractual obligations?
a. Assignment
b. Novation
c. Delegation
d. Accord and satisfaction
          (R/05, BEC, 5146L, #10, 7897)

11. Which of the following parties is liable to repay an illegal distribution to a corporation?
a. A director **not** breaching her/his duty in approving the distribution and the corporation is solvent
b. A director **not** breaching her/his duty in approving the distribution and the corporation is insolvent
c. A shareholder **not** knowing of the illegality of the distribution and the corporation is solvent
d. A shareholder **not** knowing of the illegality of the distribution and the corporation is insolvent
          (R/05, BEC, 5181L, #11, 7898)

12. Under the Revised Model Business Corporation Act, which of the following items of information should be included in a corporation's articles of incorporation (charter)?
a. Name and address of each preincorporation subscriber
b. Nature and purpose of the corporation's business
c. Name and address of the corporation's promoter
d. Election of either C corporation or S corporation status   (R/05, BEC, 9008K23L, #12, 7899)

13. Which of the following may **not** own shares in an S corporation?
a. Individuals
b. Estates
c. Trusts
d. Corporations   (R/05, BEC, A0037B, #13, 7900)

14. Which of the following activities would most likely detect computer-related fraud?
a. Using data encryption
b. Performing validity checks
c. Conducting fraud-awareness training
d. Reviewing the systems-access log
          (R/05, BEC, A0199B, #14, 7901)

15. The computer operating system performs scheduling, resource allocation, and data retrieval functions based on a set of instructions provided by the
a. Multiplexer
b. Peripheral processors
c. Concentrator
d. Job control language
(R/05, BEC, A0244B, #15, 7902)

16. Which of the following types of control plans is particular to a specific process or subsystem, rather than related to the timing of its occurrence?
a. Preventive
b. Corrective
c. Application
d. Detective   (R/05, BEC, A0261B, #16, 7903)

17. Minon, Inc. purchased a long-term asset on the last day of the current year. What are the effects of this purchase on return on investment and residual income?

	Return on investment	Residual income
a.	Increase	Increase
b.	Decrease	Decrease
c.	Increase	Decrease
d.	Decrease	Increase

(R/05, BEC, A0389B, #17, 7904)

18. The profitability index is a variation on which of the following capital budgeting models?
a. Internal rate of return
b. Economic value-added
c. Net present value
d. Discounted payback
(R/05, BEC, A0409B, #18, 7905)

19. Under the balanced scorecard concept developed by Kaplan and Norton, employee satisfaction and retention are measures used under which of the following perspectives?
a. Customer
b. Internal business
c. Learning and growth
d. Financial   (R/05, BEC, A0415B, #19, 7906)

20. If **no** provisions are made in an agreement, a general partnership allocates profits and losses based on the
a. Value of actual contributions made by each partner
b. Number of partners
c. Number of hours each partner worked in the partnership during the year
d. Number of years each partner belonged to the partnership   (R/05, BEC, A0438B, #20, 7907)

21. Which of the following procedures should be included in the disaster recovery plan for an Information Technology department?
a. Replacement personal computers for user departments
b. Identification of critical applications
c. Physical security of warehouse facilities
d. Cross-training of operating personnel
(R/05, BEC, A0548B, #21, 7908)

22. A digital signature is used primarily to determine that a message is
a. Unaltered in transmission
b. Not intercepted en route
c. Received by the intended recipient
d. Sent to the correct address
(R/05, BEC, A0582B, #22, 7909)

23. At the end of a company's first year of operations, 2,000 units of inventory are on hand. Variable costs are $100 per unit, and fixed manufacturing costs are $30 per unit. The use of absorption costing, rather than variable costing, would result in a higher net income of what amount?
a. $ 60,000
b. $140,000
c. $200,000
d. $260,000   (R/05, BEC, A0602B, #23, 7910)

24. Which of the following decreases stockholder equity?
a. Investments by owners
b. Distributions to owners
c. Issuance of stock
d. Acquisition of assets in a cash transaction
(R/05, BEC, A0624B, #24, 7911)

25. Vested, Inc. made some changes in operations and provided the following information:

	Year 2	Year 3
Operating revenues	$ 900,000	$1,100,000
Operating expenses	650,000	700,000
Operating assets	1,200,000	2,000,000

What percentage represents the return on investment for year 3?
a. 28.57%
b. 25%
c. 20.31%
d. 20%   (R/05, BEC, A0812B, #25, 7912)

26. Zig Corp. provides the following information:

Pretax operating profit $ 300,000,000
Tax rate   40%
Capital used to generate
  profits 50%, 50% equity $1,200,000,000
Cost of equity   15%
Cost of debt   5%

What of the following represents Zig's year-end economic value-added amount?
a. $0
b. $ 60,000,000
c. $120,000,000
d. $180,000,000   (R/05, BEC, A0813B, #26, 7913)

27. Food Corp. owned a restaurant called The Ambers. The corporation president, T.J. Jones, hired a contractor to make repairs at the restaurant, signing the contract, "T.J. Jones for The Ambers." Two invoices for restaurant repairs were paid by Food Corp. with corporate checks. Upon presenting the final invoice, the contractor was told that it would not be paid. The contractor sued Food Corp. Which of the following statements is correct regarding the liability of Food Corp.?
a. It is **not** liable because Jones is liable.
b. It is **not** liable because the corporation was an undisclosed principal.
c. It is liable because Jones is **not** liable.
d. It is liable because Jones had authority to make the contract.   (R/05, BEC, A0836B, #27, 7914)

28. Which of the following steps in the strategic planning process should be completed first?
a. Translate objectives into goals
b. Determine actions to achieve goals
c. Develop performance measures
d. Create a mission statement
              (R/05, BEC, A0861B, #28, 7915)

29. A divisional manager receives a bonus based on 20% of the residual income from the division. The results of the division include: Divisional revenues, $1,000,000; divisional expenses, $500,000; divisional assets, $2,000,000; and the required rate of return is 15%. What amount represents the manager's bonus?
a. $200,000
b. $140,000
c. $100,000
d. $ 40,000   (R/05, BEC, A1019B, #29, 7916)

30. What is a major disadvantage to using a private key to encrypt data?
a. Both sender and receiver must have the private key before this encryption method will work.
b. The private key **cannot** be broken into fragments and distributed to the receiver.
c. The private key is used by the sender for encryption but **not** by the receiver for decryption.
d. The private key is used by the receiver for decryption but **not** by the sender for encryption.
              (R/05, BEC, A1117B, #30, 7917)

31. In an accounting information system, which of the following types of computer files most likely would be a master file?
a. Inventory subsidiary
b. Cash disbursements
c. Cash receipts
d. Payroll transactions
              (R/05, BEC, A1274B, #31, 7918)

32. Which of the following forecasting methods relies mostly on judgment?
a. Time series models
b. Econometric models
c. Delphi
d. Regression   (R/05, BEC, A1295B, #32, 7919)

33. To address the problem of a recession, the Federal Reserve Bank most likely would take which of the following actions?
a. Lower the discount rate it charges to banks for loans
b. Sell U.S. government bonds in open-market transactions
c. Increase the federal funds rate charged by banks when they borrow from one another
d. Increase the level of funds a bank is legally required to hold in reserve
              (R/05, BEC, A1487B, #33, 7920)

34. Which of the following types of costs are prime costs?
a. Direct materials and direct labor
b. Direct materials and overhead
c. Direct labor and overhead
d. Direct materials, direct labor, and overhead
              (R/05, BEC, A1563B, #34, 7921)

35. A multiperiod project has a positive net present value. Which of the following statements is correct regarding its required rate of return?
a. Less than the company's weighted average cost of capital
b. Less than the project's internal rate of return
c. Greater than the company's weighted average cost of capital
d. Greater than the project's internal rate of return
              (R/05, BEC, A1618B, #35, 7922)

36. Which of the following is an advantage of a computer-based system for transaction processing over a manual system? A computer-based system
a. Does **not** require as stringent a set of internal controls
b. Will produce a more accurate set of financial statements
c. Will be more efficient at producing financial statements
d. Eliminates the need to reconcile control accounts and subsidiary ledgers
(R/05, BEC, A1717B, #36, 7923)

37. Which of the following risks can be minimized by requiring all employees accessing the information system to use passwords?
a. Collusion
b. Data entry errors
c. Failure of server duplicating function
d. Firewall vulnerability
(R/05, BEC, A1719B, #37, 7924)

38. Which of the following actions is the acknowledged preventive measure for a period of deflation?
a. Increasing interest rates
b. Increasing the money supply
c. Decreasing interest rates
d. Decreasing the money supply
(R/05, BEC, A1759B, #38, 7925)

39. Which of the following areas of responsibility are normally assigned to a systems programmer in a computer system environment?
a. Systems analysis and applications programming
b. Data communications hardware and software
c. Operating systems and compilers
d. Computer operations
(R/05, BEC, A1838B, #39, 7926)

40. Under which of the following conditions is the supplier most able to influence or control buyers?
a. When the supplier's products are **not** differentiated
b. When the supplier does **not** face the threat of substitute products
c. When the industry is controlled by a large number of companies
d. When the purchasing industry is an important customer to the supplying industry
(R/05, BEC, A1925B, #40, 7927)

41. An auditor is required to obtain an understanding of the entity's business, including business cycles and reasons for business fluctuations. What is the audit purpose most directly served by obtaining this understanding?
a. To enable the auditor to accurately identify reportable conditions
b. To assist the auditor to accurately interpret information obtained during an audit
c. To allow the auditor to more accurately perform tests of controls
d. To decide whether it will be necessary to perform analytical procedures
(R/05, BEC, A2008B, #41, 7928)

42. Which of the following segments of the economy will be **least** affected by the business cycle?
a. Commercial construction industry
b. Machinery and equipment industry
c. Residential construction industry
d. Healthcare industry
(R/05, BEC, A2080B, #42, 7929)

43. Which of the following inputs would be most beneficial to consider when management is developing the capital budget?
a. Supply/demand for the company's products
b. Current product sales prices and costs
c. Wage trends
d. Profit center equipment requests
(R/05, BEC, A2160B, #43, 7930)

44. An S corporation must adhere to all of the following conditions **except** having
a. No more than 75 shareholders
b. A nonresident alien as a shareholder
c. An individual as a shareholder
d. One class of stock
(R/05, BEC, C00387B, #44, 7931)

45. Most client/server applications operate on a three-tiered architecture consisting of which of the following layers?
a. Desktop client, application, and database
b. Desktop client, software, and hardware
c. Desktop server, application, and database
d. Desktop server, software, and hardware
(R/05, BEC, C00459B, #45, 7932)

46. Which of the following inventory management approaches orders at the point where carrying costs equate nearest to restocking costs in order to minimize total inventory cost?
a. Economic order quantity
b. Just-in-time
c. Materials requirements planning
d. ABC
(R/05, BEC, C01030B, #46, 7933)

47. Which of the following statements is true regarding the payback method?
a. It does **not** consider the time value of money.
b. It is the time required to recover the investment and earn a profit.
c. It is a measure of how profitable one investment project is compared to another.
d. The salvage value of old equipment is ignored in the event of equipment replacement.
(R/05, BEC, C01507B, #47, 7934)

48. Jones, Smith, and Bay wanted to form a company called JSB Co. but were unsure about which type of entity would be most beneficial based on their concerns. They all desired the opportunity to make tax-free contributions and distributions where appropriate. They wanted earnings to accumulate tax-free. They did not want to be subject to personal holding tax and did not want double taxation of income. Bay was going to be the only individual giving management advice to the company and wanted to be a member of JSB through his current company, Channel, Inc. Which of the following would be the most appropriate business structure to meet all of their concerns?
a. Proprietorship
b. S corporation
c. C corporation
d. Limited liability partnership
(R/05, BEC, C03414B, #48, 7935)

49. Which of the following statements describes the same characteristic for both an S corporation and a C corporation?
a. Both corporations can have more than 75 shareholders.
b. Both corporations have the disadvantage of double taxation.
c. Shareholders can contribute property into a corporation without being taxed.
d. Shareholders can be either citizens of the United States or foreign countries.
(R/05, BEC, C03550B, #49, 7936)

50. Smith was an officer of CCC Corp. As an officer, the business judgment rule applied to Smith in which of the following ways?
a. Because Smith is **not** a director, the rule does **not** apply.
b. If Smith makes, in good faith, a serious but honest mistake in judgment, Smith is generally **not** liable to CCC for damages caused.
c. If Smith makes, in good faith, a serious but honest mistake in judgment, Smith is generally liable to CCC for damages caused, but CCC may elect to reimburse Smith for any damages Smith paid.
d. If Smith makes, in good faith, a serious but honest mistake in judgment, Smith is generally liable to CCC for damages caused, and CCC is prohibited from reimbursing Smith for any damages Smith paid. (R/05, BEC, C03586B, #50, 7937)

MULTIPLE CHOICE QUESTION SOLUTIONS

Solution 1

Legend for Cognitive Skills
1   Understanding
2   Judgment / Application
3   Analysis

1. (b)   Since 40% of raw materials for January production is in the January 1 raw materials inventory, Johnson must purchase only 60% of the raw materials for January production during January. Johnson also must purchase 40% of raw materials for February production during January to have it on hand on February 1. Total January production requires (12,000 units × 4 lbs/unit) 48,000 lbs of raw materials. Total February production requires (11,000 units × 4 lbs/unit) 44,000 lbs of raw materials. (60% × 48,000 lbs) + (40% × 44,000 lbs) = 46,400 lbs. (Chapter 54-1-2; Skill: 3; CSO: 5.1.3)

2. (b)   The estimated material cost is $200 /unit + $30 /unit = $230 /unit. The estimated direct labor hours are 4 hours /unit × (1 - 0.25) = 3 hours. The estimated direct labor cost (DLC) is $20 / hour x 3 hours /unit = $60 /unit. The estimated overhead cost is $60 DLC /unit × 3.6 / DLC = $216 /unit. $230 + $60 + $216 = $506. $506 /unit × 10,000 units = $5,060,000. (Chapter 54-1-2; Skill: 3; CSO: 5.1.3)

3. (d)   The sales value of the breast meat is 100,000 lbs × $2 / lb = $200,000. The sales value of the leg meat is 50,000 lbs × $1 / lb = $50,000. The relative sales value of the breast meat is [$200,000 / ($200,000 + $50,000)] 80%. 80% × $600,000 = $480,000. (Chapter 53-4-3; Skill: 3; CSO: 5.3.1)

4. (c)   Material costs are 40,000 units × 100% × $5.00 / EFU = $200,000. Conversion costs are 40,000 units × 60% × $7.00 / EFU = $168,000. $200,000 + $168,000 = $368,000. (Chapter 53-2-2; Skill: 3; CSO: 5.3.2)

5. (a)   As the material usage variance is $2,500 unfavorable, $2,500 = (AQ – SQ) × SP; SP = $2,500 / (AQ – SQ) = $2,500 / (17,500 lb – 17,000 lb) = $5.00 / lb. Actual price is $70,000 / 17,500 lb = $4.00 / lb. Material price variance is (AP – SP) × AQ = ($4.00 / lb - $5.00 / lb) × 17,500 lb = -$17,500. As the actual price is lower than the standard price, the price variance is favorable. (Chapter 53-7-6; Skill: 3; CSO: 5.3.1)

6. (b)   Variable costs per unit are $21 + $10 + $3 + $6 = $40. Contribution margin is sales less all variable expenses or ($80 /unit – $40 /unit) × 4,500 units = $180,000. Editor's note: This question is identical to #69 (ID 7674) in Chapter 52, with an Area 5 CSO classification. The editors cannot explain why this question was assigned an Area 3 CSO classification; inquiries regarding this issue should be directed to the AICPA examiners. (Chapter 52-4-6; Skill: 3; CSO: 3.3.2)

7. (a)   As a matter of convention, the independent variable is assigned to the horizontal axis, which is considered "x," and the dependent variable is assigned to the vertical axis, which is considered "y." The point where the line intercepts the y axis is where the x-axis value is zero. (Chapter 54-2-2; Skill: 3; CSO: 5.3.3)

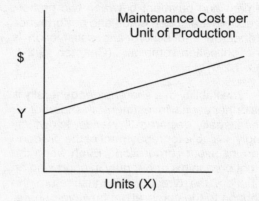

8. (c)   Software can be altered by remote access. The hardware containing physical safeguards must be accessed physically to be altered. In an online system, it is simpler to restrict access to encryption hardware than to encryption software. Locking up removable drives when not in use doesn't provide security for the information on those drives when they are being used. Segregation of duties reduces the opportunities for the same employee to both perpetrate wrongdoing and conceal evidence of it within an entity's records. Message authentication typically is concerned with both internal and external messages. Failing to provide for security at the transaction phase in an EDI system is akin to failure to provide for security over checks in a manual system; the amount of security that a service provider can provide at this level is limited, as proper and improper transactions may not have characteristics that allow the service provider to distinguish between them. (Chapter 55-4-1; Skill: 2; CSO: 4.1.4)

9. (b)   Bylaws are the rules and regulations that govern the internal management of a corporation. They need not be filed publicly. The articles of incorporation contain certain mandatory provisions, typically providing for the service of process, capital structure, and duration. They often serve to allow

creditors to know where to collect debts. The term "certificate of authority" is not commonly used. Shareholder agreements define what shareholders, not the corporation, agree to do. (Chapter 49-2-2; Skill: 1; CSO: 1.2.0)

10. (b) By definition, a novation is when a one party (the creditor) agrees to look only to a third party (the corporation) for satisfaction of a contract with a second party (the promoter) and thereby releases the second party from liability. Assignment is the act of transferring all or part of one's contractual rights. Delegation is the act of transferring all or part of one's contractual duties. Assignment and delegation generally don't eliminate the obligations of the original parties to the contract. Accord and satisfaction is an agreement and payment between two parties; after the agreement has been made and performance has been tendered, the accord and satisfaction is complete; no obligation remains. (Chapter 49-2-1; Skill: 3; CSO: 1.2.0)

11. (d) The liability of a shareholder generally is limited to his or her capital investment. A shareholder who receives illegally declared dividends, knowingly or unknowingly, is liable for repayment of the dividend amount to an insolvent corporation. Even when the director did not breach his or her duty in approving an illegal distribution, the director still must return the illegal distribution to the corporation; however, shareholders generally receive distributions, not directors. (Chapter 49-4-2; Skill: 2; CSO: 1.4.0)

12. (b) Articles of incorporation should include the nature and purpose of the corporation's business. The name of the corporation and its initial registered agent and the address of its initial registered office must be included in the articles of incorporation, as well as the name and address of each incorporator, but not the names and addresses of promoters or pre-incorporation subscribers. Election of C or S corporation status is made when filing federal tax returns, not when filing articles of incorporation with a state. (Chapter 49-2-2; Skill: 1; CSO: 1.2.0)

13. (d) Individuals, estates, and trusts may own shares in an S corporation. (Chapter 49-6-5; Skill: 1; CSO: 1.1.3)

14. (d) Reviewing the systems-access log would detect unauthorized users. Using data encryption is more likely to prevent fraud and unauthorized disclosure. Performing validity checks tends to prevent errors, and to a lesser extent, fraud. Conducting fraud-awareness training tends to prevent fraud. (Chapter 55-4-1; Skill: 2; CSO: 4.4.0)

15. (d) Job control language (JCL) is a command language that launches applications, specifying priorities, program sizes, running sequences, databases used, and files used. The term "peripheral processors" is not widely used. A concentrator combines multiple communication channels into one. A multiplexer (or multiplexor) is a device for communications that converts several low-speed transmissions into one high-speed transmission and back again. A concentrator differs from a multiplexer in that the total bandwidth of a concentrators' inputs don't necessarily equal the total bandwidth of its outputs. A concentrator temporarily stores data to compensate for this imbalance. (Chapter 55-1-4; Skill: 2; CSO: 4.2.1)

16. (c) Application controls are limited to a specific application, as opposed to system controls. Preventive controls occur before an error happens. Corrective and detective controls occur after an error happens. (Chapter 55-1-4; Skill: 1; CSO: 4.3.2)

17. (b) Return on investment (ROI) is operating income divided by average invested capital. ROI decreases when operating income decreases or when average invested capital increases. One might argue that the purchase of a long-term asset merely transfers an asset from short-term to long-term investment; however, there is no answer option that allows for no change in return on investment in this question. Therefore, to answer this question, one must assume the examiners figure that this purchase would increase average invested capital, but not affect operating income. An increase in average invested capital with no change to operating income results in a decrease to ROI. Residual income is operating income less the cost of capital times average invested capital. An increase in average invested capital with no change to operating income results in a decrease to residual income. (Chapter 51-5-5; Skill: 2; CSO: 3.1.1)

18. (c) The profitability index is calculated by dividing the present value of the cash flows by the initial investment. The profitability index was developed because is not very meaningful to compare the net present values (NPV) of different projects that differ greatly in size directly. The internal rate of return is that interest rate at which a project has a NPV of zero. Economic value-added (EVA) is operating profit after taxes less the summation of the average invested capital times the costs of that capital for each type of capital. Discounted payback is not a commonly used term. (Chapter 51-5-3; Skill: 1; CSO: 3.1.1)

19. (c) The Kaplan and Norton Balanced Scorecard is a strategic tool that enables organizations to implement a company's vision and strategy, working from four perspectives: (1) financial, (2) customer, (3) internal process, and (4) learning and growth. The **learning and growth** perspective (also referred to as innovation) includes employee training and corporate cultural attitudes related to both individual and corporate self-improvement. In a knowledge-worker entity, people are the main resource. In a climate of rapid technological change, it is necessary for knowledge workers to be learning continuously, as entities often are unable to hire new trained workers. Learning also includes things like mentors and tutors within the organization, as well as that ease of communication among workers that allows them to get help readily as needed. **Financial perspective:** Kaplan and Norton do not disregard the traditional need for timely and accurate financial data; however, they recognize that the typical emphasis on financials leads to an unbalanced situation with regard to other perspectives. Poor performance from the **customer perspective** is a leading indicator of future decline, even though the current financial picture looks good; if customers are not satisfied, they eventually will find other suppliers that meet their needs. The **internal process** (or strategic) perspective evaluates how well a business is running, and whether its products and services conform to customer requirements (the mission). Editor's note: This question is identical to #19 (ID 7668) in Chapter 54. (Chapter 54-3-1; Skill: 1; CSO: 5.1.1)

20. (b) The Revised Uniform Partnership Act provides that where a partnership agreement is silent as to the division of profits and losses, then profits and losses are divided equally among the partners, regardless of capital contributions, participation, or length of partnership membership. (Chapter 48-3-3; Skill: 1; CSO: 1.3.0)

21. (b) Identification of critical applications is important for the information technology (IT) department disaster recovery plan so that those applications can be given appropriate priorities for scarce IT department resources during plan implementation and restoration in the event of total failure. A company-wide recovery plan probably would include replacement of damaged user department equipment by the purchasing department, physical security of all facilities during and after an emergency by the security department, and cross-training of operating personnel by the operating departments. (Chapter 55-4-2; Skill: 2; CSO: 4.4.0)

22. (a) A digital signature is a guarantee that information has not been modified, like the tamper-proof seal on a bottle of aspirin. Digital signatures are used for establishing secure web site connections and verifying the validity of transmitted files. Files with digital signatures may be intercepted, nor are the contents necessarily encrypted. A digital signature does not verify the receiving person or address. (Chapter 55-4-1; Skill: 1; CSO: 4.3.2)

23. (a) Absorption costing includes fixed manufacturing costs in inventory. If there is ending inventory, the fixed manufacturing costs associated with that inventory do not get expensed on an absorption cost income statement. Direct (or variable) costing expenses all fixed costs as expenses of the period, including the fixed manufacturing costs of ending inventory. As there was no beginning inventory, the difference in the amounts of income calculated under the two methods is the amount of fixed manufacturing costs associated with the inventory on hand. 2,000 units × $30 = $60,000. (Chapter 52-4-3; Skill: 3; CSO: 3.3.1)

24. (b) Distributions to owners decrease stockholder equity. The issuance of stock by a corporation is an investment by the owners (purchasers of the stock). Acquisition of assets in a cash transaction doesn't affect equity; assets are exchanged for assets. Editor's note: The editors cannot explain why this question is designated by the examiners for the BEC exam section, rather than FAR; inquiries regarding this issue should be directed to the AICPA examiners. Given the AICPA examiner's stated intent to make the BEC exam section integrative, the editors recommend that candidates review for the BEC section after, or concurrently with, all the other exam sections. (Chapter 49-3-3; Skill: 1; CSO: 1.3.0)

25. (b) Return on investment (ROI) is operating income divided by average invested capital. Operating income is operating revenues less operating expenses ($1,100,000 - $700,000 = $400,000). Average invested capital is half of the sum of invested capital at the beginning and ending of the year [($1,200,000 + $2,000,000) / 2 = $1,600,000]. $400,000 / $1,600,000 = 25%. (Chapter 51-5-5; Skill: 3; CSO: 3.1.1)

26. (b) The economic value-added (EVA) is operating profit (P) after taxes less the summation of the average invested capital (Cn) times the costs of that capital (kn) for each type of capital. In other words, EVA is the net operating profit after tax less the opportunity cost of capital. The post-tax operating profit is $180,000,000 [$300,000,000 × (1 – 0.40)] The equity capital is $600M (50% of $1,200M) so the cost of equity capital is $90M ($600M

× 15%). The cost of debt capital is $30M ($600M × 5%). $180M – ($90M + $30M) = $60M. Editor's Note: Candidates may note that the word "debt" seems to be missing from this question in the fourth line; if something similar occurs during your exam, answer as best you can and bring the potential error to the examiners' attention. To answer this question, we must assume that 50% of the capital is debt and that the cost of equity and debt is the same as the opportunity cost of that capital. This assumption is warranted because a cost of debt is provided and no other explanation for the source of 50% of the capital is provided. If you encounter a question during your exam that you believe is in error, notify the AICPA in accordance with guidance in the AICPA's publication, *Uniform CPA Examination Candidate Bulletin: Information for Applicants.* FYI: This question is identical to #73 (ID 7670) in Chapter 51. (Chapter 51-5-7; Skill: 3; CSO: 3.1.1)

27. (d) Corporate officers have both express authority to contract for the corporation as well as that implied authority reasonably necessary to carry out their duties. By signing "T. J. Jones for The Ambers," Jones (1) discloses the principal and (2) is not liable. Jones' lack of liability doesn't eliminate Food Corp.'s liability. Editor's note: Candidates may notice that this question also is appropriate for the REG exam section, as corporate directors' rights and obligations do not differ from other agents in the sort of circumstance illustrated by this question. Given the AICPA examiner's stated intent to make the BEC exam section integrative, the editors recommend that candidates review for the BEC section after, or concurrently with, all the other exam sections. (Chapter 49-1-8; Skill: 3; CSO: 1.4.0)

28. (d) A mission is the purpose for the entity's existence. Without at least an informal mission statement, appropriate objectives, goals, and measures cannot be developed. An ideal mission statement defines the essential reason of an entity's existence, separates it from similar entities, and delineates the scope of operations in terms of products and customers. Generally, a mission statement is reviewed, created, or amended before any other strategic management steps, as the mission statement has a broad impact on goals and objectives. Performance measures typically are set after goals and objectives are determined. Editor's note: This question is identical to #32 (ID 7675) in Chapter 54. (Chapter 54-4-3; Skill: 1; CSO: 5.1.1)

29. (d) Residual income is operating income less the summation of the cost of capital times average invested capital for each type of capital. The required rate of return is another term for the cost of capital. Operating income is $1,000,000 – $500,000

= $500,000. Residual income is $500,000 – ($2,000,000 × 15%) = $200,000. The manager's bonus is $200,000 × 20% = $40,000. (Chapter 51-5-6; Skill: 3; CSO: 5.2.1)

30. (a) A private-key encryption system uses a key that is intended to be kept secret and known only by the sender and intended recipient of encrypted messages. The sender encrypts messages with the same key that the recipient uses to decrypt messages. The private key may not be transmitted in an unencrypted message or the security of the system would be compromised. Sending fragments of a key in several messages reduces, but doesn't eliminate, this weakness. One must assume that this question is asking about a symmetric (private-key) encryption system, as there is no correct answer if an asymmetric system is assumed; candidates often must make similar assumptions to answer exam questions. (Chapter 55-4-1; Skill: 1; CSO: 4.3.1)

31. (a) Cash disbursements, cash receipts, and payroll transactions are all examples of transactions; records pertaining to these events are maintained in transaction files which update master files. Editor's Note: "Inventory subsidiary" is not a common name for a master file. The editors don't expect similar questions to appear on future exams. FYI: This question is identical to #81 (ID 7676) in Chapter 55. (Chapter 55-2-2; Skill: 3; CSO: 4.3.2)

32. (c) Lacking full knowledge, decision-makers have to rely on their own intuition or on expert opinion. Expert judgment is a legitimate and useful input in generating forecasts; however, single experts sometimes suffer biases, while groups may suffer from "follow the leader" tendencies or "groupthink." The Delphi method attempts to overcome the disadvantages of conventional committee action through anonymity, controlled feedback, and statistical response. A Delphi method outcome is nothing but opinion (i.e., judgments) and is only as valid as the opinions of the experts who make up the group. Time series models provide an analysis of serially correlated data in both time and frequency domains. Econometrics is the use of mathematical and statistical techniques to study economics problems. An econometric model is an economic model formulated so that its parameters can be estimated if one determines that the model is appropriate for a given situation. Regression is a form of statistical modeling that attempts to evaluate the relationship between one dependent variable and one or more independent variables. Editor's note: This question is identical to #10 (ID 7677) in Chapter 54. (Chapter 54-2-5; Skill: 3; CSO: 5.1.2)

33. (a) By lowering the discount rate that it charges to banks for loans, the Federal Reserve Board (the Fed) lowers the interest rate, which increases the money supply and encourages borrowing. The U.S. Treasury sells U.S. bonds, not the Fed. Banks decide what rate they will charge each other when they borrow from one another. Increasing the level of funds that a bank legally is required to hold in reserve would decrease the money supply and discourage borrowing. (Chapter 50-2-6, also see Chapter 50-2-2; Skill: 1; CSO: 2.2.0)

34. (a) Prime costs are the sum of direct materials costs and direct labor costs. (Chapter 52-1-1; Skill: 1; CSO: 5.3.3)

35. (b) With net present value (NPV), a certain rate at which to compute the present value of the cash inflows is used; this rate is the cost of capital. The required rate of return is another term for the cost of capital; if a minimal rate is not attained, investors will take their money elsewhere. A project that earns exactly the required rate of return will have a NPV of zero. A positive NPV identifies projects that earn in excess of the cost of capital. In other words, the internal rate of return for these projects is greater than the cost of capital. The required rate of return generally is higher for more risky projects and lower for less risky projects; therefore, a project's required rate of return may differ from the company's weighted average cost of capital. (Chapter 51-5-3; Skill: 3; CSO: 3.1.2)

36. (c) A computerized system will be more efficient at producing financial statements. No matter what method is used to produce financial statements, the process still requires internal controls stringent enough to be effective, accurate financial statements, and reconciled control accounts and subsidiary ledgers. (Chapter 55-2-1; Skill: 1; CSO: 4.1.2)

37. (d) Requiring the use of well-developed passwords to access systems increases the effectiveness of a firewall. Passwords will not reduce collusion, data entry errors, or the failure of server duplication significantly. An appropriate environment is a better aid against collusion. Data entry errors can be minimized by various input controls, such as edit checks. As an issue of business continuity, server duplication failure is better avoided by redundant systems than by the use of passwords. Editor's note: This question is identical to #94 (ID 7681) in Chapter 55. (Chapter 55-4-1; Skill: 1; CSO: 4.1.4)

38. (b) Deflation is a decrease in the general level of prices. When the money supply increases, the general level of prices tends to rise. Inflation and deflation tends to effect nominal interest rates; interest rates tend not to effect inflation and deflation. (Chapter 50-2-7; Skill: 3; CSO: 2.2.0)

39. (c) A systems programmer normally programs operating systems and compilers. A compiler is software that translates programs from one computer language to another. Systems analysts normally analyze systems, design the overall system, and prepare system flowcharts. A datacom analyst or network administrator commonly has responsibility for developing and maintaining a data communications network; generally, a datacom analyst does more network planning than device configuration or troubleshooting. Application programmers normally program applications. Computer operators generally are assigned to computer operations (data entry, processing, and output). (Chapter 55-1-5; Skill: 1; CSO: 4.2.1)

40. (b) In a pure monopoly, the supplier is most able to influence or control buyers because the supplier is the sole source for the product. A pure monopoly has a unique product without close substitutes. Monopolistic competition is characterized by a large number of sellers and differentiated products and some influence over buyers through non-price competition (advertising, brands, etc.). In a perfect (or pure) competitive market, suppliers are least able to influence or control buyers, as buyers can go to another supplier readily. Perfect competition is characterized by many factors, including a large number of buyers and sellers acting independently and a homogeneous or standardized product. When the purchasing industry is an important customer to the supplying industry, typically, the purchasing industry has the greater influence. (Chapter 50-1-8; Skill: 1; CSO: 2.3.0)

41. (b) An understanding of the business cycle and reasons for business fluctuations is to assist the auditor to interpret information obtained during an audit. For example, the auditor must evaluate whether estimates are reasonable and must realize that estimates that are reasonable during favorable economic periods can not be expected to continue as reasonable during eventual unfavorable periods. Reportable conditions are weaknesses in internal control; while unfavorable economic periods can exert pressures that cause or further strain weaknesses in the internal controls, reportable conditions also can occur during favorable economic periods. Economic considerations have little impact on tests of internal controls. Analytical procedures (or analytics) must be performed in the planning and review stages of an audit; they may be appropriate for the evidence-gathering stage as well. When deciding whether to use analytics in the evidence-gathering stage, business fluctuations rarely are a major

consideration. Editor's note: The editors cannot explain why this question is designated by the examiners for the BEC exam section, rather than AUD; inquiries regarding this issue should be directed to the AICPA examiners. Given the AICPA examiner's stated intent to make the BEC exam section integrative, the editors recommend that candidates review for the BEC section after, or concurrently with, all the other exam sections. (Chapter 50-2-2; Skill: 2; CSO: 2.1.0)

42. (d) Industries with inelastic demand are least affected by the business cycle. Most health-care has few substitutes and rarely can be delayed until more favorable economic conditions. Health insurance also buffers healthcare decisions from economic considerations somewhat. Industries with elastic demand are most affected by the business cycle. Many economic theories explain fluctuations in the business cycle by focusing on investment expenditures such as commercial construction and investment in machinery and equipment. During recessions, employment levels shrink and individuals generally are unwilling to incur additional debt that typically is associated with residential construction. (Chapter 50-2-2; Skill: 3; CSO: 2.1.0)

43. (d) If capital expenditures are not needed, favorable contentions for the purchase of capital projects are irrelevant. (Chapter 54-1-2; Skill: 3; CSO: 5.1.3)

44. (b) Nonresident aliens, corporations, and foreign trusts generally may not be S corporation shareholders. Before the American Jobs Creation Act of 2004 (AJCA '04) became effective (October 22, 2004), a maximum of 75 shareholders was permitted for S corporations, with a husband and wife eligible to be considered one shareholder. (Provisions of the AJCA '04 are eligible to be tested starting in the July-August 2005 exam window.) Only one class of stock is allowed, although shares of stock that differ solely in voting rights are not treated as having more than one class of stock. Because of the way that the question is worded, the answer "an individual as a shareholder" also is correct, as there is no requirement that an S corporation have any individuals as shareholders, although they certainly are permissible as shareholders; however, answer (b) is a "better" answer, as a nonresident alien may not be a shareholder of an S corporation. Editor's Note: Due to the existence of two correct answers, the editors do not expect this question to appear on future exams. If you encounter a question during your exam that you believe is in error, notify the AICPA in accordance with guidance in the AICPA's publication, *Uniform CPA Examination Candidate Bulletin: Information for Applicants.* (Chapter 49-6-5; Skill: 1; CSO: 1.1.3)

45. (a) Client-server architecture generally separates the client (usually a graphical user interface) from the server (heavy-duty computing). Each computer or process on the network is either a client or a server. Server software commonly runs on powerful computers dedicated for that application. Client software typically runs on desktop computers. In three-tier architecture, application servers store data on yet a third computer, known as a database server. (Chapter 55-1-4; Skill: 1; CSO: 4.3.1)

46. (a) The economic order quantity model determines an ideal order quantity based on demand, ordering costs, and carrying costs. Just-in-time inventory management typically involves negotiating long-term contracts with a limited number of vendors who deliver quality materials on as they are needed. Material requirements planning (MRP) is a system for effectively managing material requirements in a manufacturing process, typically in a computerized environments, using bill of material data, inventory data, and master production schedules, making recommendations to reorder materials and reschedule open orders when due dates and required dates are out of synchronization. Activity-based costing (ABC) allocates overhead to products based on multiple drivers. (Chapter 51-4-3, also see Chapters 53-6-1, 54-3-2; Skill: 1; CSO: 3.3.1)

47. (a) The payback period is the length of time required to recover the initial cash outflow from incremental cash inflows after tax. Profits are not considered. It often serves a rough screening device, but the payback method doesn't compare relative profitability of different projects. The salvage value of old equipment is included as an offset to other cash outflows in determining the initial cash outflow. (Chapter 51-5-3; Skill: 1; CSO: 3.1.1)

48. (d) While a corporation has no implied power to enter into a partnership, it may do so if authorized by its charter or state corporation statute. By definition, a proprietorship has only one owner. A C corporation is subject to personal holding company tax. A C corporation may not be an S corporation shareholder. Partnership earnings are taxed at the individual partner level regardless of whether they are distributed from the partnership. (Chapter 48-1-3; Skill: 3; CSO: 1.1.2)

49. (c) Shareholders can contribute property to either type of corporation without being taxed. Before the American Jobs Creation Act of 2004 (AJCA '04) became effective (October 22, 2004), a maximum of 75 shareholders was permitted for S corporations, with a husband and wife eligible to be considered one shareholder. (Provisions of the AJCA '04 were eligible to be tested starting in the July-August 2005

exam window.) The main purpose of becoming an S corporation is to avoid double taxation. Nonresident aliens, corporations, and foreign trusts generally may not be S corporation shareholders. Because **resident** aliens may be shareholders, the answer "shareholders can be either citizens of the United States or foreign countries" also is correct; however, answer (b) is a "better" answer as it is more widely applicable. Editor's Note: Due to the existence of two correct answers, the editors do not expect this question to appear on future exams. If you encounter a question during your exam that you believe is in error, notify the AICPA in accordance with guidance in the AICPA's publication, *Uniform CPA Examination Candidate Bulletin: Information for Applicants.* (Chapter 49-6-5; Skill: 3; CSO: 1.1.3)

50. (b) When acts or omissions involve a question of business judgment, an officer who acted in good faith will not be held personally liable for "mere errors of judgment or want of prudence, short of clear and gross negligence." Officers are held to the same fiduciary standards as directors. Rarely are corporations prohibited by state statutes from reimbursing officers or directors for damages from mistakes made in good faith. (Chapter 49-1-7; Skill: 3; CSO: 1.4.0)

Simulations

The BEC exam section will not have simulations in the initial CBT exams. Simulations probably will not appear in a BEC exam section until 2007 or later. When the examiners announce that simulations will appear in the BEC exam section, the Bisk Education editors will include that information in an updating supplement. Our supplements are available at http://www.cpaexam.com/content/support.asp or through a customer service representative.

A simulation is a collection of related items. A single simulation likely will have several response types. Objective and essay responses may be included in the same simulation. Simulations probably will be 30% or less of the score for FAR, AUD, and REG exam sections.

Scenario Elements Simulations generally have one or two scenarios providing the basis for answers to all of the questions in the simulations.

Objective Response Elements Simulations may require candidates to select answers from drop-down lists or to enter numbers into worksheets or tax forms. Tax forms or schedules may appear on the REG exam section, but not all simulations on tax topics will include tax forms. Candidates don't need to know how to create a spreadsheet from scratch to earn full points on the exam; they do need to know how to categorize, determine value, and change a previously constructed worksheet.

Essay Elements Initially, essays will continue to be hand-graded. The essay score focuses primarily on writing skills. The essay content must be on topic to earn the full point value, but the examiners plan to focus on testing content in the objective response questions.

Research Elements Each simulation in the FAR, AUD, and REG exam sections will have a research element, probably for one point. With an estimated two simulations per exam section, this means that the point value on any one of these three exam sections for the research element of a simulation will total no more than three percent of that section's point value.

Simulation Appearance Simulations generally will appear as a collection of tabbed pages. Each tab requiring a candidate response will be designated by a pencil icon that changes appearance when any response is entered on that tab. Candidates should be alert to the fact that the altered icon does not indicate that all responses on that tab are entered, but rather that one response is entered.

INDEX

"On-Demand" Exam

There are four windows annually; the first one starts in January. A candidate may sit for any particular exam section only once during a window. Between windows there is a dark period of about a month when the exam is not administered. Once a candidate has a passing score for one section, that candidate has a certain length of time (typically 18 months) to pass the other three exam sections, or lose the credit for passing that first exam section. Candidates should check with the appropriate Board of Accountancy concerning details on the length of time to pass all four sections. Exam sites typically are open on Monday through Friday; some are open on Saturday as well.

January	February	March
April	May	June
July	August	September
October	November	December

More helpful exam information is included in the **Practical Advice** appendix in this volume.

CPA READY™

COMPREHENSIVE CPA EXAM REVIEW

5

PASS THE CPA EXAM IN FIVE EASY STEPS
WITH CPA READY MULTIMEDIA SOFTWARE,
GUARANTEED!

AVAILABLE BY
SECTION OR
COMPLETE SET

STEP 1
EVALUATE YOUR KNOWLEDGE WITH A DIAGNOSTIC EXAM

The **Diagnostic CPA Exam** evaluates your level of knowledge by pinpointing your strengths and weaknesses and earmarking areas for increased (or decreased) study time. This information is passed to the **Bisk Personal Trainer**™ so that the entire course outline is color-coded, identifying your individual needs.

STEP 2
LET OUR PERSONAL TRAINER SHOW YOU THE WAY

The **Bisk Personal Trainer**™ analyzes your performance on the **Diagnostic CPA Exam** by matching your weakest areas against the most heavily tested exam topics (according to AICPA specifications) and automatically develops an extensive study plan just for you. Featuring practice exams with links to over 3,400 pages of the most comprehensive textbooks on the market, this powerful learning tool even reevaluates your needs and modifies your study plan after each study session or practice exam!

STEP 3
MASTER THE CONTENT OF THE NEW COMPUTER-BASED EXAM WITH
VIDEO CLIPS, PRACTICE EXAMS AND OUR SIMULATIONS TUTORIAL

- Watch **video clips** that are built right into the self-study text so that you can get a deeper understanding of material you have just read
- Take **practice exams** that give you right/wrong answer explanations with links to the related text
- Practice **simulation questions** just as they will appear on the computer-based exam
- Plus, our new **Study Coach** feature will look at your current progress and recommend what you should study next – keeping you on the path to exam success!

www.CPAexam.com/06